Banking on Failure

Banking on Failure

Cum-Ex and Why and How Banks Game the System

RICHARD S COLLIER

Centre for Business Taxation,
Saïd Business School, University of Oxford

OXFORD
UNIVERSITY PRESS

OXFORD
UNIVERSITY PRESS

Great Clarendon Street, Oxford, OX2 6DP,
United Kingdom

Oxford University Press is a department of the University of Oxford. It furthers the University's objective of excellence in research, scholarship, and education by publishing worldwide. Oxford is a registered trade mark of Oxford University Press in the UK and in certain other countries

First Edition published in 2020

Published in the United States of America by Oxford University Press
198 Madison Avenue, New York, NY 10016, United States of America

British Library Cataloguing in Publication Data
Data available

Library of Congress Control Number: 2020933324

ISBN 978–0–19–885967–3

To JC

Sine quo nihil

Acknowledgements

My thanks are due to several people.

I am especially grateful to Christoph Spengel of the University of Mannheim, whose help and assistance included reading and commenting on some early drafts of the chapters that form Part I of this book.

I have benefitted from the discussion of various points in Part II of this book with my colleagues from the Oxford University Centre for Business Taxation, Michael Devereux and John Vella. Sophia Pietrowski and Leonie Hug kindly assisted with some of the more difficult translation points arising from the German law in Part I.

I have also received help on points relating to the tax systems of various countries from a number of people including Mike Gaffney, Dario Sencar, Alice Pirlot, and Remco van der Linden. Chris Davidson has kindly assisted me in relation to certain points relating to the OECD Intermediaries Project.

A number of other people in tax authorities, advisory firms, and banks who are not named here have also helped on a wide range of specific points.

My warm thanks are due to all who have helped me. Any errors are of course my own responsibility.

Contents

List of Figures

Introduction

This is the biggest tax robbery in European history
Christoph Spengel, reported in DW.com, 18 October 2018

What This Book Is About

This book seeks to explain why and how banks game the system. More specifically, its objective is to account for why banks are so often involved in cases of misconduct and why those cases often involve the exploitation of tax systems.[1] A case-study approach is adopted, to allow an in-depth analysis of the issues in a real-world context. The case study is presented in Part I. It concerns a flaw or malfunction in the financial markets systems of a number of countries across Europe. The flaw was embedded deep within the operating system or 'plumbing' of the capital markets where sales and transfers of shares from one party to another are effected. Specifically, its location is the point at which the capital markets infrastructure and the tax system intersect. Part I explores how that flaw was exploited relentlessly by hundreds of banks leading to losses to sovereign treasuries amounting to billions of dollars. Part II is concerned with exploring the reasons why such exploitation is actually encouraged and facilitated by existing financial and tax systems and what the case study reveals more generally about the nature of modern banks and tax systems.

The flaw allowed banks and their clients to profit from it using a scheme which was calculated to create financial claims on the government. Those claims related to the tax system and, critically, were readily converted into cash or a cash-equivalent. In other words, the scheme produced what was essentially free money. The required set of circumstances arose only on a single occasion during the course of an entire year. Even then, the opportunity was available only in certain narrow circumstances. This might suggest that in practice the flaw would have had relatively small financial consequences. However, any such conclusion would reckon without the ingenuity—and rapacity—of international banks, and

[1] The nature of 'misconduct' is considered in Chapter 5. The reference to 'tax systems' is intended as a generic reference to the bodies of rules and procedures operated by states that: define what events or transactions trigger a tax liability; stipulate which taxpayers must remit the tax and when; and detail procedures for ensuring compliance, including reporting requirements and enforcement sanctions. The nature of tax systems is discussed further in Chapter 7.

Banking on Failure: Cum-Ex and Why and How Banks Game the System. Richard S Collier,
Oxford University Press (2020).
DOI: 10.1093/oso/9780198859673.001.0001

their ability to convert the flaw into prodigious financial amounts, measured in the billions of euros, of free money.

The system flaw in fact became the foundation stone on which the banks erected an extraordinarily complex and multi-layered structure, the singular purpose of which was to exploit the anomaly to the maximum. At the heart of the structure was a trading arrangement tailored to this purpose, which came to be known as the cum-ex trade (or simply 'cum-ex'). In essence, a cum-ex trade involves the careful orchestration of a number of different financial instruments into an integrated and elaborate trading strategy. The strategy is planned and then executed just as a dividend is about to be paid on listed company shares. Understanding how this was achieved requires the intricate elements of the strategy to be carefully deconstructed and explained, a task that is given over to the first chapter of this book.

Many banks went to great lengths to exploit cum-ex. This involved the creation of hugely complex transactional structures, with chains of different parties in different countries and involving multiple separate, but coordinated, financial contracts. A wide range of financial instruments were pressed into service, including short sales, stock borrows, swaps, and futures transactions: all of it designed to extract every last penny of free money from the flaw. Hundreds of banks and investment funds were actively involved. Many funds, including hundreds of pension funds, were established for the sole purpose of participating in the arrangements. Ultimately, hundreds of thousands of trades in shares and derivatives designed to exploit the flaw were structured and executed to extract the financial benefits. Those trades involved amounts in the hundreds of billions of euros. The trades created massive claims on sovereign treasuries, allowing the banks and investment funds to siphon billions of euros from European states. In short, the flaw gave birth to nothing less than a feeding frenzy for the banks and their clients.

There was only one victim of the cum-ex scheme: the exchequers of a number of different countries, a point that is all the more striking given that many banks were entering into these cum-ex trades having been rescued by government bailouts in the depths of the Global Financial Crisis.

Part I of this book describes the nature of the cum-ex trade and how it has been exploited by banks and their clients. Examined in detail are the techniques of structured finance that were employed in both its development and execution. The book is also concerned with the wider implications of the existence and exploitation of the flaw that created the trade. In some ways, the flaw is unique. In other ways, however, the actions of the international banking sector in exploiting it bear a strong similarity to those observed in many other financial-sector scandals. As it unfolds, the story of 'cum-ex' reveals much about what banks have become and the nature of their activities in inter-bank markets, removed from the real economy. The episode also has a wider relevance in the context of the management and operation of tax systems and the degree to which complex financial products cause problems in those systems. That the cum-ex scheme pits the banks against the tax system is also no coincidence. Here again, the cum-ex transaction, though in some ways unique, can hardly be described as an isolated case of banks seeking to exploit the tax system (in this case by generating claims on the tax system). These wider systemic issues are pursued in Part II. The focus of this book is therefore concerned not only with the fascinating story of the flaw itself and how it was exploited, but also with what this case study tells us more generally about the nature of modern banks and the interaction of tax systems and financial markets.

As noted above, the flaw or malfunction in the plumbing of the capital markets has been a feature of a number of different financial markets in Europe. Those states reported as having been impacted include Austria, Belgium, France, the Czech Republic, Denmark, Germany, Finland, Italy, the Netherlands, Norway, Poland, Spain, and Switzerland.[2] In this book, I illustrate the discussion of cum-ex using the German experience as a case study. However, the parties to a cum-ex trade in the German capital markets could be anywhere in the world as long as the subject of their agreement was shares in a German company. I chose Germany for the case-study because that market has seen the highest reported level of cum-ex activity. There is some debate about the exact figure lost to the trade in Germany (a matter that is discussed in Chapter 4), but all commentators agree it is measured in the billions.[3] On a broader plane, the European-wide cost of cum-ex to taxpayers has recently been reported as €55 billion.[4] Not surprisingly, the authorities in Germany and other affected countries are currently pursuing investigations into hundreds of banks and their counterparties.[5]

Sadly, the lessons from the cum-ex episode remain all too relevant. They suggest a complete failure of the banking system and the tax system in almost every conceivable respect. Even though the transaction in its form in Germany has now been shut down, the financial 'technology' essential to cum-ex migrated to other markets. For example, no sooner was cum-ex closed down in Germany than a variant was reported to have emerged in Denmark at a loss to that country

[2] See the press release of the European Parliament, 'Cum-Ex Tax Fraud Scandal: MEPs Call for Inquiry, Justice, and Stronger Tax Authorities', 29 November 2018, available at http://www.europarl.europa.eu/news/en/press-room/20181120IPR19552/cum-ex-tax-fraud-meps-call-for-inquiry-justice-and-stronger-tax-authorities

[3] A recent estimate of the tax at stake in Germany puts the cost of the cum-ex scheme to the German state at a staggering €25 billion. See Allen & Overy, 'European White Collar Crime Report', Q2, 2017, p.8.

[4] See European Parliament, 'Cum-Ex Tax Fraud Scandal'.

[5] As at the time of writing, the first prosecution of a banker for involvement in cum-ex trading is underway in Bonn, Germany. See the report of David Segal, in the New York Times, It May Be the Biggest Tax Heist Ever. And Europe Wants Justice. 23 January 2020, available at https://www.nytimes.com/2020/01/23/business/cum-ex.html

estimated at $2 billion.[6] Elements of the cum-ex trade can also be seen in some form in certain structured trades to this day, meaning the discussion and lessons in this book remain of wide current relevance.

Why I Wrote This Book

I wrote this book on the cum-ex affair for three main reasons. First, the story of cum-ex is a fascinating, and in parts barely believable, account of the ingenuity and tenacity of banks involving massive monetary amounts, hugely complex transaction structures, and literally hundreds of banks and other financial-market participants. Second, the discussion of cum-ex throws up some important lessons on governance and control relating to the management of banks and tax systems. Third, the cum-ex affair raises a number of important policy issues relating to the existing financial and tax system, such as the implications of the proliferation of structured financial products, the role and purpose of banks, and the treatment of financial products by tax systems. These wider issues are pursued in Part II of this book.

The book demonstrates the importance of obtaining a deep understanding of what is happening at an operational and administrative level within the financial markets and tax systems. This is an area which understandably presents challenges for non-specialists. The book seeks to achieve this goal by carefully presenting in Part I the range of financial instruments and the evolution of the complex structures that were utilized to exploit the cum-ex flaw in the system. The discussion in Part II then seeks to examine the wider systemic relevance of these matters and understand how they contribute to the incidence of cases like cum-ex.

How This Book Is Organized

The book is organized into two main parts. Part I, comprising Chapters 1–4, explains the nature of cum-ex and charts its evolution and ultimately (after many years) its demise. Part II, comprising Chapters 5–7, looks at the wider implications of the cum-ex trade and especially what it tells us about banking and tax systems and how this accounts for the reasons banks 'game' those systems. Chapter 8 sets out the conclusions that may be drawn from the discussion in this book.

[6] See further the Danish DR News report, by Kresten Morten Thye Munksgaard and Katrine Birkedal Frich, of 14 December 2016, available at https://www.dr.dk/nyheder/penge/grafik-skat-snydt-123-milliarder-det-kunne-vi-have-faaet.

Chapter 1 introduces a number of financial-sector transactions and concepts (including short selling, stock borrowing, and the distinction between cum- and ex-dividend share sales), all of which are vital ingredients in the cum-ex trade. Readers that are familiar with these financial sector concepts may wish to skip the early sections of this Chapter. The discussion then explores how all these elements need to be carefully assembled and synchronized in order to deliver the basic cum-ex trade. Chapter 2 provides an explanation of how the cum-ex trade was designed to work in the German equities market. This includes a description of the relevant features of the market infrastructure and an explanation of the key 'value drivers' in the trade. (Though focused on the German market, the description is in a number of respects also relevant to any other jurisdiction.) The description includes an explanation of the basic operation of withholding tax and the impact of double tax treaties which may be skipped by readers familiar with this material. The chapter includes a step-by-step analysis of the basic cum-ex trade structuring in that market. Chapter 3 then shows how the basic cum-ex trade was subject to recurrent (and ingenious) further refinements through financial engineering in order to massively amplify its effectiveness and profitability. These refinements were continually layered onto the basic transaction, leading ultimately to the colossally complex cum-ex transaction structures which the Chapter seeks to explain. Chapter 4 deals with the closing of the cum-ex trade in Germany from 2012 and its aftermath. The discussion explains how the trade came to be challenged and ultimately (after various failed attempts) successfully defeated by the authorities. The chapter also deals with the fallout from the cum-ex trade. This is ongoing and likely to continue for several years in future.

The discussion in Chapters 2–4 focuses on the cum-ex transaction in the German equities market because it has been the biggest market which has seen the exploitation of cum-ex. However, the significance of the discussion extends well beyond the German equities market. This is because, as mentioned above, variants of the cum-ex trade have been developed and applied in a number of other European markets. The case-study discussion of the German market therefore has relevance on a broader geographical footing. A second reason concerns the participants in that trade. Though in Germany the cum-ex trade initially involved largely domestic players, for a number of reasons that are explained in this book it evolved into a cross-border structure. This means the cum-ex trade structure rapidly developed to include as key participants banks and different types of fund vehicles from around the world. Thus, in relation to any specific cum-ex trade, the various parties playing the key roles might, for example, include an American pension fund, a British investment bank, and an Irish investment fund. In some cases, there would have been very little involvement of German parties, subject only to the transaction always being settled through the capital markets settlement system used for German equities.

Based on the discussion in Part I of this book, and using the cum-ex trade as a case study or reference point, the chapters in Part II offer a wider perspective on the causes of trades like cum-ex. They seek to explain why misconduct by banks (as reflected in cum-ex and similar transactions) is not only so prevalent but is also an inevitable consequence of current financial and tax systems.

The discussion in Chapter 5 examines how the cum-ex transaction has been assessed to date before arguing that those assessments reflect a limited understanding of the real complexity and wider causes—and implications—of schemes such as the cum-ex trade. The chapter raises wider questions as to what transactions like cum-ex tell us about the nature of banks and inter-bank market activities, and what they reveal about tax systems. Those issues relating to banks and tax systems are then pursued in the following two chapters. Chapter 6 deals with the issues and implications for banks and the inter-bank market. The discussion begins by surveying the significant incidence of misconduct by banks across the globe and then presents an explanation for this based on systemic features of the banking market. This includes an account of the impact of a number of profound changes to the banking business model which have taken place in the last half-century as banks have shifted to a highly transactional business model and discovered that tax systems around the globe present fertile opportunities for exploitation. The discussion includes an analysis of why it is considered that the banks' internal and external control mechanisms have materially failed. Chapter 7 addresses various matters relating to tax systems. These include an explanation of why banks are in a unique position to exploit tax systems and why the attempts of tax systems to accommodate complex financial products have the bizarre consequence of actually facilitating the exploitation of those tax systems. Chapter 8 brings together a summary of the conclusions and lessons for the future. Specifically, it draws together the various reasons why trades like cum-ex have been encouraged and actually facilitated by existing financial and tax systems. The discussion also explores possible responses to the current situation.

Complexity and Cum-Ex

Complexity is, inevitably, a recurring theme in this book. The elaborate intricacy of the cum-ex trade has been a major asset for those seeking to unlock its benefits. It will be seen that the complexity of the multiple separate yet interlinking arrangements both concealed the transaction and also enabled it to be 'hidden' in plain sight. The complexity of the arrangements that delivered the cum-ex result was therefore relied on as a vital element in its success: in the German case-study example, the trade was facilitated not just by bringing together in an elaborate composite transaction a wide range of quite different financial instruments, but the execution of the trade also required a very detailed knowledge of the capital markets infrastructure. The trade is essentially designed to exploit the intersection of the tax system and the operational mechanics of settlement systems in capital markets. This means that, in order fully to understand the cum-ex trade, multi-disciplinary expertise in capital-market financial instruments and in the detailed operational inner workings of settlement systems and tax systems, both domestic and international, is required.

The level of complexity involved in cum-ex is not typical of capital markets transactions—but neither is it unique. It can be seen in various structured capital markets transactions. For example, it was clearly a feature of the highly structured collateralized debt obligations (CDOs) that were a causal factor in the Global Financial Crisis. It is also seen recurrently in many highly structured tax-driven financial products of which cum-ex is emblematic. Not surprisingly, this endemic complexity is as a practical matter generally better managed by banks and the bankers who originate the transactions than by the authorities who regulate them. This is an important point about which I have more to say in Part II of this book.

All this complexity is obviously a potential challenge for the reader (and therefore for the author). I have attempted to cut through any needless detail by including in the discussion only such material as is clearly necessary. Where possible, I have relegated the more detailed information to the footnotes (particularly in the discussion of the relevant tax technical issues in Chapters 2 and 4). I do not seek here to write a definitive account covering all those matters that are relevant to the cum-ex trade, such as the operation of settlement systems, the use of derivatives in the capital markets, detailed aspects of tax systems, and so on. That would require a work of vastly greater length. However, I do aim to introduce and deal with all those points that are germane to the discussion and analysis of cum-ex in Part I and the wider issues discussed in Part II that are based on the cum-ex case study.

In relation to the discussion of cum-ex in the case study dealing with the German capital markets infrastructure and tax system, I have sought to reflect the key issues arising from the experience in that country. In that regard, I have drawn on a wide variety of sources and these are referenced in the footnotes to the chapters where relevant.[7]

Though there is some illustrative (but limited) discussion of the cum-ex fallout on individual banks in Chapter 4, I have generally not sought to include detailed

[7] Some of the material relates to German-language sources, whether relating to the operation of the settlement system for German shares or the German tax rules that were exploited in cum-ex. In the limited circumstances where abbreviations of German statutes and German institutions are used in the footnotes, these are explained in the Appendix to this book. Further detail on the German settlement system and tax law is available from the material cited in the footnotes (and in any event I discuss the relevant law in English not by reference to the original German terms, which may not be identical in meaning to the concepts when expressed in English).

discussion of individually named banks. However, I have provided many examples of cum-ex transactions that were in fact executed by banks. The reason for this is that discussion of individual cases detracts from the important points relating to the staggering size of the participation of the banking sector as a whole in cum-ex.[8]

[8] There is no single authoritative listing of all the banks that have in one way or another been involved or named in relation to cum-ex trading, but various sources attest to the wide involvement of the banking sector. For example, over 120 banks are listed on the 'Wuppertal list' contained on a memory stick provided by a whistle-blower—see the German Parliamentary Report 18/12700, 18th Electoral Term, Recommendations and Report of the 4th Committee of Enquiry under Article 44 of the Basic Law, 20 June 2017, at pp.397–9. For the reader who is interested to understand more about the role in cum-ex of individual banks, the *Wall Street Journal* website is a good starting place.

PART I
THE CUM-EX TRADE

1
Cum-Ex in Concept

It was as if they had discovered the formula to produce gold
Bank insider, reported in *Handelsblatt*, 20 April 2016

Introduction

Part I of this book deals with the emergence and evolution of what came to be known as the 'cum-ex' trade, a trade in the financial markets designed to generate huge amounts of free money at the expense of the state.[1] The design of cum-ex transactions evolved to become bewilderingly complex. At its core, however, the trade hinged on a simple time delay between the point at which transactions in the capital markets are initiated and when they are considered settled and therefore complete. The delay arises from conventions which govern the manner and timing by which stock-market transactions are routed and processed in the 'plumbing' of the financial markets. In a very narrow set of circumstances, the delay could be exploited so as to allow multiple parties to appear to own the same shares at the time of a dividend payout. This made it possible to obtain multiple refunds of tax that had been paid to the tax authorities only once. At first glance, the issue might not seem especially important because of the limited circumstances in which the reclaim could be made. However, hundreds of banks and financial intermediaries have been implicated in schemes to exploit the trade. The monetary amounts involved are staggering, involving billions of euros.[2] A quirk in the system arising only in very narrow circumstances was transformed by financial engineering into one of the largest feeding frenzies of all time in the financial markets.

[1] In describing the subject matter of the cum-ex trade, I use the term 'shares', 'securities', or 'equities'. These terms may be used interchangeably. However, the practice of share borrowing (described further in this chapter) is generally described by the label 'stock borrowing and lending' and accordingly that practice is followed in this book.

[2] Given the covert nature of the transaction, the varieties of complex structuring used to implement the trade, the multiple jurisdictions involved, and the variations by country in the degree to which the trade has been investigated and pursued, it is not easy to arrive at a total figure for the cost of cum-ex. Recent individual country estimates suggest individual country costs of €25 billion for Germany (Allen & Overy, 'European White Collar Crime Report', Q2 2017, p.8) and DKK12.4 billion for Denmark in the period 2012–15 (*Zeit Online*, 17 December 2017).

Banking on Failure: Cum-Ex and Why and How Banks Game the System. Richard S Collier, Oxford University Press (2020). © Richard S Collier.
DOI: 10.1093/oso/9780198859673.001.0001

This chapter examines the essential features of the cum-ex trade and outlines the 'base template' which was the foundation for the later refinement and expansion of the trade. That evolution is charted in the following two chapters. While Chapter 2 describes the development of cum-ex in the context of one particular securities market, namely Germany, the discussion here is in more general terms. The intention is to lay out in concept the key features of the capital markets infrastructure and the tax system that together, and combined with some considerable ingenuity on the part of bankers, gave birth to cum-ex.

Before embarking on a detailed explanation of cum-ex, however, its core elements can be aptly illustrated by an event from the childhood of the author. He was about to post a letter when a friend protested 'What are you doing? Nobody pays for stamps any more. Don't you know you can send a letter for free?' The explanation followed. 'For the addressee, you write in an imaginary address on the envelope. However, in the upper left-hand corner of the envelope, where you are supposed to write the sender's address, you put the name and address *of the person you're sending it to*. Don't put any stamp on the envelope. Without the proper postage, the post office will return it to what is assumed to be the address of the sender: but it's not of course—because you've made the return address the address of the person you're sending it to. So the letter gets delivered for free.'

The childhood story is relevant to the vastly more complicated cum-ex trade because exactly the same two core elements are involved: firstly, an established, but flawed, underlying system which seems to operate as expected, day in, day out; and secondly, an inventiveness that turns the rules of the system on themselves in order to achieve a result which the designers of the system never anticipated and certainly never intended.

The system exploited by the cum-ex trade is designed to process dividend payments, a routine part of the plumbing of financial markets that participants in that system generally take for granted. The inventiveness is that of the banks[3] in profiting from a subtle flaw in the system. For a variety of reasons, the opportunity to exploit that flaw was inherently very limited. However, the banks sought out ways not only to overcome all those limitations, but also ways to multiply and leverage the opportunity presented by the flaw in the system, in the process converting it into a virtually unlimited 'free money' machine.

Through a series of careful refinements of the base template, it was not long before the cum-ex trade was developed into a 'financial product', an investment strategy in its own right that was made available, at a price, to a very large number

[3] In some jurisdictions a 'bank' is strictly speaking a deposit-taking institution which may be prohibited from dealing in shares. In others, particularly some European jurisdictions, deposit-taking banks have free rein to carry out all of the transactions necessary for the cum-ex trade. A 'bank' for the purposes of this book is a financial institution, whether part of a group of companies or a stand-alone legal entity, which has the ability and authorizations to carry out the transactions necessary for the cum-ex trade.

of banks, funds, and high-net-worth individuals. This evolutionary process added appreciably to the complexity of transactions comprising the cum-ex trade, making it increasingly hard to understand, and harder still to detect. Even in its most basic form, the cum-ex transaction is not quickly grasped. That is because there is little in its workings that might be described as intuitive. By the time the multiple refinements and reworkings from the evolutionary process are grafted onto the initial base template, it becomes a web of layered complexity, a series of steps which are both intricate and carefully choreographed as well as involving a wide range of apparently separate (but in fact connected) parties, financial instruments, and markets.

Far from being a problem for those exploiting cum-ex, this inordinate complexity was a major design benefit. The fog shrouding the workings of the cum-ex trade goes some way to account for the fact that it took those charged with regulating the market at least a decade to get to grips with both the trade and its real consequences. That fog, however, also presents a considerable challenge in explaining what the cum-ex trade is, a task to which I now turn. The approach adopted in this chapter is, first, to deal separately with a number of the individual components that are relevant to the cum-ex trade. The discussion then explains how these individual components were assembled into an integrated whole, in the process delivering a cum-ex free-money machine.

The Dividend Arbitrage Market

The cum-ex trade was born out of the 'dividend arbitrage' market, a segment of financial markets trading activity.[4] Commonly referred to within the banking industry as 'div arb', it has for many years been a significant 'inter-bank' market operated by banks and investment banks.[5] Though the cum-ex trade is in some respects different to typical dividend arbitrage transactions, there are also many similarities, including the role of banks, brokers, and the financial product

[4] The term 'arbitrage' generally refers to the practice of taking advantage of price differences between two or more markets at the same time for the purpose of generating a profit. In the case of dividend arbitrage, different effective tax rates on dividends for different groups of investors result in trades in which the dividends are received by the parties able to benefit from the highest after-tax return. Strictly speaking, unlike arbitrage profits arising outside the tax sphere, the tax differences that generate this activity are not arbitraged away (i.e. reduced) by the process of trading itself, though they may be shared between parties.

[5] The inter-bank market is a non-centralized 'wholesale' financial market for trading currencies and other financial instruments, such as securities and derivatives, among banks and financial institutions but excluding retail investors and smaller trading entities. A major factor in the early development of the inter-bank market was the development of currency trading after the collapse of the Bretton Woods agreement in 1971. Over time, the dividend arbitrage market has become to some degree constrained by measures enacted in some individual states to counter the practice of 'dividend washing' transactions, though these often have the effect of complicating, rather than precluding, such transactions.

structuring techniques used. This makes a description of the dividend arbitrage market a useful first step in the explanation of the cum-ex trade.

The dividend arbitrage market is essentially concerned with a form of trading which exploits the manner and extent to which dividends are taxed in the hands of shareholders.[6] The economic basis of the arbitrage is that the same dividend payment may have a different value depending on the circumstances or characteristics of the person receiving it.[7] The reasons why this is the case are explored further later in this chapter, but essentially the differences in value from one shareholder to another normally flow from the fact that the amount of withholding tax (a tax applied to dividend payments) varies from investor to investor and from country to country. The market exists, therefore, because investors—or at least classes of investors, such as pension funds, residents of particular countries, sovereigns, etc—have different characteristics for tax purposes. These characteristics directly affect the level of withholding tax which is applied to dividends to which they are entitled and consequently affects the amount of any after-tax dividend received by them.[8]

[6] For a general overview of techniques used in the dividend arbitrage market, see the United States Senate Permanent Subcommittee on Investigations staff report on 'Dividend Tax Abuse: How Offshore Entities Dodge Taxes on U.S. Stock Dividends', 11 September 2008, available at https://www.hsgac.senate.gov/subcommittees/investigations/hearings/dividend-tax-abuse-how-offshore-entities-dodge-taxes-on-us-stock-dividends. There is also some discussion of the market in the Financial Conduct Authority 'Market Watch' publication of June 2017, available at https://www.fca.org.uk/publication/newsletters/marketwatch-52.pdf. A narrower and more technical meaning is sometimes given to the term 'dividend arbitrage'. This relates to specific trading strategies such as the purchase of shares and a put option over the same shares, followed by the collection of a dividend on the shares and then the exercise of the put option to dispose of the shares.

[7] Any arbitrage is concerned with exploiting the value of some 'difference'. In the case of dividend arbitrage, the relevant difference is that which is created by different tax results relating to dividends from one class of shareholder to another.

[8] The following simplified example illustrates how the same dividend may, due to the impact of tax, have different economic values depending upon the identity of the recipient. Assume a fund (Fund Co.) domiciled in country X is a long-term investor in the shares in A Corp., a company in country Y. All dividends paid from companies in country Y to Fund Co. are subject to a 30% withholding tax, but not subject to any further tax when received by Fund Co. Dividends paid by A Corp. to Fund Co. are therefore subject to the 30% withholding tax in country Y. If the gross amount of the dividend (i.e. before deduction of any withholding tax) to be paid to Fund Co. is $100, the value of that dividend for Fund Co. can only ever be a maximum of $70, the amount it will receive after the withholding tax has been deducted. Assume further that an investor (Investor Co.) in country Y would not, under the tax rules of state Y, be subject to any withholding tax if it receives a dividend from A Corp. In principle, this means Fund Co. could sell the shares on which the dividend is to be paid to Investor Co. so that the dividend is then received by Investor Co. rather than Fund Co. and both parties could gain from the transaction. The gain for Fund Co. is equal to the excess over $70 that it collects by way of payment for the dividend in the sale price of the shares. The gain for Investor Co. is equal to the gross amount of the dividend (reflecting the benefit of no withholding tax, i.e. an amount of $100) less the amount paid to Fund Co. for the dividend. Thus, if the sale price of the shares in A Corp. includes an amount of $85 in respect of the dividend, the gain for each of Fund Co. and Investor Co. is $15; for Fund Co. because it receives $85 rather than $70 in relation to the dividend, and for Investor Co. because it will ultimately receive a dividend of $100 for which it has paid $85. The example illustrates the existence of different values of the same dividend in the hands of the two different parties, Fund Co. and Investor Co. It therefore demonstrates the essential economic feature that creates the dividend arbitrage market. However, it is important to recognize the example is highly oversimplified on a number of levels.

Because a dividend may have a different value in the hands of certain investors as compared to others, the dividend arbitrage market has evolved to maximize the post-tax value of market dividends. This is typically achieved by banks entering into transactions designed to redirect dividends into the hands of those who benefit the most (on an after-tax basis) from receiving them.[9] Since the right to receive a dividend derives from ownership of the dividend-paying shares, transactions in the dividend arbitrage market usually require the relevant shares to be transferred between the parties, so as to ensure that the dividend is received by the party who suffers the least withholding tax on it.[10] Financial services companies, generally banks, act as intermediaries in the market for these dividend arbitrage transactions, and their role is often to design, initiate, and facilitate the transaction, bringing those seeking to mitigate the impact of withholding tax together with those who are tax-advantaged in relation to the same dividend payment. A number of banks have organized specialist structuring and trading groups whose remit includes seeking out these differentials in the after-tax treatment of dividends and devising ways to exploit them. This means that the design of a dividend arbitrage trade in concept, the identification of suitable parties, and the execution of the required transactions may all flow from the bank's role as intermediary.

Dividend arbitrage transactions designed to move shares are normally highly structured,[11] and very often involve securities lending transactions under which a

For example, it may be assumed that, as a long-term investor in the shares, Fund Co. wishes to maintain an investment in the shares in A Corp. whereas Investor Co. does not. This means that it is likely that, subsequent to any sale of the A Corp. shares by Fund Co. to Investor Co., Investor Co. would want to sell, and Fund Co. would want to reacquire, those shares in A Corp. Further, to avoid any 'unlocked' value from the dividend being wiped out by market price volatility in the value of the shares, the parties would need to protect themselves by hedging out the risk of market price volatility during the interim period of owning (Investor Co.) or not owning (Fund Co.) those shares. A number of these issues, including examples of the complex structuring that may be developed to facilitate these types of transaction, are considered in Chapter 3. For now, the key point which is made concerns the varying economic benefits that flow from dividends according to the type of recipient and specifically from the tax treatment of the dividend in the hands of that recipient.

[9] Though it is theoretically possible to buy and sell rights to a specific dividend payment (rather than the shares in respect of which the dividend is paid), it is normally not effective to simply move or transfer dividends in isolation in the sense of selling (or buying) the right to a dividend as distinct from the underlying parcel of shares.

[10] States often seek to counter dividend arbitrage transactions in their tax law with the result that in some cases such transactions are difficult to conduct and in others may be conducted only by means of either highly complex structuring designed to sidestep the relevant obstacles or within narrow parameters. For this reason, straightforward arrangements involving a simple sale of the right to a dividend will often not be effective.

[11] By 'structured' is meant a trade that is brought about using interlocking and interdependent contractual steps including, where required, different legal entities with the object of delivering a desired result, whether tax, economic, or otherwise.

parcel of shares is initially 'lent' to a borrower and later returned to the lender.[12] An illustration of the basic structure can be seen in Figure 1.1.[13]

The diagram illustrates shares being transferred before any dividend is due to be paid. A loan of the shares takes place from one party (the disadvantaged shareholder), who would have been subject to a high level of dividend withholding tax on the dividend if the shareholder had retained the shares and received a dividend on them (Step 1). The shares are then sold (at Step 2) by the share borrower (the bank in this example) to a different party (the advantaged shareholder) who then (at Step 3) receives the dividend and whose after-tax dividend is appreciably higher (because for that shareholder the amount of dividend withholding tax is lower). After the dividend payment, the shares are then sold into the market (Step 4) and purchased by the bank (Step 5) so that it can return them to the disadvantaged shareholder to close out its open share borrowing position (Step 6).[14] The bank would pay a fee to the disadvantaged shareholder as compensation for its borrowing of the shares and the real dividend foregone by the lender (Step 7). The benefit unlocked by the transaction is equal to the reduction in the amount of withholding tax achieved by it. This amount would normally be

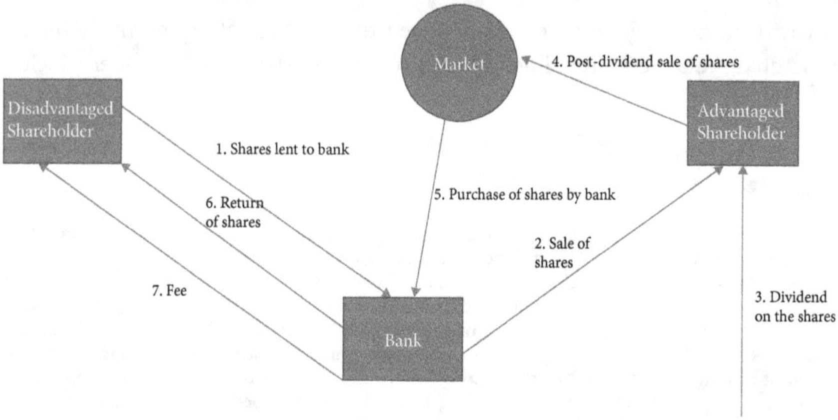

Figure 1.1. Basic dividend arbitrage structuring

[12] For example, an analysis by S&P Global Market Intelligence of five years of stock lending data for companies on the DAX 30 shows that the number of shares borrowed in the twenty days prior to the dividend record date typically climbed by 800% in comparison with levels outside this period. See Cezary Podkul, 'Wall Street Stock Loans Drain $1 Billion a Year from German Taxpayers', *ProPublica*, 3 May 2016, available at https://www.propublica.org/article/wall-street-stock-loans-drain-1-billion-from-german-taxpayers.

[13] The sequence of the steps illustrated in the example is reflected here, and in the examples given throughout this book, by the numbering of the various steps in the diagram. Accordingly, '1' should be read as 'Step 1', '2' as 'Step 2', etc. The sequencing is adopted to help explain the transactions illustrated. In practice, some of the steps may take place simultaneously or according to a different ordering.

[14] The example is simplified for similar reasons to those mentioned in the example in footnote 8 of this chapter.

shared by the parties in the pricing of the individual limbs of the transaction, typically with the savvier parties (often the banks) taking the lion's share.

In addition to being a central feature of the dividend arbitrage market more generally, securities lending is a critical component in the cum-ex trade.[15] However, it is a routine feature of securities markets.[16] It allows institutional investors such as pension funds, other investment funds, and insurance companies to 'lend out' shares which they intend to hold for the long term and in so doing earn an additional return on those shares, typically in the form of a lending fee.[17] Many jurisdictions encourage such transactions by treating stock lending transactions as tax exempt, meaning that the transfers of the shares under such transactions are not treated as giving rise to taxable disposals of the shares. The terminology used, namely the 'borrowing' and 'lending' of shares is misleading. A 'borrowing' would suggest a temporary holding or custody of the shares by the borrower, with the ownership rights remaining in the lender. That is, however, not the case. Although a loan of shares involves a simple movement of shares from lender to borrower (and not a market sale), nevertheless from a legal perspective that movement transfers full ownership of the shares to the borrower. The same is true in the case of the later 'return' of the 'borrowed' shares: full ownership in the returned shares moves to the lender upon their return, again without a market sale taking place.[18] As it does not involve any open market activity or sale of the shares, a loan of shares from one party to another can be achieved rapidly and privately, without impacting the market price of the shares. These characteristics are important to the cum-ex trade.

Because it is designed to reduce the amount of withholding tax collected, tax authorities generally do not welcome dividend arbitrage activity and will often try to counter it by legal and administrative measures.[19] Many jurisdictions have

[15] This is why the stock lending programmes run by institutional investors (such as pension funds, insurance companies, etc) to lend out the shares they own are highly relevant to the dividend arbitrage market.

[16] The practice of stock borrowing and lending is intended to add 'liquidity' to financial markets, for example by facilitating short sales (which are discussed later in this chapter). It is for this reason that stock lending transactions are normally tax exempt. Recent data suggests that, as of January 2018, the daily value of securities on loan globally has surpassed the $2.4 trillion mark, with a lendable balance of $20 trillion and some 47,000 unique securities on loan worldwide. See further the securities finance data from Datalend at http://datalend.com/services/datalend/.

[17] A typical stock lending agreement will provide for the lending and later return of the same type and class of shares as well as for a lending fee. Collateral arrangements to protect the lender against default by the borrower (such as the posting of cash collateral for the period of the loan) are also a normal feature of stock lending agreements.

[18] The shares that are returned under the securities lending agreement would normally be a different parcel of shares from those that were lent in the first place, although they are required to be 'fungible', i.e. shares of an identical issuer, nominal value, type, and ranking as those originally lent.

[19] Sudden shifts in tax authority behaviour or in the enactment of specific anti-avoidance rules are a feature of the dividend arbitrage market. Well known examples in recent years relate to the French, Italian, US, and Swiss markets. Further, Chapter 4 discusses some recent German measures. However, some tax authorities may consider these dividend arbitrage transactions to be potentially inoffensive—see OECD, 'Study into the Role of Tax Intermediaries' (OECD, 2008), at p.44.

complex tax rules which seek to prevent or limit the practice. However, the wide variety of possible transactions and structures that can be deployed to deliver a dividend arbitrage result inevitably makes the task of the tax authorities difficult.

The parties involved in cum-ex are broadly the same as those involved in the dividend arbitrage market. Many of the transaction structuring techniques, such as the critical role of securities lending and the economic value drivers behind the transactions, are also common to both dividend arbitrage transactions and cum-ex. However, there is one critical difference. Cum-ex is not concerned with moving shares from one market participant to another in order to maximize the after-tax value of the dividends paid on those shares. Rather, it involves what might loosely be regarded as a 'conjuring up' or generation of a dividend (which otherwise would never have existed) and in the process the goal is to generate value which can be converted into what is essentially free money. It is to the nature of that 'value' that the discussion now turns. This requires a more detailed discussion of withholding tax and tax credits.

Withholding Tax and Tax Credits

In many countries, dividends paid by a company are subject to the imposition of withholding tax. The withholding tax is normally deducted from the dividend and paid over to the tax authorities in the country where the company paying the dividend is based.[20] The rationale behind withholding tax is that it is intended to function as a payment of tax on account, or at least to ensure some minimum level of tax is levied on the dividend. For example, assume a company in State Y is to pay a dividend of $100 to a shareholder in the same state. If there is a 15 per cent withholding tax, then a cash amount of $85 will be paid to the shareholder and $15 of withholding tax will be paid over to the tax authorities of State Y.[21] Importantly, although the shareholder receives only $85, the $15 withheld and paid over to the tax authorities may still have value to the shareholder for one of two reasons.

First, in some cases the amount withheld may be recovered, in whole or in part, from the tax authorities by the recipient of the dividend as a cash

[20] A withholding tax obligation is typically imposed in respect of dividends where the company concerned is resident for tax purposes in the relevant jurisdiction. Withholding taxes on dividends are common to many tax systems, though the UK is one of the few jurisdictions in Europe which do not normally apply withholding tax to dividends. On the nature of withholding tax generally, see Institute for Fiscal Studies, *Dimensions of Tax Design, The Mirrlees Review* (Oxford University Press, 2010) at pp.1123–4 and 1135–7.

[21] The payment of withholding tax is usually made by the company paying the dividend payment or its agent. The amount paid to the shareholder after the deduction of withholding tax is often referred to as the 'net' dividend, whilst the amount of the dividend before withholding tax is referred to as the 'gross' dividend. Where withholding is deducted, the recipient is normally given a written statement or voucher confirming the date of the dividend payment, the amount of the dividend, and the withholding tax deducted.

reimbursement.[22] For example, an entity such as a pension fund in State Y may be exempt from tax. In that case, State Y's tax law may provide that the full amount of any dividend withholding tax suffered is to be repaid in cash to the pension fund.[23]

There are also many cases where a partial recovery of withholding tax can be made. This may be the case where the shareholder receiving the dividend and the company paying it are located in the same state, but it is also very common where those parties are in different states. Double tax treaties between states make such a partial recovery possible. Such treaties, which are concluded bilaterally between states, usually include limitations on the amount of withholding tax that would otherwise apply under the domestic law of the states signing the treaty. For example, under the Canada–Australia double tax treaty, the Canadian withholding tax of 25 per cent, which would normally be imposed on dividend payments made by a Canadian company, is reduced to 15 per cent on dividend payments to shareholders resident in Australia.[24] Therefore, if withholding at the rate of 25 per cent was deducted from the payment of a dividend from a Canadian company to an Australian resident, the Australian resident would be entitled to reclaim the excess 10 per cent of withholding tax back from the Canadian tax authorities. The level of permitted withholding tax will vary from tax treaty to tax treaty and may also vary under a single tax treaty, according to the specific attributes of the recipient of the dividend in some cases.[25] Where there is no double tax treaty in place between two states, the maximum rate of domestic withholding tax in the state of the company paying the dividend will normally be levied.[26]

The second reason that withholding tax suffered may still have 'value' for the recipient of the dividend derives from its function as a 'tax credit'. That is, withholding tax (assuming it is not repayable in cash as discussed above) is often treated in effect as a prepayment of tax and so may be 'credited', that is, subtracted—from the income tax which is due on all income of the recipient, including the dividend income itself. For example, suppose a net dividend payment of $85 is made to a shareholder, with $15 of withholding tax deducted by the tax authority. Suppose further that no part of that $15 in withholding tax is repayable in cash. Assume that the taxpayer has a total tax liability for the tax

[22] The amount of any such cash recovery typically varies from taxpayer to taxpayer according to its specific status for tax purposes.

[23] As an operational matter, such a rule may operate either by permitting the withholding tax deducted to be reclaimed from the government or alternatively by overriding the imposition of withholding tax in the case of payments to the recipient concerned in the first place.

[24] See Article 10 (2) (b) of the Canada–Australia double tax treaty. Certain detailed conditions apply.

[25] Double tax treaties may provide that certain recipients in one state, such as pension funds, may recover *all* of the withholding tax levied in the other state. An example of this would be the provision to this effect in Article 10 (3) (b) of the 2001 US–UK double tax treaty.

[26] This is particularly relevant to investors resident in tax haven states (such as the Cayman Islands) as those states will often have a very limited tax treaty network or no tax treaties at all. As many hedge funds are based in such tax havens, their global dividend income would—in the absence of dividend arbitrage strategies—therefore be subject to the highest rates of withholding tax.

year of $500 on its income from all sources, including the dividend. In such a case, the taxpayer may be entitled to reduce that total income tax bill by the amount of tax already suffered and not repaid in cash on the dividend. In the example, that would mean that the total tax liability of $500 is reduced by a 'tax credit' representing the withholding tax suffered of $15. The effect is that the withholding tax suffered at the time of payment of the dividend ultimately leads to a dollar-for-dollar reduction of the taxpayer's income tax bill, leaving a total tax liability of $485 in this example.

It is also possible that the two cases discussed above might be relevant simultaneously—for example, where the shareholder receiving the dividend may be able to recover part of the withholding tax deducted in cash and receive a tax credit for the remainder of the withholding tax suffered.

For present purposes, the details of any state's domestic tax rules and the workings of double tax treaties are much less important than the fundamental principle: to the extent that withholding tax can either be reclaimed in cash or used as a tax credit (or both), monies deducted from the dividend in the form of withholding tax and paid to the state tax authorities are not lost in economic terms. Rather, the amount of tax withheld has *value* to the shareholder receiving the dividend. This also explains the differences in the value of the same dividend from one shareholder to another, given that some investors will be entitled to nil or reduced rates of withholding and/or a tax credit for any withholding tax suffered, while others may have neither entitlement.

As noted earlier, efforts to optimize the tax value of dividends in the dividend arbitrage market are normally based on these same two elements of value.[27] The extraction of economic benefit from both of these elements of 'tax value' was also the most fundamental economic driver behind the cum-ex trade. However, cum-ex represents an entirely novel mechanism for that exploitation.

Introduction to the Cum-Ex Trade

As in the dividend arbitrage market, the economic value that cum-ex transactions sought to generate was centred on the twin elements of (1) a cash repayment of some or all of amounts deducted as withholding tax and (2) the use of tax credits relating to that withholding tax. However, in contrast to the dividend arbitrage

[27] There may also be other (though much less common) features of certain dividends that may be tax-optimized. For example, formerly states such as Italy and France treated certain recipients of dividends in specific cases as entitled to additional tax credits (over and above the gross amount of the dividend, with the tax credits partially refundable in cash) and inevitably these were the subject of considerable activity in the dividend arbitrage market. For example, UK recipients of dividends from Italian companies were formerly entitled to an additional amount (*credito d'imposta*) of 56.25% (less a withholding tax at the rate of 15%) on top of the gross dividend paid.

techniques discussed so far, the objective of cum-ex was to generate these benefits by creating a fundamental *asymmetry:* on the one hand to generate or cause the system to create withholding tax benefits in the hands of the *recipient* of a dividend, whilst at the same time avoiding the cost of withholding tax on the *payment* of a dividend, which means avoiding the imposition of withholding tax altogether. This might seem an impossible task given that the value of withholding tax for any recipient of a dividend would normally be related to the withholding tax actually deducted by the dividend-paying company. However, precisely that result was claimed in the cum-ex trade. How this was achieved will become clearer in the explanation that follows.

Turning to the exploration of the ingredients of the cum-ex trade, the first point to deal with is the name of the trade, 'cum-ex'. This is important because the name itself incorporates two concepts that are integral to the design of the trade.

Cum-Dividend and Ex-Dividend

The name 'cum-ex' combines an abbreviated reference to both 'cum-dividend' and 'ex-dividend' shares. These terms, cum- (meaning 'with') dividend and ex- (meaning 'without') dividend are used in financial markets to describe whether a parcel of shares carries a right to receive an upcoming dividend (as in 'cum-dividend') or whether it does not (as in 'ex-dividend').[28]

The terms are especially relevant when a parcel of shares in a company is sold very close to (or on) the company's 'dividend record date'. The dividend record date is the date on which the company (or alternatively the company's registrar) examines the company's share register to confirm the identities of the current shareholders in the company who are entitled to receive a prospective dividend.[29] This is the normal way to identify those shareholders who are entitled to receive a dividend from the company concerned.

However, there is one situation in which it is not possible to establish the entitlement of a shareholder to a dividend simply by inspecting the names on a company's share register on the dividend record date. This exception arises where a parcel of shares is sold *immediately prior* to a dividend record date. The reason

[28] Under established stock exchange practice, shares are traded with dividend rights attached (cum-dividend) up to a certain day. Shares purchased on the following day (which is often referred to as the ex-date) no longer carry dividend rights (meaning they trade ex-dividend) and the share price generally experiences a decline corresponding to the amount of the dividend. For simplicity, the discussion here will generally assume that the dividend record date is the day prior to the ex-date (as is the case in Germany). A 'cum-ex' trade is a trade that is entered into before the shares concerned cease to trade with dividend rights attached, but which nonetheless is settled on or after the ex-date.

[29] The registrar functions will normally be carried out by the company's secretarial team unless a third-party specialist provider has been engaged to operate the company's share register. The registrar functions include maintenance of the share register, payment of dividends and interest, and dispatch of shareholder communications such as annual and interim reports.

for this is that there will often be a delay or 'time lag' in registering the shares in the name of the new shareholder, the buyer of the shares, on the share register and in removing the name of the seller. The delay is similar to the delay that often occurs between entering into a contract to buy a house or car and being formally registered in the vehicle or property register as the new owner. In share trading, where shares are sold immediately before the dividend record date, the entitlement to the dividend to be paid by the company will normally be determined not by the name of the shareholder shown on the share register but instead by the terms of any share sale agreement between buyer and seller.

Where, immediately prior to the dividend record date, shares are sold on a 'cum- dividend' basis, it normally means the *buyer* will be entitled to receive the upcoming dividend on the shares, and so will be buying the parcel of shares together with the right to receive the accrued or impending dividend on those shares. This is true even though the time lag in registering the name of the buyer on the company's share register means the buyer's name will not be registered until after the dividend record date. If, however, the shares are sold instead on an 'ex-dividend' basis, this normally means that the *seller* will be entitled to that dividend with the result the buyer is buying the parcel of shares only and *not* the right to receive the dividend, which will be paid to the seller. Consequently cum-dividend purchases of the shares together with the right to receive a dividend on them, will be more expensive than corresponding ex-dividend purchases where the right to receive the dividend remains with the seller.

An example will help to illustrate these points.

> Suppose that the dividend record date for shares of a particular company, X Co., is Wednesday 26 May. If a parcel of shares in X Co. is sold by an existing shareholder on Tuesday 25 May, the buyer will legally become the owner of those shares immediately and therefore will normally be entitled to receive the upcoming dividend. The fact that there may be insufficient time for the buyer's name to be registered on X Co.'s share register by Wednesday does not change the position. In this example, because the buyer has bought the parcel of shares on Tuesday (the 25th), i.e. *before* the dividend record date on Wednesday (the 26th), that buyer would be buying on 'cum-dividend' terms in this situation. Buying on 'cum-dividend' terms means that the amount paid for the shares will reflect the buyer's right to the shares *and also* the right to receive the imminent dividend payment. If the buyer had instead bought the shares on Thursday (the 27th), the day after the dividend record date, the purchase would normally be on ex-dividend terms. This is because the dividend record date (the 26th) would already have passed at the time the sale was made. The seller would therefore have been entitled to receive the dividend payment before the sale of the shares was agreed.

This example illustrates that whether shares are sold on a 'cum-' or 'ex-dividend' basis is generally determined by the date of the sale: if the sale is made before the dividend record date, it will normally be a 'cum-dividend' sale of shares and carry an entitlement to receive the imminent dividend; on the other hand if the sale is made after the dividend record date it will generally be on 'ex-dividend' terms.[30]

The Settlement Time Lag

The X Co. example describes a time lag in the process by which a buyer of shares first becomes recognized on the company's register of shareholders following a purchase of shares in the market. In securities markets, this time lag is due to the operation of clearing and settlement systems. Legally, the ownership of a parcel of shares usually moves from seller to buyer at the time when a binding sale and purchase agreement is entered into—and not when the parcel of shares later arrives in the buyer's account. Once such a binding sale and purchase agreement is concluded, the job of the clearing and settlement systems is then to process the transfer of the securities from the account of the seller to the account of the buyer and to transfer the purchase monies from the account of the buyer to the account of the seller.[31] The company's register of shareholders will then be updated to reflect the buyer as a new shareholder. Processing these transfers generally involves the agents, typically custodian banks, acting for the seller and buyer matching the respective buy and sell orders of the seller and buyer in relation to the type and class of securities, the quantity of securities purchased, the price, etc. In some cases, it also involves the parties dealing with the interposition of a central clearing counterparty which is inserted into the arrangement as part of the clearing process.[32]

[30] For simplicity, references in the example are to sales of shares on a date before or a date after the date of the dividend record date. In practice, it is possible that sales of shares may be made on the same day as the date of the dividend record date. This explains why there will typically be a cutoff point on the specific dividend record date itself, such as 2 p.m., by reference to which the entitlement to the relevant dividend is established. For completeness, it should be noted that it may be possible to enter into a contract for the sale of shares just prior to a dividend record date on 'special ex' terms under which, even though the sale agreement is agreed before the dividend record date, the entitlement to the dividend remains with the seller. The corollary, a 'special cum' agreement is also possible. Such agreements are rare and are irrelevant to the matters discussed in this book.

[31] In strict terms, clearing is the process which ensures that buyer and seller have agreed on an identical transaction and that the seller is selling the securities which the buyer is intending to purchase. It therefore includes the processes by which the buyer and seller trades are matched. Settlement is the process of movement or 'delivery' of the securities and the corresponding cash consideration, from each party to the other. The settlement process is also referred to as delivery versus payment ('DvP'). In certain cases, delivery may be made free of payment (for example, where securities are gifted).

[32] The role of a central clearing counterparty (often referred to as a 'CCP') is to mitigate counterparty and settlement risk for the parties entering into a transaction together. This is achieved by the CCP becoming a counterparty which stands between the parties so that it is a counterparty to the seller and a counterparty to the buyer. In so doing, it guarantees the trade even if one of the parties defaults on the agreement.

There are market-wide conventions which apply to ensure the processing and transfers are carried out within a uniform time period. A sale of shares in European markets, for example, will normally be subject to 'T+2' settlement, meaning that the movement of the shares (e.g. from the account of the seller to that of the buyer) and the payment of the purchase price will ordinarily be completed within two days of the date of the sale transaction (the trade date, or 'T'). The settlement time lag is therefore a common feature of many transactions in the financial markets. Importantly, however, there are circumstances where the time lag is not present, for reasons discussed further below. The existence of the settlement time lag as well as its absence in certain circumstances are critical features of market practice upon which the cum-ex trade depended.

The settlement time lag has an important consequence. This concerns the circumstances discussed in the example above where, immediately before the dividend record date, a buyer of shares has (1) entered into a 'cum-dividend' purchase transaction (and so is entitled to an impending dividend), but (2) due to the settlement time lag, that buyer is not yet formally recognized as a shareholder in the company by the time of that dividend record date. In such a case, it is the buyer who is entitled to the dividend, because the buyer has bought the shares 'cum-dividend'. However, during the settlement time lag, the clearing and settlement system will continue to formally recognize the seller as the owner of the shares and therefore as the person entitled to the dividend. Where this time lag straddles a dividend record date, an adjustment is therefore necessary to reflect the correct position, namely, that it is the buyer that is entitled to the dividend. This adjustment is made in the clearing and settlement processing of the transaction between buyer and seller. Specifically, a 'dividend adjustment mechanism' in the settlement system is designed to move the dividend from the person who, due to the time lag, receives it but is legally not entitled to it. In the above example, that person is the seller. In such a case, the job of the settlement system is to transfer the dividend to the person legally entitled to it, in the example, this is the buyer. This mechanism is critical to the cum-ex trade and is discussed further below.

Though the clearing and settlement systems in established markets are seen as little more than the basic 'plumbing' of the financial markets, the operation of these systems—and, in particular, the operation of this dividend adjustment mechanism—became the linchpin of the cum-ex trade.

The Base Template of Cum-Ex

Fundamental Dividend Rules

It follows from what has been said above that, if shares are bought and sold in financial markets immediately before the dividend record date, the buyer 'cum-dividend' will be entitled to the impending dividend, notwithstanding the fact that the seller will still be formally recorded as the party entitled to the dividend on the shareholders register of the company paying the dividend. This simply represents the norm across securities markets globally and calls for little further comment beyond noting that it reflects what might be regarded as two fundamental Dividend Rules:

> Dividend Rule 1—*Symmetry between dividend payment/withholding tax deducted and dividend receipt/tax credit*: Dividend Rule 1 holds that for each dividend received by a shareholder, there is a corresponding dividend payment made by the company concerned (i.e. the company that originally issued the shares). This rule also means that in order for any person to claim a tax credit representing withholding tax suffered on a dividend there must have been a corresponding deduction of withholding tax by the company paying the dividend; and
>
> Dividend Rule 2—*One dividend, one shareholder*: In the event that a parcel of shares is sold close to a dividend record date, Dividend Rule 2 provides that either the buyer or the seller will be entitled to that dividend, but not more than one person can be entitled to the same dividend.

These two rules might seem such obvious statements of fact as hardly to be worth stating. Remarkably, however, the cum-ex trade claimed a result which violated both of these dividend rules such that:

- Contrary to Dividend Rule 1, a dividend payment, together with the associated tax credit benefit reflecting withholding tax suffered, could under the cum-ex trade be received without being matched by a corresponding payment of a dividend by the dividend-paying company; and
- Contrary to Dividend Rule 2, and in connection with share sales immediately before the dividend record date, *two* (or more) parties could under the cum-ex trade *each* be entitled to the 'same' dividend.

The results claimed by the cum-ex trade seem logically impossible. How could they be true? The answer lies in a weakness in the settlement systems of a number of different European share markets. In these markets, there was a faulty assumption in the plumbing of the clearing and settlement system. That faulty assumption was open to exploitation, just like the simple example of the postal 'return to sender' convention discussed earlier, though only in very narrow circumstances.

The narrow circumstances where exploitation was possible are those that have already been discussed above (see the X Co. example), namely, where there is (1) a sale of shares immediately prior to the relevant dividend record date and (2) the buyer of those shares agrees to purchase them 'cum-dividend' and (3) due to the settlement time lag, a dividend adjustment mechanism is applied in the clearing and settlement process to move a dividend from the seller to the cum-dividend buyer. Having regard to the narrow circumstances in which the faulty assumption in the system even became relevant, one might think this to be a very limited issue in practice. However, to make such an assessment would be to overlook both the ingenuity and audacity of the banking industry to capitalize on this weakness.

Dividend Adjustment Mechanism

To explain the faulty assumption and the systems malfunction it gave rise to, it is necessary to explore the detailed operation of the dividend adjustment mechanism in the clearing and settlement process. This mechanism lies at the heart of the cum-ex trade. The following explanation will show why that mechanism is needed and how it is intended to operate, before considering how it was, in effect, hijacked.

It will be helpful to return to the example given above. In that example, a seller, who has owned a parcel of shares in X Co. for some time, sells them cum-dividend on 25 May, the day before the dividend record date (which is on 26 May). At law, the buyer of those shares becomes the owner of the shares immediately on the conclusion of the purchase agreement on 25 May. The buyer is therefore entitled to receive the upcoming dividend. X Co. will make the dividend payment to those shareholders shown on the company's register of shareholders on the dividend record date, 26 May. Although the buyer will be the legal owner of the shares from the 25th, the time lag in the settlement system means that there is insufficient time for the shares to be registered in the name of the buyer on the dividend record date. Instead, because of the time lag, the shares will remain on the share register in the seller's name. Put differently, the buyer has, by virtue of the purchase of the shares immediately before the dividend record date, a legal entitlement to the dividend but is not actually registered to receive the dividend from X Co. On the dividend record date of 26 May, the seller is still registered on the shareholders register. The seller therefore receives the actual cash dividend from X Co., but, because of the earlier cum-dividend sale to the buyer, has no legal entitlement to it. Adjustments are therefore required in the clearing and settlement process to reverse the effect of the settlement time lag and deliver the dividend to the correct party, the buyer.

The need for such adjustments in relation to the dividend payment is made even clearer if the relevant cash flows are considered. In Figure 1.2, the facts of our example are supplemented with details of the relevant cash flows.

In Figure 1.2, the buyer is at Step 1 agreeing to pay cash for the cum-dividend shares bought from the seller on 25 May. The €520 consideration is therefore paid

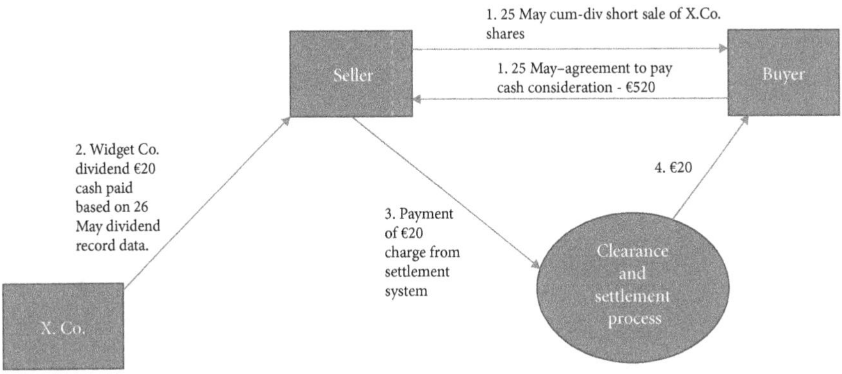

Figure 1.2. Dividend adjustment mechanism

for the shares *and* the right to the dividend. Assume that of the €520 purchase consideration, €20 is attributable to the purchase of the upcoming dividend with €500 attributable to the shares. However, in the narrow circumstances with which the example is concerned, the settlement time lag results in the actual dividend being paid, on the basis of the company's shareholder register on the dividend record date, to the seller (see Step 2 in Figure 1.2). This means that the seller has both received the dividend from X Co. *and* been paid for it by the buyer. Conversely, the buyer has paid for the dividend in the purchase price of €520 but not received it. The adjustments in the clearing and settlement process back out this payment of the dividend to the seller and ensure instead that the buyer receives the dividend it paid for in the cum-dividend purchase (see at Steps 3 and 4 in Figure 1.2).[33]

There are two elements to the dividend adjustment which is made in the settlement process. First, there is a reattribution of the cash amount of the dividend from seller to buyer.[34] This is what is illustrated in steps 3 and 4 of Figure 1.2. Before any adjustment is made, the seller receives the cash amount of the dividend, i.e. €20 (see Step 2 of Figure 1.2). The effect of the dividend adjustment on the seller is that a charge (expense) of €20 is generated in the clearing and settlement process (see Step 3 in Figure 1.2). The economic effect is to take away the dividend (€20) from the seller. Having received the dividend in the purchase price of €520 and having then had it deducted by the clearing and settlement system, the seller is now 'flat' on the dividend and so receives no

[33] The financial numbers used in Figure 1.2 to reflect the cash flows relating to the dividend are simplified and it is assumed in this illustration that no withholding tax is charged on the payment of the dividend. A withholding tax is added in Figure 1.3.

[34] Since this is simply a cash adjustment between the parties, there are no particular implications beyond the practical issue that the seller will need to price in the cost of the dividend adjustment charge in the settlement process in setting the sale price of the shares under the short sale agreement (this should happen automatically if the seller charges a cum-dividend price for the shares).

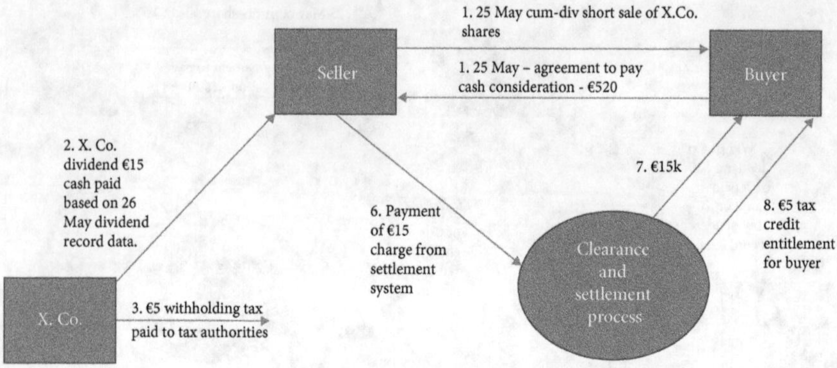

Figure 1.3. Dividend adjustment mechanism dealing with withholding tax

cash benefit from the dividend (shown by the combined effect of Step 2 and Step 3). The settlement system adjustment then credits the cash amount of the dividend, €20 to the buyer (see Step 4 in Figure 1.2). The result is that the buyer now has the cash dividend. The intended result has now been delivered by the settlement system.

Figure 1.3 uses the same facts of Figure 1.2 but now adds in the existence of a dividend withholding tax so that the effect of the second element of the dividend adjustment mechanism can be illustrated. The second element of the dividend adjustment is concerned with that withholding tax.

The only difference from Figure 1.2 is that in Figure 1.3 the dividend paid by X. Co. of €20 is subject to a 25 per cent withholding tax. This means a net amount of €15 has been paid after the deduction of €5 in withholding tax (see Figure 1.3 at steps 2 and 3).[35]

Since the clearing and settlement adjustment is designed to put the buyer in the same position as if it had received the dividend, and since the dividend is paid net of withholding tax, the second element of the dividend adjustment process recognizes the buyer as having suffered the withholding tax. It therefore issues to the buyer a tax voucher representing the tax credit attributable to the withholding tax. This is illustrated at Step 8 in Figure 1.3.[36] For completeness, Figure 1.3 also illustrates the cash adjustments that have already been explained

[35] As a practical matter, the existence of a dividend withholding tax (and therefore a possible tax credit in respect of that withholding tax) would probably influence the pricing of any cum-dividend share sale given that some buyers would value the dividend above the cash amount of the net dividend. The point is irrelevant to the matters discussed here and accordingly the same simplified assumptions as to pricing the transaction are made in Figure 1.3 as were made in Figure 1.2 where there is no such dividend withholding tax.

[36] The tax voucher is produced by the buyer's custodian bank. There is no need for any corresponding adjustment relating to the seller because, given that tax vouchers are normally produced by the custodian banks, the custodian bank acting for the seller would in this circumstance recognize the seller has no entitlement to a tax voucher.

above and which are illustrated by Figure 1.2. The seller is charged with the cash cost of the dividend. The same cash amount is credited to the buyer. These are shown in steps 6 and 7 of Figure 1.3, and the only difference from the previous example is that the cash flows representing the dividend are now reduced because of the dividend withholding tax charged.

The result of these two adjustments, relating to the cash amount of the dividend paid and the tax voucher representing the withholding tax suffered on the dividend, is that the buyer is put in the same position it would have been in had the settlement system recognized the buyer as the rightful owner of the dividend in the first place. The result is that the dividend adjustment in the settlement system has now successfully reattributed the dividend to the buyer.

Intended Operation of the Dividend Adjustment Mechanism

The dividend adjustment mechanism illustrated in Figure 1.3 would clearly work as intended where, as in that example, the seller sells shares which, prior to the sale, were *actually owned* by the seller. In such a case the dividend would, in the absence of any adjustment, be paid to the seller. Given the seller would not be entitled to the dividend (by virtue of having sold the shares 'cum-dividend' to the buyer immediately prior to the dividend record date) the adjustment is required to get the dividend into the hands of the correct party. This is what is illustrated in Figure 1.3 and it is exactly the situation that the dividend reattribution adjustment was designed to deal with. It is also clear that in these circumstances the intended result of that mechanism reflects the two fundamental dividend rules that were referred to earlier, namely:

(1) although not yet shown on the company's register of shareholders, the buyer is legally regarded as the owner of the relevant net dividend paid by X. Co., and the buyer's tax credit relating to that dividend represents the withholding tax paid over to the tax authorities by X. Co. (Dividend Rule 1); and
(2) the buyer and only the buyer is regarded as the owner of that dividend. The seller is regarded for all purposes as receiving no dividend (Dividend Rule 2).

However, whilst the dividend adjustment mechanism discussed above works as intended where the seller owns shares and enters into an agreement to sell them immediately prior to the dividend record date, this is not the same as saying that it works in *all possible* circumstances. One possible scenario (though apparently not one that was contemplated in the actual design of the clearing and settlement system) is that, at the time of entering into the sale agreement, the seller does *not* own the shares which it agrees to sell. In other words, it sells the shares short. It is in this situation that the dividend adjustment mechanism can potentially be manipulated to operate in a wholly unintended way. Given the significance of the point to the cum-ex trade, it will be useful to clarify what is involved in a short sale.

Short Selling

Selling shares which one does not own (known as 'shorting' or 'going short') is an everyday occurrence in financial markets. Commonly, shares are shorted where the seller expects the shares to fall in value. The obligation to deliver the shares after a short sale (often referred to as the obligation to 'fulfil' or 'fill' the contract) requires the seller to borrow similar[37] shares from a lender who already holds them, such as a large pension fund. The borrowed shares are then delivered to the buyer. The short seller's intended profit is achieved at a later date where the short seller can buy back in the market a similar parcel of shares when they have fallen in value. Once repurchased by the short seller in the market, those shares are transferred (or 'returned') to the lender to close out the loan arrangement. The profit of the short seller would be equal to difference between the amount of the sale proceeds realized in the short sale and the cost of the later repurchase of the shares in the market, less the amount of any stock lending fee paid to the lender during the time that the loan of shares was outstanding. This sort of composite shorting and stock borrowing transaction is illustrated in Figure 1.4.

It is important to note that in order for a seller to enter into a short sale agreement, it is essential that the seller has the ability to borrow shares of the same type as those that are 'shorted'. If it is not possible to borrow sufficient shares of the same type, it will not be possible for the seller to deliver shares to the buyer under the short sale agreement. This means that agreement could not be fulfilled.[38] It might be the case, for example, that there is considerable demand among short sellers to borrow the shares, depleting the supply of shares available to be lent. The seller's ability to borrow shares may therefore operate as a real constraint on the ability of that seller to enter into a short sale, particularly in

[37] The term 'similar' as used here is shorthand. Technically, the shares must be identical in type, nominal value, and description, in industry parlance 'equivalent securities'.

[38] Conventions on this point differ by market. In the United States, a short seller must, among other requirements, identify or 'locate' a parcel of shares available to borrow from a lender, prior to entering into the short sale, as prescribed by Regulation SHO, a collection of US Securities and Exchange Commission rules relating to short selling, see 17 CFR Parts 240, 241, and 242, available at https://www.sec.gov/rules/final/34-50103.pdf. In other markets, a short sale which is not completed or fulfilled by the delivery of borrowed shares will constitute a 'fail' and may attract market fines imposed by the relevant regulator.

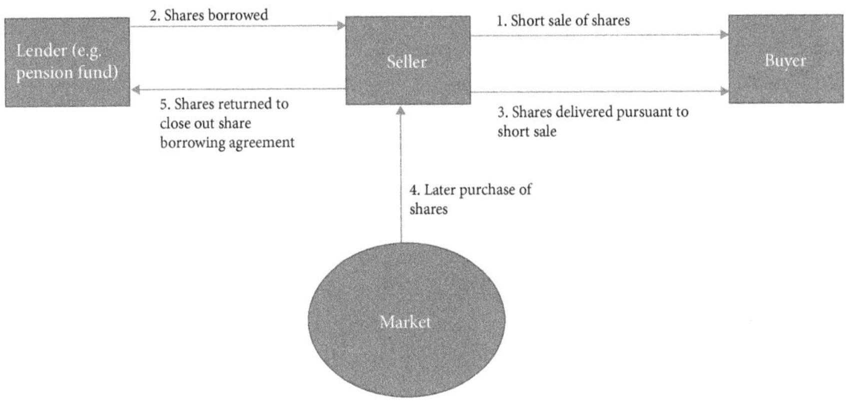

Figure 1.4. Short selling

relation to a large quantity of shares. As will be seen, this is also an important point in the development of the cum-ex trade.

By definition, if a short seller enters into a cum-dividend short sale, this means that the seller, despite not being an owner of the shares, agrees to sell the shares concerned, together with the right to receive the dividend on them. However, as is the case with any short sale of shares, the short seller, when entering into a cum-dividend sale, would not be the owner of the shares on which the dividend will be paid. The short seller, since it is not the shareholder shown on the company's register of shareholders will also not be entitled to receive the dividend. This contrasts with the position of a seller who in fact owns the shares prior to the sale, and who would, in the absence of the sale, receive the dividend.

Nonetheless, despite short selling being a common feature of financial markets, the clearing and settlement systems of a number of markets do not distinguish between sellers that already hold and own shares and sellers that are selling the shares short. This in turn means there is no way that the dividend adjustment mechanism discussed in the earlier examples can be restricted to situations where the seller of shares in fact owns the relevant shares at the time of sale. The consequences of this, which provides the foundation or 'base template' for the cum-ex trade, are explored below.

Unintended Operation of the Dividend Adjustment Mechanism

It has been seen above that the dividend adjustment process operates to transfer a dividend from one party (who receives it, but who is not entitled to it), to another party (who is entitled to it, but who would not receive it in the absence of the dividend adjustment mechanism). Having noted the difference between sales of shares that are already owned by the seller and short sales where the seller instead borrows shares to sell, the question arises as to how this dividend adjustment mechanism works in the context of short selling. Specifically, where a seller has sold short immediately before the dividend record date and so does not hold any shares at the time of sale (nor has any prospect of receiving the dividend), how does the adjustment mechanism operate?

For reasons which are explained below, the answer exposes a major malfunction in the settlement system, a malfunction on which the cum-ex trade is founded. This is because the system does not recognize any difference at all. Whether a seller is selling shares short or selling shares it already owns, the dividend adjustment mechanism operates in exactly the same manner. The result is equivalent to the settlement system 'assuming' that the short seller does, at the time of the sale agreement, own the shares it is selling. This is in spite of the fact that by definition the short seller does not own them. It therefore also assumes that the seller will be receiving a dividend that needs to be rerouted to the buyer. As shown below, these assumptions represent a critical flaw in the settlement system. That flaw represents one of the two most important building blocks of the cum-ex trade.

The dividend adjustment process in respect of a cum-dividend short sale will consist of the same two adjustments discussed earlier and illustrated in Figure 1.3. The first adjustment is that the short seller is charged the net cash amount of the dividend and the buyer is credited with the same amount. This is simply an adjustment between the parties to move the cash amount corresponding to the net dividend.[39] It is the second element of the adjustment that is considerably more important in a cum-dividend short sale situation. The second adjustment is the creation of a tax voucher for the buyer. The tax credit evidences the withholding tax that the settlement system assumes has already been withheld. That makes perfect sense in the situation where the seller *already owns* the shares at the time of the sale agreement: in that case it is necessary for the adjustment to reattribute (i.e. move) the tax credit from the seller who receives the dividend (and so suffers the withholding tax on it) and deliver a voucher, representing a credit for that withholding tax in the hands of the buyer, as discussed earlier.

The position is completely different where there is a short sale. In that case, the seller does not own the shares at the time of sale and is therefore not shown on the register of shareholders of the company paying the dividend. As a consequence, the seller cannot receive the cash dividend, and therefore cannot suffer any withholding tax on it. As there is no dividend received, there is no dividend which needs to be moved between seller and buyer. There is therefore no rationale

[39] As illustrated in the earlier Figure 1.2, the cash amount moved to the buyer by this settlement adjustment will correspond to an amount paid out by the buyer in respect of the dividend and included in the cum-dividend purchase price.

for the dividend reattribution adjustment in this short sale situation. Nonetheless, as a consequence of the faulty assumption in the system, the dividend adjustment process operates automatically, just as it normally does. This means that any reattribution of the tax credit to the buyer under the settlement system process has the potential for a 'one-sided' adjustment, i.e. to create or manufacture an additional tax credit in the hands of the buyer, in a situation where there has never been any corresponding withholding tax paid.[40] Whether this potential for a one-sided adjustment can be achieved depends on how the cum-dividend short sale is actually settled. This is the second critical building block of the cum-ex trade.

As discussed above, a short seller's obligation to deliver shares under a short sale agreement is discharged by the delivery to the buyer of shares which have been borrowed by the short seller. Where shares are borrowed, the settlement process required to transfer those shares from lender to the short seller/borrower is straightforward and simply involves a transfer or movement of the shares from the account of the lender's custodian to the account of the borrower (or the borrower's custodian).[41] Because the participants involved (i.e. banks and custodians) operate the financial system, that transfer can in fact be achieved on a 'T+0' or same-day basis. In other words, unlike the T+2 lag which is the convention for purchases and sales of shares in the European market, transfers of shares under stock lending arrangements can occur with no settlement delay.[42] The same is true where those borrowed shares are in turn delivered to the account of the buyer in fulfilment or settlement of the short sale. This is possible because all of the initial tasks associated with share purchases—for example, matching the sell and buy orders of the parties, or identifying each party's relevant custodian account details—for which the T+2 settlement period is designed, will by this stage of the transaction already have been dealt with by the parties. This allows the delivery of the borrowed shares to be achieved by a simple transfer of the shares from the account of the seller (or seller's custodian) to the account of the buyer (or buyer's

[40] There would be such an asymmetric effect if, contrary to the intended purpose of the dividend adjustment mechanism, the operation of that mechanism in a specific case does not address, much less adjust, the position of any other actual recipient of a dividend.

[41] If, as is usual, the borrower is a bank, the lender may have already appointed the bank as its custodian to hold the shares in any event. In such a case, a simple internal account transfer within the bank would be required.

[42] The shorter settlement cycle generally required for stock lending transactions is a consequence of the simpler mechanical processes that are required to complete a stock loan, but there are also important policy factors supporting it. Further, these policy factors favour a shorter settlement cycle for stock loans of securities than is applicable to the outright purchase and sale of the same securities in the same market. This shorter settlement cycle reflects the purposes of securities lending, for example to avoid settlement fails on outright trades, to support short selling and market-making activities, and to provide immediate liquidity to the market. See 'Securities Lending Transactions: Market Development and Implications', report prepared by the Technical Committee of the International Organization of Securities Commissions and the Committee on Payment and Settlement Systems of the central banks of Group of Ten countries, July 1999, at p.35.

custodian). Critically, the acts of borrowing the shares by the seller and the subsequent delivery of those borrowed shares to the buyer can both be processed within a single day (the T+0 basis). It is therefore possible for the borrowing and delivery to take place up to two days after the initial agreement for the short sale, in other words, at the end of the two-day window created by the T+2 settlement period relating to the short sale. Where the date of the short sale agreement *precedes* the dividend record date, meaning that the settlement of the short sale takes place *after* the dividend record date, something of special importance becomes possible. With careful attention to the timing of the transaction, *ex-dividend* shares (shares that have already paid out the dividend to their owner) can be borrowed to meet the settlement obligation under an earlier *cum-dividend* short sale agreement.[43] As noted, this ability to borrow ex-dividend shares to satisfy the initial cum-dividend short sale is the second fundamental building block of the cum-ex trade. The dramatic result that follows from this possibility is illustrated in Figure 1.5, using the same facts as used in our X Co. example and in figures 1.2 and 1.3.

By entering into a lending contract in relation to *ex-dividend* shares, the lender is expressly confirming that no dividend entitlement is transferred with the parcel of lent shares. Instead, the lender retains the dividend. This can be seen clearly in Figure 1.5 at Step 2 . There is no sense in which the dividend adjustment mechanism in the settlement system (illustrated at Steps 6,7 and 8 in Figure 1.5) will therefore 'move' the dividend and tax credit from any party. The result is that, in this specific case, where *ex-dividend* shares are borrowed and then delivered to the buyer to satisfy an earlier cum-dividend short sale, the system-generated tax credit in the hands of the buyer may be seen as 'created' or generated from nothing. As can be seen in Figure 1.5, the outcome is that, despite there being only one real parcel of shares (the shares that are borrowed from the lender at Step 4 and delivered by the seller to the buyer at Step 5) and only *one* real dividend in respect of which withholding is levied (the dividend paid from X. Co. to the lender at Step 2), there are nonetheless *two* tax credits (see at Step 2 and Step 8). The second tax credit (at Step 8) has been 'generated' by the routine operation of the dividend adjustment mechanism. This means that, despite a single payment of withholding tax (at Step 3), there will be two parties that will seek to benefit from

[43] For completeness, it should be noted that a borrowing of cum-dividend shares is also a possibility, though given that it would not be effective in delivering the cum-ex trade, it was not a possibility that was generally pursued. The possibility of borrowing cum-dividend shares would require the seller to agree on the stock borrowing transaction with the lender *before* the dividend record date, though *after* the short sale transaction had been entered into. In such a case, the position would be in line with the intended operation of the dividend adjustment mechanism in the settlement system: that mechanism would move the dividend—and tax credit—from the person who is actually the registered owner of the shares on the dividend record date (here, that person would be the lender) to the person legally entitled to that dividend on that date (this would be the buyer, as a result of the short sale and share borrow agreements entered into by the seller). There would therefore be no separate 'creation' of the tax credit by the settlement system in such a case.

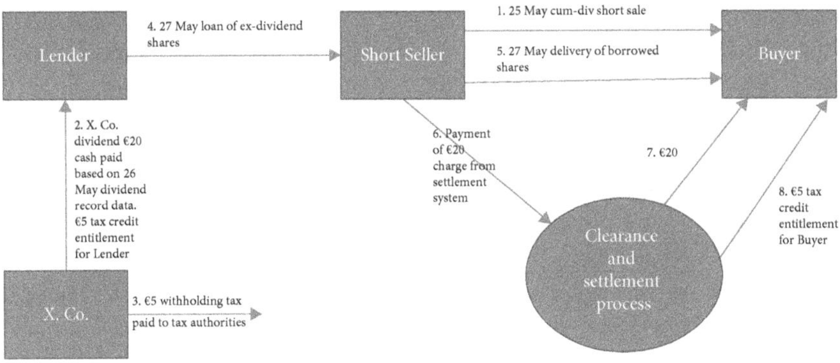

Figure 1.5. The cum-ex trade (1)

that tax credit, whether by way of full or partial cash repayment of the withholding tax deducted or by using the tax credit to reduce an existing tax liability. In Figure 1.5, the total withholding tax paid is €5 yet the two tax credits in respect of this withholding tax (from Steps 2 and 8) sum to €10. Further, neither of those two parties that are able to benefit from the tax credit has caused this result, nor even necessarily knows this result has been caused. The result is of course caused by the seller, who receives no tax credit. This is the alchemy of the cum-ex trade.

Figure 1.5 illustrates the cum-ex trade, a carefully-timed cum-dividend short sale satisfied with the delivery of ex-dividend shares (hence, 'cum-ex'). The 'magic' of the trade is derived from the faulty assumption in the settlement system, which can be exploited due to the seller's ability to bring about same-day delivery of ex-dividend shares to the buyer to fulfil a cum-dividend short sale which took place two days earlier. The goal of the trade is therefore to generate valuable tax credits without the payment of any corresponding withholding tax. However, that goal is delivered only if all of the elements that have been discussed so far in this chapter are carefully integrated in a single composite trade which includes: the short sale, the later share borrowing, the cum- and ex- structuring, the exploitation of the settlement time lag, and the mechanics of the dividend adjustment mechanism.

Returning to the two fundamental dividend rules discussed earlier, it can be seen that both are contradicted by the cum-ex trade. Dividend Rule 1 states that any tax credit benefit simply corresponds to some or all of the withholding tax already paid over to the tax authority by the company which paid the relevant dividend. This rule does not hold true for cum-ex in relation to the settlement-system-generated credit, because in that situation the system-generated tax credit is not matched by any corresponding withholding tax paid over to the tax authority as a result of the payment of any real dividend. The tax credit is instead brought into existence purely by the operation of the system, as a result of the assumptions as to share ownership made by the settlement system itself. Dividend Rule 2 is contradicted by the fact that, although there is only one real dividend payment subject to withholding tax, there are two parties that consider they are the recipient of that dividend and the rightful owner of the accompanying tax credit.[44]

It is open to question whether a sale agreement in respect of cum-dividend shares can properly be settled with ex-dividend shares. This is because the legal nature of what is contractually promised in the short sale agreement (i.e. cum-dividend shares) and what is actually delivered on settlement of the contract (ex-dividend shares) are clearly different. However, the effect of the dividend adjustment mechanism is to blur any such difference. As described earlier in this chapter, that dividend adjustment mechanism works in exactly the same way irrespective of whether the seller is transferring cum-dividend or ex-dividend shares to settle the contract. Given the nature of the dividend adjustment mechanism, the two situations will look exactly the same from the perspective of the buyer: in both cases there will be transferred to the buyer a parcel of securities and, through the dividend adjustment mechanism, there will be both a dividend and a tax credit. The buyer will have no way of knowing whether a cum-dividend sale agreement involves a short sale by the seller or a sale of shares already held by that seller and therefore whether the sale is satisfied with cum-dividend shares or with ex-dividend shares.

The Consequences

It is clear from the above discussion that, in the narrow circumstances where shares are sold short immediately before a dividend record date and the sale is fulfilled using ex-dividend shares borrowed after the dividend record date, any market where the dividend adjustment mechanism in the settlement system functions in the manner described above can be exploited to generate valuable tax credit benefits through the cum-ex trade.

This may seem some a rather obscure or mundane point with little practical relevance. However, to the extent the settlement system can be stimulated to generate tax credits in this manner, it is economically equivalent to printing (free) money. This is because the amount of the tax credit is potentially reclaimable in cash or can be deducted against an existing tax bill, meaning that in either

[44] It might be objected that, in the special case of the cum-dividend short sale satisfied with ex-dividend shares, the buyer is in fact not receiving a dividend payment as such through the operation of the settlement system. Rather, in this case, the system-generated payment is some form of payment in compensation for the non-delivery of the real dividend (which is paid to a third party, such as the lender—as seen in Figure 1.5). This possible characterization of the payment is relevant to the case-study discussion in Chapters 2–4 and is therefore discussed further in those chapters.

case it is readily convertible to a cash equivalent. Another way of looking at it is that it represents a 'negative' tax.[45]

It is obvious from the above discussion that the cost of any such 'manufactured' tax credits is borne by neither of the parties to the sale and purchase transaction, nor by the entity lending the shares to the buyer, nor by the company whose shares are the subject of the short sale transaction and that paid out the real dividend. Rather, the cost of all of the generated benefit is borne by the state. It is the state that will be repaying in cash some or all of the tax credit where this is due, and it is the state that will be offsetting, where relevant, some or all of the tax credit to reduce the amount of a taxpayer's existing tax liability in the manner explained above.[46]

The discussion so far clarifies the fundamental weakness in the settlement systems of a number of European markets and also indicates the potential benefits from that weakness that could be exacted. A rapacious exploitation by the banks is exactly what followed in a number of markets. The ability to exploit the flaw at the heart of the system was in practice magnified by a range of factors, such as various structural features in the tax rules, the uncoordinated nature of market rules and conventions, and the sclerotic administration of the system by regulators and those responsible for exercising business judgment and control. Extracting the maximum benefit from the weakness in the system involved a continual evolution of financial structures which were designed to overcome a number of different obstacles that constrained the degree to which the benefits could be maximized. Ultimately, this involved highly complex transactions, designed so as to expose no party to any risk, and without constraints imposed by market size, market liquidity, or even limited by the amount of real dividends actually paid out by European corporates.

Having set out the fundamentals of the system weakness that created the platform for the cum-ex transaction to be exploited, the dramatic evolution of the transaction, including the different generations of structures that were used in the process, will be pursued in the following chapters by reference to the specific case of the German market.

[45] The term is coined in Christoph Spengel, 'Expert Opinion pursuant to s. 28 PUAG for the 4th Investigative Committee of the 18th Legislative Term', 28 July 2016, at p.14.

[46] As a general matter, the cost of any cash refund of the withholding tax deducted/tax credit would fall on the state in which the company paying the dividend is resident for tax purposes. It is to that state that the withholding tax on the dividend would have been paid. That state may also bear the cost of any offset of the tax credit against an existing tax liability, though, if different, the state in which the recipient of the income is resident would normally bear this latter cost.

2
The Emergence of Cum-Ex

> Whatever form the present difficulties take, it is clear that the general tax principles of national jurisdictions are inadequate to meet the challenge of modern financial instruments.
>
> OECD, *Taxation of New Financial Instruments* (OECD, 1994)

Introduction

Chapter 1 explained the concepts that are central to the cum-ex trade. This chapter explores the practical application of those concepts in the cum-ex trade and how it worked in concrete terms in the context of the capital markets infrastructure and a functioning tax system of a specific country.

The Introduction noted that the cum-ex trade has been executed in a number of European markets. Here the trade is illustrated in the context of the German market and in relation to transactions involving German shares. However, for reasons that will be explained, this leads directly to a discussion of connected activity in a number of other jurisdictions, notably the US and the UK.[1]

The German Equities Market

There are various reasons why this chapter focuses on the German market. The reasons are the same as those which made the German market attractive to those seeking to exploit the potential of the cum-ex trade.

First, in terms of the total market value of shares listed, the German market is the largest in which the settlement systems malfunction exploited in cum-ex was present.[2] The size of the German stock market means that there is a high volume

[1] The infrastructure of both the US and UK share market lacked the essential prerequisites for the cum-ex transaction to be carried out in relation to transactions in US and UK equities. However, many banks and funds in both states were in various ways active participants in the cum-ex trades. This is discussed further in Chapter 3.

[2] Deutsche Börse AG, which is one of the world's largest exchange operators, runs the Frankfurt Stock Exchange, the largest of Germany's seven stock exchanges and one of the ten biggest exchanges in the world, with a market capitalization of $1.76 trillion as of April 2017 according to the statistics portal Statista at https://www.statista.com/statistics/270126/largest-stock-exchange-operators-by-market-capitalization-of-listed-companies/. (The term 'market capitalization', or 'market cap', refers to the

Banking on Failure: Cum-Ex and Why and How Banks Game the System. Richard S Collier, Oxford University Press (2020). © Richard S Collier.
DOI: 10.1093/oso/9780198859673.001.0001

of shares traded, with large pools of German shares held by both domestic and international investors.[3] The market also includes a number of very large dividend-paying German companies, such as those that comprise the DAX,[4] a blue-chip stock-market index consisting of the thirty major German multinationals on the Frankfurt Stock Exchange and including companies such as Allianz (insurance), BASF (chemicals), Bayer (pharmaceuticals), BMW (automotive), Daimler (manufacturing), Deutsche Telekom (communications), and Siemens (industrial).

Two other features of this particular market attracted cum-ex traders: the size of dividends paid out by German companies, and the size of the withholding tax charged as a proportion of those dividends. At the time that the cum-ex trade was in full swing, many German shares had dividend yields of more than 3 per cent, with some as high as 5 per cent. This is reflected in the findings of a recent study that identifies that 20 per cent of the world's biggest dividend-paying companies are German.[5] The withholding tax charged on dividends paid by German companies was deducted at the hefty rate of 26.375 per cent of the gross dividend. The withholding tax due was payable to the German tax authorities by the corporation paying the dividend or, in practice, by its agent.

All of these factors, the large German share market capitalization, the relatively high level of dividends paid by the biggest German companies, and the large percentage of withholding tax levied on those dividends, taken together explain why the German market was an attractive and potentially lucrative market for exploitation of the cum-ex mechanism. The sheer size and liquidity of the German stock market opened the door to the possibility of a significant volume of transactions, each of which could involve high-value dividends and therefore also a significant withholding tax benefit which could be exploited by the trade.

A further feature of the German market was also helpful in practice. Unlike shares which pay dividends quarterly (as is the case for shares listed on the US and

total value of tradable shares of a listed company. It is calculated by multiplying the share price by the number of outstanding shares.) With a share in turnover of more than 85 per cent, the Frankfurt Exchange has virtually all of the turnover in Germany and a substantial share of the turnover in all of Europe. The Exchange's fully electronic trading system Xetra is one of the most widely used electronic trading platforms in the world. See further http://deutsche-boerse.com/dbg-en/about-us/frankfurt-stock-exchange.

[3] The significance of the large pools of German securities held by investors will become apparent later in this chapter in the discussion of the stock borrowing of German shares from long-term investors.

[4] The unabbreviated name is the Deutsche Aktienindex.

[5] See the Janus Henderson, 'Global Dividend Index', Edition 15, August 2017, at p.11, available at https://az768132.vo.msecnd.net/documents/109355_2017_11_21_11_44_28_033.gzip.pdf. The survey lists the world's twenty biggest dividend-paying companies, four of which (Allianz, Daimler, Deutsche Telekom, BASF) are German companies. The relatively high rates of dividend may also be in some measure attributable to the lower use in Germany (say, in comparison with the US) of share buy-backs as a means of passing profits to shareholders.

Canadian stock exchanges), or semi-annually (as in the case of shares listed on the UK and Japanese stock exchanges), the overwhelming majority of German shares pay only a single dividend each year, which in most cases occurs in April or May.[6] The significance of this point is that any benefit derived from the exploitation of the cum-ex mechanism could be concentrated in a single high-value transaction, rather than in lower-value quarterly or semi-annual transactions. This helped the cum-ex trade in two ways. First, the single annual dividend payment cycle provided a longer period of time in which to arrange in advance all of the elements required to execute the cum-ex trade—arranging the parties, financing, structuring, pricing, etc. As the structure of the cum-ex transaction grew more complex, this preparation period was therefore of practical benefit. Second, given that the typical annual dividend payment of the big German companies led to the concentration of the cum-ex benefit into a single transaction, the costs of the cum-ex trade could be kept to a minimum. The execution of the trade would have been costlier if the same annual tax credit benefit had been spread over multiple smaller dividend payments in the year, as this would have required multiple cum-ex trades (each with their own costs of overhead) to achieve the same level of benefit.[7]

The factors discussed above meant that the German share market provided fertile ground for the cum-ex trade. They also explain why individual cases of cum-ex trading caused losses to the German state in particular of tens to hundreds of millions of euros, and why these losses were created by underlying share transactions counted in the tens of billions of euros.[8]

The Market Infrastructure

The market infrastructure in Germany is similar that of most established securities markets.[9] Shares in German companies can be listed and traded on a number of stock exchanges in Germany but the shares of the bigger German companies are

[6] According to a recent study, German companies pay a single dividend in 97 per cent of the cases considered, with 3 per cent paying dividends on a semi-annual basis. See Stephen Ferris, Gregory Noronha, and Emre Unlu, 'The More the Merrier: An International Analysis of the Frequency of Dividend Payment', *Journal of Business Finance and Accounting* 37:1–2 (2010), 148–70. The April–May period is often referred to as the dividend 'season'. The practice of paying a single annual dividend is common in other European markets.

[7] For example, repeated cum-ex trades over the course of a year would have led to multiple stock borrowing costs in respect of each cum-ex transaction. Where shares need to be borrowed only once in the year, there is only a single stock borrowing fee charged by the lender.

[8] See Spengel, 'Expert Opinion', at p.IV.

[9] A useful discussion of the objectives and functions of market infrastructure generally is given in European Central Bank, *The Payment System: Payments, Securities and Derivatives and the Role of the Eurosystem*, ed. Tom Kokkola (European Central Bank, 2010). The discussion of securities markets is at pp.65–92. The publication is available at https://www.ecb.europa.eu/pub/pdf/other/paymentsystem201009en.pdf.

typically listed and traded on the Frankfurt Stock Exchange.[10] Trading takes the form of traditional open outcry trading on the floor of the exchange or, as is now more common, on the Xetra electronic trading system. The trading of German shares would also be possible on an 'over-the-counter' (OTC) basis, which involves 'off-exchange' transactions between two parties, without the supervision of an exchange.

Investors in German shares, such as investment funds and pension funds, will normally hold their shares through a custodian bank. Such an investor will normally appoint the custodian bank on a global or regional basis with the result that its shareholdings in different markets are then held by local sub-custodians in each market. These are usually local nominee companies or branches of the global custodian bank. Consequently, the custodian bank, typically through its local nominee company, will usually appear as the formal owner of the shares. This allows the custodian bank to deal with matters such as collecting the dividend income on the shares, converting it into the currency of the investor (if different to the currency in which it is paid), dealing with any corporate actions relating to the shareholding, etc.[11] The custodian bank will usually hold the shares in the relevant central securities depository or 'CSD'.[12] The primary function of a CSD is to provide collective safekeeping and custody of shares on behalf of its customers, which are usually regulated financial institutions. The CSD acts therefore as a central hub, holding the shares of its customers in book entry form. Transfers of securities between customers can then take place within the CSD, again by book entry, removing the need for physical transfers of certificates. This centralized holding of securities within a CSD allows it to function as an integral part of the securities settlement system. In the German market, the CSD is Clearstream Banking AG (referred to here as 'Clearstream').[13] Virtually all banks that engage

[10] The German name is the Frankfurter Wertpapierbörse, frequently referred to as the 'FWB'. The shares and bonds of a large number of German and international issuers can be traded on the Frankfurt Stock Exchange.

[11] Corporate actions are events or processes which relate to the issued securities of a company, such as dividends, rights issues or bonus issues of new shares, spin offs, mergers and acquisitions, etc.

[12] The role of custody banks as customers with accounts with a central securities depository means that they are often referred to in this capacity as 'depository banks'.

[13] A useful overview of the role and processes within Clearstream is available from the Clearstream 'Customer Handbook in English', available at http://www.clearstream.com/blob/10702/535f4eb198e06d8c641baf6b100fe14f/hbecomp-pdf-data.pdf. The general terms on which Clearstream acts are set out in the Clearstream General Terms and Conditions of Clearstream Banking AG, which may be accessed at http://www.clearstream.com/blob/91388/c9fd9bef5670de408635af483f476442/gtcs-cbf-en-sept-2017-data.pdf. Part VIII of the Terms and Conditions document provides that Clearstream will perform various services, including custody of securities, administration of securities and rights to securities, and performance of orders for the transfer of securities and claims to surrender of securities or of rights which shall be performed by means of book entry. It should be noted that online Clearstream documents, guides, manuals, etc are constantly updated. Where relevant, I have tried to use earlier versions of these documents from the period under discussion. Where this is not possible, I have cited the updated versions.

in the trading of German securities or which conduct custody business involving such securities maintain customer accounts with Clearstream. Investors with no direct link to Clearstream are able to make use of the services offered by Clearstream indirectly through parties who are Clearstream participants, who thus act as the investor's appointed custodian. German shares are therefore typically held using the structure illustrated in Figure 2.1.[14]

Figure 2.1 also shows the link between Clearstream and the issuer of the shares. Investors in shares of the major German companies are normally recorded in a share register maintained by the share issuing company or, more commonly, a

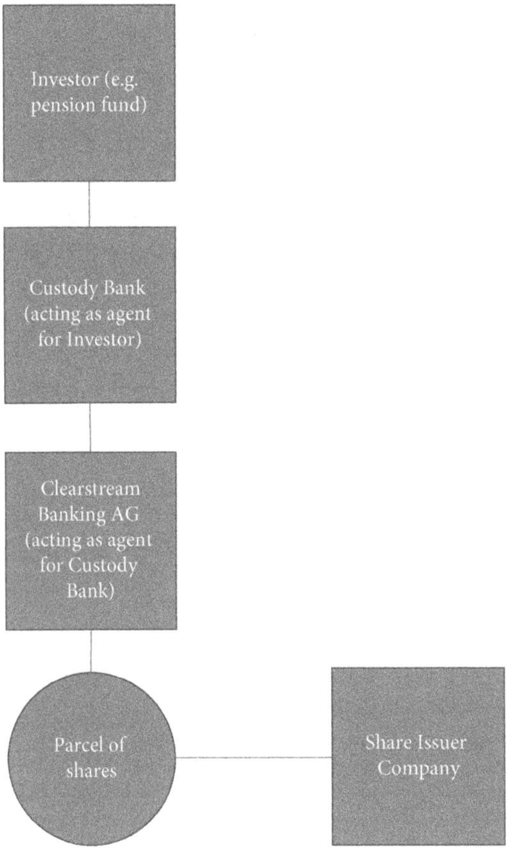

Figure 2.1. Typical holding structure for shares

[14] In the case of collective safe custody, such as that provided by Clearstream in its role as CSD for German shares, the investor is a fractional co-owner—based on the nominal amount or the number of securities it holds—of the collective holding of a class of securities. Collective safe custody is the standard form of custody in Germany.

specialist company providing registrar services to the company. It is the entry onto the share register that grants a shareholder rights over the company. Figure 2.1 illustrates the use of Clearstream to register and transfer the shareholder data on behalf of the share issuing company.

Where investors wish to buy or sell shares on the German share market, they will typically use broker-dealers. Broker-dealers will typically be members of the stock exchange on which the share is traded (which for current purposes means the Frankfurt Stock Exchange) and they will act based on client instructions. They will typically enter into buy or sell trades with specialist market makers or other broker-dealers through the Xetra electronic trading service, although broker supported floor trading is also possible. Alternatively, a seller may sell shares 'off exchange' in the OTC inter-dealer broker market. Any such sale would be entered into directly with an inter-dealer broker acting in a principal capacity.[15] The seller would therefore normally not know the identity of the buyer on the other side of the transaction. Clearing and settlement of the transaction would be handled by Clearstream.[16]

The processes that are required to complete a transaction on the exchange are relatively complex. Figure 2.2 illustrates the parties involved (and their relationships) in a simple buy/sell transaction and summarizes the key processes involved in a Frankfurt Stock Exchange trade.[17]

The first step is the placing of orders by the buyer and seller with their respective brokers and informing their custodian banks (Step 1). The orders are then executed on the exchange by the brokers (Step 2). Once the trade is agreed or 'executed' on the Frankfurt Stock Exchange, the counterparties to the trade enter the respective sell and buy instructions (including the type of shares, nominal value, and equivalent amount) into the Frankfurt Stock Exchange dealing system where they are 'matched', meaning that buy orders are paired with corresponding sell orders.[18] The Exchange will then automatically send to the brokers and to Clearstream details of the executed transaction (Step 3), which then allows the

[15] Inter-dealer brokers will generally carry out these transactions on a 'riskless principal' basis, meaning that the buy trade between IDB and seller matches the sell trade between IDB and buyer, apart from some element of profit or commission taken by the IDB.

[16] Clearstream clears and settles transactions that are both entered into on the stock exchange and that are entered into on an 'OTC' (over-the-counter, or off-exchange) basis between the parties. Clearstream may also be required to clear and settle transactions that do not involve payment in consideration for the movement of shares, such as stock lending or collateral transactions. These are referred to as 'free of payment' ('FoP') transactions. The nature of clearance and settlement functions is discussed in footnote 31 of Chapter 1.

[17] The step-by-step description of the processing of the trade is based on the description in European Central Bank, *The Payment System* at pp.88–9 and the description of the role of Clearstream Banking AG in the settlement process which is available from Clearstream at http://www.clearstream.com/blob/8320/ddf63b2bc8e8c91802549b8ddd3e67c7/bis-iosco-cbf-2013-data.pdf, Section V at pp.22–9.

[18] The process of matching will often by complicated by the use of algorithms which determine how orders are matched and subsequently completed or 'filled'.

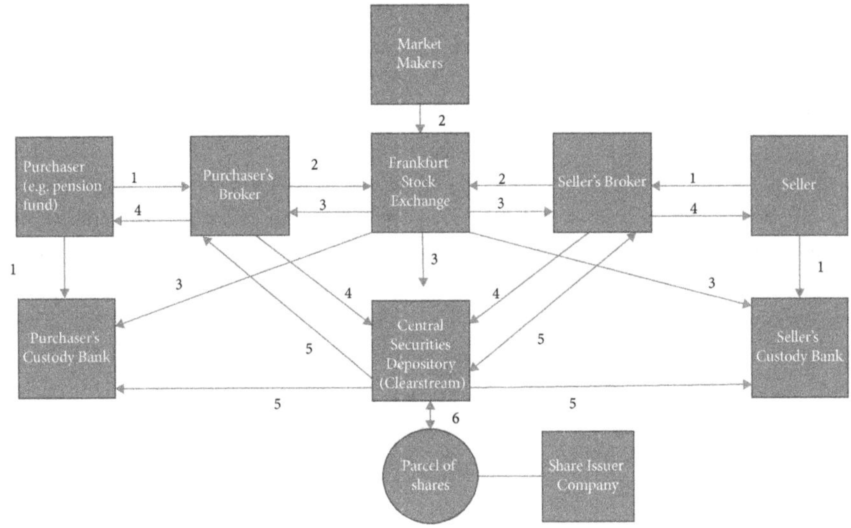

Figure 2.2. Processes in an on-exchange buy–sell transaction

commencement of the clearing phase. The brokers will send details of the trade to Clearstream and to their respective clients (Step 4). Clearstream will identify the two sides of the trade and confirm the relevant details to each broker and custodian. The information flow is designed to ensure there are no errors or differences in the details of the buy and sell sides of the trade. Once the trade has been captured, matched, compared, and confirmed, the calculation of the settlement obligation commences. Clearstream sends details of the securities and funds balances to the brokers and custodians (Step 5). This is followed by the actual settlement processes, the final delivery of the securities and funds (Step 6).[19] This takes place on an automated basis within Clearstream's settlement system.[20]

[19] For completeness, it should be noted that, since 2003, the settlement process in Clearstream involves the interposition of a central counterparty, Eurex Clearing AG, between the two parties to a securities trade. The central counterparty becomes the seller to the buyer and the buyer to the seller, with two new contracts created to replace the original single contract between the two parties to the trade (the legal process of replacing one contract with two in this way is called 'novation'). The benefits of the role of the central counterparty are the netting of trades (reducing settlement fees charged) and improved risk management given that the parties can rely on the new contract with the central counterparty and so are in consequence insulated from any default of their counterparty.

[20] From the customer's perspective, the processing of security transfers and the calculation of the corresponding funds to fulfil security transactions are both performed within Clearstream's settlement system. The ownership of securities is transferred by book entry within Clearstream in the case of instruments in collective safe custody, or by physical delivery of the certificates in question. However, cash settlement itself will be carried out using cash accounts held outside the clearance system, and central bank accounts at the Bundesbank are used for this purpose. The securities are transferred by accounting entries on the books of Clearstream. Clearstream also maintains an internal representation of the cash accounts for bookkeeping purposes which mirrors the accounts held at the Bundesbank.

A 'delivery versus payment' ('DvP') basis of settlement applies within Clearstream, meaning that the cash consideration and the shares concerned are delivered concurrently between the parties involved if and only if both the cash and the shares are each available.[21] The settlement of the transactions, and the transmission of legal ownership in the shares and cash, takes place after the successful confirmation of all debits and credits (representing share and cash movements) on the respective accounts of the customers. After the clearing and settlement process has been completed within Clearstream, the change of the name of the owner of the shares sold is communicated to the holder of the company's register of shareholders. As noted, this could be the company itself but in practice will often be a service company providing this service. The shares may be registered in the name of the beneficial owner or, as is more common, in the name of a nominee. The cycle for clearing and settling shares bought and sold on exchange in the German market is required to fall within a two-day or 'T+2' requirement.[22]

With the basic features of the German equities market described in brief, it is now possible to proceed to the German cum-ex trade itself. As outlined in Chapter 1, in markets such as Germany where the cum-ex trade has been exploited, the 'value' or benefit which the trade is designed to generate hinges on the creation and treatment of tax credits representing dividend withholding tax. During the period in which cum-ex trades were being executed in Germany (i.e. up to 2012), the tax treatment of a dividend paid by a German company was as set out in the following section.

[21] The mutual interdependency of each side of the transaction minimizes counterparty risk of each party to the other. The concurrent delivery is achieved by ensuring in Clearstream that the purchaser of the shares has confirmed all securities transfers with payment of the relevant consideration by way of matching instructions before the securities may be processed for settlement. This obviously requires that Clearstream customers have both sufficient securities cover in their custody accounts (sellers) and sufficient cash cover in their Deutsche Bundesbank accounts (buyers). If this is not the case, it is possible for sellers to engage Clearstream's automatic securities lending facility and for buyers to draw on the central bank's lending facilities, given that the cash amounts are settled via central bank accounts.

[22] Since 2014 this has been agreed as a general standard by the twenty-eight European Union states—see http://www.clearstream.com/clearstream-en/products-and-services/settlement/settlement-services/european-markets-settlement-cycle-migration-to-t-2/65826. The German T+2 standard has applied to stock-exchange transactions for some years, including the period in which cum-ex trades were carried out in the German markets (see https://www.ecb.europa.eu/pub/pdf/other/escb-cesr-standardssecurities2004en.pdf at p.26). The T+2 standard is mandated by the Conditions for Transactions on the Frankfurt Stock Exchange, which, at Section 4, require settlement of exchange transactions according to the T+2 limit (an English language version of the Conditions document is available at http://www.xetra.com/blob/1187644/650ffb91622c2637cc30c85ce8b2598b/data/2018-01-03-Conditions-for-Transactions.pdf). The T+2 standard is not required in the case of privately agreed OTC trades and a different delivery time may be agreed by the parties.

The Tax Treatment of a Dividend Paid by a German Company

(1) Withholding Tax Levied on Payment of a Dividend

Dividends paid by companies that are resident in Germany for tax purposes are subject to a flat rate withholding tax on dividends of 25 per cent together with an additional 'solidarity charge' of 5.5 per cent applied to this 25 per cent to give a final rate of 26.375 per cent.[23]

In the period leading up to 2012, the obligation to pay the withholding tax due on a dividend fell on the dividend-paying company.[24]

On the payment of a dividend, the dividend-paying company would itself, or via its paying agent (such as a bank), pay the required amount of withholding tax over to the German tax authorities. The amount of the dividend after the deduction of that withholding tax (i.e. the 'net' amount of the dividend) would then be transferred into Clearstream, where it would be passed on to the custodian banks holding accounts with Clearstream and from there to the underlying owners of the relevant shares.[25] The arrangements are illustrated diagrammatically in Figure 2.3.

(2) Taxation of the Recipient

The tax consequences which flow from receiving a German company dividend vary according to the characteristics of the recipient. The types of recipients that

[23] A company is resident in Germany for tax purposes if it maintains its registered office (as determined by its articles of incorporation) or central place of management in Germany (Section 1 (1) Corporation Tax Act). The solidarity surcharge was introduced in 1991 to finance the reunification of Germany and applies as an additional fee to German income taxes and withholding taxes. The dividend withholding tax charge is deducted at source under Section 43 (1) No. 1 and Section 50 (2) Clause 1 of the Income Tax Act as required by Section 36 (2) (2) Sentence 1 Income Tax Act. The withholding tax is technically a capital gains tax but it is referred to throughout this book as simply the 'withholding tax' on the dividend. A useful English-language version of German tax law, which also explains basic concepts and principles, is available in the volume edited by Otto H. Jacobs, Dieter Endres, Christoph Spengel, Andreas Oestreicher, Andreas Schumacher, Hannah Nusser, Pia Dorfmüller, and Barbara Zuber, *Internationale Unternehmensbesteuerung* (C.H. Beck, 2016).

[24] Section 44 Paragraph 1 Income Tax Act. Various exemptions from withholding tax would apply in specific circumstances. For example, under the EU Parent–Subsidiary Directive, no withholding tax is payable on dividends paid by a German company to another EU corporation, where the latter has held 10 per cent of the shares in the former for an uninterrupted period of twelve months preceding the distribution of dividends. As will be discussed in Chapter 4, the operation of the German withholding tax system was fundamentally reformed from 2012 with the primary goal of closing down the cum-ex trade.

[25] Information on the detailed processes within Clearstream is set out in Clearstream, 'Compensation Handbook, Corporate Action Transaction Management for Customers of Clearstream Banking AG', Frankfurt document number F-CMG04, January 2018. The Clearstream note, 'Income Processing CSD', available at http://www.clearstream.com/clearstream-en/products-and-services/asset-services/income-processing/income-processing-csd is also helpful. Further detail on the process is explored further below in connection with the manner in which sales immediately prior to dividend record date are dealt with.

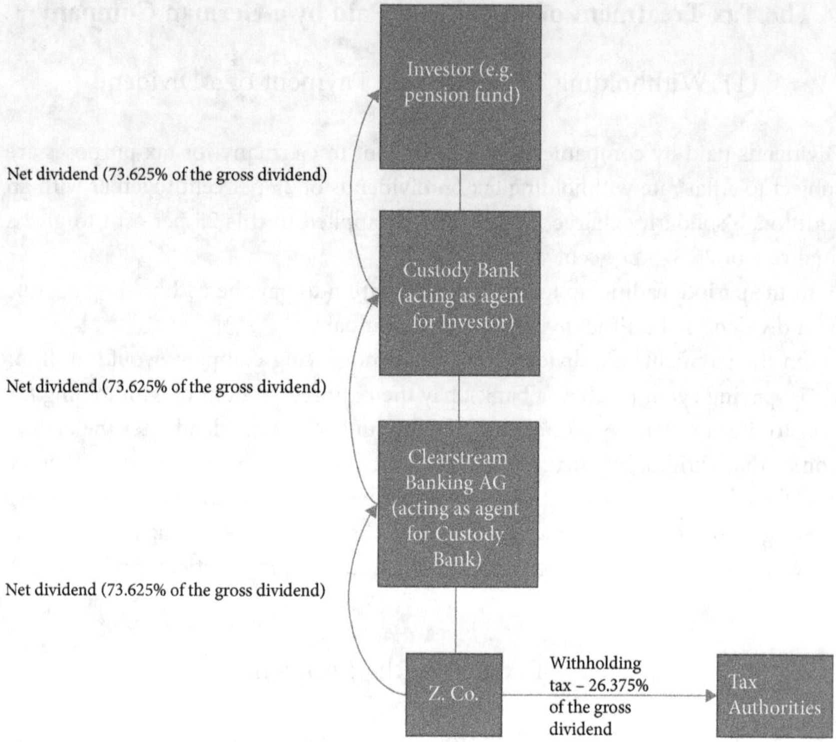

Figure 2.3. Dividend payment process

are of particular interest for the purposes of the discussion in this book are companies (particularly banks and other financial traders) and investment funds, both in Germany and overseas.

As a general matter, the deduction of the withholding tax is evidenced by a tax voucher prepared by the custodian bank acting for the owner of the shares.[26] The tax voucher itself has value, in the sense that it can be used to demonstrate an entitlement to cash reclaims and/or tax credits, as described further below.

(i) Recipients in Germany

German domestic entities regularly investing in and trading in shareholdings in German companies (investors) include banks and other financial institutions (traders) and funds such as investment funds, pension funds, and insurance companies.[27]

[26] The voucher is issued pursuant to Section 45a (2) or (3) Income Tax Act.

[27] The tax compliance affairs of taxpayers in Germany are generally overseen by the relevant local tax offices/administrations of the German states (Länder) which act on behalf of the Federal Government. The state tax administrations are managed by the state ministries of finance or senate administrations.

Companies (Banks and Financial Traders)

German banks and other financial traders are subject to tax on dividends from companies in Germany (as well as on profits from trading in German shares) and would typically pay tax at effective rates up to 33 per cent.[28] The determination of taxable income is based on the results of commercial accounting according to the German Commercial Code. Where an investor receives from a German company a dividend from which withholding tax has been deducted, a tax credit is available.[29] Where the credit mechanism cannot operate because tax is not payable, such as where the taxpayer has incurred trading losses, a refund of an amount corresponding to the withholding taxes may be made.[30] However, for the tax credit (or refund) to be available, German law requires that three conditions be satisfied. These are: (1) the recipient must have received investment income which is either taxable income or, in certain designated circumstances, exempted from tax;[31] (2) income tax must have been levied on the income by 'tax deduction'; and (3) a valid certificate must have been submitted to the tax authorities.[32] As will be seen later, the requirement in (2) that the taxpayer is entitled to a credit or refund

[28] Companies in Germany are subject to the corporate tax rate at the rate of 15%, plus a 5.5% solidarity surcharge, which results in a combined rate of 15.825%. Municipal trade tax, typically at rates between 14% and 19%, also is imposed. The effective corporate tax rate (including the solidarity surcharge and trade tax) typically ranges between 30% and 33%. The taxation of dividends in the hands of German banks and financial traders and arising from trading activity (under Section 8b Paragraph 7 of the Corporation Tax Act) stands in contrast to the general tax treatment of dividends in Germany: dividends from (and profits from the sale of shareholdings in) a domestic or a foreign corporation are exempt from taxation if at least 10 per cent of the relevant share capital is held. In cases where the shareholder is a corporation, the receipt of the dividends is exempt from taxation according to the Section 8b Paragraph 1 of the Corporation Tax Act in Germany, though a 5% amount of any dividend income is considered a non-deductible expense and is added to the profit of the company, resulting in an effective exemption of 95%. The exemption is not granted in respect of dividends received in the course of carrying on a financial trading business by banks, financial service institutions, and financial enterprises, including holding companies (in respect of shares acquired with the intention of realizing a short-term profit from trading, 'held for trading exception'), life and health insurance companies, and pension funds. German companies receiving dividends under the effective dividend exemption of 95% referred to above were not used as buyers in cum-ex trades for technical reasons that are explained in Chapter 3.

[29] The withholding tax (strictly, capital gains tax) can be considered as a kind of advance payment on the personal income tax or corporation tax under Section 31 (1) Corporation Tax Act. For this reason, Section 36 (2) of the Income Tax Act states that withholding tax on capital income tax can be credited or refunded.

[30] The circumstances in which a refund may be made are contained in Income Tax Act, Section 44a (7) and (8) though the requirements of Section 36 Paragraph 2 Number 2 of the Income Tax Act must be met—see further below at footnotes 32 and 40 (which deals with the particular case of German special funds).

[31] The general principle under German tax law is that a tax credit may be credited against taxable income. However, a tax credit is also available where the dividend receipt is specifically exempted from tax in the hands of a German corporate recipient pursuant to Section 8b Paragraph 1 of the Corporation Tax Act.

[32] The conditions are imposed by Section 36 (2) Number 2 of the Income Tax Act. The tax certificate is issued pursuant to Section 45a (2) or (3) of the Income Tax Act.

of dividend withholding tax only if that withholding tax has actually been paid is of particular significance to cum-ex trades.[33]

Funds

The tax rules applying to German investment funds are complex, though in general a principle of 'transparency' has been applied for tax purposes (though this approach has been replaced from 2018 with an entirely new tax regime for German funds).[34] This transparency principle meant that the investment fund itself was not subject to corporate income tax or trade tax. Instead, the investor in that fund is treated for tax purposes in the same way as if it had invested directly in the investments held by the fund.[35] In short, a transparent tax treatment means that the tax authorities 'look through' the investment fund, taxing the investor directly. Investors are therefore taxed according to their usual tax regimes on the fund income. For example, a corporate investor would regularly be subject to 15 per cent corporation tax plus 5.5 per cent solidarity surcharge (in total, 15.825 per cent) though would usually be exempted on dividend income.[36]

A good example of such a German investment fund, which was regularly employed in cum-ex structures, is the so-called 'special fund'.[37] A special fund is a regulated collective investment vehicle set up under the German Investment Act and subject to the supervision of the German Federal Financial Supervisory Authority (BaFin).[38] It is usually established as an unincorporated contractual type of investment scheme, meaning it has no separate legal personality. The fund would usually be managed by a German investment management company which provides the infrastructure for the special fund.[39] Special funds may be marketed to a limited number of not more than 100 institutional investors who must not be individuals. The transparent treatment of the fund is reflected in the Investment Tax Act, which provides that the same tax provisions apply to the income of an investor in a special fund as would apply to income which an investor received

[33] The requirement is imposed by Section 36 Paragraph 2 Number 2 Sentence 1 of the Income Tax Act.

[34] The new regime replaces the broad transparency of funds for German tax purposes with a new regime of taxation. The effect, given that certain investment funds will continue to be treated as transparent, is that funds will be divisible for German tax purposes into two categories: opaque funds (taxable at the fund level for the first time together with a partial exemption for investors) and special funds which will remain subject to a transparency approach.

[35] The tax-exemption is delivered by Section 11 of the Investment Tax Act.

[36] The fund income may comprise distributions, deemed distributions, and capital gains from the sale of fund shares. The semi-transparent treatment of funds for German tax purposes requires complex accounting in order to calculate correctly the amount of 'deemed distributions'.

[37] In German, Spezialfond. Under the new investment tax reform, a special fund is accorded exceptional treatment provided it meets certain regulatory and investment restrictions, allowing it to remain subject to the traditional system of semi-transparency.

[38] BaFin is a federal institution charged with the oversight and supervision of financial markets with a role that includes the supervision of banks, insurers, and other financial service providers.

[39] The management company is known as a Kapitalanlagegesellschaft, or 'KAG'.

from a direct investment in the assets held by such a fund. A special fund is tax exempt for corporate income tax and German trade tax purposes, with the result that any withholding tax suffered on dividends received from German companies is refundable.[40] Dividends from German companies would be paid to a special fund after deduction of the 26.375 per cent withholding tax. However, arrangements normally in place with the German tax authorities would allow the immediate repayment of the withholding tax to the fund's custodian bank (say, within two to three weeks). Where distributions to investors are made by a special fund, withholding tax at the same rate of 26.375 per cent falls due. If no distribution is made, the tax rules will operate to deem a distribution to have taken place at year-end.

(ii) Overseas Recipients

If a recipient (whether a bank, fund, etc) of a dividend from a German company is not resident in Germany for tax purposes and does not carry on a business through a branch in that country, then the German taxation of the recipient is limited to the withholding tax levied.[41]

Germany has an extensive double tax treaty network consisting of bilateral treaties between Germany and about ninety countries. Such tax treaties often reduce the level of permitted German withholding tax on dividends paid out of Germany. The level of the reduction varies from treaty to treaty and may also vary under a single treaty by reference to the particular type of taxpayer. In the case of Germany's double tax treaty with the United States, for example, the amount of dividend withholding tax is usually limited to 15 per cent of the gross amount of the dividend. However, where dividends from German companies are paid to US pension funds, they are paid gross, i.e. the withholding tax charge is removed completely.[42]

[40] Investment Tax Act, Section 11 (2).

[41] Under Section 49 (1) Number 5, dividend payments from a German company to a foreign resident shareholder involve a limited German tax liability, with the German tax imposed via withholding tax under Section 43 (1) Number 1 and Section 50 (2) Clause 1 of the Income Tax Act.

[42] See Article 10 of the 1989 double tax treaty between the US and Germany, available at https://www.irs.gov/businesses/international-businesses/germany-tax-treaty-documents. The exemption for pension funds was introduced by revisions to that treaty which were introduced by a protocol to the treaty in 2006. The specific provision relating to the exemption for pension funds is now in Article 10 (3) (b) of the treaty, as amended by the protocol. The theory behind the withholding tax exemption for pension funds rule is based on the fact that pension funds normally do not pay tax so cannot benefit from a foreign tax credit for withholding tax suffered. Further, since distributions from a pension fund generally do not maintain the character of the underlying income, the beneficiaries of the pension are not in a position to claim a foreign tax credit when they finally receive the pension, in many cases years after the withholding tax has been paid. Accordingly, in the absence of the exemption, the dividends would be subject to unrelieved double taxation. Though not relevant to the discussion in this book, a new German withholding tax regime for foreign investment funds came into effect on 1 January 2018 following changes made by the German Investment Tax Act. Under the new rules, and subject to certain rules, the German withholding tax will be reduced to 15% at source irrespective of the location of the fund.

Where dividend withholding tax is charged to a resident in a country with which Germany has a double tax treaty and the amount charged is in excess of the permissible rate agreed under that treaty, the German tax authorities operate a treaty refund process under which that excess is repaid in cash.[43] This requires that certain paperwork be completed and submitted in support of such a tax reclaim.[44]

The treatment of any amount of German withholding tax which is not refunded will depend on the rules of the domestic tax system in the recipient's state. It would therefore be the local tax law in the recipient's state that would determine whether any German withholding tax which has been applied but not refunded is allowed as a tax credit in the state of the recipient.

(3) The Value of German Withholding Tax

As described above, the value of German withholding tax will vary according to the status of the party who receives the dividend to which it relates. The greatest value the withholding tax can achieve is obtained by German residents able to utilize the withholding tax in full by credit or by repayment. However, the status of some overseas investors under double tax treaties with Germany may produce similar results (for example, as in the case mentioned earlier of US pension funds which suffer no German withholding tax). At the other end of the spectrum, investors resident in states with no double tax treaty with Germany may be subject to the German withholding tax in full, with no ability to make a reclaim. In some cases, they may also have no ability to claim a credit for the withholding tax suffered in their home state, meaning that the full amount of German withholding tax is an outright cost to them.

These wide variations in the treatment of German withholding tax, coupled with the relatively high level of dividends (and therefore also correspondingly high amounts of withholding tax) that have been noted earlier, have led to dividend arbitrage activity of the type discussed in Chapter 1. Dividend arbitrage, it will be recalled, involves the transfer of cum-dividend shares from parties that cannot reduce the incidence of German withholding tax, or cannot benefit from a tax

[43] The withholding tax is refunded to non-residents pursuant to Income Tax Act, Section 44a (9) and Section 50d (1). The system of dealing with refunds to non-residents is administered by the Federal Central Tax Office (the BZSt), which is a subordinate authority of the Federal Finance Administration (the BMF), the latter being the highest authority in the federal administration of finance whose responsibilities include setting tax, financial, and financial-market policies.

[44] The documentation includes a formal claim form; evidence of receipt of the dividend, including details on the security type, gross amount of payment, date of payment, and amount of tax withheld; a power of attorney where the claimant is completing the claim form on behalf of the beneficial owner; and a questionnaire. Detailed information on the process for reclaims is available from the German federal tax authorities via the link http://www.steuerliches-info-center.de/EN/SteuerrechtFuerInvestoren/steuerrechtFuerInvestoren_node.html.

credit where it is suffered, to parties that can. In Germany, such dividend arbitrage transactions are sometimes also referred to as 'cum-cum' transactions to distinguish them from cum-ex. Cum-ex transactions are founded on the specific dividend adjustment mechanism discussed in Chapter 1 and in that sense cum-ex and cum-cum transactions are quite different. However, one important similarity is that both strategies are aimed at directing tax credits to the most tax advantaged parties. In practice, this means that the cum-ex trade would be structured so as to ensure that the tax credit generated by it arises in the hands of a party best able to extract the maximum value from it.

Introduction to Cum-Ex in the German Market

As Chapter 1 has explained, the settlement system malfunction exploited by cum-ex arises in a relatively narrow set of circumstances, namely where (1) shares with the right to receive the dividend (cum-dividend) are sold short immediately before a dividend record date and (2) after the dividend record date, shares that have paid out their dividend (i.e. ex-dividend shares) are then borrowed by the seller and delivered to the buyer in order to fulfil that earlier cum-dividend agreement.[45] In such a situation, the objective of the cum-ex trade is to trigger the operation of the dividend adjustment mechanism in the settlement system so that it generates valuable tax credits which are not matched by any actual payment of withholding tax. All these essential points are encompassed in the cum-ex trade in the German market, where the settlement mechanisms operated in Clearstream.

Following the approach adopted in Chapter 1, the discussion below contrasts the *intended* operation of the relevant mechanisms in the settlement system within Clearstream before considering the situation targeted by the cum-ex trade. The discussion draws on the explanation of the clearing and settlement role of Clearstream that has been explained earlier in this chapter.

Intended Operation of the Clearstream System

Where an existing investor sells shares it already holds in a German company on one of the two business days immediately prior to the dividend record date, the

[45] As will be discussed in Chapter 3, these two elements (the cum-dividend short sale and the ex-dividend borrowing of shares) are commonly seen in cum-ex trades but are not prerequisites to the triggering of the systems malfunction. Alternative mechanisms can be used to replicate the same effect of each element. For example, a carefully timed but deliberately 'failed' trade can in certain instances be used as a surrogate for the short sale. It is also possible to dispense with the stock borrowing in some cases by buying in (rather than borrowing in) the ex-dividend shares and then using those shares to deliver to the buyer in the cum-ex trade.

transaction cannot settle in Clearstream in time for the buyer to become the shareholder of record on the dividend record date. This is because of the time lag created by the T+2 settlement cycle. That cycle means that, where the transaction is agreed on the day before the dividend record date, it will not settle in Clearstream until the day after the dividend record date. Nonetheless, the buyer is buying on cum-dividend terms and so is legally entitled to the relevant dividend. In such a case, the steps involved in the sale of the shares (whether on the Frankfurt Stock Exchange or in an 'off-exchange' sale of shares) will follow the process described earlier.[46] The dividend payment on the shares which are the subject of the sale agreement will also be paid within Clearstream and via the custodian banks, again in the manner set out above. However, because the seller actually holding the shares remains formally recognized as the recorded owner of the shares on the dividend record date (and so is listed as an owner entitled to a dividend on the shares sold), an adjustment relating to that dividend will need to be made within the Clearstream settlement system. The nature of that dividend adjustment mechanism in Clearstream is at the heart of the cum-ex trade.

In this situation where there is a sale of shares immediately prior to the dividend record date, the dividend processing within Clearstream involves what is in effect a two-step approach. First, having had the cash amount of the net dividend transferred into Clearstream by the dividend paying company or its agent, Clearstream allocates the dividend based on the listing of owners of the shares booked in Clearstream at the end of the dividend record day (which is often the day of the dividend-paying company's annual general meeting). Where, as is often the case, the shares are held by Clearstream customers for underlying owners, the net dividend would then be paid up the chain of ownership until it is paid to the underlying owner. This is exactly what is illustrated by Figure 2.3 above.

The second step in the Clearstream process adjusts for trades which are both (1) entered into just before the dividend record date (these are therefore 'cum-dividend' trades) and (2) settled after the dividend record date.[47] The adjustment is obviously necessary because of the time lag caused by the T+2 settlement period, as explained earlier. The purpose of this second-step adjustment is to cancel the seller's entitlement to the dividend and instead to substitute a new dividend entitlement created in the name (and account) of the buyer. As described earlier

[46] Where sales are made on the Frankfurt Stock Exchange, the operation of the T+2 settlement cycle follows from Frankfurt Stock Exchange rules. 'Off-exchange' or 'over-the-counter' (OTC) sales are not bound by the Exchange rules and so are not necessarily subject to T+2 settlement as the parties may agree shorter or longer settlement periods, though in practice the parties would in cum-ex trades use Clearstream to settle the trades adopting the T+2 settlement period.

[47] A number of relevant details relating to the process may be found in Clearstream's 'Compensation Handbook'. The latest version of which (July 2019) is available online at https://www.clearstream.com/resource/blob/1316782/08a424c5b61fe77d19385e550a56a842/compensation-handbook-cata-en-data.pdf

in connection with the process for clearing and settling trades, Clearstream will be able to identify trades which require this second-step adjustment based on the trade data that comes to Clearstream automatically from the Frankfurt Stock Exchange (or from the parties or their custodian banks in the case of an 'off-exchange' transaction).

Where the Clearstream settlement process identifies a trade date just before what is described in Clearstream as the 'entitlement' date (i.e. the dividend record date), the adjustments will be made automatically in the settlements system through postings in the clearing members' accounts. This is achieved by the posting of a 'market claim' in Clearstream for the dividend from the seller's custodian bank.[48] The amount specified under the market claim would be debited (i.e. expensed) to the Clearstream account of the seller's custodian bank. As a result of the adjustment, the amount of the claim would correspondingly be credited as income to the Clearstream account of the buyer's custodian bank.[49] As with the initial allocation of the dividends under the first step described above, any adjustments required under this second step are made on a 'net' basis meaning that the market claim is for the net cash amount of the dividend after deduction of the withholding tax or, put another way, in the form of 73.625 per cent of the gross (pre-withholding-tax) dividend.

The adjustments considered above deal with the cash element of the dividend. It is also necessary that the process deals with the tax credit element of the dividend. The withholding tax triggered by the payment of a dividend would be paid over to the tax authorities by the dividend-paying company. A tax voucher, evidencing that withholding tax has been withheld, would then be produced for the buyer by the buyer's custodian bank under this second-step adjustment process. Given the operation of the Clearstream settlement system and the participation of both the buyer's and seller's custodian banks in the claim/reverse claim process described above, the seller's custodian bank would be aware of the right of the buyer to the dividend (and the reversal of the seller's dividend receipt). It would therefore recognize that the seller is not entitled to any tax voucher.

It is helpful to illustrate this dividend adjustment process in a worked example. Figure 2.4 shows the seller agreeing to sell a parcel of shares it holds in, for example, the German company Siemens. The sale is entered into on 15 January, the day before the dividend record date the next day, on 16 January (Step 1). The resulting process to transfer the shares and cash consideration in order to settle the sale transaction is not shown in this diagram but is exactly the same as the

[48] A market claim will be made wherever a security is traded 'cum' but is delivered (i.e. settled) after the entitlement (dividend record) date—Clearstream, 'Compensation Handbook', at p.1-1. The detailed process for market claims and reverse claims is set out in the Compensation Handbook.

[49] The dividend adjustment process is often referred to by market participants as 'auto-comp' (auto-compensation). This is derived from the description generally used in Clearstream guidance as 'automatic compensation managed by local CSD'.

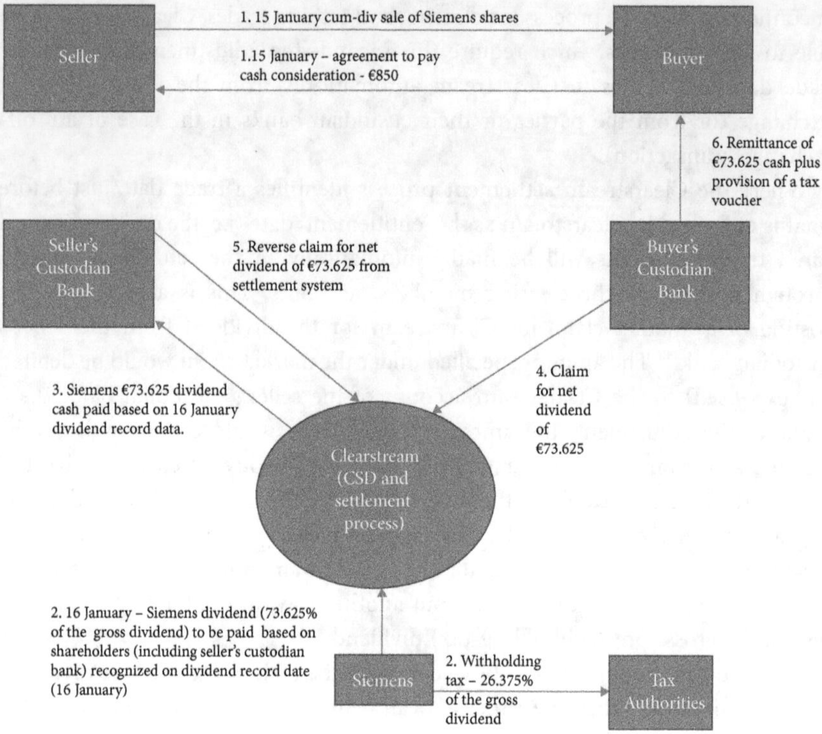

Figure 2.4. Dividend adjustment process in Clearstream

process steps shown earlier in Figure 2.2. However, the detailed cash movements relating to the dividend and dividend adjustment are shown in Figure 2.4. At Step 2, Siemens pays out the dividend. This involves two separate movements of cash. Siemens pays the withholding tax due in respect of the dividend to the German tax authorities. At the same time, the net dividend is paid to Clearstream by Siemens for onward distribution to the shareholders shown on the company's register on the dividend record date. Parties appearing on the register include the seller's custodian bank (acting for the seller) and so (at Step 3) that custodian bank receives the amount of the net dividend due. For simplicity, the amount of the gross dividend is assumed to be €100, meaning the net dividend paid will be €73.625, after the withholding tax of €26.375 is deducted. The buyer's custodian bank will recognize that the trade was booked before the dividend record date but settled after it and so a claim will be generated within the Clearstream system on behalf of the buyer for the net dividend (Step 4). At Step 5, a 'reverse claim' will be generated, again within Clearstream, against the seller's custodian bank, which will be debited €73.625, the amount of its net dividend receipt at Step 3. The seller has now been both credited and debited €73.625, thus flattening its cash position on the dividend to zero. The effect of steps 4 and 5 is that the seller is debited, and the buyer is credited, €73.625, the net amount of the dividend. The credit for the buyer is recorded in the Clearstream system and in the books of the buyer's custodian bank as dividend income. Finally, at Step 6, the cash amount collected representing the net dividend is made available to the buyer. A tax voucher would also be prepared by the buyer's custodian bank and made available to the buyer at Step 6. This tax voucher evidences the withholding tax already suffered on the dividend (see Step 2). That tax voucher would be indistinguishable from the tax voucher that is created in respect of any dividend on German shares that is passed through the chain of ownership as described earlier.

As Figure 2.4 shows, the overall result delivered by the settlement system is to make the required adjustments given that it is the buyer who is (rightly) recognized as the owner of the dividend, having purchased the shares cum-dividend in advance of the record date relating to the dividend. Correspondingly, the seller has no entitlement to any dividend at all.[50] The settlement system merely attempts to close a gap in the formal recognition of share ownership created by the two-day lag between a share purchase taking place and its later registration in the settlement system. Having set out the intended operation of the settlement system in Clearstream, it is now possible to examine how this intended result was turned on its head in the creation of the cum-ex trade.

The Short Sale Situation—Unintended Operation of the System

What happens if the seller is selling 'short', i.e. selling a parcel of shares which the seller does not own at the time of the sale? As discussed in Chapter 1, short sales are routinely seen in the capital markets, so the mere fact of a short sale would not be unusual. However, given that the seller has sold the shares short, the seller would need to be able to obtain a parcel of shares to fulfil the contract with the buyer.[51] In this situation, the shares would normally be obtained by a borrowing of the shares, as explained in Chapter 1. By virtue of the size of the German equities market, there are significant holdings of German shares in the hands of institutional investors. This means there will be lenders of large pools of shares.[52]

[50] The result delivered accords with the requirements of Section 20 of the Regulations for Transactions on the Frankfurt Stock Exchange. Section 20 requires, in relation to the delivery obligation, that securities be delivered with all rights and obligations pertaining to them at the time at which the transaction has been entered into. See http://www.xetra.com/blob/1187644/650ffb91622c2637cc30c85ce8b2598b/data/2018-01-03-Conditions-for-Transactions.pdf at p.11.

[51] If the seller cannot locate such a parcel of shares, the short sale contract cannot be fulfilled and the seller may could be subject to fines and, for repeat infractions, regulatory sanctions.

[52] In 2016, for example, there were $290 billion of lendable German shares. In 2015, revenues from stock lending activity in Germany totalled $632 million. See Datalend, *The Purple: A Datalend Research Publication* Issue 1, September 2016, available at https://issuu.com/equilend/docs/data_magazine_digital_issuu?e=25574162/38985667.

If large pools of German shares are available and can be lent out to fulfil short sales, the next question relates to the mechanics, and particularly the timing, of any lending transaction and the onward delivery of the borrowed shares to the buyer. Any shares borrowed by a short seller must be capable of being moved from the lender to the short seller (in borrowing the shares) and onwards from the short seller to the buyer (in fulfilling the short sale) within the required T+2 settlement cycle. The critical question is therefore what time period is needed to transfer shares under a borrowing arrangement (i.e. from lender to borrower) and also needed to transfer the shares on to the buyer? The answer, surprisingly, is that shares can be transferred from a lender to the seller, and from the seller to the buyer, on an immediate basis (i.e. on a T+0 basis) in the case of each limb of the transaction. In other words, the shares can both be borrowed by a short seller and then delivered to a buyer within the space of a single day.

It may seem initially puzzling that, within a single day, shares may be both transferred from a lender to the short seller (as borrower), and then again transferred from the short seller to the buyer given that the underlying contract for the sale of shares is subject to the more protracted T+2 settlement period. The obvious question is why the share-purchase settlement cycle is so relatively long compared to the time it takes to move the borrowed shares from the account of the lender to the account of the short seller and then from the account of the short seller to the account of the buyer. The answer to this question lies in the functions and processes that are involved in share purchases as compared to share lending arrangements. Significantly, what is involved in the borrowing of the shares and the delivery to the buyer is much simpler than the processes involved in the T+2 settlement cycle.

The T+2 settlement cycle which applies to the agreement originally struck between seller and buyer is a market convention designed to give sufficient time for the completion of all the clearing and settlement processes described earlier in this chapter. These include the processes of capturing, matching, comparing, reconciling, and confirming the trade, calculating the settlement obligations and giving effect to the simultaneous movements of cash and securities. In common with a number of developed capital markets where there is significant trading by foreign institutions, it may be difficult to confirm trades in a timely manner due to differences in time zones, differences in national holidays, and the involvement, as is very common, of multiple parties and intermediaries. By design, the T+2 settlement cycle allows the time to accommodate all these constraints. Although standardized settlement cycles such as T+2 and T+3 are widely adopted in global markets, they are purely a convention and do not indicate the highest speed at which a parcel of securities can actually be transferred. Whilst the period of settlement cycles has narrowed in recent years, a concern has been that without sufficient time being allowed for all of the formalities involved in a transfer, a settlement cycle which is too short may cause an increase in settlement failures, interrupting the smooth running of the market and triggering penalties for market participants.

The functions involved in borrowing shares and then delivering them to a buyer are generally much simpler than those involved in the T+2 cycle for share purchases and settlements referred to above. When a short seller intends to borrow shares, the short seller's custodian bank would normally check either manually or through an automated locate service whether a potential lending agent has the relevant shares available to lend. This is usually a bank acting as lending agent for one or more institutional lenders. Assuming the shares are available, the lending agent will book a delivery of the shares to the seller's custodian bank and that custodian bank will book an expected receipt for the parcel of shares. The parties will generate accompanying messages in the inter-bank SWIFT messaging system containing all the necessary information relating to the transfer (i.e. identity of the shares, quantity, price, account details, etc). The settlement staff at the lending agent will then approve, usually through an automated tool, all the matching deliveries and the delivery of the lent shares will have been achieved.[53] The subsequent onward delivery of the shares by the short seller to the buyer is simply one of the many processes that are dealt with in the T+2 settlement cycle. When the parcel of borrowed shares arrives at the seller's custodian bank, it will be matched off against the separate short sale transaction which was set up earlier to reflect the settlement obligations under the trade between the short seller and the buyer. With the shares now available in the short seller's account, the exchange of cash for shares will take place, involving a transfer of the shares to the account of the buyer. This is achieved by book entries.

At one level, the ability of the seller to both borrow the shares and deliver them to the seller on a same-day basis means that the short sale can comfortably be settled within the T+2 period by the borrowing of shares, even if the seller is not able to find a lender of the shares until as late as two days after the short sale to the buyer. However, the ability for same-day settlement of both the stock loan and the delivery of the borrowed shares to the buyer also has much more profound implications. Specifically, it means that, in certain narrow circumstances, a cum-dividend short sale can be settled by an *ex-dividend* borrow of shares—i.e. by a borrowing of shares on which the person owning those shares has *already received* the dividend. That person lending the shares is neither the short seller nor the

[53] This description of the lending process is somewhat summarized but contains the essential steps. Since no exchange is involved in a securities lending transaction, the parties are able to move securities at will and very rapidly. The relevant deliveries of the shares will be booked as free of payment (FOP) deliveries even though there will be collateral obligations which the borrower has in respect of its borrows from the lender. Each of the seller's custodian bank and the lending agent will record in their systems the corresponding return obligation relating to the borrowed shares. This is the liability of the borrower and the lending agent's receivable. These will remain open until the shares are returned.

buyer but a person who, at the time of the short sale two days earlier, actually held the shares.

These narrow circumstances can be illustrated using exactly the same facts as given in Figure 2.4, but with the critical difference that the seller is not selling shares it already holds but rather is selling short and so must borrow the shares it delivers to the buyer.

In the example as now modified (shown in Figure 2.5) the seller is on 15 January (Step 1) selling short the shares (on cum-dividend terms) to the buyer. The buyer may not be aware that the seller is selling short and so, as in Figure 2.4, would expect to become the owner of the shares from the time of that agreement of the 15th and so be entitled to the upcoming dividend. However, as before, the time lag in the settlement system means that the shares cannot be registered in the name of buyer on the record date. As explained in Figure 2.4, this triggers the dividend adjustments in Clearstream. These dividend adjustments in Clearstream (illustrated as steps 4 and 5 in Figure 2.5) are exactly the same as those shown in Figure 2.4. Specifically, no difference is caused to the operation of those adjustments by the short sale, a point which is of critical significance to the success of the cum-ex trade. At Step 6, the amount of the net dividend is paid to the buyer together with a tax voucher, exactly as in the earlier example.[54] However, the net

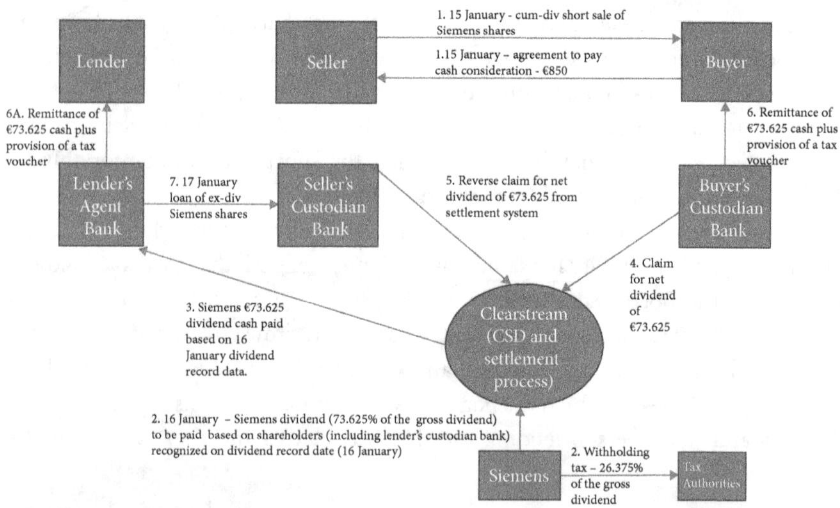

Figure 2.5. The cum-ex trade (2)

[54] However, given that the lender of the shares receives the real 'net dividend' the payment to the buyer of what appears in systems terms to be a net dividend might more appropriately be regarded as a form of system-generated 'dividend' or dividend compensation payment.

dividend and tax voucher are also passed simultaneously (at Step 6A) to the lender of the shares before they are later lent on *ex-dividend* terms to the seller. The borrowing of the shares is shown separately at Step 7.[55] The seller's custodian bank will then use those borrowed shares and deliver them to buyer (this step is not included in Figure 2.5).

The critical differences in the facts illustrated in Figure 2.5 as compared to those illustrated in Figure 2.4 are (a) the short sale and (b) the borrowing by the seller of ex-dividend shares to fulfil the short sale to the buyer. In Figure 2.4, the seller sold shares it already held so there was no short sale and therefore no need for a borrowing of shares. As Figure 2.5 demonstrates, the impact of these differences is profound. The result (shown at steps 6 and 6A in the diagram) is that a tax voucher representing a tax credit is now available to the buyer *and also* to the lender of the shares. There is only one parcel of shares in Figure 2.5, but there are now *two* tax credits: *two* parties are each getting what seems to be the same dividend on the same parcel of shares—namely the real dividend received (before the stock loan) by the lender and the system-generated dividend received by the buyer.[56] This result is made possible by the operation of two features of the settlement system. One is the ability of the seller to borrow the shares ex-dividend (due to the 'T+0' or same-day settlement of the borrowed shares) and the second is the operation of the dividend adjustment process in Clearstream. The settlement process, including the dividend adjustment process, operates in exactly the same way in both examples. However, the effect of this operation in the circumstances shown in Figure 2.5 is completely different. Here the settlement process in Clearstream does not operate to take a dividend from a seller who was not entitled to it (because of a cum-dividend sale) and put it in the hands of the entitled party (the buyer) (as in the previous Figure 2.4). Rather, in this situation the dividend adjustment process creates and moves what is in effect a 'system-generated' dividend within Clearstream.[57] Clearstream operates as if it were *transferring* a dividend from the seller to the buyer. However, because of the shorting and subsequent borrowing of ex-dividend shares, the short seller was never going to receive a dividend in any event. The effect is that the system generates or manufactures a dividend and, critically, a valuable tax credit receipt. Given that, as described earlier, such a tax credit could give rise to

[55] The share borrowing is illustrated as Step 7 in Figure 2.5 but in practice may not take place in the sequential order indicated. The share borrowing is independent of the Clearstream dividend adjustments and so might be made prior to or at the same time as those adjustments.

[56] This situation breaches the fundamental dividend rules discussed in Chapter 1. As noted above, this system-generated dividend may be regarded as a dividend compensation payment. A payment equal to the amount of the net dividend is taken from the seller's custodian bank and credited to the buyer's custodian bank which issues what is in effect a second tax voucher.

[57] The system-generated nature of what is referred to here as the 'dividend' which is transferred to the buyer might be interpreted as the reason for construing the payment as not a dividend as such but some form of compensation payment for the absence of a real dividend. As will be discussed more fully in chapters 3 and 4, this interpretation was pursued in the German law designed to regulate these payments.

a cash refund or be used to offset an existing tax bill, this is equivalent to the system-generation of free money.

In this situation the seller has by contract promised the buyer that it will deliver shares 'cum-dividend' but obviously by borrowing and delivering ex-dividend shares it cannot fulfil that promise. Instead the seller relies on the automatic operation of the dividend adjustment mechanism in the Clearstream system to complete the cum-dividend terms of the contract.[58]

It is notable that the Clearstream dividend adjustment processes put the responsibility for creating the withholding tax certificate on the buyer's custodian bank. Obviously, this is a different party to the party which deducts withholding tax in the first place (i.e. the dividend paying company—which in the example is Siemens- or its bank) and different to the seller entering into the short sale. Given that the dividend adjustment mechanism in Clearstream could not distinguish between real holders selling shares they own and short sellers selling shares they do not own, the buyer's custodian bank would have no way of knowing whether there has been any actual payment of withholding tax corresponding to the tax voucher it creates for the buyer.[59]

In spite of these uncertainties for the buyer and the buyer's custodian, it is the seller, not the buyer, which benefits from the 'system-generation' of a dividend tax credit within the Clearstream system. This is because the cash amount of the net dividend, together with the amount of the tax credit, would normally be reflected in the cum-dividend sale price agreed between the parties at the time of the sale. The buyer would therefore have paid the seller for the shares and the dividend (plus the amount of the tax credit) in agreeing to buy the shares on cum-dividend terms. The gain or benefit from the settlement system malfunction which is realized by the seller stems from the difference between what the buyer will include in the purchase price to reflect the impending dividend (say, 100 per cent of the gross dividend) and the amount the seller will be charged in Clearstream under the operation of the dividend adjustment (73.625 per cent of the gross dividend). That difference is of course an amount equal to the tax credit (26.375 per cent of the gross dividend), and it is pocketed by the seller.

The implications of this situation are fundamental and create the opportunity for the cum-ex trade: a short seller is apparently able to engineer the result that *both* buyer and lender will each derive a 'dividend' on the same (single) parcel of

[58] Clearstream provides securities lending and borrowing programmes to its customers. There is an automated fails lending service (Automated Securities Lending Programme, ASL) which is available for OTC and stock-exchange transactions that are to be settled against payment. There is also a strategic lending service (Strategic Securities Lending Programme, SSL) where loans are initiated on a case-by-case basis upon request to Clearstream from the borrower. See http://www.clearstream.com/blob/8320/ddf63b2bc8e8c91802549b8ddd3e67c7/bis-iosco-cbf-2013-data.pdf at p.4.

[59] The settlement system operates as if it simply assumed a dividend has flowed to the (short) seller, and it therefore makes adjustments to the assumed position of the parties to reflect their assumed cum-dividend sale.

securities as described above, thus generating additional valuable tax credits.[60] The vital ingredients of the trade are two: (1) a short sale just before the dividend record date, and (2) a settlement of that short sale using ex-dividend borrowed shares obtained two days later.[61]

Position under German Tax Law

The discussion so far sets out how the Clearstream settlement system operated. The immediate question, however, was whether the system-generated dividend—and particularly the tax credit which accompanied it—would be respected in the hands of the buyer for German tax purposes. This would be essential if the apparent tax credit was to be repaid in cash or allowed as a credit to reduce an existing tax liability.[62] The view generally adopted by German tax specialists advising on the cum-ex trade was that the dividend and tax credit should indeed be respected for all relevant tax purposes in Germany.[63]

The German tax technical analysis to support this characterization of the cum-ex trade was generally provided in legal opinions from German tax consultants or law firms addressing the position of the buyer or the seller. The main conclusions typically reflected in those opinions were as follows:[64]

(i) In Relation to the Buyer

The critical issue in the German tax analysis was the status of the system-generated dividend payment in the hands of the buyer. The tax position on that

[60] As noted in footnote 57 of this chapter, given that the real dividend would have been paid to the lender of the shares, the apparent 'dividend' paid to the buyer might more correctly be regarded as some form of system-generated dividend compensation payment. This analysis, and its implications for the cum-ex trade, later became a significant focus of the analysis of the trade and is discussed further in Chapter 4.

[61] As a practical matter, it would be possible for a seller to enter into a short sale immediately before a dividend record date having already lined up a share borrowing transaction after the dividend record date. This would remove any risk of not being able to arrange a suitable borrowing of the relevant shares after entering into the short sale.

[62] See the earlier discussion in this chapter on the availability and permitted uses of a tax credit relating to withholding tax suffered in respect of a dividend paid by a German resident company. In principle, the implications of the system-generated dividend (including the status of the withholding tax credit) would also be an issue for the tax systems of other states to the extent buyers in those states receiving the system-generated tax credits sought to use those credits against their tax liabilities in those states. This is a point which is discussed in Chapter 3.

[63] The position generally adopted would be later reassessed and also subject to litigation as discussed in Chapter 4.

[64] Much of the German tax authority for the German tax analysis was not specifically derived from judgments, legislative notes, etc that dealt specifically with the situation of shares that are cleared and settled through an official clearing system such as Clearstream, but generally it was concluded that the principles of the analysis should be the same.

point was determined by analysing the time at which the buyer should properly be regarded as the owner of the shares purchased.[65] Where shares are purchased from an *existing* holder, it was taken as clear under German law that the buyer should be regarded as the true economic or 'beneficial' owner of the shares from the time the shares are purchased. This meant that if the shares are purchased just before the dividend record date, the dividend is owned by, and should be allocated to, the buyer. This raised the question whether this analysis would still apply to the rather different situation where the seller was shorting the shares to the buyer, as in the cum-ex trade. The question arose because a short seller, at the time of entering into the contract, would generally be in no position to deliver any ownership rights in shares to the buyer given that there are then no shares in the seller's hands to deliver. However, in the case of short sale transactions executed on the exchange, it was concluded that the same analysis should apply.[66] In reaching this conclusion, reliance was generally placed on a decision of the Federal Finance Court of 15 December 1999.[67] The court decided that the beneficial ownership passes at the time of the conclusion of any sale contract. The view taken was that the decision was equally relevant to short sale contracts.[68] Further support for this interpretation was derived from a clarification in the legislator's notes to the Annual Tax Act of 2007, to the effect that the legal position is exactly the same whether the seller is selling short or not.[69] The reliance on those

[65] The attribution of dividend income is dealt with by Section 20 (2a) Income Tax Act up to and including 2009 and then from 2009 pursuant to Section 20 (5) Income Tax Act, whose wording is identical. These provisions stipulate that it is the relevant shareholder that derives any dividends and that the shareholder is determined by asking to whom the shares are attributable pursuant to Section 39 of the General Tax Code at the time of the dividend decision. It is that person who is to be regarded as receiving the dividend income within Section 20 (1) (1) Income Tax Act. Section 39 contains the tax provisions relating to the German concept of beneficial ownership ('wirtschaftliches Eigentum'). Under Section 39, ownership for tax purposes is generally based on the civil-law ownership, though this is overridden and ownership is assigned to a person other than the legal owner if such a person is able to exclude the legal owner from the risks and rewards of the asset (e.g. in relation to the dividend entitlement, voting, etc).

[66] The ability to enforce the specific performance of the seller's delivery obligations under the relevant Exchange regulations was interpreted as equivalent to holding the underlying shares.

[67] See BFH of 15/12/1999, IR 29/97, Federal Tax Gazette, II 2000, p.527.

[68] As will be explored in Chapter 4, the later technical assessment of the cum-ex trade by the tax authorities and the courts would lead to a fundamental distinction between system-generated 'dividends' paid in the period until the end of 2006 as distinct from those paid in the period 2007–11. This was attributable to the interpretation of those system-generated payments as being in reality dividend compensation payments. In the period to the end of 2006, there were no rules dealing with such payments and they would not qualify as investment income on which withholding tax could be reclaimed. From 2007, however, such rules were introduced treating dividend compensation payments broadly like dividend payments and subject to their own withholding regime. The 2007 rules are discussed further in chapters 3 and 4, though are of less relevance to the tax opinions discussed here, as these opinions rested generally on a particular interpretation of Section 39 of the General Tax Code (which has been discussed in footnote 65 of this chapter) based on the decision of the Federal Finance Court of 15 December 1999.

[69] The relevant 2007 legislative provisions represented an early attempt to regulate cum-ex trades. The notes in the Annual Tax Act 2007 relating to the new provisions are discussed further in chapters 3 and 4. The conclusion that the buyer is the beneficial or real owner of the shares from the time of

legislator's notes was also a factor in the extension of the conclusion to include trades executed off exchange, i.e. OTC trades.[70]

The view that under German tax law the buyer should be regarded as the true economic or beneficial owner of the stock from the time of the contract (i.e. the trade date) was regarded as not being affected by the fact that the actual settlement date occurs later (under the T+2 settlement cycle in Germany, two days later).[71] This was so even though the materially later settlement date meant it might be possible for a third party (such as the lender of ex-dividend shares in a typical cum-ex transaction) to have received the real dividend on the shares that were ultimately delivered to the buyer. No significance was attached to the materially later settlement date because, first, as from the moment of the sale of the shares, all risks and rewards in them are fixed, and, second, the settlement delay is attributable to the standardized technical rules of the market.[72]

If, according to this analysis, the buyer can be regarded as the true or economic owner of the shares as from the date of purchase, the consequence is that the buyer should be treated for German tax purposes as the owner of the (system-generated) dividend and entitled to exploit the full benefit from the ownership of the dividend and accompanying tax credit.[73]

concluding the purchase contract might seem somewhat odd where the seller is selling short as clearly the real owner of the shares in such a situation could not be the seller given the nature of the 'short' sale. The seller would not have borrowed the shares until a later time, typically after the dividend record date, and so would not yet be the owner of shares or in a position to exercise control over the shares—see Section 20 (5) Income Tax Act. However, as a practical matter, it would normally be expected that a buyer would be unable to differentiate between situations where shares are bought from an existing shareholder and where shares are bought from a short seller. As noted in footnote 68 of this chapter, the introduction of the 2007 rules dealing with dividend compensation payments would later prove to be of critical relevance in the assessment of cum-ex trades by reference to the two periods, namely up to the end of 2006 and from 2007 to the end of 2011.

[70] In the case of OTC sales and purchases, where the Exchange regulations do not apply and there is no such right to specific performance, support for a similar conclusion was taken to follow from the scheme of the 2007 rules imposing withholding tax on dividend compensation payments, given that the buyer receiving the dividend would be regarded as receiving 'other dividend earnings' irrespective of whether the transaction was executed on exchange or OTC. The 2007 rules are discussed further in chapters 3 and 4.

[71] In cases where the shares were acquired by the buyer under a physically settled derivatives transaction such as under a futures contract, the relevant date would be the date of the expiry of the contract. Such derivatives contracts were employed in varieties of the basic cum-ex transaction illustrated in Figure 2.5 and often have longer settlement cycles (up to T+4). These contracts are discussed in Chapter 3.

[72] The significance in this context of the trade date was considered to be confirmed by the Federal Fiscal Court decision of 15 December 1999, I R 29/97 (Federal Tax Gazette II 2000, 527). The judgment of the Federal Fiscal Court in 2007 was taken to reaffirm this view (see judgment of 20 November 2007, I R 85/05, BFH/NV 2008, 551). Some tax opinions also took comfort from the later Federal Ministry of Finance tax circular of 5 May 2009 (IV C 1 S 2252/09/10003, DOK 2009/0288260, Federal Tax Gazette I 2009, 631) on the basis that this decree also indicates the decisive nature of the trade date. It was recognized that the analysis would be different in the case of OTC trades given that the Exchange rules would not apply, but a similar conclusion was reached as explained above.

[73] The position adopted was that the proper time to allocate the dividend to the buyer was at Clearstream's close of business on the dividend record date given that, under Clearstream's general

In the earlier discussion of the requirements that must be met before a tax credit (or refund) is available in respect of a dividend, it was noted that one of the preconditions is that withholding tax must actually have been deducted and paid over to the tax authority.[74] This led to the question whether, in the absence of the actual deduction of withholding tax, there was a risk that the buyer might have no ability to seek a credit (or refund) for the amount recorded as withholding tax. However, it was generally concluded by those writing the tax opinions in support of the cum-ex trade that the seller (or seller's agent) had complied with all applicable withholding tax laws, was at law to be regarded as the owner of the dividend (for the reasons discussed above), and that the withholding tax certificate had been issued in compliance with German tax legislation. Accordingly, it was concluded that a tax credit or refund should be available. For various reasons, tax advisers typically also took the view that the German anti-tax-avoidance rules should not adversely impact this position. For example, it was generally concluded that the general anti-abuse rule in Section 42 of the General Tax Code, which operates to derecognize a legal structure if its design is an abuse of law,[75] should have no application to the cum-ex trade.

(ii) In Relation to the Seller

In principle, a domestic taxpayer entering into a sale of German shares would be taxed or exempted according to the general German tax regime applicable to the taxpayer concerned. However, where the shares were sold by a domestic seller pursuant to a short sale agreement, the seller would probably be a German bank or financial trading institution with the result that any gain arising from the sale would form part of the profits from running the business and so be taxed at

terms and conditions, this is when the dividend coupons are detached from the shares. Such an approach aligned the tax position with the civil-law position as required by the relevant legislative intention.

[74] As will be explored in Chapter 4, a later assessment of cum-ex trades by the tax authorities and the courts addressed the withholding tax issue in the context of the tax rules that applied to dividend compensation payments and this led to a significant distinction in the technical analysis between the period to the end of 2006 and the period from 2007 to 2011.

[75] Under Section 42 (1) clauses 1 and 3, the relevant legal structure of a transaction would be regarded as abusive if (1) the chosen structure is not 'appropriate' and (2) the taxpayer concerned cannot show adequate non-tax reasons for entering into the transaction. It was also concluded that there should be no abuse by reference to the stated views of the Federal Tax Authority itself. This conclusion was based on a Decree on the General Tax Code dated 2 January 2008 (Federal Tax Gazette, I 2008, p.26) to the effect that an abuse arises where there exists: a legal structure which is not appropriate given the nature of the particular economic transaction, a tax benefit generated by that structure that is not expressly provided for in the law, and the absence of proper business reasons for the course adopted. The view taken was that in relation to cum-ex trades buyers would be motivated by sound commercial motivations.

normal rates. For reasons that follow from the discussion in the previous section, any such seller would not be the beneficial owner of the shares sold at the relevant dividend record date and so would not be subject to German dividend withholding tax.[76]

Any overseas seller (again, most likely to be a bank or financial trader in the case of a short sale) would typically have no business presence in Germany and so no liability to German corporation tax or trade tax. As for domestic sellers, any overseas seller selling short would not, for German tax purposes, be the beneficial owner of the shares at the relevant dividend record date and so would not be subject to German dividend withholding tax.

(iii) In Relation to the Lender

The position of any German lender of ex-dividend shares was relatively straightforward. The tax treatment of the dividend and accompanying tax credit received in advance of any lending of the relevant shares would follow the normal tax rules. Where the lender was a German bank, the dividend would be subject to tax and the tax credit would be available to reduce the German tax due on the income of the bank. The share lending transaction would be ignored for German tax purposes by reason of a stock lending tax exemption.[77]

The comments above on the German tax position reflect the basic German tax analysis that supported the tax-effectiveness of the cum-ex trade. As will be seen, this paved the way for a tidal wave of cum-ex transactions to exploit the system weakness in Clearstream.

The opinions given by German tax advisers which laid out this analysis and arrived at these conclusions would be subject to certain general assumptions: for example, that the transactions entered into would be genuine market transactions and not prearranged between the parties. The detailed tax analysis changed over time as the cum-ex trade structure itself evolved, a process which is described further in Chapter 3. However, until the structure was finally closed down, the main points of the basic German tax analysis set out above were commonly regarded as supporting the legal validity of the cum-ex trade.

[76] The shares to be used for settling the trade would, at the dividend record date, not yet have been borrowed from the lender and so on that date the seller would have no possession of the shares or other rights relating to them. The seller could only become the beneficial owner of the borrowed shares when these are borrowed after the dividend record date.

[77] Where the stock loan is governed by a standard lending agreement, neither the initial transfer of securities nor the subsequent retransfer of equivalent securities are disposals for the purposes of the German corporate tax. The fact that a securities lending transaction is not considered as a taxable disposal for German tax purposes follows from its German civil-law treatment according to Section 607 Paragraph 1 of the German Civil Code. Transfers of collateral are similarly treated.

The Cum-Ex Trade Created

The benefit created by the cum-ex trade lies of course in the generation or 'manufacturing' of the withholding tax credit of 26.375 per cent of the gross dividend, as reflected in the tax voucher which would be produced by the buyer's custodian bank. As noted, such tax certificates could in some cases be immediately turned into cash (where there is a cash reimbursement of some or all of the credit) or a cash equivalent (where the tax credit could be offset to reduce an existing tax bill). In both cases, that 'benefit' from the manufacturing of the withholding tax credit was funded by the German state.

The early exploitation of cum-ex generally involved transactions between domestic parties in Germany. An example is illustrated by the Rafael Roth case relating to transactions in the years 2006–8.[78] The case involved the basic cum-ex structure, namely the purchase of cum-dividend shares by a German limited liability company on the relevant dividend record date, with ex-dividend shares acquired by the seller to fulfil the short sale.[79] The acquired shares were then resold by the seller via the OTC market. (The structure is similar to that illustrated in Figure 2.5 above.) The financial amounts involved in the case give an indication of the scale of benefit that was targeted by even these early trades: the subject matter of the relevant transactions was shares valued at approximately €15 billion, with tax credit benefits (equal to the intended profit generated by the transactions) of €125 million.[80]

With time, these domestic structures were modified to include the use of German investment funds, such as the special funds that were considered earlier in this chapter. Such funds would act as the buyer in the cum-ex structure. As well as potentially widening the range of possible participants in cum-ex trades as a result of the fund structure, there was also a technical difference achieved by the use of such fund vehicles. This related to the speed with which any tax credit generated in a cum-ex trade could be accessed by the buyer. With a standard limited-liability German company, the tax credit mechanism operated by reference to the company's year-end assessment procedure, meaning there could be an appreciable delay between the payment of the dividend and the actual use (or refund) of the tax credit. In contrast, German funds that were treated as transparent (such as a special fund), could often recover the cash amount of the

[78] The case was heard in the regional financial court of Hesse and is discussed in Spengel, 'Expert Opinion', at pp.28–9. See FG Hessen from 8.10. 2012, 4 V 1661/11, EFG 2013, from p.47.

[79] The price risk of the shares acquired by the buyer was in this case hedged by futures contracts. This type of hedging strategy is discussed in Chapter 3.

[80] The decision in the case was in fact to deny the validity of the relevant tax credits. The case is discussed further in Chapter 4.

withholding on a much shorter time-scale, typically within two to three weeks of the dividend payment.[81]

A further development was the increasing use in cum-ex trades of parties outside Germany (whether acting as buyer, seller, broker, or custodian bank for the parties). If the buyer were located in another country, any cash reimbursement of the German withholding tax would normally depend on the type of investor purchasing the shares and the terms of any applicable double tax treaty between Germany and the state of that investor. The most common maximum level of dividend withholding permitted under double tax treaties with Germany is 15 per cent, meaning that many investors located in states benefitting from those tax treaties with Germany would be able to reclaim the excess 11.375 per cent of the 26.375 per cent[82] withholding tax from the German tax authorities.[83] Investors in such a position would where possible seek to treat the 15 per cent German withholding tax suffered as a tax credit in their home jurisdictions. In certain special cases, there would be no withholding tax ultimately suffered. For example, as mentioned earlier, a US pension fund would be entitled under the US–Germany double tax treaty to receive a dividend from a German company without any deduction of withholding tax and so could reclaim from the German tax authorities the entire amount of the withholding tax.[84] This exemption for US pension funds was the basis of the transaction structuring in the Bank Sarasin case. The case is discussed in Chapter 3, but it is again useful to note here that it involved transactions in shares valued at €6.3 billion with a tax-credit-generated amount of €54 million.

In all these situations, involving both domestic and cross-border investors, it can be seen that the 'manufacture' of the withholding tax credit by the cum-ex trade clearly generated real tangible value—ultimately, literally billions of euros worth of real tangible value—which would be shared out among the parties to a cum-ex trade.

The transactional steps that were used in the cum-ex trade did not remain static. Over time, a number of changes were made to the basic structure of the transaction used to execute the cum-ex trade. The cumulative effect of these

[81] Spengel, 'Expert Opinion' at p.32 discusses certain other benefits that accrue from the use of investment funds in the structuring of the cum-ex trades, including (in comparison to limited-liability companies) the more flexible rules that apply to investment funds for increasing and reducing their capital and their ability to time redemptions to reduce the tax payable by the fund.

[82] i.e. 26.375%–11.375% = 15%, the maximum allowable rate of withholding.

[83] For example, the 15% rate applies for most UK investors under Article 10 (2) (c) of the 2010 UK–Germany double tax treaty, and the same level of withholding applied under the earlier 1964 treaty.

[84] See Article 10 (3) (b) of the US–Germany double tax treaty. The treaty was signed originally in 1989 but the specific provision dealing with pension funds was inserted by a 2006 protocol. Tax treaties do not always exempt pension funds from withholding tax. Some tax treaties may make no special provision for pension funds. In others, the rate of withholding tax may be set at a different level. For example, under Article 10 of the 2010 UK–Germany double tax treaty, pension funds would be subject to a 10% withholding tax on dividends received from German companies.

changes was to greatly complicate the structure of the trade. Some of the simpler changes were made to sidestep anti-avoidance measures taken by the German tax authorities to block the structure. For example, the tax authorities made material changes to the tax law and the administration of the rules in 2007 and 2009. Both changes led to modifications to the design of the cum-ex transaction. However, in both cases it proved relatively easy for the cum-ex transaction structure to be successfully adapted to overcome these developments. Other changes made to the transaction steps were designed to boost the financial benefits from the trade, whether by expanding the pool of participants in the trade or by mechanisms adopted to multiply the benefits or reduce the costs of the transaction, or both. Some of these changes led to the introduction of very complex changes to the cum-ex trade structure.The many modifications that were made to the cum-ex structure as it evolved are explored in the next chapter.

3
The Evolution of Cum-Ex

[Such] complexity creates numerous opportunities for planners that have resources that far eclipse the ability of the government to police them.

Mihir Desai, Testimony before the US Senate Committee on Finance, 10 March 2015

Introduction

The basic cum-ex trade identified at the end of the previous chapter required significant further financial engineering in order to overcome a range of limitations imposed by the marketplace, which would otherwise restrict the profitability of the trade for the banks and their fund clients. Other modifications and refinements were needed in order to ensure that the trade could generate returns of a size which could accommodate institutional demand. Consequently, the potential of the trade needed to be maximized through what was essentially a process of industrialization. To complicate matters further, the cum-ex transaction structure had to adapt over time in order to circumvent efforts by the tax authorities to close the trade down. Collectively, these changes can be seen in a continual evolution and refinement of the trade. The goals of this evolution were multifaceted: namely, to enhance the returns from the trade; to open participation in the trade to a broader range of financial actors; to greatly increase the total capital deployed in the strategy; to reduce transaction costs; and to sidestep changes in tax law. All of these developments are explained in this chapter.

Mechanisms to Exploit Cum-Ex

Chapter 2 explained how the cum-ex trade could generate what would be essentially free money in the form of claims on the state, using German shares settled in the Clearstream settlement system. The immediate question for the banks was how cum-ex trades involving German shares could best be exploited at scale.

As seen in the preceding chapter, the creation of the cum-ex benefit relies on the actions of one party alone, namely, the short seller. In order to generate that

Banking on Failure: Cum-Ex and Why and How Banks Game the System. Richard S Collier, Oxford University Press (2020). © Richard S Collier.
DOI: 10.1093/oso/9780198859673.001.0001

benefit, the short seller must take two actions which straddle the dividend record date. It must first sell the relevant shares short immediately before the dividend record date and then must settle that short-sale with ex-dividend shares borrowed after dividend record date.[1] The automatic operation of the system then does the rest, creating tax credits in the account of the buyer. These credits are, of course, the source of profit in the cum-ex trade.

The fact that the actions of the seller alone can activate the benefits of the cum-ex trade means that it would be possible for a seller, such as a trader or trading team within a bank, to exploit the trade without making any prior arrangements with any other party, in other words, on an entirely independent or 'stand-alone' basis. This could be achieved by entering into cum-dividend short sales of cum-dividend shares in the open market with third parties, and then settling those short sale agreements with borrowed ex-dividend shares. The short sales transaction would be indistinguishable from countless other short sales taking place every day in the capital markets. Such a stand-alone approach would have a number of important advantages for the seller. By acting alone to exploit the cum-ex trade, the seller could potentially capture all the profit from the trade. As discussed in Chapter 2, the reason for this is that the tax credits, although generated by the cum-ex trade in the account of the buyer, have value which would be priced into any market transactions. Consequently, when selling the shares on a cum-dividend basis, the value of those tax credits would have been incorporated into the sale price received by the seller, thereby allowing the seller to 'monetize' the cum-ex benefit. The stand-alone approach would have other benefits. To an external observer located outside the bank, a standard open-market short sale would help to obscure the cum-ex mechanism that generated the profit in the trade. It is true that such a trading strategy would require careful management of the short sales in the period of one or two days before the dividend record date. However, if it were possible to execute the strategy using everyday share-dealing transactions, a cum-ex short sale would be hard to distinguish from any other short sale.[2] A normal on-exchange trade in the open market, carried out on standard terms and dealing at arm's length with a buyer as counterparty, would also be unlikely to require specific approval under the bank's internal controls.[3]

[1] As is mentioned in footnote 45 of Chapter 2, it is in some circumstances possible to effect a cum-ex trade in the absence of these two elements of a short sale and a borrowing of shares.

[2] One difference to be expected, however, though discernible only within the bank concerned, would be the relative higher profitability of cum-ex trading when compared to ordinary market or 'flow' business transacted on behalf of clients. Also, within the bank, such an approach to trading might be viewed as having some similarity with dividend arbitrage trading. This would be on the basis that the trading simply involved pricing in the relevant tax features of the transaction which had value to the buyer and that the system was operating as intended (or, if not as intended, at least as constructed).

[3] Whilst structured transactions generally require approval under a bank's internal controls, ordinary proprietary trading transactions most often do not—or at least did not, prior to the 'Volcker Rule'—see The Dodd–Frank Wall Street Reform and Consumer Protection Act, § 619 (12 U.S.C. § 1851), effective 21 July 2015. See further the discussion in Chapter 6.

Also, in order to execute it, no additional steps would be necessary and there would be few complications to deal with beyond finding a willing buyer for the shares and a lender to lend them.[4]

Figure 3.1 shows what would be involved in the stand-alone approach to trading cum-ex from the short seller's perspective. At the inception of the trade there would be three separate transactions: the short sale of the shares to the buyer prior to the dividend record date (Step 1 in Figure 3.1); the later borrowing of the shares from the lender (Step 2); and the derivatives hedging transaction (Step 3). The derivatives hedging transaction, considered in more detail below, removes the risk associated with market fluctuations in the price of the shares until they are later repurchased in the market by the short seller and returned to the lender.

Looking at such a transaction from the buyer's perspective, it would have purchased securities at fair market value (including the value of the impending dividend), apparently suffered a withholding tax deduction on that dividend when it was paid, and received tax credits evidencing that deduction. Because the purchase would be in all respects completely standard and on open-market terms, it would be indistinguishable from any other purchase of those shares in the market. Consequently, the buyer would be completely unaware that the seller was selling short. Specifically, the buyer would be oblivious to the fact that it had in fact received the withholding tax credits due only to the operation of the settlement mechanism exploited by the cum-ex trade and without the dividend being subjected to any actual withholding tax.

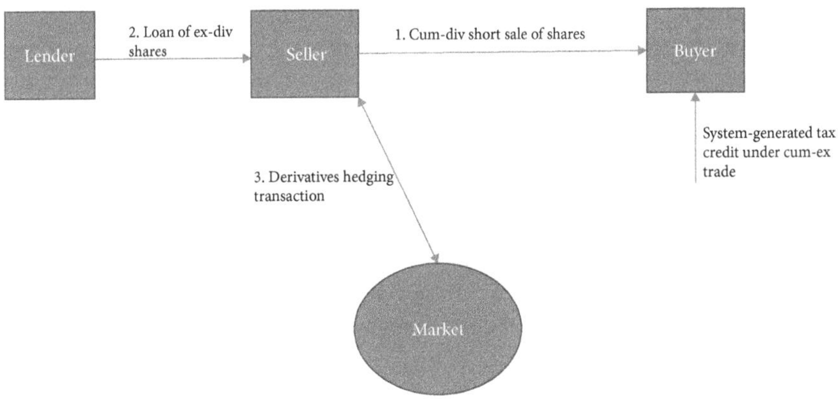

Figure 3.1. Stand-alone approach to cum-ex

[4] Notwithstanding the relative simplicity of this trading strategy for cum-ex trades and the fact that trades would be entered into on normal market terms with an entirely independent buyer, there is some significant controversy in Germany as to the status of any such approach to cum-ex trading under German law. The issues emerged largely after cum-ex trading in Germany was closed down. The issues are discussed in Chapter 4.

The discussion above shows that in principle it would have been possible for a seller to enter into cum-ex trades on open-market terms and at arm's length from buyers who would have been wholly unaware that the purchase of shares was part of a cum-ex strategy operating in the background.[5] However, from the perspective of the banks, such an approach would quickly encounter a number of difficulties or constraints. The biggest of these would be the inevitably limited scale of trading activity and therefore also the limited financial benefits that would be possible. This is because the trading opportunity would by definition be confined to the very short time period prior to the dividend record date in which short sales could activate the strategy. There would also be a natural limit to the number of third-party buyers seeking to become owners of the shares in this brief period.

A short seller wishing to exploit the cum-ex trade on an entirely stand-alone basis would also have faced transactional constraints which would become more acute as the size of any cum-ex trading was increased. These limitations are highly relevant to the current discussion because the efforts of the banks to expand the revenues from the cum-ex trade meant that a solution was required to overcome each limitation. The nature of these constraints is therefore considered in the next section of this chapter.

Constraints on the Expansion of the Cum-Ex Trade

The discussion below identifies six separate constraints on a seller implementing a 'stand-alone' approach to cum-ex trading in the open market. These are discussed in turn, before an exploration of the responses or 'solutions' to these issues which were adopted by cum-ex traders.

Constraint 1: Finding Buyers and the Problem of Trade Size

For banks eager to implement the cum-ex strategy, the task of locating willing buyers is a critical obstacle standing in the way of an open-market approach to cum-ex trading. It has two aspects. First, given that German shares typically pay a single dividend annually and that cum-ex trades need to be executed immediately before the relevant dividend record date, there is a very narrow window of time within which cum-ex trading can take place. Second, the profit from a cum-ex trade is derived from the total value of transactions comprising the trade. In other words, the extraction of a large profit from the strategy requires the size of the

[5] A number of banks entering into cum-ex transactions have claimed they were doing so on this basis of dealing on open-market terms and at arm's length with buyers who would have been unaware of the relevant cum-ex structuring involved in the trade.

trades also to be large. Within a bank, this second factor would usually be exacerbated by an expectation that any transaction such as cum-ex which involves structured or complex features should contribute meaningfully to the bank's profits. As discussed in Chapter 2, the financial benefit associated with the cum-ex trade is directly proportional to three variables: the quantity of the shares traded, the size of the dividend paid on those shares, and the amount of withholding tax levied on that dividend. Given that withholding tax rates are determined by governments and dividend rates are decided by corporations, there remains only one variable that can be influenced by the decisions of the cum-ex trader: the trader must increase the quantity or volume of shares traded in order to increase the financial benefit generated by the strategy. This requires that there must be buyers able and willing to enter into large trades.

The pressure to find sufficient willing buyers in quantities which greatly exceed the daily volume of shares ordinarily traded means in practice that buyers would need to be incentivized to enter into the trade. The profits from the cum-ex trades would thus need to be shared to some extent with the buyers in order to induce them to purchase the shares.[6] This leads to two immediate effects. First, and most obviously, it means that the banks acting as short sellers would not in practice be able to retain all of the profits from the exploitation of cum-ex trading. Because sharing the profits further lowers the profits available to the bank from the strategy, there is a second consequence: the quantity of shares traded must be even larger to deliver the level of profits targeted by the cum-ex trading strategy.

A bank looking to engage in cum-ex trading will compare the revenue the strategy is expected to generate with the costs associated with implementing and managing the trade. As the cum-ex trade is relatively complex, the resources consumed by it within a bank are correspondingly high. A minimum level of profit is required to justify those expenses and achieve a meaningful level of profit for the bank. Medium to large sized banks will require prospective profits of a minimum of €10 million to consider embarking on an undertaking as involved as the cum-ex trade. Costs typically consume approximately 50 per cent of revenue at such banks. Further, if half the revenue from the trade is shared with the counterparty in any cum-ex trades executed, that means €40 million in revenue will be needed to sustain a €10 million contribution to yearly profit, after taking account of costs and the sharing of revenues. Generating €40 million in revenue from cum-ex trading requires a total volume of shares in the order of €2 billion per year.[7] Locating a sufficient number of buyers wishing to purchase billions of euros

[6] One possible mechanism for sharing the benefits in the transaction (which, of course, arise from the system-generated tax credit) would be for the seller to reduce the cum-dividend sale price charged to the buyer. The price paid by the buyer for the tax credit might thereby be less than 100 per cent of the value expected to be derived from the tax credit.

[7] As discussed in Chapter 2, the Bank Sarasin case produced tax credits of €54 million from a share value traded of €6.3 billion, meaning that the market value of shares traded was 116 times the tax credit

worth of shares in the narrow window of two days prior to the dividend record date would, to put it mildly, pose a major impediment to the profitable implementation of the strategy in the open market. Nonetheless, empirical academic research shows that cum-ex trading drove volumes of shares traded well beyond their normal levels.[8]

The two-pronged problem of increasing trade size and identifying buyers willing to engage in them is in fact more extensive than the above discussion indicates. Banks are, or at least are supposed to be, financial intermediaries. When traders within a bank enter into transactions carrying significant trading risk (such as short sale transactions) they will be expected to lay off the risk either by using hedges or by limiting their risk-taking to as short a period as possible, or preferably both. In the specific case of a short sale, the risk that is created by the transaction stems from the fact that the short seller will at some future stage need to purchase shares in the market so that they can be returned to the stock lender. The risk lies in the possibility that the market price of the shares may rise between the time that they are sold short and the later time at which they are purchased and returned to the lender. As a risk-management imperative, therefore, short sales of the size demanded by the cum-ex strategy would need to be hedged. A derivative position, economically equal and opposite to the short sale, is the usual instrument of choice for banks.[9]

Entering into derivative trades to hedge its risk would require the bank to find suitable counterparties prepared to take the other side of those trades, and in a transaction size or value matching that of the short sale. This of course doubles the

realized by the strategy. The Rafael Roth case described in Chapter 2 required a trade size 120 times the tax credit realized. As the benefit was presumably shared between the parties to the trade, it suggests a transaction multiplier of at least fifty times the expected profit. This explains the above illustrative figure of €2 billion.

[8] In the few days leading up to the once-yearly dividend date for a German company, Buettner et al show that shares traded would often exceed by 66–68 per cent the average quantity of that share regularly traded for the rest of the year. See Thiess Buettner, Carolin Holzmann, Felix Kreidl, and Hendrik Scholz, 'Stock Market Behavior on Ex-Dividend Dates: The Case of Cum-Ex Transactions in Germany', 13 March 2018, p.27, available at https://ssrn.com/abstract=2960015 or http://dx.doi.org/10.2139/ssrn.2960015. The paper also shows that in the absence of the doubly generated tax certificates, the trades would be unprofitable. The discussion that follows explains how these sharply increased volumes were in practice made possible.

[9] For example, a possible form of derivative in this context might be an equity swap. In a simple equity swap, the party who is 'long' the swap pays amounts equivalent to any market value falls, and receives amounts equivalent to any market value rises, in the market price of the shares referenced by the swap, while the counterparty (who is 'short' the swap) receives equal and opposite cash flows. Such a transaction would allow a party that has sold the shares short to lay off their risk by entering into a long swap over the same quantity of those same securities. They would then be 'short' the securities but 'long' the swap, in equal quantities. The hedging transaction provides the opportunity to eliminate market risk, which would here flow from movements in the price of the shares. Any loss from holding the shares would be made whole by amounts received on the swaps contract hedge and equally any gains from the shares would be equal to amounts paid out under the swap contract. A number of different types of hedging contracts (for example, forwards, futures, etc) could be used to deliver the same economic function as a swap.

total value of transactions necessary to execute the cum-ex trade: if the bank is short-selling €2 billion of shares, it must find counterparties prepared to enter into €2 billion of offsetting long derivative transactions. Moreover, the counterparties to these hedging trades would need to be available and willing to trade at exactly the same point in time as the short sale transactions are entered into by the bank.[10] In other words, *buyers* of huge volumes of shares have to be ready and able to purchase shares from the bank at precisely the same time as there are *sellers* of an equal volume of related derivative trades. Reverting back to the example above, if the short sale was to be sized at €2 billion in order to generate €40 million in shared profit, then counterparties prepared to enter €2 billion in equal and opposite derivative trades would also need to be found.

Constraint 2: Market Risk and the Execution of Trades

It is clear from the above discussion that a bank seeking to execute cum-ex trades as a short seller would require sufficient willing buyers of shares, and sufficient willing counterparties to derivatives hedging transactions, to make the activity possible. The bank must also have access to those share buyers and derivatives counterparties simultaneously. However, even if such buyers and counterparties were available at the same time to enter into trading and hedging transactions with the bank, the potential risk issues are by no means resolved. Even with hedging trades of equal and opposite size in place, losses could still emerge in a number of ways.

First, sales of a large quantity of stock into the market can be expected to cause the price of the shares being sold to fall. The trading desks at large investment banks regularly sell such large blocks of shares on behalf of their clients. For example, an institutional investor might be looking to exit a significant holding in the shares of a particular company. The investor will naturally want to try to dispose of the shareholding at the best attainable price. Investment banks have traders who specialize in 'working' such block trades. Working a block trade means seeking out interested buyers for the shares through the trader's market contacts or employing a sophisticated computer program to manage the timing of the share sales, or both. Either way, the process takes time. If a seller is looking to dispose of a block of shares which exceeds the amount that is regularly traded in those shares for a given day, it could take several days for the sale to be 'worked'. But short sales in the cum-ex strategy by their very nature could not take days. They *had* to take place on one of the very few days each year leading up to the dividend record date of the shares used in the cum-ex trade. All the major

[10] The requirement for the simultaneous execution of the short sales and the derivative hedging positions is attributable to issues relating to market pricing risk. These are explained further below.

investment banks have computer programs which can provide an estimate of the proceeds that might be expected on the rapid sale of a block of shares valued at, say, $500 million. One thing is certain: those proceeds would normally fall short of $500 million because such a supply of stock hitting the market would saturate short-term demand for the shares.[11] Very simply, the price of those shares would need to fall[12] in order for the shares to be absorbed by buyers in a short space of time, bringing supply and demand into equilibrium.

Similar issues to those discussed above are relevant to any hedging transaction: in attempting to hedge large short sales by entering into offsetting derivatives transactions, a bank can expect the cost of those hedging transactions to rise as its demand for those hedges puts pressure on the price. Thus, while it is theoretically possible to short-sell a block of shares valued at $500 million or to enter into offsetting hedging transactions of an equal size, in practice, managing either one of these feats is a risky, delicate, and time-consuming operation.

A further problem is that if the hedging transactions are not entered into on an exactly simultaneous basis with the short sales, the bank may have a mismatch in price. For example, a bank might have sold short 10 million shares at 11 a.m. at the then prevailing market price per share of €11.75. Given that prevailing market prices fluctuate second by second, those shares might trade a moment later at a different price. If in that time the bank is unable to find a counterparty to the hedging transaction for 10 million shares at that same price of €11.75, there will be a mismatch. That mismatch might lock in a gain on the short sale, as where, for example, the market price has fallen, to say €11.50 in the time it took to enter into the hedging trade.[13] But it might equally lock in a loss if the price has risen. In short, if hedging trades are not available on terms both as to price and quantity which precisely match the short sales, not only is there no assurance of a profit on the strategy, but there are likely to be large and frequent losses. Such losses could wipe out the benefits generated by the cum-ex strategy over time. In practice, however, losses were very rarely, if ever, encountered in the cum-ex strategy, whereas very large and persistent profits were the norm.

The real implications of the two constraints discussed so far are best illustrated by an example. The example also shows the relationship between the tax benefits generated by the cum-ex trade and the size of the share sale and hedging transactions required to generate that benefit.

RWE AG is a German utilities company whose shares were particularly popular with cum-ex traders because of its rich dividend yield. In 2009, shares in RWE AG

[11] The Wall Street saying 'there is one price to sell and another to sell quickly' is in this context apt.

[12] The extent of the fall in value would depend on the size of the company whose shares are being sold.

[13] There would be a gain of €2,500,000 (10,000,000 × 25 cents) in this example.

traded at approximately €60 per share. Its annual dividend was €3.50 per share, giving its shares a very high dividend yield of about 5.8 per cent.[14]

Assume that a cum-ex trader has the ability to borrow €300 million of RWE shares. The total yearly dividend paid out on the stock would be 5.8 per cent of €300 million, or approximately €17.4 million. The total withholding tax credit available is 26.375 per cent of the dividend, or €4,589,250. Implementing the cum-ex strategy, the trader enters into a short sale of €300 million in RWE shares the day prior to the dividend record date. Two business days later, after the shares have paid out their dividend to the holder of record, the trader borrows those (ex-dividend) shares and delivers them to settle the short-sale. Ignoring transaction costs involved in both the sale of the shares and the purchase of a hedging transaction, the maximum potential value of the tax credits is 1.5 per cent of the size of the short sale transaction (being €4.589 million/€300 million).[15] Including a hedging transaction of equal and opposite size, the tax credits available are only 0.75 per cent of the combined size of the short sale and hedging transactions combined. Put another way, for each €10 million of profit from a cum-ex transaction, at least €650 million in shares must be sold short and another €650 million hedged. Or again, 1.7 per cent of RWE's then market capitalization of €38 billion would need to be sold short, just to produce a €10 million profit.[16] That profit would, of course, need be shared between the short seller and the buyer.

As well as showing the scale of the cum-ex trades, the example underlines the potential risks inherent in a cum-ex trade carried out on open-market terms: the tax credit generated in a cum-ex transaction, although significant, cannot be secured without underlying share trades and hedging transactions involving prodigious amounts. Even then, the margin of error is exceedingly thin. A 0.75 per cent fluctuation in the price of a share is a common occurrence in the stock market. However, it is a fluctuation that would present enormous risk to a cum-ex trader pursuing the 'stand-alone' approach to the cum-ex trade. The trader must find a buyer for an immense block of shares, which is a difficult undertaking in itself. Hedging that short sale with a derivatives trade effectively doubles the total size of the transaction.

However, these two transactions initiating the cum-ex trade are only half of the story. After the tax benefits that are the focal point of the strategy have been

[14] The dividend yield is a measure of the amount of the dividend as a percentage of the traded price of the shares, in this case €3.50/€60.

[15] In practice, the percentage amount would be smaller owing to transaction and hedging costs.

[16] Putting this number into context, in 2007 European and US investment banks had combined revenues of $53 billion in their equities divisions. See http://www.tricumen.com/wp-content/uploads/downloads/2016/03/Tricumen_European-vs-US-i-banks_revenue-dynamics-2007-15_210316.pdf. In 2017, the 10 largest global investment banks had equity capital markets revenue of over $6 billion. See https://www.statista.com/statistics/273080/revenue-of-the-worlds-largest-investment-banks-by-product-group/. Therefore, to be of any interest at all to the large investment banks, the profits generated from trading strategies such as cum-ex needed to be significant.

captured, the whole transaction must then be unwound, i.e. all the initiating steps reversed. The shares must be repurchased by the short-seller so that they can be returned to the stock lender. The derivative trade that was entered into must be terminated (or 'closed out'). Combining these two further closing transactions with the opening transactions means that the total size of all purchases and sales (of both derivatives and shares) is four times the size of the initial short sale. Returning to the earlier example, at the inception of the trade, €300 million of RWE shares must be sold short and €300 million of derivatives over RWE shares purchased. On the termination of the trade, €300 million of RWE shares must be repurchased and €300 million of derivatives over RWE shares sold. A total of €1.2 billion in RWE shares and related derivatives contracts are caught up in opening and later closing a trade which can produce a maximum tax benefit of €4,589,250 or 0.38 per cent of that total. Here again, effecting these closing trades brings risks. The precarious steps taken in entering into the transactions would now need to be carefully retraced: the short seller must close the short position as well as the hedging transaction, and on a precisely synchronized basis.[17] If all of these opening and closing transactions collectively incurred losses of little more than one third of one per cent of the amounts traded, there would be no profit in the trade.

Constraint 3: Stock Borrowing Issues

Since the cum-ex strategy is first activated by precisely timed short sales, the seller must of course be able to borrow the relevant shares.[18] The stock loan market is an institutional market, dominated by the investment banks and agent lending banks which loan out shares on behalf of their clients, who are generally large pension and investment funds. It is also a market which, since its creation, has been opaque. Stock loan agreements are entered into bilaterally between banks and stock lenders or bilaterally between banks and the agent lending banks. Fragmented by these private bilateral arrangements, there is no central hub such as an exchange where stock borrowers can compete for shares. In the absence of a common platform for participants, stock borrowing fees have also historically not been widely published. Nevertheless, there is competition for shares and a price for borrowing them which evolves through repeated interactions between demand and supply. Borrowing shares on the scale required by a cum-ex trading desk puts

[17] The open borrow would be closed by the seller by buying shares in the market to return to the lender, and the intention would be that the hedging transaction would insulate the seller from any financial risk in relation to the cost of those shares. For example, if the price of the shares when bought in the market had gone up, any additional cost would be equal to the gain derived from the derivatives hedging contract (and vice versa).

[18] The need for stock lending to facilitate short selling is discussed in Chapter 1.

upward pressure on stock borrow fees, raising the costs of executing the cum-ex trade and therefore lowering its profitability.

There are also further hazards associated with large stock borrowing transactions. Given that the short seller has borrowed shares and sold them, the main economic risk associated with the short sale is that the price of the shares rises, making them more expensive to later repurchase and return to the lender. Since the possible market price rise of a share is theoretically unlimited, short sellers are extremely sensitive to increases in the share price. Any significant depletion of the pool of shares available for borrowing by short sellers can itself create the conditions for a violent rise in the price of the shares concerned, known in the financial industry as a 'short squeeze'. A short squeeze is a self-reinforcing cycle in which short sellers, while attempting to control losses from a share price rise, collectively bring about a vertical ascent in the price. Many conditions can bring about a short squeeze, but one example is as follows. As discussed earlier, significant lenders of stock are typically large pension and investment funds, which will often hold significant positions of shares in individual companies. Such a fund might at any time decide to permanently reduce or eliminate its holding of shares in a specific company. This could include the shares in a German company, such as BMW. If the fund's BMW shares have been loaned out to a short seller in a cum-ex trade, the lent shares need to be first returned to the lender in order for the lender to be able to sell them.[19] If the borrower of the shares (the short seller) cannot return them to the lender because they are tied up in the cum-ex trading strategy, then in order to obtain shares to return (and assuming borrowing further shares is not possible),[20] the borrower will be required to purchase replacement shares on the open market, a step known as a 'buy-to-cover'.[21] Given that purchases are involved, buys-to-cover can spark a surge in the price of the affected shares. This is because any other market participants who are short begin to suffer losses as the price of the shares rise. In order to manage their risk, they would need to cut their losses. To do so, they must close their short positions and so must also buy back shares in the market. If a large number of participants are short in the shares, their collective efforts to control losses by buying back shares can result in a monumental surge in the share price as short sellers scramble to buy back and return the shares. Immense losses for short sellers can be the result.[22]

[19] This risk that a lender may need its shares back is known as 'recall risk' and is a very real threat to any short-selling strategy (because short selling is normally possible only where, and for as long as, shares are available to be borrowed). Where, as in cum-ex, the strategy involves large short sales and so in turn the borrowing of significant quantities of shares, the risk is amplified.

[20] For example, because a widely pursued cum-ex strategy has exhausted the supply of stock available to borrow.

[21] A similar transaction carried out by the lender of shares would be a 'buy-in'.

[22] Famously, on Tuesday 28 October 2008, a short squeeze took place in the shares of Volkswagen AG. Although it was not related to cum-ex trades, the spike in the share price at one point caused

While these market pricing issues relating to the stock loan represent important limitations on the ability to execute the cum-ex strategy on a large scale, there is also a more routine issue connected to the loan of the required shares. In order to carry out the cum-ex trading strategy on the scale illustrated by the examples at the end of Chapter 2,[23] the short seller would need the ability to borrow hundreds of millions, if not billions, of euros worth of a company's shares. While the market for stock lending is large, measured globally in the trillions of dollars of securities available for loan, it is not without limit.[24] The supply of stock available to be loaned out in a particular market, such as Germany, is dispersed among numerous lenders, each having privately negotiated lending arrangements with one or more preferred banks. The fractured nature of the market places a limit on the shares available to be borrowed by any one short seller. On the demand side of the equation, however, the number of banks and investment funds engaged in the cum-ex strategy was measured in the hundreds. Keeping in mind that the availability of the cum-ex strategy in relation to any particular share was restricted to a few days in each calendar year, there was a clear potential for borrowing demand from short sellers to greatly outstrip the supply from lenders.

Constraint 4: Credit Limits

In order to ensure a bank is not overly exposed to a single market counterparty, the bank's credit department will establish limits or 'lines' for each party with which the bank has a business relationship.[25] These are effectively credit limits. Amounts owed by or to each counterparty by the bank will be aggregated and monitored to ensure that the exposure stays within the line or limit that has been set by the bank's credit department. This ensures that the risk of a party failing to perform its financial obligations is contained within acceptable bounds. Where the bank is the party owing the financial obligation, the line or limit is still applied to ensure that the bank is diversified across its lenders. Consequently, whether the counterparty is a buyer of shares from the bank or a lender of shares to the bank, there will always be a limit above which it may not deal. Where a bank sells shares

Volkswagen AG to become the most valuable company in the world by market capitalization. For further information on the short squeeze and its effects, see https://www.reuters.com/article/us-volkswagen/short-sellers-make-vw-the-worlds-priciest-firm-idUSTRE49R3I920081028.

[23] See the reported transactions discussed at the end of Chapter 2 for illustrations of the size of the relevant share transactions. These would require similarly sized stock borrowing transactions.

[24] See Paul Walsh, 'Global Securities Lending Hits $2 Trillion Mark', *Global Custodian*, 13 March 2017, available at https://www.globalcustodian.com/global-securities-lending-hits-2-trillion-mark/.

[25] In addition to being commercially prudent, counterparty limits and the management of counterparty risk are considered essential components of sound risk management by banking regulators around the world. See, for example, https://www.bis.org/bcbs/publ/joint37.pdf.

short, the key risk is of course that the buyer fails to deliver the purchase monies on the settlement date.[26] Equally, where shares are borrowed by a bank to settle that short sale, the credit department of the stock lender will also establish a limit on the amount of business which can be carried out with the bank. This means that the credit departments of all of the parties involved in a cum-ex trade will aggregate and monitor each other's activity to ensure that these counterparty limits are respected. Holding to these counterparty risk limits places a significant quantitative constraint on any bank's ability to carry out a strategy that involves trades amounting to billions of euros.

Constraint 5: The Demand for Collateral

Transactions between market participants that create significant financial exposure will generally need to be collateralized.[27] For example, a bank that borrows shares from a stock lender creates an exposure equal to the value of those shares. The lender of shares is exposed to the bank that has borrowed them. Collateralization of a transaction simply means that the party with the financial obligation is required to deliver cash or other securities to the party to whom the obligation is owed, i.e. the exposed party. The purpose of the arrangement is that the party receiving such cash or securities then has an obligation to return them to the delivering party when the underlying transaction has been closed out. If a bank borrows $100 of shares but delivers $103 of cash collateral to the lender of those shares, the consequence is that the bank has a net exposure of $3 to the lender.[28] Receiving collateral in this way across its book of business, a lender of stock is able to reduce its exposure to borrowers.

In the context of cum-ex trading, the obligation to deliver collateral to a stock lender will be substantial. The stock lender of shares worth €350 million to a bank short selling those shares in a cum-ex trade might require the bank to deliver cash or high-quality government bonds of perhaps €360 million to collateralize the loan of shares. Although it is true that each short sale of shares generates cash proceeds from the sale which could then be delivered back to the stock lender as

[26] Where the sale of shares takes place on an exchange, a clearing house associated with the exchange may assume the buyer's obligation to the seller. However, even here, the banks will monitor counterparty risk to central counterparties, such as a clearing house.

[27] Where the risk of a counterparty failure, or the amount of exposure involved, is low, market participants can, of course, assume uncollateralized exposure to each other. An exposure which is not collateralized is referred to as a 'gross' exposure.

[28] Typically, the exposure of a lender of shares is over-collateralized by the borrower in this way. The excess collateral cover is intended to introduce a buffer, offering some level of protection in the event that the exposure increases or the value of the collateral falls (or both) by virtue of market price fluctuations. The lower the quality of collateral, the higher the level of overcollateralization that will be required. Stock loan exposures are normally collateralized by developed country government bonds and cash which, being of high credit quality, will have the lowest level of overcollateralization.

collateral for the borrowing of stock, in practice it is not always so simple. A core activity in which banks are engaged is financing, whether it be the takeover of one company by another or a loan to finance a customer's purchase of securities. Much of the financing undertaken by banks ties up cash for significant periods of time. Consequently, business lines in a bank must compete for cash, a process which is managed by a bank's internal treasury group. The treasury group will normally place limits on the amount of cash each business can consume, as well as charging each line of business within the bank for the total amount of cash it utilizes. This creates a further practical constraint on how much cash a single business line engaged in cum-ex trading can have at its disposal to deliver as collateral for its stock borrowing obligations.

Constraint 6: Dealing with Operational Risk

Even in its simplest form, the cum-ex trade is complex. The trade consists of a carefully timed set of transactions, each of which must be precisely executed in order for the trade to achieve its purpose. If the transactions comprising the trade, including those transactions unwinding the trade at the end of its term, do not marry up with each other in terms of quantity of shares traded, price, and timing, they will not come together to achieve their goal and financial losses may result. The same is true for the hedging transactions. If these are not matched precisely with short sales and purchases, and later unwound in a similar frictionless fashion, a significant loss may occur. Operational error may also be relevant where large cash amounts, such as the purchase price for a block of shares, are transferred between parties (for example, as a result of 'fat-finger' errors where the financial amounts are miskeyed into the system). Further, for the shares of any particular company, there are at most three days of the year upon which the cum-ex trade can occur, compressing intense trading into a short period of time. All of these factors reflect the high level of operational risk—the risk of financial loss through operational error—that is involved in the cum-ex trade.[29] The presence of

[29] Operational risk is explained by the Basel Committee as being the risk of loss resulting from inadequate or failed internal processes, people and systems, or from external events. This definition includes legal risk, but excludes strategic and reputational risk. See Basel Committee on Banking Supervision, 'Principles for the Sound Management of Operational Risk', (Bank for International Settlements, June 2011), available at https://www.google.com/url?sa=t&rct=j&q=&esrc=s&source=web&cd=1&ved=0ahUKEwirxKSs7LnbAhXBLlAKHfXVAxUQFggpMAA&url=https%3A%2F%2Fwww.bis.org%2Fpubl%2Fbcbs195.pdf&usg=AOvVaw0OA46f8_T2HkpZodWhZ8XG. The Basel Committee on Banking Supervision, whose definition of Operational Risk is quoted at the beginning of this footnote, is comprised of central banks and bank supervisors from twenty-eight jurisdictions. The committee sets standards for regulation and supervision of banks around the world. Its recommendations and policy prescriptions become embodied in the laws and regulations of state authorities such as the Federal Financial Supervisory Authority ('BaFIN') in Germany and the Financial Conduct Authority ('FCA') and Prudential Regulatory Authorities ('PRA') in the United Kingdom.

operational risk also imposes significant regulatory requirements on the bank's board of directors and its management to understand, monitor, and address the specific elements of the risk.[30]

Given the enormous sums involved in cum-ex trades and the weighty regulatory requirements to manage the operational risk, a bank could not embark on the cum-ex strategy lightly. The potential operational hazards associated with the cum-ex trading scheme thus placed a significant restriction on a bank's capacity to engage in it.

Dealing with the Constraints and Limitations

The discussion in the previous section of this chapter identifies some material constraints on the expansion of the cum-ex trade. However, none of these issues proved in practice to be a problem, as evidenced by the enormous scale of the cum-ex transactions that were entered into over a long period and apparently without market losses. Not only were solutions found for the various issues identified so far, but the trade was expanded in a number of other ways. The financial engineering skills deployed by the banks were by any standard ingenious.

The main priority for the cum-ex trade was locating shares of German companies. Apart from the essential requirement that such shares were traded in the German market, they had only one thing in common. This had nothing to do with which industry sector the shares related to, nor with the profitability of the company that had issued the shares. Not even their identity had any special significance. To the cum-ex trader, none of these details mattered. The only thing of importance was that the company paid as large a dividend as possible in the current year. The share was merely the vehicle or delivery mechanism for the cum-ex strategy. Given that the tax credit was a fixed percentage of the dividend, the larger the dividend, the greater the tax credit which could be extracted from each cum-ex short sale of shares. Isolating the tax credit and the maximizing its value on big dividend-paying shares in the largest German companies therefore became the sole object of the banks seeking to exploit cum-ex.

The discussion that follows explains how the constraints described in the previous section were overcome by banks in the course of devising large trading

[30] These include: the requirement for an operational risk management system with clear responsibilities assigned to an operational risk management function; an operational risk assessment system by which the bank systematically tracks relevant operational risk data including material losses by business line; regular reporting of operational risk exposures, including material operational losses, to business unit management, senior management, and to the board of directors; an operational risk management process and assessment system subject to validation and regular independent review (with reviews including both the activities of the business units and of the operational risk management function); and an operation risk assessment system (including the internal validation processes), which must be subject to regular review by external auditors and/or banking supervisors.

schemes to capitalize on the cum-ex opportunity. These schemes were refined to enhance their effectiveness, including also some changes to sidestep the efforts by tax regulators to close down cum-ex trading. All of these developments led to a number of distinct evolutionary steps in the cum-ex trade.[31] These steps are discussed separately below to show the evolution of the trade over time, though in practice some steps may in particular cases have followed a different sequence and some steps may also have been implemented simultaneously. The structures which ultimately were devised reveal as much about the general machinery of the structured finance capability of banks as they do about the ingenuity of the trading staff who implemented them in the specific case of cum-ex.

Overcoming the Market Constraints

Risk Neutralization—Executing the Transactions

From the discussion above, it is clear that, if a bank acted on a 'stand-alone' basis in exploiting the cum-ex trade (i.e. acting independently as a short seller in entering into open market trades), it would run the risk of creating financial losses which could dwarf the amount of any tax benefit. This risk flowed from the inherent difficulty of managing market price fluctuations associated with short sales of shares and the execution of the accompanying hedges. In order to achieve an 'optimized' exploitation of the cum-ex flaw in the settlement system, this problem had to be solved. The first step was therefore to insulate the trade from the uncertainty created by market price risk.

It should be clear from what has been said above that very large blocks of shares in German companies would need to be traded to generate what would for a bank be material profits from the cum-ex trading strategy. However, short selling large blocks of shares is a risky undertaking. When a seller goes into the open market to sell shares, the process of finding a price at which buyers will trade and strike a bargain is something financial regulators call 'price discovery'. To traders on a structured finance desk, price discovery means unpredictable and volatile results in real market trading conditions. Uncertainty of outcome attracts attention from within the bank because market volatility creates the potential for loss which, quite apart from the losses it may inflict on the trading desk, may eat into the capital

[31] Given that banks will not accept unnecessary risks, each constraint described above had to be carefully examined and a solution for it found. Overcoming all of the constraints was a complex undertaking. Each transaction or step in the structure needed to operate harmoniously with each of the others. The final trading structure would also have to pass through the bank's controls and receive approval.

base of the bank and therefore restrict the bank's activities.[32] If a transaction involves large amounts and uncertain results, the credit, risk, and treasury groups will scrutinize and may well reject it.[33] If the transaction creates actual losses of any significance, the consequences for the trading staff range from dismissal to the incident being reported to the bank's board of directors. A large financial loss would trigger a full-scale investigation in which the bank's regulator would probably be involved or at least informed. It would also lead to a detailed investigation including the chronology of events, steps taken in mitigation, any lessons for the future, and the identification of the accountable parties.

Optimization of the cum-ex strategy therefore sought to take away as much risk as possible, and preferably all risk. An obvious way to do this is for the short seller, at the end of the trade, to buy the shares back from the same party that bought the shares under the short sale agreement at the trade's commencement. Such an approach would remove risk from the seller because it would mean the seller is assured that it will receive back the shares, enabling it to return them to the stock lender. The buyer would also be relieved of risk because the arrangement would mean that it could buy and sell the shares relatively quickly, being confident it had a buyer to repurchase the shares at the conclusion of the trade. Eliminating market risk also means the price at which the shares are sold and later repurchased would need to be agreed between the parties in advance. Such an approach would facilitate the isolation of the cum-ex benefit. However, it would also mean the abandonment by the seller of any attempt to exploit the cum-ex benefit by the 'stand-alone' use of ordinary short sales in the market. It would also transform the nature of the role of any buyer involved in the trade, as that party would obviously have no interest in retaining any investment in the shares. Instead, the buyer would be the temporary recipient of the shares as they travelled their circular course around the settlement system (from seller to buyer and back again), collecting tax credits as they went.

Given the earlier discussion of the possible consequences of market trades going wrong, and the fact that the author is not aware of any reported incidents of cum-ex trades actually going wrong in this way, the implication at a practical level seems obvious: cum-ex traders must have known in advance who was going

[32] Banks are inherently leveraged, meaning that their shareholder's equity is a small proportion of their total assets. Maintaining the integrity of banks' processes, maintaining visibility to the value and composition of their assets, and controlling their ready access to sources of funding are all goals of financial regulation. However, none of these objectives can be effective if losses are not contained, as losses erode capital, thereby increasing leverage and undermining confidence in both the bank and the wider financial system.

[33] The bank's credit group will be concerned to know that the counterparty on a large value transaction has the resources to perform its obligations under the transaction, while the risk group will aim to assess what the quantum of those obligations is likely to be under a number of scenarios. The treasury group will be concerned to know that the bank itself has sufficient funds available to finance the transaction, in the context of the other financing obligations the bank has assumed in aggregate across its business lines.

to purchase the shares, and also when, in what quantity, and at what price. Thus, when €350 million shares of Allianz AG, for example, were going to be sold short, the short seller would know exactly which party was going to buy those shares, and also how they were going to be repurchased. All of the shares could then be sold to, and repurchased from, the ready buyer without any fluctuation in their price. In order to ensure that there were no losses whatsoever, the bank and its counterparty would also enter into hedging transactions with each other.[34] For example, the bank would wish to enter into a long derivative transaction with the buyer. That would offset any losses on its short position in the shares. From the buyer's perspective the same derivative contract would hedge the risk on the shares which it bought under the short-sale agreement.[35] In ordinary circumstances, a hedging trade of such size would be difficult and expensive to achieve. However, since the buyer has an equal and opposite need to hedge its exposure to the purchase of the shares through what for it is a 'short' derivatives transaction, the bank can be assured of a counterparty to the hedge. In a kind of financial suspended animation, each party then becomes both economically long and short the same quantity of shares (and the same derivatives contract) at exactly the same price and at exactly the same time. Apart from the profit shared among the parties from the cum-ex tax benefit, the net economic effect of the arrangement was precisely zero.

In concept, the result can be seen in the simplified Figure 3.2. The diagram shows a cum-div short sale of shares and a hedging transaction entered into between buyer and seller (Step 1) as well as a loan and return of shares between seller (likely in practice to be a bank) and the lender (steps 2 and 5). The shares that are returned to the lender are acquired by the seller from the buyer (Step 4) after having delivered the system-generated tax credit under the cum-ex trade (Step 3). The simplified example reveals the significant change in the role of the buyer when the position is compared to Figure 3.1. In the earlier example, the buyer would have no knowledge the seller was selling short, nor that any tax credit

[34] As explained earlier, selling the shares short leaves the bank exposed to a rise in the price of the shares because a parcel of shares will ultimately need to be purchased in the market to return to the lender whose shares were used to fulfil the short sale. Conversely, the buyer is exposed to a fall in the price of the shares for as long as they are held. This is why both parties will normally hedge their respective exposures with derivative positions.

[35] It is the buyer's need for a hedge that explains why a German buyer in a cum-ex transaction would need to be a bank or other financial institution holding the shares and the hedge on its trading book. For such a buyer, the income and expenses from the shares and the hedge would be treated in the same way, namely as taxable (in the case of income) or deductible (in the case of expenses). In practice, this would mean any gain or loss on the shares would be offset for German tax purposes by an equal and opposite loss or gain on the hedge. For other corporate buyers, there would be no such symmetrical tax treatment. Instead, any dividend income derived would be subject to an effective 95 per cent exemption, as explained in Chapter 2 (with any gain on the shares also exempt), but the hedge would have been fully taxable, yet with restrictions on the use of any losses. This means that, for such a buyer, a fall in the value of the shares between purchase and resale would lead to a non-deductible loss on the shares and a taxable gain on the hedge. The risk of such a tax charge precluded the use of such buyers.

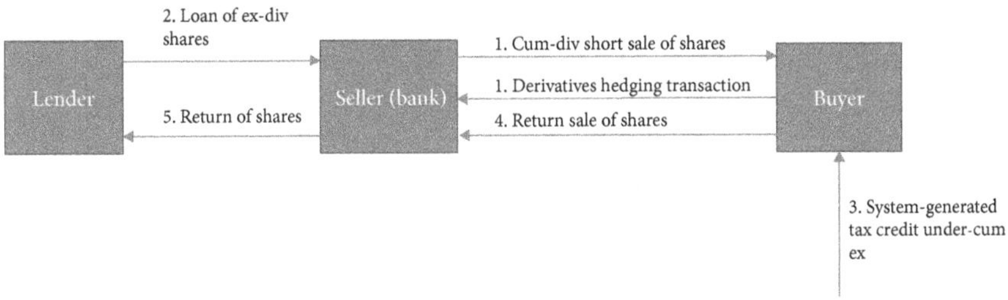

Figure 3.2. Removing market risk from the cum-ex trade

would be system-generated. The actions of the buyer in Figure 3.2 on the other hand indicate the buyer has no intention of being economically exposed to the shares—the position of a normal buyer wishing to own the shares—and the buyer's role now enables a risk-free execution of the cum-ex trade, sharing the profits generated with the seller.

The example shows a single large transfer of shares. In practice, the transfers might be broken up into smaller parcels. By agreeing a sale price which was at, or somewhere near, the then current market price, and breaking the sale up into a number of smaller parcels (or, in Wall Street parlance, 'shapes'), the intention was that the trades would not attract adverse attention. They would be unremarkable among the trillions of dollars of shares sales and purchases that pass through the financial markets each business day.

There is another important advantage to the trade structure and this is also illustrated in Figure 3.2. Having first sold the shares short and then later borrowed ex-dividend shares to finalize the sale, the seller is left with an obligation to return the borrowed shares to the lender at some point. Even if it can reduce or eliminate its price risk by a hedging transaction, the seller must still reacquire the shares at the end of the trade so that they can be returned to the lender. This potentially puts the seller in the awkward position of having to repurchase the shares in the market (probably causing a rise in their price) while simultaneously closing down the hedging transaction designed to protect against those same prices rises. A major advantage of the structure illustrated in Figure 3.2 lies in the fact that the buyer has an interest in disposing of the shares which the seller needs to repurchase. This is because each of the seller and the buyer are strongly incentivized to ensure that the hedging trade is closed out on favourable terms. This will be possible if buyer can sell the shares, and seller can buy the shares, on terms that align with the hedging contract at the time it expires, thereby removing any risk from market price volatility.[36] In fact, once the scheme is agreed, a profitable outcome is mutually assured. Neither party has an interest in deviating from the terms of the deal, for to do so would expose it to severe risk of loss. Of course, such

[36] For a more detailed explanation of the approach see footnote 46 below.

interdependency between the parties also means that the profits of the trade need to be shared in a mutually satisfactory way.

Obscuring the Identity of the Parties: The Role of Inter-Dealer Brokers

Although the simplified structure illustrated in Figure 3.2 deals effectively with the market risk issues at a conceptual level, it introduces a fundamental problem. The problem is so foundational that it explains why a structure in the form of Figure 3.2 would not be seen in practice. Structured in the way depicted in Figure 3.2, the short sale would generally not be respected for tax or accounting purposes. In other words, it would not be treated by reference to the intended transaction executed by the parties and nor would it be accepted as having the intended consequences (including, critically, the tax consequences and in particular the entitlement of the buyer to a tax credit). The reason, not surprisingly, is that it is generally not possible to sell (or buy) a parcel of shares under a pre-agreed arrangement that the same shares will later be repurchased from the original buyer (or resold to the original seller) and then expect to be treated for tax purposes as having made an outright disposal of them (or acquisition of them). Under German tax law, for example, if the transaction had been structured in this way then the arrangement would have been seen as abusive and it would not have been effective in capturing the system-generated tax credit at the heart of the cum-ex scheme.[37] For example, the general tax anti-abuse rule in Section 42 of the General Tax Code and the German repo rules would have come into play and defeated the aims of the trade.[38] There could have also been adverse tax consequences in the jurisdiction of a non-German party to a cum-ex trade.[39] Such an overt circular arrangement would leave little prospect of the buyer in a cum-ex trade being regarded as entitled to the tax credit on any system-generated dividend payment.

[37] Structuring the transaction as illustrated in Figure 3.2 would also have other implications, for example a different accounting for the results of the transaction may have been required.

[38] The general anti-abuse rule is discussed in Chapter 2. The entitlement to a tax credit is also policed by specific anti-abuse requirements stipulated in Section 36a of the Income Tax Act. In a repo transaction, the beneficial ownership of the shares remains with the original seller for accounting purposes (Section 340b of the German Commercial Code) and the provisions of the German Commercial Code relating to the ownership of assets and liabilities are intended to be consistent with the tax notion of ownership in Section 39 of the General Tax Code.

[39] For example, a UK short seller that repurchases the shares or similar shares on the unwind of a transaction would have been vulnerable to the recharacterization of the transaction as a repo transaction under complex UK tax law dealing with manufactured dividends. The result would be that the seller would be deemed to be in receipt of a manufactured dividend payment subject to a 'reverse charge' withholding tax under ICTA 1988, Schedule 23A Paragraph 4 (4), (later rewritten into CTA 2010, Section 794). The UK law referred to here is discussed later in this chapter.

This obvious conflict between eliminating market risk issues and preserving the intended tax credit benefit of the trade had to be resolved.

In order for the cum-ex trade (as now modified to take care of the market risk issues) to work, the buyer had to appear in all respects to be a genuine or *bona fide* purchaser of the shares or it would not be entitled to the tax credits. To do this, it was necessary to break any visible connection between seller and buyer. Some kind of mechanism was required to allow the shares to be sold 'into the market' by the seller, and later repurchased by it through the same apparent open-market mechanism, without disturbing the arrangements which neutralized market risk. The same approach was needed for the buyer. The solution, in the form of a 'market' for these purposes, came largely to mean a type of third party known as an inter-dealer broker. Inter-dealer brokers or 'IDBs' as they are commonly known, are niche brokerage firms which intermediate orders between other brokers or financial institutions.[40] The theory behind the existence of these 'brokers of brokers' is that they provide privacy and liquidity in markets for financial instruments, enabling larger brokers to acquire or dispose of shares without revealing their identity to the other party selling or purchasing those instruments.

Whatever their purpose in other market transactions, inter-dealer brokers were critical to the success of the cum-ex strategy for a number of reasons. First, they represent an opaque layer between the short seller of shares in a cum-ex trade and the ultimate buyer. When a large block of shares is sold immediately before the dividend record date to an inter-dealer broker, the link between seller and ultimate buyer is obscured. Since the role of the inter-dealer broker is to ensure anonymity and privacy, it is in theory not possible to look through the inter-dealer broker to discover the identity of its confidential client. Second, because there are numerous inter-dealer brokers, buying the shares back at the conclusion of the cum-ex trade becomes a simple matter of approaching a different inter-dealer broker to that used for the initial sale. Again, the identities of both buyer and seller are in this way concealed. The revised structure of the trade using inter-dealer brokers can be seen in Figure 3.3.

Obscuring the circularity of the steps in the transaction was critical. With inter-dealer brokers interposed in all the steps, any casual challenge to the transaction could be met with the response that the shares were sold through an open-market transaction with an inter-dealer broker (IDB1, in Figure 3.3), with a parcel of shares later bought in the market via a different inter-dealer broker (IDB2, as

[40] IDBs intermediate through standardized processes and systems for concluding financial transactions. For example, secure communication systems such as Bloomberg or recorded voice conversations can be used to enter into binding transactions to buy and sell shares, while secure messaging systems such as SWIFT transmit the instructions by which cash and securities are moved from party to party. IDBs, as described further in this chapter, also have at their disposal trade entry systems which can be used to transact purchases and sales of securities and derivatives on exchange.

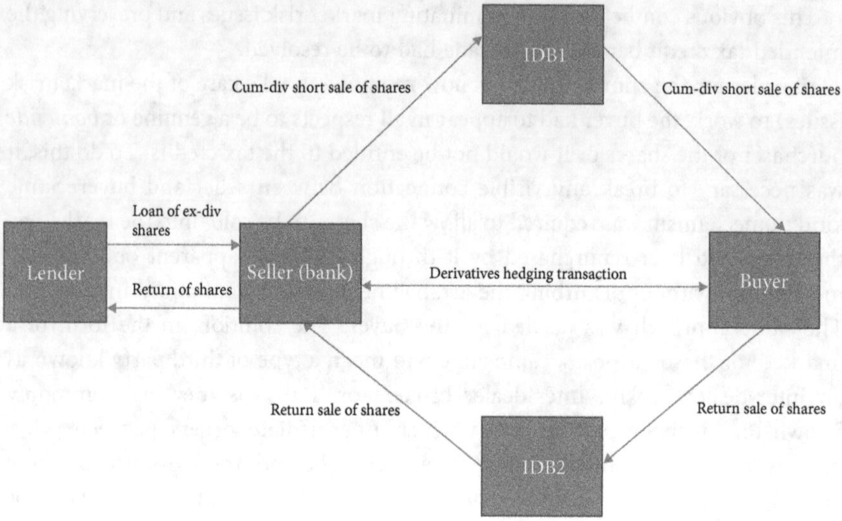

Figure 3.3. Use of IDBs (1)

shown in Figure 3.3). It could then be said that those trades were with disinterested third-party brokers working for their own clients in the market. With these measures in place, the participants could contend that the transactions should be regarded as genuine market trades conducted in the market at arm's length. The short seller of the shares might then be presented as having completely divested itself of the shares sold, parting with any control over them and having in place no discernible prearrangements to repurchase them.

One problem with inserting multiple parties into the trade in order to conceal its circularity is this: how does one coordinate all the steps so that each party knows how many shares to buy (or sell) and when? In practice, various approaches could be used to deal with this issue. One possible technique was that, at some time prior to trade date, the parties (buyer, seller, and inter-dealer brokers) would meet, call, or text message each other to agree a trade size.[41] On the trade date, the short seller, generally the bank, would, in addition to placing an order to short-sell the shares through an inter-dealer broker (say IDB1), call up a different inter-dealer broker (say IDB2), responsible for the derivatives hedging transaction, and place a buy order for the hedge reflecting the pre-agreed trade size.[42] IDB2 would contact a number of market counterparties, using Bloomberg or a similar messaging service. Although that would seem to be a step which offered the derivatives hedging contract up to anyone, in fact, all the market counterparties to whom it

[41] Using secure means such as pay-as-you-go phones, mobile phones not registered with the bank, or secure messaging services such as WhatsApp.

[42] For reasons that are explained later in this chapter, the most commonly used hedging instrument was a single stock futures contract.

was sent would be cum-ex traders. Each would know that (1) it was intended to be taken up by only one of their number, and (2) that, representing a hedge on a trade over a designated number of shares in a specific company, it had to match the pre-agreed transaction details. Only one of them would be dealing in this particular number of shares in relation to the company specified and it would be only that party which would then pick the trade up. The buyer of shares, seeing the derivatives hedging contract order put out for offer, would know that it was time to lodge its share purchase order with IDB1. The buyer would simultaneously accept the derivatives hedging contract offered by IDB2.

Not all cum-ex trades were organized in this way. Another possibility was that the inter-dealer broker managing the share purchase for the buyer could put out a message broadcast on an electronic dealing service such as: '5.25 million shares Siemens to buy, *subject to hedge*'. The unique share quantity and the key words 'subject to hedge' told all of the bank trading desks receiving the message (cum-ex traders) that this was a share purchase order which was intended to be matched by an offsetting futures hedge. Those words offered another level of protection, in the sense that the attachment of a condition, 'subject to hedge', ensured the purchase of shares would not be confused with a straightforward buy order. It was understood by cum-ex traders across the market as code for a prearranged trade taking place between one buyer and one short seller. The buyer and short seller could then deal with each other via their preselected inter-dealer brokers and consummate the purchase and sale of shares and the related derivatives hedging contract.

Overcoming Collateral Constraints

As noted earlier, collateral constraints on the constituent transactions of a cum-ex trade represent a possible impediment to trading. For example, the short seller in a cum-ex trade may be a financial trader which is using a bank to finance and arrange the transactions.[43] If the financial trader intended to short-sell large quantities of shares, this would give rise to significant market risk and therefore margin requirements would quickly come into play. Returning to the example of a €300 million short sale of shares in RWE AG, the amount that a bank would require its client to deliver as collateral for a routine[44] short sale of such size would generally be in the order of 10 to 15 per cent of the transaction value, i.e. €30–45 million. With multiple cum-ex trades being run at once, the cum-ex trader would quickly run out of cash.

[43] In such a case, the financial trader may be relying on the bank to arrange for the borrowing of the shares concerned and to finance the transaction by lodging collateral with the lender of those shares.

[44] The reference to a routine short sale is intended to mean a transaction that is not connected with a cum-ex trade and not hedged by an offsetting derivative transaction.

The solution to this issue comes from two sources that have already been discussed: the use of a derivatives transaction to reduce market risk and the use of inter-dealer brokers to obscure the involvement in the transaction between seller and buyer.

The market risk problem is solved by hedging the short sale with derivatives transactions, as described earlier in this chapter. If the client of the bank were to short-sell €300 million of the RWE AG shares while at the same time entering into a €300 million 'long' derivatives contract linked to those shares, it could immunize itself from any market price movements in the price of those shares. In Wall Street terminology, it would be both 'short' the shares, and 'long' an equal and offsetting exposure to the shares through the derivative. However, whilst a bilateral derivative transaction entered into directly with the buyer of the shares would solve the market risk issue, it would, if entered into directly between the seller and buyer, expose the identity and relationship between the parties, drawing a direct link between them. The danger would be that this would expose the circularity of the trade over the shares and, as explained above, nullify the effectiveness of the intended cum-ex trade.

What was needed was a way for the seller to 'buy' the derivative and the buyer to 'sell' the derivative without them dealing directly with each other. If it were possible to eliminate the economic risk using an apparently open-market mechanism, the bank could justify applying a very small collateral requirement to the trades, notwithstanding their size. The collateral requirement would be reduced to perhaps 1 per cent, or even less. On a €300 million short sale, this might only require the cum-ex short seller to post €3 million in cash as security for the trade. Not surprisingly, this was also a situation where inter-dealer brokers could be used to deliver the intended benefits of the trade. With an inter-dealer broker inserted between the parties, the short seller can simply buy a derivative from the inter-dealer broker.[45] The inter-dealer broker would then enter into an equal and opposite derivatives trade with the buyer, as shown in Figure 3.4.[46]

The hedging transaction serves a further purpose which goes beyond isolating the buyer and the seller from market risk and greatly mitigating collateral constraints. It is the conduit by which the profits of the cum-ex trade can be shared between the parties. Alternatives to the parties sharing the profits through the

[45] The collateral issue explains why the approach discussed would normally be preferable to the alternative approach of bifurcating the composite transaction between related parties—i.e. using one group company to sell short and another group company to take a long derivative position.

[46] Upon expiry of the cum-ex trade, the seller would pay or receive under the derivatives hedging trade what it lost or gained, respectively, from the market price movements of the shares that were sold under the short sale. This would allow the seller to repurchase the shares at the then market price through IDB2. This ensures that none of the problems involved in buying and selling large blocks of shares on the open market, discussed earlier in this chapter, emerge. Once the shares are bought back in this way, the short seller can return the shares to the stock lender. For its part, the buyer, now that it has its original purchase monies back, can repay any loan it drew down to buy the shares.

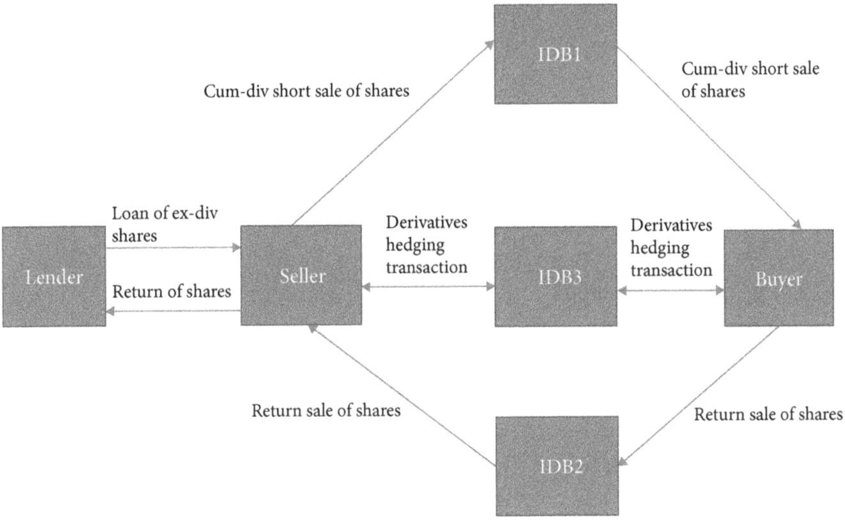

Figure 3.4. Use of IDBs (2)

derivative hedging trade would be both limited and risky. Any separate cash flow passing directly between seller and buyer, such as a profit-sharing fee for the cum-ex trade, would draw attention to the direct relationship between them, something the involvement of the inter-dealer brokers was designed to disguise. It would also be most unusual for a market transaction of this sort. Neither would it be attractive to share profits through the short sale of the shares.[47] That transaction would need to be carried out at a price as close as possible to the price prevailing in the open market for the shares. It was important that the prices at which shares in cum-ex trades were sold and bought did not differ from their price quoted on the stock exchange. If they did, it would be difficult for the parties to argue that the transactions were open-market transactions at arm's length. Derivative transactions, on the other hand, can have more variation in their pricing. This is because there is no immediate sale and purchase of an item of property such as a share which has a readily ascertainable traded value. The share has ascertainable value by reference to its price on the stock exchange on which it trades. However, the derivative transaction would often be a contract with customized terms such as time to expiry of the contract, amount of premium paid at inception of the contract, etc, and there would therefore be no obvious benchmark against which a third party could compare the pricing terms of the derivative transaction. But

[47] A further advantage of the derivative is that cash flows under the contract would normally not be subject to German withholding tax as they would not fall within the designated items subject to withholding in Section 49 (1) Income Tax Act.

embedded in its large transactional size would be the comparatively small element of profit representing the profit from cum-ex.

Dealing with Operational Risk

Within a bank, the management of operational risk associated with trading (i.e. the risk of errors which might undermine the profitability of trades) is normally delegated to the bank's main middle-office operations group.[48] However, this was not an especially attractive proposition for cum-ex traders. The concern was that the diverse transactional elements of cum-ex were not typical of the standard functions carried out by middle- and back-office operations within the bank. There was a risk that there would be insufficient capacity to deal with the trade or that there would be a failure to appreciate the high degree of vigilance needed in managing all the components of trade. The solution adopted by a number of cum-ex trading desks was to build out and staff a separate middle office within the bank which could be dedicated to the cum-ex traders. In order to obscure their function and justify their presence on the trading floor, they might be described as 'desk support'. For convenience, they might even sit near the bank's structured equity desk. Responding to directions from the trading desk and isolated from the bank's operations group, this dedicated middle office could be focused on dividend-related trades. That focus meant the team would develop specialist expertise in handling cum-ex trades and not be distracted by the general business of the bank.[49]

A second means of controlling operational risk associated with cum-ex was, to the extent possible, to internalize and standardize all the elements of the trade. Instead of dealing with a third-party trading cum-ex at a distance, the cum-ex trading counterparty—usually an investment fund—would often become a client of the bank. As a client, it could hold substantially all of its shares and its hedging transactions at the bank and deal with the bank more or less exclusively, albeit through the intermediation of inter-dealer brokers. This greatly narrowed the number of third parties coming into contact with the client, reducing dependency on others. Having agreed the trade size and pricing with the bank, the client could

[48] 'Middle office' is a term used to describe the group within a bank's operations function which manages the transactions agreed to by the bank's front office. Whereas the 'back office' will ensure the outcome of the transactions is properly recorded in the bank's books and that any discrepancies are identified, the middle office will assist in managing the trades, interacting with third parties such as clients and brokers to ensure the transactions are consummated and ultimately closed.

[49] Operations functions, because of the perceived lower value of their work, are generally allocated less expensive office space within a bank or possibly are located in a different building. However, this dedicated middle office supporting the cum-ex traders would be critical to the success of the trades and their higher-value work meant that they could occupy costly space on the trading floor. The creation of a dedicated middle-office function for cum-ex transactions is discussed further in Chapter 6.

then authorize the trading staff of the bank to carry out the necessary transactions on its behalf. The arrangement meant that the bank wore two hats: a client hat (where it acted as the client's agent in dealing with the IDBs) and a bank trading hat (where it acted on its own behalf in dealing with the IDBs). This allowed the bank to carry out its own side of the cum-ex trade, then take the bank hat off and put on a client hat to carry out the other side of the trade on behalf of the client. If an organization is effectively dealing with itself in this way, the scope for error is substantially reduced. Minimizing operational risk would allow the bank to offer even higher levels of leverage to the cum-ex fund client. Higher leverage translated directly into higher returns for the client and the bank from the cum-ex strategy. Further, since the bank would charge interest on the funds advanced to the client to buy the shares being short sold, the more money was loaned, the higher were the bank's profits.[50]

Nevertheless, cum-ex could not operate without some involvement of third parties, particularly the inter-dealer brokers. Lowering operational hazards associated with their involvement meant standardization. The same inter-dealer broker would therefore often be used by a bank for the same transaction each time a cum-ex trade was executed. For example, one inter-dealer broker would be responsible for the derivatives trades, while another would look after short sales, etc. Standardizing the roles of the parties meant that all parties knew exactly what they were doing. Their functions became highly routinized, further reducing the scope for error.

All these measures were intended to ensure that the operational risk of cum-ex was minimized. Their implementation was a further step in the industrialization of the trade.

Refining the Cum-Ex Trade

The preceding discussion explains how the various market constraints were dealt with whilst simultaneously trying to ensure that the tax credit benefit at the heart of the cum-ex trade was protected. A number of further modifications to the cum-ex structure are discussed in this section. These are refinements made to the design and implementation of the trade to achieve various goals including: expanding the parties (and therefore the sources of capital) that could be involved in the cum-ex trade in order to broaden the scale of trading activity; improving the cosmetics of the trade; making the structure more efficient; and boosting

[50] The bank would typically take a security interest over the shares, further cementing its position to ensure that the client could not remove the shares involved in the strategy without the bank's consent and giving the bank the right to sell the shares to repay the loan in the event of a default. In this situation, the bank would be lending money to the party purchasing the shares the bank is selling.

profitability, both by devising a way to permit multiple repetitions of the basic trade between the same counterparties and also by cutting the costs of implementing the trade. By exploiting flexible features of the settlement system, particularly in relation to the timing of share deliveries, cum-ex traders were able to use and then reuse a single parcel of borrowed shares in executing multiple cum-ex trades. While the owner from whom the shares were borrowed would suffer withholding tax on the dividend only once (and thereby receive only a single tax credit), the parties trading cum-ex could recycle that same parcel of shares between them repeatedly, creating tax credits which were not only unrelated to any actual withholding tax but also which represented many multiples of the withholding tax actually suffered by the party who owned the shares prior to dividend record date. Some further changes were also made to the cum-ex structure to sidestep efforts by the tax authorities to close down the cum-ex trade. A number of the modifications made to the trade delivered multiple benefits simultaneously. Examples of all these modifications to the structure of the cum-ex trade are discussed below.

Multiplying the Cum-Ex Trade

One way in which the benefit of the cum-ex trade could be boosted is by arranging multiple trades (in effect, trades within trades), timed by reference to the same dividend record date and using the same parcel of (ex-dividend) shares to settle the various short cum-dividend sales. This is what is illustrated in Figure 3.5. To illustrate the complex nature and effect of the successive transactions within a short space of time, each individual step in the diagram includes information on

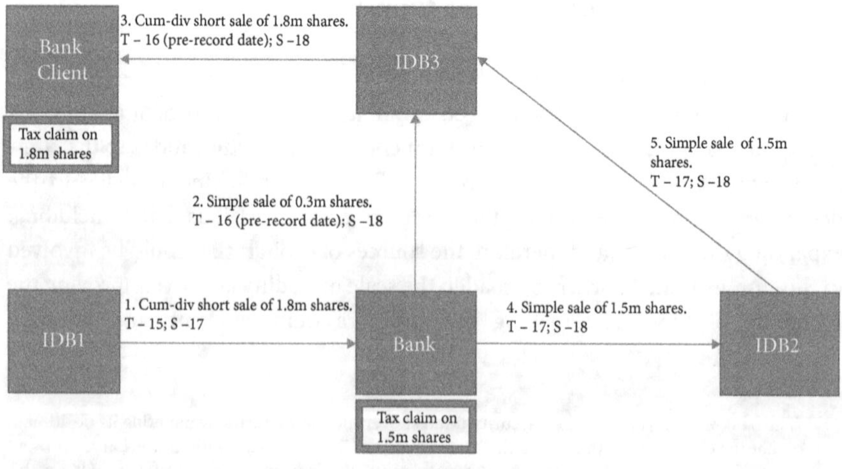

Figure 3.5. Trades within trades

the trade date and settlement date. These dates are denoted by "T" and "S" respectively in Figure 3.5. In the example, the relevant dividend record date (around which the various sale transactions are structured) is the 17th day of the month. This means that a cum-ex tax benefit may be delivered in any case where the relevant trade date of a sale is before that date and the relevant settlement date is on or after that date. (Where a sale is not made before the dividend record date and so does not achieve the cum-ex tax benefit, it is referred to in Figure 3.5 as a simple sale).

Figure 3.5 demonstrates two main points. The first is the ability to immediately recycle a cum-ex trade to allow one or more successive cum-ex trades which are designed to also deliver the cum-ex tax benefit. This can be seen in Figure 3.5 by following through the sequence of transactions following the first cum-ex trade at Step 1 to a second cum-ex trade at Step 3. It can be seen that the parcel of shares used to settle the transactions comprises a parcel of 1.8 million shares. Nonetheless, the arrangements depicted in Figure 3.5 are designed to generate a tax claim under the two cum-ex trades entered into by Bank and Bank Client in respect of 3.3 million shares in aggregate (Bank makes a tax claim on 1.5 million shares and Bank Client a tax claim on 1.8 million shares). This is possible because of the multiplication of the cum-ex benefit achieved by this "trade within a trade" structure. Having (at Step 1) bought shares cum-dividend from IDB1 (which is the short seller), Bank sells on the shares to IDB3 (Step 2) and IDB2 (Step 4). The sale to IDB3 is made by Bank before the record date (which explains why Bank's tax claim is restricted to 1.5m shares), but the sale to IDB2 takes place after that record date. At Step 3, and prior to the record date, IDB3 short-sells cum-dividend 1.8 million shares to Bank Client and uses the shares it will acquire from Bank and IDB2 to settle the trade. The short sellers in this example are therefore IDB1 and IDB3. The role of IDB2 arises after the relevant record date for the dividend and therefore IDB2 is involved simply to move ex-dividend shares to IDB3. The multiplication benefit is illustrated in Figure 3.5 by reference to a second cum-ex trade but in practice the sequence could be repeated to generate further tax credit benefits.[51]

The second point illustrated by Figure 3.5 is the use in practice of contracts over different sized parcels (or 'shapes') of shares and the use of intermediated entities (such as IDB2). Both features are designed to obscure the real purpose of the structure. It can be seen that Bank has chosen to reduce its tax claim under the cum-ex trade at Step 1 by structuring the onward sale of shares to IDB3 at Step 2 prior to the dividend record date. This means that its record date entitlement

[51] Although the process described is capable of multiple iterations, there were practical limits to the number of cycles which could be carried out in a working day. Beyond a certain point, which will depend among other things on the operational sophistication of the participants involved and the systems they use, the repeated recycling of securities becomes too complicated to manage, creating the risk of a failure to complete the related trades in the chain.

would be for the net amount of the two transactions, i.e. 1.5 million shares. This is designed to obscure the prearranged circularity of the arrangements by indicating there is no necessary connection between the number of shares bought at Step 1 and the later tax claim. After the record date, Bank sells on its remaining 1.5 million shares to IDB2, which immediately on-sells them to IDB3. This allows IDB3 to settle the cum-ex trade over 1.8 million shares it entered into with Bank Client (see at Step 3). The interposition of IDB2 is again designed to obscure the circularity of the arrangements.

Expanding Participation in the Cum-Ex Trade

The massive scale of cum-ex trading is explained by a number of factors but arguably the most important of these is the expansion of participation in the trade to include parties from around the world. Wider participation proved important for a number of reasons. Most obviously, it led to a vast increase in the number of participants seeking to enter in to cum-ex trades, the volume of executed trades, and thus the value of the tax credits generated. It also led to fresh sources of capital to finance the trading activity[52] and new sources of revenue for banks managing or executing cum-ex trades on behalf of this enlarged client base.

The following discussion considers various aspects of this wider participation in the cum-ex trade, a trend that was relevant to all parties—buyers, sellers, lenders, and their agents.

1. The Involvement of Overseas Sellers and Buyers and Industrialization of Cum-Ex

The cum-ex trade was exploited initially on a largely domestic basis, with buyers and sellers located in Germany. However, there was in reality no requirement for the parties to be present in Germany. The seller and the buyer would of course need to have access to a Clearstream account, but this was easily accomplished if each of those parties used a custodian bank which itself was a customer of Clearstream.[53] The seller (and lender) could be almost anywhere in the world. The buyer also had no reason to be located in Germany provided the tax credit

[52] New sources of capital to finance cum-ex activity would have been important as funding is required in respect of collateralizing the short sale and the stock borrowing under the cum-ex trade.

[53] The vital role of the Clearstream settlement system in turn led to the requirement for German shares which were settled in that system (and preferably high-dividend-paying German shares) as the subject matter of the cum-ex trade. Provided such shares were available and they paid a reasonably high dividend, the identity of the particular corporate whose shares they were was largely irrelevant.

could be used effectively.[54] For non-German buyers, this usually meant that a large amount of the tax credit would be repaid in cash under the terms of an applicable double tax treaty between Germany and the country in which the buyer was resident.[55] Ensuring the most effective use of the tax credit required the identification of those states with which Germany had tax treaties and then ascertaining which of those treaties provided for the application of the lowest rate of German withholding tax on dividend payments from German corporates. A party located in such a state would then be able to make a reclaim in cash from the German tax authority, being the difference between the rate of withholding ordinarily applied to dividends in Germany (26.375 per cent) and the (lower) rate prescribed by the double tax treaty with that state. In some cases, all the credit was refundable in cash because of specific features of the buyer (as in the case of a US pension fund, discussed further in Subsection 2 below.).

For an overseas buyer in a cum-ex trade, the general approach was to use the tax treaty with the lowest rate of permitted withholding tax as this would maximize the amount of cash that could be reclaimed. For example, whilst German treaties often permit a 15 per cent rate of withholding tax, the treaty between Germany and Ireland caps the permitted withholding tax on dividends paid from German companies to Irish residents at 10 per cent. The effect of the cap would be that, of the 26.375 per cent withholding tax deducted in Germany, the Irish resident could reclaim 16.375 per cent (26.375 per cent minus 10 per cent) in cash from the German tax authority. This made it attractive to establish and use Irish parties as cum-ex buyers. Not surprisingly, a number of cum-ex structures were designed using an Irish vehicle as the buyer, for example, Irish investment funds.

Thus, although the use by German taxpayers (acting as buyers) of the German tax credit was a common feature of the earlier cum-ex structures, as time went on there was an increasing presence of non-German buyers and sellers. There were in fact a number of incentives for foreign parties to participate in cum-ex. For example, a foreign short seller, such as a bank based in the United Kingdom, could generate the key tax benefit under the cum-ex trade but would not be subject to any German corporate income tax or trade tax.

The process by which participation in the trade was 'internationalized' was also fuelled by some specific developments that are explored in more detail below. The efforts of the German tax authorities to close the cum-ex trade down proved to be an important factor. The details are discussed later in this chapter, but for current purposes what is worth noting is that these efforts to close down the trade were largely ineffective, succeeding only in shifting participation in the cum-ex trade

[54] Given that the withholding tax certificate needed by the buyer could be provided only by a German financial institution, the buyer's custodian bank would need to be resident in Germany.

[55] The relevance and operation of double tax treaties in this context is explained in Chapter 2.

away from German domestic players to overseas players. Another factor, also discussed below, was the growing sophistication of methods to extract value from the portion of the tax credit that was not refunded in cash, as this enhanced the attractiveness of the cum-ex trade to certain non-German participants.

The wider involvement in cum-ex of parties from around the globe was achieved in part by the efforts of the banks to distribute the trade to their clients as a 'financial product' offering. Such financial products are normally highly structured transactions or arrangements, commoditized by the bank for ease of implementation. The process for devising a 'financial product' usually involves five stages: design, structuring, packaging, distribution, and implementation. The process of transforming the cum-ex trade into a financial product involved standardized slide packs being presented to clients worldwide with a view to enticing them to participate in the cum-ex trade, usually in the role of the buyer. The selling effort was normally supported by opinions from legal and tax advisers. If the client was persuaded to take up the offer and participate in the strategy, the bank could play the traditional role of intermediary, picking up profits from facilitating the various transactions along the way.

2. The Role of Funds

Over time a number of types of funds (including domestic German funds and overseas pension and investment funds) became increasingly involved in cum-ex trades, again normally in the role of the buyer. Structuring the cum-ex trade to include a fund inevitably brought additional complexity to the cum-ex trade structure.

The use of funds could enhance the cum-ex trade in two different ways. First, fund vehicles were an efficient mechanism to channel into the trade additional participation—and therefore capital—which would not otherwise be possible in the absence of the fund. For example, the capital of a variety of investors such as existing pension or investment funds or high-net-worth individuals might be brought together in a new fund specially created for participation in the cum-ex strategy.[56] Second, the attributes of the fund vehicle itself could bring greater economic efficiency to the operation of the cum-ex trade. For example, as discussed in Chapter 2, the use of a German special fund proved popular in cum-ex structures because of the accelerated arrangements to reclaim the tax credit in cash which would normally apply to those funds. Similarly, US pension funds were used as the buyer in cum-ex trades because of their privileged status under the

[56] Given the nature of the cum-ex trade, the participation—and funding—could be for very short periods. Spengel refers to arrangements involving fund financing of no more than three to four days. See Spengel, 'Expert Opinion', at pp.36–7.

US–Germany tax treaty. They could reclaim in cash from the German tax authority 100 per cent of the German withholding tax. It is, of course, also possible that both of these features might be used simultaneously in the same cum-ex trade structure, as shown in Figure 3.6.[57]

Figure 3.6 shows (at Step 1) how a Luxembourg fund could be used to collect capital from multiple investors, including from high-net-worth individuals and other funds (the latter having in turn gathered capital from different sources). The capital of the Luxembourg fund is then made available (at Step 2) to a US pension fund which acts as the buyer in cum-ex transactions (Step 3). As noted, a US pension fund is entitled to reclaim 100 per cent of any German dividend withholding tax in cash. In principle, a pre-existing pension fund could be used or a dedicated pension vehicle established specifically to act as the cum-ex buyer.[58] The profits made by the pension fund buyer from the cum-ex trade would then be used

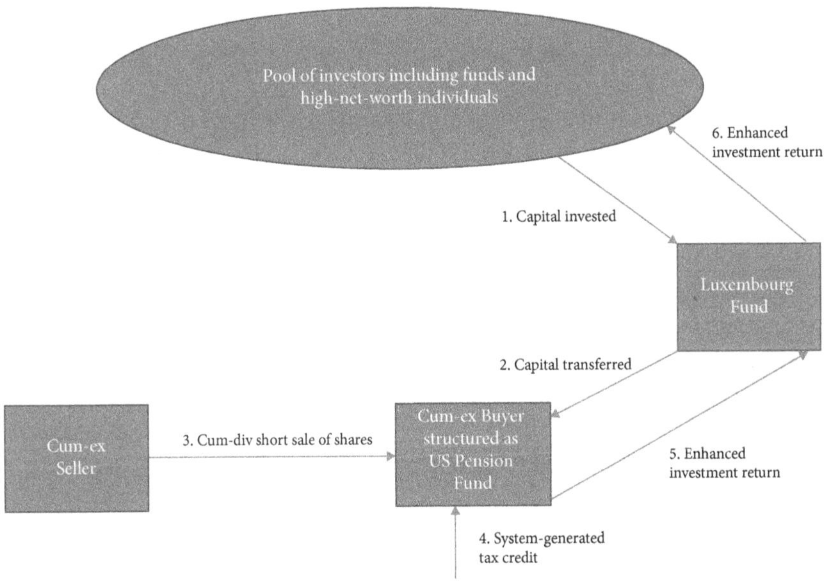

Figure 3.6. Use of funds in cum-ex

[57] Figure 3.6 is a simplified example based on the Bank Sarasin case. See OLG Köln from 11 December 2014, 7 U 23/14, juris, Document number JURE150004324.

[58] The fund may also enter into hedging arrangements, such as swaps or other derivatives. The result may be that withholding tax reclaimed from Germany is then passed, via settlement of the relevant derivative contract, to another vehicle or taxpayer, such as the party creating the captive fund in the first place.

to offer an enhanced return to the ultimate investors, via the intermediate fund (steps 5 and 6).

3. Spin-Offs

Participation in the cum-ex trade was also expanded by what may be termed 'spin-offs'. Aware of the profitability of the trade, cum-ex trading staff from some of the large investment banks left to start up their own cum-ex trading shops, often establishing new funds to pursue the strategy. Given that the trade was perfectly hedged and carried essentially no market risk, some banks provided exceptionally high levels of leverage on the cum-ex trade to such newly established cum-ex funds.[59] The close relationship between the 'spin-off' traders and their former bank employer made it much more likely that the bank would approve the fund as a counterparty, authorize it to borrow large amounts on the strategy, and offer it other favourable terms. With such vast leverage at its disposal, a fund would not need much in the way of start-up capital to be successful but would nonetheless be able to hold out to its investors the promise of lucrative returns from the cum-ex strategy.

Moving the strategy into a 'spin-off' fund managed by former employees of the bank had additional benefits. It shifted the risks associated with the cum-ex trade, including reputational risk, to the spin-off structure, instead of concentrating these risks at the bank. It also meant that gaining an understanding of the complex cum-ex structures that were executed required a comprehensive picture of the separate activities of the spin-off trading entity, two or more inter-dealer brokers, and the bank itself. That made the trade much more difficult for the authorities to understand and detect.

4. Securing the Supply of Stock Lenders

Efforts to expand participation in the cum-ex trade were not restricted to potential buyers and sellers. They also extended to potential lenders of high-dividend-paying German shares. It was noted earlier in this chapter that the availability of shares which could be borrowed in order to carry out the cum-ex trade was one important constraint on the ability to execute the strategy on a large scale.

[59] The cum-ex fund might for example have \$20 million in monies raised from investors. If the fund purchased \$1 billion of German shares, it would be leveraged fifty times (50 × \$20 million = \$1 billion). The bank could loan the fund \$980 million based on the view that there was minimal risk in the trade given that the bank itself was not only the trading counterparty for the fund but it carried out the transactional steps for both itself and the fund. See further the discussion of the double-hatted role of the bank on pp.96–7.

Accessing sufficient quantities of lendable shares to allow the cum-ex trade to take place at scale is itself a major undertaking. Stock lenders with large pools of German shares need to be identified but, even if they have a sizeable quantity of shares available, a number of problems can arise in practice. One is that they may make an investment decision to sell some or all of the relevant shares around the time that the cum-ex trade is put on. A second issue is that they may lend the securities out to another party, reducing the supply available to others. Finally, competition for the shares in the market drives up borrowing fees, driving down the profitability of the trade.

A great deal of effort was therefore expended in locating lenders, negotiating terms with them, and signing stock lending agreements.[60] To ensure dependable access to the securities, an 'exclusive lending agreement' (or 'exclusive') was used. Under this arrangement, the lender of shares would, in return for a fixed yearly fee, agree to make a whole pool of shares available for borrowing by a particular bank. That bank was selected by a process of submitting bids to the lender for the fixed annual fee, the highest bidder winning the exclusive. Exclusives were signed with stock lenders all over the world, including some highly regulated pension funds, for example, in the United States.[61] Although the lender was still free to alter its portfolio by selling shares of particular companies, these exclusive arrangements gave the bank sole access to large quantities of shares in the various cum-ex markets, including Germany.[62]

The pressure on the banks to secure a ready supply of securities that were suitable for cum-ex trading drove them to seek out more remote sources of supply. For example, the author is aware of efforts to use German shares held in the American Depositary Shares (also known as 'ADS', or in physical certificated form, the American Depositary Receipt or 'ADR') market. These are certificates listed and traded in the United States which represent an ownership interest in a number of underlying foreign shares. By a process known as pre-release or 'cracking', the ADS can be converted back into the underlying shares for use in cum-ex trades before the shares would be reconstituted in their ADS form. This made further pools of lendable shares traded in cum-ex markets available to the banks.

[60] The contract normally used in the stock lending markets is the Global Master Securities Lending Agreement or GMSLA. Some domestic German lenders may have preferred to use the German domestic market equivalent contract, the Rahmenvertrag für Wertpapierdarlehen.

[61] Many large United States pension funds are subject to the Employee Retirement Income Security Act of 1974 ('ERISA'), enforced by the United States Department of Labor. The legislation places stringent controls on the investment and use of these pension fund assets. In 2013, such plans held $7.6 trillion in assets for more than 141 million workers and beneficiaries. See the United States Department of Labor, 'Employee Benefits Security Administration Fact Sheet', available at https://www.dol.gov/agencies/ebsa/about-ebsa/our-activities/resource-center/fact-sheets/what-is-erisa.

[62] Exclusives have also been used for similar reasons to support dividend arbitrage activities.

Improvements to the Optics and Efficiency of the Cum-Ex Trade

Improvements to the optics—the apparent, rather than real, nature of the arrangements—and the economic efficiency of the cum-ex trade were delivered in a number of ways. The discussion that follows considers the use of on-exchange financial instruments and the use of physically settled derivatives, though some of the other developments discussed in this chapter would also contribute favourably to the optics and efficiency of the trade, for example, the use of inter-dealer brokers discussed above and the stock lending 'looping' arrangement discussed later in this chapter.

1. The Use of On-Exchange Instruments

Before turning to the specific use in cum-ex trades of on-exchange financial instruments, some general background on the purpose and functioning of forward contracts and their exchange-traded equivalent, the futures contract, is required. Forward contracts were originally conceived to allow buyers and sellers of a commodity such as, for example, wheat, to hedge their respective exposures to that commodity. Assume a flour manufacturer requires a certain amount of wheat in September, and a wheat farmer will harvest a certain quantity of wheat for sale around the same time. Until the time of the harvest and sale of the wheat, the purchaser (the flour manufacturer) would be exposed to a rise in the price of wheat while the seller (the farmer) might fear a decline in price. A forward contract could assist the parties in mitigating their respective risks. In spite of the terminology, it is quite simple in concept, being a contract to buy and sell a specified asset or commodity at a future date. Hence, it is bought and sold 'forward'. Earlier in the year, say, in January, the flour producer could arrange to buy wheat forward from the farmer, for delivery in September. The price would be agreed in advance but not paid until later, at the time of delivery. By entering into that forward sale and purchase contract, each party's risk or exposure to the price of wheat would be locked in or hedged. When the wheat was harvested, the farmer and the flour manufacturer would be assured of a certain price, irrespective of whether the price of wheat had fallen or risen between January, when the forward contract was agreed, and September, when the wheat was delivered. While the use of forward contracts as a means of locking in or hedging prices on commodities for future delivery was useful, it suffered from certain deficiencies. One of these was a mismatch in the quantity of a product that a particular pair of buyers and sellers wanted to buy and sell (i.e. the seller may produce more wheat than the buyer wanted to buy or vice versa). That meant having to find another party to lay off the unmatched part of the risk. Another difficulty was that individual buyers and sellers could agree on a wide variety of terms as to quality, place of delivery, timing of delivery, and the like. With highly variable terms, finding other buyers and sellers to participate in a given forward sale contract becomes more cumbersome.

The innovation came with the development of the futures market, which enabled standardized terms such as quantity and quality of the product and delivery date. A future is simply an exchange-traded forward. A clearing house associated with the exchange[63] may be inserted between the buyer and seller, taking over each of their obligations to each other and calling for collateral from each of them against their respective obligations. If the seller did not sell what was agreed to be sold or the buyer did not pay over the cash price on settlement date, the exchange would assume the obligation to deliver the goods or pay the price. What was previously a bilateral 'forward' transaction became a listed 'future', traded on exchange. Because the futures contract had standardized terms, it was liquid. In other words, numerous buyers and sellers could enter into similar standardized contracts of varying size and those contracts could easily be traded. The standardization attracted yet more participants creating a network effect. As a result, participants were concentrated into these standard hedging contracts. Soft Red Winter Wheat on the Chicago Mercantile Exchange, as an example, trades contracts that expire in July, September, December, March, and May (on the last business day prior to the 15th day of each such month), with daily volumes on the Chicago Mercantile Exchange alone reaching 15 million tons of wheat per day.[64] The key point is that standardization of terms drives volume and liquidity, one of the main objectives of the futures market.

The reason for reviewing the origin and purpose of futures exchanges is to contrast their general purpose and use with a variant which the cum-ex trading community exploited. This was the flexible single stock future, created in 2005, around the time when the cum-ex trade was growing in popularity.[65] A single stock future functions in exactly the same way as the wheat future described above, in the sense that the buyer of the future agrees to pay a price for a quantity of shares of a specific company to be delivered at a future date. However, there was a crucial difference. The flexible single stock future allowed participants nearly infinitely variable contractual terms. Instead of one contract expiry date in July, September, December, March, and May, the participants could pick any day of any month. The price to be paid for the share, expiry date of the future, and other terms could all be altered at will to whatever was required by the parties. That

[63] See, for example, the timeline of development of the Chicago Exchange and the establishment of its clearing house to guarantee trades in 1926, at 'Timeline of CME Achievements', available at https://www.cmegroup.com/company/history/timeline-of-achievements.html.

[64] http://www.cmegroup.com/trading/agricultural/wheat-futures.html

[65] See further http://www.marketswiki.com/wiki/Bclear. Primary source press releases relating to BClear appear no longer to be available online.

variability would appear hard to reconcile with the key functions of a futures market described above, namely standardization and liquidity.

While it may have had value to market participants in other contexts, the flexible single stock future was ideal for one particular situation: namely, where two parties wished to trade a futures contract over hundreds of millions of euros worth of shares in, for example, a single German company.[66] It was therefore ideally suited to the needs of the cum-ex trade. As discussed earlier, any seller entering into a short sale of German shares would need to simultaneously hedge the risk of that transaction. With a single stock futures contract, a short-seller of Siemens shares, for example, could agree to sell, say €250 million worth of shares while simultaneously entering into a 'long' single stock futures contract on those shares expiring at the agreed end-date of the cum-ex trade. The result would be that any fluctuation in the market value of the short sale of shares would be matched by equal and opposite movements in the long single stock futures contract.[67]

An important advance in the industrialization of the cum-ex trade stemmed from the particular nature of the hedging contract. BClear, for example, a facility for the trading of single stock futures contracts on the LIFFE exchange, allowed two parties to a cum-ex trade to hedge their short sales and purchases of shares with a futures contract on exchange.[68] Inserting an exchange in this way between the two parties might be taken to indicate that they would be anonymous to one another. That inference would be drawn from the fact that the parties were trading 'on exchange', and therefore not with each other. In addition to being 'transacted' on an exchange, each party's single stock futures hedging trade would be assumed

[66] An example of such a contract is the BClear 'Flex' single stock futures contract, though this was not the only means of entering into such hedging arrangements. A similar functionality was also available via Eurex, allowing parties to execute and clear bilateral trades using their Trade Entry Services, which were said to deliver 'anonymity' and 'safety'. See further http://www.eurexchange.com/blob/236908/0a3d3cfb2bdd5dfc9a7335f35b27e8ca/data/presentation_eurex-single-stock-futures-oct2017.pdf. The BATS ETR service currently provides a similar service, allowing parties to bring 'pre-negotiated trades' on exchange, see http://www.eurexchange.com/blob/236908/0a3d3cfb2bdd5dfc9a7335f35b27e8ca/data/presentation_eurex-single-stock-futures-oct2017.pdf. See also http://newsroom.icap.com/icap-routes-212-billion-notional-equity-baskets-into-bats-europes-etr-service-since-the-launch-of-their-cleared-basket-solution/.

[67] Single stock futures contracts were generally used with relatively short durations (say, up to two weeks). The cash flows under the contract would be euro-denominated, with a single net cash settlement amount paid on maturity of the contract. The cash flows are determined by reference to the 'forward price' under the contract. This forward price would typically be the spot price of the shares at the inception of the contract less the dividend (or more likely a percentage of the dividend) plus the cost of funding the shares over the life of the contract. A party that is long under such a contract would receive payments representing the appreciation in the price of the shares as compared to the forward price and pay amounts representing the depreciation in the price of the shares as compared to the forward price.

[68] BClear futures were transacted through the London International Financial Futures Exchange (LIFFE) and cleared through LCH.Clearnet Ltd. This 'reduced the counter-party credit, legal and operational risks associated with OTC deals'. See http://www.mondovisione.com/news/liffe-expands-bclear-stock-range-further-no-other-exchange-offers-more-european-/.

by the clearing house associated with the exchange. The role of the clearing house is to sit in the middle between the buyer and the seller of the future, assuming the obligations of each on the futures contract. Consequently, as far as their hedging trades were concerned, neither the short-seller nor the buyer would apparently be dealing with each other and so neither would they have direct risk to each other. Instead, each would have a contract with the clearing house. The result is illustrated in Figure 3.7.

By all outward appearance, these flexible single stock exchange-traded futures would be seen as an 'exchange', and therefore 'market' trades.[69] However, although described as exchange-traded futures transactions and sharing the legal form of such a transaction, the flexible single stock futures contract was in reality a bilateral contract that was integrated into an exchange clearing mechanism. This can be seen from the mechanics of entering into the contract and the fact that the parties to a cum-ex trade could agree in advance the identity of the inter-dealer broker they wished to use for the transactions involved in the trade. Returning to the example of RWE shares discussed earlier, having settled on using inter-dealer broker IDB1, for example, as well as on the price and other terms of the hedging transaction, the short seller would contact IDB1 with a view to entering into a long single stock futures contract to hedge its simultaneous short sale of €250 million of RWE shares. The buyer would also contact IDB1 to enter into a corresponding short RWE single stock futures of €250 million (which would hedge its simultaneous purchase of €250 million of RWE shares). With the buyer and seller agreed, a broker at IDB1 would open up, for example, a BClear flexible single stock futures trading screen. This screen allowed the broker working at IDB1 to enter the details of the buyer and the seller, the agreed price and the date at which the futures

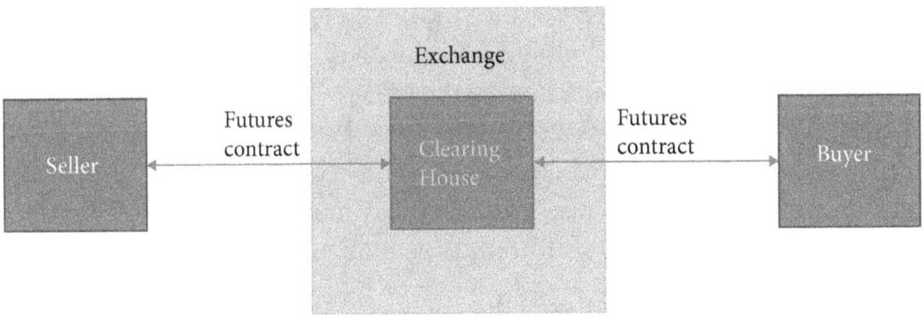

Figure 3.7. On-exchange clearing-house transactions

[69] Various alternative mechanisms to improve the optics of the trade were also possible. For example, some cum-ex trades were arranged by shorting baskets of shares (including in relation to the DAX 30) which would include one or more parcels of German shares. These shorts would then be hedged with a derivative over the basket. The net effect would be the same as delivered by the simpler version of the cum-ex trade.

contract would expire. By submitting those details on the BClear order entry screen, the pre-agreed terms of a bilateral trade between a given buyer and seller could be 'transacted' as a futures trade on the exchange. This had three immediate benefits. First, to anyone not intimately familiar with how BClear worked, the transaction appeared to be an exchange-traded transaction, carried out like any other 'on-exchange' transaction. That gave it the imprimatur of legitimacy as an apparently normal open-market transaction carried out at arm's length. Second, it also concealed what would otherwise have been a direct connection between the parties to the cum-ex trade. These first two features of flexible single stock futures contracts clearly improve the appearance or 'optics' of the arrangements. Third, the use of this mechanism eliminates counterparty risk for the parties involved. Once the exchange's clearing house accepted the trade, it split it into two parts: a hedging contract between the buyer and the exchange on the one hand, and an equal and opposite hedging contract between the seller and the exchange on the other. It then fell to the clearing house to manage that counterparty risk and, if necessary, collect collateral from the buyer and the seller.[70] As a result, the IDB would not have to manage the counterparty risk associated with all these derivative contracts.

2. The Use of Physically Settled Derivatives

Removing market risk on the short sale and purchase of the subject security can be achieved by the parties hedging with each other in the way described above. However, such hedging contracts would not generally solve a fundamental problem relating to the shares that the short seller has borrowed and delivered to the buyer. While the hedge will offset the price risk of the short sale, the hedging contract does not usually do anything to help with the seller's obligation to return shares to the lender at the conclusion of the trade.

One development to address this problem was the use of a hedging transaction which is 'physically settled'[71]. Derivative contracts are normally cash-settled, which means that any difference in the market price of the commodity or item covered by the contract during its term is paid by one party to the other at the

[70] In collecting collateral, a clearing house will generally look at the totality of a party's transactions with it. If that party is a seller of certain futures contracts with one party and a buyer of other identical or similar contracts with another party, those equal and opposite transactions may net down, meaning that the clearing house requires a reduced amount of collateral.

[71] As well as their use in the context described in this section, physically settled futures contracts were also used in another context in some cum-ex trades. This was to introduce, or at least to appear to introduce, an element of risk at the initiation of a cum-ex trade. Instead of selling shares short, the seller would sell a physically settled future which expired one day later. The idea was the buyer of that physically settled future might not exercise it (i.e. might not take delivery of the shares), thereby creating the appearance that the short sale was not inevitable.

conclusion or expiry of the contract. However, where a derivative contract is physically settled, the actual item referenced by the contract is delivered upon its expiry. In the case of the cum-ex trade, the physically settled single stock futures contract would provide for the shares to move back to the seller on termination of the contract, in much the same way that wheat would be delivered at the expiry of a physically settled commodities futures trade. This has the major attraction of ensuring that the seller can obtain the shares without having to repurchase them in a separate transaction.

It would have been important that this improvement in efficiency from the use of physically settled derivatives transactions was not gained at the expense of creating any direct and visible route by which the shares moved back from the buyer to the seller upon the termination of the hedging trade.[72] For this reason, the physically settled hedging contracts used in the cum-ex trade could be arranged through back-to-back contracts with inter-dealer brokers interposed in the contracting arrangements. Being exchange-traded contracts, the clearing house associated with the exchange would manage the delivery of shares. Thus, it would not be possible to observe the party from whom the shares were obtained.

Multiplying the Profitability of the Cum-Ex Trade

1. Looping

A further innovation made available an effectively unlimited, reliable, and free supply of shares. An understanding of the innovation requires a description of how regular (i.e. non-cum-ex) share purchases are settled during the course of a day. Suppose a buyer, not involved in a cum-ex trade, purchases a quantity of 300,000 shares. Assume further that this is a high-value amount of shares and a quantity which exceeds the average daily amount of that share which is ordinarily traded on the market. It is rare, as mentioned earlier in this chapter, for the open-market purchase of a large block of shares to be satisfied by a single seller. In the process of purchasing 300,000 shares, numerous sellers will have had the opportunity to offer their smaller lots of shares towards the buyer's total purchase. Each seller will have a price at which it is prepared to part with its shares. Consequently,

[72] As has been seen in Figure 3.4, an alternative approach is for the seller to short-sell the shares to the buyer through one inter-dealer broker while simultaneously purchasing a hedging transaction through a second inter-dealer broker. This is a possible alternative approach to structuring the cum-ex trade using a cash-settled hedging trade. Where the transaction has been prearranged, the purpose of using different inter-dealer brokers is to mask the fact that the underlying buyer on the short sale is the same party as the underlying seller on the hedging trade. Using two inter-dealer brokers makes these connected transactions appear independent. The possible difficulty in a physically settled hedging transaction is that it creates a direct and visible linkage between the movement of shares back from the buyer to the seller and the termination of the physically settled hedge trade.

the buyer will normally acquire a number of smaller parcels of shares which collectively add up to the total amount purchased. These smaller parcels, or 'shapes', would arrive in from the various sellers over the course of a trading day. A total purchase of 300,000 shares might be satisfied by one shape of 40,000 shares, two of 60,000, another of 53,000 and so on, until the desired quantity of 300,000 is reached.

The cum-ex trader exploited this mundane feature of the daily settlement process to create what may be described as a cum-ex equivalent of the spin cycle in a washing machine.

Assume, in the above example, that the purchase of 300,000 shares is part of a cum-ex trade and that the short seller (say, a bank's trading desk) is working closely with the buyer, a fund client of the bank. Immediately prior to the relevant dividend record date, the bank short-sells a quantity of 300,000 shares to the fund. Two business days later, in order to complete the cum-ex trade, the bank will have to deliver 300,000 ex-dividend shares to the buyer. The bank could borrow these shares, but it may prove difficult to borrow a block of shares in that size and at a reasonable cost (in terms of borrowing fee charged).

The response to this situation relies on two features of the financial markets. First, within Clearstream, shares can be moved between the accounts of Clearstream member firms more or less instantaneously. Second, once a share is delivered to a Clearstream participant, whether in relation to a borrow of shares or a purchase, that participant is then free to do with it as it wishes. If the assistance of a third party, such as an inter-dealer broker, could be relied on, then these features of the market infrastructure could greatly reduce both the quantity of shares required to settle the short sale of 300,000 shares as well as the cost of borrowing the shares.

The mechanism devised (often referred to as 'looping') is illustrated in Figure 3.8, and it worked as follows. Two days after the short sale by the bank (Step 1 in Figure 3.8), and once the dividend record date has passed, it is

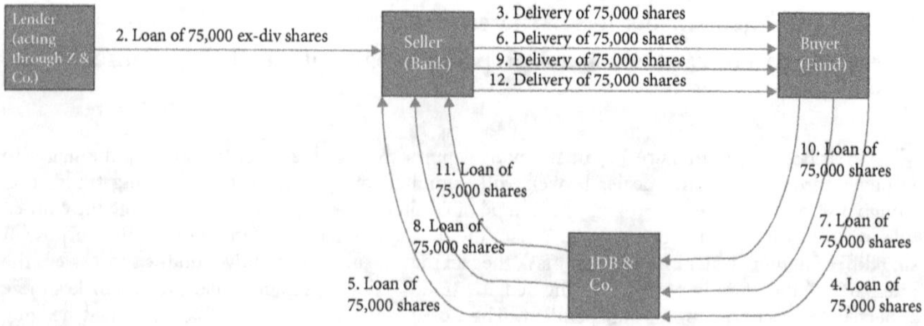

Figure 3.8. Looping

settlement day, the time for the bank to deliver 300,000 shares. All shares now borrowed will be ex-dividend, having paid out the dividend to their owners. The bank approaches Z & Co., a lender of shares on behalf of major pension funds, and borrows 75,000 shares (Step 2). The bank and Z & Co. agree that the borrow of shares will not be recallable on demand but instead that the borrow will be a committed or 'term' borrow, only recallable by Z & Co. at the expiry of two weeks.[73] The shares then move from Z & Co.'s account in Clearstream to the account of the bank, Account V111. From there, at 10:00 a.m. on the settlement date, the bank delivers the shares to the buyer's account in Clearstream, Account V222 (Step 3). Upon arrival in the buyer's account, two things are true. First, part of the seller's delivery obligation of shares is satisfied. In other words, the seller now has an obligation to deliver only 225,000 shares to the buyer (i.e. 300,000 less the 75,000 delivered). Second, now that this parcel of 75,000 shares has been delivered to the buyer, the shares are the property of the buyer, which is free to use those shares as it sees fit. Specifically, the shares are now available for the buyer to lend out.[74] At 10:15 a.m. on settlement date, the buyer approaches IDB & Co., an inter-dealer broker familiar with the business operations of both the bank and the buyer. IDB & Co. agrees to borrow the buyer's parcel of 75,000 shares (Step 4). The buyer transfers these shares into IDB & Co.'s account in Clearstream, Account V333. From there, IDB & Co. on-lends the shares to the bank, delivering the shares into its account at Clearstream, Account V111 (Step 5).

With 75,000 shares back in its possession, the bank delivers the shares again into the buyer's account at Clearstream, Account V222, thereby satisfying a further 75,000 tranche of its 300,000 share delivery obligation (Step 6). Having delivered this additional parcel of shares (which is of course the same parcel of shares as used in the first delivery), the bank's delivery obligation is further reduced to 150,000 shares (i.e. 225,000 less 75,000). Because they are all 'fungible' or completely interchangeable, the settlement system is unable to distinguish between individual parcels of shares. This means that the same parcel of 75,000 shares can be put to use in this manner repeatedly. The settlement system does not track where the shares came from or where they go after delivery to the buyer's account. Moving the same parcel of 75,000 shares two more times from the bank's Account V111 to buyer's Account V222 to IDB & Co.'s V333 and back to Account V111 over the course of the settlement day completes the seller's obligation to deliver 300,000 shares (Steps 7-12). The reason this scheme is so effective is that the continual arrival of shares over the course of the day mimics the normal pattern and tempo by which shares arrive on a large purchase. Operations and

[73] Typically, borrowed shares may be recalled at any time, hence 'on demand'. A 'term borrow' is the phrase used to describe a borrowing of shares for a fixed period of time.

[74] In practice, the buyer may not choose to lend directly to the seller. Instead, it may introduce a third party through which the shares can be routed in order to obscure the direct relationship between buyer and seller and the circular nature of the stock lending transactions.

control personnel at Clearstream, the bank and the buyer would all expect to see this regular flow of securities. It is unremarkable.

Employing this technique, it can be seen that a single parcel of shares can be used and reused to fulfil a much larger share delivery obligation. The settlement system is a machine, and as such cannot discern the cycling and recycling of shares. Being a machine, all it requires is that a total of 300,000 shares arrive in the buyer's account over the course of the day. The seller's delivery obligation is thereby discharged.

In addition to relieving the constraint on stock borrowing capacity, the 'looping' mechanism has another major benefit. It dramatically reduces the cost of borrowing the shares. In Figure 3.8, instead of incurring borrowing fees on a total borrow of 300,000 shares needed to satisfy the short sale, fees are only incurred in respect of a borrowing of 75,000 shares. From a cost-benefit perspective, this greatly improves the economics of the trade.

Notwithstanding this refinement, the need to rely on third parties, such as inter-dealer brokers, introduces undesirable risks. Each time a parcel of shares is moved around, there is a chance that an error, human or otherwise, may cause a delivery to be delayed or missed. Also, each party acting as a stock borrower in the series of transactions would be expected to deliver collateral to the party from which it borrowed the stock. Performing borrows of stocks and deliveries of collateral repeatedly over the course of a trading day becomes difficult to manage and track from an operational perspective. Fortunately, and under a further refinement, it turns out that a third party is not necessarily needed for looping to be successful.

Banks, like any other fiduciary, operate in a proprietary capacity (i.e. for their own account) as well as for the account of clients. The expression 'broker-dealer' embodies these two distinct functions. Reflecting these separate roles and the different motivations associated with them, a bank which is a participant in the Clearstream settlement system will have at least two accounts. One will be the proprietary or 'house' account of the bank in respect of its own dealings in securities. The second will be the client account. Into the house account will go all the shares which the bank borrows from lenders of shares. If one of the bank's clients has a need to borrow shares as a consequence of entering into a short sale, the shares will normally be borrowed by the bank from the lender and delivered into the bank's house account. They will then be loaned to the client by delivery from that house account to the client account.[75] The account separation achieves a number of things. First, it separates legal ownership so that it is clear which shares belong to the bank and which belong to its clients. Second, it separates the accrual of fees so the bank can track and distinguish between its own costs and expenses

[75] In practice, there might be a single delivery of shares into the client account, but best industry practice is for the house account and the client account to record the two steps described here.

and those of its clients. The bank might borrow 100,000 shares from a stock lender at a fee of 0.40 per cent per annum. The shares will be recorded in the house account, as will the fee expense associated with the borrow. When those same shares are loaned out to a client, the shares and the higher fee reflecting a mark-up by the bank on its cost of the borrow, say 0.50 per cent per annum charged to the client, will be recorded in the client account.

It is not difficult to see how these distinct accounts could be put to work in the service of looping. Instead of interposing an inter-dealer broker, as shown in Figure 3.8, the bank, acting as a short seller on a cum-ex trade, can deliver the parcel of 75,000 shares to its client, acting as buyer, on that same trade. The client can then lend those 75,000 shares back to the bank. With those shares back in its account, the bank can deliver 75,000 shares once more to the client. Again, the satisfaction of a 300,000 shares settlement obligation associated with a short sale becomes a matter of simply moving the shares around between the account of the bank and the account of the client, successively lending and relending.

A scheme which is so simple, and contained within the two related accounts operated by the bank at Clearstream, might appear to be highest form of looping model. In fact, a further enhancement was devised. The problem with the repeated loans of shares between the client and the bank is twofold. First it requires a system to track each of those loans and borrows. Banks have such systems, but managing numerous looping transactions on a large number of cum-ex trades puts additional operational risk pressure on them. Second, there would again normally be cash collateral to be delivered by the party borrowing stock to the lender of the stock. At the end of the cum-ex trade after the dividend record date, the whole sequence of transactions would have to be played backwards. All of these stock borrowing transactions and collateral delivery transactions would have to be reversed until all the transactions were unwound and the single parcel of 75,000 shares was back with the bank. From there the shares could be returned to the lender.

The answer to this problem can be found in the terms of the legal agreement into which a bank enters with its fund clients, the International Prime Brokerage Agreement.[76] Under the standard form of this agreement, the fund client grants the bank a right over the fund's shares, known as a 'right of rehypothecation'. This right gives the bank the power to use the fund's shares for whatever purposes the bank chooses, at no charge to the bank and often without any limit[77] on the

[76] This agreement is used for hedge funds trading any kind of strategy: in other words, it is not limited to cum-ex trading.

[77] In the international context, clients now typically impose limits, most often expressed as a percentage of the client's indebtedness to the bank, e.g. the broker-dealer can rehypothecate shares to a value not exceeding 100 or 200 per cent of client indebtedness. In the United States, rehypothecation of client shares by the broker-dealer is limited to 140 per cent of that client's indebtedness to the bank.

quantity of shares the bank can use. The grant of this right to the bank by fund is part of the compensation for the bank agreeing to finance the share trading activity of the hedge fund. Free use of the fund's shares is valuable: the bank can take the shares and lend them out, receiving a fee. Importantly, the bank is not required to deliver any collateral when it uses the client's shares in this way. Nor does it pay the fund any fee for their use. There is another final benefit: no involvement from the fund is required whatsoever. With the lawful authorization of the client to do so by written agreement, the bank removes the shares from the client's account, delivers them to the bank's house account and can then return them, as many times as it sees fit. With this power of rehypothecation, the bank is able to manage the whole cycle of looping without the involvement of other parties, at no cost to itself, and without the need to track and fulfil collateral delivery requirements.

If Account V111 is the bank's house account at Clearstream and Account V222 is the bank's client account at Clearstream, shares can be moved back and forth between these two accounts freely and nearly instantaneously. What is more, with this capability at its disposal, the bank and its client can trade with each other in both directions. In other words, the bank can short-sell to the client fund (via an inter-dealer broker), and on settlement date deliver shares to the client, borrow those shares, and loop those shares back to the client, each time fulfilling part of its share delivery obligation. But there is no reason that the client must always act as buyer. It can short-sell to the bank, while the bank, again employing looping, manages the client's settlement obligations to it (i.e. to the bank itself). With looping operating in both directions between bank and client, activity on the client's trading statement will be a mix of (1) share purchases (of the bank's short sales), with inbound deliveries of ex-dividend shares from the bank after dividend record date, and (2) short sales (by the client) prior to dividend record date and their related outbound deliveries, also after dividend record date. The whole scheme is concentrated in Clearstream accounts controlled exclusively by the bank, with the client fully captive in the process. Operational risk is now contained to an absolute minimum. And because of the intermix of short sales and purchases by the bank to the client and the client to the bank, it becomes nearly impossible to tell from looking at the client's trading statement what exactly is going on.

2. Alternative to Borrowing

The search for further ways to minimize the cost of borrowing shares needed to satisfy the settlement of the short sale did not end with looping. One option developed was to dispense with borrowing altogether. In a normal short sale that has nothing to do with cum-ex trading, the short seller's profit is typically derived from the difference between the proceeds received from selling the borrowed shares (say €100,000) and the price the short seller pays at a later date to buy the shares back and return them to the lender (say €90,000, assuming there has been a fall of €10,000 in the market price of the shares). That difference (here, €10,000) is the profit.[78] However, a short seller engaged in the cum-ex trade is not interested in variations in the price of the shares over time but rather seeks to insulate the trade from all effects of price movements. For the cum-ex trader, the short sale is merely the mechanism by which the operation of the cum-ex flaw in the settlement system is activated. Viewed in this light, there is in principle no need to follow the traditional short seller's route of borrowing shares. Instead, the cum-ex short seller could simply buy ex-dividend shares after dividend record date and deliver them to the buyer.[79] For the strategy to work, the shares would need to be bought under an agreement that provided for expedited settlement, whether on a T+1 or T+0 basis (which is why this approach was often referred to as the 'T+1' trade). This scheme is illustrated in Figure 3.9. Such an approach removes the need to borrow (and pay a borrowing fee). It would also remove the risk from a later buy-in of shares to close an open borrow position and so would also be less risky from an operational risk perspective.

One particularly useful application of this approach is in circumstances where a party holding German shares does not want to be seen to be participating in cum-ex trading but wants nevertheless to profit from the strategy. The party (for example, an investment fund) could approach a bank, instructing it to carry out

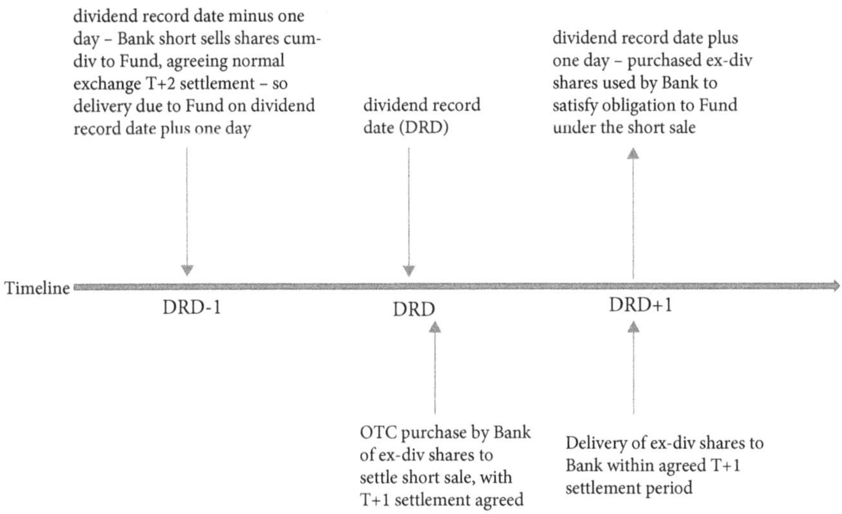

Figure 3.9. 'T+1' trades

[78] In this case, the profit would be before any fees, commission, or other charges.

[79] It is assumed that the buyer under such an arrangement may not wish to retain the shares and so could simply sell the shares, whether to the seller or to an inter-dealer broker.

a cum-ex short sale of, say, €250 million of BMW shares. The bank might charge 3 dividend percentage points (by reference to the gross dividend) for this service. Two days later, after dividend record date, when the time comes to settle the short sale, the fund could approach an inter-dealer broker, indicating that it is interested in selling its €250 million of BMW shares. The inter-dealer broker would then contact the bank short seller and sell it those shares. Having purchased the BMW shares, the bank can now settle the short sale. Taking an isolated view of the activities of the investment fund, it has simply sold shares after dividend record date, a transaction which in isolation has no appearance of being a cum-ex trade as it lacks both the usual two key features of a cum-ex trade, namely, a short sale and a borrowing of ex-dividend shares. In practice, however, the investment fund would participate in the profits generated by the cum-ex trade through its arrangements with the bank. This transaction structuring allows the fund as holder of shares to benefit from the cum-ex strategy, without being seen to do so. The position of the bank is arguably also improved optically because, although the bank has entered into a short sale, it is not a party to any borrowing of the shares shorted.[80]

3. Alternative Recycling Arrangements

A further refinement of the above approach (again removing or reducing the need for the short seller to borrow shares) provided a further mechanism to recycle the shares and thereby to boost the profitability of the cum-ex trade. Lenders, recognizing the value their shares had to cum-ex trading, began to charge lending fees for German shares based on a percentage of the dividend or 'dividend points' in industry parlance.[81] With stock lending fees required by lenders climbing to levels of around 6 percentage points of the gross amount of the dividend, borrowing the stock for a cum-ex trade became expensive. This meant that maximizing the use of any borrowed shares became the subject of intense focus and effort. One response in addition to the looping of the shares was to be found in the further use of exchange traded single stock futures. These contracts could be used, not merely as the hedging contract (as discussed earlier in this chapter), but also as a flexible

[80] The example illustrates the point that, though a borrowing of shares is normally regarded as a staple feature of cum-ex, it was still possible to execute a cum-ex trade without a borrowing of shares. The same is true of the other feature normally regarded as required in a cum-ex trade, namely a short sale. Where an owner of shares agrees to sell them cum-dividend on or just before the dividend record date but then deliberately orchestrates a delivery failure in the settlement system (for example, by inputting incorrect details into the settlement process or delaying that process) the result is that ex-dividend shares would be delivered after the cause of the failure had been rectified. It was therefore still possible to execute a cum-ex trade in the absence of a short sale. An instance of cum-ex trading involving deliberate late deliveries is referred to in the German Parliamentary Report at p.173.

[81] The approach generally applied in the stock loan market is to charge a stock loan fee expressed as a yearly percentage of the value of the shares.

means by which the short sale could be achieved and the shares subsequently recycled.

Since, as described above, single stock futures can be physically settled, a sale of a flexible single stock futures contract which expires just prior to dividend record date acts exactly like a short sale of the shares. Instead of a contract to sell shares, the seller could therefore enter into a single stock futures contract which, on later expiry, resulted in a sale of the shares to the buyer of that contract. Although a futures contract would normally be expected to endure for some time to a date in the future (as the name of the contract suggests) these contracts were often entered into on the same day that they expired.

The main benefit of short selling in this way (i.e. selling a single stock future which is physically settled) relates to the settlement convention for such contracts.[82] Critically, the settlement period for the physically settled future is four days instead of the two days settlement period for a short sale. This means that the short seller had twice the amount of time between entering into a short sale agreement and being obliged to deliver the shares to the buyer. The reason those additional settlement days were important is revealed by the worked example shown in Figure 3.10 below.

Figure 3.10 depicts a timeline centred around the relevant dividend record date (DRD) and a series of transactions between Bank (the short seller) and Fund (the buyer). A BClear futures contract ('Trade 1' in the example) which expires four days prior to the dividend record date (DRD–4) can be settled four days later on

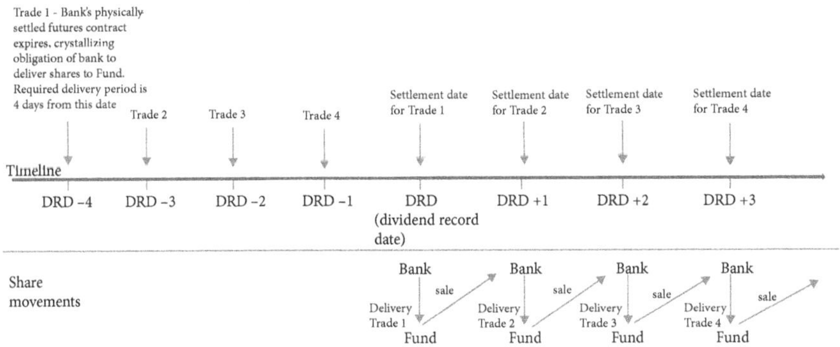

Figure 3.10. Physically settled single-stock futures trades

[82] The BClear example again demonstrates the role played by market practices in relation to settlement days in the various forms of the cum-ex trading strategy. The T+2 settlement period for straightforward sales of shares and T+4 settlement period for BClear futures settlement derive from conventions adopted by the Frankfurt Stock Exchange and LIFFE respectively, on which these contracts traded. Much shorter settlement periods including same-day (T+0) settlement were also possible by agreement between institutional parties to a trade.

DRD, with ex-dividend stock.[83] The extended settlement period has the effect of expanding the amount of time for cum-ex trading from the usual two days prior to ex-date to four days prior to ex-date. Bank and Fund enter into three additional flexible physically settled single stock futures contracts. Trade 2 expires on DRD–3 and therefore settles on DRD+1; Trade 3 expires on DRD–2 and therefore settles on DRD+2; and Trade 4 expires on DRD–1, settling on DRD+3. Four trades are executed between the parties which have the critical cum-ex characteristics: they involve an obligation to transfer shares *prior* to the dividend record date, with a corresponding obligation to deliver those shares *on or after* that date. Because the obligation to deliver shares falls on or after the dividend record date, they can all be settled using ex-dividend shares.[84]

Apart from increasing the timeframe in which the cum-ex trade can be implemented, this daily succession of futures trades has an important advantage. Trade 1, which expires on DRD, results in a transfer of shares from the seller of that futures contract to the buyer. By way of example, assume that on DRD, this results in €250 million of shares of RWE passing to the buyer of that physically settled futures transaction. Being the DRD, these are now ex-dividend shares which Bank has borrowed from a lender on that day and delivered (via Clearstream) to the buyer, Fund. On DRD+1, the second futures trade is due for settlement. Bank could of course borrow an additional parcel of €250 million of RWE shares to deliver to Fund, but that would involve a further stock borrow and additional stock borrow fees. In any event, Fund already has €250 million shares from Trade 1 in its possession which completed their purpose in the service of the first cum-ex trade and so are no longer needed. By immediately selling those shares back to Bank (for example, via an inter-dealer broker), Fund puts Bank back into a position to settle Trade 2 on DRD+1 using the same parcel of €250 million shares. Similarly, when Trade 3 settles, on DRD+2, Bank can then redeliver those €250 million of RWE shares back to Fund. Once again, Fund can sell the shares back to Bank so that Bank is able to settle Trade 4, settling the next day on DRD+3.

In the manner illustrated in Figure 3.10, a whole series of physically settled single stock futures can be settled in sequence using the same parcel of stock. The arrangements require close cooperation between buyer and seller. Each time the

[83] In the example given, a settlement using ex-dividend shares is made on the dividend record date (DRD) itself. From an operational perspective, this required precise timing in order to obtain the shares on a same-day basis (T+0) immediately after they had paid out their dividend. As such, it was considered an aggressive tactic. Nevertheless, the practice was widespread.

[84] This approach to structuring the trade would often form part of a 'calendar spread' method of futures trading. It is so called because it was implemented using the sale of one futures contract which was shorter in length than the other futures contract purchased as the hedge. Having two futures contracts of different lengths allowed the cum-ex trader to position the trade as an arbitrage, designed to pick up any difference between the price of the thing sold (the short-dated futures contract) and the price of the thing purchased (the longer-dated futures contract).

buyer receives shares in settlement of a futures trade, it must resell the shares quickly so that the next successive futures contract can also be settled.

4. Optimizing the Non-Refundable Credit

Over the life of the cum-ex trade there were continual efforts applied to ensure that the buyer would derive the highest possible benefit from the trade. This often involved two different issues: first, maximizing the available cash reclaim from Germany and, second, extracting maximum value or 'optimizing' that portion of the tax credit which was non-refundable. The first of these issues has been discussed earlier in this chapter. As regards the second issue, optimizing the non-refundable portion of the German tax credit would normally bring into play the tax rules in the country of the buyer (assuming a non-German buyer). The key issue would be whether a tax credit would be available under the tax rules in the buyer's country for any non-refundable portion of the German tax credit. Obviously, the availability of such a local tax credit would enhance the benefits from the cum-ex trade.

A good (but admittedly complex) example of the scope for such optimization concerns the UK. For UK buyers, and as a result of the maximum permitted 15 per cent rate of withholding tax on dividends paid to holders of German shares contained in the UK–Germany tax treaty, the cash reclaim from Germany would be 11.375 per cent, i.e. the amount by which the actual rate of withholding tax (26.375 per cent) exceeds the maximum permissible rate of 15 per cent. This is a smaller cash reclaim than is available to residents of certain other states (e.g. Ireland, where a lower tax treaty rate of 10 per cent applied, giving a cash reclaim of 16.375 per cent). However, if it were possible in the UK to derive value from the remaining portion of the German tax credit—that part of the withholding tax credit which was not refundable in cash—then the UK would be an attractive location for buyers in the cum-ex structure. This is exactly what certain cum-ex structuring sought to deliver. Under some extraordinarily complicated UK tax rules, a German tax credit in the hands of a UK-based buyer could be 'recycled' into a different form of tax credit in the hands of a third party. This solution was made possible by certain UK tax rules that had been enacted to deal with what had been seen in the UK as the problem of 'manufactured dividends'. This UK problem was in some ways similar in concept to the issues raised by cum-ex, though it arose in a completely different context.

The manufactured dividend problem for the UK tax system arose in the late 1980s and involved UK lenders of shares. Where loans of shares would cross a dividend date, the lender would not receive a real dividend on those shares (such real dividends would otherwise normally be received 'net', after the deduction of any withholding tax applicable in the country of the dividend-paying company).

Instead, the lender would receive from the borrower of the shares a compensation payment in the place of the dividend income foregone during the time that the shares had been lent out.[85] However, in practice the compensation payment would often be equal to only the net amount of the real dividend (which would otherwise have been received, had the shares not been loaned out).[86] The concern for the UK tax authorities was that this practice of lenders of shares receiving a 'net' compensation payment might result in the lender then treating that net payment as if it were the net payment of the *real* dividend. In other words, the lender might assume from the fact that the compensation payment was net as implying that a withholding tax had been applied to it. The problem was that lenders might then include the assumed tax credit in their tax return, reducing the UK tax otherwise payable by the amount of the 'assumed' tax credit. A solution came in the form of a new set of tax rules which regulated compensation payments made in relation to stock lending activity.[87] The UK tax authorities introduced one of the most complicated tax regimes on the UK statute book: the 'manufactured dividend' rules.[88] Reflected in the operation of the rules was the principle that when a compensation payment for a dividend foregone on shares lent out was paid by a borrower to a lender, a withholding tax was charged and paid over to the tax authorities.[89] This same rule equally applied to any other situation where such a 'manufactured dividend' was paid by a UK party.[90] The intention was that the manufactured dividend would then be treated by the lender in the same way as the real dividend on the shares would have been treated, with the recipient (the lender) able to claim a tax credit corresponding to the withholding tax that had been paid over on the manufactured dividend under these new rules. A particular (and, in the present context, highly relevant) feature of these tax laws is that they

[85] This payment was also commonly referred to as an 'in lieu of' payment or as a 'manufactured' or 'substitute' payment.

[86] In some instances, this was because the taxpayers concerned could not use any tax credits on the dividends, for example because they were exempt from UK tax.

[87] The concerns arose largely due to the lack of familiarity on the part of lenders with the then nascent stock lending market, coupled with accounting and control systems that were poorly equipped for distinguishing between shares that were owned and shares that had been lent out.

[88] The UK's manufactured dividend rules were introduced in 1993 and enacted in UK statute in ICTA 1988, Schedule 23A, which was later rewritten as CTA 2010, Part 17. Perhaps not surprisingly, given the complexity of the rules (coupled with the difficulties for the UK tax authorities of staying on top of the administration of the highly detailed regime), they were the subject of very many tax avoidance schemes. The rules were ultimately abolished from 1 January 2014 because of the intense difficulty for the tax authorities of making them work in the face of the serial avoidance activity. Prior to their abolition, the rules were continually amended to block off avoidance schemes, but many of these amendments simply fuelled additional avoidance activity. See further Richard Collier, 'Section 77 and Schedule 29—Manufactured Payments: General', *British Tax Review* 4 (2013), 473–4.

[89] The amount of the withholding was determined by the withholding tax rate suffered on the relevant real dividend by a UK resident investor. If the payor of the manufactured dividend was not located in the UK, the rules applied a 'reverse charge' withholding tax on the first receipt of the manufactured dividend in the UK.

[90] There were a number of important exemptions from the charge to tax, but these are not relevant here.

contained a set of complex provisions designed to permit the netting off of amounts due from banks to the UK tax authority in respect of withholding tax on manufactured payments on the one hand against the amount of withholding tax already suffered on dividend (and manufactured dividend) income on the other.

In optimizing cum-ex trades with UK buyers, these UK manufactured dividend rules were brought into the service of structuring a cum-ex trade in order to 'recycle' the tax credit received by a UK buyer in respect of the system-generated dividend from Clearstream. The recycling would have two broad results. First, the tax credit could be monetized in a very flexible way by the bank concerned.[91] Second, the process of recycling would transform the German tax credit so that it would no longer be regarded for UK tax purposes as a German tax credit. These manufactured dividend rules operate in a complex way, but the basic result can be illustrated by a simple example, which is depicted diagrammatically, initially by Figure 3.11 and then as further developed in Figure 3.12.

The steps in Figure 3.11 are intended to illustrate the basic operation of the UK tax rules dealing with manufactured dividends. Figure 3.11 shows a third-party

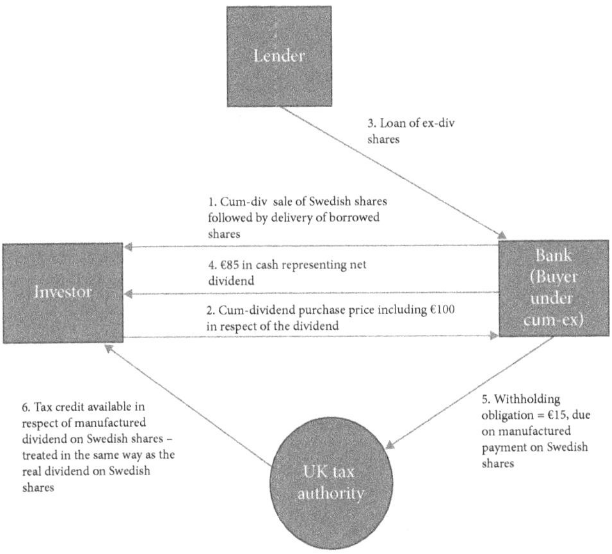

Figure 3.11. Operation of UK manufactured dividend rules

[91] The flexibility was delivered first through the initial choice available to the bank concerned as to whether to use the relevant tax credit by way of offset against the bank's own tax liability. However, this was often not possible due to accumulated losses from the Global Financial Crisis, which wiped out any profits in the year with the result that no tax was actually paid. A second use of the tax credit came in the manner shown in Figure 3.11, in which case the tax credit could be recycled in a wide range of transactions involving shares from a large number of different markets.

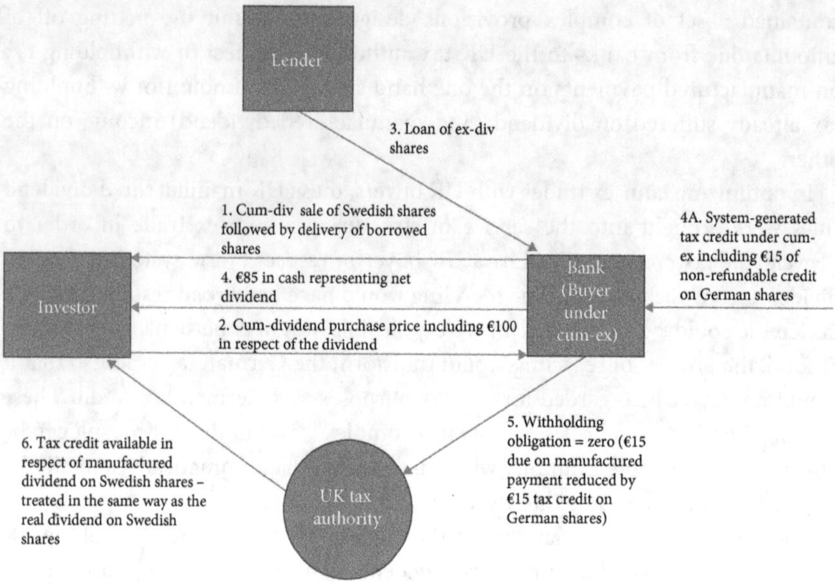

Figure 3.12. Recycling the German tax credit

investor (assume also located in the UK) that buys a parcel of Swedish shares, cum-dividend from the bank (Step 1). The real dividend on the Swedish shares would normally be paid to such an investor after deduction of withholding tax of 15 per cent, so assuming a gross dividend of €100 there would be a cash payment of €85 in cash after €15 withholding tax. Assume that the investor in the Swedish shares is able to benefit from the tax credit on the dividend and so included in the cum-dividend purchase price (at Step 2) is an amount of €100 in respect of the dividend (equating to the cash amount of €85 and the €15 withholding tax which the investor expects to use as a tax credit to reduce tax otherwise payable). Later, and to settle the trade, the bank borrows shares which it delivers to the investor (Step 3). By the time of the share borrowing transaction, the relevant dividend record date has passed and so the shares borrowed are ex-dividend. Under the agreement at Step 1, the shares were sold 'cum-dividend', meaning that the bank must pay the investor a manufactured dividend of €85 as compensation for the net dividend on the shares which the investor, by virtue of receiving ex-dividend shares, did not receive (Step 4). In the hands of the investor and under the UK rules that are being discussed here, the manufactured dividend is taxed in the same way as if it were a real dividend on the Swedish shares. Under these UK manufactured dividend rules, the bank is obliged to pay an amount of withholding tax on the manufactured dividend directly to the UK tax authority (Step 5), and this amount corresponds to the tax credit the investor will claim in respect of the manufactured dividend (Step 6). The UK rules operate here exactly as intended. Their main goal is to ensure that any tax credit claimed in respect of a receipt of a manufactured dividend corresponds to withholding tax actually paid over to the tax authorities by the payor.

The example can now be extended to show what happens if the bank is also a buyer under a cum-ex trade. This is illustrated in Figure 3.12.

Here, the first four steps remain as depicted in Figure 3.11. The difference comes from the receipt of the cum-ex dividend generated by the cum-ex trade. This is received with a German tax credit of €26.375. Of this, €11.375 will be reclaimed from the German tax authority in cash, leaving a non-refundable portion of €15 (Step 4A). The tax structuring in this case sought to exploit the complex netting-off rules contained in the UK manufactured dividend rules. Specifically, the design objective was that the €15 tax credit arising in Step 4A (representing non-refundable German withholding tax) would be offset against the liability of the bank to pay €15 of withholding tax on the Swedish manufactured dividend. This wipes out the obligation on the bank to pay any withholding tax to the UK tax authorities (Step 5) without affecting the entitlement of the investor to a credit in respect of the manufactured dividend on the Swedish shares (Step 6).

The result is that two things have happened by the combination of these rules and the two unrelated share transactions. First, the non-refundable portion of the German tax credit has been in effect converted into cash by the bank concerned: it has received €100 from the buyer of the Swedish shares and this amount incorporates the value of the net dividend *and* the withholding tax credit. Second, the process of recycling has transformed the non-refundable portion of the underlying German tax credit so that it no longer would be regarded as a German tax credit at all. In the hands of the investor, the manufactured dividend received would be treated by the UK tax system as equivalent to a Swedish dividend on which *Swedish* withholding tax has been levied. In effect, the non-refundable portion of the German tax credit received by the bank has been transferred and simultaneously 'recycled' so that it is treated as a tax credit on a Swedish dividend.

A detailed exposition of these UK manufactured dividend rules is obviously beyond the scope of this book, but what the example demonstrates is the cross-border layering of complexity on top of complexity, with quite different rules in different states being intricately brought together with the sole aim of delivering the most profitable tax-optimized financial outcome.[92]

[92] There are real questions as to whether the UK rules considered here should ever apply in the manner discussed, as it seems highly doubtful whether a valid tax credit is created for UK tax purposes by the system-generated tax credit mechanism in Clearstream. However, possibly due to an incomplete understanding of the cum-ex mechanism in Germany and perhaps also of the practices of some banks in generating the tax credit, this was not the view taken by some UK banks and tax advisers.

Culmination of Efforts to Improve Profitability and Efficiency of Cum-Ex

The culmination of efforts to improve the efficiency and profitability of the cum-ex trade is probably best illustrated by cases where both seller and buyer were established within the same taxpayer group. In such cases, the short seller would often be a bank or financial trader and the buyer would be structured as a fund, typically established for the purpose of cum-ex trading. The situation is illustrated in Figure 3.13.

Such cases were not common but arguably reflected a high point in the degree to which the cum-ex mechanism was exploited as well as a very high degree of confidence in the reliability of legal entity structuring. The structure was motivated by a number of factors. Primarily, the use of entirely 'in-house' structures limits significantly the profits that need to be shared with other parties, as would be the case where the seller and buyer are unrelated.[93] However, as illustrated in

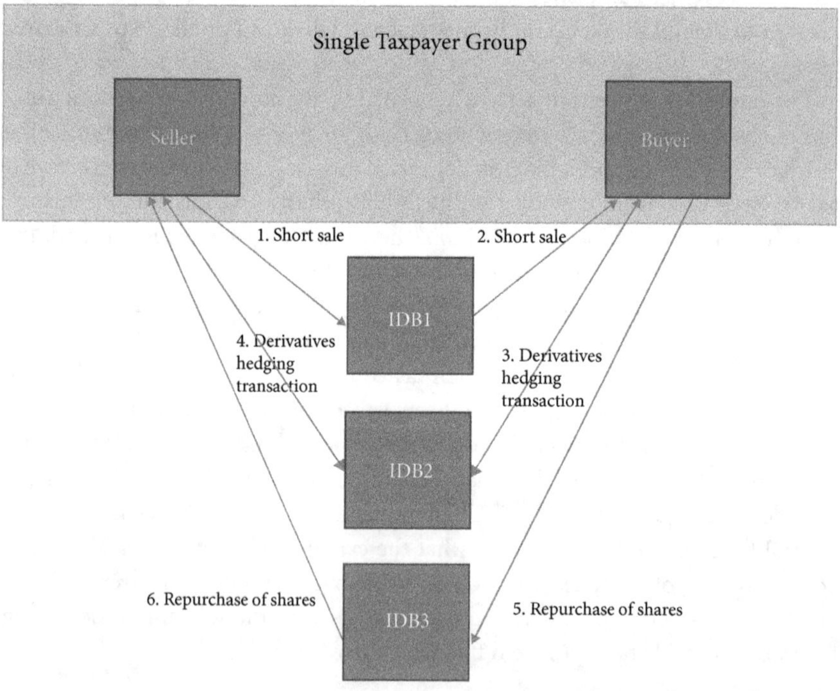

Figure 3.13. In-house buyer and seller

[93] In addition to intra-group trades, cum-ex trading could also be made more lucrative where a group entity acted as the relevant custodian for itself or an affiliate and so could make its own declaration to the tax authorities—see the German Parliamentary Report at p.348.

Figure 3.13, there would remain the costs arising from the use of inter-dealer brokers. Nonetheless, the common control of both of the main parties to the trade facilitated a high level of automation of the cum-ex trade process, as well as making it easier to cut costs such as stock borrowing fees, given that the captive nature of the parties would also make it easier to implement looping and similar practices.

Structure of the Cum-Ex Trade in Practice

So far, the discussion has considered a number of separate refinements of the basic cum-ex structure in isolation. In practice, many of these elements would together have been incorporated into the actual structures implemented. An illustration combining the involvement of a fund, the use of IDBs, and a looping arrangement is illustrated in Figure 3.14.

Even though the structure remains a simplified illustration of the main elements of a cum-ex trade, it shows the high level of structural and transactional complexity of cum-ex trades in practice.

Sidestepping Attempts to Close the Cum-Ex Trade

The cum-ex trade was also adapted to work around some attempts by the German regulators to close down the opportunity for the trade. However, until this result was finally achieved in early 2012, the efforts of authorities were almost totally

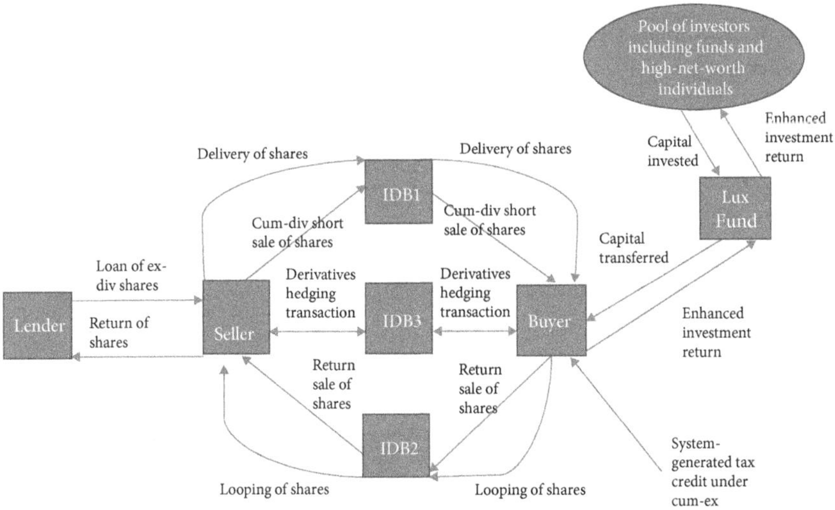

Figure 3.14. Cum-ex in practice

ineffective in curbing the scale of cum-ex trades. Somewhat ironically, the effect of these failed attempts arguably encouraged cum-ex trading, given that they were interpreted as defining by implication the broad bounds in which such trading would be accepted by the tax authorities.[94]

2007—Imposition of Withholding Tax on the Dividend Compensation Payment

As will be explored in more detail in Chapter 4, the tax authorities became aware of the factors that gave rise to the cum-ex trade over German shares from the 1990s at the latest.[95] However, the first major attempt to close the trade was not until 2007. In that year, a new law was introduced to target arbitrage opportunities from short sales in German shares around dividend date.[96] The new law was clearly aimed at cum-ex. Legislation in 2007 introduced a new withholding tax obligation intended to fall on the payer of a dividend compensation payment. Specifically, the withholding obligation was introduced to apply to the 'entity executing the sales order' for the cum-dividend short seller.[97] According to this new law, the dividend adjustment (or compensation) payment received by the buyer where shares have been purchased cum-dividend but with ex-dividend settlement is recognized for the first time as 'other dividend income'[98] with the result that the buyer is entitled to a withholding tax certificate from its custodian bank.[99] Significantly, this entitlement was not made conditional on the actual imposition of withholding tax at the seller's end of the transaction, nor does the law make any reference to such imposition.

The intention of the law change was clear: for cum-ex transactions carried out after 1 January 2007, the seller's bank, though not receiving any real net dividend, would as before continue to be charged under the Clearstream dividend settlement process for an amount equal to the net dividend. However, in addition, the seller's bank would also now be obliged to collect and pay the withholding tax

[94] The point is discussed further below.

[95] See further the discussion in Chapter 4 on the early history of the cum-ex trade and also Spengel, 'Expert Opinion', at p.13.

[96] The law change was effected by changes to the Income Tax Act, sections 20, 44, and 45a (and see especially Section 44(1) Clause 3).

[97] Income Tax Act, Section 44 (1) Clause 3. Technically, the obligation under Section 44 (1) Clause 3 would arise only where there is a short sale around the dividend date falling within Section 20 (1) No.1 Sentence 4 of the Income Tax Act.

[98] Income Tax Act, Section 20 (1) No. 1 Sentence 4. The effect of this change was to ensure that the dividend compensation payment would rank as designated investment income for the purposes of the first limb of Section 36 (2) (2) Income Tax Act (which imposes the three tests required to be met before a tax credit is available). Prior to this change, such income would not have been recognized as a separate type of income but rather would have been treated as normal operating income.

[99] The entitlement to a tax credit is given by a certificate prepared pursuant to Section 45a (3) of the Income Tax Act.

introduced by this change in the law.[100] The buyer would continue to receive an amount equal to the net dividend through the Clearstream settlement system and be issued with a withholding tax certificate.[101] In the context of a cum-ex trade, the intended result would be two instances of withholding—one on the real dividend (as before) and one on the dividend adjustment (or dividend compensation payment) (under the new law). Correspondingly, there would be two tax certificates issued, one relating to the real dividend and one relating to the dividend compensation payment. The tax law was therefore intended to restore symmetry between the imposition of withholding tax in the hands of the seller and the availability of a tax credit in the hands of the buyer.

Unfortunately, while this may have been the result intended by the new law it was not the result that was delivered by its application in practice. Critically, the law was framed to apply the new withholding tax charge to the 'entity executing the sales order' for the seller of the German shares. That entity was then defined to be the relevant *domestic* credit institution or domestic financial services institution concerned.[102] The view widely adopted by German lawyers and tax advisers was that the 'entity executing the sales order' should be interpreted as the entity with a direct contractual relationship with the short seller, i.e. the short seller's custodian bank. This was on the basis that the custodian bank was the only entity acting 'for' the short seller and also because only the custodian bank was in a position to determine whether the seller, at the time of the sale, owned the shares, or was a short seller.[103] Therefore, other parties in the settlement chain, such as sub-custodians, clearing agents, etc were regarded as entirely unaffected by the new law. This included Clearstream Banking Frankfurt as central clearer, and any other sub-custodian in Germany, meaning that there would be no liability for any of these parties under the 2007 withholding tax rule.[104] Also, the law imposed no

[100] The withholding tax charge under Section 44 (1) Sentence 3 Income Tax Act introduced by this 2007 change would be applied up to 31 December 2011, when the cum-ex trades were finally closed down.

[101] However, as noted, the law provided no express and direct interaction between the new withholding tax charge under Section 44 (1) and the provisions in Section 45a (3) Sentence 2 of the Income Tax Act dealing with the issue of a tax certificate. Dividend compensation receipts would rank as taxable business income if the shares were held as business assets. If not, they were exempt from tax. See German Parliamentary Report at p.78.

[102] The definition is in Section 44 (1) Clause 3 of the Income Tax Act. That definition would include German branches of non-German credit or financial-services institutions.

[103] Academic commentaries seemed to support this restrictive view of the 'entity executing the sales order' but identified the obvious loophole or failure in the law as the withholding tax could only be collected from domestic institutions. It was also argued that the interpretation made sense on the basis of (1) being administratively workable, given that the German tax authorities would not have been readily able to collect tax from a non-resident and (2) was in line with the approach already taken in the law to the definition of a paying agent of interest.

[104] It seems that in July 2007 Clearstream Banking Frankfurt took tax advice as to whether it was a 'domestic credit organization executing the sales order for the seller' according to the legal test in Section 44 Paragraph 1 Income Tax Act and the conclusion was that it was not—see German Parliamentary Report at p.348.

obligation on the seller to inform any of those entities or agents as to the arrangements it had entered into.

In the context of what is likely the most internationalized (and adaptable) business sector, this was an extremely odd development. It was obviously defective. By restricting the new withholding tax charge to *domestic* entities (custodian banks) 'executing the sales order', it is (and was) immediately obvious that the new charge would be irrelevant to *non-domestic* custodian banks acting for the seller. Further, such non-domestic entities could nonetheless still use the Clearstream settlement system and be substituted at a moment's notice for any domestic custodian bank that was already being employed in the structure. The result was entirely predictable. Invariably, the cum-ex structure was adapted from the end of 2006 to ensure that the seller's custodian bank would always be a *non-domestic* 'entity executing the sales order' so that it would not be subject to the German withholding tax imposed on the dividend compensation payment. In other words, the seller would simply engage a custodian bank located outside Germany. Not only was this step effective to avoid any withholding tax charge but also the general view adopted by tax advisers was that the clear statutory restriction of the withholding tax rule to *domestic* institutions meant that the deliberate use of a *non-resident* institution could not be seen as an abuse of the law. This was on the basis that, since the scope of the law was so clearly limited in its application to domestic institutions, adopting a structure which excluded such domestic institutions constituted an arrangement that the legislator was (presumably) deliberately accepting should not be seen as an 'abuse'. Accordingly, anti-avoidance rules would not be triggered.[105]

The practical consequence of this law change was that it had little discernible effect on the incidence of cum-ex trading. It did, of course, cause a wholesale shift to the use of non-domestic custodian banks by cum-ex sellers so that the account in which the short position was entered would be held outside Germany. In all these cases, the short seller's custodian would then not be a domestic German entity 'executing the sales order' and so would not be obliged to deduct withholding tax.

2009—BMF Cum-Ex Circular of 5 May 2009

The next development requiring adaptation of the cum-ex trade structure did not follow until two years later. This time, a different approach was adopted. There was no change in the law but rather an administrative change, targeted at the

[105] This line of argument was used to justify the inapplicability of anti-avoidance provisions such as the general anti-avoidance rule in Section 42 of the General Tax Code.

procedure for issuing withholding tax certificates to buyers in cum-ex trades; the parties who would be claiming tax credits or refunds. The goal was to impose additional constraints on any buyers seeking to claim withholding tax credits arising from cum-ex transactions.

A letter of 5 May 2009, often referred to as 'the Cum-Ex Circular', was issued by the German Ministry of Finance (BMF).[106] The circular required the tax certificate produced by the buyer's custodian bank to identify on its face those dividends, together with the corresponding withholding tax, which arose from cum-dividend share purchases where the settlement of the purchase was made after the dividend record date. The purpose was of course to identify cum-ex tax credits. Further, the circular stated that there would be no credit or refund in respect of such identified amounts unless an authorized tax professional, such as a tax adviser or lawyer,[107] provided a written confirmation that the taxpayer had not, broadly, entered into any collusive 'arrangement' relating to the acquisition of the shares over the dividend date which avoided the withholding tax imposed on short sales over dividend record date (i.e. the withholding tax imposed by the 2007 law change discussed above).[108]

Where tax credits were generated by cum-ex transactions, the BMF Circular was therefore seeking to put the burden of proof as to whether there had actually been a payment of withholding tax associated with the withholding tax credit onto the taxpayer concerned (i.e. the buyer in a cum-ex treade). The relevant custodian bank was required to report the relevant dividend income, associated tax credits and whether the above certification had been filed to the Federal Central Tax Office. If no such certification had been filed, the Federal Central Tax Office could assume that withholding taxes had been refunded incorrectly and therefore reclaim them.[109]

There were material limitations on the scope of the BMF Circular. First, it was relevant only to certain German taxpayers where dividends were part of a taxpayer's business income, which initially included German banks and special

[106] BMF IV C 1-S 2252/09/09, 10003, Federal Tax Gazette I 2009, p.631. Later updates to the Cum-Ex Circular were published on 21 September 2010 and 3 March 2011. The circular was initially issued for the 2009 tax year only but later it was extended to dividends arising after 2009 by an update in the form of a Federal Ministry of Finance letter of 21 September 2010 dealing with 'withholding tax in the case of short sales over dividend record date'.

[107] It was later clarified that, if the accounts of the taxpayer concerned are subject to an audit, then the confirmation should be signed by the taxpayer's statutory auditor—see BMF clarification of 11 November 2009 (BMF 2009/0701214).

[108] The required certification process for German special funds was slightly different and involved the manager of the fund making a similar declaration to the custodian bank of the fund.

[109] In the absence of any change of law, the circular was interpreted as an expression of the view of the Federal Ministry of Finance that the buyer would have no entitlement to a tax credit or refund in the event of a collusive arrangement between the short seller and the buyer resulting in the buyer being aware that no withholding tax was paid to correspond to the tax voucher received.

funds.[110] Second, the circular applied only in the event of an 'arrangement' between the short seller and the purchaser relating to the acquisition of shares settled over the dividend record date by a corresponding short sale on which no withholding tax was levied. In the absence of any such arrangement, the terms of the circular would not apply. Further, the circular had no impact on the tax position of any short seller, including any German short seller, nor on the position of non-German custody banks acting for short sellers. It would not therefore deal with the obvious flaw from the 2007 law change by extending the withholding tax charge on dividend compensation payments to deal with non-German custodian banks.

Not surprisingly, the consequences of these scoping issues led to a much greater use of non-German buyers in the structuring of cum-ex trades. There was also a consequence relating to German buyers potentially within the scope of the BMF Circular, namely the creation of uncertainty (and dispute) as to the exact scope of the arrangements that were caught by the circular and those that were not.[111]

The effect of both these changes was not to close down the cum-ex trades but rather to push them further offshore.[112] The 2007 legislative change meant the short seller's custodian bank would invariably be located outside Germany, while the 2009 administrative change weighed the scales heavily in favour of the use of unaffected non-German buyers in cum-ex trading.[113] The unintended effect of these successive attempts to close the cum-ex trade down was therefore to internationalize the opportunity it presented.

Almost two years after the release of the Cum-Ex Circular, and a few months before the cum-ex trade was finally closed down, the German tax authorities announced in March 2011 that they were extending the scope of the 2009 Cum-Ex Circular to non-residents.[114] This meant that non-German claimants,

[110] The focus on special funds (which included the requirement for professional certification) also included special investment stock corporations which made refunds pursuant to Section 11 (2) Investment Tax Act. At the time of the first BMF letter, domestic mutual funds were excluded from its scope as these were considered unlikely to be participating in cum-ex activity. See German Parliamentary Report at p.201. The scope of the circular was later extended to include certain German public/mutual funds by a Federal Ministry of Finance decree of 18 August 2009, IV C 1 – S 1980 – 1/08/10019, Federal Tax Gazette 1 2009, 931, 972, annotation no. 242.

[111] For example, it is understood that 'fail' transactions giving rise to cum-ex transactions were regarded as not strictly falling within the scope of the Cum-ex Circular. ('Fail' transactions are discussed in footnote 80 of this chapter). There was also uncertainty as to whether and how far it was possible to use brokers and/or on-exchange dealings to break the direct connection with a German counterparty and therefore sidestep the terms of the 2009 circular. Some of the difficulties are referred to in the 2017 German Parliamentary Enquiry into cum-ex—see German Parliamentary Report at p.357.

[112] Volumes of cum-ex trades increased after the BMF Circular—see German Parliamentary Report at pp. 216, 466.

[113] It is also significant that the letter of 5 May 2009 was widely interpreted as signaling that the tax administration did not regard cum-ex trades as illegal.

[114] An English-language version of the letter was released and is entitled 'Refunding withholding tax pursuant to Income Tax Act § 44a and § 50d for shares acquired after the key date for dividend payments to non-residents', IV B 3 – S 2411/07/10015-14, doc. 2011/0259303, 29 March 2011.

including non-domestic buyers in cum-ex trades, seeking refunds of tax were required to document when they purchased the relevant shares. Further, if the shares were acquired on or immediately before the dividend record date, a treaty refund would be available only if an independent professional party confirmed the absence of collusive arrangements.[115] This extension of the original 2009 BMF letter indicated the authorities were finally getting to grips with the cum-ex trade, well over a decade after first becoming aware of the cum-ex flaw in the system. However, even at this stage, the approach remained far from perfect: for example, it created the difficult task of policing the veracity of the professional certificates from overseas tax professionals.[116]

The cum-ex trade was finally closed down from 1 January 2012, although, as will be seen, the developments through 2011 which include the extension of the Cum-Ex Circular to non-residents had already signaled the increasing difficulties facing cum-ex trades. The process which led to the closing of the cum-ex trade over German shares, together with the resulting fall-out, is discussed in the next chapter.

[115] The letter drew particular attention to any claims to refunds made by foreign funds and required that any claims should be reported to the Federal Ministry of Finance, broken down into the specific countries in which the respective funds have been set up.

[116] See German Parliamentary Report at pp. 215, 232.

4
The Closure of Cum-Ex and the Aftermath

> Never before have so many actors been involved in a case of financial crime and the network of scammers been so big. Alarmingly, many joined in: domestic and foreign banks, private and public financial institutions, fund managers, stock traders, accountants, banking associations, tax consultants, lawyers, professors.
>
> German Parliamentary Report on Cum-Ex, 20 June 2017

Introduction

The ability to execute cum-ex trades in Germany was finally brought to an end in early 2012, after the failure of previous attempts to close down the trade in 2007 and 2009. Once cum-ex had become more widely understood by the tax authorities, a reappraisal of the trade, starting in 2009, led to a reassessment of some major aspects of the tax analysis that had underpinned its legality.[1] As the technical position was being reconsidered, details of the practices in which participants in cum-ex trades had engaged began to emerge. This led to a wide-ranging investigation into cum-ex trading, from which the scale of the collusive behaviour amongst market participants soon became apparent. The resulting fallout prompted major recriminations on a number of levels. New arguments were advanced about who was to blame and who should be held to account for the financial damage the trades caused. All these matters are pursued in this chapter.

The Period Leading up to the Closure of Cum-Ex

What is striking about the period leading up to the shutdown of cum-ex in 2012 is the length of time it took the authorities to get to grips with cum-ex.

Discussions within the banking industry about share transactions executed around the dividend record date go back as far as the 1970s.[2] For example, there

[1] For an outline of the tax analysis that supported cum-ex, see the discussion in Chapter 2.

[2] For an interesting discussion of the early emergence of these issues, see German Parliamentary Report at pp.112–31. The 830-page report, written in German, provides a detailed account of the historical developments relevant to cum-ex as well as of the manner in which the incidence of cum-ex trades has been addressed by the German authorities.

Banking on Failure: Cum-Ex and Why and How Banks Game the System. Richard S Collier,
Oxford University Press (2020).
DOI: 10.1093/oso/9780198859673.001.0001

was a discussion in 1978 about 'accidental' short sale transactions (created by a broker selling shares it did not own) and sale transactions that were not completed before the dividend record date. These discussions raised issues which lie at the heart of cum-ex, such as the time at which ownership of the shares passes in the case of a short sale and thus as to which of the seller, broker, or buyer would be entitled to the dividend and the tax certificate. Even at this early stage, there was also a recognition of the need to avoid the duplication of tax certificates. Associations of the banking industry took up the issue.[3] A number of pragmatic mechanisms, targeted at the seller, were explored by individual banks in order to avoid the double use of tax credits in these situations. Such mechanisms included imposing on the seller a gross 'dividend compensation' charge, applicable to the amount of the net dividend plus the amount of the tax withheld. An alternative approach involved requesting from the seller a confirmation that any (duplicated) withholding tax credit on the dividend would not be used by way of tax credit or refund. Whilst these improvised mechanisms lacked a clear basis in law and were in any event not well understood by foreign sellers, they do demonstrate an early recognition of the tax problems raised by transactions around the dividend date.[4]

Such matters continued to be discussed periodically.[5] A desire to find a solution led in 1997 to the creation of an ad-hoc working group of the Federal Association of German banks to address the tax problems associated with share transactions taking place on or before the dividend date.[6] The approach adopted by the working group was that the buyer should always be regarded as the beneficial owner of the shares from the date of the contract to purchase and so should be regarded as the owner of the dividend. This meant that ownership of the shares should not be attributed to the seller or, if this were not possible operationally (because the shares were not held by the seller's custodian bank), the seller should be subject to a 'gross' dividend compensation charge to cancel out any possible double benefit from the tax credit.[7]

[3] See German Parliamentary Report at pp.113–17.

[4] See German Parliamentary Report at pp.116–21. The discussion also refers to early cases where a gross charge in respect of dividend compensation was applied, with the monies corresponding to the withholding tax remitted to the Federal Office of Finance, only for it to be sent back for want of a legal liability—see at pp. 121, 335.

[5] In 1992, for example, the Central Landesbank in Hesse dealt with dividend-stripping in an edition of the Frankfurt Financial Market Report. The discussion also included consideration of abusive efforts to produce tax certificates by trades involving short sales before dividend record date where only a net dividend was charged, with the relevant tax certificate being 'produced out of nothing'. See German Parliamentary Report at p.118.

[6] The Federal Association of German Banks is one of five banking associations in Germany and represents over 200 private member banks and eleven state associations—see German Parliamentary Report at p.112.

[7] See German Parliamentary Report at pp.123–5. The view assumed was that the buyer is always the beneficial owner of the shares under the provisions of Section 39 of the General Tax Code. As an operational matter, the shares in question might not be held by the seller's custodian bank either because a different bank was holding the shares for the seller or because the sale was short.

The need for a clear legal basis for any approach led to some informal discussions with the tax administration in 1998 and, later, to a letter being sent in 2002 from the Federal Association of German Banks to the Federal Ministry of Finance.[8] That letter clearly identified the problem of cum-ex transactions carried out with short sales and the need for a legislative response.[9] A second letter sent shortly afterwards suggested some draft legislation.[10] At this stage, the matter was not regarded by the tax authorities as requiring an urgent response, which is ironic given that it was at about this time that significant cum-ex trading activity was gaining momentum.[11]

Efforts to address the anomaly by a legislative response did not get under way until late 2005. The result was the announcement of a change in the manner of dealing with what was characterized as a 'dividend compensation payment'. This was the amount of the dividend-equivalent payment, received where the purchaser acquired shares in a cum-dividend sale but with settlement taking place using ex-dividend shares. The proposed measures would take effect in relation to sales of German shares from 1 January 2007, some five years after the Bankers Association had drawn attention to the issue.

The policy aims of the 2007 law were therefore (1) to characterize the nature of the 'dividend-related' amount paid by the seller to the buyer in a cum-ex trade as a 'dividend compensation payment'; (2) to leave the position of the recipient of that dividend compensation payment (i.e. the buyer in a cum-ex trade) unaffected; and (3) to charge withholding tax on the payor (i.e. the short seller), though only when the transaction settled through a domestic custodian bank. The operation of these 2007 rules has already been discussed in Chapter 3 but, in summary, they involve (1) a withholding charge on any domestic bank paying a dividend compensation payment and (2) a stipulation in the law that the dividend compensation receipt

[8] See German Parliamentary Report at pp. 126, 140–1.

[9] See further Spengel, 'Expert Opinion', at pp. 13, 104–6, 111. The letter was sent on 20 December 2002. Spengel (at p.104) speculates that the letter was motivated by concerns of a liability issue on the part of German custodian banks relating to the production of incorrect certificates of withholding tax, a view that is repeated in the report of the parliamentary enquiry—see German Parliamentary Report at pp. 333, 510. The original plan had been to apply a gross charge to all short sellers through Clearstream, but when it emerged that short positions could not necessarily be identified in Clearstream the proposal put to the Federal Ministry of Finance was modified so that the withholding tax charge would be applied by the seller's custodian bank (and it was expressly recognized that the withholding obligation would not apply to foreign banks acting for the seller). See German Parliamentary Report at pp. 132–7, 336.

[10] The later letter of 9 January 2003 suggested a possible legislative response in the form of the imposition of a withholding tax on the dividend compensation payments made through domestic banks. See German Parliamentary Report at pp.332–3.

[11] It seems that the issue was difficult for the tax authorities to understand and in the absence of any material presented on volumes or amounts it was treated as requiring merely a technical adjustment to the tax law—see German Parliamentary Report at pp. 142, 337, 342. There is little to indicate any systematic exploitation of cum-ex in the period 1977–2000, though cum-ex trades may have been executed on an isolated basis in this period. See Spengel, 'Expert Opinion', at p.25. By 2002, significant cum-ex trades were clearly taking place—see German Parliamentary Report at p.291.

(in the hands of the buyer) should be regarded as a separate item of 'other dividend income'.[12] The basic intention of the 2007 law was therefore to impose a new withholding tax on cum-ex trades so that any claim to a tax credit by the cum-ex buyer would be matched (and offset) by an amount of tax paid over to the tax authorities under the new withholding tax obligation.[13]

The German rules of 2007 were ineffective for two reasons: first, with the new withholding tax charge being limited to 'domestic credit institutions' it was obviously overly narrow. As discussed in Chapter 3, it was all too easy for the seller to avoid the rules simply by using an agent bank outside Germany.[14] Second, contrary to their clear intention, the new measures were interpreted as an *encouragement* of cum-ex activity on the theory that because they defined the boundaries (which as it turned out were in practice extremely narrow) within which cum-ex activity would *not* be acceptable to the tax authorities, activity outside of these boundaries was regarded as tacitly approved. From this, cum-ex participants and their advisors drew the inference that transactions structured so as to fall outside the application of the new rules would be respected and not challenged.[15]

[12] In a development that anticipated the direction of discussion in later years on cum-ex trades, it is notable that, as part of the work on the 2007 law, the Ministry of Finance of the State of North Rhine-Westphalia challenged the proposals on the basis there could be only *one* owner of the shares—rather than, as the proposed rules implied, two: the receiver of the 'real' dividend and the receiver of the 'artificial' dividend (or dividend compensation payment) which was system-generated by the cum-ex trade. The Ministry argued that the assumption that the buyer was the beneficial owner was misconceived: the short seller could not be the legal or economic owner at the point of shorting the shares and so could not transfer ownership, meaning that the legal status of the claim acquired by the buyer must be investigated. See German Parliamentary Report at pp.145–7. The consequence of this view is that the 2007 reform was not necessary. This is because the buyer in a cum-ex trade would never have been entitled to claim a tax credit given that, in the period up to the end of 2006 (i.e. before the reform took effect) the buyer would not have received any real dividend and any dividend compensation payment received would have been taxed as ordinary income but carried no entitlement to a tax credit.

[13] A similar conceptual approach to the 2007 German law had been seen in earlier tax legislation in the United Kingdom dealing with dividend compensation payments in that country. However, the corresponding UK law was significantly more robust and not so readily sidestepped as the German rules. The corresponding UK law, introduced in the early 1990s and enacted in Schedule 23A of ICTA 1988, had two features in particular that made it significantly more robust than the German rules. First, the withholding tax charge on the payment of dividend compensation payments was not restricted to payments by agents. Second, where the compensation payment was made by an overseas payor but received by a recipient in the jurisdiction, a supplementary 'reverse charge' withholding tax charge would arise. The relevance of the UK law on dividend compensation payments to the structuring of cum-ex trades is discussed in Chapter 3.

[14] The 2007 rules were based on the blueprint provided by the Federal Association of German Banks and this point on the scoping of the new rules was brought to the attention of the authorities in the original Banking Association proposals and also at the time of the enactment of the rules in 2007 by tax advisers. See German Parliamentary Report at pp.164–5.

[15] As noted in Chapter 2, the official notes to the 2007 legislation were also taken to support the view that the true beneficial ownership in shares (and therefore the ownership of the relevant dividend) is acquired by the buyer from the date of contract even if the seller is a short seller. From 2007 onwards, this statement in the official notes is of less importance given that dividend compensation payments were given the same treatment as real dividends in relation to withholding tax and tax credits. However, as regards the period up to 2006, the statement supports an interpretation which was ultimately rejected, as explained further below.

As cum-ex trading volumes increased and discussion of the strategy started to appear in the tax specialist literature, a second attempt to deal with cum-ex came in 2009.[16] This was the BMF (German Ministry of Finance) letter (or 'Cum-Ex Circular') of May 2009. The details of the Cum-Ex Circular have been discussed in Chapter 3, but the circular may be summarized as having introduced three elements: (1) a modification of existing tax certificates relating to dividend payments by the separate identification of tax credits arising from cum-ex transactions; (2) the requirement for a confirmation by a tax professional of the absence of any collusive arrangement before a tax credit or refund would be available; and (3) a particular focus on the activities of domestic special funds.[17]

The Cum-Ex Circular was in fact triggered by an email in March 2009 from a whistle-blower alerting the BMF to the ineffectiveness of the 2007 legislative change and outlining the scale of the cum-ex activity that was taking place.[18] The email also included an estimate of the resulting financial costs to the state, which the whistle-blower put at €12 billion.[19] The Cum-Ex Circular was therefore a rushed response made in the midst of the 2009 dividend season with the aim of showing the market that the BMF knew about the trade. It was also designed to introduce a mechanism in the form of the separate identification of cum-ex tax credits on the relevant tax certificate in order to bring cum-ex cases to the attention of the tax authorities.[20]

Unlike the earlier 2007 attempt to close cum-ex, the 2009 Cum-Ex Circular was directed at the party actually deriving the immediate benefit from the trade, namely the buyer. However, as with the 2007 legislative change, there were a number of problems with the action taken. The main problem was the scope of the

[16] According to Christoph Spengel, the earliest article in the tax specialist literature appeared in 2007—see Spengel, 'Expert Opinion', at p.13. The first general press report on cum-ex (in the magazine *Der Spiegel*) appeared in July 2009 and in the same year parliamentary questions were raised about cum-ex. See German Parliamentary Report at pp.16–17.

[17] As noted earlier, the circular was also widely interpreted as reflecting a tax authority view that the cum-ex trade was not generally illegal. See further the discussion of the Cum-Ex Circular in Chapter 3.

[18] This was not the first instance of whistle-blower activity. Though the available details are limited, there had been a whistle-blower communication to a German federal agency in May 2007 outlining the double use of the tax credit in cum-ex as well as explaining how the benefit would be shared between the parties to the cum-ex trade and the use of overseas parties to sidestep the 2007 legislation. There had also been an earlier whistle-blower report in April 2008 to the Hessian Ministry of Finance just prior to the 2008 dividend season of April–July. There was also further activity involving whistle-blowers in 2010 and 2011. See German Parliamentary Report at pp. 168, 191–2, 194–5.

[19] The estimate of €12 billion was a four-year estimate of financial damage based on the fact that the use of tax credits could be as much as five times what it should be due to repeated trades over the same shares and also on the basis that the DAX 30 paid €3 billion dividends annually. Therefore, the duplicated tax credits were equal to €3 billion ÷ withholding tax rate of 25% × 4 (duplicated use) × 4 (years) = €12 billion.

[20] The reasoning behind the use of tax professionals to certify the absence of collusion was to secure an independent view of the arrangements in light of the limited knowledge and resources of the authorities. See German Parliamentary Report at pp. 194, 200, 355.

measure, as it applied to German residents only.[21] It is therefore hardly a surprise that it did not stop cum-ex trading, but rather had the effect of shifting the buy side of the cum-ex trade outside Germany. This led to significant activity involving non-residents, particularly funds, acting as buyers in cum-ex trades.[22]

Also, because it expressly targeted collusive arrangements, the circular was interpreted by some market participants and tax advisers to suggest that cum-ex trades where there was no such collusion would not be subjected to scrutiny. Further, the standards required to assess the absence of collusive activity were themselves uncertain.[23]

By 2011, it had become clear that there would be a further legislative response to deal with cum-ex. There were also other significant developments both within and outside Germany.[24]

Within Germany, a major development was the further extension from March 2011 of the scope of the Cum-Ex Circular of May 2009 and its required procedures (including certification of the absence of collusion by tax professionals in appropriate cases) to include not only domestic taxpayers but also reimbursements to foreign claimants based on the provisions of applicable double tax treaties.[25] The consequence was a more detailed investigation of refund claims made by overseas taxpayers, particularly funds, by the tax authorities.[26] This change signaled a significant extension of the efforts of the tax authorities to get to grips with cum-ex. It was by no means a comprehensive solution given that, for example,

[21] The parliamentary report indicates that this design defect was brought to the attention of the authorities in November 2009 by tax advisers—see German Parliamentary Report at p.164.

[22] Also, within Germany there was evidence of exploitation of the exemption available to domestic mutual funds from the requirements of the 2009 BMF letter—see German Parliamentary Report at p.203. To deal with the use of domestic mutual funds, the scope of the original BMF letter was expanded (by a later BMF letter of 21 September 2010) to include German mutual funds.

[23] Discussions took place in October 2009 between the tax authorities and the Federal Chamber of Tax Advisers about uncertainties relating to the process of issuing professional certificates as stipulated in the BMF letter. The discussions addressed the standards to be applied, the data that should be collected, etc. See German Parliamentary Report at p.357.

[24] As discussed in the next section, work on a new legislative response had commenced by Autumn 2009 and was widely known in the market by 2010, though the measure only became effective from 1 January 2012.

[25] The change was announced in the BMF letter of 3 March 2011. The change of practice was a response to growing concerns on the part of the tax authorities relating to Irish funds and Dutch treaty claimants. There was also a concern about the increased use of US pension funds—see German Parliamentary Report at pp. 205, 235, 237. It was also evident by this time that the volumes of trades in the 2010 dividend season were significant, suggesting the measures announced in the original BMF letter of May 2009 had not been effective—see German Parliamentary Report at p.216.

[26] The Federal Central Tax Authority, which was responsible for administering the treaty refund process would routinely request detailed information including the date of acquisition of the shares giving rise to the reclaim, the related transactions in the shares, hedging arrangements, etc, with special attention given to cases involving foreign investment funds. This led to the development of criteria being applied to identify cases warranting particular attention. These criteria included the existence of claims in excess of €750,000, first-time claimants with high reimbursement requirements, and the presence of tax-exempt funds such as US pension funds. Training of the tax authority staff was also instituted. See German Parliamentary Report at pp. 205, 232–6.

the tax authorities in Germany were hardly able to assess whether the requested professional certificates issued by overseas tax professionals and confirming the absence of collusive arrangements corresponded to the truth of the matter in any particular case.[27]

Another very significant development in 2011, though probably not one that was appreciated by the authorities in Germany, was the issue by the London International Financial Futures Exchange (LIFFE) of a notice entitled 'Dividend Entitlements in Relation to Physically Delivered Universal Stock Futures and Individual Equity Option Contracts'.[28] The 1 April notice concerned LIFFE futures contracts which catered for physical delivery of securities in settlement of obligations under the contract.[29] From the 2009 dividend season, for the reasons explained in Chapter 3, these contracts had been used frequently to transfer shares from the seller to the buyer in cum-ex trades. The extensive use of these contracts, particularly during the 2010 dividend season, had led to a settlement logjam causing a large number of settlement failures. The notice was issued in order to help remedy the situation.[30]

Although very short in its terms, the LIFFE notice clarified that where securities were delivered under a LIFFE contract with an entitlement to a dividend 'the delivery by the Seller must include the associated entitlement to any tax credit'.[31] Whilst it was not explicitly spelled out in the notice, LIFFE made it known that if ex-dividend shares were delivered in settlement of contractual cum-dividend obligations under the futures contracts, it would represent a default in performance of the contract. In practice, this meant that any delivery of shares with a dividend entitlement would need to be accompanied by a tax voucher: this would prevent the normal cum-ex structuring of the trade.

Following the notice, there was an immediate—and dramatic—decline in the use of the LIFFE physically settled futures contracts to effect cum-dividend transfers of German shares. The notice also had a chilling effect on the wider

[27] The process of investigating the dates of cum-ex trades was also highly burdensome for the tax authorities. See German Parliamentary Report at pp. 215, 232.

[28] NYSE LIFFE Euronext Derivatives Markets, London Notice No. 3418, Dividend Entitlements in Relation to Physically Delivered Universal Stock Futures and Individual Equity Option Contracts, 1 April 2011.

[29] The notice referred specifically to four separate LIFFE contracts involving physical delivery that could be traded and referred specifically to the individual terms in each of those contracts.

[30] On investigation it emerged that some buyers and some sellers had conflicting views on the requirements of the settlement process relating to these contracts: some sellers argued that the 'market claim' requires a cash indemnity payment equal to the amount of the net dividend; some buyers argued that market claims for physical settlement of cum-dividend physically settled derivative contracts should consist of both the net dividend and also a proof of payment that tax has been withheld, thus allowing the buyer to make a tax refund claim.

[31] In technical terms, the clarification made was that the legal entitlement to any tax credit associated with a dividend is 'necessarily captured' in the 'relevant entitlement' to a dividend when a security is delivered with a dividend entitlement (cum dividend) on physical settlement. In consequence, the implication was that using ex-dividend shares to settle a cum-dividend obligation would trigger a default of the contractual terms.

cum-ex market. From this point, market participants started to accept that their budgeted cum-ex revenues for the year were unlikely to be achieved.

By late 2011, some of the tax advisers in Germany that had hitherto been extensively involved in advising on cum-ex trades were no longer writing tax opinions in support of the trade. At the same time, the first cases challenging cum-ex related tax credits were beginning to come before the German courts.[32]

When examining the actions of the tax authorities up to 1 January 2012, the date on which cum-ex was finally closed down, it may be concluded that the authorities were not only slow to appreciate the significance and scale of cum-ex trades but also ineffective in their attempts to bring the trade to an end.[33] As mentioned earlier, one direct consequence of their initial efforts to close the trade down was that, in drawing too narrowly the boundaries of activity they sought to prohibit, they unwittingly encouraged cum-ex activity.[34] It is also hard to resist the conclusion that there was a basic compliance and accounting failure on the part of the German tax authorities given that they refunded or gave credit for vastly more withholding tax than they had actually collected.

The 2012 Action to Close Cum-Ex

The change in law that finally brought an end to the cum-ex trade involved a fundamental—yet nonetheless simple—modification of the rules governing the obligation to apply dividend withholding tax. The effect of the change was to bring together the two functions whose separateness under the preceding rules had provided the opportunity for the cum-ex trade to flourish, namely the process of deducting withholding tax from a dividend on the one hand and the process for the production of a tax certificate for the investor (or buyer, in a cum-ex trade) on the other. The tax certificate written by the cum-ex buyer's custodian bank was produced essentially in a vacuum: there was no necessary correspondence or linkage between the tax certificate created and the imposition of any actual

[32] The first case to come to the courts was the 2011 Roth case. The first raids on suspected cum-ex participants were not to begin until 2012.

[33] It is clear that the tax authorities knew about the problem creating the technical possibility for cum-ex from at least the 1990s, if not appreciably earlier. However, this is not the same as saying they appreciated the practical realities of the scale and seriousness of the problem. It seems unlikely that the authorities appreciated the full extent of the cum-ex problem until 2009 or later, and, even then, the true scale and implications of the cross-border structuring may not have been fully appreciated. Even in 2009, the authorities' knowledge of cum-ex trades was very limited and it seems to have been only in the Spring of 2010 when the UK tax authorities sent the German tax authorities a UK bank's detailed 'strategy paper' on cum-ex from 2007 that the German authorities obtained for the first time a concrete idea of what the market was doing and the mechanisms that were being used (see German Parliamentary Report at pp. 205, 209, 354). It was probably not until 2011, with the extension of 2009 BMF letter arrangements to non-residents, that the tax authorities truly began to get to grips with cum-ex trading.

[34] This is certainly the view of Spengel—see 'Expert Opinion', at pp. 109, 111.

withholding tax on a real dividend (or, from 2007, on a dividend compensation payment).

The need for a change in the law was recognized from mid-2009 and a detailed proposal was in place by the autumn of that year.[35] However, it was not until June 2011 that the law was passed, though with a deferred effective date of 1 January 2012, some two and a half years after the need for the law was accepted.[36] The law was changed to bring an end to the separation of (1) the responsibility for deducting withholding tax on the payment of a dividend (which previously lay with the dividend-paying company or its agent) and (2) the responsibility for producing the tax credit certificate evidencing withholding tax on the receipt of a dividend. This was achieved by the new law which, from 1 January 2012, shifted the obligation to withhold tax on dividend payments from German companies paying the dividend to the relevant 'paying agent', which was either the custodian bank of the final beneficiary or the last German bank paying the dividend abroad.[37] This meant that the German depository or custodian bank acting for the recipient of the dividend would be responsible *both* for levying the dividend withholding tax and issuing the tax certificate relating to that withholding tax. As a result, the separate, and entirely independent, exercise of producing the tax credit certificates without reference to whether withholding tax had actually ever been paid, came to an end.

In order to permit the withholding tax obligation to shift to the relevant custodian bank, the obligation to deduct withholding tax from the dividend was taken away from the issuer of the shares. In consequence, a gross payment (i.e. 100 per cent) of the dividend would be made by the dividend paying company's paying agent, with that amount being credited to Clearstream. That gross payment would then flow through the Clearstream system to the German custodian banks. The last bank in the chain acting for the investor entitled to the dividend (or, where intermediate non-German custodian banks were also used by the underlying

[35] The discussions on the new law also involved consultation with the banking industry in June 2009. Two alternative approaches were discussed initially, being (1) an extension of the withholding tax to foreigners making compensation payments and (2) a shift of the dividend withholding obligation to the level of the paying agent. The approach of the new law (based on (2)) was agreed in October 2010. See German Parliamentary Report at pp. 206–7, 210–17, 357–61.

[36] The reasons for the slow enactment process are considered in the German Parliamentary Report at pp. 207, 221–3.

[37] The change in the identity of the party obliged to levy withholding tax was delivered by Article 7 (8) of the UCITS IV Implementation Act, the law transposing European Union Directive 2009/65/EC on the coordination of laws, regulations, and administrative provisions relating to undertakings for collective investment in transferable securities, 22 June 2011, Federal Law Gazette, I, p.1126. The change involved a shift from the 'debtor principle', under which the issuer of the shares and the payor of the dividend was obliged to account for withholding tax, to the 'paying agent' principle (also referred to as the 'number of points' principle), under which the obligation to deduct and account for the withholding falls on the dividend-paying custodian acting for the shareholder pursuant to Section 44. (1) Sentence 4, Point Number 3 of the Income Tax Act.

owner, the last custodian bank in Germany) would be required to deduct the withholding tax and pay it over to the tax authorities.

In addition to these new withholding tax arrangements, changes were also introduced to the withholding tax reclaim procedure under German tax treaties. The procedure was changed to require the reclaim application to be accompanied by the formal tax voucher issued by the German paying agent. Where requested by the owner of the dividend income, the tax voucher would be produced by the paying agent bank (which would have deducted withholding tax as explained above).

The principle thereby established was that tax certificates would be issued only by the bank which had also paid the withholding tax to the tax office for the certified position.[38] The result of the change in law is that any reclaim of German withholding tax must now always be matched by actual payments of withholding tax on the dividends concerned. This simple change closes down the mismatch in the system that was exploited by the cum-ex trade.

Legal Reassessment of Cum-Ex Structures

Once the German authorities had begun to understand the full scale of cum-ex activity, their response was: (1) to close the opportunity for cum-ex trades through the legislative response discussed above; (2) to challenge the legality of tax claims by a careful reassessment of the legal analysis upon which cum-ex trades had previously relied; and (3) to investigate past transactions and, where relevant, to pursue criminal sanctions against the participants in cum-ex trades. The previous section has already dealt with the legislative change in (1) and the approach to the investigations of cum-ex trades in (3) will be considered in the next section. The discussion in this section is concerned with (2), the reassessment of the legal basis of cum-ex trades.

As the public profile of cum-ex trades increased from around 2009, there began what was to become an ongoing intensive discussion in the technical literature and emerging court cases on the legality of the design of the cum-ex structures. This happened in various ways: arguments raised by the tax authorities leading up to 2012 and subsequently; court cases dealing with cum-ex issues; discussion of the relevant technical issues in the professional and academic literature; special

[38] The relevant custodian bank would be permitted to issue vouchers only where the withheld tax recorded on the voucher did not exceed the total amount of the withholding taxes actually paid. For more detail on the relevant tax voucher process and the tax reclaim processing requirements, see the Clearstream release at http://www.clearstream.com/clearstream-en/products-and-services/asset-services/tax-and-certification/germany–reminder—tax-voucher-process-and-tax-reclaim-processing-requirements/63342.

reports and investigations on cum-ex; and in the course of work relating to the 2017 German parliamentary enquiry (discussed later in this chapter).[39]

The primary line of argument challenging the legal basis of cum-ex trades which emerged from this reassessment centred on the fact that in cum-ex trades there is never any withholding tax deducted on the payment of the dividend (or, from 2007, the dividend compensation payment) which the buyer receives. In the absence of any withholding tax ever having been paid, there could not, according to this line of argument, ever be a valid tax credit or refund. In other words, cum-ex could never work.[40] According to this reasoning, it is not sufficient that a tax certificate be merely issued to the recipient of the relevant income: it must also meet certain legal requirements before a tax credit can become available to a taxpayer. As discussed in Chapter 2, these legal requirements are: (1) that the income concerned must be a dividend (or alternatively, and from 2007, a dividend compensation payment) and (2) in respect of this income, *income tax must have been levied by way of tax deduction*.[41] Cum-ex trades over German shares were designed so that a withholding tax certificate would be issued without there being any withholding tax actually paid.[42] This was, of course, the whole point of cum-ex trades. Their aim was to create a claim for a tax credit in the hands of the buyer in the absence of any actual withholding tax being applied to the payment received by that buyer.[43] The direct implication of this line of argument advanced by the German tax authorities is that the tax certificate issued is incorrect and the conditions for a tax credit or refund are not met: the absence of any actual withholding tax means that the buyer's tax certificate could never be duly completed.[44]

[39] The various technical arguments and disputes that are discussed below are examined in more detail in the expert report prepared for the parliamentary enquiry. See Spengel, 'Expert Opinion'. The issues are also discussed in detail in the parliamentary report itself.

[40] This line of argument can be seen emerging in the approach of the authorities. In the BMF letter of 2009, the Finance Ministry seems to be implying that cum-ex trades would work provided there is no collusion between the parties. However, by the time of the later supplement to the letter in 2011, the Finance Ministry expressly states in the release that a tax certificate may have been issued without the amount of withholding tax specified in it having been levied or paid. The statement then goes on to say that the withholding tax stated in the tax certificate may not be credited because it has not been paid and the requirements for refund have not been met. See German Parliamentary Report at pp. 232, 356.

[41] The requirements that must be met for a tax credit to be available (under Section 36 (2) Number 2 of the Income Tax Act) are discussed in Chapter 2 and require that: certain stipulated income is derived by the taxpayer; income tax was levied on that income by deduction; and a valid tax certificate is submitted to the tax authorities.

[42] From 2007, the trades were structured so that there would be no withholding tax under the dividend compensation rules on the payment of a dividend compensation payment by virtue of the use of foreign custodian banks.

[43] Prior to the introduction of the withholding tax charge on domestic credit institutions in respect of dividend compensation amounts that took effect from 1 January 2007, there was no mechanism under German tax law for withholding to be applied to these payments. After the introduction of that law, cum-ex trades were generally structured to ensure the relevant withholding tax charge introduced in 2007 was avoided by using non-domestic custodian banks. Accordingly, withholding tax was not applied in respect of the dividend compensation payments to the buyer in a cum-ex trade.

[44] See Section 45 (3) of the Income Tax Act.

This interpretation was subject to considerable discussion in the technical literature, with a number of arguments being presented as to why the tax certificate, and the tax credit, should nonetheless be regarded as valid.[45]

The contention that cum-ex trades should fail because of the lack of any actual withholding tax having been applied was completely at odds with the interpretation of the law that had originally been assumed in the tax opinions which supported cum-ex trades. In those opinions, the position generally adopted was that the buyer became the owner of the shares on the date the contract for the purchase of the shares was entered into, rather than on the later (T+2) date on which settlement of that contract took place. On this view, the buyer therefore also became the owner of the dividend rights that attached to the shares, having contracted to buy the shares *before* the date upon which the right to receive the dividend arose (i.e. the dividend record date). These opinions, therefore, took the view that withholding tax deducted was thus properly attributable to the dividend which was paid.[46]

A major issue of the debate was therefore whether it was correct to conclude that the income received by the cum-ex buyer should be regarded as being a *dividend*. Under German law, the time at which the buyer becomes the owner of the shares is determined by the provisions of Section 39 of the General Tax Code, which deal with how ownership should be interpreted.[47] The original view that had been adopted in the opinions supporting cum-ex trades was later attacked by the tax authorities on the basis of a lengthy analysis of this provision. The argument was that Section 39 provides that the owner is either the legal owner *or* a person that excludes the ownership rights of the legal owner. However, the critical point on this approach was that there can be only *one* owner. Yet in a case such as cum-ex involving a short sale, the earlier analysis in support of cum-ex trades would lead to the existence of *two* owners: one was the lender of the shares who was the legal owner on the dividend record date and received the dividend before the shares were later lent on ex-dividend terms. The second was the cum-ex

[45] These included the arguments that: the dividend compensation amount was paid net of tax, not gross, indicating tax had been deducted, even though it may not have been paid over to the tax authorities; the relevant tax that had been deducted was the tax deducted by the issuer of the shares on the payment of the dividend; the tax deduction was in effect deemed by operation of the relevant law (in Section 45a (3) Sentence 2); and that the certificate itself was sufficient and proper evidence of the tax deduction. These arguments are considered, and rejected, in Spengel, 'Expert Opinion', at pp.79–85. However, a significant body of authors and legal scholars holding a contrary view is cited (at p.64, footnote 175). The importance of the requirements for a valid tax credit was emphasized in the Higher Regional Court of Cologne in its decision of 12/11/2014, 7 U 23/14, Rn. 59, juris, document no. JURE150004324.

[46] The view that the buyer is always the beneficial owner from the contract date was also reflected in the 2002 letter from the Federal Association of German Banks. It is stated in a footnote to that letter that the Federal Finance Court in a 1999 judgment also came to the same conclusion. See German Parliamentary Report at p.332.

[47] See further the discussion in Chapter 2 at pages xxx–xxx.[this should refer to what is now C2.P57-C2.P60 and in particular footnote 65]

buyer as the 'beneficial owner' of the shares, who by virtue of that ownership excluded the ownership rights of the legal owner as from the contract date.[48] It was argued that the suggestion that there could be two owners of the same parcel of shares would violate fundamental principles of German law.[49]

These debates led to significant controversy amongst academics as to the proper interpretation of the ownership rules under German law.[50] The arguments also featured much reference to the government's stated justification for the introduction of the withholding tax charge on dividend compensation payments and also to specific statements in the 2009 Cum-Ex Circular. In both cases it has been argued by market participants and their advisers that the relevant statements actually seem to support the original view taken in the opinions supporting cum-ex trades.[51]

The discussion above addresses the question whether or not the cum-ex buyer can properly be regarded as the owner of the dividend on the shares in a cum-ex trade. It was a key issue in the period to the end of 2006. From 1 January 2007, it became necessary also to take account of the dividend compensation payment rules. Those provisions were designed to introduce a new form of withholding tax on such compensation payments and also provide that dividend compensation

[48] Contrary to the supportive position adopted in the earlier opinions, it was argued by the tax authorities that, firstly, it is clear that lender of the shares is the owner because that person is the shareholder on the dividend record date—and clearly on that date the ownership of the lender is not excluded by buyer (the lender might be completely unaware of the buyer and seller on the dividend record date). This means that the lender must have unfettered rights on the dividend record date. Secondly, as there is no authority for the view there can be multiple owners of the same asset (such as a parcel of shares), the cum-ex buyer is excluded on this approach as the owner of the dividend. This means the buyer is not entitled to a dividend but merely derives a dividend compensation payment under the short sale. It is the lender, as owner of the shares, who receives the dividend. This line of argument makes a distinction between owner sales (i.e. sales of shares that are already owned by the seller, or "long" sales) and short sales—owner sales are different because the real dividend economically is derived by the buyer and no-one else, whereas in short sales the buyer cannot exclude the ownership rights of the legal owner (typically, the lender in cum-ex transactions).

[49] This argument was confirmed in the case FG Hessen from 10/02/2016, 4 K 1684/14, EFG 2016, pp.761 et seq. It is also referred to in Spengel, 'Expert Opinion', at p.67. The line of argument was first developed in Christoph Spengel and Thomas Eisgruber, 'Die nicht vorhandene Gesetzeslücke bei Cum/Ex- Geschäften', *Deutsches Steuerrecht* 16 (2015), 785–848.

[50] This included significant discussion of a 1999 judgment of the Federal Finance Court concerning a (cum-cum) dividend stripping trade and in which the court concluded the buyer was the beneficial owner (BFH of 15/12/1999, IR 29/97, Federal Tax Gazette, II 2000, p.527). The position adopted in legal opinions supporting the cum-ex trade was that legal authority for the buyer to be regarded as the owner of shares from the contract date clearly derived from that case and that this interpretation should apply also in the case of short sales. The counterview (proposed by the tax authorities) was that the case contemplated a single owner of shares and did not provide any authority for the view that there could be multiple owners of the same parcel of shares. Spengel argues that the Federal Fiscal Court comments preclude as the owner a person who does not know the legal owner and has no relationship to them. See Spengel, 'Expert Opinion', at p.71. The position of the Federal Government stated in 2013 is that the transfer of ownership from the time of the contract applies to 'owner' sales, but not to short sales. See Spengel, 'Expert Opinion', at p.70.

[51] For example, though not effecting an express change in the law, the explanation of the 2007 measure indicates that dividend compensation withholding tax was needed to correspond to the credit claimed by the buyer *as the acquirer of the shares and beneficial owner entitled to the dividend.*

receipts were a form of 'other dividend income' in respect of which a tax credit may be available.[52] However, here again the primary argument countering the legal position adopted in support of cum-ex trades was based on the absence of withholding tax actually paid – the argument being that if tax has been deducted from dividend compensation payments by a domestic custodian, then that tax is creditable in the hands of the buyer. Conversely, if no tax has been deducted, for example because of the use by the seller of a foreign custodian bank, then no credit could ever be available.

This line of argument based on the absence of any actual withholding tax represents a complete rejection of the effectiveness of all cum-ex trades over German shares, whether entered into before or after 2007. For cum-ex trades carried out before 2007, the argument is that the cum-ex buyer did not become the owner of the shares at the time of entering into the contract with the short seller so cannot be regarded as receiving a 'dividend', and in any event there was no actual withholding tax which could justify the availability of a tax credit.[53] For cum-ex trades executed after 1 January 2007, when dividend compensation payments were recognized in the law for the first time as a separate item of income, no withholding tax would have been deducted in the usual case where a foreign custody bank was used by the cum-ex seller.[54]

The argument outlined above, based on the absence of any relevant withholding tax, has been adopted by the tax authorities in dealing with cum-ex cases, and denies the existence of any 'loophole' in the law that could legitimately have been exploited: on this view, the taxpayer must be able to prove the fact of actual withholding tax having been deducted before a credit (or refund) could be available. If the taxpayer cannot prove this, there is no tax credit.[55]

[52] From 1 January 2007, the withholding tax charge on dividend compensation payments is imposed by Section 44 (1) Number 2 Income Tax Act. Also, dividend compensation payments are made a new category of income within Section 20 (1) 1 by Section 20 (1) (1) Sentence 4. The relevant tax credit requirements remain those in Section 36 (2) Number 2 Income Tax Act.

[53] Technically, the argument is that the cum-ex buyer never received income from capital assets within Section 20 (1) (1) of the Income Tax Act (and so fails the first limb of the tax credit requirements in Section 36 (2) (2)) because the dividend is paid to the actual shareholder, as determined by Section 39 of the General Tax Code, and the ownership rights of the actual shareholder are never excluded by the cum-ex buyer. This approach takes it as axiomatic that there can only ever be one owner and it is argued that there is no inconsistency with the 1999 judgment of the Federal Finance Court on the basis that case concerns only the situation of an 'owner' seller. Further, the absence of actual withholding means the second limb of the requirements of Section 36 (2) (2) is also not satisfied.

[54] Here again, the tax authorities argued that the second limb of the tax credit tests in Section 36 (2) (2) Income Tax Act (the requirement for the actual deduction of withholding tax) has not been fulfilled. This view was confirmed by a Hessian Finance Court decision of 8 October 2012 (ref. 4 V 1661/11).

[55] On this approach, the certificate in accordance with Section 45 (3) Income Tax Act is required but it is not in itself a sufficient discharge of the burden of proof. Rather, the taxpayer must show that the criteria for a valid credit in Section 36 (2) Number 2 are met. For cum-ex trades, this would usually mean (post 2006) that tax had been deducted under Section 20 (1) Number 1. This inevitably led to arguments that the buyer might not know the seller was short-selling (which was argued to be especially relevant if the purchase is executed on exchange) and so cannot deal with burden of proof issue, delivering a result that lacks 'any sense of justice' where the buyer relies on the tax certificate as evidence

There is one further important consequence which arises from tax credits being claimed in the absence of actual withholding tax being applied. This concerns the production of what is in consequence an invalid tax credit certificate. Under German tax law, the domestic custodian would strictly be liable for the tax advantages conferred by such a certificate, irrespective of whether the error was understood by it.[56] This gives a harsh result for any domestic custodian bank unaware of the existence of short sales, though there seems to have be little sympathy for the position of such banks in relation to this point.[57]

To date, there has been no Supreme Court case to resolve beyond all further debate the technical matters discussed above.[58] However, the debate on the technical legal issues was predicated largely on the assumption of a lack of collusion between the parties. As the number of investigations into cum-ex trades has expanded, it has becoming increasingly—and pervasively—evident that there was in fact a very high level of planning, cooperation, and coordination amongst the parties to cum-ex trades. This can hardly be regarded as surprising given the discussion in Chapter 3. As a practical matter, therefore, the discussion on the technical issues that has been explored above has now been supplanted by a large-scale criminal investigation. It is to that investigation that the discussion in this chapter now turns.

Ongoing German Tax Authority Challenges and Impacts

At a very early stage of their response to cum-ex trades, the tax authorities determined that the trades were unlawful, largely for the technical reasons

of the tax withheld. However, many commentators have little sympathy for such an objection on the basis that the transactions were obviously targeted around dividend date, involved stock transactions in the billions of euros, and involved little or no real risk, meaning that the participants must have been advised of the technical requirement for tax deduction under Section 36 (2) Number 2 Income Tax Act, in addition to the fact that the burden of proof falls on the claimant.

[56] Section 45 (7) Income Tax Act. This would be relevant generally in the period to 2006 and in the period 2007–11 if foreign custodian banks were used by the seller.

[57] For example, the view taken by Spengel is that such banks must have seen the trading activity around dividend dates and must have been aware of the possibility of cum-ex trading. Custodian banks could also have checked the trading pattern with their customers. Spengel also comments on the obvious failure of internal controls for banks and concludes that their role turns out to be a much riskier business than first thought. See Spengel, 'Expert Opinion', at p.101.

[58] As at the time of the publication of this book in Summer 2020, the latest major development in the consideration of the tax technical position relating to cum-ex is the Cologne Tax Court decision of 19 July 2019, 2 K 2672/17, https://www.justiz.nrw.de/nrwe/fgs/koeln/j2019/2_K_2672_17_Urteil_20190719.html. This decision is further confirmation of the position reflected in the legal arguments advanced by the German tax authorities. The decision of the court unambiguously rejected arguments in support of the cum-ex trade that "double ownership" of a parcel of shares could be possible and stipulated that there can only ever be one owner for tax purposes. The decision also suggested a reversal of the burden of proof in respect of the short sale, adopting the position that it is for the claimant of a tax credit to show the relevant income receipt is not generated by a short sale, rather than for the tax authorities to demonstrate the existence of a short sale. The decision of the court has been appealed.

explained above.[59] This transformed the nature of their response. Instead of having to rely on anti-avoidance rules which might be relevant in the event the trades legally exploited a loophole in the law, the sanctions relevant to criminal tax evasion were potentially brought into play.[60] For such a criminal action to be relevant, both an *objective* and *subjective* element would need to be present in relation to the actions of the taxpayer concerned. The objective element would normally consist in the declaration of entitlement to the tax benefit arising under a cum-ex trade. This element would typically be satisfied by the filing for a reclaim of the tax credit with the tax authorities. The subjective element would require a knowledge on the part of the taxpayer (and any accomplices) that the action was contrary to the law. In practice, this subjective element normally consists in there being some collusive arrangement between the parties to bring about the intended result under cum-ex trading, i.e. the creation of an entitlement to a tax credit in circumstances where it was clear that no withholding tax had been deducted from the relevant payment. The relevant law provides for a prison sentence up to five years or a fine where inaccurate facts or incomplete information is given deliberately to the tax authorities and tax is thereby reduced or an unjustified tax benefit is taken.[61] However, the length of the potential prison sentence is extended to ten years where the financial damage caused is significant and the relevant actions are carried on by 'members of a gang' acting in concert whose purpose is the continued commission of forgery or fraud.[62] These provisions are potentially relevant not merely for claimants of tax credits generated by cum-ex trades (i.e. buyers in cum-ex trades) but also other parties who were complicit in such schemes.[63]

[59] Broadly, the position adopted by the tax authorities was that the tax certificate produced in most cum-ex trades would be incorrect and it was then to be explored on a case-by-case basis whether the actions of the parties to procure its existence amounted to criminal fraud.

[60] German tax law makes a distinction between the (legal) misuse of design, which may be countered by, for example, the general anti-abuse rule in Section 42 of the General Tax Code, and (criminal) tax evasion within the meaning of Section 370. The tax authorities' approach of seeking to apply Section 370 has been supported by the courts. The Cologne regional court in its decision of 16 July 2015 (LG Cologne on 7 July 2015, 106 Qs 1/15, juris document no. JURE 150011775) suggested that Section 370 is relevant if there has been a claim for tax credit in a cum-ex case.

[61] The legal provisions of primary relevance in such a case are Section 370 of the General Tax Code and Section 263 of the German Criminal Code.

[62] See Section 370 (3) Number 5 and Section 376 (which stipulates a ten-year limitation period) General Tax Code and Section 263 (3) of the German Criminal Code.

[63] There is a discussion of Section 370 in Spengel, 'Expert Opinion', at pp. 56–7, 97–9, 107–8, 115. Spengel argues that the conditions for Section 370 to apply are fulfilled merely by the cum-ex buyer's claim of a tax credit given that no withholding tax was actually levied. Spengel notes the counter-arguments to the application of Section 370 put forward by a number of commentators (see footnote 285 on p.98 and the discussion on pp.98–9) and concludes that ultimately it is for the courts to decide if Section 370 applies in individual cases. This discussion of the application of Section 370 does not take full account of what has emerged from many of the cum-ex trades that have been investigated in individual cases, namely the collusive nature of the agreed transactions (see further below). The possibility of a secondary tax liability risk for the short seller (or other parties) in relation to any unlawful tax credit in the hands of the buyer potentially arises where a tax fraud has been aided or abetted pursuant to Section 71 of the General Tax Code.

The approach of the tax authorities meant that the focus shifted from a more abstract discussion of the relevant technical issues relating to cum-ex (and their strict legal and transactional effect) to a much more detailed forensic analysis of the *conduct and collaboration* of the parties entering into individual cum-ex trades. The scale of the ensuing investigation started with some of the smaller players but rapidly evolved into a full international undertaking, involving banks and financial institutions around the globe.

Given the inevitable detail of the investigations in any particular case, the sheer volume and sophistication of the transactions concluded, the lengthy time period over which this activity was conducted, and the large numbers of banks and their clients involved, it is very likely that this investigation will continue for years. The discussion in this section charts the main developments that have been seen in the period from 2011 to Spring 2020.[64]

An early indication of the authorities' approach to dealing with cum-ex trades entered into prior to 2012 was the use of raids on suspected parties. The earliest reported cum-ex raid, on the German bank HVB, took place in 2012, following reports from a whistle-blower.[65] The raid was coordinated by the Frankfurt prosecutor's office. While the bank in question was not particularly large, the team which was assembled for the raid revealed the scale and complexity of investigating cum-ex. The raid was carried out nationwide in Germany on thirteen separate premises, with sixty prosecutors, police officers, and tax inspectors in attendance.[66]

The bank involved had cooperated extensively with the authorities.[67] It had already repaid the tax authorities a provisional amount of €65 million in relation to tax credits previously claimed from certain cum-ex trades and had undertaken a thorough internal investigation assisted by external counsel.[68] In doing so (and underlining the detailed nature of investigating cum-ex trading in practice), it was required to analyse nearly 2.7 million transactions in equities and other

[64] The cooperation on investigations between the Ministry of Finance, the Federal Central Tax Office, and the state financial authorities was sharply increased in the course of 2012, though the Federal Central Tax Office had started systematic investigations in 2011. See German Parliamentary Report at pp. 224, 231.

[65] 'HVB' (HypoVereisbank) is the brand name used by UniCredit Bank AG.

[66] See the report in Handelsblatt, 29 November 2012, available at: https://www.handelsblatt.com/finanzen/banken-versicherungen/verdacht-auf-steuerhinterziehung-razzia-bei-der-hypo-vereinsbank/7455354.html. It was reported that eight people were suspected of involvement in a scheme to defraud the public purse of €124 million with some of their number suspected of tax evasion. See the report in Juve, 29 November 2012, available at: https://www.juve.de/nachrichten/verfahren/2012/11/hvb-razzia-wegen-cum-ex-trades-vorstand-und-aufsichtsrat-wappnen-sich-mit-strafrechtlern.

[67] See the report in Handelsblatt, 29 November 2012, available at: https://www.handelsblatt.com/finanzen/banken-versicherungen/verdacht-auf-steuerhinterziehung-razzia-bei-der-hypo-vereinsbank/7455354.html

[68] See the report in Juve, 29 June 2012, available at: https://www.juve.de/nachrichten/verfahren/2012/06/umstrittene-steuerprodukte-hvb-wehrt-sich-broker-erhebt-schwere-vorwurfe-gegen-clifford

securities.[69] Such was the seriousness of the matter that each of the management board of the bank and the supervisory board appointed separate counsel to represent them.[70] In December 2016, the bank was fined €10 million for its German cum-ex business. Its cooperation with prosecutors was noted as a reason that the fines and consequences for the bank were not higher, although, even with this leniency, the affair would cost the bank over €250 million.[71] These losses prompted the bank to sue directly three former members of its management board, claiming €180 million for their failures in relation to cum-ex trades.[72] The materiality of the issue also led to its disclosure in the bank's annual report.[73]

The scope of the investigations and raids expanded to include banks, investment funds, intermediaries (such as brokers that executed trades and prime-brokers that financed the trades), and tax advisory firms.[74] For example, an unnamed investment fund was raided in October 2014, this time under the auspices of the Munich public prosecutor's office. Five current and former managers of the fund were under investigation. The amount alleged to be involved was reported at €350 million, nearly double the amount at issue in the 2012 HVB raid. At the time, this made it the largest cum-ex case in Germany. Persons of interest were reported to include those responsible for operating the financial infrastructure of the German equities market, making their employers, including Clearstream AG, the subject of raids.[75]

The investigation of cum-ex trades raises a number of practical issues. Chapter 3 noted a number of features that would complicate the task of any investigation, including the different roles in a cum-ex trade that might be assumed by an individual bank (including, as buyer, seller, custodian, and trading platform for clients), the multiple securities accounts (including the bank's

[69] See the report in Süddeutsche Zeitung, available at: http://www.sueddeutsche.de/wirtschaft/cum-ex-deals-dubiose-geschaefte-teure-folgen-1.2509369.

[70] See the report in Juve, 29 November 2012, available at: https://www.juve.de/nachrichten/verfahren/2012/11/hvb-razzia-wegen-cum-ex-trades-vorstand-und-aufsichtsrat-wappnen-sich-mit-strafrechtlern

[71] See the report in Süddeutsche Zeitung, available at: See http://www.sueddeutsche.de/wirtschaft/hypovereinsbank-muss-millionen-euro-strafe-zahlen-1.2766099.

[72] See the report in Süddeutsche Zeitung, 14 September 2016, available at: http://www.sueddeutsche.de/wirtschaft/cum-ex-hypo-vereinsbank-verklagt-vorstaende-auf-millionen-euro-1.3161143

[73] See the report in Juve, 29 November 2012, available at: https://www.juve.de/nachrichten/verfahren/2012/11/hvb-razzia-wegen-cum-ex-trades-vorstand-und-aufsichtsrat-wappnen-sich-mit-strafrechtlern

[74] A leading legal firm was raided in October 2017 in connection with its role in advising on the tax aspects of cum-ex. See the report in Süddeutsche Zeitung available at: http://www.sueddeutsche.de/wirtschaft/umstrittene-anwaelte-freshfields-und-der-wohl-groesste-deutsche-steuerbetrug-1.3720509.

[75] In September 2017, an investigative team arrived at the offices of the German stock exchange, Deutsche Börse, in Eschborn. Its subsidiary Clearstream is one of the world's largest providers of securities services and holds assets of around €13 trillion for customers, handling more than 100 million transactions per year. A Clearstream manager was reported to be under investigation in relation to cum-ex. See the report in Handelsblatt, 4 April 2018, available at: https://www.handelsblatt.com/finanzen/banken-versicherungen/cum-ex-geschaefte-staatsanwaltschaft-nimmt-manager-der-deutsche-boerse-tochter-clearstream-ins-visier/21140286.html

proprietary accounts and the accounts maintained for its customers) in which the transactions might be booked, the different business units that might be involved (including the derivatives desk, the financing business, the stock loan desk, and the share dealing desk), and the different directional flow of the trades (given that a bank might act as buyer in relation to some transactions and as seller in relation to others). Making the matter even more difficult to penetrate, arrangements relating to some or all of the trades would often have been deliberately concealed. For example, a bank's traders might blend cum-ex trading in with thousands of other legitimate transactions, while a fund might embed cum-ex trading within a broader investment strategy, making the cum-ex trades extremely difficult to detect. All of these matters, coupled with the steep learning curve that faced investigating officials, placed significant constraints on the German investigators. Beyond Germany lay multiple countries where still other intermediaries, banks, and funds had been involved in carrying out cum-ex trades. Pursuing entities in those countries would require both a legal basis for any enquiry and the cooperation of foreign authorities. This fragmented and inter-jurisdictional backdrop to cum-ex trading inevitably made for slow progress.

Finally, there was also the task of ensuring coordination amongst the various investigating bodies themselves, given that the German states (or Länder) normally have responsibility for investigations of taxpayers within their jurisdiction, whilst the Federal Central Tax Office is responsible for administering and policing the reimbursement of German withholding tax internationally pursuant to double tax treaties. Overall supervision of these bodies is exercised by the Federal Ministry of Finance.[76]

Notwithstanding the practical difficulties of pursuing cum-ex investigations, significant progress was made in some of the early cases in establishing the nature of the arrangements that operated among participants in the trades. It became clear that the trades had been well-planned. For example, in one case it was discovered that detailed Excel spreadsheets (significantly, prepared in advance of the dividend season) captured the details of the planned trades and counterparties and showed how the profits generated would be split among the parties through the pricing of the hedging instruments used. The investigations confirmed the existence of a high level of collusion amongst participants, particularly where evidence was unearthed showing that they communicated covertly with each other through messaging services such as Bloomberg chats or emails, etc.[77] The

[76] These bodies would also work with prosecutors and specialist criminal law units. For example, the Federal Central Tax Office would work closely with its criminal and penal section and the Prosecutor's Office in Cologne. See German Parliamentary Report at pp.233–4. The administrative responsibilities of state and federal institutions in relation to issues raised by the cum-ex trade and responsibilities for the administration of the law relating to tax crimes are discussed in the report at pp.83–5.

[77] Evidence of the collusion of parties in cum-ex trades is also discussed in the German Parliamentary Report at pp. 173–5 and 280.

role of whistle-blowers has also played a key role in alerting authorities to the nature and scale of the collusion among the parties.[78]

Cum-ex investigations began to extend beyond German borders. In October 2014, Swiss police, acting at the behest of German authorities, searched the offices of Bank Sarasin in Zurich and Basel.[79] Prosecutors and police also conducted raids in a number of cantons across Switzerland: Basel-Stadt, Basel-Landschaft, Zurich, Zug, Graubünden, St. Gallen, and Schwyz, with more than twenty offices and apartments searched. The public prosecutor's office in Zurich coordinated the operations on behalf of the prosecutor's office in Cologne.[80] It was the first time that Switzerland had assisted German authorities with a bank raid, made all the more unusual by virtue of Switzerland's historically strict approach to bank secrecy.[81]

The cooperation between the German and Swiss authorities was the first step in the expansion of the cum-ex investigation to other countries around the world. By late October 2014, German authorities had reportedly enlisted the assistance of HM Revenue & Customs, the UK tax authority, in seeking information from British-based banks relating to cum-ex activity carried out by them or their clients.[82] As the geographical reach of the investigation widened, German-based prosecutors were compelled to seek the cooperation of a growing list of national

[78] The role of whistle-blowers in the early development of cum-ex trades has been noted above. Whistle-blowers also played a significant role in the investigation phase of cum-ex. As is discussed above, the first raid, in November 2012, came about in a case involving a whistle-blower. There are various further instances of the actions of whistle-blowers. In October 2016, for example, a person suspected by the authorities of involvement in cum-ex trading became a key witness for the prosecution, hoping for leniency from the Cologne prosecutor's office. The witness described the close coordination between the parties, including the fact that the perpetrators had established action plans to manage the tax office were it ever to carry out an audit. See https://www.tagesschau.de/wirtschaft/cum-ex-skandal-101.html. A further case was reported in April 2018. See http://www.sueddeutsche.de/wirtschaft/cum-ex-geschaefte-mitwisser-packen-aus-ring-von-bankern-und-boersen-haendlern-aufgeflogen-1.3468112.

[79] See the report in Handelsblatt, 24 October 2014, available at: https://www.handelsblatt.com/finanzen/banken-versicherungen/umstrittene-steuergeschaefte-steuer-razzia-bei-schweizer-bank-sarasin/10885518.html. Bank Sarasin's connection to cum-ex was by this time well known. It had introduced clients to a number of Luxembourg-based funds that invested in cum-ex trades. The clients suffered losses from these investments and sued Sarasin, a matter which is discussed later in this chapter.

[80] See the report in Handelsblatt, 24 October 2014, available at: https://www.handelsblatt.com/finanzen/banken-versicherungen/umstrittene-steuergeschaefte-steuer-razzia-bei-schweizer-bank-sarasin/10885518.html

[81] See the report in Süddeutsche Zeitung by Thomas Knellwolf and Klaus Ott, available at https://www.sueddeutsche.de/wirtschaft/steuerfall-schweiz-hilft-deutschen-ermittlern-mit-razzia-1.2187897.

[82] See Jenny Strasburg, 'European Probe Widens into Tax Maneuver', *Wall Street Journal*, 29 October 2014, available at https://www.wsj.com/articles/european-regulators-expand-probe-into-tax-avoidance-stock-trades-1414604558. The exchange of information between states for tax purposes is provided for in Article 26 of the OECD Model Tax Convention. The relevant provisions (which cater for a broad information exchange) are a standard feature of comprehensive bilateral double tax treaties between states as well as incorporated into bilateral tax information exchange agreements. Certain multilateral agreements are also relevant, including the European Union Directive on Administrative Co-operation in the Field of Taxation (which has been repeatedly updated) and the Joint Council of Europe/OECD Convention on Mutual Administrative Assistance in Tax Matters.

authorities and in doing so navigate the scope of differing regulatory and legal regimes governing the permitted exchange of information between country authorities.[83]

The legal impediments were not confined to foreign matters. Within Germany, statute-of-limitation constraints applied to some of the older cases under investigation. The long delay by the German authorities in tackling cum-ex cases meant that some of the earliest cases could not be pursued, while in other cases, the limitation period for pursuing them was close to expiry.[84]

Practical difficulties posed by the statute of limitations were exacerbated by an exploding caseload. For example, by 2014, the German state of Hesse alone had thirty proceedings under way, while authorities in North Rhine-Westphalia, Germany's most populous state, were managing between 300 and 400 investigations.[85] A shortage of resources resulted in some ad-hoc approaches to managing the load, such as the imposition of a financial floor of €750,000 below which reclaimed amounts would be regarded as *de minimis* and so not trigger an investigation.[86]

In June 2015, several offices of Germany's flagship bank, Deutsche Bank, were raided in relation to cum-ex trading.[87] The raid was reported to relate to a number of former bank employees, who had established entities and managed cum-ex-deals from Luxembourg. Reports revealed that the raids pertained to serious charges of attempted tax evasion. Seventy officials of the Federal Criminal Police Office were involved.[88] Deutsche Bank was reported to have been active in financing the strategy as carried out by its clients. It would later withdraw tax certificates which it had issued for certain cum-ex trades.[89]

[83] Some of the difficulties of pursuing cross-border investigations (including the protracted nature of such investigations and the need for taxpayer cooperation or, where this is not forthcoming, the use of information obtained through international information exchange under mutual assistance regimes) are discussed in the German Parliamentary Report at p.238.

[84] The impact of the limitation period issues is discussed further below and also in the German Parliamentary Report at pp.247–9.

[85] See the report on Welt, 24 November 2014, available at: https://www.welt.de/wirtschaft/article134651541/Fiskus-fordert-jetzt-erbarmungslos-Geld-zurueck.html

[86] The informal floor of €750,000 was initiated by the Federal Central Tax Office in March 2011 and applied to investigations, though this floor was applied flexibly and varied according to the nature of the claimant in certain cases. The practical operation of this floor is discussed in the German Parliamentary Report at pp.235–7.

[87] See further the report in Handelsblatt, 9 June 2015, available at: https://www.handelsblatt.com/finanzen/banken-versicherungen/deutsche-bank-die-naechste-razzia-/11889712.html. Deutsche Bank is Germany's largest bank with assets of €1.4 trillion, nearly 100,000 employees and a presence in fifty-eight countries.

[88] See the report in Süddeutsche Zeitung available at: http://www.sueddeutsche.de/wirtschaft/deutsche-bank-von-wegen-kleingeld-1.2516219.

[89] These amounted to a reported €35 million for 2009 alone. See the report in Süddeutsche Zeitung available at: https://www.sueddeutsche.de/wirtschaft/aktiendeals-spaete-einsicht-der-deutschen-bank-1.3650964.

Deutsche Bank's shares fell 3 per cent on news of the raid.[90] This was not an isolated development, and in a number of other cases, some of which involved global banks, the cum-ex raids had a similar adverse effect on the share price of the bank concerned.[91] For one bank, the financial consequences proved much more severe. In the autumn of 2015, a small German bank was to be overwhelmed by its cum-ex liabilities.[92] That bank was Maple Bank GmbH, a subsidiary of the Maple Financial Group Inc., a Canadian bank holding company 28 per cent owned by the Ontario Teachers' Pension Plan[93] and 25 per cent owned by the National Bank of Canada, the sixth largest commercial bank in Canada.[94]

In September 2015, in a raid coordinated by the Frankfurt prosecutor's office, a task force of 300 German government employees searched the business premises of the bank.[95] Prosecutors accused eleven current and former employees of tax evasion employing cum-ex trades in the years 2006 to 2010. Eight of the employees were also accused of money laundering.[96] Maple was reported to have claimed more than €450 million in cum-ex tax credits, on share trades having an aggregate value of more than €50 billion.[97] To give context to the scale of this cum-ex trading, its own balance sheet amounted to only €5 billion.[98] By early 2016 it was clear that Maple Bank did not have sufficient own funds to repay the liabilities associated with its cum-ex trading activities (in fact, the cum-ex claims far exceeded the bank's entire equity capital, reported at €378 million). On 7 February 2016, the German supervisory authority, BaFin, enforced the closure of the bank.[99] While BaFin (which learned of the prosecutor's raids from press

[90] See the report in Frankfurter Allgemeine, 9 June 2015, available at: http://www.faz.net/aktuell/wirtschaft/unternehmen/ermittlungen-gegen-deutsche-bank-razzia-in-frankfurt-13637368.html

[91] For example, in March 2016 Citigroup stock fell on reports that it was the subject of enquiries in relation to cum-ex. The bank stated that it had never been a trader, broker, or structurer of cum-ex trades, but instead had acted only as a settlement agent for client trades. See https://www.reuters.com/article/us-citigroup-germany-taxes-idUSKCN0WO127.

[92] A data stick acquired from a whistle-blower by the North-Rhine Westphalia authorities revealed that a very large number of smaller banks were involved in cum-ex. On that data stick alone were listed 129 banks trading cum-ex. See https://www.n-tv.de/wirtschaft/Wie-der-Fiskus-Cum-Ex-Insider-abblitzen-liess-article19897200.html. As exemplified by the Maple Bank case, it quickly became apparent that the fact a bank was modest in size did not mean that its cum-ex participation or exposures were correspondingly small.

[93] The plan is one of the largest pension schemes in the world, with net assets of Can$191 billion. See https://www.otpp.com/corporate/about-teachers.

[94] Further information on the bank is available from its website, nbc.ca

[95] See the report on Berliner Morgenpost, 26 September 2015, available at: https://www.morgenpost.de/wirtschaft/article205797893/Razzia-bei-der-Maple-Bank.html

[96] See German Parliamentary Report at p.266.

[97] See the report in Süddeutsche Zeitung, 22 June 2016, available at: http://www.sueddeutsche.de/wirtschaft/aktienskandal-cum-ex-und-hopp-1.3045885

[98] See the report on Handelsblatt, available at https://www.handelsblatt.com/finanzen/banken-versicherungen/cum-ex/maple-bank-bafin-schliesst-bank-in-deutschland/12931046.html

[99] See the report in Süddeutsche Zeitung, 7 February 2016, available at: https://www.sueddeutsche.de/wirtschaft/maple-bank-keine-gnade-bei-dubiosen-aktiendeals-maple-bank-muss-schliessen-1.2853796.

reports three days after they occurred)[100] noted that Maple had 'no systemic relevance',[101] it was in fact one of the largest bank failures in German history. There were 236 creditors with claims of more than €3.3 billion against the bank, and by 2016 no less than €2.6 billion had been paid out of the deposit insurance fund of the Association of German Banks.[102] Maple Bank's insolvency, and the realization that cum-ex alone could destabilize a financial institution, prompted BaFin to undertake a survey of nearly all of Germany's 1800 banks in order to determine which of them had been involved in cum-ex trading and to what extent.[103]

The failure of Maple Bank demonstrated that the scale of cum-ex liabilities could not only overwhelm banking entities but could also place significant burdens on deposit insurance funds. It revealed, with echoes of the Global Financial Crisis, that the effects of cum-ex could be felt across the world. National Bank of Canada's first-quarter 2016 profits fell 37 per cent as it took a $145 million charge associated with writing off its stake in Maple Bank.[104]

A further dimension to the investigations and raids has been the increasing political sensitivity of the developments. Concerns about the adequacy of the response of state institutions to cum-ex trading have been a constant theme in the press and were a primary factor behind the parliamentary enquiry which is discussed later in this chapter. However, the nature of some participants in cum-ex trades also raised politically sensitive issues. For example, in the autumn of 2017, by which time a steady stream of raids had been seen, the offices of Commerzbank were reported to have been searched in cum-ex raids by Frankfurt prosecutors together with German federal criminal police and tax officials.[105] Five persons were the subject of the enquiry, some of whom had been former heads of the bank.[106] Commerzbank's involvement was politically charged, as the bank had been rescued with €18 billion of taxpayer financial support during the financial crisis of 2008–9, even apparently as its traders and clients were involved in cum-ex transactions whose source of profit was the state

[100] See German Parliamentary Report at p.266.

[101] See the report in Süddeutsche Zeitung, available at See http://www.sueddeutsche.de/wirtschaft/maple-bank-keine-gnade-bei-dubiosen-aktiendeals-maple-bank-muss-schliessen-1.2853796.

[102] See the report on Handelsblatt, Exclusive: Maple Bank Creditors Demand €3.3Billion from German Subsidiary, available at https://global.handelsblatt.com/exclusive-maple-bank-creditors-demand-e3-3-billion-from-german-subsidiary-677041

[103] See the report on Reuters, 26 February 2016, available at https://de.reuters.com/article/deutschland-banken-cum-ex-idDEKCN0VZ28O

[104] See the report, National Bank profits down 37% as lender writes off $145M Maple Bank stake, 23 February 2016, available at https://www.cbc.ca/news/business/national-bank-earnings-1.3460433

[105] A number of private homes were also reported to have been searched. See https://de.reuters.com/article/deutschland-commerzbank-idDEKBN1DA1VV.

[106] See the report in Bild, 10 November 2017, available at https://www.bild.de/bildlive/2017/15-commerzbank-53817798.bild.html

itself.[107] Earlier in 2017, Commerzbank had been the subject of a separate enquiry in relation to cum-ex. Eight years previously, it had taken over Dresdner Bank. In a case before the Hessian tax court, Dresdner's trades in cum-ex were at issue.[108] It was reported that Dresdner's cum-ex trading involved more than €10 billion in securities, with €75 million having been extracted from the German treasury in tax claims.[109]

Similar, if not more acute, sensitivities have been raised by the participation in cum-ex trades of the state-owned Landesbanks,[110] particularly as the authorities of those same states have been actively investigating cum-ex trading.[111]

By early 2018, the number of cum-ex cases was reported to have expanded to 417, involving tax evasion totalling €5.3 billion. As recently as October of the previous year, there were 259 cases.[112] The Ministry of Finance reported that €2.4 billion had so far been recovered.[113] A further important development, in May 2018, was the filing of criminal charges by the Grand Duchy of Frankfurt against a leading tax adviser and five other defendants in Germany, the UK, and New Zealand. The indictment itself was 948 pages long, and it alleged the theft of €113 million employing cum-ex trades in shares valued at €15.8 billion.[114] It was the first reported indictment of foreign-based persons in the cum-ex scandal.[115]

[107] See the report in Süddeutsche Zeitung, 9 May 2016, available at http://www.sueddeutsche.de/wirtschaft/finanzbranche-commerzbank-in-dubiose-aktiendeals-verwickelt-1.2986157. Commerzbank said it had conducted a voluntary investigation at the end of 2015 into all trades between 2003 and 2011, which revealed that there were cum-ex trades at Commerzbank. Commerzbank said it pro-actively notified the authorities with the preliminary results of that investigation and was cooperating fully. See the report in Handelsblatt, 9 May 2016, available at https://www.handelsblatt.com/finanzen/banken-versicherungen/cum-ex-affaere-steuer-razzia-bei-der-commerzbank/20567960.html?ticket=ST-1346192-V7Mea5jrLxd9o6uRZX1l-ap3.

[108] See the report on reuters by Hans Seidenstuecker, 10 November 2017, available at https://de.reuters.com/article/deutschland-commerzbank-idDEKBN1DA1VV

[109] See the report in Juve, 10 November 2017, available at https://www.juve.de/nachrichten/namenundnachrichten/2017/11/razzia-wegen-cum-ex-steuerfahnder-durchsuchen-commerzbank

[110] The Landesbanks are state-owned banks of a type unique to Germany. They are similar to wholesale banks and act as the head banking institution in their respective states and are charged with responsibility for the pursuit of public purposes.

[111] For example, the investigation in 2017 of Portigon (successor to the bankrupt Landesbank West-LB, and owned by the state of North-Rhine Westphalia) by Dusseldorf prosecutors was triggered by data the North-Rhine Westphalia authorities procured from a whistle-blower on a data-stick. See https://www.handelsblatt.com/finanzen/banken-versicherungen/westlb-nachfolger-portigon-verschiebt-jahresabschluss-wegen-cum-ex-verdacht/19586634.html. See also the comments on the participation in cum-ex of the Landesbanks in the German Parliamentary Report at p.546.

[112] See the report at NTV, 11 January 2018, available at https://www.n-tv.de/wirtschaft/Cum-Ex-Schaden-geht-in-die-Milliarden-article20224694.html

[113] See the report at NTV, 11 January 2018, available at https://www.n-tv.de/wirtschaft/Cum-Ex-Schaden-geht-in-die-Milliarden-article20224694.html

[114] See the report on Bloomberg by Karin Matussek, London Investment Bankers Charged in German Cum-Ex Tax Case, 22 May 2018, available at https://www.bloomberg.com/news/articles/2018-05-22/london-bankers-charged-by-german-prosecutors-in-cum-ex-tax-case

[115] See the report in Süddeutsche Zeitung by Hans Leyendecker and Klaus Ott, 8 May 2018, available at http://www.sueddeutsche.de/wirtschaft/cum-ex-geschaefte-steuertrickser-bleibt-frei-1.3972304

The first criminal trial for tax evasion relating to cum-ex commenced in September 2019 in the Regional Court in Bonn.[116] The accused were two former London bankers. The decision of the court was delivered on 19 March 2020.[117] The court found that the cum-ex trade could not properly be characterized as a mere legal loophole but had always been illegal. The guilty verdict in the case means that the profits (in the hundreds of millions of euros) that accrued to various banks from the relevant cum-ex transactions may now be subject to confiscation and repayment to the German authorities on the basis they arise from acts that have been determined to be unlawful. The judge in the case is reported to have referred to the cum-ex trade as "a collective case of thievery from state coffers" and also to have noted that all of the parties involved (and not just the short seller) had known what they were doing.[118] Two further criminal trials (in Frankfurt and Wiesbaden) are now proceeding, more are expected by the end of 2020 and many more will follow in subsequent years.

Estimates of Financial Damage Caused by Cum-Ex

For a number of reasons, an accurate figure of the total monies lost to the German state from cum-ex remains somewhat elusive.

First, and as mentioned earlier, cum-ex trades in some form may have started as early as the 1970s. Whilst there is no evidence of large-scale exploitation of the cum-ex trade in Germany until the early 2000s, cum-ex volumes increased sharply from that point. However, no data is available from Clearstream before 2005.[119] There are also doubts as to whether some cum-ex cases before 2009 have been lost due to the lack of any systematic investigation of this period.[120]

[116] For a discussion of the case at its inception see the report in Handelsblatt, 4 September 2019, available at thttps://www.handelsblatt.com/finanzen/banken-versicherungen/cum-ex/landgericht-bonn-cum-ex-strafprozess-gewaehrt-einblicke-in-die-abgruende-des-steuerskandals/24978556.html?ticket=ST-673082-h4EY9lUnwIFWYlbjZ4lb-ap3. English language commentaries on the trial are available. See: David Segal, It May Be the Biggest Tax Heist Ever. And Europe Wants Justice. New York Times, 23 January 2020, available at: https://www.nytimes.com/2020/01/23/business/cum-ex.html. and Philip Oltermann, The men who plundered Europe: bankers on trial for defrauding €447m, The Guardian, 21 September 2019, available at https://www.theguardian.com/business/2019/sep/20/the-men-who-plundered-europe-city-of-london-practices-on-trial-in-bonn#img-1

[117] See Philip Oltermann, Former London bankers convicted after Germany's "greatest tax robbery", The Guardian, 19 March 2020, available at: https://www.theguardian.com/world/2020/mar/19/former-london-bankers-convicted-after-germany-greatest-tax-robbery. It is understood that the decision in the case has been appealed. The appeal will be heard by the Federal Court of Justice in Karlsruhe.

[118] See footnote 117, ibid. See also the report on the judgement by Manuel Daubenberger and Felix Rohrbeck in Zeit Online, 25 March 2020, available at https://www.zeit.de/2020/14/cum-ex-urteil-bewaehrungsstrafe-justiz/seite-2.

[119] Concerns have also been raised about other forms of cum-ex transaction that may not have been included in the estimates made to date. See the German Parliamentary Report at pp. 466, 468–9, discussing free-of-payment and options transactions.

[120] See German Parliamentary Report at pp. 248–9, 472–3.

Second, even if the records of those first trades were to be available, they may be of little interest to the authorities. Tax evasion, even in particularly serious criminal cases, is subject to a statute of limitation in Germany, restricting the ability of tax authorities to pursue false claims which are more than ten years old. Because the investigations did not begin in earnest until 2011, the money extracted through older cum-ex trades is now lost.[121]

The complexity of the cum-ex scheme and the fact that, particularly in later years, it involved banks and their clients around the world makes it hard to know the full extent of participation in the scheme and the financial amounts that were extracted by it. Investigations are not only still in process,[122] but, as more defendants agree to give evidence for the state, the investigative forces can be expected to both widen their nets and strengthen their grip.[123]

Finally, the estimate of the losses to the state caused by cum-ex trades in Germany has itself become a hotly contested political issue, with arguments surfacing among the different political parties as to whether the official estimates of financial damage have been deliberately kept low to minimize political fallout.[124]

Nevertheless, there have been attempts to quantify the size of the cum-ex trade in Germany. Dr Christoph Spengel, an expert witness to the German parliamentary enquiry in 2017, estimated the losses to the German state to be at least €7.2 billion.[125] Spengel's estimates are based on the data provided by the settlement system operator, Clearstream.[126] That data, however, suffers from a number of shortcomings which may significantly underestimate the extent of the loss. These include the fact that Clearstream was not involved in a number of cum-ex transactions and the data it collected did not include certain transactions of German domestic custodians. Spengel goes on to include an estimate of the relevant transactions of those latter institutions, adding €2.14 billion and bringing

[121] The limitation period for cases found not to involve tax evasion is appreciably shorter. See German Parliamentary Report at p.279.

[122] As at June 2018 there were 417 cases involving €5.3 billion in claims. See the report of the *Suddeutsche Zeitung* dated 13 June 2018 by Margot Gibbs et al., available at http://www.sueddeutsche.de/wirtschaft/steuerflucht-brisante-spur-nach-dubai-1.4012419. This same article indicates that Austria and Spain also incurred financial costs from cum-ex trading.

[123] See the report of the *Tagesschau* by Massimo Bognanni, available at https://www.tagesschau.de/wirtschaft/cum-ex-skandal-101.html. It is also true that the absolute cost of cum-ex to the German state has been reduced by recoveries from banks and funds of amounts already paid out and by the refusal of outstanding treaty claims for the refund of the German tax—see German Parliamentary Report at p.400. These actions obviously reduce the direct financial costs from cum-ex, but necessarily incur the cost associated with hundreds of highly detailed investigations by numerous tax, criminal, and civil authorities.

[124] See, for example, German Parliamentary Report at pp. 456, 505–6, 532, 540.

[125] Christoph Spengel et al., 'Estimate of Tax Liability Incurred by Cum / Ex short Selling Transactions', University of Mannheim report, 31 March 2017, p.8, available at https://spengel.bwl.uni-mannheim.de/fileadmin/files/spengel/Dokumente/PDF/Projekte_u_Gutachten/Steuerschaden_Cum-Ex__2017-03-31_.pdf.

[126] Spengel et al., 'Estimate of Tax Liability', p.1.

the lower bound of his total estimate of loss to nearly €10 billion.[127] Other estimates are much higher.[128]

In the case of Maple Bank, the small Canadian-owned German bank discussed above, tax claims exceeding €450 million were generated by cum-ex trades over a five-year period. With investigations into banks running into the hundreds, and many of the banks involved being larger (or much larger) cum-ex participants with balance sheets hundreds of times that of Maple Bank, it is likely that total losses will be enormous by any measure.[129]

When evaluating the size of losses from cum-ex, it is also important not to lose sight of the fact that this book is centred around Germany as a case study. Other countries have been affected too. Even in a much smaller economy such as Denmark, arrangements reported to be similar to cum-ex schemes are reported to have deprived the state of at least €1.6 billion.[130] The European-wide cost of cum-ex has recently been reported as a staggering €55 billion, with the countries said to be affected including Austria, Belgium, France, the Czech Republic, Denmark, Germany, Finland, Italy, the Netherlands, Norway, Poland, Spain, and Switzerland.[131]

Fallout from Cum-Ex

The aftermath of the cum-ex affair has a number of repercussions which go well beyond those persons directly participating in the trades themselves.

For the banks which have owned up to their involvement, if not always for the individual cum-ex traders themselves, the affair has been extremely costly with huge financial damage inflicted. The costs include: repaying what have turned out to be invalid tax credits or earlier cash refunds; taking charges to income in the financial statements; fines and interest on additional tax due; as well as the cost of internal forensic investigations, legal advice, and the management of raids and investigations by the authorities. As noted above, developments in the course of investigations by the authorities have, on a number of occasions, had a tangible and adverse effect on the share price of a number of banks. Concerns have been expressed about the potential impact of the affair on the stability of the banking

[127] Spengel et al., 'Estimate of Tax Liability', p.5.

[128] For example, Allen & Overy put the figure closer to €30 billion—see Allen & Overy, 'European White Collar Crime Report', Q3 2017, p.10, available at http://www.allenovery.com/SiteCollectionDocuments/Allen-Overy-European-White-collar-Crime-Report-Q3-2017.pdf.

[129] The larger global banks have balance sheets of nearly $2 trillion, while Maple Bank's balance sheet was €5 billion. See, for example, Federal Reserve, 'Statistical Release: Large Commercial Banks', 31 March 2018, available at https://www.federalreserve.gov/releases/lbr/current/default.htm.

[130] See the report of the *Suddeutsche Zeitung* dated 13 June 2018 by Margot Gibbs et al., available at http://www.sueddeutsche.de/wirtschaft/steuerflucht-brisante-spur-nach-dubai-1.4012419. This same article also refers to the financial costs incurred in Austria and Spain.

[131] See the press release of the European Parliament, 'Cum-Ex Tax Fraud Scandal.

sector.[132] Not surprisingly, in Germany it has contributed to an extremely negative public perception of the financial sector in general and banks in particular, bringing the reputation of banks to a low ebb. Tax advisers too have been the subject of excoriating criticism over cum-ex.[133]

Beyond the direct impact on the banks and their advisers, the collateral effects of cum-ex include a proliferation in law suits. In addition to tax authorities and regulators, fund investors and private individuals have brought significant claims, in many cases with claims and counterclaims involving a wide range of parties. The scale of financial damage inflicted has also raised questions as to how blame should be apportioned. This has made cum-ex a political issue at the highest levels. The affair has triggered similar direct and indirect effects in those countries which have also seen cum-ex trading. Some of these wider collateral impacts from cum-ex are explored in the discussion below.

Regulatory and Tax Authorities

Certain features peculiar to the cum-ex scandal have led to a number of questions being raised about the conduct of the relevant tax and regulatory authorities. In relation to the tax aspects of cum-ex these include the lengthy period over which cum-ex trades were carried on despite the tax authorities' knowledge of the issues at a very early stage, as well as the sequence of responses by the authorities which were intended to curtail cum-ex but which proved ineffective and arguably encouraged even greater levels of cum-ex trading. There is also the size of the financial benefits generated by the multiple use of tax credits including the enormous credits and refunds generated for banks and their clients. One of the chief questions for the regulatory authorities (such as the German federal supervisory authority, BaFin) has been how it could be that, across the market, shares worth literally hundreds of billions were being regularly cycled in and out of trades clustered around dividend dates with no apparent awareness of what was happening on the part of the regulators. The point is all the more striking given the highly detailed financial reporting obligations operated by the regulatory authorities. Those regulatory reporting requirements have as their purpose the surveillance by regulators of market transactional activities.[134] Concerns relating to these questions were a significant factor behind the launch of a German parliamentary enquiry into the handling of cum-ex, which is discussed below.

[132] The German Parliamentary Report at p.17 notes that banks, financial institutions, and their senior executives may be vulnerable to tax fraud proceedings and that in an extreme case a bank might also lose its banking licence.

[133] See German Parliamentary Report, for example at pp. 346–8, 353.

[134] See, for example, Spengel, 'Expert Opinion', at pp.101–3.

Similar questions have been raised about the conduct of statutory auditors, particularly given the potentially enormous financial risks to custodian banks, which under German law have liability for the production of incorrect tax certificates.[135]

Role of Academics

A surprising development in the denouement of the cum-ex affair was the involvement of a number of academics. It emerged that academic experts, some of whom occupy prestigious tax law chairs in Germany's public universities, had written opinions in support of individual taxpayers' participation in cum-ex trades. The concern was especially pointed in cases where some academics had published these opinions as academic papers without disclosing that they had been paid to do so by interested parties, particularly as those papers were later cited by taxpayers in discussions with the tax authorities.[136]

Investors Suing for Lack of Promised Returns

As discussed in earlier chapters, cum-ex evolved from a trading strategem into a fully fledged 'financial product'. In many cases, it was adopted as a trading scheme directly by banks' clients. In others, it was incorporated into investment funds as a strategy and sold to high-net-worth individuals. In either case, when the tax authorities began to demand repayment of monies extracted through cum-ex transactions, large losses emerged for the clients. Litigation quickly followed.

A good example is the Roth case (which also led to the 2012 raid on HVB, as discussed earlier in this chapter). In February 2011, a tax assessment was carried out on the affairs of Rafael Roth Financial Enterprises, a company owned by the German real estate billionaire Rafael Roth. Following that assessment, the tax office sought to recover €113 million in tax credits generated by cum-ex trading,

[135] Spengel, 'Expert Opinion', at p.102. As discussed earlier in this chapter, the liability accruing to custodian banks for the production of incorrect tax certificates arises under Section 45 (7) Income Tax Act.

[136] See Volker Votsmeier and Sönke Iwersen, 'Tax Law Experts Played Along', *Handelsblatt Global*, 1 August 2017, available at https://global.handelsblatt.com/finance/tax-law-experts-played-along-806313. The position is discussed in the parliamentary enquiry. See German Parliamentary Report at pp.352–3. The judgement in the first criminal trial of bankers involved in cum-ex trades was also sharply critical of these opinions by law professors – see further the discussion at and the report on the judgement by Manuel Daubenberger and Felix Rohrbeck in Zeit Online, 25 March 2020, available at https://www.zeit.de/2020/14/cum-ex-urteil-bewaehrungsstrafe-justiz/seite-2.

plus another €10 million in interest.[137] The company had acted as a buyer in cum-ex trades, but the authorities determined that it was neither the legal nor economic owner of the shares on the dividend record date. They also alleged that the trades constituted an 'improper purposeful and planned action'.[138]

HVB Bank, which had repaid significant interim sums to the tax authorities in relation to the assessment, sued Roth, its own legal advisers, and the inter-dealer broker through which the transactions were conducted.[139] Roth then countersued the bank, claiming that it had structured the cum-ex transactions and given its assurance that the transactions were legal.[140] It also appeared that the bank had carried out the trades on Roth's behalf. Roth claimed that those trades were carried out without his full knowledge and consent. As the case progressed, it emerged not only that HVB had carried out cum-ex trades on its own account, but that its internal lawyers were aware of the strategy. Consequently, the court doubted that the bank's external lawyers could be held accountable in such circumstances.[141] In August 2014, HVB settled the matter with all parties, extinguishing all but a fraction of its €123 million alleged claim against Roth. In addition, the bank had reportedly spent €100 million on its internal investigation and legal advice in dealing with the cum-ex affair.[142]

Another example of such litigation, which also shows the risks from the industrialization and packaging of cum-ex as a financial product, concerns Erwin Muller, a German drugstore chain billionaire. Muller brought an action against Sarasin Bank for approximately €45 million in 2013.[143] Sarasin had introduced Muller to a Luxembourg investment fund called the 'Sheridan Solution Equity Arbitrage Fund'.[144] According to Muller, the bank had promised

[137] See the report in Handelsblatt, 16 March 2016, available at https://www.handelsblatt.com/finanzen/banken-versicherungen/cum-ex/rafael-roth-immobilienmogul-mit-renditehunger/13037158.html?ticket=ST-4876876-iVLJn07p0QaniXPFyffD-ap5

[138] See the report in Juve, 29 June 2012, available at https://www.juve.de/nachrichten/verfahren/2012/06/umstrittene-steuerprodukte-hvb-wehrt-sich-broker-erhebt-schwere-vorwurfe-gegen-clifford

[139] See the report in Juve, 31 January 2012, available at https://www.juve.de/nachrichten/verfahren/2012/01/klageerweiterung-clifford-mandantin-hvb-nun-wegen-steuertricks-auf-155-millionen-euro-verklagt

[140] See the report in Juve, 21 August 2012, available at https://www.juve.de/nachrichten/namenundnachrichten/2012/08/vorwurf-des-interessenkonflikts-clifford-legt-hvb-mandat-nieder-gleiss-lutz-ubernimmt

[141] See the report in Juve, 3 July 2014, available at https://www.juve.de/nachrichten/verfahren/2014/07/cum-ex-prozess-ernuchternder-start-fur-gleiss-mandantin-hvb-gute-aussichten-fur-ex-dewey-partner-berger

[142] See the report by Marc Young in Handelsblatt, HypoVereinsbank Settles Dividend Stripping Case,21 August 2014, available at https://global.handelsblatt.com/finance/hypovereinsbank-agrees-to-settlement-in-tax-dodging-cum-ex-trading-case-9245

[143] See the report in Süddeutsche Zeitung by Stefan Mayr, 24 June 2018, available at http://www.sueddeutsche.de/wirtschaft/bank-sarasin-cum-ex-und-weg-1.4027471

[144] See the report in Süddeutsche Zeitung, available at http://www.sueddeutsche.de/wirtschaft/cum-ex-geschaefte-drogeriekoenig-mueller-bekommt-millionen-zurueck-1.3516842. There was no suggestion, however, that either Muller or Sarasin on his behalf had carried out cum-ex trades.

him a 12 per cent return.[145] The Sheridan investment, however, was not a success. It was based on cum-ex and, as in the Roth case, the tax authorities refused to recognize the tax credits generated by the trades. Muller's case against the bank turned on whether the bank had provided him with proper investment advice. In court, Muller succeeded, winning a claim for €44.8 million with a further €8 million in interest payments.[146] There have been similar claims by other investors in the Sheridan funds.[147]

Directors and Officers Insurance Issues

Those seeking to sue banks and their clients in relation to cum-ex are not limited to parties external to the bank. The potential exists for claims to be brought by company supervisory boards against management boards (where such separate boards exist, as in Germany), company boards against directors (both past and present), and company directors against each other. Such claims relating to cum-ex activities have already been pursued.[148]

Both the nature of the claim and the parties who may be subject to a claim raise important issues for insurance companies. While it has a lower level of penetration across Europe than, for example, in the United States,[149] directors and officers ('D&O') insurance is nevertheless common among European banks and corporates. It is a form of liability insurance payable to a company or to its directors and officers for losses or costs arising as a result of legal or regulatory actions brought against the insured. While D&O insurance may be available to cover some or all of these sources of claim, the nature of the claim may have a significant bearing on whether the insurer will pay out. Typically, D&O policies do not cover losses arising from criminal or fraudulent conduct. Thus, as the investigations into

[145] See the report in Süddeutsche Zeitung by Stefan Mayr, 23 May 2017, available at http://www.sueddeutsche.de/wirtschaft/cum-ex-geschaefte-drogeriekoenig-mueller-bekommt-millionen-zurueck-1.3516842

[146] See the report in Süddeutsche Zeitung by http://www.sueddeutsche.de/wirtschaft/cum-ex-geschaefte-drogeriekoenig-mueller-bekommt-millionen-zurueck-1.3516842

[147] Americo Amerim, a billionaire and Portugal's richest man, together with Carsten Maschmeyer, a businessman and television celebrity in Germany, both suffered heavy losses through investments in Sheridan funds introduced to them by Sarasin. Like Muller, both claimed that while the bank offered high returns with little risk, it had not adequately explained the strategy and that as a result they did not understand it. See http://www.sueddeutsche.de/wirtschaft/deutscher-investor-carsten-maschmeyer-verklagt-schweizer-bank-1.2211276, and https://global.handelsblatt.com/finance/billionaires-battle-over-dividend-stripping-losses-499350.

[148] For example, in 2017 UniCredit, the parent company of the German bank HVB, a participant in cum-ex schemes, brought an action for damages amounting to €140 million against three former board members for their alleged role in cum-ex trading. As noted above, HVB itself incurred significant costs in carrying out internal investigations, repaid amounts which were determined to be wrongly reclaimed from the tax authority, and was ultimately subjected to fines.

[149] Advizen, 'European D&O Insurance Market', October 2011, available at https://www.advisenltd.com/wp-content/uploads/europeanDandO.pdf.

cum-ex centre increasingly on collusion, it becomes less likely that companies and their directors will be afforded protection by D&O policies. In addition to exclusions for fraudulent or criminal conduct, most D&O policies will also not cover losses arising from amounts illegally obtained by the company (in other words, claims for the return of monies to which the insured was not entitled, such as cum-ex tax credits).[150]

The German Parliamentary Enquiry

An enquiry into the cum-ex affair, demanded by certain of Germany's opposition parties, was initially opposed by the government but was finally agreed to after a period of political wrangling. The work of the enquiry from 2016 led to a report issued in June 2017.[151]

The enquiry was tasked with identifying the final cost of cum-ex and determining whether the response by the state institutions was appropriate. Members of the committee of enquiry had quite varied perspectives on these issues.

Largely for the reasons covered in the earlier section on the technical reassessment of the trade, the committee members concluded that cum-ex trades had always been unlawful and that there was never a loophole in the law that could legitimately be exploited.[152] Not surprisingly, cum-ex participants were subjected to thorough condemnation: the report severely criticizes the collusive behaviour of the banks and their clients and the manner in which they deliberately masked their activities.[153] The report concludes that although there is no Supreme Court decision which deals with certain relevant technical issues, there are clear reasons to pursue criminal investigations against those involved.[154] The Federal Association of German Banks, which raised the cum-ex issue with the Federal Ministry of Finance in 2002, is portrayed as having contributed to the problem,

[150] Where D&O insurance is available to cover claims arising out of cum-ex, the amounts involved will probably be large in the context of the market for D&O claims in Europe. For example, in 2014, total EU premiums collected by European insurers were nearly €2.3 billion. See Finaccord, 'D&O Insurance in Europe', December 2014, p.4, available at http://www.finaccord.com/documents/rp_2014/series_prospectus_dando_insurance_europe.pdf. There is therefore the potential for successful D&O claims to strain the insurance capacity in the market, causing future premiums to rise.

[151] The enquiry commissioned a detailed expert report from Professor Dr Christoph Spengel and heard from some seventy-five witnesses over forty-six sessions. The resulting report is 830 pages long and includes a detailed analysis of the history and developments in Germany relating to the cum-ex trade. The discussion includes an analysis of the various state institutions that were involved in the cum-ex affair and also discusses the relevant financial costs.

[152] German Parliamentary Report at pp. 320, 326.

[153] German Parliamentary Report at pp.346–53.

[154] German Parliamentary Report at p.379. The committee endorses the view of the law enforcement authorities that the objective facts of a tax evasion under Section 370 General Tax Code are present and it is left to those authorities to investigate the conduct of the parties on a case-by-case basis (see at p.326).

not having helped to solve it.[155] The report is also highly critical of the role played by some academics.[156]

However, on the more political aspects of the enquiry, there is a sharp divide of opinion. Reflecting the views of the then incumbent administration, the majority report concludes that the enquiry was never needed and that the allegations justifying the inception of the enquiry are refuted: rather, the state authorities clearly did their job in an exemplary fashion and worked together in a coordinated and speedy manner with dedication and with few exceptions.[157]

The two minority reports (reflecting the views of the opposition minority parties) take a completely different view.[158] They agree with the majority's two criticisms of the unrestrained greed in the financial services industry and the fake legality supporting the trades. To that they add a third: massive state failure. Theirs is a scathing critique of the actions taken by state institutions.[159] This is based on what is described as the inordinate delay in dealing with the issues, the self-evidently inadequate responses to cum-ex in 2007 and 2009, and the incompetence and absence of the necessary expertise in the tax and regulatory authorities.[160] The minority reports also allege that the work of the enquiry is a cover-up of the true financial damage caused by the affair in an effort to dodge political responsibility for what transpired, that the amounts lost are appreciably larger than is stated in the majority report, and that there will be no final reckoning of the actual financial loss because of the state's late intervention and the presence of earlier cases which are lost or time-barred.[161] There is some particularly severe criticism in the minority report of the former and then current federal finance ministers, Peer Steinbrück and Wolfgang Schäuble.[162] The German states (Länder) are also heavily criticized, including for apparently being unaware that their state banks (the Landesbanken) were participating in cum-ex transactions whilst the state finance ministries were simultaneously trying to combat the trades.[163]

Cum-Cum Trades

The momentum of the negative reaction to cum-ex also came to embroil so called 'cum-cum' trades in Germany. These are simply dividend arbitrage trades of the kind that were discussed in Chapter 1. Broadly, they involve the cum-dividend

[155] German Parliamentary Report at pp.336–8.

[156] German Parliamentary Report at pp.352–3.

[157] German Parliamentary Report at pp. 315, 379–80, 433–4.

[158] These are the reports of Richard Pitterle and Gerhard Schick. See German Parliamentary Report at pp. 381–458 and 458–546 respectively.

[159] German Parliamentary Report at p.504.

[160] German Parliamentary Report at pp.413–15.

[161] German Parliamentary Report at pp. 466, 506. The criticisms (at p.505) include the observation that the Federal Finance Ministry is not serious about quantifying the financial damage from cum-ex.

[162] German Parliamentary Report at p.456.

[163] German Parliamentary Report at pp.546–7.

sale (and also delivery) of German shares before the relevant dividend record date from a non-resident to a German resident entity, typically with the shares being returned some time after the dividend has been received.[164] The aim of the transaction is normally to generate a profit by ensuring the most efficient use by the parties of the German withholding tax.[165] The profit is then divided amongst the parties to the trade. Such cum-cum trading activity had been carried on for many years in Germany. Whilst in some specific cases these trades could be regarded as abusive under the general anti-abuse provisions in the German tax code, there was a widespread view within the banking sector that they were not illegal.[166]

As details of the cum-ex trades emerged, the focus on cum-cum trades intensified, increasing the reputational concerns of banks carrying on such activity.[167] A 2015 decision of the Federal Fiscal Court denied the effectiveness of a stock lending transaction over record date in a cum-cum transaction, further fuelling the pressure on these trades and leading to increased scrutiny of cum-cum trades by both federal and state fiscal administrations.[168] Cum-cum trades were also discussed in the parliamentary enquiry into cum-ex. Not surprisingly, that enquiry was sharply critical of these trades and the financial amounts at stake.[169]

Legislation to curtail cum-cum trades was introduced by the Investment Tax Reform Act of 27 July 2016.[170] The new provisions do not preclude cum-cum transactions as such but stipulate that a full tax credit for the withholding tax will not be available unless the taxpayer concerned has satisfied certain conditions. The first is that the taxpayer must have held the shares for at least a forty-five-day period in which the dividend income is received (the economic ownership test). Next, the taxpayer must also bear at least 70 per cent of the risk in fluctuations in

[164] The shares may also be delivered initially under a stock loan in place of a sale.

[165] They are referred to as cum-cum trades because both the sale contract and settlement delivery are made on cum-dividend terms (whereas cum-ex trades involve a cum-dividend sale contract but an ex-dividend settlement delivery of the shares). As explained in Chapter 1, such dividend arbitrage transactions are common in many countries.

[166] The anti-abuse provision generally considered potentially relevant to cum-cum transactions is Section 42 of the General Tax Code. Testimony at the parliamentary enquiry into cum-ex trades confirms the widespread view of the banking sector that such trades could be structured in an entirely lawful manner. See German Parliamentary Report at pp. 287, 314.

[167] See, for example, German Parliamentary Report at p.288.

[168] See German Federal Fiscal Court decision of 18 August 2015, BFH, I R 88/13. The case was decided on the basis that the ownership of shares should be denied if facts show that a formal legal ownership or 'empty shell' alone was acquired. The case involved a pre-tax negative stock lending transaction over record date. It was determined that ownership of the shares remained with the non-resident transferor.

[169] Cum-cum trades were included within the scope of the enquiry on the basis they are 'similar designs' to cum-ex trades. There is a detailed discussion of cum-cum trades at pp.281–314 of the enquiry report. There is also specific reference to the German banks bailed out in the financial crisis yet nonetheless entering into cum-cum trades with foreigners at the expense of the German treasury. See German Parliamentary Report at p.377. Cum-cum trades are also discussed, and their financial consequences explored, in the expert report prepared by Spengel—see Spengel, 'Expert Opinion', at pp. 4, 5–13, 16, 39–63.

[170] The 2016 legislation introduced a new provision, Section 36a, into the Income Tax Act to deliver the intended result.

the value of the shares (the minimum risk test). Finally, the taxpayer must not pass on the income derived wholly or predominantly, directly or indirectly, to other persons (the pass-through test). If these three tests are not met, the available tax credit amount is limited to 10 per cent—the same economic result that applies to non-residents subject to a 15 per cent German withholding tax.[171] The imposition of the three tests has the effect therefore of putting German residents and non-residents on a similar footing, greatly constraining the scope for dividend arbitrage over German shares.

Subsequent to the new legislation, the Ministry of Finance took further action in relation to cum-cum transactions.[172] In its circular letter of 17 July 2017, it went to some lengths to describe cum-cum transactions and set out stricter guidelines for permissible transactions.[173] The day after the issue of the circular letter, the financial supervisory authority, BaFin, sent out a questionnaire on the topic of cum-cum to 1800 German banks and saving banks. This was designed to allow an assessment of the impact on the banking sector of the Ministry of Finance letter by reference to any future charges from the disallowance of cum-cum tax credits, including penalties, as well as possible effects on their risk-bearing capacity.[174] The survey by BaFin was prompted by concerns as to the stability of banks (particularly smaller banks), and the consequences for their solvency, due to the impact of overall liabilities from cum-cum trades (and in the light of the financial damage already caused to Maple Bank and others in relation to cum-ex).

Impacts in Other Countries

It has already been seen that the German investigation into cum-ex involved steps taken by the German authorities in order to pursue foreign parties involved in specific cum-ex trades. As well as these further actions there have been two other

[171] The rules in Section 36a apply with retroactive effect from 1 January 2016 but are not applicable if the relevant income in the period is €20,000 or less, or if the shares have been already held for at least a year without interruption.

[172] It seems that there had previously been some disagreement between state and federal authorities as to the circumstances in which cum-cum trades should be regarded as abusive. See the article in the *Suddeutsche Zeitung* of 18 July 2017, available at http://www.sueddeutsche.de/wirtschaft/cum-cum-geschaefte-bafin-sorgt-sich-um-stabilitaet-vieler-banken-1.3592721.

[173] Broadly, a cum-cum arrangement was assumed to be abusive if an economically legitimate reason is missing for the legal transaction and the arrangement as a whole reflects a tax-induced design. It was clarified that there would be a lack of an economically legitimate reason if the only benefit to emerge from the arrangement is a tax one. The exclusion of risk of changes in value in the prices of shares would be a further indication of abuse. See https://www.bundesfinanzministerium.de/Content/DE/Downloads/BMF_Schreiben/Steuerarten/Einkommensteuer/2017-07-17-Steuerliche-Behandlung-von-Cum-Cum-Transaktionen.pdf;jsessionid=BEDD833E3B5BB633F0D1D12A0AF7CC39?__blob=publicationFile&v=2.

[174] See the report in Süddeutsche Zeitung by Mike Schreiber, 18 July 2017, available at http://www.sueddeutsche.de/wirtschaft/cum-cum-geschaefte-bafin-sorgt-sich-um-stabilitaet-vieler-banken-1.3592721

developments in countries outside Germany. First, tax authorities of certain other countries were influenced by the situation in Germany when it became public to look into the possible impact of cum-ex in their own country. Second, some banks shifted their focus from Germany to other states in an effort to continue generating returns from the cum-ex strategy or strategies similar to it. Examples of both developments are considered below, drawing on the position in Austria and Denmark respectively.

Countering Cum-Ex in Austria

The size of the Austrian capital market is, of course, nowhere near that of the German capital market and so the scale of cum-ex trading in Austria was inevitably appreciably lower than in the German market. Austria is nonetheless a significant economy with some large companies.[175]

Once cum-ex trades over Austrian shares were identified as being a problem, the response of the Austrian tax authorities was to introduce an immediate and blanket moratorium on the repayment of claims for refund of Austrian withholding tax.[176] This meant that from 2012 claims generated by cum-ex trades in Austrian shares were in practice simply not paid. The nature of the response reflected the primary concern of the Austrian tax authorities that cum-ex trading activity over Austrian shares was being driven by foreign, not domestic, claimants.

The imposition of this moratorium was intended to give the Austrian tax authorities time to develop a response to the cum-ex issue. It was not until September 2014 that the response was forthcoming and it came in the form of an 'Information Letter' issued by the Austrian Ministry of Finance.[177] The Information Letter clarified that only the person who held the relevant shares in a securities account *before* the ex-date (the date from which shares are traded with no dividend rights) would be entitled to ask for a refund of Austrian dividend

[175] A number of key indicators for the Austrian economy are available from the Austrian National Bank publication, 'Facts on Austria and its Banks', October 2015, available at https://www.oenb.at/dam/.../Fakten%20zu%20Oesterreich_e_October_2015_mon.pdf. Significant companies include the oil and gas sector's OMV Group and Red Bull GmbH, a drinks company.

[176] The refunds related to the Austrian Capital Yields Tax (Kapitalertragsteuer) on dividends paid by Austrian companies on the basis of Section 94 Paragraph 2 of the Austrian Income Tax Act (Einkommensteuergesetz 1988—EStG); Section 6 of the Austrian Corporation Tax Act (Körperschaftssteuergesetz—KStG); Section 21 Paragraph 1, Subparagraph 1a KStG or pursuant to the terms of an applicable double tax treaty. It is significant that all treaty reclaims were put on hold as the Austrian tax authorities had no ready mechanism to distinguish between claims with cum-ex indicia (i.e. buys and sells around the dividend date) and those without.

[177] 'Information on Capital Yields Tax Refunds for Dividends Received by Taxpayers with Limited Tax Liability (Non-Resident Taxpayers)'. The Information Letter is available at https://english.bmf.gv.at/taxation/Relief_Austrian_Withholding_Tax_on_Dividends_2.pdf?67rqd9.

withholding tax.[178] This reflected the view taken by the Austrian Federal Ministry of Finance that, for tax purposes, a shareholder qualifies as the beneficial owner of income derived from Austrian shares only when those shares have actually been transferred into their securities account. This meant that investors purchasing shares immediately before the dividend record date would be ignored.[179] The approach was effective in stopping any cum-ex abuse, though it had some adverse side-effects.[180] Following the release of the Information Letter, the processing of unpaid claims (which by then numbered 15,000) was resumed in 2014, though subject to the submission of additional information and documentation such as securities account statements showing relevant holdings to substantiate any claims to a refund.

Shift of Trading Activity to Denmark

Unabashed by the experience in Germany and in spite of the fact that raids were taking place by German authorities, some banks and their clients sought out new markets in which to pursue variants of the cum-ex strategy once it had been closed down in Germany. Their efforts in one such market would not be uncovered until three years had passed.

In the autumn of 2015, it emerged that tax authorities in Denmark, apparently acting on the basis of two tips, were pursuing investigations into 'a large network of companies abroad [that had] apparently sought to receive income tax on the basis of fictitious stockholdings and counterfeit documentation'.[181]

The Danish tax investigation initially focused on more than 2,100 requests for tax reclaims involving an amount of DKK6.2 billion.[182] As in the case of Germany,

[178] The assumption made in the Information Letter was that if the relevant shares had not been delivered to the securities account of the buyer by the time of the end of the day before the ex-date, the seller of the shares would still have the beneficial ownership of the shares and the buyer would not be entitled to make a reclaim of Capital Yields Tax.

[179] Given that the Vienna Stock Exchange, like the Frankfurt Stock Exchange, operates a T+2 settlement cycle, shares would normally be delivered to the buyer's account two days after the trade is executed. In consequence, buyers of shares immediately before the ex-date (including cum-ex buyers, at whom the measure was targeted) would normally not be recognized as owning any dividend under this new test.

[180] The Information Letter recognized the possibility that this approach might mean that neither the seller nor the buyer could obtain a refund of the tax, for example where the seller had clearly sold the shares before the dividend record date or 'cum' date, and the buyer had not been able to transfer the shares into its securities account before the ex-date. In such an 'exceptional' case, the Information Letter leaves open the possibility of proving the beneficial ownership of the shares, though in practice the situation would be resolved with the tax authorities only after very lengthy discussions and the provision of significant documentation. Various procedural and operational difficulties of the approach in the Information Letter are referred to in the letter from the British Bankers Association dated 19 June 2015 addressed to the Austrian Federal Ministry of Finance.

[181] One tip came from a Danish lawyer, the other from British authorities. See the report of DR News of 25 August 2015, available at https://www.dr.dk/nyheder/indland/skat-anmelder-aktie-svindel-over-seks-milliarder.

[182] See the report of DR News of 25 August 2015, available at https://www.dr.dk/nyheder/indland/skat-anmelder-aktie-svindel-over-seks-milliarder.

a clearer picture of what had occurred emerged only gradually. As an understanding of what had happened grew, so too did estimates of the scale of the impact. The depiction was graphic: from the time of the shutting down of cum-ex in Germany, claims for tax refunds against the Danish treasury exploded, as illustrated in Figure 4.1.

From a base of approximately DKK1.5 billion in 2012, tax refund claims had grown to DKK8.7 billion by 2015. The Danish estimated that of the DKK1.5 billion of refunds in 2012, DKK0.03 billion was attributable to dubious reclaim activity. By contrast, of the DKK8.7 billion in 2015, DKK3.2 billion (40 per cent of all reclaims) was reported as being fraudulent.[183] The sum at issue represented an amount of DKK2,500 for each man, woman, and child in Denmark, which not surprisingly led to a hostile public reaction to the affair.[184] The estimate of the loss to the Danish treasury was later revised to €1.6 billion (DKK12.4 billion).[185]

The source of the reclaim activity was traced to actors across the globe including the United States, the UK, and Malaysia.[186] As in Germany, the slow process of

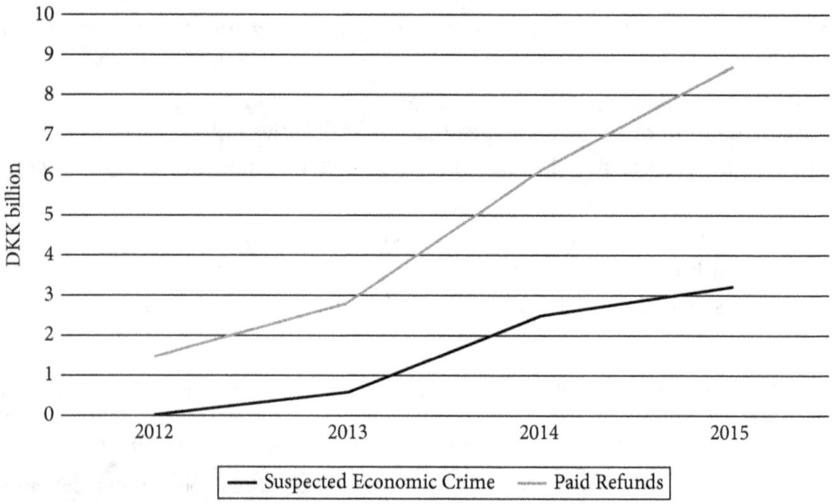

Figure 4.1. Tax Payments, Denmark 2012–15.
Source: DR News/Danish Tax Authority[187]

[183] See the report of DR News of 25 August 2015 by Mette Simonsen, available at https://www.dr.dk/nyheder/penge/40-procent-af-skats-refusionsudbetalinger-skatteudbytte-gik-til-svindlere.

[184] See the report of DR News of 27 August 2015 by Barbara Christensen, available at https://www.dr.dk/nyheder/penge/grafik-skattesvindel-det-kan-vi-faa-62-milliarder-kroner.

[185] See the 'Webfeature' report of DR News by Niels Fastrup and Thomas Svaneborg, undated, available at https://www.dr.dk/nyheder/webfeature/milliardkuppet.

[186] See the report of DR News of 1 November 2015 by Thomas G Svaneborg, available at https://www.dr.dk/nyheder/penge/milliardsvindel-mod-skat-dansk-politi-mistaenker-finansmand-i-london. In the Summer of 2017, the German press reported that a bank in Mainz was alleged to have been involved in arrangements relating to €153 million of Danish tax reclaims, further underscoring the cross-border nature of the scheme.

[187] See the report of DR News of 25 August 2015 by Mette Simonsen, available at https://www.dr.dk/nyheder/penge/40-procent-af-skats-refusionsudbetalinger-skatteudbytte-gik-til-svindlere.

litigation for recovery of monies appropriated by this activity is now under way in Denmark. A major development came in June 2018. The Danish treasury brought legal actions in nine US states against no fewer than 277 pension funds, each such fund having only a single beneficiary.[188]

Within a few months, it became apparent that Denmark was not the only victim. Reports emerged that authorities in Belgium and Norway had uncovered similar tax reclaim schemes and that Denmark, Belgium, the United Kingdom, and Germany had established a joint task force (JIT) to investigate cum-ex. Concurrently, through the international organization Eurojust, based in The Hague, coordination between Danish and United States authorities began.[189]

Expected Future Developments

At the time of writing, investigators in Cologne, Frankfurt, Dusseldorf, Hamburg, Berlin, Stuttgart, Stuttgart, Munich,[190] and elsewhere throughout Germany are managing parallel actions in an effort to reclaim monies lost through cum-ex trading. A particular feature of the investigations is the emerging use of key witnesses, being primarily former participants in cum-ex trades who are now cooperating with the investigating authorities. It seems inevitable that the investigations will continue for many years with banks, intermediaries, and financial institutions outside Germany increasingly drawn into the proceedings.[191] It is also likely that new fronts will open up. For example, one possibility that has already been identified concerns ERISA funds, the vehicle used by many US individuals for their pension savings. ERISA funds were large lenders of shares to cum-ex trades and derived healthy stock lending fees from this activity. However, if any ERISA fund knowingly profited from illegal trading—which is now the characterization of cum-ex trades by the authorities in Germany—there may be severe sanctions under the relevant ERISA rules, given the high standards of conduct to which managers of ERISA funds are held.[192]

[188] See the report of DR News of 26 June 2018 by Thomas Svaneborg, available at https://www.dr.dk/nyheder/penge/skat-paa-mission-i-new-york-kraever-milliarder-tilbage-til-statskassen.

[189] See the report of DR News of 12 December 2016 by Niels Fastrup and Thomas Svaneborg, available at https://www.dr.dk/nyheder/penge/politi-i-fire-lande-jagter-sanjay-shah.

[190] https://dip21.bundestag.de/dip21/btd/18/127/1812700.pdf, at p.278.

[191] On 7 November 2018, the *Financial Times* reported that the Munich offices of BlackRock, one of the world's largest fund management groups, had been raided by criminal prosecutors investigating cum-ex trades. On 9 April 2019, *Handelsblatt* reported that approximately 180 prosecutors, tax inspectors, and police searched nineteen business and residential premises in Hesse, Lower Saxony, Baden-Wurttemberg, and Bavaria for information relating to cum-ex trades which garnered some €42.7 million in profits. See the report of Soenke Iwersen and Volker Votsmeier, 10 April 2019, available at https://www.handelsblatt.com/finanzen/banken-versicherungen/cum-ex/steuerhinterziehung-razzia-im-cum-ex-skandal-hauptverdaechtiger-soll-43-millionen-euro-hinterzogen-haben/24203002.html?ticket=ST-1007876-Ri99bLkgioeN5ToqpTf4-ap2.

[192] For an overview of the ERISA regime, see United States Department of Labor, 'History of EBSA and ERISA', available at https://www.dol.gov/agencies/ebsa/about-ebsa/about-us/history-of-ebsa-and-erisa.

As noted earlier in this chapter, the first criminal trial has now been concluded, opening the way to very many more criminal trials including actions to recover profits derived from cum-ex trades. There are already some 600 individual suspects identified in cases which involve at least 130 banks.[193] It seems likely there will be an impact from the decision on the financial services industry worldwide, for example as banks assess whether they are vulnerable to actions to recover profits from cum-ex trading and regulators around the world investigate whether firms were involved in cum-ex or similar schemes and whether they had sufficient systems and controls in place to flag such transactions.[194] The likelihood is that it will be years before the full impacts of the cum-ex affair are finally clear.

[193] Footnote 117, ibid.

[194] The expectation of such action by regulators across the world is discussed in GreenbergTraurig, German Cum-Ex Verdict: What This May Mean for UK Firms, March 26, 2020, available at https://www.gtlaw.com/es/insights/2020/3/german-cumex-verdict-what-this-may-mean-for-uk-firms. The article also discusses in more detail possible actions by the UK Financial Conduct Authority. Further, as a result of a resolution on cum-ex of 29 November 2018, the European Parliament asked the European Securities and Markets Authority (ESMA) and the European Banking Authority (EBA) to conduct an investigation into cum-ex and similar schemes in order to: assess potential threats to the integrity of financial markets and to national budgets; to establish the nature and magnitude of actors in these schemes; to assess whether there were breaches of either national or European Union law; to assess the actions taken by financial supervisors in Member States; and to make appropriate recommendations for reform and for action to the competent authorities concerned. The resolution also makes a number of other calls or appeals in relation to the affair (see European Parliament resolution of 29 November 2018 on the cum-ex scandal: financial crime and loopholes in the current legal framework ("https://oeil.secure.europarl.europa.eu/oeil/popups/ficheprocedure.do?lang=en&reference=2018/2900(RSP)" 2018/2900(RSP)), available at https://www.europarl.europa.eu/doceo/document/TA-8-2018-0475_EN.html

PART II

POLICY ISSUES

5

Assessing the Cum-Ex Trade

> . . . in real life, financiers, lawyers, accountants and tax experts tend to work together in teams, starting from large banks and down to boutique asset management firms. As to be anticipated, they take full advantage of existing conceptual, analytical and regulatory 'blind spots'.
>
> Nesvetailova et al, 'Tax Evasion and Avoidance Through Financial Engineering: The State of Play in Europe', October 2018

Introduction

The second part of this book is concerned with assessing the root causes behind the cum-ex trade and similar tax-driven transactions that are routinely entered into by banks and their clients.

In common with other instances of misconduct, the cum-ex trade has to date been assessed in a somewhat narrow manner, largely on the basis that it consists of isolated and anomalous conduct on the part of those within the banks who brought it about and on the part of the regulators who failed for such a lengthy period to understand what was going on. However, as will be demonstrated, misconduct on the part of banks is not just common but is literally an everyday occurrence.[1] This includes very many cases where the abuse of tax systems is a central feature in that misconduct.[2] However, the typical reaction to individual cases of misconduct such as the cum-ex trade generally fails to make any link with this wider pattern of behaviour. Rather, in virtually all such cases, the usual explanation offered is, just as in the cum-ex trade, centred on the individuals (the 'bad apples') who either perpetrated or failed to deal with the misconduct. Given the broad incidence of misconduct cases involving banks and tax, the obvious question arising is whether this 'bad apples' explanation gives an adequate account of the forces at play. The discussion in this part of this book is therefore concerned with assessing the causes of the cum-ex trade and other similar cases of

[1] Chapters 6 and 7 each discuss the serial incidence of misconduct by banks from a different perspective.

[2] The nature of misconduct by banks is discussed later in this chapter.

Banking on Failure: Cum-Ex and Why and How Banks Game the System. Richard S Collier, Oxford University Press (2020). © Richard S Collier.
DOI: 10.1093/oso/9780198859673.001.0001

misconduct relating to tax systems. In particular, the discussion seeks to understand why bank misconduct is so pervasive and persistent and why the abuse of tax systems is so often at the heart of these cases.

This chapter reviews briefly the public and official responses to the cum-ex trade before proceeding to look at what is missing in those responses. The discussion opens the way to the wider issues discussed in the following two chapters relevant to the questions of why banks (Chapter 6) and why tax systems (Chapter 7) so often feature in these misconduct cases. This chapter also considers the scope of what is meant by 'misconduct' on the part of banks.

As the discussion throughout Part II will seek to show, there a number of systemic factors that explain why banks are drawn to the exploitation of tax systems, as in the cum-ex trade and similar transactions. These factors concern the nature of banks, the conditions in which they operate, and what they have become. They also concern the nature of tax systems and the position of banks in relation to those systems. Collectively, these factors make it practically inevitable that tax systems will be serially exploited by banks in the manner illustrated by the cum-ex trade.

Nature of the Response to Cum-Ex

As indicated in the discussion of cum-ex in Chapter 4, the response to cum-ex has, at all levels, been dominated by concerns over the large financial numbers involved as reflected primarily in terms of the financial loss to the states which were targeted by the strategy. Central to the inquiry has been the identity and culpability of the wrongdoers such as the banks, financial intermediaries, investment funds, and traders that carried on cum-ex business. Special attention has been paid to the individuals involved, especially their lifestyles and the money they made from the trade. These aspects of the affair have been common features of the reporting of cum-ex in the press and are also major themes in the German parliamentary report into cum-ex. They are also evident in the response of the German state.

With regard to the general reporting of the cum-ex affair, much of the reporting has been presented in terms of shock and outrage and the arrogance and conceit of the bankers who have been involved and their subsequent fall from grace.[3] The reporting style often resembles a modern form of morality tale.[4] A second

[3] For example, see the account of the life of 'Frey', a banking insider at the centre of Correctiv's undercover investigation into cum-ex, part of the 'Cum-ex Files, A Cross Border Investigation'. In his interview, he describes his rise from a modest provincial background in Germany to a lifestyle involving lavish parties and the accumulation of vast wealth before his arrest by police and subsequent fall from grace. The interview, which is in German but with English subtitles, is available at https://www.youtube.com/watch?time_continue=3350&v=J1XA320LiUk.

[4] Michael Levi observes that white-collar and financial crimes are often treated by the mass media as an extension of what he refers to as 'infotainment', with a particular emphasis on, inter alia, the position

significant theme in the reporting has been the enormous size of the financial amounts involved and the resulting costs that fall on the state.[5] This reaction is not surprising given the anti-bank/anti-banker sentiment which has been prevalent since the Global Financial Crisis and the concomitant bailout of the banking sector. There has also been a significant focus on identifying the parties that may have caused or exacerbated the issue by their incompetence (e.g. tax administrators and regulators).

These same two themes of the response to cum-ex, namely the focus on the financial loss to the state and the culpability of individuals are also strongly evident at the political level, though in that sphere the dominant feature of the response has (not surprisingly) been concerned with the question of who within the government is to be blamed for the whole affair. This can be seen, for example, in the German parliamentary report into cum-ex. That report reflects the absence of any agreement between the political parties on a common response to cum-ex. Instead, separate responses, organized along factional party lines, are set out, and with strikingly different conclusions. Whilst the main government-backed conclusion is that the authorities did their job and worked well and that the blame falls squarely on the banks,[6] the minority reports are significantly more scathing, citing the cluelessness of the regulatory and tax authorities over a ten-year period. Further, they ultimately place the blame for the whole affair at the highest level, that of the German Federal Finance Minister.[7]

As discussed in Chapter 4, the response of the German state and regulatory authorities has been to finally close down the trade, stemming the losses to the state, and to pursue those regarded as responsible for the trades. The latter objective is made difficult by the sheer number of banks and investment funds that have been involved in executing or participating in the trade and the challenges presented by the process (particularly in relation to the pursuit of cross-border investigations) that must be followed in carrying out this task.

The overall response to cum-ex can therefore be seen to involve relatively little focus on the nature of the transaction itself nor on how it was that it came about. In addition, there has been virtually no attention paid to the wider ramifications of the trade, such as what it might reveal more generally about the financial system or

of high-profile individuals leading lavish lifestyles in difficulties or acting as hypocrites and the existence of the long-term concealment of fraud as demonstrating that the relevant business or its regulatory authority are incompetent. See Michael Levi, 'The Media Construction of Financial White-Collar Crimes', *British Journal of Criminology*, 46:6 (2006), 1037–57.

[5] See, for example, the report in the Austrian newspaper *Addendum*, part of the 'Cum-ex Files, A Cross Border Investigation', available at https://www.addendum.org/steuerraub/oesterreich-steuermafia/.

[6] German Parliamentary Report at pp.379–80.

[7] German Parliamentary Report at pp. 413–15, 433–4, 456 (contained in the minority report of Richard Pitterle of The Left) and at pp. 505, 526, 530, 532, 537, 540, 546–7 (contained in the report of Gerhard Schick of the Green Party).

about tax systems. This means that some of the key features of the cum-ex trade, such as its complexity and the fragmentation of the components that comprise it, have been subjected to no serious analysis in their own right. While the complexity of the cum-ex trade is touched on in the reporting, it is presented as being an obstacle to any careful explanation of the nature of the trade rather than as a deliberate design feature of the arrangements that in itself calls for particular comment or further examination.[8]

In the academic legal literature there has also been little or no significant discussion of whether there are wider or systemic factors that lie behind the trade. Instead, the bulk of the response in that circle has been concerned with the technical analysis of the rules that were thought to support the trade, including in particular an intricate legal dissection of the issues surveyed in Chapters 2 and 4. The relevance of these issues has dimmed as the extensive involvement of the fraudulent collusion among the parties has become more apparent.[9] There have also been concerns voiced about the role (and culpability) of the regulators.[10] Much discussion condemns the role of the lawyers and academics who wrote technical opinions, articles, and papers in support of the trade.[11]

What is Problematic in the Response to Cum-Ex?

The popular and political reaction described above is at least partially explained by the significant difficulty of getting to grips with the detail of exactly what the cum-ex trade entails. The response is perhaps also to be expected in the context of the difficult economic environment (often referred to as 'austerity') that has prevailed since the 2008–9 Global Financial Crisis, particularly as the banks were widely seen to have played a significant role in bringing about the crisis yet were in large measure shielded from its effects.[12]

[8] The difficulties of encapsulating and clarifying the nature of the cum-ex trade in sufficiently brief terms for the purposes of newspaper reporting are demonstrated in the explanation given by one of the leading journalists investigating cum-ex, Jenny Strasberg of the *Wall Street Journal*: 'The transactions are dizzyingly complex. They hinge on a gap between when stock loans and other trades are initiated and when they are considered completed, which is the result of wrinkles in the way many stock-market transactions are routed and processed. The result is that multiple parties can appear to simultaneously have owned the shares at the time of the dividend payout.' Jenny Strasberg, 'Officials Expand Probe of Tax Move', *Wall Street Journal*, 30 October 2014.

[9] See further the discussion in Chapter 4.

[10] For example, the role of the German regulatory authority BaFin in missing the huge share movements around the dividend date is discussed by Christoph Spengel. See German Parliamentary Report at p.501.

[11] See Votsmeier and Iwersen, 'Tax Law Experts Played Along'.

[12] There is an extensive literature on the financial crisis and the role of the banks, including the point that bank losses from the crisis were socialized whilst profits were privatized. For example, see Ewald Engelen et al, *After the Great Complacence: Financial Crisis and the Politics of Reform* (Oxford University Press, 2011) at pp.27–32.

It is not suggested here that the response to cum-ex discussed above is inappropriate but rather that it is simply not sufficient or complete as an exercise in the proper assessment of the scheme. In the view of the author, the response to the cum-ex trade discussed above limits the insights and learning points from the cum-ex affair, though it is typical of responses to similar cases of industry-wide misconduct. In particular, the almost exclusive emphasis on the financial scale of the losses to the state and the culpable parties (though these are certainly important issues) has shut out from the discussion a number of other issues such as (1) taxpayer equity; (2) the sharply contrasting positions of professional traders compared to retail investors; (3) distortions to competition, capital allocation, and the operation of markets (for example, in the creation of significant operational risk); (4) instability in the domestic and international system;[13] and, arguably most important, (5) a consideration of the relevant root causes relating to the role of banks and the involvement of tax systems. Given the widespread scale of the misconduct, an alternative possibility is that it is the system as a whole, and less the particular individuals concerned, that stands most in need of examination and reform.

As well as being an inadequate explanation of cum-ex in its wider context, a fixation on the costs to the state amounts to an oversimplified response to the nature of fraud, since it fails to take account of a number of other important issues. Put another way, addressing the costs to the state is not the same as addressing the fraud.[14] Rather, the reduction of the affair to a concentration on its outcome expressed in financial numbers and culpable individuals precludes any discussion or analysis of possible systemic causes with wider implications.[15] One immediate consequence of this is that important lessons are not being recognized or are being

[13] Notwithstanding the focus on the financial losses to the state, there has been relatively little analysis relating to the truly colossal money flows and the gigantic movements of securities that, over a period measured in years, passed through the financial system in order to deliver the cum-ex trade.

[14] A similar argument, presented in the context of VAT fraud, is put forward in Rita De La Feria, 'Tax Fraud and the Rule of Law', Oxford University Centre for Business Taxation, Working Paper 18/02, January 2018, available at https://www.sbs.ox.ac.uk/sites/default/files/2018-08/WP1802.pdf.

[15] Recent developments, however, suggest an increased emphasis in addressing the culpable parties. For example, the recent draft report of the European Parliament's Special Committee on Financial Crimes, Tax Evasion and Tax Avoidance proposes that financial institutions, advisers, and other intermediaries that knowingly, systematically, and repeatedly facilitate, engage, or participate in money laundering or tax evasion activities should face effective, proportional, and dissuasive penalties, and, where applicable, be restricted from operating in the single market. See European Parliament, 'Draft Report on Financial Crimes, Tax Evasion and Tax Avoidance' (2018/2121(INI)), 9 November 2018, at paragraph 179 (p.30), available at http://www.europarl.europa.eu/cmsdata/156723/TAX3%20Final%20draft%20report.pdf. There are similar developments at a domestic level—for example the new UK criminal law rule dealing with the corporate offences of Failure to Prevent Facilitation of Tax Evasion, on which see Part 3 of the Criminal Finances Act 2017, which came into force on 30 September 2017, and the accompanying guidance at https://assets.publishing.service.gov.uk/government/uploads/system/uploads/attachment_data/file/672231/Tackling-tax-evasion-corporate-offences.pdf. A similar, but broader, Italian rule, Legislative Decree no. 231 of 8 June 2001, which provides for a direct liability of legal entities in respect of certain crimes committed by their representatives, is referred to later in this chapter.

ignored. For example, there is obviously a significant difference between simple tax fraud such as deliberate concealment or misrepresentation (often associated with smaller taxpayers) and organized fraud involving large networks of people implementing sophisticated transactional structures in plain sight and operating on a cross-border basis. These two distinct categories of fraud not only give rise to different costs but also have different effects: organized fraud involves much larger amounts and represents a subsidy to the organized network involved.[16] Those costs may include the costs of responding to fraud, distortions to competition, taxpayer inequity, and the like.[17] Nonetheless, white-collar crime generally, let alone the variant involving organized networks and sophisticated structures, is a poorly researched and poorly understood area.[18] This arguably makes it all the more important to take the opportunity to fully understand the forces at work with a view to responding in a comprehensive and rational manner, rather than merely highlighting some features of what are taken to be isolated cases. In the present context, that seems all the more important as, first, tax fraud is estimated generally to be a far more significant source of economic loss than any other single area of public- or private-sector fraud, and, second, because work on frauds in the financial sector typically examines frauds perpetrated *on* the regulated financial sector rather than *by* it.[19]

The concern is therefore that not only is the response to cum-ex inadequate or incomplete but that it is also failing to capture all the relevant costs and is hindering the development of insights into the nature and operation of the banking sector which may be useful in preventing similar episodes in future. In the view of the author, the real causes are much less to do with the individual banks and bankers (the 'bad apples' explanation) and more concerned with systemic factors, which have so far been largely ignored.

A number of significant matters are clearly not addressed at all, much less explained, by the official or public response to cum-ex actually seen, yet seem

[16] De La Feria, 'Tax Fraud and the Rule of Law', at pp.6–7.

[17] These costs are discussed in De La Feria, 'Tax Fraud and the Rule of Law', at pp.11–15. There is also a more detailed discussion of the costs and other impacts of fraud, though in a UK context, in M. Levi and J. Burrows, 'Measuring the Impact of Fraud in the UK', *British Journal of Criminology* 48:3 (2008), 293–318.

[18] The analysis of white-collar crime is often lumped in with street crime. See Levi and Burrows, 'Measuring the Impact of Fraud', at p.298. At a more general level, the existing understanding of the field is strongly criticized in recent work of the European Parliament's Special Committee on Financial Crimes, Tax Evasion and Tax Avoidance (TAX3), which published its first findings in November 2018. The draft report deplores 'the lack of reliable and unbiased statistics on the magnitude of tax avoidance and tax evasion' and stresses 'the importance of developing appropriate and transparent methodologies to quantify the scale of these phenomena, as well as their impact on countries' public finances, economic activities and public investments'. See European Parliament, 'Draft Report', at p.6.

[19] Levi and Burrows, 'Measuring the Impact of Fraud', at pp.308–9. It is also relevant that in the case of cum-ex there is and has been for some time appreciable media and political pressure which has led to significant resources being deployed to investigate the cum-ex trades. Given the lengthy period and high level of costs needed to investigate and prosecute in cases like cum-ex, it seems doubtful if all other similar cases would be similarly resourced.

essential to a proper understanding of the cum-ex affair. For example, what factors explain the significant extent of collusion between banks, brokers, and their clients and the scale of the cum-ex activity? If 'bad apples' were at work, how is it possible that there were so many of them operating all at once and at so many institutions? What factors contributed to the very long period of time before the cum-ex trade was properly understood by the regulators and successfully stopped? How was it possible that, within the extensive (and multiple) internal control systems operated by banks, vast numbers of cum-ex trades involving colossal capital movements could be regularly executed (and apparently approved) in plain sight of the relevant internal control mechanisms? What are the lessons for bank governance structures, financial regulation, and tax systems?

As the discussion in Part II of this book will seek to demonstrate, cum-ex is not a one-off aberration but the predictable outcome of a syndrome of conditions which has led to a long series of similar cases of misconduct by banks.

The Nature of Misconduct

It is necessary to clarify at the outset what is meant by referring in the discussion here to cases of 'misconduct'. The primary focus in this book relates to misconduct in relation to tax systems (particularly in the context of the intersection of financial market systems and tax systems), and the scope of what is meant by references to misconduct in that context are discussed further below. However, the prevalence of misconduct by banks outside the sphere of tax systems is also germane to the discussion here given that it is relevant to a more general understanding of the nature of banks.

In referring to cases of misconduct by banks which do not involve tax systems, it is intended to denote cases involving illegality or cases where regulatory requirements central to the proper and safe operation of the financial system and the protection of its constituency are clearly infringed.[20]

Within the field of taxation, the notion of defining relevant 'misconduct' for the purposes of the discussion is not straightforward, though the topic has been extensively canvassed by tax professionals, academics, governments, and international institutions.[21] Conduct that is unlawful under the applicable rules of a tax

[20] Banks are, of course, subject to extensive regulatory requirements which concern a wide range of matters including safe and sound operation, capital requirements, use of customer deposits, protection of customers and their assets, management of conflicts of interest, and codes of conduct (e.g. market abuse rules) governing their interactions with other market participants. This extensive regulatory regime reflects the unique role of the banking sector in the wider economy (a role that is also reflected in the 'too big to fail' characterization of the larger banks).

[21] In the international sphere, the topic of international tax avoidance and evasion has been the subject of discussion by fiscal authorities and international institutions for the last century. The League of Nations first considered the matter in the 1920s. See League of Nations, 'Double Taxation and Tax

system is clearly to be included in any notion of tax system misconduct. This is usually referred to as tax evasion. Tax evasion is normally considered to refer to actions by a taxpayer which entail breaking the law and which were taken wilfully, with the intention of escaping payment of tax, the result being that the payment of tax is evaded but the tax liability is not.[22] However, evasion does not require wilful intent on the part of the taxpayer in all jurisdictions where it is recognized as a legal concept.[23] In others, the specific intent of the taxpayer to evade taxes leads to a particular form of tax evasion, namely tax fraud.[24]

In framing the breadth of relevant misconduct in relation to tax systems, some consideration should also be given to conduct which may not be illegal as such, but which subverts the intended operation of the tax system (for example, the exploitation of a 'loophole' in the law). This conduct is usually referred to as tax avoidance. Explored further below, the concept raises a number of difficulties.[25] In broad terms, a tax avoidance transaction is one which: avoids or reduces tax; is entered into with that purpose; is carried out within the law but is not a

Evasion', Report and Resolutions submitted by the Technical Experts to the Financial Committee of the League of Nations, Document F.212 (League of Nations, 1925).

[22] Cases of tax evasion are not limited to instances where a payment of tax due is not made. They may also concern cases where a tax benefit or tax reclaim is claimed in circumstances where the relevant tax requirements are not satisfied.

[23] OECD Committee on Fiscal Affairs, 'Tax Evasion and Avoidance' (OECD, 1980), p.5. A 'wilful' or 'bad faith' act by a taxpayer is not necessarily required, as tax may be evaded by a taxpayer's negligence or failure to exercise proper care, for example where a tax return is not submitted by a specific date. See also V. Uckmar, 'General Report', in International Fiscal Association, *Tax Avoidance and Evasion*, Cahier de Droit Fiscal International 68a (Kluwer, 1983), at p.22.

[24] The distinction between evasion generally and tax fraud can be significant. An example of the relevance of the distinction is given by recent litigation in the US. The litigation concerns the pursuit by the State of Denmark of millions of dollars which it regards as secured by fraudulent tax reclaims on the part of a large number of US pension funds. The point at issue in the litigation was whether the claims of the State of Denmark constituted efforts to pursue tax evasion (therefore representing direct enforcement of Danish tax law) or whether the claims amounted to the recovery for 'money stolen from the plaintiff by fraud'. The former would be prevented by the 'revenue rule' (which prohibits courts from hearing actions by foreign states to enforce their foreign tax laws and which is discussed in Chapter 7), whereas the latter would not. The decision in the litigation was in favour of the State of Denmark. See In Re Skat Tax Refund Scheme Litigation, Memorandum Opinion, No. 1:2018cv04047—Document 80, US District Court, Southern District of New York, 2019, 18-md-2865 (LAK), available at https://law.justia.com/cases/federal/district-courts/new-york/nysdce/1:2018cv04047/493285/80/. If the logic of the reasoning in the case is accepted more widely, it is likely to lead to states seeking redress for tax evasion by a wider use of theft/fraud claims.

[25] The tax avoidance concept is widely recognized in common-law and civil-law countries. It is reported in Ana Paula Dourado, 'Tax Avoidance Revisited in the EU BEPS Context', in Ana Paula Dourado, ed., *Tax Avoidance Revisited in the EU BEPS Context*, EATLP International Tax Series, Volume 15 (IBFD, 2016), at section 1.1.1.1, that the tax avoidance concept is acknowledged and identifiable by the courts and the legal doctrine in most of the twenty-two states surveyed in the book. This includes common-law jurisdictions such as the UK, US, and South Africa, and continental jurisdictions such as Austria, Belgium, France, Germany, Greece, Luxembourg, Italy, the Netherlands, Portugal, Spain, the Czech Republic, Croatia, Poland, Russia, and Turkey, and also other jurisdictions belonging to different (sub-)families of law such as the Nordic countries (Denmark, Finland, Norway, and Sweden).

transaction the legislature intends to encourage.[26] As will be apparent from what follows, references to tax avoidance may include a wide spectrum of activity. Within that spectrum, the more aggressive form of avoidance activity is potentially relevant to the notion of misconduct in relation to tax systems for two reasons. First, the legitimacy of such avoidance activity under the law may be determined on an *ex post* basis and declared to be ill-founded, as where an avoidance arrangement is challenged by the tax authorities and determined by a court to be invalid under the law.[27] Second, the more aggressive form of tax avoidance is widely perceived to be an abuse, or misuse, of tax systems and is commonly opposed by states which seek to counter it at both a domestic level and through the work of international bodies such as the OECD.[28]

It is usually assumed that there is a clear distinction between evasion and avoidance. This is on the basis that the former is illegal while the latter is legal.[29] Unfortunately, the distinction between tax evasion and tax avoidance, as well as

[26] The definition is derived from G.S.A. Wheatcroft, 'The Attitude of the Legislature and the Courts to Tax Avoidance', *Modern Law Review* 18 (May 1955), 209–30. A similar definition—'an arrangement leading to tax advantages, the granting of which is not intended by the legal system'—is given in Dourado, 'Tax Avoidance Revisited'. For a general discussion of the concept of tax avoidance, see Michael Devereux, Judith Freedman, and John Vella, 'Tax Avoidance', report commissioned by the UK National Audit Office (Oxford University Centre for Business Taxation, 2012).

[27] Where such an arrangement is not explicitly dealt with under the law, a number of different anti-abuse standards may be applied judicially, such as a purposive interpretation of the law, a sham doctrine, a substance over form test or business purpose or economic substance test. Other forms of tax non-compliance involving the violation of an explicit tax rule (as in cases of tax evasion, for example) are in contrast illegal on an ex ante basis. See further Kyle D. Logue, 'Optimal Tax Compliance and Penalties When the Law is Uncertain', *Virginia Tax Review* 27:2 (2007), 241–96. It is, of course, also possible that the court may uphold the validity of the arrangements under the law, for example where the law is defectively drafted or due to some other failure in the way the legislation is written. In some cases, though not necessarily all, this may itself lead to the enactment of anti-avoidance legislation. The fact that some avoidance arrangements may be struck down by the courts (while some such arrangements may not) has led some writers to draw the more general distinction between 'effective' and 'ineffective' avoidance. See Devereux, Freedman, and Vella, 'Tax Avoidance'.

[28] A recent example of efforts at countering corporate avoidance activity through international bodies is given by the OECD BEPS project. As noted, the use of international bodies in this way dates back to the work of the League of Nations in the 1920s. The concerns at that time were with tax 'evasion', a concept that was used then to encompass what arguably now would be included in the notions of tax evasion and, broadly, aggressive tax avoidance. See League of Nations, 'Double Taxation and Tax Evasion', Part III. International bodies (and states) have often sought to counter the evasion and avoidance of taxes on a similar footing—see for example United Nations Department of International Economic and Social Affairs, 'International Co-operation in Tax Matters', Guidelines for International Co-operation Against the Evasion and Avoidance of Taxes (with Special Reference to Taxes on Income, Profits, Capital and Capital Gains) (United Nations, 1984). Similarly, the Convention on Mutual Administrative Assistance in Tax Matters was developed jointly by the OECD and the Council of Europe to tackle evasion and avoidance—see further the explanation on the OECD website at http://www.oecd.org/ctp/exchange-of-tax-information/convention-on-mutual-administrative-assistance-in-tax-matters.htm.

[29] Malcolm Gammie casts the distinction between tax avoidance and tax evasion in different terms: tax avoidance being a function of the tax base (namely, what it is you are trying to tax), and tax evasion being a function of the mechanisms by which tax is collected and enforced. See Malcolm Gammie, 'Moral Taxation, Immoral Avoidance—What Role for the Law?' *British Tax Review* 4 (2013), 577–90, at p.577.

the notion of tax avoidance itself, is not so clear-cut.[30] This inevitably complicates the task of identifying the scope of misconduct under tax systems for the purposes of the discussion in this book.

Although some general distinction between evasion and avoidance is recognizable in many legal systems, the bounds of the concepts from one tax system to another are by no means identical.[31] This may mean that, as a result of variations in legal standards, what may be illegal and therefore evasion in one country may be treated as avoidance in another, and vice versa, making it impossible to establish common criteria with any reasonable degree of certainty.[32] Not surprisingly, the OECD has concluded that although the tax avoidance–tax evasion distinction is frequently made, it is in reality impossible to apply it as a paradigm and in any consistent way as between countries.[33] Even within a single tax system, there are other factors that undermine the clear distinction between evasion and avoidance. For example, there may be cases where it is not always clear if the relevant activity amounts to evasion or avoidance, because of the inherent unpredictability of the response of the state concerned.[34] Further, it may be difficult to

[30] The distinctions may be very significant from a legal perspective given they may lead to different remedies and sanctions under the relevant local law. However, the evasion–avoidance distinction has little significance in economic terms. Economically, avoidance and evasion are hardly distinguishable since it is of minimal importance in terms of economics whether a particular activity or transaction falls within the law or not. Malcolm Gammie notes that the distinction between evasion and aggressive avoidance is a distinction at law but suggests that for many it is a distinction without a difference as instances of aggressive avoidance represent an affront to sensible taxation and the question is what to do about it—see Gammie, 'Moral Taxation, Immoral Avoidance', at p.579. A similar view is expressed in Agnar Sandmo, 'The Theory of Tax Evasion: A Retrospective View', *National Tax Journal* 58:4 (December 2005), 643–63, at pp.645–6. The problematic nature of tax avoidance is explored from a number of different perspectives in the volume edited by Judith Freedman, 'Beyond Boundaries: Developing Approaches to Tax Avoidance and Tax Risk Management' (Oxford University Centre for Business Taxation, 2007), available at http://eureka.sbs.ox.ac.uk/3563/. Domestic efforts to counter aggressive tax avoidance are seen in the enactment of domestic anti-avoidance legislation, such as targeted and general anti-avoidance rules, etc.

[31] One Japanese commentator has characterized the activity of treaty shopping as evasion whereas it is more normally considered an avoidance activity—see Professor H. Ishi, 'National Report on Japan', in International Fiscal Association, *Tax Avoidance and Evasion*, Cahier de Droit Fiscal International 68a (Kluwer, 1983), at p.484. For a broader contemporary discussion, see Dourado, 'Tax Avoidance Revisited', which also (at Section 1.1.1.1) discusses some of the difficulties from the lack of alignment in the concepts (and words) used to describe avoidance activity.

[32] Uckmar, 'General Report', at p.22. It is noted in a more recent study that 'each revenue body faces a different environment within which they administer their taxation system. FTA countries differ in respect of their policy and legislative environments and their administrative practices and cultures'. See OECD, 'Study into the Role of Tax Intermediaries', at p.7.

[33] This is because not only do tax laws differ from country to country, but 'to frustrate the intentions of the tax law is, in some countries, already to break the law, so that in such countries there is no clear-cut distinction between tax avoidance and tax evasion'. See OECD Secretariat, 'OECD Work on Tax Avoidance and Tax Evasion', in Council of Europe, *International Tax Avoidance and Evasion* (1981), p.13. Similar observations are made in OECD Committee on Fiscal Affairs, 'Tax Evasion and Avoidance', p.5. The blurry nature of the dividing line between evasion and avoidance is also discussed in Joel Slemrod and Christian Gillitzer, *Tax Systems* (MIT Press, 2014).

[34] For example, in Italy it is generally the case that only individuals can be considered responsible for criminal acts as such. However, Legislative Decree no. 231 of 8 June 2001 provides for a direct liability of legal entities in respect of certain crimes committed by their representatives. Since its introduction in

apply the law to the facts in any particular case. To take a simple example, the payment of an intra-group management charge by one group company for services not in fact supplied by a group affiliate is clearly evasion. If services are actually provided by the one group company to the other but the payment is slightly above comparable market rates, that would normally be treated as avoidance. However, there is presumably some point at which the fee may be so disproportionately large and the service so minimal that avoidance becomes evasion. Similar practical difficulties may arise in identifying the motives or mental state of a taxpayer or, as in cum-ex and similar transactions, the real nature of a very complex composite transaction involving numerous steps and multiple parties.[35] It is also true that courts have struggled with the distinction.[36]

The concept of avoidance is problematic for a number of reasons. Some jurisdictions deny a legal meaning to 'avoidance' on the basis that if the relevant activity is legal, any notion of avoidance is legally immaterial. Where the relevant activity is illegal it would be regarded as evasion and any notion of avoidance would again be legally immaterial.[37] There are also significant concerns about the imprecision of the notion of 'avoidance' due to the breadth of what may potentially be included in the concept. This breadth of the notion of avoidance has led to various attempts to categorize gradations of what may loosely be termed 'avoidance' activity under tax systems, with a continuum from relatively benign activity at one end of the spectrum which hardly warrants the description 'tax avoidance' (taking advantage of a specific relief or exemption in circumstances intended by

2001, the scope of the provision has been continually widened by the legislator and now includes a number of broadly based (and arguably imprecise) categories such as 'crimes to the detriment of the State or public bodies', 'market abuse', and 'corporate crimes'. The provision was used unexpectedly by the Italian tax authorities in the period 2005–8 in relation to certain tax-driven dividend arbitrage transactions executed by global investment banks and involving shares in Italian companies. The relevant transactions, often involving stock lending transactions, were geared to exploit the additional tax credit relating to dividends paid by Italian companies that was available under certain tax treaties (such as the Italian tax treaties with the UK and France). The Italian tax authorities regarded these transactions as artificial and designed to defraud the Italian state of €4.2 billion. Various factors may contribute to the unpredictability of a state's response to cases of evasion and aggressive avoidance. For example, if the reasoning in the recent US litigation discussed in footnote 24 of this chapter is adopted more widely, this may also have the effect of encouraging states to pursue cross-border evasion and aggressive avoidance cases as constituting theft or fraud.

[35] In the case of cum-ex, it was only after a lengthy period of investigation that the real nature of the arrangements between the parties involved in executing many of the trades became clear and led to the introduction of criminal tax fraud sanctions—see the discussion in Chapter 4.

[36] In the UK, for example, 'the courts have not always been too careful in drawing the distinction, sometimes saying "evasion" when "avoidance" is intended', A.J. Easson, *Cases and Materials in Revenue Law* (Sweet and Maxwell, 1973), p.26. Easson cites a number of illustrative cases to which may be added the example given by Lord Scarman in referring to 'the limit beyond which the safe channel of acceptable tax avoidance shelves into the dangerous shallows of unacceptable tax evasion'—see Furniss v Dawson, 1984 STC 156.

[37] See Uckmar, 'General Report', at p.23. It is also true that notions of avoidance may shift over time within a single country, depending on the attitudes of government, public opinion, the tax authorities, and the courts.

the relevant law, sometimes referred to as 'tax saving') to cases of 'aggressive' avoidance at the other, for example, complex tax arbitrage transactions using financial products such as derivatives.[38]

The difficulties discussed above mean that it is not possible to arrive at any common international definition of 'tax evasion' or 'tax avoidance' nor, where relevant, at any clear notion of where the line is to be drawn in relation to the more benign form of tax avoidance.

These difficulties have not prevented governments and tax authorities from actively seeking to counter a range of tax-driven activity by corporates, both on a domestic basis and by coordinated international action aimed at tax avoidance activity.[39] This clearly encompasses activity that ranks as tax evasion in the relevant jurisdiction but also includes activity that is regarded as involving avoidance activity at the more aggressive end of the scale. The latter activity is often referred to as amounting to 'unacceptable' tax avoidance.[40] As to specifically what is meant by the reference to 'unacceptable' tax avoidance, the general tendency is to define given attributes of that activity or specific areas of concern, rather than rely on some prescriptive definition or categorization of 'tax avoidance'.[41]

[38] For example, Arthur Shenfield classifies avoidance into the following four categories: (1) the decision not to acquire capital or accept taxed employment, etc taken in order to avoid a tax liability; (2) the acceptance of tax exemptions, tax privileges, or tax holidays offered by a government; (3) the pursuit of normal commercial objectives but with an eye to the selection of that method which provides the least unwelcome tax result; and (4) the pursuit of tax avoidance as the main or sole aim of a transaction. See Arthur Shenfield, 'The Political Economy of Tax Avoidance', IEA Occasional Paper 24 (IEA, 1968). That range is also sometimes described as involving 'unacceptable tax avoidance' at one end and 'acceptable tax avoidance' at the other, though it is not clear how this particular distinction is to be drawn. A similar approach is the distinction between 'proper' and 'improper' tax planning/tax avoidance—see J. Shafer and J. Solursh, 'National Report on Canada', in International Fiscal Association, *Tax Avoidance and Evasion*, Cahier de Droit Fiscal International 68a (Kluwer, 1983), at pp.296–7.

[39] In 1980, the OECD acknowledged that common definitions of avoidance and evasion could not be reached but maintained that this did not imply governments were not in agreement on what constitutes the range of tax evasion and avoidance they wished to combat or that they had problems identifying it. See OECD Committee on Fiscal Affairs, 'Tax Evasion and Avoidance', at p.6. This conclusion is somewhat mystifying (if there is no agreement on the basic concepts then it is hard to see how there could be general agreement on the range of avoidance and evasion to be countered), but it should probably be interpreted as meaning there is a broad-based agreement on specific types of transactions or arrangements that are widely perceived as unacceptable. In this context, avoidance activity akin to 'tax saving' activity is generally of little concern to tax authorities and governments. See OECD Committee on Fiscal Affairs, 'Tax Evasion and Avoidance', p.6.

[40] However, as noted, a variety of similar terms have also been used to mean much the same thing, such as in references to avoidance that is improper, illegitimate, artificial, or abusive. See Brian Arnold, 'Responses to Tax Avoidance', in Malcolm Gammie, ed., *Striking the Balance: Tax Administration, Enforcement and Compliance in the 1990s*, Conference Report of the Institute for Fiscal Studies Sixth Residential Conference, 1993 (Institute for Fiscal Studies, 1996), at p.205, available at https://www.google.com/search?client=safari&rls=en&q=Striking+the+Balance:+Tax+Administration,+Enforcement+and+Compliance+in+the+1990s,+Conference+Report+of+the+Institute+for+Fiscal+Studies+Sixth+Residential+Conference+1993&ie=UTF-8&oe=UTF-8. With some exceptions, terms such as 'abusive' or 'aggressive' tax planning are generally not recognized as legal concepts.

[41] This development seems to date back to the 1980s. See, for example, OECD Committee on Fiscal Affairs, 'Tax Evasion and Avoidance', at pp. 5 and 7; and United Nations Department of International Economic and Social Affairs, 'International Co-operation in Tax Matters', at pp. 11 and 12. More

A recent example of this approach is given by the OECD-sponsored Forum on Tax Administration (FTA) in relation to its 'Study into the Role of Tax Intermediaries'.[42] This study was designed to address the concerns of the then forty or so states represented within the FTA relating to non-compliance with tax laws in an international context. The particular focus of the project was on the spread of aggressive tax planning promoted by tax intermediaries, such as legal and accounting firms and other tax advisers. Financial institutions, including particularly banks, were included in the category of tax intermediaries covered by the work. The Seoul Declaration, which gave the mandate for the project, identified the need to understand the role of intermediaries in 'unacceptable tax minimization arrangements'.[43] However, there was early consensus that because of the differences in the legal framework between states, it would not be appropriate or feasible to attempt to reach a definition of this phrase 'unacceptable tax minimization arrangements'. Instead, two types of arrangements were identified as representing the areas of common concern. The first was tax planning 'involving a tax position that is tenable but has unintended and unexpected tax revenue consequences'. This was explained by the FTA as involving misuse of the tax legislation to achieve results which were neither foreseen nor intended by the legislators. This area of concern might be paraphrased as referring to 'loopholes' in the law. The second type of concern identified was 'taking a tax position that is favourable to the taxpayer without openly disclosing that there is an uncertainty whether significant matters in the tax return accord with the law'.[44] The two concerns together are referred to in the study (and in later related work of the FTA) as 'aggressive tax planning' (often referred to by the acronym 'ATP').[45]

recently, the European Parliament's Special Committee on Financial Crimes, Tax Evasion and Tax Avoidance (TAX3) has called for the adoption of a comprehensive definition of aggressive tax planning indicators. See European Parliament, 'Draft Report', at p.7. It is also notable that, in some countries, administrative rulings may describe the types of arrangement that may be considered avoidance. See, for example, the discussion of Austria, Belgium, and the Netherlands in Dourado, 'Tax Avoidance Revisited', at Section 1.1.1.2.

[42] OECD, 'Study into the Role of Tax Intermediaries'. The Forum on Tax Administration (FTA) was created in 2002 as a forum for tax commissioners from OECD and non-OECD countries. Its membership currently comprises tax commissioners from fifty-one OECD and non-OECD countries. The 'Intermediaries' study (and further related work by the FTA) is discussed in Chapter 7.

[43] The Seoul Declaration was made following the third meeting of the Forum on Tax Administration in Seoul, Korea, in September 2006. For the full Seoul Declaration and a list of countries that attended Seoul, see www.oecd.org/ctp/ta/seouldeclaration.

[44] OECD, 'Study into the Role of Tax Intermediaries', p.9.

[45] The 'aggressive tax planning' concept has also been taken up and used extensively by the European Commission. See, for example, European Commission, 'Aggressive Tax Planning Indicators', Taxation Papers, Working Paper No. 71 (European Union, 2017), available at https://ec.europa.eu/taxation_customs/sites/taxation/files/taxation_papers_71_atp_.pdf and European Commission, Study on Aggressive Tax Planning and Indicators, Final Report, Taxation Papers, Working Paper No. 61-2015, (European Union, 2016) Ramboll Management Consulting and Corit Advisory, available at https://ec.europa.eu/taxation_customs/sites/taxation/files/resources/documents/taxation/gen_info/economic_analysis/tax_papers/taxation_paper_61.pdf

The first of the two types of arrangement referred to above has in particular proved contentious. This is because it seems to place a significant emphasis on the tax authorities' expectations of the revenue consequences of a transaction, the objection being that the test of what is 'acceptable' tax planning should be determined by the law, as interpreted by the courts.[46] Nonetheless, though the aggressive tax planning concept is relatively new, it arguably represents—with all its flaws—an old aspiration of any legal and tax system, namely that transactions must have not only a form but also a (legal) substance that permits them to be considered as legitimate and founded.[47] Strictly, of course, the nature and range of anti-avoidance standards are to be derived from the domestic tax laws of individual tax systems rather than by some 'international standard' of avoidance deriving from the action of international organizations.[48] The FTA's assessment that tax planning based on achieving 'unintended consequences' of the law is tantamount to a misuse of the law cannot, therefore, be regarded as representing anything more than a broad (but imprecise) correspondence with the prevailing approaches seen in many states.

The discussion in this book of misconduct by banks in relation to tax systems does not rest on any precise definition or forensically delineated notion of aggressive tax avoidance activity. However, it is considered that the notion of 'aggressive tax planning' discussed above offers a reasonable proxy test for the scope of the tax avoidance concern on the part of governments and tax authorities relating to the misuse or abuse of tax systems. It combines the two elements identified in the above definition of aggressive tax planning (namely tax planning arrangements that deliver an unintended result under the tax rules and contentious or debatable interpretations of the tax law that are kept secret) and so reflects long-standing and widely shared areas of concern for tax authorities.[49]

[46] A key criticism is that revenue authorities are seeking in effect to correct defective legislation with references to notions of unforeseen results or the wider 'spirit of the law'—see Devereux, Freedman, and Vella, 'Tax Avoidance', at pp.15–17.

[47] This view is expressed in Adolfo Martin Jimenez, 'Tax Avoidance and Aggressive Tax Planning as an International Standard—BEPS and the "New" Standards of (Legal and Illegal) Tax Avoidance', in Ana Paula Dourado, ed., *Tax Avoidance Revisited in the EU BEPS Context*, EATLP International Tax Series, Volume 15 (IBFD, 2016), 25–62, at paragraph 2.2. Jimenez also argues that the concept is indicative of the fact that a certain degree of harmonization in the international context is needed to prevent taxpayers having easy options for avoiding the tax levels of their domestic tax systems.

[48] An examination of whether the OECD standard of 'aggressive tax planning' might be taken as a new international standard is contained in Jimenez, 'Tax Avoidance and Aggressive Tax Planning'. For various reasons, Jimenez rejects the idea that 'ATP' is a new international standard that draws the line between what is permitted and what is prohibited to taxpayers. Rather, he argues that any new anti-avoidance standards have to be defined by reference to the OECD BEPS actions, though recognizes that this is problematic as those actions do not use a unitary concept or single conceptual tool to define avoidance. That BEPS-centric approach is of limited relevance to the discussion here as the BEPS actions have little to say about the use of the financial products and arrangements of the sort discussed here.

[49] These features were being aired as key characteristics of 'avoidance' and avoidance schemes some forty years ago—see OECD Secretariat, 'OECD Work on Tax Avoidance and Tax Evasion', p.7.

Accordingly, 'misconduct' in relation to tax systems is here regarded as conduct which represents an abuse or misuse of tax systems, encompassing conduct which broadly corresponds to the FTA notion of aggressive tax avoidance in addition to conduct that would qualify as tax evasion in any particular jurisdiction.

Notwithstanding the difficulties of defining the bounds of avoidance (or aggressive tax avoidance) activity and delineating the borderline between evasion and avoidance activity, there is one practical point that may be made in relation to avoidance activity by banks. This relates to the specialist structuring groups within banks whose remit specifically includes identifying differentials or gaps in the tax law and devising ways to extract value from them for the bank as well as its clients.[50] Such groups generally operate on the basis of exploiting tax legislation by structuring techniques that are considered to be within the law. Accordingly, their activities would normally be regarded as having an avoidance or aggressive tax avoidance character. In some of the bigger banks, the profile and activities of these groups has changed since the Global Financial Crisis. In particular, the intense pressure on banks and especially on the standing and reputation of banks since the financial crisis has led the senior management of some banks to seek to voluntarily curtail the activities of these groups. However, whilst this has led to a reduction in these activities on the part of some banking groups, it remains true that much of the tax structuring activity discussed in this book occurred well after the financial crisis. This includes the cum-ex trade, which involved literally hundreds of banks.[51] It is also true that some of these specialist groups were restructured, for example by being segmented into smaller groups of individuals working within other business lines rather than being closed down entirely. Some of the tax structuring expertise has also shifted to smaller, niche players who are less sensitive to reputational issues, though the trades and activity of these smaller players may still be facilitated, including financed, by the bigger banks. These developments have been brought about by a senior-management response to the significant reputational pressure on banks in a kind of informal self-regulation, rather than in response to specific legislative developments.[52] While it does

[50] Such groups are discussed briefly in Chapter 1 at p.15.

[51] It also includes a number of the other cases of misconduct that are referred to in this book, such as the 'pre-release' mechanism and the after-tax hedging structures discussed in Chapter 7 (at pp. 253 and 264 respectively).

[52] This development might suggest that measures intended to counter tax-system-based misconduct by banks should focus on some form of reputation-based sanction, such as a 'naming and shaming' approach. This is the approach adopted by the UK's Code of Practice on Taxation for Banks, which is discussed in Chapter 7. The code is policed by an annual report which identifies publicly banks that have not adopted the code or banks which have breached the code. However, the reputation issues raised for a bank in the context of the code are arguably of a different order to those raised globally across the sector in the wake of the Global Financial Crisis. Further, it seems likely that overseas headquartered banks will find the sanction of the code less of a concern than UK-headquartered groups. HMRC guidance on the code is available at https://assets.publishing.service.gov.uk/government/uploads/system/uploads/attachment_data/file/566119/The_Code_of_Practice_on_Taxation_for_Banks___HMRC_consolidated_guidance.pdf.

suggest that bank senior management are both capable of understanding these activities and suppressing them, it raises the question of whether this state of affairs is sustainable and permanent. For all these reasons, it cannot be concluded that the problem of banks exploiting tax systems has somehow gone away.

Why Banks and Why Tax?

The central questions addressed in the next two chapters deal with why it is that banks are so often involved in cases of misconduct such as cum-ex and why so many of these cases involve exploitation of tax systems. The discussion is particularly concerned with examining these questions in the context of the intersection or overlap of financial market systems and tax systems.

Chapter 6 deals with the first of these, addressing the question—why banks? The chapter outlines the significant incidence of misconduct by banks before investigating a number of systemic factors that comprise a syndrome of causes which tend to lead to this situation. Included is a consideration of how, at an operational level, banks are able to implement trades such as cum-ex within the apparent plain sight of the relevant governance structures, including those that are both internal to the bank and external to it. The chapter compares the position of the banking sector to other business sectors as regards the degree to which misconduct may actively be engineered by industry participants. The discussion is illustrated by a high-level comparison of the Volkswagen emissions scandal ('Dieselgate') with the cum-ex affair.[53]

The second major question—why tax?—is pursued in Chapter 7. This explores the role of banks in tax systems and considers why, in comparison with all other tax intermediaries, banks might be regarded as having a unique ability to exploit tax systems. The chapter also explores the features of tax systems that recurrently provide a magnet for banks and why it might be said that the rules in tax systems actually facilitate their own exploitation, particularly in relation to the tax rules applying to financial products and financial markets. This involves a discussion of the structure of tax legislation, the impact of derivatives and the difficulties posed for the administration of complex tax rules dealing with financial products.

Chapter 8 sets out the overall conclusions that may be drawn from the discussion in this book. This includes offering an account of the ways in which the business of banks and financial-market and tax systems actually encourage and facilitate schemes like the cum-ex trade.

[53] The Volkswagen emissions scandal, which is often referred to as 'Dieselgate', began in September 2015 when the US Environmental Protection Agency (EPA) issued a notice of violation under the Clean Air Act to the Volkswagen group.

6
Banks and Misconduct

The Best Way to Rob a Bank is to Own One

William K. Black

Introduction—Why Banks?

This chapter is concerned with the question of why banks are so often involved in misconduct and also why much of this misconduct involves complex transactions or arrangements involving financial products.[1]

The discussion begins by considering the nature and extent of misconduct by banks. In examining the extent of such misconduct, a number of recent studies and examples in the banking industry are considered. These would appear to indicate that misconduct in the banking industry is pervasive. As discussed in the previous chapter, the cause of such misconduct is often attributed to the acts of the individuals concerned in their particular facts and circumstances. However, on closer examination it is possible to identify a number of recurrent themes that are also visible in the cum-ex case study. These themes contribute to a better understanding of the root causes of misconduct by banks. The hypothesis presented is that misconduct by banks has less to do with individuals and much more to do with both the nature of banking business and industry conditions in the financial services sector.

To explore this hypothesis, the analysis in this chapter is broken down into three parts. First, there is a consideration of how the modern bank has changed radically in recent decades. It can be seen that material changes in the business model of banks have taken place. These have relevance to the propensity of banks to participate in misconduct, including schemes such as cum-ex. The discussion is concerned essentially with what the modern bank has become.

The second part of the analysis builds on the first. This is achieved by a review of the mechanisms that operate in practice to permit or deliver trades like cum-ex within the banking sector. Some of these mechanisms are internal to banks, while

[1] The meaning of references to 'misconduct' is explained in Chapter 5. Chapter 7 will address the question of why tax is a regular component of such misconduct involving transactions or arrangements entered into by banks.

Banking on Failure: Cum-Ex and Why and How Banks Game the System. Richard S Collier, Oxford University Press (2020). © Richard S Collier.
DOI: 10.1093/oso/9780198859673.001.0001

others are external, such as certain features of the market infrastructure or its regulatory framework.

The final section of this chapter compares the nature of misconduct in the banking sector to other business sectors, taking the case of the car industry's 'Dieselgate' as a reference point. The analysis suggests a number of ways in which the banking sector, and particularly misconduct in the banking sector, is unique.

The Incidence of Misconduct in the Banking Sector

Whilst studies addressing the nature and extent of misconduct in the banking industry are almost non-existent, cross-industry reviews of the most serious form of misconduct, namely fraud, are conducted on a regular basis. In such cross-industry studies of fraud, banking features prominently. In 2014, for example, the Association of Certified Fraud Examiners (ACFE) carried out a study of 1500 cases of fraud around the world. Their report reveals that fraud is nearly twice as common in banking as in any other industry.[2] The finding is not particularly surprising given that instances of bank misconduct are reported almost daily in the press and every major bank seems to have been involved in a long litany of misconduct cases.[3]

One possible barometer of the scale of bank misconduct is the level of the fines imposed on banks by regulators. These reflect the extent and seriousness of misconduct by banks, as the fines vary according to the duration of the misconduct, the number of violations, and the amount involved.[4] A recent report estimated those fines that have been incurred since the Global Financial Crisis at a whopping $243 billion.[5]

[2] Association of Certified Fraud Examiners, 'Report to the Nations on Occupational Fraud and Abuse, 2014 Global Fraud Study', available at https://www.acfe.com/rttn/docs/2014-report-to-nations.pdf. Banking frauds represented 17.8 per cent of all frauds considered in the study. The next highest incidence of frauds occurred in the following sectors: government (10.3 per cent), manufacturing (8.5 per cent), healthcare (7.3 per cent), and education (5.9 per cent). The limitation of this study is that the fraud under examination is occupational, defined as 'the use of one's occupation for personal enrichment through the deliberate misuse or misapplication of the employing organization's resources or assets' (Association of Certified Fraud Examiners, 'Report to the Nations', p.6). As such, the study does not enumerate cases where the bank either knowingly, recklessly, or otherwise, permitted systematic fraud to be carried out by its employees against others. It does, however, suggest that banks offer significant opportunities for fraud.

[3] In 2017, the CCP Research Foundation reported on the 'conduct costs' of the world's twenty leading banks between 2012 and 2016. Including provisions for such costs, these banks incurred conduct costs exceeding £264 billion during this period. See the Conduct Costs Project at http://conductcosts.ccpresearchfoundation.com/conduct-costs-results.

[4] See Jon Eisenberg, 'Brother Can You Spare $8.9 Billion? Making Sense of SEC Civil Money Penalties', K&L Gates Legal Insight, 13 February 2014, available at https://www.jdsupra.com/legalnews/brother-can-you-spare-89-billion-maki-87533/.

[5] It is particularly notable, as the report makes clear, that just thirteen banks incurred 93 per cent of the total amount fined. These banks are universal global banks operating in the inter-bank market. They are of particular interest to the subject matter of this book, because it is in that market that many

While banking regulators carry out thematic reviews from time to time (for example, in relation to a whether banks are mis-selling a particular type of financial product), neither the industry nor its regulators normally compile comprehensive statistics on misconduct across the sector, whether domestically or on an international basis. However, from time to time, a particular event may prompt an inquiry into such misconduct in the sector. A recent example of this can be seen in Australia. A number of separate but high-profile instances of misconduct by different Australian banks prompted the government to establish a Royal Commission on banking misconduct in December 2017.[6] The Royal Commission report surveys a wide range of misconduct, including in banking sub-sectors as diverse as mortgage broking, car financing, consumer credit, and credit cards. The misconduct recorded in the report ranges from banks charging fees to customers while in fact providing them with no services at all, to various instances of fraud.[7]

The Australian Royal Commission investigation is relevant to the discussion here for two main reasons. First, it clearly evidences the large scale of the misconduct issue in the banking sector. In the initial stages of the work of the Royal Commission, the Commissioner wrote to a number of banking institutions, including Australia's largest banks, asking for a 'detailed and comprehensive list of all conduct' in the preceding five years that the institution considered amounted to 'misconduct'. Tellingly, two of the banks complained that the task assigned them by the Commissioner was too large and the time allowed too short. While they could not readily assemble a comprehensive list of all relevant cases of misconduct, what did emerge was that each of these large banks had hundreds of incidents of relevant misconduct to report.[8]

A second reason this Australian Royal Commission is relevant is that the Royal Commission highlighted the tendency of the banks to treat incidents of

tax-driven arrangements, such as the cum-ex trade, are implemented. See the report of Michael Chavez in *Forbes*, 31 July 2018, available at https://www.forbes.com/sites/michaelchavez/2018/07/31/the-power-of-purpose-in-financial-services/#361c0152323f.

[6] See Royal Commission into Misconduct in the Banking, Superannuation and Financial Services Industry, 'Final Report', 1 February 2019, available at https://financialservices.royalcommission.gov.au/Pages/reports.aspx#final. The prompt for the Royal Commission included various issues that arose out of the investigation by journalists of mis-selling within the financial planning division of the Commonwealth Bank of Australia, a major Australian bank (see the report of Adele Ferguson of ABC News, Australia, 'Banking Bad', 5 May 2014, transcript available at https://www.abc.net.au/4corners/banking-bad/5433156). In 2015, National Australia Bank (NAB), another large Australian bank, was caught up in a scandal also involving inappropriate financial advice. In 2017, the Australian bank Westpac was alleged to be involved in rigging the Australian bank bill swap rate along with both Australia and New Zealand Banking Group Limited (ANZ) and NAB (see Sarah Danckert, 'Westpac to Fight ASIC Allegations after ANZ, NAB Settle Rate-Rigging Case', *Sydney Morning Herald*, 20 October 2017).

[7] See Royal Commission into Misconduct in the Banking, Superannuation and Financial Services Industry, 'Interim Report', 28 September 2018, Volume 1, at pp. 73, 117, and 171.

[8] Royal Commission, 'Interim Report', Volume 1, pp.7–9.

misconduct as isolated events and so not capture them or attempt to understand them in any comprehensive or systematic way. The Commissioner noted the 'disjointed series of bits of information framed by reference to particular events' provided by two of the banks, indicating that it created a risk that these apparently disparate incidents are recurrently explained as 'a small number of people choosing to behave unethically' or as the product of 'people, policies and processes that existed with a pocket of poor culture in that area at that time'.[9] As discussed in Chapter 5, a similar approach was adopted in Germany in response to cum-ex trades. As noted earlier, this seems to be the usual response in such cases, with the analysis focusing on the conduct of the specific actors and institutions (the 'bad apples') that were directly involved. However, as the Australian Commissioner has warned, this leads to a tendency to see individual cases, even if recurrent or symptomatic across the industry, as confined to their own facts.[10] The same tendency can be seen in a number of recent, and well-known, examples which are discussed briefly below. These examples also reveal a number of important themes that are developed in this chapter.

Wells Fargo

The problems of Wells Fargo & Company[11] have been well publicized.[12] Leading up to 2016, Wells Fargo's US retail bank had implemented a cross-selling scheme within its retail bank. Employees at the bank received sales commissions according to how many accounts were opened for customers. The sales commission was based purely on the *number* of new accounts, not the revenue associated with those accounts. Unsurprisingly, customers were pressured into opening new accounts; existing but unused accounts were left open; and, over time, accounts were simply opened fraudulently by the bank's sales staff in the names of customers. By August 2017, the number of accounts at Wells Fargo which had been opened improperly (or maintained as open when they were no longer required)

[9] Royal Commission, 'Interim Report', Volume 1, p.10.

[10] Royal Commission, 'Interim Report', Volume 1, p.87.

[11] Wells Fargo & Company is an American diversified financial services company headquartered in San Francisco. Information about the company and its banking operations is available at https://www.wellsfargo.com/about/investor-relations/annual-reports/.

[12] The case of Wells Fargo discussed here concerns a single bank and relates to a single jurisdiction. There are also many examples of a single bank being involved in cases of misconduct in multiple jurisdictions. For example, Deutsche Bank's problems in a myriad of schemes which include money laundering, market manipulation, sanction busting, and others are well documented. See, for example, the report of Mayra Rodriguez Valladares, 'Deutsche Bank Needs Serious Laundering', *Forbes*, 7 April 2019, available at https://www.forbes.com/sites/mayrarodriguezvalladares/2019/04/07/deutsche-bank-needs-serious-laundering/#4465c7bd42d4. Another example is the Swiss bank UBS, which is discussed in footnote 2 of Chapter 7.

had risen to 3.5 million.[13] As a result of the affair, the bank paid $185 million in fines and refunded customers $5 million.[14]

The direct cause of the misconduct at Wells is plain to see. A sales incentive system sponsored by the senior management of the bank induced employees to find ways to game the system. Few observers have asked what caused the faulty system of incentives in the first place. The answer to that question is that low revenue growth and narrow profit margins in retail banking had persisted for some years, caused at least in part by low interest rates set by the US Federal Reserve.[15] Retail banks, in order to increase profit, had to either push costs down or find a way of driving revenue up—or both.[16] Industry conditions posed an external set of constraints which the Wells Fargo CEO sought to overcome through the account-opening sales mandate. While that sales commission system was itself poorly structured, it can only be properly understood against the backdrop of highly constrained industry operating conditions.

The case of Wells Fargo demonstrates that difficult industry conditions can drive poor corporate behaviour in an effort to improve financial performance. It also shows that any explanation centred around a small number of 'bad actors' ('bad apples') or 'poor culture' is unconvincing (and at best descriptive rather than causal). The misconduct at Wells was so widespread that such a 'bad apples' theory seems rather implausible: by September 2016, 5,300 employees had been fired for fraudulent sales practices.

LIBOR

A second well-known recent example of banking misconduct concerns the LIBOR scandal which emerged in 2012 and which involved a number of different banks located primarily in one financial centre, namely London. LIBOR, the London Interbank Offered Rate, is the benchmark interest rate from which interest payments on trillions of dollars of financial liabilities around the world are calculated. The rate is set by a number of banks based on an average of the reported rate at which the banks loan money to each other.

[13] See the report of Peter Conti-Brown, 'Why Wells Fargo Might Not Survive Its Fake Accounts Scandal', *Fortune*, 31 August 2017, available at http://fortune.com/2017/08/31/wells-fargo-fake-accounts-scandal-2017-tim-sloan/.

[14] See the report of Matt Egan on CNN Business, '5,300 Wells Fargo employees fired over 2 million phony accounts', 9 September 2016, available at https://money.cnn.com/2016/09/08/investing/wells-fargo-created-phony-accounts-bank-fees/index.html.

[15] Susan McGee, 'Wells Banking Scandal a Crisis We Can Finally Understand', *The Guardian*, 7 October 2016, available at https://www.theguardian.com/business/us-money-blog/2016/oct/07/wells-fargo-banking-scandal-financial-crisis.

[16] McKinsey & Co. 'Retail Banking Insights', March 2015.

During the Global Financial Crisis, there were indications in the press that the banks were not reporting the LIBOR rate correctly.[17] The International Monetary Fund and the Bank for International Settlements, both supranational monetary organizations, issued reports directly contradicting this suggestion.[18] Following the subsequent investigation by the authorities, it turned out that a number of banks had been allegedly misreporting their borrowing rates for years.[19] The direct cause was collusion to manipulate LIBOR by traders responsible for reporting their bank's lending rate. In the case of one bank, its traders had made over 2000 written requests to other banks for alterations in rates from at least January 2005 to at least June 2010.[20] According to transcripts released by the UK's Financial Services Authority, that bank's traders also offered financial inducements to inter-dealer brokers to help manipulate rates by spreading false information. The inter-bank market was therefore also involved.[21]

While collusive conduct was the direct cause of the scandal, it is not, as in the Wells Fargo example, an adequate explanation of the fraud in itself. How and why was it that a large group of people, employed by a number of different banks, were able to cooperate in the fraud in the way that they did and were able to do so for a significant number of years?[22] The motivation becomes more obvious when taking account of the fact that while the LIBOR rate has been used to set market interest rates generally, it was also used to calculate the contractual obligations of the banks themselves.[23] In other words, by underreporting the rates at which they

[17] See the report of Carrick Mollenkamp and Mark Whitehouse, 'Study Casts Doubt on Key Rate', *Wall Street Journal*, 29 May 2008.

[18] See Bank for International Settlements, 'International Banking and Financial Market Developments', *BIS Quarterly Review* (March 2008), p.70, available at https://www.bis.org/publ/qtrpdf/r_qt0803.pdf, and International Monetary Fund, 'Global Stability Report: Financial Stress and Deleveraging', October 2008, p.76, available at https://www.imf.org/en/Publications/GFSR/Issues/2016/12/31/Financial-Stress-and-Deleveraging-Macro-Financial-Implications-and-Policy.

[19] See, for example, the report of Douglas Keenan, 'My Thwarted Attempt to Tell of LIBOR Shenanigans', *Financial Times*, 26 July 2012, available at https://www.ft.com/content/dc5f49c2-d67b-11e1-ba60-00144feabdc0.

[20] See Commodity Futures Trading Commission, 'CFTC Orders UBS to Pay $700 Million Penalty to Settle Charges of Manipulation, Attempted Manipulation and False Reporting of LIBOR and Other Benchmark Interest Rates', CFTC Release Number 6472-12, 19 December 2012, available at https://www.cftc.gov/PressRoom/PressReleases/pr6472-12.

[21] In September 2013, an inter-dealer broker settled allegations that they had manipulated LIBOR. See the report of Kirstin Ridley, Clare Hutchison, and Aruna Viswanatha, 'ICAP Fined $87 Million over LIBOR, Three Former Staff Charged', Reuters, 25 September 2013, available at https://www.reuters.com/article/us-icap-libor/icap-fined-87-million-over-libor-three-former-staff-charged-idUSBRE98O0BX20130925.

[22] The British Banker's Association, a trade association consisting of banks, had as early as 1986 recognized the problem and put in place a process 'formalizing the collection and governance process'. In the thirty years which followed, the collusive conduct hardened into what seems to have been routine behaviour.

[23] The LIBOR scandal may have erupted into public view in the aftermath of the Global Financial Crisis, but the self-referential nature of the LIBOR-setting process had been known for years. In the mid-1980s it was realized that some of the largest borrowers to whose loans the LIBOR applied were the same banks submitting the interest rate used in the LIBOR rate calculation. See Christopher J. Click, 'Death of a Benchmark: The Fall of LIBOR and the Rise of Alternative Rates in the United Kingdom

borrowed, these banks could reduce the cost of funding their own loans. The structure of the market was such that the price of borrowing money was determined by reference to the rate at which major borrowers—the banks themselves—borrowed money. This meant that, not only did the banks control and operate the system of interest rate-setting, they had a further power. They could operate the rate-setting system directly for their own benefit. It therefore seems hardly surprising that this self-referential aspect of the system would be manipulated. Because the rate-setting process was run by the banks, regulators did not, or were not able to, subject that scheme to rigorous control, examination, or challenge.[24] Operating in secret and unchecked by the surveillance of an independent body, it seems inevitable that a cooperative system of rate-setting would devolve into a collusive enterprise which the banks exploited for profit (which is exactly what happened). As in the Wells Fargo case, laying blame for the misconduct at the door of a small number of individual bankers (the relevant 'bad apples')—and possibly also as stemming from a 'weak corporate culture'—seems a rather feeble explanation which neither identifies the root cause of the scandal nor explains how it was carried out, possibly over decades.

The Mortgage Frauds of the Global Financial Crisis

The final example relates to the creation by a large number of banks of vast numbers of new mortgage loans in the run-up to the 2008 Global Financial Crisis.[25] The mortgage business is, of course, a significant revenue stream for banks, particularly when mortgages are 'securitized' (the process by which mortgages are parceled up and transferred into a securitization vehicle which issues tradable bonds to investors, with the return on the bonds based on the underlying return from the mortgages).[26] These bonds date back to the 1970s when United

and the United States', *North Carolina Banking Institute* 22 (2018), 283–307, available at: http://scholarship.law.unc.edu/ncbi/vol22/iss1/16.

[24] The regulatory failure is a point which the LIBOR scandal has in common with the case of cum-ex. There are also other similarities given the widespread inter-bank cooperation to participate, the effective hijacking of the financial system infrastructure, the minimal punishments and sanctions in response to the affair, the role of investigative journalism in highlighting the issues, etc.

[25] The events leading up to the crisis have been examined extensively in literature dealing with the causes of the Global Financial Crisis and so are not pursued here, beyond noting that the mushrooming of credit that is referred to here is widely regarded as being one of the significant causes of that crisis. See, for example, Financial Crisis Inquiry Commission, 'Crisis Inquiry Report: Final Report of the National Commission on the Causes of the Financial and Economic Crisis in the United States', Submitted by The Financial Crisis Inquiry Commission Pursuant to Public Law 111-21', January 2011, available at http://fcic-static.law.stanford.edu/cdn_media/fcic-reports/fcic_final_report_full.pdf.

[26] Banks derive revenues by way of fees on the creation of any mortgage loans and the built-in spreads on the lending. Where mortgages are securitized, the pricing and terms of the bonds also give a

States government-sponsored entities (GSEs) first issued them.[27] Because they were government-sponsored, the GSEs came to be thought of as having the 'implicit' backing of the United States government. Their bonds consequently traded at interest rates approaching those on US government bonds, the least costly interest rate available. The various mortgage frauds in the run-up to the Global Financial Crisis were to a large extent concerned with the securitization of mortgages as described above.

This chain of mortgage security issuance running from the highly-rated GSEs through the banks and down to the lower credit rating of the individual mortgage borrower represented a stair-step sequence of declines in credit quality. In an open competitive market and in the absence of securitization, these changes in credit quality would be reflected in the cost of financing applicable to each participant in the mortgage loan and bond creation chain. Instead, the GSEs, carrying the implicit backing of the US government, purchased and guaranteed pools of mortgages and issued bonds at interest rates approaching those of the government itself. In other words, the effect of the implied government backing of the GSEs acted like a gravitational force on the mortgage market, pulling all the interest rates along the chain down towards the sovereign borrowing rate. That created a set of *differences* between the lending terms which would prevail in a free market and those which could exist in the government-sponsored market. These were differences conferred upon the mortgage market by government action, in effect a privilege which the banks could and did exploit.

Through continual innovation in packaging up mortgages into structures which achieved the highest rating, money could be loaned to (and therefore revenues generated from) an ever-expanding population of homeowners who could borrow at rates which would, absent the government effectively co-signing the mortgage loan, not be available to them. Banks, as well as other mortgage market participants, were able to extract fees for their involvement in each step of the chain, with the GSE scheme meaning that loans could be made to borrowers of increasingly lower credit quality. In the presence of an implied government guarantee, obtaining proof of borrower income or other qualification to obtain financing became perfunctory steps. By the time of the Global Financial Crisis,

further opportunity for a bank to generate revenues in the form of fees and monetized spreads. The process of securitization is described in more detail later in this chapter.

[27] The first mortgage bonds emerged when the Government National Mortgage Association ('Ginnie Mae'), a US government-sponsored entity (GSE), first sold securities the return on which was backed by mortgages. While the banks would originate the mortgages to homeowners and package them up into bonds, the GSEs would purchase those bonds. To finance that purchase, the GSEs would themselves issue bonds to investors such as pension funds. Ginnie Mae was sponsored by the government to both increase the flow of credit to the housing market and to lower the cost of that credit.

banks were originating 'liar loans' based on little to no proof of borrower income at all.[28]

It was not simply financial engineering by the banks which transformed individual borrowers' mortgages into highly-rated bonds. The fragmented nature of the regulatory regime was also an important factor. For example, as state regulators attempted to impose restrictions on mortgage lenders who offered higher-risk mortgages to homeowners, some banks simply surrendered their state lending licences. Instead, to carry out riskier mortgage lending, they relied on their federal banking charters, whose rules were laxer.[29]

The mortgage scandal also demonstrates how banks are able to overcome constraints in the market to suit their ends. For example, rising house prices strained affordability by buyers. The simple response to this constraint from the banks was to relax the credit terms of the mortgages. The banks also modified the market itself, creating new mortgage products to lower initial mortgage payments.[30] The result was mortgages with much higher default risk, though this did not prevent the banks from finding a way of packaging them up into securities and selling them. Lower-rated tranches of mortgage securities which could not easily be sold to investors were themselves pooled together and used as the collateral for yet further tranches of mortgage securities, known as collateralized debt obligations (CDOs). Structured in the right way, these securities could achieve investment grade credit ratings much higher than the credit of the underlying borrowers.[31] Further restructuring was employed by the banks when the GSEs, by virtue of their government-sponsored charter, refused to purchase mortgage bonds backed by borrowers who made low down-payments on their home purchases. The banks responded by innovating the problem away: with a 'piggyback' mortgage, the bank could offer a first mortgage to the value of 80 per cent of the property and a second mortgage for a further 10–20 per cent. This meant that the first mortgages could then be packaged up and sold to the GSEs. These examples show how the banks could and did innovate rapidly to change the nature of the market itself.[32]

[28] Financial Crisis Inquiry Commission, 'Crisis Inquiry Report', p.9.

[29] Financial Crisis Inquiry Commission, 'Crisis Inquiry Report', p.113.

[30] Adjustable-rate mortgages (ARMs) and negative amortization mortgages (NegAm) were among the products of that financial innovation.

[31] Achieving the right ratings on bonds was critical to the process. The agencies setting the criteria by which ratings were judged were themselves regulated by the SEC, itself a branch of the government. The amount of capital banks had to hold against their proprietary risk on mortgage securities in their possession was tied to the mortgage securities' ratings. Investors also depended on the ratings, with many pension funds being forbidden from buying securities with sub-investment-grade ratings.

[32] Government had an important role in financial regulation, which assisted banks directly in originating and securitizing mortgage bonds. In November 2003, the SEC introduced the Consolidated Entity Supervision (CES) programme. In brief, the effect of the programme was to allow certain federally regulated banks to opt into a new regime for calculating the capital which they were required to hold against their holdings in securities. The CES had the effect of permitting banks to calculate their own regulatory capital requirements using internal models. Capital

While the banks' process of innovating and industrializing mortgage securities iteratively lowered the credit quality of borrowers, weakened the mortgage market, and contributed materially to the Global Financial Crisis, those outcomes are not the subject of this book.[33] What is important for current purposes is that the various instances of the pre-Crisis mortgage misconduct by banks provide a compelling example not only of the ability of banks both to exploit differences in fractured markets and regulatory regimes but also to modify the characteristics of the market in which they themselves conduct business.

The above three examples suggest that, far from being isolated incidents of misconduct, many cases of banking misconduct are best understood as the practically inevitable outcomes of a set of conditions which prevail in the banking industry. The next section of this chapter seeks to explore how banks have, over time, changed the way in which they operate, and in the process contributed to the creation of that set of conditions.

Transformation of the Banking Business Model

The previous section has shown that the incidence of misconduct is a frequent feature of the business carried on by banks. The discussion which follows considers why this is true.

The hypothesis put forward by this book is that cum-ex and similar schemes are not random 'accidents' or anomalies that are the consequence of the behaviour of individual 'bad apples' employed by the banks. Rather, the discussion below advances the view that they are a direct consequence of the nature of the existing financial system and, in particular, an inevitable result from a number of factors, of which two critical factors are considered below. These are: (1) the current business model operated by banks; and (2) the weaknesses of the relevant control and governance structures that apply to banks.[34] These issues are discussed in turn, though it will be helpful (and relevant) to preface the discussion of the transformation of the banking business model with a brief survey of the wider changes that have taken place in the financial markets more generally. As will be

requirements fell by an average of 40 per cent as a consequence, meaning that with the same amount of capital in the bank's business it could lend even more.

[33] Arguably, a particularly low point of the banks' approach to this market is reflected in the period prior to the financial crisis when banks were creating more mortgage loans to borrowers of ever poorer credit quality so that they and their clients could short those same bonds, benefiting from a decline in their price as they went into default. See, for example, the report of Gretchen Morgenson and Louise Story, 'Banks Bundled Bad Debt, Bet Against it and Won', *New York Times*, December 23 2009, available at https://www.nytimes.com/2009/12/24/business/24trading.html.

[34] A third factor, the powers and privileges enjoyed by banks, is considered later in the book.

seen, cum-ex and other schemes like it have been facilitated by the consequences of this sea change in the banking business environment.[35]

Shifts in the Financial Sector Environment

The business of banking, and the financial system in which banks operate, is virtually unrecognizable from the banking industry that prevailed some forty to fifty years ago. There are many changes that have radically transformed the banking sector in recent years, but in this context three formative themes are of particular relevance. These are: (1) shifts in thinking on the nature, operation, and purpose of financial markets, specifically as reflected in certain academic developments in the 1970s; (2) changes in the political climate which gave rise to economic policies which embraced much of this academic thinking; and (3) a number of technical, product, and legal innovations which transformed the nature and capabilities of financial products and the means by which such products could be traded.

With regard to shifts in academic thinking on the nature, operation, and purpose of financial markets, there were various lines of thinking on economic theory that emerged in the period leading up to the late 1970s. This included the proposition that the capital markets were the efficient means of the optimal allocation of resources, between economic agents and over time, because prices perfectly reflected all available information.[36] There was also the more general idea that markets, left to operate relatively unfettered by government, would not only be more productive but would generate higher returns (in the form of taxation yields and higher employment) for government.[37] Detailed technical work was

[35] Given the enormous scale of change that has taken place over this period, the discussion here is inevitably summarized. This section therefore deals in very brief terms with the evolution of the business of banking and financial markets, yet that transformation might more appropriately be contained in one or more books on the topic. For a more detailed treatment of the themes discussed here, see John Kay, *Other People's Money* (Profile Books, 2016) and (in the context of an analysis of the financial crisis) Engelen et al., *After the Great Complacence*—see in particular Chapter 4, 'Banks Misunderstood'. A more detailed historical analysis is available in Youssef Cassis, Richard Grossman, and Catherine Schenk, *The Oxford Handbook of Banking and Financial History* (Oxford University Press, 2016).

[36] See, for example, E. F. Fama, 'Efficient Capital Markets: A Review of Theory and Empirical Work', *Journal of Finance* 25:2 (1970), 383–417, and E. F. Fama and M. Miller, *The Theory of Finance*, (Holt, Rinehart and Winston, 1972).

[37] For example, in 1970, Milton Friedman wrote a renowned article arguing that businesses with a 'social conscience' are less competitive and put shareholders' profits at risk. See Milton Friedman, 'The Social Responsibility of Business Is to Increase its Profits', *New York Times*, 13 September 1970, 32. Arguments that markets should not be unduly fettered claimed support from the theory expounded by the supply-side economist Arthur Laffer to demonstrate the concept of taxable income elasticity, i.e. the more an activity is taxed, the less of it will take place (The 'Laffer curve' sought to demonstrate that as tax rates rose, tax revenues increased, but only up to a certain high point, after which high tax rates would cause tax revenues to decline). See Arthur Laffer and Jan Seymour, *The Economics of the Tax Revolt: A Reader* (Harcourt Brace Jovanovich, 1976).

undertaken on the interrelationship between risk and return in the form of modern portfolio theory which meant that risks associated with pools of assets could in theory at least be measured, priced, and sold.[38] Finally, there were also significant developments relating to corporate finance policy and equity valuation,[39] as well as significant developments in the understanding of how complex financial products such as options and other derivatives could be priced.[40] Collectively, these theories pointed to the benefits of financial innovation (the broad notion that includes everything that makes markets more efficient and/or extends their sphere of influence to deliver higher growth)[41] and to the need for financial and capital markets to be as extensive and as integrated as possible. The theory was that the larger the number of participants in financial markets, the greater the liquidity and therefore the greater the efficiency with which they could allocate economic resources. In short, these theories came together to form a roadmap for the expansion of financial and capital markets, the removal of restrictions constraining the operation and integration of those markets, and the differentiation and proliferation of financial products on a global scale.

While the above strands of new thinking on the role of markets were theoretical and abstract, they were taken up at a political level as a policy prescription in the territories of the world's two biggest financial markets, the US and the UK.[42] This thinking found its expression in the supply-side economic policies expressed and instituted through the 1980s by Ronald Reagan in the US and Margaret Thatcher in the UK. They envisioned a new economic order, opening up market

[38] The early development of modern portfolio theory (the use of mathematical models to designate a portfolio of assets with a maximized expected return for a given level of risk) is often attributed to H. Markowitz, 'Portfolio Selection', *Journal of Finance* 7 (1952), 77–91 and W.F. Sharpe, 'Capital Asset Prices: A Theory of Market Equilibrium Under Risk', *Journal of Finance* 33 (1964), 425–42.

[39] Developments on corporate finance policy and equity valuation stem from the work of Modigliani and Miller on capital structure and dividend policy choices. See Franco Modigliani and Merton Miller, 'The Cost of Capital, Corporation Finance, and The Theory of Investment', *American Economic Review* 48 (1958), 267–97 and Merton Miller and Franco Modigliani, 'Dividend Policy, Growth, and the Valuation of Shares', *Journal of Business* 34 (1961), 411–33.

[40] On how complex financial products such as options and other derivatives could be priced, see for example F. Black and M. Scholes, 'The Pricing of Options and Corporate Liabilities', *Journal of Political Economy* 81:3 (1973), 637–54 and R.C. Merton, 'The Theory of Rational Option Pricing', *Bell Journal of Economics and Management Science* 4:1 (1973), 141–83. Together, the developments discussed here played a major role in the development of financial economics which would later pave the way for the development of 'Var' or Value at Risk, a metric to measure the level of financial risk within a firm, though this emerged in 1990s—see Philippe Jorion, *Value at Risk, The New Benchmark for Managing Financial Risk*, 3rd edition (McGraw Hill, 2007).

[41] P.L. Bernstein, *Capital Ideas: The Improbable Origins of Modern Wall Street* (The Free Press, 1992).

[42] In the US, the Treasury Report of 1991 and the Financial Services Modernization Act of 1999 encouraged these developments, as did the 1986 Financial Services Act in the UK. Other countries also encouraged the development of their financial markets on the basis of the expected contribution to the local economy. The European Union's Second Banking Directive of 1989 encouraged universal banking in its member states, and in Japan the Financial Services Agency's Financial Reform Programme had similar aims—see the discussion in Engelen et al., *After the Great Complacence*, at pp.100–1.

mechanisms to create jobs and wealth with the goal of thereby boosting the economy.[43] The policy prescription was that markets, if left broadly unfettered, could unlock capital and resources and deliver socially optimal outcomes in the form of both an increase in general prosperity and a higher tax base. It followed that whatever stood in the way of the free operation of capitalism was an impediment to be set aside.[44] A wave of deregulation followed in the two largest financial markets in the world, centred in New York and London.[45]

Although the growth and liberalization of global financial markets had support from these academic and political circles, a number of technical, financial product, and legal developments were critical catalysts for the change. Chief of these was a revolution in information and communication technologies. This also began in the 1970s: Intel released the first programmable microprocessor,[46] the first email was sent,[47] and the Ethernet (an early form of the Internet) was first developed.[48] These innovations, which gathered pace through the 1980s and 1990s, meant that rapid and efficient global communications, the processing of very large numbers of transactions, and the computing power for complex risk calculations, all became possible. They also opened the door to remote screen-based electronic trading.

In both wholesale and retail markets, new products, services, and distribution channels, combined with new techniques for pricing and risk management, to rapidly and radically transform financial markets. Derivatives markets emerged in the late 1970s and early 1980s in response to the lifting of exchange controls,

[43] The thinking on the theory of rational and efficient markets therefore became an imperative in the development of economic policy and formed part of a wider initiative to reconstruct political, social, and economic institutions from the late 1970s in the image of a deregulated system of free-market capitalism.

[44] The belief in the power of this free-market thinking can be seen most clearly in the execution of two actions an ocean apart, which were both politically sensitive. The Professional Air Traffic Organization (PATCO) in the United States, a union of air traffic controllers, declared a strike in August 1981. When they refused to return to work after three days, President Reagan fired 11,345 of them. In the UK, three years later, Margaret Thatcher took on the striking trade unions and defeated them. For a more detailed discussion, see the report of Paul Wilenius for the BBC on Friday 5 March 2004, available at http://news.bbc.co.uk/1/hi/3067563.stm.

[45] Significant reforms included the Financial Services Act 1986 in the UK and the ongoing erosion of the Glass–Steagall Act in the US.

[46] The Intel 4004, the first general-purpose programmable processor was released in 1971. See 'The Story of the Intel 4004', available at https://www.intel.co.uk/content/www/uk/en/history/museum-story-of-intel-4004.html.

[47] Ray Tomlinson sent the first email on the US Government network, ARPANET in 1971. See the report of Sarah Skidmore Sell, 'Ray Tomlinson: Programmer Who Invented the Email System and Chose the @ Symbol to Connect Senders and Addresses', *The Independent*, 7 March 2016, available at https://www.independent.co.uk/news/obituaries/ray-tomlinson-programmer-who-invented-the-email-system-and-chose-the-symbol-to-connect-senders-and-a6917536.html.

[48] Ethernet, the first widely accepted networking standard allowing computers to interconnect on a local area network was developed at Xerox's Palo Alto Research Center in 1972. Charles E. Spurgeon, 'Ethernet: The Definitive Guide', available at https://www.oreilly.com/library/view/ethernet-the-definitive/1565926609/ch01.html. Widespread public use of the Internet by the public did not develop until the early 1990s.

deregulation and globalization of markets, and the developments in information technology described above.[49] The result was not only an array of new (and often interchangeable) financial derivative products[50] but also an expansion in the rise of complex structured finance techniques and related securities (such as structured notes)[51] and the more extensive use of certain financial contracts such as stock lending and repo.[52] Another very significant factor which is highly relevant to the discussion in both this chapter and the next was the new-found ability to securitize and trade previously illiquid financial assets such as loans.

The securitization process which, as discussed earlier, lay at the heart of the Global Financial Crisis, is important because it enables assets such as bank loans which would otherwise be illiquid and bilateral to be made economically liquid and transferable by transforming them into a tradable product. This is achieved by the process of pooling such illiquid assets under the ownership of a separate legal vehicle which issues securities or tranches of securities, the return on which is linked to the return on the underlying 'securitized' assets. The newly-issued securities can then be sold and traded in the market. The basic structure is illustrated in Figure 6.1.

The securitization process is considered to lead to a broader distribution of risks across the financial system, thus reducing the risk of market failure from traditional banking, for example, stemming from the mismatch between long-term and illiquid assets in the form of loans made on the one hand and overnight and liquid liabilities, for example, bank deposits, on the other.[53] The securitization

[49] Derivatives in some form can be traced to the fourth millennium BC. See E.J. Weber, 'A Short History of Derivative Security Markets', in W. Hafner and H. Zimmermann, eds, *Vinzenz Bronzin's Option Pricing Models* (Springer, 2009), 431–66. Though derivatives have existed for some considerable time, the way in which they are now traded and used has changed considerably in the modern era. The real growth in the derivatives markets began in the mid-1980s. There are now trillion-dolllar markets in derivatives (such as futures and forwards, options and swaps) relating to currencies, commodities (such as oil and gas), financial assets, interest rates, share and other indices, creditworthiness, etc. The nominal value of derivatives outstanding is many times greater than value of underlying securities they might have hedged. A raft of BIS triennial and regular OTC derivatives market statistics showing the enormous size of derivative markets is available at https://www.bis.org/statistics/derstats.htm. A thorough discussion of the nature and uses of derivatives is available in Satyajit Das, *Swaps and Financial Derivatives*, 3rd edition (John Wiley, 2004).

[50] For instance, the Chicago Mercantile Exchange launched futures contracts written on financial instruments in 1972 and the Chicago Board of Trade introduced the first interest rate futures contracts in 1975. A more recent example is the emergence of credit derivative contracts and a bourgeoning credit derivatives market from the mid to late 1990s.

[51] A structured note is a debt obligation (usually a tradable security) that contains some form of embedded derivative component that adjusts the risk/return profile and associated cash flows of the instrument.

[52] The nature of stock lending has been discussed in Chapter 1. A repurchase or 'repo' transaction is structured in a broadly similar manner (meaning that securities are transferred from the owner to an interim owner before equivalent securities are later transferred back to the original owner), but these are normally entered into as a financing transaction, the 'sale' price of the securities normally constituting the amount of the loan, with the transferred securities held as collateral.

[53] International Monetary Fund, 'Global Financial Stability Report, April 2006'. The same argument could apply generally to structured financial products on the basis that these products could package

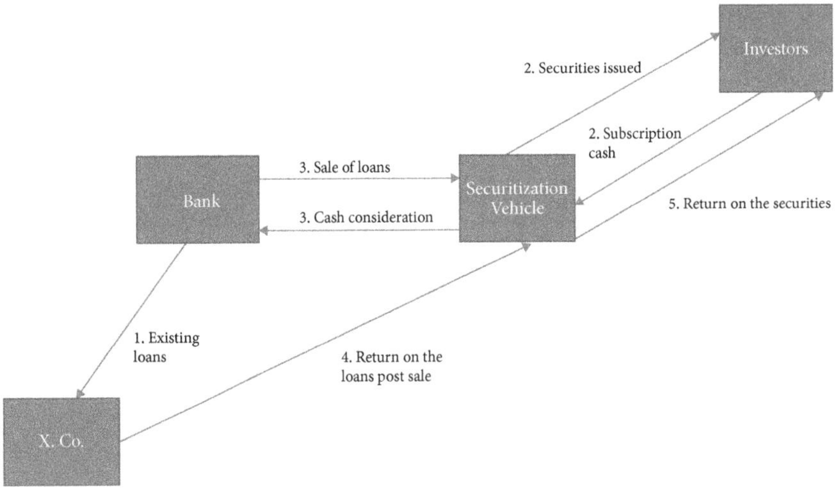

Figure 6.1. Securitization

process also enables banks to lay off risk by packaging up assets (e.g. loans) into securities and selling them off to investors freeing up capital to be redeployed in the making of further loans.[54] Legal innovations have also played an important role. As the markets grew and became global, the use of New York and English law as the governing law of choice for financial products and transactions became the norm.[55] The contracts for numerous traded financial instruments were standardized both in their terms and in their adoption of one of these governing laws. This fostered a better market-wide understanding of the rights and obligations attaching to those products, promoting confidence in their broader acceptance and accounting treatment.[56] The overall result is that it became much easier to originate and trade these products in the financial markets.

up, hive off, and embed risk in securities and other contracts whose future performance could be modelled and therefore priced, giving rise to an efficient distribution of risk across the financial markets.

[54] A further argument in support of the securitization process was the claim that it led to social improvement through liquidity creation and a market for trading obligations which would otherwise be bilateral in nature between lender and borrower. This was on the basis that it led to the creation of more loans for more people, enabling further consumption or investment. See European Parliament, 'Understanding Securitisation: Background – Benefits – Risks' (European Parliamentary Research Service, October 2015), available at http://www.europarl.europa.eu/RegData/etudes/IDAN/2015/569017/EPRS_IDA%282015%29569017_EN.pdf.

[55] Technically, references to UK law should be understood as references to the law of England and Wales and references to US law means the law of the State of New York, which is the US jurisdiction most commonly used in international financial transactions.

[56] The standardization of financial products does not apply in all cases, but there are important areas where market-standard documentation has become the market norm. For example, 'ISDA' (International Swaps and Derivatives Association) documentation is normally used in relation to derivatives contracts, 'GMSLA' (Global Master Securities Lending Association) documentation will

Collectively, these developments have transformed markets in financial products around the world, initially laying the foundations for, and then delivering, an integrated global system.[57] The process by which this has occurred since the mid-1970s has been described as one of 'financialization', meaning that financial considerations have occupied a position of increasing importance and influence over the behaviour of banks, corporates, and individuals during this period.[58] A consequence of the market reforms was an influx of new players in the financial markets, but the reforms also resulted in some smaller players going out of business or being combined into larger firms.[59] The volume of international transactions, as well as the opening up of new markets, has burgeoned.[60]

Impact on the Banking Sector Business Model

The innovations discussed above relating to academic thinking, political policy, and information technology, financial products, and law have had a wide range of effects on the financial markets in general and the banking sector in particular. The focus here is on their impact on the banking business model.

In the traditional banking business model, which prevailed until at least the 1970s, banks acted as intermediaries. In creating credit (in the form of simple loans), they entered into arrangements to connect the surplus cash of depositors with the funding requirements of borrowers. This business model is usually

often be used for securities lending transactions, and 'GMRA' (Global Master Repurchase Agreement) for repo agreements.

[57] This has led to the breakdown of separate or 'compartmentalized' markets and their replacement by the 'transnationalism' of bond, equity, and derivative markets—see Engelen et al., *After the Great Complacence*, at p.49.

[58] See, for example, Kay, *Other People's Money*, Part I.

[59] For example, the US banking group J. P. Morgan has acquired or merged with the UK investment bank Cazenove, the US securities dealer Bear, Stearns, and the US bank Chase Manhatten. Likewise, the US Citigroup has acquired the US brokerage firm Smith Barney, the insurance group Travelers (though this was later spun off in 2002), Salomon Brothers (a bond dealer and investment bank), Shearson Lehman (a retail brokerage and asset-management firm), Morgan Stanley wealth management, and Banamex (the second-largest bank in Mexico).

[60] As early as 1986, the US Central Intelligence Agency remarked on this rapid growth in international finance, noting '... foreign exchange transactions now exceed $100 billion per day; interbank deposits stood at $1.4 trillion last year, twice the 1981 level...'—see United States Government Directorate of Intelligence, 'Globalization of Financial Markets: Implications, Vulnerabilities and Opportunities', October 1986, at p.(iii), declassified in part, available at https://www.cia.gov/library/readingroom/docs/CIA-RDP87T01127R001100940003-0.pdf. These numbers were dwarfed by the later growth in the global derivatives market, which, in less than a decade, expanded in terms of the notional value of transactions outstanding from $87 trillion in June 1998 to $454 trillion in June 2006—see Stephanie Curcuru, 'U.S. Cross-Border Derivatives Data: A User's Guide' (United States Treasury Board Division of International Finance, May 2007), available at https://ticdata.treasury.gov/Publish/frbulmay2007.pdf. As at June 2018, this number stands at $595 trillion—see Bank for International Settlements, 'Statistical Release: OTC Derivatives Statistics at End June 2018', 31 October 2018, available at https://www.bis.org/publ/otc_hy1810.pdf.

referred to as the 'originate to hold' model of banking.[61] Under this model, the bank would originate loans and fund them using deposits, extracting profit from its relationships with both the depositor and the creditor (borrower) over time. That profit would be taken in the form of a 'spread' or margin, reflecting the difference between the loan interest received from the creditor and the loan interest paid to the depositor. Critically, the bank would act in the role of the lender from origination through to maturity of the loan. The model meant that the original decision to make the loan remained, over the life of the loan, directly relevant for the bank given that any default by the creditor to repay the loan would have an immediate and negative financial impact on the bank. This explains the traditional importance of the customer relationship and the bank's knowledge of its customers developed through local ties, etc. The simple nature of the traditional banking intermediation model therefore bound the fortunes of a bank to the loans it originated. This inevitably meant that the activity of the bank was necessarily limited by the amount of capital which the bank had at its disposal to originate new loans. It also meant that the profitability of the bank would be limited by available spreads on lending business.[62]

Over the last half century, nearly everything related to this business model that could change has changed, including both the scale and the manner in which banks carry out their core business of lending.[63] In the UK, the Financial Services

[61] See David T. Llewellyn 'Fifty Years in the Evolution of Bank Business Models', in Morten Balling and Ernest Gnan, eds, *Fifty Years of Money and Finance—Lessons and Challenges* (Suerf, 2013), 319–54, available at https://www.suerf.org/books-and-colloquium-volumes/217/50-years-of-money-and-finance-lessons-and-challenges.

[62] Given that a bank's sources of funding and capital were limited, revenues and profits were consequently constrained. The model was therefore inherently self-limiting.

[63] The discussion of banking business models here describes a significant shift which represented a broad tendency rather than a change that applied to all the loan transactions of every single bank, irrespective of the bank's size and market. There were in practice different business models operated by different types of entity and these would have been affected in different ways by the increasing importance of the trading-based business model discussed here. For example, some investment banks shifted the focus of their business from deriving fee income on mergers and acquisitions business and from arranging the issuance of equity and bonds to put much greater emphasis on proprietary trading. The universal banks shifted from longer-term margin business to the 'originate to distribute' model (discussed below), also with a focus on proprietary trading. Many of the investment banks and universal banks would later also set up hedge funds and private equity funds and/or businesses such as 'prime brokerage' that were designed to meet the trade financing needs and operational/infrastructure requirements of hedge funds. Some of the smaller retail banks resisted major changes to their traditional business model. What is discussed here is therefore the general trend towards the adoption of a trading model by the banks. A good example of this general tendency is provided by the activities of the German Landesbanks, the regional state-owned banks whose role was traditionally restricted to wholesale markets lending to support the domestic German banking industry. Many of these Landesbanks adopted an essentially trading-based model and took on significant additional leverage and traded/invested in highly structured assets, including complex derivatives products. As a result of the Global Financial Crisis, many of these banks suffered catastrophic losses and had to be bailed out by the German state. See Laura Noonan, 'The Landesbanken: Inside Germany's Trillion Euro Banking Blind Spot', Reuters, 17 September 2013, available at https://www.reuters.com/article/us-banking-germany-landesbanken/the-landesbanken-inside-germanys-trillion-euro-banking-blind-spot-idUSBRE98G06720130917?feedType=RSS&feedName=topNews.

Act of 1986 and, in the US, the erosion and later final abolition of Glass–Steagall in the United States[64] meant that the way was opened up for a bank—at single-entity level—to be involved in a broad range of transactions concerning financial products. This could include not just the traditional role of deposit-taking and lending but a wide range of other activity including trading in financial instruments such as equities and bonds, share-broking, writing and trading derivatives, creating and trading structured products, etc. Further, banks became entitled to participate in these markets not only in the capacity of acting for their clients (broking) but also on their own behalf (dealing), originating and trading principal risk as a proprietary trader.[65]

These developments, which led to a general rise in the significance of proprietary trading by banks, had a significant impact on the banking business model. Making a loan or 'originating' it and then, rather than holding it to maturity, selling it off became possible on a significant scale. This possibility was opened up by the theoretical and practical innovations that have been discussed above and, in particular, by the ability to securitize a loan (or a portfolio of loans) described earlier.[66] To the bank, there were some important benefits to this ability to securitize loans. By selling off its loans immediately after making them, the bank could realize (and book in its accounts) the sale price for the loan, which would include the profits associated with the future revenue stream from those loans.[67] Further, the bank's own funding requirements for any loan that was securitized would fall away, meaning the bank's balance sheet would be freed up to permit new loan business or other transactions. The costs of monitoring and administering the loan might be transferred to a mortgage-servicing company and also saved.

If banks could be described as acting in the role of intermediaries at all under this new model, they became at best impermanent intermediaries. This 'originate to distribute' model meant that the credit relationship between the bank and its

[64] The Glass–Steagall Act, which imposed the complete separation of commercial banking and investment banking, was originally enacted in 1933 in the wake of the of the banking crises in the 1920s and early 1930s. In 1999 Congress passed the Gramm–Leach–Bliley Act, also known as the Financial Services Modernization Act of 1999, to repeal the law. Prior to its abolition in 1999, there had already been various incremental changes, starting in the 1960s, which had the effect of eroding the limitations imposed by Glass–Steagall. See Oonagh McDonald, 'The Repeal of the Glass–Steagall Act: Myth and Reality', Policy Analysis No. 804 (Cato Institute, November 2016), available at https://www.cato.org/publications/policy-analysis/repeal-glass-steagall-act-myth-reality.

[65] Hence the term 'broker-dealer', which denotes the two capacities in which such an entity may engage.

[66] Portfolio theory laid the theoretical groundwork for this securitization, computing power enabled the necessary financial modelling to be conducted on the portfolio's expected behaviour (including expected defaults, etc) to determine its financial value, and the global distribution networks operated or accessed by the banks enabled the securities to be sold to investors around the world. Different classes of security, with different rights and entitlements to income, could also be created based on the underlying 'securitized' loans.

[67] In very broad terms, the profit would be derived from the net present value of the spread or margin on the loans over their expected life.

borrowing customer from origination to maturity of the loan, which was central to the predecessor 'originate to hold' model, diminished greatly in importance. As a transactional business model which existed to generate a steady stream of profits for the bank from the process of distribution, the new 'originate to distribute' model became inherently bank-centric rather than, as formerly, customer-centric: the primacy of what was once the bank's 'customer' gave way to the 'counterparties' with whom it would sell securities and lay off its risk.[68] The implications of the new model were that transactions entered into by the bank would have a different risk profile than its former long-duration credit relationships, in the sense that once the loan or other product is wrapped up into a security and sold off to a counterparty it becomes the risk of that buyer. This in turn means that the focus of the bank's internal product risk management must correspondingly change. The customer looking for credit becomes a vehicle or means to an end, that end being to originate the loan and consummate its sale. The efforts of the bank thus become relatively more directed to the short-term outcome of selling the loan off to a counterparty (a successfully closed deal) than the ongoing process over the life of the loan of managing the customer (a successful long-term relationship).

A bank that relies on a flow of transactions for its revenue will inevitably have a different culture to one operating under the traditional 'originate to hold' model, as the latter is relationship-based. Central to the 'originate to distribute' model is the need for transactional flow and volume. This in turn creates a continual need to generate more transactions/sales, meaning that the bank becomes committed to a perpetual transaction-based business model for immediate profit, and with a strong preference for volume-based business to maximize shorter-term profits. The operation of this model is assisted where the bank has a significant geographical scale of operation and the ability to constantly innovate. Geographical scale is important because it allows the bank to sell the widest variety of products (in industry parlance, 'reach') in the largest possible physical domain ('footprint'), with the largest possible number of customers ('wallet'). This accounts for the rise of the universal bank with multiple business lines and the importance within a bank of cross-selling between its products.[69] The ability to innovate is significant because it leads to the rapid development of new financial products and markets.[70]

[68] It is also true that the connection of the retail and wholesale markets through the securitization model reduced the importance for funding of a bank's retail deposit base. This was because the securitization of assets and access to the inter-bank market gave new funding opportunities to the bank.

[69] The 'poster child' for the creation of a 'supermarket' global bank providing the widest range of financial products was arguably created by the Citicorp merger with Travelers in 1998, creating the largest financial services organization at the time, with operations in 100 countries. See the *New York Times* report by Martin Mitchell, 'Citicorp and Travelers Plan to Merge in Record $70 Billion Deal: A New No. 1: Financial Giants Unite', 7 April 1998.

[70] The innovation process can be, and often is, speedy because, essentially, banks create, process, and trade contractual *claims*. Given that the financial product is essentially a legal/contractual construct

It became important for a bank to be able to combine these two features in what may be termed a 'scalable differentiation' to generate volume revenues, achieved by an assembly line of new financial products combined with an ability to upscale and distribute them.

By the time of the 2007–8 Global Financial Crisis, the business model of international banks was arguably a real-world expression of the theory of capital markets articulated decades earlier by the Chicago School economist Eugene Fama:[71] nearly anything that had a cash flow associated with it could now be packaged up into a security and sold off. Anything which could be assigned a daily price could be the subject of a tradable contract, such as a derivative or other structured transaction.[72] However, as each new market or product became established and new participants came to join the process of 'financialization' and globalization, there was a strong tendency for financial-services businesses and their products to become commoditized, leading to falling returns as each new endeavour or product became gradually saturated by transactional volume.[73] Nonetheless, the process of saturation can be mitigated where there are differences that may be built into financial product design which have a direct impact on product pricing.[74] The greater the number of such differences, and the more they are complex and opaque, the greater the opportunities (that are not easily saturated by competitor activity across the market) for the bank and its customers. Such differences might be created based on a wide variety of factors such as those relating to specific sectoral characteristics, local regulation, exchange control

which governs cash flows and other rights and obligations, banks can innovate at speed through the process of the legal design of contracts.

[71] See further footnote 36 in this chapter.

[72] The Global Financial Crisis beginning in 2008 had the effect of drastically slowing rather than stopping this process. In 2007, immediately prior to the crisis, the volume of securitizations carried out in the United States was approximately $11 trillion. In Europe it was €595 billion. By 2015, these had fallen to $1.9 trillion and €214 billion, respectively. The fall-off in volume was widely attributed to a loss of confidence in a market which had been at the centre of the mortgage scandal. See Steven L. Schwarcz, 'Securitization Ten Years after the Financial Crisis: An Overview', *Review of Banking and Financial Law* 37:2 (2018), 757–69, available at https://papers.ssrn.com/sol3/papers.cfm?abstract_id=3169839. The response to the crisis by regulators was to subject securitizations to significant new regulation. Nevertheless, new securitization issuance continued to recover, such that global issuance volume had by 2018 increased 50 per cent over 2015 volumes. See Tom Schopflocher et al., 'Global Structured Finance 2019 Securitization Energized with $1T in Volume', S&P Global Ratings report, 7 January 2019, available at https://www.spglobal.com/en/research-insights/articles/global-structured-finance-outlook-2019-securitization-continues-to-be-energized-with-potential-1-trillion-in-volume-expected-ag.

[73] Witness, for example, the ever-falling cost of commissions to trade shares, culminating with the recent launch of robinhood, a financial technology firm offering an app through which share trading is commission free—see https://robinhood.com/. The phenomenon of falling margins has also been exacerbated by the decline in nominal interest rates from the 1990s.

[74] The example of banks paying millions of dollars for access to a line which made arbitrage between New York and Chicago faster by reducing 'latency', the time between placing a transaction and its execution, by three milliseconds is featured in Michael Lewis, *Flash Boys* (Penguin, 2015).

regimes, accounting rules, or, as is explained further below, tax differences.[75] Financial products based on these kinds of bespoke characteristics would be attractive to a bank because the product created might be very attractive to its customers and, for a time at least, not easily replicable by its competitors.

The purpose of this brief survey of the evolution of the modern bank business model and its restless preoccupation with generating new transactional business is now evident. The modern bank must constantly seek out new and varied types of business if it is to both grow and remain profitable. Any financial instrument or aspect of the financial system which features some difference, whether in terms of timing, location, or embedded characteristic will be scrutinized as a potential source of new business. It is in this context that tax systems can be understood as potentially offering fertile ground for a bank in relation to the exploitation in financial products of differences which are both systemic and systematic. A single country will typically have multiple types of taxes within a single tax system, comprising income taxes, taxes on capital gains, withholding taxes, stamp and transfer taxes, turnover taxes, etc. Though there may be some general features that are common in tax systems from country to country (or, exceptionally, taxes such as a VAT which are applied in a broadly similar way across Europe), individual taxes (such as the corporate income tax) will normally vary in many detailed ways due to the bespoke and highly country-specific manner in which individual taxes are designed and evolve. Each will have its own rules on: scope, specific taxpayer exemptions, items that are deductible, the relevant measure of income, foreign exchange differences, etc. The result is that the tax system in any one jurisdiction will often create a myriad of different taxes and different treatments of individual taxpayers. As will be discussed in more detail in the next chapter, the impact of tax will therefore often create major differences in the value (specifically, the after-tax value) of financial products and transactions from one party to another under any individual tax system. Those differences may also be further multiplied by the series of different bilateral agreements (in the form of double tax treaties) that further vary those differences from one category of taxpayer to another. In this complex picture, the tax profile of every country, every financial product, and every customer may vary in some way. These tax differences are considered in more detail in the next chapter, but for now it is enough to note (1) the potential relevance of tax systems to the business model of banks and (2) that the greater the global reach of the financial institution, the greater is the ability to access the opportunities such differences present in local markets and the ability to bring to

[75] The search for profitable business and constant product innovation based on complex financial modelling which could include elements of legal and tax systems also explains why, over time, the trading side of the organization grew to incorporate accountants, lawyers, and tax advisers among its ranks, since the continual innovation, particularly as it pertains to new products or markets, required these skills.

bear the required mix of products, expertise, and financial machinery that are needed to unlock them.

Weaknesses in the Control and Governance of Banks

Before turning to consider the impact on cum-ex and similar schemes of the themes discussed above, it is necessary to take note of some specific effects which the new trading-based model had on control and governance issues. Under this model, the ability to create transaction flow (i.e. originate new business) becomes the critical skill for an individual banker/trader in a what is now a sales-driven (rather than a relationship-driven) organization, with that ability typically deriving from a banker's skills, specialist knowledge, or market contacts (and in practice often all three together). This has a number of implications, chief of which is the increased role and importance of the individual 'producer' banker. Such an individual can command a higher wage than in the predecessor 'originate to hold' model, where the static relationship between the intermediary bank and its lenders and borrowers renders the source of profit relatively immobile over time. It also becomes common for individuals in a 'front-office' role to be paid according to the volume of business that they generate (allowing them effectively to command a share of the bank's business revenue)[76] and in consequence the producer will be both highly paid and highly mobile.[77] To be effective in generating new transactions for the firm, the banker must be able to command and direct the resources of the firm. Doing so requires and, through the operation of the process, vests, power and authority in the individual concerned. If successful in generating significant revenue from transaction origination, the banker will be promoted and then manage a group of individuals (and be paid more). With time, the individual will rise up the ranks of the firm, becoming the head of a trading desk or overseeing the whole trading operation, possibly even the bank.[78]

[76] It is common for major banks and investment banks to refer to their employee compensation expense in terms of share of revenue for this reason. A major bank financial metric is the compensation-to-revenue ratio. In the investment banks and trading/wholesale departments of the major banks, it is common for something in the order of 40–50 per cent of net revenues to be paid out as compensation to staff. See Engelen et al., *After the Great Complacence*, at pp.122–4.

[77] There has been a dramatic growth in financial-sector wages over recent decades—see, for example, Joanne Lindley, 'Wage Growth and Human Capital in the UK Finance Sector', University of Surrey, School of Economics Discussion Papers 0313, March 2013, available at https://ideas.repec.org/p/sur/surrec/0313.html. From 1997 to 2009, the finance-sector ratio of wages to other private sectors rose from 1.81 to 2.75. In order to reduce the risk of individual bankers moving firms, the bank may feel compelled to offer a compensation package which incentivizes the banker to remain.

[78] Through the process, the banker becomes credentialized and able to attract ever higher levels of pay, and potentially able to move whole teams to other banks along with captive customer accounts and business.

The rise in importance of the individual banker/trader, including the increase in compensation based on successful trading, puts more pressure on the governance model of banks. This is because it makes it much more likely for there to be a conflict between the interests of the individual bankers/traders and the interests of the ultimate owners of the business, the bank's shareholders. Conflicts between the interests of shareholders in a company and the agents that run the company on their behalf are normally described as raising problems relating to the economic theory of agency.[79] The shift within banks to a transaction-based and sales-led culture, coupled with the industry-wide importance (and compensation) assigned to the role of the individual traders and bankers, meant that the banking industry exacerbated the agency problem as it shifted towards a proprietary trading-based model, as reflected in the 'originate to distribute' business model.

The firm's dependency on the banker to achieve its business objectives brings two immediate consequences. First, the firm must accommodate the needs of the banker and make resources (such as trade execution staff, back-office and support staff, etc) available to facilitate the implementation and completion of transactions originated by the individual concerned.[80] Second, the firm must simultaneously place controls on the banker's efforts to originate and execute new business because, if not subject to scrutiny, the proposed transactions may present undesirable financial or reputational risks to the firm. In an effort to create a counterbalance to front-office staff consisting of bankers and traders (collectively, the 'line of business'), whose often significant compensation was driven by the successful generation of transactions, the governance structure adopted by most, if not all, banks was an adversarial model comprising two pillars: a management structure exercising 'control' in one pillar and the line-of-business 'producers' in the other.[81]

[79] See, for example, S.A. Ross, 'The Economic Theory of Agency: The Principal Problems', *American Economic Review* 63 (May 1973), 134–9. A significant theme in the discussion of agency is that if the shareholders (principal) and agents are each 'utility maximizers' the agents may not always act in the best interests of the principal. The agency problem is usually discussed in the context of the separation of ownership and control represented by large corporations and by reference to the top managers within a firm (as in Michael Jensen and William Meckling, 'Theory of the Firm: Managerial Behavior, Agency Costs and Ownership Structure', *Journal of Financial Economics* 3 (1976), 305–60). The agency problem was famously referred to by Adam Smith in his description of the directors of joint-stock companies: 'being the managers of other people's money rather than their own, it cannot well be expected that they should watch over it with the same anxious vigilance with which the partners in a private copartnery frequently watch over their own…Negligence and profusion, therefore, must always prevail, more or less, in the management of the affairs of such a company.' Adam Smith, *The Wealth of Nations* [1776], ed. Edwin Cannan (Modern Library, 1937), at p.700.

[80] In practice, there will of course also be other bankers with other competing business that must also be accommodated, meaning that resources would need to be allocated based on the relative merits (chiefly, profitability) of competing proposals. However, the importance of bringing the capabilities of the firm to bear on effecting the banker's transactions can be seen most clearly in the rise of 'Transaction Management' and 'Special Execution' groups, whose role it was to marshal the firm's resources.

[81] The adversarial model of 'line of business' and 'controls' was a simple structure adopted by banks formally or informally for many years since the OECD in 2004 articulated a principles-based approach to corporate governance in the aftermath of the Enron and WorldCom scandals. See OECD, 'Principles

It was the responsibility of the former to understand the risks being assumed by the latter and to manage the nature and extent of those risks. These two pillars were largely independent but became fused at the highest levels of the firm, where senior management is exercised and where each pillar reported into the board of directors of the firm.[82]

However, the checks that were intended to be delivered by this two-pillar approach were undermined by certain *interdependencies* and also by what may be termed *intermingling* issues that are inherent in the model.

The *interdependency* problem relates to both financial and competency issues. The financial issue consists in the fact that not only does the bank rely on the bankers/traders for the origination of revenue-generating business, but the staff employed in the control functions also rely on these same individual producers, since their own compensation is derived from that same revenue. The competency issue is that the dependence of the bank on the banker derives from his or her specialized skill and expertise, knowledge of markets, and market contacts to deliver revenue. In the absence of the banker, the bank lacks that specialized expertise, knowledge, and skill. By contrast, staff within the bank's control functions are very unlikely to have had any direct experience of the line of business. For example, bank accountants and lawyers acting in the control line will have been drawn from large private practices, where their experience (and interests) will often largely consist in dealing with abstract contractual problems. They will often not understand the detailed workings of market infrastructure or the day-to-day operations of the firm.[83] However, the task of applying effective controls over

of Corporate Governance' (OECD, 2004), available at http://www.oecd.org/corporate/ca/corporategovernanceprinciples/31557724.pdf. Since 2013, some banks have moved to a structured 'Three Lines of Defence' model. The first line of defence consists of controls embedded into the daily conduct of the business and charged with the task of evaluating and managing risks as they emerge. The second line of defence lies in risk-management and compliance functions, among others, designed to evaluate the effectiveness of the controls being managed by the first line of defence. The third line of defence represents assurance that the model is operating and consists of the audit function. It is also true that some financial regulators now support the use of a fourth line of defence in the model, that being the external audit function as an independent validation of the first three lines of defence. For example, see Isabella Andorfer and Andrea Minto, 'The Four Lines of Defence Model for Financial Institutions', Financial Stability Institute, Occasional Paper No 11 (Bank for International Settlements, December 2015), available at https://www.bis.org/fsi/fsipapers11.pdf.

[82] The two-pillar model simplifies for the purpose of exposition what is inevitably a much more elaborate control structure within a large bank consisting of dedicated market risk, credit risk, model validation, operational risk, compliance, legal, and treasury risk functions (among others).

[83] The expertise on trading desks is normally of a high order. Securitization and structured products require a high concentration of financial product and professional skills, including experienced product specialists, quants, and legal, tax, and accounting specialists. Desk expertise is more focused, energetic, and motivated (due to the front-office incentive structure) and typically is superior to the knowledge of professionals in control functions, often to the point where the controls function may defer to the desk's superior understanding of particular issues. Thus, highly specialized skills and knowledge in the business lines will usually run far ahead of the abilities of both internal controls and external regulators to understand the issues and resource the control function.

the front-office bankers requires persons with commensurate knowledge and skill. One side effect of the two-pillar model, therefore, is that it made the operation of control functions in the bank (for example, the implementation of business risk assessments) reliant to a large degree on the specialized product/business knowledge of the front-office producers. The three- and four-lines-of-defence governance models now in vogue may tacitly acknowledge the existence of this problem.[84]

The *intermingling* problem also consists of two elements. First, there is 'leakage' from the control pillar to the line-of-business pillar. This is because the need for specialized knowledge in the line of business (such as accounting treatment, legal structuring knowledge, or tax expertise to devise transactions and prepare them for approval by the controls function) creates a strong incentive for control staff to transition to the line of business where the pay and prospects are perceived to be materially better. This further strengthens the skill-set advantage of the business line. Second, there is also a leakage, or progression, from the line of business up and into management. The executive roles of the senior management function are overwhelmingly filled from the ranks of the bankers and traders, with the consequence that the senior management function may be predisposed to sympathize with the demands of the line of business. That tendency is also again supported by the fact that the compensation of the senior management within the bank is funded by the business generated by the front-office bankers.

The result is therefore hardly surprising: while the formal structure posits a control pillar exerting review, challenge, and risk-mitigation authority over the bank's business line in the opposing pillar, the substantive financial power and competency weaknesses initially embedded in the structure (as also further weakened over time by the interdependency and intermingling problems) introduce formidable impediments to the control structure's intended operation.

The two-pillar adversarial governance structure described above has another feature. It is related to the 'originate to distribute' business model but is less obvious. That control structure is designed to deal with 'origination', which in the 'originate to distribute' model describes the bank's contractual relations with its transactional counterparties. Apart from credit or risk decisions which relate to the firm's quantitative and qualitative 'appetite' for the transactional business in the context of a particular counterparty or market instrument,[85] the active control functions focus by design on the novel elements of a transaction, namely either

[84] See footnote 81 to this chapter.

[85] Reference in this context to the 'appetite' of a firm could describe a variety of features of a transaction, or class of transactions, which are attractive or unattractive to the bank. For example, the bank may have a negative view of the prospects of a particular company, industry, or country and may therefore seek to limit the total business carried out with such an entity, sector, or country. Alternatively, the bank may already have entered into very significant amounts of business with a counterparty and so wishes to place limits on how much further business it is prepared to do with that counterparty. In the context of a structured trading business which exploits different tax anomalies, the

completely new business (such as a new market, or a new financial instrument) or the evolution of existing business but with novel features embedded (such as a medium-term note whose payoff is linked to a new formula or a credit event rather than a simple interest payment). In other words, the active controls focus on the counterparty-facing or 'front-end' of origination with a particular predisposition to examine features in the business that may be novel. The presence of novelty is taken as signaling a change in business terms which requires attention, just as the emphasis on transactions driven by the needs of the bank's customers or counterparties conceives of risk as primarily exogenous rather than endogenous to the bank. This means that there are material parts of the business conducted by banks that fall outside the normal ambit of those active control functions. For example, unless some unusual issue arises by way of exception to the normal course of dealing,[86] the control functions do not generally review and examine: (1) proprietary or market transactions, where the trading desks enter into market-standard transactions such as buying and selling securities, entering into derivatives trades, arranging stock loans, etc for the firm's own account;[87] and (2) the middle- and back-office functions which comprise the day-to-day operations of the firm and include the settlement of proprietary and client transactions, the transfer and receipt of payments, the collection of dividends or reclaims of tax credits, or the management of the effects of other corporate actions such as the outcome of a corporate takeover, and the like. These are all generally regarded as both inherent and routine to the business and therefore as involving non-controversial functions.[88]

The control or governance of a bank is, of course, not exercised only by mechanisms and structures that are internal to the bank. In the banking sector in particular, and owing to the unique role of banks in the economy and the

bank may take a portfolio approach, limiting its exposure to each strategy in an effort to compartmentalize the attendant risks.

[86] An exception in this context might be a dispute with a trading counterparty as to what terms of a transaction were agreed during a conversation closing a deal, or an outsized transaction which may require specific internal approvals or notifications to regulators.

[87] It will be in the nature of the bank's charter, its regulatory registrations, and a wide set of internal approvals to carry out these transactions. If it is a market-maker, it may even be under an obligation to stand ready to buy and sell securities. Adopting a risk-based approach, the legal and compliance controls of a bank could legitimately regard these functions as low risk, unlikely to be violative in nature, and not therefore subject them to significant scrutiny.

[88] It is true that the middle- and back-office operational functions of the bank will incorporate controls, consisting of policies, procedures, processes, routines, and periodic review, but their working will not be subject to regular analysis or challenge, save in exceptional circumstances. The low-profile nature of the control processes stems from the normal view of legal and compliance functions that middle- and back-office functions are little more than required, but nonetheless mundane, post-transaction processes, such as the confirmation and formal completion of transactions.

privileges accorded to them,[89] the role of external regulators is also very significant.[90] However, as with the bank's internal control mechanisms, there have been some evident difficulties in the exercise of this external control by regulators that are relevant to the discussion here.[91] These difficulties were also highlighted in the German parliamentary enquiry into cum-ex.[92] Some of these problems are well understood—for example, the scale and complexity of the business operations conducted by banks that are subject to external regulation. The largest banks will typically have tens of thousands of employees,[93] and hundreds, if not thousands, of subsidiaries (many of which they control, some of which may be jointly controlled with others). They will also enter into hundreds of thousands (if not millions) of individual transactions daily, with the transactional landscape crossing multiple markets, transaction types, and counterparties, and with no necessary correspondence between a given transactional activity on the one hand and an approved entity or permitted jurisdiction on the other. There is also the volume

[89] These privileges are a critical feature of the banks' ability to exploit market anomalies and are considered further in Chapter 8.

[90] In the UK, banking regulation has historically been principles-based and this has led to a self-consciously light touch in UK regulatory regime with a significant element of self-regulation. In the US, the regime has generally been rather more rules-driven, but it is argued in Engelen et al., *After the Great Complacence*, pp.135–8 that, due to pressure to soften any adversarial stance from the time of the Reagan administration and a pressure on resources, the US regime has operated to produce a similar result (though after the Global Financial Crisis, the Turner review determined that a more intrusive, adversarial approach was needed—see Financial Services Authority, 'The Turner Review: A Regulatory Response to the Global Banking Crisis' (Financial Services Authority, 2009), at pp.88–9. Referring to examples in Germany and France, that review also discusses (at p.232) how national interest has led to a lengthy lead time for the phasing in of new regulatory protections. One further consequence of the developments discussed earlier in this chapter is also relevant here. Because at its core the policy prescription for financial markets was laissez-faire, there has been a tendency for financial innovation to run ahead of regulation, reflecting a widespread view that the state which pursued the most market-friendly regulatory regime would prosper or gain a comparative advantage. There has also been a belief that financial innovation is itself a powerful protection against market failure.

[91] Different states may operate different approaches to the external regulation of the banking sector. However, the issues discussed here, which are concerned with the operation, and particularly the effectiveness, of external controls by the regulator, seem to be generally relevant to external regulatory regimes. A number of recent studies have discussed the weaknesses of bank regulatory regimes, particularly in light of the Global Financial Crisis. See, for example, Andrew Haldane, 'Rethinking the Financial Network', speech given at the Financial Student Association, Amsterdam, 28 April 2009, and 'Small Lessons from a Big Crisis', Federal Reserve Bank of Chicago 45th Annual Conference, 8 May 2009. There is also G. Tett, 'Silos and Silences. Why So Few People Spotted the Problems in Complex Credit and What That Implies for the Future', *Banque de France Financial Stability Review* 14 (July 2010), 121–9. The matter is also addressed in Dan Awrey and Kathryn Judge, Why Financial Regulation Keeps Falling Short, Cornell Law School Legal

Studies Research Paper No. 20-03; European Corporate Governance Institute (ECGI) Law Working Paper No. 494/202; Columbia Law and Economics Working Paper No. 617 (2020). Available at: https://scholarship.law.columbia.edu/faculty_scholarship/2604

The US Government enquiry into the Global Financial Crisis concluded that widespread failures in financial regulation and supervision were a primary factor in the financial crisis. See Financial Crisis Inquiry Commission, 'Crisis Inquiry Report'.

[92] See further the discussion in Chapter 4.

[93] For example, the largest US banks have between 20,000 and 23,200 employees. See the relevant data on the statistics portal, Statista, available at https://www.statista.com/statistics/250220/ranking-of-united-states-banks-by-number-of-employees-in-2012/.

and complexity of the laws and regulations with which banks must comply. Consequently, in addition to the day-to-day activities in which the bank is involved, the scope of matters under regulatory jurisdiction is potentially vast. Nor may it be assumed that any mischief lies in proportion to the scale of either those laws and regulations, or the transactions into which the bank enters. From a legal or regulatory perspective, a small set of transactions (or even a single transaction) may have a significance or financial impact that greatly exceeds the revenue or profit associated with the transaction itself.[94] A further challenge for the regulatory bodies is that of securing and retaining suitably qualified and market-experienced staff given the constraints of the regulators' pay scales and the 'revolving-door' movement of seasoned regulatory staff to banks in an effort to obtain materially higher compensation as a consequence of their experience of working at a regulator.[95]

For all these reasons, the reach of regulatory supervision and examination is inevitably based on a high-level approach and/or the adoption of a closer risk-based inspection of a narrow range of specified matters.

Difficulties also arise by virtue of the fragmented nature or 'patchwork' of external regulation. While the bank's operations may be global, external regulation is generally confined to the country in which the relevant bank operates. For example, the London operation of a large non-UK bank will be subject to the regulatory authorities in the UK. If the bank conducts business in a third country, business carried out in that state through branches or subsidiaries there will also generally be subject to review by that country's regulator. However, though there are exceptions, a regulator in one country does not generally have broad power to examine business carried out by the branch or subsidiary of the bank in another state.[96] In addition to this geographical limitation, external regulation may be

[94] For example, certain United States pension funds are subject to the Employee Retirement Income Security Act of 1974 (29 U.S.C. §1001 et seq.) which imposes strict fiduciary duties on persons who manage pension-fund assets or to whom such money management is delegated (such as some hedge funds). Breach of these rules can give rise to high penalties if a transaction is prohibited by ERISA. A fine, referred to as an 'excise duty' of 15 per cent of the amount involved in the offending transaction is applied and reapplied for each successive year the transaction is outstanding. See Internal Revenue Code §4975. Under certain circumstances a 100 per cent excise duty may also be applicable as may criminal penalties. The penalty is not proportionate to the profit the bank derives from a breach.

[95] Regulators are not well paid compared to the bankers they regulate. For example, an examiner from the Office of the Comptroller of the Currency (OCC), which regulates and supervises US banks as well as federal branches and agencies of foreign banks, might make in the region of $42,000 while a very senior OCC executive might make as much as $280,000 (the data is taken from the OCC website at https://careers.occ.gov/pay-and-benefits/salary/index-occ-salary-structure.html). At the Securities and Exchange Commission (SEC), an SEC employee's salary at the most senior level is capped at $243,500 (see the data on the SEC website available at https://www.sec.gov/ohr/sec-compensation). These salary levels are materially lower than corresponding levels within the banks.

[96] An example of an exception is that the US Federal Reserve has authority, as part of its consolidated examination responsibility, to review the foreign operations and foreign subsidiaries of bank holding companies subject to its supervision. See further Division of Supervision and Regulation, 'Bank Holding Company Supervision Manual' (Board of Governors of the Federal Reserve, as supplemented in January 2017), available at https://www.federalreserve.gov/publications/files/bhc.pdf.

further fragmented by the fact that banking activities are also subject to regulation by reference to specific financial products traded by banks (see further below) and by reference to specific attributes or features of the bank's business, such as the capital it holds, the amount of business it carries out, or the conduct of its staff. This fragmentation can be illustrated by reference to the case of the United States. There, banks are regulated by a host of regulatory bodies. In some cases, the nature of the bank entity itself attracts the regulator in question, in other cases, it is the nature and extent of the entity's activities which invoke the jurisdiction of the regulator. For example, the US Federal Reserve examines bank holding companies (BHCs) (which would commonly be the corporate entity whose shares are listed and traded on one or more large stock exchange). The US Securities and Exchange Commission (SEC) will regulate the subsidiary of a BHC which is a broker-dealer. The SEC will also regulate a subsidiary if it sells securities to the public, or if it transacts certain swaps over securities. The US Commodity Futures Trading Commission (CFTC) may regulate that same subsidiary if it deals in futures contracts and has a parallel regulatory authority over other types of swap.[97] The upshot of this patchwork of regulation is that a universal bank with operations in the United States might be regulated by four or more of these regulatory agencies, each interested in different or possibly overlapping aspects of the activities of the bank and its subsidiaries. To complicate the picture further, financial industry self-regulatory organizations such as a FINRA also engage in rule-making, carry out examinations of bank broker-dealer subsidiaries, and bring disciplinary actions against their members.[98]

The focus and objectives of external regulation will vary by regulator. Some regulators will have a mandate to examine the bank for its safety and soundness; they may take a holistic approach and examine the adequacy of its accounting, its policies and procedures, and its associated controls. Other may be more focused on the effects of the financial firm's behaviour in the context of the wider market. In the UK, for example, the two main regulatory organizations are the UK's Financial Conduct Authority (FCA) and the Prudential Regulation Authority (PRA). The FCA's objectives revolve around the 'conduct' of the financial firms

[97] The CFTC regulates interest rate swaps and foreign exchange swaps, among others. The SEC also has authority in relation to swaps, for example, swaps over shares. Although efforts are under way to improve coordination between the agencies and reduce the complexity associated with the regulatory regime in which the CFTC and SEC operate, it is fair to say that it is an extraordinarily difficult regime to comprehend, much less operate within. See US Securities and Exchange Commission and US Commodity Futures Trading Commission, 'Memorandum of Understanding Between the U.S. Securities and Exchange Commission and the U.S. Commodity Futures Trading Commission Regarding Coordination in Areas of Common Regulatory Interest and Information Sharing', 11 July 2018, available at https://www.cftc.gov/sites/default/files/2018-07/CFTC_MOU_InformationSharing062818.pdf.

[98] FINRA, the Financial Industry Regulatory Authority, is a private corporation that acts as a self-regulatory organization, whose aim it is to oversee the affairs of broker-dealers in an effort to protect investors and safeguard efficient markets. For more information, see finra.org.

it regulates in an effort to safeguard the fairness of markets and the proper functioning of markets and to foster competition in the marketplace.[99] By contrast, the PRA is a 'prudential' regulator, meaning that it focuses its efforts on the 'safety and soundness' of the firms it regulates, meaning the adequacy of their capital and controls.[100] It is notable that, in the two of the world's most important financial markets, the US and the UK, a fragmented approach to regulation is applied on a national basis. As a general matter, external regulators are therefore not embarking on an exercise to understand why or how transactions or structures (including highly complex composite arrangements) function in detail or why they are profitable. One obvious consequence of this fragmented regulatory regime is that it permits a bank to choose one regulatory regime over another by booking business into a particular legal entity and thereby determining the external regulator. In the process it may be able to ring-fence the activity from other possible regulators.[101]

The difficulties discussed above are compounded by weaknesses in the day-to-day process of regulatory supervision and examination. For example, regulators place a high level of reliance on banks being forthright with them about illegal or improper conduct by the bank. In industry parlance, banks are expected to 'self-report' to their regulator material issues they discover in the course of their business. If there was a material risk issue or a significant loss or operational failure, the bank would be expected to make the regulator aware of it promptly.[102] The self-reporting regime presupposes that the relevant department within the bank has correctly identified the issue, properly assessed its severity, and raised it fully and forthrightly to bank senior management.[103] Where the issue relates to

[99] For more about the FCA's purpose and objectives, see https://www.fca.org.uk/about/the-fca.

[100] See further https://www.bankofengland.co.uk/prudential-regulation.

[101] For example, a bank headquartered in one country can constrain the ability of a given regulator to understand, regulate, examine, and enforce an activity by establishing an operating subsidiary in a second country which transacts with clients in third countries. If the activity is improper, recourse of affected parties may not only be confined to the subsidiary, but regulators in the third countries will require the energetic participation of the second country to enforce or prosecute the operating subsidiary. The more tightly circumscribed the mandate of the home-country regulator and the less effective the level of international cooperation among regulators, the more effective such a technique will be.

[102] In the UK, the Financial Conduct Authority's handbook of rules and guidance provides a set of principles. These are designated 'PRIN 2.1.1' and marked with 'R' to indicate a binding rule. Principle 11 states: 'A firm must deal with its regulators in an open and cooperative way, and must disclose to the FCA appropriately anything relating to the firm of which that regulator would reasonably expect notice.' See https://www.handbook.fca.org.uk/handbook/PRIN/2/1.html.

[103] The reporting of suspicious transactions which come to the bank's attention is also specifically mandated. In the United States, these are transactions which a financial institution 'knows, suspects, or has reason to suspect' relate to funds derived from illegal activity or which appear to serve no business purpose, among other criteria. See, for example, United States Department of the Treasury, 'Treasury Announces Final Suspicious Activity Rule for Broker-Dealers', 28 June 2002. In the United Kingdom, persons working in the financial-services sector are required to file a Suspicious Activity Report (SAR) 'if they know, or suspect or have reasonable grounds for knowing or suspecting, that a person is engaged in, or attempting, money laundering or terrorist financing'—see Part 7 of the Proceeds of Crime Act 2002. Although these SAR requirements were intended to combat money laundering by

misconduct by the bank itself, there are strong disincentives of staff to self-report issues.

The formal examination process is more limited than might appear to be the case.[104] In a typical formal examination, the bank's senior management will be informed of the examination several weeks in advance. The thrust of the examination will be described in advance by the regulator and a questionnaire prepared by the regulator may be sent on areas of interest containing specific questions for the bank to address. Questions asked of the bank by the regulator are expected to be answered fully and forthrightly. The bank will prepare formal replies and/or presentations which are directly responsive to the regulator's questionnaire. These will be submitted to the regulator. A series of meetings will follow during which the regulator will follow up orally on the bank's written answers. Prior to regulators arriving at the bank to discuss the questionnaire, bank employees who will participate in the oral examination may be coached on how to answer the regulator's questions. In that process, they will typically be directed to answer the questions directly, but not to speculate or offer up information which is not within their direct knowledge. Above all, the bank employee is instructed not to go beyond the perimeter of the precise question being asked and not to offer up additional information. During the examination, the regulatory examiners ask follow-up questions of the bank, to which bank employees respond. As the responses are strictly coterminous with the questions (in accordance with the coaching of bank employees prior to the examination) the scope for examiners to probe further is limited.

Even if a regulator uncovered some activity by a bank which was suspect or amounted to clear misconduct, there may be a number of reasons why the regulator might seek to minimize it (whether through limiting sanctions, avoiding publicity through a private settlement with the bank, or other actions and inactions). These reasons may, for example, include embarrassment to the regulator. The regulator is responsible for ensuring that the bank is well-managed and compliant. If it is not, then arguably the regulator has failed to some extent in its mission. There is, therefore, an incentive to work with the bank to ensure any identified issues are resolved quickly so that all parties can move on. There may alternatively be political consequences of any publicly identified problem. If the problem is material, confidence in the bank could be undermined. For systemically important banks, the consequences could affect the economy, the prospects of

criminal organizations external to the bank, they would equally apply to illegal conduct carried out by bank employees and suspected by other employees of the bank in the course of their duties.

[104] Formal examinations of banks can be either regular or ad-hoc. Regular examinations involve a review of the business, any major issues particularly of the risk variety, market developments of note, and the bank's business plan for the coming years. Ad-hoc examinations may stem from a particular issue with the bank which the regulator has identified, or they may be thematic, stemming from industry developments which the regulator wants to ensure are being properly addressed.

other banks (because of extensive inter-bank market dealings creating exposures between banks), and in extreme cases may result in a bailout or some other recourse to public resources, which may attract adverse political attention. At the level of an individual regulator, there may also be more personal factors that influence outcomes. Taking a hard-nosed approach and imposing significant sanctions upon the bank concerned is unlikely to improve future employment prospects for regulatory staff should they ever wish to move to a highly-paid job in the banking sector. These factors present further incentives for, and assist in explaining the existence of, a system in which violations are investigated, enforced, and settled in secret with only cursory facts and reasons provided ex post.[105]

Impact on Facilitation of Cum-Ex and Similar Schemes

Having discussed the consequences of the changed banking business model and the general weaknesses in control functions, it is now possible to turn to the question of how, in practice, these two factors created the environment for the cum-ex trade to be executed.[106] The discussion that follows concentrates on their specific impact in the case of cum-ex, but the points made have a more general relevance by analogy to other transactional schemes carried out by banks which involve misconduct of one kind or another.

Assembling the Elements of the Cum-Ex Trade

Once the possibility of generating tax credits through the cum-ex trade had been identified,[107] the task for the cum-ex trader was to transform the idea into a marketable trading strategy. The motivation was, of course, to generate a highly profitable product for the bank and thereby a large bonus for the trader.[108] Such an

[105] This is an important issue which is discussed further in Chapter 8.

[106] There is a detailed discussion in Chapter 3 of the mechanics of cum-ex trades, but the focus here is on explaining what was done in the context of the incentives of the business model and the controls and governance weaknesses. It should be acknowledged that not all banks implemented the cum-ex trade, so it cannot be claimed that the discussion here applies to all banks. Some banks chose not to enter into the trade at all, and some chose to cease cum-ex activity after a certain period (though in some cases continued to assist and finance their clients with cum-ex trades). However, it is clear that a very large number of banks did conduct cum-ex business.

[107] The precise origins of cum-ex as a trading strategy are not known for certain. It is sometimes suggested that the trade was discovered by accident (as a result of difficulties in reconciling the financial movements involved in a routine securities lending transaction) in approximately 2001 and at one of the US investment banks. However, it is clear that the nature of the cum-ex anomaly had been known of for some time before this (see further Chapter 4), though the exploitation of the anomaly in a highly organized and structured form did commence from around 2001.

[108] The amount of the trader's 'take' from the trade would vary according to the status of the individual and group concerned and the terms of any negotiations with the bank. As noted earlier in

opportunity would usually be identified and pursued by the tax-structuring and trading group at the bank. Such groups would be responsible for identifying and exploiting tax anomalies and they would also have the skills and specialist disciplines required to bring cum-ex as a strategy into being.[109] The primary control function applicable to new products developed by this group would be the bank's new products or 'approvals' process which is discussed later in this section.

As has already been seen in Part I of this book, a cum-ex trade involves a bank or investment fund entering into a composite transaction consisting of a number of different transaction types involving a variety of financial instruments. Whilst the overall 'choreography' of the composite transaction might be designed by the tax-structuring and trading group, any actual execution of the trade would require the cooperation of the specialist groups or 'desks' charged with responsibility for dealing in each of the relevant instruments.[110] Accordingly, before any cum-ex trade could be considered as a practical possibility, these different specialist groups would need to be lined up to assist with any implementation of the trade. At a minimum, the different specialist groups required would include the stock loan desk[111] (which would manage the supply of borrowed shares for the strategy, ensuring that all short sales executed under the cum-ex trade were fulfilled in good time using borrowed shares),[112] the derivatives trading desk (which would be responsible for executing and managing equity swaps contracts to hedge precisely the terms of any purchase or sale contracts relating to the underlying shares),[113] the equities trading desk (to enter into the short sale contract), a futures trading desk (whose responsibility it would be to manage any single stock futures contract employed in the strategy), and the prime brokerage business (which could leverage the trade as well as act as an additional supply of borrowed securities).[114] The

this chapter, something in the order of 40–50 per cent of net revenue might be paid out to staff in the form of regular pay and performance bonuses.

[109] Tax strategies such as dividend arbitrage (discussed in Chapter 1) would have used in part similar techniques and structures, so the tax structuring and trading group would be fluent in managing the cum-ex strategy and its associated processes.

[110] The segregation of individual financial product types by trader group or 'desk' is largely driven by the need for an appropriate level of product specialism to deal in those products.

[111] Individuals on the stock loan desk would have deep relationship contacts with large custodial banks who lend out securities of large holders of shares (such as pension funds), but the desk would also have access to shares from such lenders directly.

[112] This would require delivery of the borrowed shares by the settlement date of the short sale after the dividend record date.

[113] In practice, a bank would usually have various separate derivatives desks. The derivatives desk dealing with cum-ex transactions would have responsibility for single stock equity swap contracts. These are so-called 'delta-one' swaps, because the bank's obligations under the swap contract correspond one for one with the hedge that it holds in the underlying security.

[114] The prime brokerage desk would typically have the right to borrow or 're-hypothecate' at will shares held by its clients and these could then be made available as borrowed shares to fulfil a short sale in a cum-ex trade.

ability to secure the cooperation of these groups was premised on the profitable nature of the business for the bank and the expectation that each desk would be rewarded for the specific transactions they would execute in the implementation of the trade.[115]

As will be discussed further below, for the trade to be viable, it would also need the involvement of back- and middle-office personnel within the bank. The middle office would coordinate with counterparties engaged in the trade, such as the funds executing the strategy, generally as buyer, and inter-dealer brokers and exchanges. The back-office groups would ensure payments and movements of shares were completed on a timely basis and follow up with custodians to ensure that the tax credit reclaim process was completed.[116]

The New Products or Approvals Process

Turning to the main control mechanism, if a transaction is new or has some novel element, it is required to be reviewed by one or more committees consisting of bankers and relevant control personnel from across the bank.[117] The transaction will be assessed to ensure that it complies with the bank's policies and presents well-understood risks which are properly compensated. This approval and commitment process is the bank's primary mechanism of control over business that is either entirely new to the bank or which has some novel feature.

Numerous groups would participate in this process. The approval of the tax department would need to be sought to confirm that the transaction would not contravene any tax laws or involve unacceptable reputational damage and would achieve the tax effect described by the proposal put forward. The legal department would be asked to confirm the trade was both legal as well as reputationally sound. The compliance function would address whether the trade would violate

[115] The distribution of money to desks and their trading staff associated with a trade is generally achieved by a system of 'production credits' which broadly equate to the revenue associated with business either brought in by a trader directly or a transaction to which the trader contributed in some way. The more production credits a trader has to his or her name, the higher the proportion of the amount allocated for bonuses (the 'bonus pool') that person will take. There is usually no science equating a person's contribution with the number of their production credits. The share of the pie will depend not only on the revenues associated with specific transactions in any one year but also on how the bank perceives that person's 'value' to the organization. Consequently, the process of awarding production credits and therefore shares of the bonus pool is a politically charged process. For a first hand account, see the report of Joris Luyendijk, 'Former Private Banker: "Making Money is the Easy Part"', *The Guardian*, 19 September 2013, available at https://www.theguardian.com/commentisfree/2013/sep/19/private-banker-investment.

[116] As the middle and back offices are seen as a support service to the front-office desks, they would not normally be rewarded on a transaction-by-transaction basis in a similar way to the rewarding of front-office desks.

[117] A proper process is required to ensure the institution concerned understands the business it undertakes.

applicable regulatory requirements or rules of market practice (e.g. market abuse) or of an exchange. Operations staff would be required to confirm that they could manage to process the proposed number of transactions, and treasury would be called upon to confirm that sufficient funds could be made available to deliver as purchase monies or as collateral to stock borrows. Still other groups would focus on technical rules, for example, the bank's accounting policy group would check to ensure that the bank had taken the necessary measures to ensure that any shares sold or purchased were treated correctly for accounting purposes. Complicating the picture further, control groups within a bank typically specialize in particular types of instrument. There will be a group within the legal department that focuses purely on derivative transactions, just as there may be an operations group that is expert on the minutiae of settling such transactions. All relevant groups would be involved in the commitment and approvals process.

As discussed in Part I, cum-ex trades involved the movement of hundreds of millions of euros of company shares moving in and out of the bank multiple times a day. If there were a significant risk of loss involved in the transaction it could threaten the financial safety of the bank, even a large bank. Consequently, at least two risk groups would be involved in the approvals process: first, the bank's market risk function, to assess the appropriateness of the risks being undertaken in the transaction, not only in terms of the type and size of transactions being employed, but also the amount of leverage involved in the transaction;[118] and second, the credit risk function, a further control group of the bank, which would assess the ability of the counterparty (such as an inter-dealer broker) to meet its financial commitments under the financial transactions in question. Each of these groups would need to be satisfied that the risks were well-understood and contained.[119] In order to ensure that the market and credit risk control groups gave their approvals in a timely fashion and to curate discussions with them about the trade, the bank would typically employ an 'in-business' risk officer. That person would understand the precise criteria the risk control groups imposed. It would often be part of that officer's job to make sure that the approvals came through.

Though the approvals process is normally discharged through a formal approvals meeting attended by all the groups involved, in practice, the approval of each

[118] In some cases, very high levels of leverage would be involved in cum-ex trades. That obviously creates a risk to the bank because it is typically the bank that would be providing the leverage in the form of loans to its clients to fund their participation in the trades.

[119] Securing the approval of a number of compartmentalized control groups may seem an administratively cumbersome process. However, the bank's businesses, controls, and operational functions are separated in this way by design: first, because specialization is necessary for efficient operation at large scale, but also, second, because bank governance (and bank regulation) specifically mandates compartmentalization to achieve a 'segregation of duties'. This is to ensure that those transacting business for the bank are subject to controls to ensure they do so on terms which are appropriately priced in the light of all the risks being assumed.

group or function would normally be secured in advance of that meeting, with discrete discussions between the team structuring the cum-ex trades and each group individually. This makes the segregation of duties, a control concept designed to separate distinct tasks, a helpful feature in obtaining approval of trades like cum-ex: since each control group is specialized, for example, in the oversight of a particular aspect of the transaction, the promoter of the proposed trade will in such meetings tend to concentrate on that aspect of the transaction in isolation, notwithstanding that it is a component of the larger composite cum-ex trade. The result can be illustrated by reference to the cum-ex trade and involving, for example, the legal function controlling derivatives transactions.[120] The relevant legal staff in such a role will generally be drawn from large law firms where solving complex problems using analytical skills is highly prized. They will be less interested in (and typically have a limited understanding of) the details of how, practically speaking, a transaction is delivered or settled. Obtaining approval from such a lawyer will often be straightforward for various reasons. First, there is nothing controversial about an equity swap or single stock future. In isolation, each of these contract types forms part of the everyday business of the bank. Second, the specialized control function may well not comprehend the overall purpose and effect of the particular transaction presented to them for approval in the context of the larger trading strategy. Arguably, no control group would understand the coordination of these disparate transactions including their timing, the manner in which they were executed among numerous counterparties, or their precise manner of settlement within market infrastructure. Third, the transaction being assessed is, at the approvals stage, merely contemplated and theoretical. Since it is to take place in the future, the approver will not know *how* it will take place. In particular, if there is a high degree of coordination among the parties at the time it is actually executed, that future fact will not be apparent at the time of any approval. Finally, the transaction in question, together with the wider set of transactions comprising the trade, will be described in a legal opinion, generally from a prestigious law firm (the role of legal opinions in the approvals process is significant and is discussed further below). For these reasons, when presented with the proposed trade and the opinion confirming its validity, the control staff member will often have neither the grounds nor the means to mount any significant challenge to the trade.

[120] As discussed, the cum-ex trade is a composite trade, comprised of a number of cash securities transactions (short sale, stock borrow) and derivative transactions (swaps, futures). Each of these is the subject of separate control by a specialist group at the bank. For example, legal control in a bank is generally organized around categories of financial instrument, e.g. a derivatives lawyer covering derivative trades, a futures lawyer covering futures trades, and stock lending lawyers responsible for that area of activity.

The issue of approval raises different issues in the context of staff responsible for risk and credit approval. Risk managers will have often come from a trading background and will be expected to understand not merely the form of a transaction but also its effects and attendant risks. As mentioned above, an 'in-business' risk manager was typically employed to manage conversations with the market and credit risk control groups. That person, paid as a front-office member of staff and therefore financially interested in the trades carried out by the line of business, would provide carefully prepared explanations as to the motivation for the trade. To the risk control group, the in-business risk manager would explain that the trades are simply 'flow' business (i.e. carried out in the ordinary course of participating in the marketplace) and are intended to achieve a level of profitability based on the market 'mispricing' of a dividend. In other words, the trade is simply an open-market dividend arbitrage opportunity.[121]

The day-to-day functioning of this approvals process is also hardly helpful to an effective control assessment. The cum-ex team would work up a presentation which would be circulated to the control functions. The presentation would contain information which the bankers decide is appropriate for inclusion. In practice, bankers used specific techniques to limit the scope for challenge of cum-ex trades and restrict the number of bank personnel involved in the approval process. One technique is to impose urgency upon the transaction, limiting the time for challenge. The trade is positioned as a time-sensitive market opportunity, calling for immediate approval. Also, code or project names for transactions were often used. The use of project names is common in investment banking to isolate sensitive private-side transactions from public exposure, for example, an impending corporate acquisition on which the bank is advising. Bankers arranging cum-ex trades were able to borrow this investment-banking protocol, which had the effect of conferring legitimacy and importance on the trade as well as cloaking it in a veil of secrecy. Another technique used was to pitch the proposed trade as merely requiring an extension of prior approvals that had already been signed off for similar trades. This engendered in control staff a predisposition to understand and accept the proposal in the context of what had previously been approved.

[121] The in-business risk manager would also deal with other matters such as, for example, the effect of the hedging trades and the ability to reacquire the securities to meet the commitment to redeliver to the share lender. On the first issue, though it was true that the size of the trades involved were very high, the in-business risk manager would explain that the bank's exposure on the short sale of shares was perfectly hedged by the derivative trade, with the consequence that the actual amount of risk was exceptionally low or nil. On the second point, the business risk manager might deal with the apparent problem (for the credit approval for the transaction) that the shares sold short by the bank need to be retrieved and returned to the lender of shares at the end of the trade by explaining that the counterparty buyer in the trade was also a client of the bank. The purchased shares would therefore move directly into the account of the fund controlled by the bank, making them readily available to discharge the later requirement to return shares to the lender.

The Legal Opinions

Because of the significant reliance placed upon them, legal opinions play a decisive role in the approvals process.[122] Their importance goes beyond a declaration that the trade is legal. The opinion also confirms that the transactions will allow amounts to be netted off against each other or cause property rights to pass in a way which is enforceable should the transactions ever become subject to challenge in court.

Depending upon the transaction being approved, there may be a variety of legal opinions that are required in any one case—for example, with separate opinions on each of the following: the tax aspects of the transaction (with a separate opinion dealing with the tax systems of each country involved in the transaction); the legal aspects of the transaction (again, with separate opinions for each country involved in the transaction); the accounting aspects of the transaction (ensuring that accounting rules recognize the bank's disposal of the shares as wholly separate from their later repurchase); and regulatory matters providing comfort that the trade as contemplated will not breach market trading regulations in the countries involved. It is also possible that there may be multiple tax and legal opinions relating to the same country, for example each dealing with different taxes, or different legal issues, within the same jurisdiction. Such opinions can in some cases deal with extremely complex matters and be very lengthy. These opinions are normally given by one or more external law or accounting firms with specialist legal and tax experience.

Control weaknesses may arise from the process of simply requesting opinions. For example, the opinions required in support of a tax trade are normally commissioned by the line of business at the bank and not by the control groups.[123] This is because the line of business will have ready access to the funds to pay for the opinion. It is well-known that they will be reluctant to pay for negative opinions.[124] More fundamentally, there is arguably a mutual reliance in the opinion process which is often poorly recognized in practice. In the case of cum-ex, the positive opinions which the bank sought and received were the cornerstone upon which internal approvals rested.[125] However, whilst it is obvious

[122] This was certainly true in relation to cum-ex transactions in the securities of German companies as the tax opinion provided by external tax advisers was widely regarded as validating the strategy.

[123] In the case of tax opinions on cum-ex, for example, it was almost invariably the front-office tax structuring and trading group, being regarded within the bank as the locus of skill and expertise in relation to tax-driven structures and trades, that would take control of the process of obtaining opinions (rather than the tax department representing the internal control function). This was often on the basis that only they had the requisite expertise to manage this process, coupled with the necessary budget to deal with the relevant costs.

[124] In practice, this means that an opinion is normally taken from a trusted external adviser who can be relied on to identify and develop solutions for any problems, and that there would usually be initial discussions with that adviser to confirm the expected outturn of any detailed technical tax analysis.

[125] The tax opinions taken in cum-ex and dealing with German tax issues are discussed in Chapter 2.

that the bank relies very heavily on the opinion of the specialist outside counsel, it is also true that the opinion of the external opinion-writer relies heavily on the bank. This latter reliance is manifest in two related areas: first, the opinion-writer depends on the bank for a complete and accurate description of the facts, including specifically the constituent elements of the transaction. Second, virtually all opinions, including especially tax opinions, set out a variety of assumptions which are critical to the detailed analysis and conclusions. These assumptions, if incorrect, would normally invalidate the conclusions drawn in the opinion. The opinion-writer is implicitly relying on the bank to ensure these assumptions are valid in any particular case. Further, since tax opinions are usually written without any reference to transaction sizes, and with only limited information on the mechanical/settlement issues, there is also a reliance on the point that these missing elements will not enter the equation so as to undermine or conflict with the conclusions reached in the opinion.[126]

In the cum-ex case, and as is demonstrated by the scale and nature of the investigations in Germany discussed in Chapter 4, all of these matters have proved highly problematic. On the first point, certain steps, in particular the fact that the trades were closely coordinated with intermediaries and counterparties, typically leading to a later return to the bank of the securities which were shorted (so that the bank could return the shares to the lender), were omitted. On the second point, a critical assumption made in the tax opinions written on cum-ex was the absence of such prearrangements. It seems evident that the control functions of banks have either not recognized at all the critical nature of the degree to which the external opinion-writer relies on the bank, or that they have recognized it but failed to reflect the point in the operation of their control processes.[127]

Implementation of Cum-Ex Trades

Partly as a result of the degree of reliance on the one-off approvals process, controls on the day-to-day implementation of transactions by traders are somewhat limited. In the last two decades, the compliance function at many banks has become distanced from the task of tying back actual practice (including the implementation of individual trading strategies) to the policies and related procedures established and approved by the bank. Instead, possibly in an effort by

[126] The absence of data on expected transaction sizes would have made it difficult for any opinion-writer to consider the practical realities of market risk and the difficulties of executing perfect hedges over very-large-sized equities transactions. However, many opinion-writers, being expert in their specialist technical area of the law but not in the realities of market execution, may have struggled on this point even if such information had been available.

[127] These points emphasize further the significance of the operational detail that is normally highly relevant in the case of such transactions, but which is typically not covered by the opinion (ironically, precisely because it is 'operational detail').

the legal and compliance functions to divide their respective workloads, the compliance group began to assume an 'advisory' function.[128] The legal group would provide guidelines on the applicability of laws and regulations to categories of transaction, while the compliance group would assess in any particular case whether a transaction was in conformity with those guidelines. As illustrated in the comments above on cum-ex, this meant that there was in that case limited or no active monitoring of transactions in order to ensure that they were being carried out in line with the approvals sign-off parameters or that the manner of their execution did not contradict the assumptions contained in the opinion supporting the trade.[129] In any event, given that cum-ex involved the execution of proprietary trades (e.g. the short sales and the related stock loans), the cum-ex traders could take advantage of the fact that these trades are rarely reviewed. In consequence, certain non-standard features of the day-to-day implementation of cum-ex trades went largely unremarked on by the internal control functions. These non-standard features included the existence of significant manual intervention in the trading process due to the use, in large volume, of non-standard instruments. For example, because the terms of the flexible and variable futures contracts[130] used in many cum-ex trades were tailored on a transaction-by-transaction basis according to the precise requirements of the contracting parties, it was not a futures contract which the bank's automated processes could process automatically. Instead, the settlement of its terms had to be adapted to the particular quantity, pricing, and dates of a single cum-ex trade. This requires human intervention,[131] which would be carried out by the bank's middle and back office.[132] Another example is the short-selling and stock borrowing elements of the

[128] A further issue is that staff in the compliance function are generally not required to have specific qualifications. Experience is typically gained by on-the-job learning in the financial-services sector and receiving training and acquiring certificates over time. See International Compliance Association, 'Begin a Career in Compliance', available at https://www.int-comp.org/careers/a-career-in-compliance/begin-a-career-in-compliance/.

[129] Realistically, if a control function did raise a concern or a question, it would have been very difficult to challenge the immensely complex cum-ex trade, many of whose component transactions were apparently conducted with third parties and on the market. There was a material amount of revenue at stake for the bank and its clients, and the transaction would also have passed through the approvals process. If a challenge were raised, who would win that argument?

[130] See further the discussion of these contracts in Chapter 3.

[131] A transaction which requires intervention and/or careful monitoring and management is a 'manual' transaction. In the BClear example, this means that the non-standard terms of the BClear futures contract need to be documented and entered into bank and counterparty systems correctly. Similarly, the deliveries of borrowed securities, instead of settling on the normal T+2 basis, would need to be carefully handled to ensure that shares that have already paid out their dividend are delivered and that the delivery can be achieved on T+0 terms.

[132] The middle office would liaise with counterparties to ensure that the transaction has been recognized by each party involved in the trade and is being properly processed, including ensuring that, at all steps of the transaction, the transactional details processed by both parties match. This ensures that the transaction will take effect as planned. The role of the back office is to ensure that the movements of large amounts of cash and securities actually take place, or in other words that the transactions 'settle' on a timely basis.

trade. While it may not be unusual to short securities and borrow shares prior to dividend date, doing so in immense quantities of shorted shares (with the short sale and the borrow designed to straddle the dividend record date), and on a tight timeline, is unusual and the process required careful management. This is particularly true when the borrowed shares had to be moved on a same-day basis. The problem is exacerbated when shares are, as explained in Chapter 3, 'looped' given that deliveries, returns, and onward deliveries must be very carefully sequenced.

The above examples are features of the cum-ex trade which require precise planning and very active operational management and intervention in order to ensure that the transactions comprising a cum-ex trade did not 'fail'.[133] The significance of this (as well as being somewhat unusual in its own right) is that, once trading patterns and arrangements sidestep ordinary market mechanisms and tempo, it raises a question as to what lies behind the arrangements. It may also imply a reliance on another party or parties entering into matched trades on a basis which is necessarily coordinated. Far from signifying any control concerns, the operational intensity involved in cum-ex trades (arising from the large number of transactions and their carefully coordinated nature) actually led to a response in some banks that underlined the power of the cum-ex trader to marshal the resources of the bank to deal with any issues that might otherwise constrain the cum-ex opportunity. In the cum-ex dividend season, the focused effort required to deliver cum-ex transactions was of such a high degree that the bank's regular middle office might struggle to manage it alongside its other daily work. At some banks, the response was to accommodate this problem by offering the cum-ex traders the widest latitude. Specifically, in order to ensure that the bankers carrying out these trades had the support they needed, they were permitted to install and manage what was in effect a separate and dedicated middle-office group, which would work next to the bankers on the trading floor. What was extraordinary about this development was the degree to which the juxtaposition of the front and middle office on a trading floor violated fundamental bank procedural safeguards. The middle office of a bank operates under the supervision and control of the operations group. It has no interest in the outcome of any particular trade but is instead there to manage the operation of the bank's affairs generally. Placing operations staff under the day-to-day management and control of a single group whose mission it was to carry out cum-ex and dividend arbitrage trades meant that the prospects for pay and promotion within the bank of these

[133] A 'fail', as the word suggests, would mean that the bank did not meet its obligations to deliver or receive shares or cash when due. A 'fail' can bring about significant adverse monetary consequences, for example, fines by market regulators, a counterparty not being able to complete a transaction, or obtaining undelivered shares from another source at a significant cost borne by the party responsible for the fail.

operations staff were tied directly to those of the traders they supported. Over time, the risk is that such a group will deviate from bank procedure, cut corners, or achieve outcomes in ways that are not consistent with bank policy. Banks normally isolate functions, a measure known as 'segregation of duties' precisely to avoid such risks from emerging.

A feature of the implementation of cum-ex trades is that it led to a proliferation of cum-ex trading in the inter-bank market. Banks will often attempt to keep structures like cum-ex secret from their competitors, but in practice this is rarely possible due to bank staff skilled in the trade moving between banks. For example, a junior member of a cum-ex team in one bank might find their status and earning power materially increased by moving to another bank and exploiting the experience gained prior to the move. Information about the trade may also be dispersed due to the use of market intermediaries, such as inter-dealer brokers. In practice, therefore, structures such as cum-ex soon become widely known in the industry.

One aspect of the practical execution of cum-ex trades was the ability of the banks to utilize powers and privileges reserved to them[134] in the form of features of the financial system which are not available to non-professional participants in the financial markets. An example of this is the ability to move securities for immediate settlement.[135] It is necessary to exercise a high level of control over the operation of the settlement system in order to execute a cum-ex trade, and this is not something which is available to such non-professional participants. Another example is the use of the flexible futures contracts that have been discussed in Chapter 3. These were bilaterally tailored in much the same way as occurs with an OTC or off-exchange contract and yet they qualified as on-exchange contracts. Further, because the banks, together with custodians and inter-dealer brokers, *are* the financial system, they can modify the manner of its operation to suit their purposes. For example, the single stock futures contract employed in cum-ex developed two characteristics which greatly facilitated the trade: one was that the terms of the future (unlike futures regularly traded on large futures exchanges) had terms which were infinitely variable; the second was that the futures contract had a settlement period which, at four days, was twice as long as the regular settlement period. That doubled the cum-div period for a given share, providing additional days in which the cum-ex trade could be executed.

[134] The powers and privileges enjoyed by banks are considered in detail in Chapter 8.

[135] For the cum-ex trade to be made to work, it is necessary to deal with two movements of securities (relating to (1) the borrowing of the shares from the lender and (2) the delivery of the borrowed shares to the purchaser under the short sale). Given that shares cannot be borrowed until the ex-dividend date has passed, these two share movements need to be accomplished in materially less time than is provided for in the standard T+2 period allowed for settlement of the short sale. This is achieved through the privileged role for market professionals in the process and specifically their ability to choose the timing for these two share movements in a way not open to non-professionals.

External Controls

The external regulator was, for the reasons discussed earlier in this chapter, poorly equipped to identify, let alone deal with, cum-ex trading. As confirmed by the German parliamentary report into the cum-ex affair discussed in Chapter 4, the German bank regulatory authorities (as opposed to the German tax authorities) were broadly unaware of the cum-ex transactions until some time after they had finally been stopped.[136]

Summary

Based on the above discussion, it is concluded that bank controls are not well-suited to dealing with trades such as cum-ex. It is therefore not surprising that in many cases no serious challenge to cum-ex trading was presented by the operation of governance and control mechanisms either internal or external to the bank. In particular, the approvals process, which is central to the bank internal control apparatus, suffers from a number of defects. The outcome was that the control function did not have the specialized knowledge to understand how the trade worked, had at best a limited understanding of the result which flowed from the aggregation of transactions needed to deliver cum-ex, relied very heavily on the legal opinions from outside advisers (which as noted are problematic in certain fundamental respects), and would in practice have found it difficult to challenge the trade. For their part, external bank regulators never came close to penetrating the layers necessary to understand the trade.[137] Arguably, these outcomes are to be expected, and perhaps are even inevitable, given the incentives embedded in the banking business model and the architecture of the control systems in place.

Misconduct in the Banking Sector in Comparison with Other Sectors

The discussion in this chapter has so far been concerned with misconduct in the banking sector. A question not so far pursued is how misconduct in the banking sector compares with that in other sectors. Other industries of course experience

[136] There are many references in the German parliamentary report to the financial market regulators being completely unaware of what was going on despite the reporting of share movements in the billions of euros around dividend dates, and to the lack of cooperation between the regulators, and to the difficulties of the regulators in even understanding the nature of the cum-ex trade. See German Parliamentary Report at, for example, pp. 262–4, 500, 501, 520–1, 526, 530.

[137] In some rare cases where the cum-ex strategy was discussed with external regulators it would have been presented as a market arbitrage opportunity, supported by legal opinions, and that would have been the end of the matter.

misconduct,[138] yet some features of misconduct in the banking sector seem to the author to be unique, or at least materially different from other sectors. It is therefore instructive to compare the nature of misconduct in banking with misconduct in other sectors. However, such a cross-industry comparison of misconduct is a subject which could occupy one or more books in itself. The point is therefore taken up in a more limited way by contrasting cum-ex with an example of a fraud from another industry, with a view to gauging important differences as well as similarities. The example selected is the Volkswagen emissions scandal, often referred to as 'Dieselgate'. This example is of value because it consists of misconduct which, both in its nature and scale (and for other reasons which are discussed in more detail), might reasonably be regarded as in some ways broadly comparable to cum-ex. By coincidence, the example also has German roots.[139] It is not claimed here that the example chosen is necessarily representative of all or even some fraud in other industries, but nonetheless the comparison illustrates some important respects in which misconduct in the banking sector is materially different to misconduct in other industries. It will help to first summarize the key facts of Dieselgate.

Dieselgate—The Facts

The name 'Dieselgate' refers to a scheme by which a number of vehicle manufacturers,[140] most famously Volkswagen, evaded diesel emission standards.[141] In 2013, the International Council on Clean Transportation (ICCT), an independent non-profit organization, engaged a team of research engineers at a University of West Virginia laboratory, the Center for Alternative Fuels, Engines and Emissions (CAFEE), to undertake emissions tests on a number of diesel cars.[142] The ICCT sought to understand why it was that diesel cars were apparently able to comply

[138] See the discussion earlier in this chapter of Association of Certified Fraud Examiners, 'Report to the Nations'. It is notable that in addition to banking, three of the four industries with the largest incidence of fraud (government, healthcare, and education) are sectors where, in many states, the public sector is involved directly or which are sectors that have strong ties to, and interactions with, government.

[139] Germany was the largest market in which the cum-ex trade was carried out, though the trade was by no means limited to that market. The fact that the Volkswagen example concerns a German company, Volkswagen AG (known internationally as the Volkswagen Group), is therefore purely coincidental.

[140] See the report of Damian Carrington, 'Four More Carmakers Join Diesel Emissions Row', *The Guardian*, 9 October 2015, available at https://www.theguardian.com/environment/2015/oct/09/mercedes-honda-mazda-mitsubishi-diesel-emissions-row.

[141] For a series of essays on the background, emergence, and legal aspects of the scandal, see Marco Frigessi di Rattalma, ed., *The Dieselgate: A Legal Perspective* (Springer Nature, 2017).

[142] See the 'Frequently Asked Questions' page of the International Council on Clean Transportation, 25 September 2015, available at: https://www.theicct.org/news/faq-use-nox-emissions-diesel-passenger-cars.

with emission standards in the US that were widely regarded as more stringent than their European equivalents. The hope was that this would uncover ways in which the emissions of diesel cars operating in Europe could be improved.[143] Instead, tests by CAFEE of three diesel vehicles revealed that emissions of nitrogen oxide (NOx) from two of the cars exceeded US permissible levels by between nine and thirty-eight times. In early 2014, the University of West Virginia engineers presented their findings at a conference in San Diego. In the audience were members of the California Air Resources Board (CARB), a department of the California Environmental Protection Agency (EPA) charged with defining and enforcing emissions standards in that state.[144] The agency was immediately interested in the university team's findings and pursued an investigation into the matter.[145] Around ten meetings were then convened between CARB and Volkswagen,[146] until in December 2014 Volkswagen proposed a recall of the affected cars to correct the emissions problem on the basis this was due to some sort of technical fault in the system. The recall process was to be completed in Spring 2015. Not surprisingly, the recall was unsuccessful in solving the problem. Only when it became clear that the EPA and CARB would not approve Volkswagen's cars for certification and sale in the 2016 model year did Volkswagen admit to the presence and use of a so-called 'defeat device'. The Environmental Protection Agency issued, on 18 September 2015, a notice of violation against Volkswagen. In the notice, the agency stated its finding that Volkswagen had installed defeat devices in vehicles sold in the United States over a number of years.[147] The defeat device consisted of software which was designed to detect whether the vehicle was undergoing an emissions test.[148] If it was, the software would then immediately (and for the purposes of the test) modify the vehicle's emission controls to cause it to pass the test. On 23 September 2015, five

[143] See the report of Patrick McGee, 'How VW's Cheating on Emissions Was Exposed', *Financial Times*, 11 January 2017, available at https://www.ft.com/content/103dbe6a-d7a6-11e6-944b-e7eb37a6aa8e.

[144] For a comprehensive description of the work of the California Environmental Protection Agency, see their website at https://ww2.arb.ca.gov/our-work.

[145] See the report of Jack Ewing, 'Researchers Who Exposed VW Gain Little Reward from Success', *New York Times*, 24 July 2016, available at https://www.nytimes.com/2016/07/25/business/vw-wvu-diesel-volkswagen-west-virginia.html.

[146] See the report of Geoffrey Smith and Roger Parloff, 'Hoaxwagen', *Fortune*, 7 March 2016, available at http://fortune.com/inside-volkswagen-emissions-scandal/.

[147] United States Environmental Protection Agency, Office of Enforcement and Compliance Assurance, 'Notice of Violation by letter to Volkswagen AG, Audi AG and Volkswagen Group of America', 18 September 2015, available at https://www.epa.gov/sites/production/files/2015-10/documents/vw-nov-caa-09-18-15.pdf. By 2 November 2015, the EPA issued a further Notice of Violation, specifying a number of additional Porsche, Audi, and Volkswagen models also incorporating the defeat device.

[148] This was achieved by programming the software to identify the existence of a number of conditions, such as speed and position of the steering wheel, which would be present in the event of a formal testing of the emissions system. Volkswagen software engineers labelled the relevant software as 'acoustic condition', apparently to cause an observer to believe that the relevant 'defeat' code related to engine noise.

days after the Environmental Protection Agency notice of violation, the CEO of Volkswagen was forced to step down.[149] In January 2016, former FBI director Robert Mueller was appointed to bring the parties involved in more than 500 lawsuits against Volkswagen to a financial settlement.[150] In 2016, the vast majority of Volkswagen car owners in the US agreed to participate in a $25 billion settlement which included buyback offers and additional compensation for about 500,000 owners. Volkswagen later settled a US class action lawsuit by a further 2000 owners who opted not to participate in the 2016 settlement.[151] By March 2019, Dieselgate had cost Volkswagen approximately $31 billion.[152]

Comparability of Dieselgate to Cum-Ex

There are a number of reasons why Dieselgate may be regarded as having some broad comparability with cum-ex, at least for the purposes of the discussion here: each crossed national boundaries and had widespread effects around the world, particularly in Europe; and each involved a very specific manipulation of an important control system. In Dieselgate the defeat device was designed to overcome the applicable vehicle emission controls, creating low-emission results, while in cum-ex the cum-dividend short sale was intended to manipulate the financial infrastructure for the payment of dividends so as to generate positive outcomes in the form of system-generated tax credits. The two cases are also broadly comparable in their financial scale, involving double-digit billions of dollars. Whether measured in terms of cars sold that were affected by the emissions scandal (475,000 in the US alone[153] with 10.5 million affected worldwide[154]), or the cost to Volkswagen of the scandal ($25 billion, including $7 billion spent repurchasing cars), the scale of Dieselgate is similar to cum-ex.[155] Although the schemes were

[149] See the report of Jack Ewing, 'Volkswagen CEO Martin Winterkorn Resigns Amid Emissions Scandal', *New York Times*, 23 September 2015, available at https://www.nytimes.com/2016/07/25/business/vw-wvu-diesel-volkswagen-west-virginia.html.

[150] See the report of Reuters, 'This Former FBI Director Will be Volkswagen's "Settlement Master"', reported in *Fortune*, 19 January 2016, available at http://fortune.com/2016/01/19/volkswagen-robert-mueller/.

[151] See the report of David Shepardson, 'Volkswagen Settles U.S. Diesel Owner Lawsuit on Eve of Trial', *Forbes*, 23 February 2018, available at https://uk.reuters.com/article/uk-volkswagen-emissions/volkswagen-settles-u-s-diesel-owner-lawsuit-on-eve-of-trial-idUKKCN1G72SY.

[152] See the report of Joe Miller, 'Mopping up Dieselgate: The Boss Transforming Volkswagen', BBC News, 17 March 2019, available at https://www.bbc.co.uk/news/business-47524588.

[153] At an average cost of approximately $20,000 per car (see https://www.cars.com/research/volkswagen/) this would equate to $9.5 billion in total sales.

[154] See Reuters, 'VW Has Still Not Fixed One in Three Dieselgate Cars in Britain', 8 November 2017, available at https://uk.reuters.com/article/uk-volkswagen-emissions-britain/vw-has-still-not-fixed-one-in-three-dieselgate-cars-in-britain-idUKKBN1D828L.

[155] See the report of Robert Stumpf, 'VW Dieselgate Graveyards Grow to Over 300,000 Cars Across U.S.', *The Drive*, 30 March 2018, available at http://www.thedrive.com/news/19768/vw-dieselgate-graveyards-grow-to-over-300000-cars-across-u-s. As might be expected, a financial motivation was

executed in very different industries with quite different products (contrast the tangible nature of a car with the abstract nature of a financial product), there are some strong similarities between the schemes in both the level of complexity and the manner of its implementation. In Dieselgate, the fraud was targeted at the most abstract level of the manufactured product, where multiple vehicle-management software systems and millions of lines of code converge to achieve an operational outcome, namely, the testing of vehicle emissions. Diagnosing the fraud required multidisciplinary skills crossing numerous physical vehicle sub-systems, computer code, and a knowledge of both regulatory emission guidelines and testing techniques. As implemented by Volkswagen, it was an immensely complex fraud.[156] Cum-ex is similarly complex, particularly after the product refinements discussed in Chapter 3 were applied to the trade. There were also some commonalities relating to the relevant regulatory regime. EU regulations applicable to the car industry placed reliance on the car manufacturer to ensure its own compliance with emission standards.[157] As already discussed, banks have an extensive self-policing regime, consisting of self-regulatory organizations which act as regulators and self-reporting regimes which require the banks to promptly and forthrightly alert regulators to internal control failures. A further point of comparison is that in neither case was the miconduct uncovered through routine governance mechanisms, regulatory examinations, or monitoring channels designed to expose compliance weaknesses.[158] Finally, it is also notable that both the cum-ex and Dieselgate scandals resulted, initially at least, in a 'bad apples' explanation of the misconduct. Before the United States Congress, Michael Horn, Volkswagen's US Chief Executive, commented that the software code designed to defeat the emissions test was created by 'a couple of software

also key in both cases. Like the banking sector, the consumer car business is highly competitive. Profit margins range between 4.5 and 8 per cent, with Volkswagen falling at the lower end of that range. This created the environment in which Volkswagen was incentivized to find ways of extracting higher profits through illegal means. One solution that had been available to Volkswagen for managing NOx emissions was to license technology from Daimler and Bosch (this was the Bluetech solution), but, at a cost of €300 per vehicle, it was considered prohibitively expensive. See Michael Moffett, 'Volkswagen's Defeat Device Debacle', Thunderbird School of Global Management, 2017, available at https://thunderbird.asu.edu/faculty-and-research/case-series/id/a07-17-0009-author-michael-moffett.

156 It took a year-long investigation by an international team of researchers to isolate the code. See the report from University of California–San Diego, 'Researchers Find Computer Code that VW Used to Cheat Emissions Tests', 22 May 2017, available at https://phys.org/news/2017-05-code-volkswagen-emissions.html.

157 For example, in judging compliance with emission rules, Germany's Federal Motor Transport Authority relied on emission testing results from the manufacturers themselves. See further Marcus Schuetz, 'Dieselgate – Heavy Fumes Exhausting The Volkswagen Group', The University of Hong Kong, Asia Case Research Centre, Ref: 16/572C (ACRC, 2016).

158 As noted earlier, in 2013 the International Council on Clean Transportation, a non-profit organization with offices in Europe, the US, and Asia, engaged a team of research engineers at a University of West Virginia laboratory to undertake tests on a number of diesel cars. See https://www.theicct.org/news/faq-use-nox-emissions-diesel-passenger-cars.

engineers who put this in for whatever reason' and that it was not a corporate decision. However, when Volkswagen introduced an amnesty allowing non-managers to come forward with information about the fraud without fear of dismissal, approximately fifty did so. It also emerged that the deception was an 'open secret' within Volkswagen and had been raised by at least one internal whistle-blower in 2011, refuting the claim that the cause was a couple of errant software engineers acting in isolation.[159]

Relevant Differences

While Dieselgate and cum-ex have a number of shared characteristics, there are also some very telling differences which are illustrative of the attributes of the financial sector as compared with other sectors. These differences go a long way to explaining why misconduct in the financial sector is not only pervasive but why it presents some unique problems in comparison with other industries.

Knowledge of the Misconduct

One obvious difference is that, whilst the existence and broad outline of the Dieselgate fraud is now very widely known across the world, the existence of cum-ex is very largely unheard of, at least outside a handful of European states.[160] This reflects a much broader set of obstacles in understanding the financial sector and the companies which operate in it. Notwithstanding the central and even critical role in the economy played by the banking sector, the business of banks is poorly understood.[161] A major factor in this state of affairs is probably the striking asymmetry between the relative simplicity of the financial affairs of most businesses and individuals on the one hand, and the complexity of the financial operations of most banks on the other. As discussed further below, large swathes of the financial system operate independently of the non-financial economy with, for example, complex structured instruments being traded primarily between

[159] See the newspaper report by the *Sueddeutshe Zeitung*, 'Volkswagen report finds manipulation was open secret in department: newspaper', 22 January 2016, available at https://www.reuters.com/article/us-volkswagen-emissions-investigation-idUSKCN0V02E7.

[160] The existence of the cum-ex scheme is more widely known in Germany, though even there the basic facts of cum-ex are not widely understood, and, as noted earlier, even the specialist journalists following the case have difficulty in articulating the essential nature of the cum-ex trading structure.

[161] This theme is pursued in Engelen et al., *After the Great Complacence*. The discussion there (at pp.43–4) includes the comment that in 2006, before the Global Financial Crisis, the global issuance of collateralized debt obligations (CDOs) reached $5.2 trillion yet this warranted just 116 articles in the *Financial Times* over the whole year. The automobile industry generated over 4000 articles in the *Financial Times* over the same period yet represented just one quarter of the size of the CDO market in revenue terms.

banks and other financial institutions (such as inter-dealer brokers and hedge funds), creating a closed and detached system which can be understood only by insiders working within the sector. This creates an obvious barrier to the detection of misconduct in the sector. In the case of cum-ex, for example, not only was the scheme targeted at an obscure part of the clearing system and its interaction with the tax system, but the manner by which the tax credits were monetized and distributed among the participants was concealed by the use of private derivative contracts.

As with many sectors, the position of the automobile industry is very different. The product that is produced, and the manufacturing process itself, is tangible and easy to grasp, at least in concept. This normally means that any defect in the product due to misconduct on the part of the producer will quickly become apparent. In the case of a defective car, for example, consumers experience the subject matter of the fraud directly in owning and operating an affected car. Environmental effects, such as emissions pollution, may not be observable, but nonetheless they present readily understandable health issues: the prospect of owning an excessively polluting vehicle is for a number of reasons unattractive to potential purchasers. There are also direct and negative financial consequences associated with the value of a car which, owing to its true level of emissions, is now illegal and/or subject to higher emission taxes, not to mention the palpable emotional disappointment and anger which an owner might feel from having been deceived.

The position in relation to the bulk of the operation of the banking sector is very different. It is true that there are some situations, usually involving the direct interaction of banks with the public,[162] where what is said above about the automobile industry bears some similarity to the banking sector. However, overwhelmingly, these features are absent from the banking sector due to the layered complexity of financial markets.[163] The contrast is reflected in the nature of cum-ex: the result generated from the trade cannot be experienced and is not observable except to the perpetrators who carried it out. Understanding the trade requires specialized knowledge of several things: a range of complex financial instruments; the detailed settlement conventions of the market and how they might be varied in particular circumstances; the law and practice of the specific

[162] It is true, however, that in the context of retail banking, credit cards, and perhaps commercial lending, episodic failures of customer service, revelations of improper fees, and the mis-selling of financial products do of course elicit similar public reactions and disapprobation. Large financial scandals involving inter-bank dealings such as LIBOR and cum-ex, while raising awareness about the conduct of banks and bankers, cannot be said to have a direct impact on individual citizens' lives.

[163] The complexity also means that a bank will often have a long lead time between the point at which a hazard is created and the point when it comes to light—and that lead time may often be longer than the lifespan of the relevant employee.

dividend withholding regime as well as its operational features, including the mechanics of tax reclaims embedded in the operation of the clearing and settlement system; and so on. Finally, cum-ex might be perceived as a victimless crime on the basis that no person is directly affected or directly harmed by it, yet a number of states and millions of European taxpayers were impoverished substantially as a result of the tax reclaims generated by the trade.

Modus Operandi of the Misconduct

Partly as a result of the differences referred to above, a major distinction between the two cases lies in the steps taken to conceal each of them. In the case of Dieselgate, the fraud was (and depended for its effectiveness on being) elaborately concealed, with Volkswagen executives admitting to it only after they had been confronted with the evidence.[164] If, in the planning stage, the arrangements had ever been described and subjected to open scrutiny (which, of course, they were not), it seems inconceivable they would ever have been blessed by a suite of legal opinions in support of the arrangements. By contrast, it is difficult not to be struck by the openness with which the cum-ex trade was planned and implemented within the banks. It was drawn up overtly as a business 'strategy'. It was then presented to, and analysed by, the relevant control groups and, following their review, it received explicit approval. It was successfully pitched to investment funds around the world as a strategy. This marketing and execution of cum-ex in plain sight, by hundreds of financial institutions, is noteworthy and reveals the confidence within banks that the scheme would not be challenged, and, even if it were, that there would be a low probability of serious consequence.[165]

The Abstract Nature of Banking Business

The points discussed above stem largely from the abstract and complex nature of banking business. On this matter, there is a point of similarity between Dieselgate and cum-ex which, paradoxically, identifies a way in which the respective sectors

[164] Only when US officials threatened to withhold approval for the 2016 model year did Volkswagen executives admit to the fraud. See Jack Ewing, 'Volkswagen Denied Deception to EPA for Nearly a Year', *Houston Chronicle*, 21 September 2015, available at https://www.houstonchronicle.com/business/article/Volkswagen-denied-deception-to-EPA-for-nearly-a-6520476.php.

[165] Many in the financial industry thought the German authorities would not act retrospectively. See further,Clancy Yeates, Sönke Iwerson, and Volker Votsmeier, 'Germans Don't "Blame and Shame"; Emails Reveal Macquarrie's Mind over Tax Deals', *Sydney Morning Herald*, 22 July 2019.

are completely dissimilar. In Dieselgate and cum-ex, the misconduct was in each case designed to exploit the weakest point in the relevant system. It is no coincidence that, in both cases, this was where the complexity of the system at work was at an especially high point. In the case of Dieselgate, that point of weakness was the emissions control system, where numerous elements of the car's functional capability were controlled by computer code. That location is an extremely difficult area of the vehicle to understand given that in modern cars it may comprise over 150 different sub-systems, digital interfaces, and connections, managed by as many as 100 million lines of code and representing in abstract form the designs and technology of a raft of different engineering and software disciplines.[166]

Comparison with the banking sector exposes a stark difference between the two industries. Whilst this level of complexity may be relatively exceptional in the automobile industry, in the banking sector it is the norm. In banking, the only tangible elements in the business are the offices, people, furniture, and computer hardware. All the other elements are abstract and intangible: much of a modern bank's business is carried out using electronic systems over private connections with counterparties. Further, to the extent a bank must carry out transactions on public exchanges or report its transactions to regulatory authorities, it will do so through systems which require transactions in individual financial instruments to be disclosed. They display *what* the transaction consisted of, but not how or why it was conducted, nor how it might relate to any other transaction or transactions. Not only are there millions of such reported transactions daily, but, being separate, their combined effect cannot possibly be discerned from the available public information. The transactions themselves are executed on a large number of exchanges, trading platforms, multilateral trading facilities, and through 'dark pools' and over-the-counter markets. The transactions may involve a range of different types of intermediary, and involve a very wide array of different (and sometimes highly esoteric) financial products, many of which are either readily interchangeable with each other or can be tailored to deliver that effect. As an abstract, intangible, impenetrable, and closed system, the entirety of the banking system is, in the terms of Dieselgate, arguably itself one enormous emission control system, potentially available to be configured and operated to defeat its purpose.

[166] See Bob O'Donnell, 'Your Average Car is a Lot More Code-Driven than You Think', *USA Today*, 28 June 2016, available at https://eu.usatoday.com/story/tech/columnist/2016/06/28/your-average-car-lot-more-code-driven-than-you-think/86437052/. In fact, it took a group of researchers from Ruhr-Universitat Bochum and the University of California, San Diego a year to precisely locate and map the operation of the Volkswagen defeat code, underscoring the ease with which a fraudulent device can be concealed within a highly complex system. See Moritz Contag et al., 'How They Did It: An Analysis of Emission Defeat Devices in Modern Automobiles', IEEE Symposium on Security and Privacy (SP), 22–26 May 2017, available at https://cseweb.ucsd.edu/~klevchen/diesel-sp17.pdf.

Wider Implications

The highly abstract nature of financial business carried on by banks has a number of implications that are of particular relevance in the context of the discussion in this book.

Malleability of the Banking Product

As in most business sectors, the carmaker is bound by the physical means of production, including land, labour, machines, and the limits of the relevant technology/automation to deliver that production. The production process transforms, through physical operations, raw materials such as steel, leather, aluminium, and plastic into finished products, with the 'inputs' in the process being directly referable to the finished product or 'outputs'. The car manufacturer's life cycle to develop and introduce a new product is measured in years and requires large commitments of capital,[167] meaning it is necessary to design its products years ahead of their ultimate build and release date. Once in production, the product has a limited lifespan meaning that the design, development, testing, and release cycle with all of its attendant risks and high investment costs must begin anew.[168] Captive to physical laws which involve all the means of production, the carmaker follows a process which is transformational, combining components and assembling them into a finished physical good. Supporting the production process is a supply chain which is global in nature, stretching from extractive industries to semiconductors. The basic manufacturing operations may be capable of relocation, but this would be an expensive and slow undertaking and means that the basic business conditions are not easily modified. That picture is broadly the same in most industries, but it is quite different in the banking sector. The banks comprise their own supply chain. Further, from a transactional perspective, the essential nature of a bank's business is to design, structure, originate, and trade *claims.* These claims are created by financial product contracts between banks and third parties and consist in rights and obligations to cash flows or assets under those contracts. This means that the financial products of a bank are highly

[167] The cost of developing a new car is in the region of $1 billion. See the report of Terry Shea, 'Why Does It Cost So Much for Automakers to Develop New Models?', *Autoblog*, 27 July 2010, available at https://www.autoblog.com/2010/07/27/why-does-it-cost-so-much-for-automakers-to-develop-new-models/.

[168] The lifespan of a new model of car is typically in the order of seven years. See Center for Automotive Research, 'Automotive Product Development and the Need for Balance with the Regulatory Environment', 20 September 2017, available at https://www.cargroup.org/automotive-product-development-cycles-and-the-need-for-balance-with-the-regulatory-environment/.

malleable and can readily be modified through legal transformation, that is to say, simply by varying the terms of contracts. Therefore, unlike industries such as car manufacturing, product innovation in the financial sector can be and is extremely rapid.

Ability to Trade and Re-Trade the Claim

It follows from the nature of the banking business product—a set of claims—that it may be traded and re-traded multiple times. In the automobile industry, the vehicle that is the business product is valuable due to the assembly of all the component parts into a single unit, which may then be sold. However, there are some obvious external constraints on the process. The manufacturer can only book revenue from the car production and sales process once because of the limitations on the population of potential customers. Customers are people outside the industry. It is not a sustainable strategy to sell the product to other car manufacturers or to the car manufacturer's suppliers, etc. This is not the case with banking-sector business. The nature of the business product as one or more financial claims means that simultaneous trading and re-trading of the same underlying claim is possible. There is in principle no limit to the number of times that given cash flows and/or risks relating to those cash flows may be repackaged in financial products. For example, a single underlying loan may give rise to multiple credit default swaps which relate to the default risk relating to that single loan, and each of those swaps may then be traded and re-traded (tiering derivatives contract on derivatives contract) effectively without limit.[169] This feature of financial trading has already been seen to be directly relevant to cum-ex. As discussed in Chapter 3, the same cum-ex trade could be instantly 'repackaged' to create another trade (or 'a trade within a trade') over the same parcel of shares.

[169] Two recent examples amply demonstrate this feature of the industry. The number of exchange traded funds (ETFs)—which are funds created by financial services firms containing shares of public companies—now exceed in number the total number of public company issuers. Put another way, if ETFs are baskets and public companies are eggs, the number of baskets exceeds the number of eggs. The number of public companies stands at approximately 3600—see the Editorial Board report 'Where Have All the Public Companies Gone', *Bloomberg Opinion*, 9 April 2018, available at https://www.bloomberg.com/opinion/articles/2018-04-09/where-have-all-the-u-s-public-companies-gone. The number of exchange traded products, such as ETFs and similar products exceeds 5000. See the report of Todd Shriber, 'The Best ETFs 2019: A Comprehensive Guide' *Investopedia*, 22 April 2019, available at https://www.investopedia.com/investing/best-etfs-2018-comprehensive-guide/. Another example lies in the credit derivatives market. In the context of the credit derivative swaps market, it is not uncommon for the notional value of contracts referencing a particular company's bonds to exceed the actual outstanding amount of those bonds. The financial industry has free rein to create such untethered mushrooming of claims.

Impact of Network Effects

The earlier discussion of the 'originate to hold' model of traditional banking business model places the bank as an enduring intermediary between parties in the real economy (i.e. between the debtor/borrower and the lender/depositor). The growth of the 'originate to distribute' model broke these linkages to the real economy by allowing the bank to sell off the loans to special purpose vehicles funded by third party investors. As noted above, however, the modern banking model also *deconstructs* financial claims, disaggregating them into their constituent components. The theory is that this allows certain undesirable risks to be laid off to others, assuming that there are others willing or able to assume them. In order to achieve this result, additional counterparties must be brought into the picture, or further contracts entered into with existing parties. The end result of this process is that what in the simple banking model is a series of cash flows and simple credit exposures to entities and assets in the real economy becomes under the modern banking model an elaborate web of interdependencies between highly complex chains of transactions and actors. Given the proliferation of tradable contracts and specific forms of deconstructed cash flows, market infrastructure in the form of exchanges and clearing houses become necessary to process and manage the numerous claims. At the same time, there is an escalating need for exchanges of collateral between the parties or between the parties and the clearing houses to mitigate all the resultant credit exposures created among market participants. The relevance of this is that it has converted the traditional conduit for intermediating credit into a vast global network, components of which come into existence to allow the network to operate and to support interactions between all of its various elements. Consequently, much of the financial system finds its purpose in serving other parts of the financial system, and the link to the real economy becomes ever more remote. Further, because of all the complex interdependencies, the network cannot easily be disentangled, meaning that single points of failure are hard to identify and, as risks are continually laid off to others, that dependency on other participants to manage risk appropriately makes it more likely that the interrelated components could fail in a domino fashion.[170] The modern 'financial system' which consists of this network is therefore poorly understood, crosses jurisdictional borders, manages and modifies its own operating conditions, and creates linkages and interdependencies which contribute to its fragility. Collectively, these features make both isolating and addressing misconduct within the system, including through investigation and prosecution, exceptionally difficult. Further, the systemic importance of the system's largest participants appears to have made prosecution in particular politically

[170] Compare to the position under the simple banking model where a failed entity's assets (loans) and its liabilities (deposits) could be assumed by a financially strong bank.

unpalatable, greatly lessening the deterrent effect of serious legal action against those participants in response to their misconduct.[171]

Ability to Modify the System

The intricate interdependent infrastructure of the modern financial system leads to another very significant difference between the financial sector and other sectors of the economy. Specifically, the complex and fragmented nature of the system creates opportunities for banks to 'repurpose' or 'hijack' transactions or attributes of the system, essentially modifying its operation through deliberate changes to the manner in which they employ its infrastructure and capabilities. This might be achieved in various ways, a number of which are illustrated by cum-ex. For example, exemptions or reliefs designed for one purpose in the system may be redeployed for another, as where the tax exemption for transfers of shares under a stock loan[172] was a crucial element in delivering the tax benefit under the cum-ex trade. Cum-ex also illustrates how the operation of the settlement system could be varied by design, in that case to achieve an instant settlement of the borrowing of the stock and the onward delivery to satisfy the short sale yet within the context of what was otherwise a settlement system driven by an apparently rigid T+2 settlement convention.[173] It is also true that financial products, sometimes with their own specific settlement terms, were created and these made the task of executing cum-ex trades appreciably easier. Again, in the cum-ex case there was the ability under the flexible futures contracts that were used to convert what was essentially a private, bilateral off-market forward trade into an 'on-exchange' futures agreement, potentially masking the real nature of the agreements entered into. Certain futures contracts were constructed with a four-day settlement feature, critically expanding the period in which cum-ex trades could executed. This ability to modify the business environment at will is not present in industrial

[171] Hence the comments of the US Attorney General: 'But I am concerned that the size of some of these institutions becomes so large that it does become difficult for us to prosecute them when we are hit with indications that if we do prosecute—if we do bring a criminal charge—it will have a negative impact on the national economy, perhaps even the world economy. I think that is a function of the fact that some of these institutions have become too large.' See further 'Transcript; Attorney General Eric Holder on "Too Big to Jail"', *American Banker*, 6 March 2013, available at https://www.americanbanker.com/news/transcript-attorney-general-eric-holder-on-too-big-to-jail.

[172] Recall that in a stock loan transaction legal and beneficial title passes to the borrower of the shares through simple delivery and without a sale or execution taking place in relation to the shares. The lender, however, is not treated as having disposed of the shares for tax purposes and so does not realize a capital gain or loss on the delivery of lent securities.

[173] It is also relevant to note that under a forward sale or short sale, ownership rights normally vest in the purchaser from the time the trade is agreed. However, under a forward stock loan, the movement of ownership rights is usually dictated by the (later) settlement date. The difference in conventions by reference to the form of the transaction was another factor relied on in facilitating cum-ex.

sectors grounded in the real economy. It is not even available to the non-professional participants (such as retail investors) in the financial sector.

Regulatory Response and Resolution

The observations above go a long way to explain what might be regarded as the most remarkable difference between the two cases, namely both the speed, and the severity, of the response of the relevant regulator. Once the outlines of the fraud became clear, the resolution of Dieselgate was both rapid and decisive. Six days after the notice of violation was served by the Environment Protection Agency, the CEO of Volkswagen was forced to step down.[174] By 28 June 2016, less than a year after that notice had been served, Volkswagen had agreed to a package of $14.7 billion in car buybacks ($10 billion) together with compensation and penalties ($4.7 billion).[175] In June 2017, Volkswagen AG entered a guilty plea to charges including fraud, and also admitting to cheating in a 'statement of fact', effectively a set of written admissions to the US Department of Justice.[176] By June 2018, a number of Volkswagen executives were in prison, either in the United States or in Europe.[177] Oliver Schmidt, a Volkswagen executive, was arrested in the United States and sentenced to seven years in prison and fined $400,000 for joining a conspiracy to commit fraud. Rupert Sadler, the CEO of Audi, was in custody in Bavaria. Further, prosecutors in Braunschweig, Munich, and Stuttgart were investigating more than seventy Volkswagen defendants including members of the company's supervisory board.[178] The European Commission was also investigating Volkswagen, Daimler, and BMW for collusion.[179] On 10 September 2018 investors filed a $10 billion lawsuit in Braunschweig seeking compensation for the

[174] See Ewing, 'Volkswagen CEO Martin Winterkorn Resigns'.

[175] See the report of Sam Thielman, 'Volkswagen to Pay $14.7bn Settlement and Buy Back Cars from Consumers', *The Guardian*, 28 June 2016, available at https://www.theguardian.com/business/2016/jun/28/volkswagen-settlement-buy-back-cars-emissions-rigging.

[176] United States Department of Justice, 'Volkswagen AG Agrees to Plead Guilty and Pay $4.3 Billion in Criminal and Civil Penalties; Six Volkswagen Executives and Employees are Indicted in Connection with Conspiracy to Cheat U.S. Emissions Tests', press release, 11 January 2017, available at https://www.justice.gov/opa/pr/volkswagen-ag-agrees-plead-guilty-and-pay-43-billion-criminal-and-civil-penalties-six.

[177] See the report of Hugo Miller and Karin Matussek, 'VW Executive Tally in VW "Dieselgate" Grows with Stadler Arrest', *Bloomberg*, 18 June 2018, available at https://www.bloomberg.com/news/articles/2018-06-18/vw-executive-tally-in-vw-dieselgate-grows-with-stadler-arrest.

[178] See the report of Rene Bender in *Handelsblatt*, 19 June 2016, available at https://www.handelsblatt.com/unternehmen/industrie/vw-audi-porsche-fuenf-mal-haft-70-beschuldigte-diese-manager-sitzen-wegen-dieselgate/22708740.html?ticket=ST-735853-1ihC9bxci36dbHerxzdE-ap5.

[179] See European Commission, 'Antitrust: Commission Confirms Inspections in the Car Sector in Germany', press release, 23 October 2017, available at http://europa.eu/rapid/press-release_STATEMENT-17-4103_en.htm.

37 per cent fall in the company's share price.[180] All of these events took place within a timeframe measured in months.[181] The actions of regulators and criminal authorities were by any measure a swift, severe, and decisive response to the emissions cheating scandal.[182]

The contrast with the banking sector in general, and cum-ex in particular, could hardly be greater. The different standards of accountability in the financial sector may be seen in the stark disparity in the treatment and punishment of mistakes by, say, a junior social worker, as compared to the senior bankers and traders whose malfeasance played a role in the global financial crisis. The comparison suggests a generalized and material difference in standards of accountability, competence, and performance. In the financial sector, there is also a regular pattern of private out-of-court settlements between banks and authorities, without admission or denial of liability.[183] As for cum-ex, Chapter 4 has already discussed how the nature of the trade, including the very large number of related and unrelated parties, the variety and large number of legal entities through which hundreds of thousands of linked transactions were executed and/or booked, the large number of different jurisdictions involved, and other factors all combine to make it inevitable that the process of regulatory response and resolution will be costly, difficult, and protracted.[184]

[180] See William Boston, 'Investor Test Case in Volkswagen Emissions Scandal Goes to Court Next Week', *Wall Street Journal*, 6 September 2018, available at https://www.handelsblatt.com/unternehmen/industrie/vw-audi-porsche-fuenf-mal-haft-70-beschuldigte-diese-manager-sitzen-wegen-dieselgate/22708740.html?ticket=ST-735853-1ihC9bxci36dbHerxzdE-ap5.

[181] It seems that Volkswagen had expected a more lenient approach in the event that it was ever caught out on the fraud. The treatment by regulators for infringements in the sector in the past (even in the case of so-called 'defeat device' infringements) had consisted of a settlement, negotiated in private and not made public, and with a manageable fine attached: 'And in this case, the employees of Volkswagen of America had the impression on the basis of constructive talks with the EPA that the diesel issue would not be made public unilaterally but that negotiations would continue.' See Agence France-Presse, 'We Didn't Expect EPA to Go Public So Quickly', *Industry Week*, 7 March 2016, available at https://www.industryweek.com/corporate-culture/vw-we-didnt-expect-epa-go-public-so-quickly. In previous cases, relatively modest fines had been levied. Volkswagen itself was fined $120,000 in 1973 for installing an emissions-control defeat device. Ford and Chrysler had also been involved in circumventing industry rules through similar tactics—see K. McKelrath, 'The Volkswagen Scandal Wasn't Exposed by Regulators, but by Two Engineers Working at a Small Non-Profit Lab', *Alternet*, 6 October 2015, available at https://www.alternet.org/2015/10/volkswagen-scandal-two-engineers-who-exposed-massive-deception/.

[182] For example, by February 2017, the European Union had assembled a number of measures to prevent a recurrence of Dieselgate, including real driving condition onboard tests to more accurately measure vehicle emissions and a May 2016 regulation requiring carmakers to seek approval for any emission-abatement procedures in vehicles. See the report of Sara Lewis, 'New EU Guidance Meant to Prevent Dieselgate Repeat', *WardsAuto*, 10 February 2017, available at: https://www.wardsauto.com/engines/new-eu-guidance-meant-prevent-dieselgate-repeat.

[183] This issue, together with a number of relevant examples, is discussed further in Engelen et al., *After the Great Complacence*, at pp.124–5.

[184] In addition to the difficulties referred to here, there are also other problems that stem from the mechanics of the cross-border investigative process. These are discussed in the next chapter.

Conclusion

This comparison of the cum-ex scheme and Dieselgate, from two very different business sectors, suggests some fundamental differences between the financial services industry and nearly all other industries. These sectoral differences are highly relevant to the respective nature and incidence of misconduct. The financial claims of a vehicle manufacturer are, as is common in most other industries, tied directly to the factors of production: plant, labour, materials, and the finished product. It is costly and time-consuming to modify or move these factors, and the opportunities to extract some benefit by engaging in misconduct in relation to them is relatively limited.[185] It is therefore not surprising that the Dieselgate fraud consisted in exploiting one of the more abstract, complex, and concealed locations in the system (the emissions control mechanisms comprising the relevant hardware and software), which, from the perspective of the perpetrator, represented the weakest point in the system.

In the financial sector, opportunities to exploit similar abstractions (similar weak points in the system) are potentially vast, owing to the sheer number of financial instruments traded, the different legal attributes they possess, the different legal systems which govern them, the manner in which they trade, the nature of each state's settlement systems, and so on. As will be seen in the next chapter, there is also another immense dimension of variation and complication which stems from the treatment of this array of financial instruments under the many and unique tax systems of the world. The *opportunity set* available to the banks is a function of the combinations and permutations of all of these factors. Those opportunities are of course not grounded in, or restricted by, physical and immovable factors of production. Innovation can occur rapidly because the products are contractual claims which can be easily modified, repurposed, used in combination, or split into their constituent cash flows. The business of banking can therefore be seen generally to offer up significant potential for misconduct across a global set of claims which are abstract, and often abstruse and barely observable. It is in that context that the next chapter discusses the relevance of tax systems.

[185] Though the impact of tax is considered in the next chapter, it is nonetheless relevant to note here that cases of aggressive tax planning in the automobile/industrial-vehicle sector often rely on the use of financing structures or, as in the well-known case of the US company Caterpillar, through re-invoicing arrangements. See United States Permanent Subcommittee on Investigations, 'Caterpillar's Offshore Tax Strategy', Majority Staff Report, 1 April 2014, available at https://www.hsgac.senate.gov/imo/media/doc/Caterpillar's%20Offshore%20Tax%20Strategy%20(4-1-14,%208-28-14%20FINAL).pdf.

7
Banks and Tax Systems

> It is difficult to overstate how poorly our tax system deals with financial products. The rules are incredibly complex, under- and over-inclusive, ineffective in some respects and outdated in others. They give rise to wasteful tax planning, revenue losses, and unappealing distributional consequences. They may impede legitimate business hedging transactions, and they certainly fail to stop aggressive tax reduction strategies.
>
> Professor Alex Raskolnikov, before the Joint Hearing of the US House Committee on Ways and Means and US Senate Committee on Finance, 6 December 2011

Introduction—Why Tax?

This chapter[1] is concerned with the question why tax is so often at the heart of highly structured trades entered into by banks.

Chapter 6 has explained the recurrent instances of misconduct involving banks. As this chapter will demonstrate, tax has played a role in many of these cases, with tax-driven arrangements being a regular focus of activity pursued by banks for themselves and for their clients. Tax, of course, provides the rationale for cum-ex, because it was in essence a tax trade: the 'value' it generated was created out of nothing by the tax credits manufactured by the trade. Any argument that cum-ex was a one-off aberration or anomaly lacking wider implications for the tax system is misplaced. It is contradicted by the existence of a long line of cases in which banks have sought to exploit features of the tax system to generate 'opportunities' and 'value' for the banks themselves or for their clients, or, more often than not, both.

Some of these tax trade cases involve evident tax evasion similar to the cum-ex experience in Germany (as well as in other countries) discussed in Part I of this

[1] The reference here to 'tax systems' is intended as a generic reference to the bodies of rules and procedures operated by states that define what events or transactions trigger a tax liability, stipulate which taxpayers must remit the tax and when, and detail procedures for ensuring compliance, including reporting requirements and enforcement sanctions. See Slemrod and Gillitzer, *Tax Systems*, at p.10.

Banking on Failure: Cum-Ex and Why and How Banks Game the System. Richard S Collier, Oxford University Press (2020).
DOI: 10.1093/oso/9780198859673.001.0001

book. There are also numerous other cases where banks enter into transactions or arrangements, whether on their own account or for the account of their clients, which are investigated or challenged on tax evasion grounds.[2]

As well as these cases involving tax evasion activities, there are also numerous cases of aggressive tax avoidance being pursued by banks. Recent examples include the concerns of the tax authorities in Switzerland relating to market-wide treaty abuse issues from the use of total return swaps and futures.[3] The issues are similar to those that arose in the US markets in 2008, again involving widespread practices.[4] In some jurisdictions, there have been multiple generations of such tax-driven products or tax structuring.[5] Other well-known examples include the UK action in 2012 to introduce retrospective legislation in order to counter a bank tax scheme relating to buy-backs of debt securities that was

[2] Many banks will have been involved in a litany of such cases. For example, this can be seen in the case of the largest Swiss bank, UBS AG. Following a US Department of Justice investigation in 2007, the bank was fined $780 million and reached a limited deferred prosecution agreement in respect of its activities in helping wealthy US individuals evade taxes through the use of offshore accounts. A number of other Swiss banks were also implicated in the investigation—see further United States Senate Permanent Subcommittee on Investigations, 'Tax Haven Banks and U.S. Tax Compliance', Staff Report, 17 July 2008, available at https://www.hsgac.senate.gov/imo/media/doc/REPORTTaxHavenBanksJuly1708FINALwPatEliseChgs92608.pdf. The same bank has been investigated recently by the German tax authorities from 2012 (see David Crawford, 'Germany Probes UBS Staff on Tax-Evasion Allegations', *Wall Street Journal*, 8 November 2012), the French tax authorities from 2013 (see Robert Wood, 'French Criminal Tax Probe Of UBS—Talk About Déjà Vu'. *Forbes*, 4 June 2013, available at https://www.forbes.com/sites/robertwood/2013/06/04/french-criminal-tax-probe-of-ubs-talk-about-deja-vu/#1db14e8a5ccd), and the Belgian tax authorities from 2014 (see VRT nieuws, 'Topman UBS België in verdenking wegens fraude', 19 June 2014). Following the actions of a whistle-blower, UBS has also been the subject of a more recent US investigation (from 2015) into its use of bearer bonds (see Robert Wood, 'New UBS Tax Evasion Probe, Again Over Americans', *Forbes*, 5 February 2015). It was reported on 20 February 2019 that UBS has been fined €3.7 billion in relation to a tax fraud case in France. See the BBC report, 'UBS Fined €3.7bn in Tax Fraud Case', available at https://www.bbc.co.uk/news/business-47305227.

[3] See, for example, Marcus Desax and Martin Busenhart, 'Swiss Tribunal Rules on Ownership and Treaty Abuse Issues regarding Total Return Swaps', *Tax Notes International*, 7 May 2012, 557–64.

[4] See further the investigation into the practices of six banks highlighted in the report of the US Senate Permanent Subcommittee on Investigations, 'Dividend Tax Abuse'.

[5] For example, in Switzerland stock lending transactions were structured in the period 2004–6 to facilitate double claims of withholding tax in relation to shares in Swiss companies (by the stock lender and by the party holding the borrowed shares). The practice was curtailed by changes to the tax reclaim administration arrangements. In the period 2006–8 cum-ex trading activity was undertaken until this was stopped by a circular issued by the Federal Tax Administration. From the mid 2000s, there was also the international dividend washing using total return swaps and futures that has been referred to above. The position is similar in Italy. Throughout the 1980s arbitrage transactions were structured between corporate taxpayers and investment funds to exploit the imputation tax credit that could not be used by (non-taxable) Italian investment funds; in the latter half of the 1990s the emphasis shifted to treaty-based structures (often based on stock lending transactions) to exploit the additional tax credit relating to dividends paid by Italian companies that was available under certain tax treaties (such as the Italian tax treaties with the UK and France); and from 2004 to 2006 dividend washing transactions were structured using the anonymity of the 'open auction' system of the Italian stock market, the Borsa Italiana, and involving total return swaps, futures, and options.

described as 'highly abusive' and 'designed to work around legislation that has been introduced in the past to block similar attempts at tax avoidance'.[6]

Some of the cases referred to above share some of the vital ingredients seen in the cum-ex trade, namely an apparent flaw in the market infrastructure which is rapaciously exploited by the banks through complex structuring of transactions designed to unlock benefits or 'value' based on systemic tax attributes. For example, a recent spate of cases has involved the exploitation of an ADR 'pre-release' mechanism.[7] The cases illustrate one of the key attributes of the cum-ex trade: a market mechanism (in this case, as in cum-ex, a relatively obscure financial market mechanism) which was hijacked and manipulated by the banks in a manner that had never been intended by the creators of the mechanism in question. In order to generate significant tax benefits, the banks and their clients exploited the feature on a broad scale involving literally tens of thousands of transactions.[8]

These comments might be taken to suggest that all these cases can be divided neatly between those that involve tax evasion and those that do not, but which instead involve aggressive tax avoidance. However, for the reasons explored in Chapter 5, the distinction is not always easy to maintain in practice. Rather, the common tendency in all these cases is that, irrespective of whether the arrangements amount to tax evasion or aggressive avoidance of tax, the particular tax-driven activity conducted by the banks is regarded (by the tax authorities at least) as having not been intended by the law and it is generally challenged by the state when the reality of the situation comes to be understood.[9]

[6] See HM Treasury, 'Government Action Halts Banking Tax Avoidance Schemes', press release, 27 February 2012, available at https://www.gov.uk/government/news/government-action-halts-banking-tax-avoidance-schemes.

[7] The nature of American Depositary Receipts ('ADRs') (and American Depositary Shares ('ADSs')) was discussed briefly in Chapter 3. ADRs are dollar-denominated certificates listed and traded in US markets which represent an ownership interest in a designated number of underlying foreign shares. The relevant underlying foreign shares must normally be held by the ADR issuer (the depositary) before the ADR certificates may be issued and traded. However, in order to deal with settlement timing disparities relating to the delivery of the underlying foreign shares to the depositary, it has, subject to certain conditions, been possible to obtain ADRs from the depositary through a 'pre-release' mechanism. This enables ADRs to be obtained in advance of the actual delivery of the underlying foreign shares. In the case referred to in the present discussion, that pre-release mechanism was being used in a manner that was contrary to the intention behind the facility and in a manner which did not clearly fulfil the required conditions.

[8] The relevant tax benefits in this case were derived from withholding tax benefits from the countries whose shares underlay the ADR. There were many thousands of transactions considered in the case. See United States of America Before the Securities and Exchange Commission, 'Order Instituting Cease and Desist Proceedings, Pursuant to Section 8A of the Securities Act of 1933, Making Findings, and Imposing Remedial Sanctions and a Cease-and-Desist Order', Administrative Proceeding File No. 3-18605 In the Matter of Deutsche Bank Trust Company Americas, 20 July 2018, available at https://www.sec.gov/litigation/admin/2018/33-10523.pdf. A similar case involving Citibank N.A. from November 2018, again involving thousands of transactions, is available at https://www.sec.gov/litigation/admin/2018/33-10571.pdf.

[9] The difficulties associated with notions of 'avoidance' (including reliance on the 'intention' of the law) are discussed in Chapter 5.

Two wider questions arising out of the interaction of banks and tax systems are pursued in this chapter, namely (1) whether there are specific factors that explain the role of banks in exploiting tax systems and (2) whether there are features of tax systems that lend themselves to exploitation by banks.[10]

The view presented below is that banks are in a unique position to exploit tax systems because of their specific nature and attributes. It is also considered that there are features of the tax system which lend themselves to such exploitation. Further, whilst these features are arguably present across the tax system, they are especially relevant to the taxation of financial products and financial markets.

The discussion that follows will start by considering the position of the banks and set out the reasons why they are considered to have a unique ability to exploit tax systems. It will then discuss the features in a tax system that have a tendency to contribute to, or facilitate, the process by which rules in that tax system are exploited. This will include both the substantive tax rules of tax systems and the arrangements for the administration of tax systems.

Banks and Tax Systems

Tax considerations have some impact on virtually all economic decisions, but that impact is especially significant in relation to banks.[11] This is because, unlike most other businesses, the effect of tax is embedded in, or highly relevant to, much of what may be termed the banking business product. In particular, it is inevitable that banks that carry on the business of financial intermediation or trading (rather than merely simple lending business) will be attuned to the impact of taxation on financial markets and adept at managing, including optimizing, that impact for themselves and their clients. This is because the yield from many financial instruments is routinely affected directly by taxation.

Given that asset prices reflect expected future returns, they also reflect expected future tax payments. At the most basic level of corporate finance, the cost of servicing debt is normally tax deductible, whereas financing by equity is not. Similarly, in the hands of investors the income or coupons on an investment in debt will often be taxable yet a return from an equity investment may be exempted or subject to a lower rate of tax by the tax system. Further, some types of entities will be generally exempt from income tax on their income from financial

[10] As explained in Chapter 5, references to the 'exploitation' of the tax system are intended to include both cases involving tax evasion and those involving aggressive tax avoidance.

[11] Generally, banks are subject to the same tax rules that apply to non-financial companies, but the different nature of their business is normally recognized by the tax rules. For example, for tax purposes greater levels of leverage will normally be permitted in the case of a bank or financial trader; a mark-to-market basis of income recognition will often be used for assets held on the trading book; and there may be separate rules dealing with tax provisioning on loan assets.

products, meaning that their after-tax yield from financial products will differ from yields derived by other entities which are subject to tax. Also, with rates of withholding tax on certain types of income such as dividends and interest reaching as much as 30 per cent or more in some cases, the impact of taxation can be a major determinant of yield on those instruments and therefore on investor choices. There are also transfer duties or taxes which apply to some financial instruments but not others.[12]

In all these cases, the impact of tax on the return from financial products will often vary from one type of investor to another and, in the hands of the same investor, from one form of financial instrument to another. This may be true even if the cash flows from differing forms of financial instrument are the same. Further, the availability of a tax exemption for one type of investor (such as a pension fund) may apply to one tax but not another imposed by the same domestic tax system.[13] There are also businesses such as leasing that are carried on within a bank, where the impact and allocation of tax depreciation allowances on the asset or item financed are critical to the business and the effects are consequently embedded in the pricing of the relevant transactions. All of this means that, in practice, a bank will need to address the impact of taxation on an investor-by-investor and product-by-product basis. These issues explain why banks are accustomed to consider carefully the effect of taxation on financial products on a day-to-day basis and why the impact of tax is an important element in their proprietary and customer business.

Given the variability of the incidence of taxation on financial product yields, as explained above, coupled with the highly competitive nature of the market for financial services, it follows that banks are commonly drawn into the active management of the impact of taxation on financial products, both for themselves and their clients. The result is that tax is often a potent value driver of the business of banks. Further, the variable impact of tax on different types of investor and different types of financial product (each with its own tax features) inevitably leads to attempts at innovation, usually in the form of attempts to minimize the incidence of taxation or attempts to find a way of bringing a financial activity within a tax exemption. This in turn is enabled by the large number of different financial products (for example an equity swap) which can in economic terms be used to replicate the effect of other financial products (for example, a holding of a share).

[12] For example, the impact of UK transfer tax (stamp duty, or stamp duty reserve tax) on the purchase of UK shares (but not on the corresponding derivatives) is a major reason why many institutional investors wishing to invest in UK shares will choose to invest in the form of a derivative over the shares rather than directly in the shares themselves.

[13] For example, under the UK tax system pension funds are generally exempt from income taxation on their income from investments but are subject to UK stamp tax (stamp duty or stamp duty reserve tax) on their purchases of shares.

For a bank, it is a small step to see tax, and specifically innovative tax planning or tax arbitrage, as a source of value in its own right, with the ability to generate revenue streams for the business. It is therefore no surprise that some banks have developed business teams with a mandate for tax optimization, whether relating to financial products alone or on a wider basis of exploiting cracks and mismatches in a domestic tax system or between tax systems.[14] A specialist team assisting clients in managing tax issues is often considered a 'key differentiator' which may attract clients to the bank.

The significance of tax to the business of a bank may be contrasted to the position of other taxpayers. Other taxpayers, such as non-financial-sector multinationals (MNCs), may see tax as contributing value (sometimes significant value) through the adoption of tax planning strategies to lower the effective tax rate on the profits of the business of the MNC group.[15] The same use of tax planning is available to a bank.[16] However, a bank is different in that the impact of tax is embedded in many of its front-office business products and revenues, as explained above, making tax relatively more important in the day-to-day running of a banking business.[17] That difference is also reflected in the role that banks have as a 'tax intermediary'. An OECD study, discussed later in this chapter, used that term to refer collectively to financial institutions (mainly banks) and other tax advisers which represent the promoters or 'supply side' of aggressive tax planning.[18]

Significantly, amongst intermediaries, banks are distinguished by their unique ability to exploit weaknesses or mismatches in, or between, domestic tax systems. In common with the larger tax advisory firms, such as the global legal and accounting firms that provide tax advisory services, banks have certain relevant attributes: a ready insight into the requirements of their clients (as a result of ongoing client relationships); the ability to develop and distribute tax arbitrage products or techniques to their clients; and the footprint or reach to replicate such products across national borders. However, banks also have certain attributes that other tax advisers do not have. The most important of these is the ability to access capital and financial markets and provide financial leverage. This is significant for a number of reasons. Most obviously, financing is very often a component of tax-driven products and structures. This means that the financial amounts involved in such products and structures and the tax issues at stake are likely to be very large,

[14] The degree to which a bank will maintain specialist business units or resources to exploit revenue streams from tax mitigation strategies will, of course, vary from bank to bank.

[15] A well-known example of this can be seen in the report of the US Senate Permanent Subcommittee on Investigations, 'Caterpillar's Offshore Tax Strategy'.

[16] The position of banks and other financial-sector businesses may, however, be less flexible in some respects in comparison to MNCs due to the effect of the regulatory restrictions that apply in the financial sector.

[17] Banks whose business is restricted to a simple domestic loan business are likely to be much less affected by tax than those carrying on more complex trading business, and therefore their position in relationship to tax is likely to be closer to that of non-financial sector MNCs.

[18] See OECD, 'Study into the Role of Tax Intermediaries', at p.4.

often in the hundreds of millions of dollars.[19] This was seen in cum-ex with the significant leveraging of the trade. For a bank, the ability to integrate the provision of financing with tax planning presents a huge advantage over other tax advisers/intermediaries. As seen in the cum-ex trade, leverage can magnify what might otherwise be a small tax benefit. It also means that the financial cost of exploring and implementing any tax-driven stratagem for the bank (as reflected in the cost of obtaining tax opinions, etc) is likely to be small, or insignificant, in comparison with the resulting financial benefits. The reason of course is that, for a bank, the benefits which flow to it typically consist of some percentage-based proportion of the total deal size, rather than in the form of the hourly-based fees which are usually charged by tax advisers.

Banks are in a unique position compared to other tax intermediaries in three other respects. First, there is within the banks a deep expertise in a variety of disciplines (e.g. legal, regulatory, operational, tax, etc), in financial products. The continual innovation in financial products which is a hallmark of the modern day 'originate to distribute' model of banking has brought together and concentrated these disciplines in the modern bank. In order to marshal the specialized financial instruments (including derivatives) which play a significant role in strategies which exploit asymmetries and mismatches in the tax system, this multidisciplinary expertise is essential. Second, the business of modern banking is problematic for the tax authorities. Notwithstanding efforts to make the activities of banks and their clients more transparent, for example through reporting requirements, much of what is transacted, particularly in the inter-bank markets is, as has been discussed in the previous chapter, opaque, complex, and difficult to understand.[20] For example, a lack of product knowledge on the part of the tax authorities may make it hard to discern the source of benefits in financial transactions or comprehend the degree to which instruments can be used interchangeably. The sheer volume of transactions and that the fact that a single strategy may make use of numerous individual financial transactions simultaneously can make the identification of particular structures or arrangements very difficult. Further, highly structured financial products may be used in tax-driven strategies but may also form part of other commercial arrangements where a tax benefit is neither the purpose nor result. Third, a bank is the only type of tax 'intermediary' that carries out transactions for its own benefit rather than simply promoting tax-driven products and structures to its clients. The combination of banks engaging in aggressive tax planning and in trading in the inter-bank market for their own

[19] The statement by HM Treasury relating to the UK debt buy-back scheme mentioned earlier (see at pp.252–3) illustrates the large amounts that are often involved. In that case, the consequence of legislation to counter a bank's debt buy-back scheme was to 'ensure the payment of over half a billion pounds in tax, [and to] protect further billions of tax from being lost'. See HM Treasury, 'Government Action Halts Banking Tax Avoidance Schemes'.

[20] See OECD, 'Study into the Role of Tax Intermediaries', at p.5. This study is discussed below.

account (as well as on behalf of their clients) has been identified as being of particular concern to the tax authorities.[21] All the factors discussed above mean that the position of banks is different to other MNCs and different to other tax intermediaries.[22]

Whilst there have been some periodic concerns raised, the unique and systematic challenges posed to the tax system by banks have not been widely recognized by tax authorities and the major international bodies charged with responsibility for developing international tax policy.[23] There are various reasons for this. In relation to studies on aggressive tax avoidance, banks are less commonly the subject of such enquiry than other taxpayers as (1) the business model of banks is materially different to that of other taxpayers and so banks are often omitted from the scope of such studies and (2) most large datasets on banks cover only subsidiaries and not branches, yet banks use branches extensively, meaning that the underlying statistical data for banks is less useful than that available for other taxpayers.[24] Further, and as illustrated by the discussion of cum-ex in Part I of this book, a bank's participation in tax-driven arrangements will not always lead to a simple reduction in its own tax bill and therefore its effective tax rate. Yet a marked reduction in the effective tax rate of a corporation is a measure that is often used by tax authorities as a possible indication of aggressive tax avoidance. Whilst it is true that a bank in the role of a buyer in a cum-ex trade will generally reduce its effective tax liability through the use of the tax credit generated by the

[21] Concerns about the lack of transparency in dealings in the inter-bank market have been emphasized as an issue relevant to the position of banks as tax intermediaries. See OECD, 'Study into the Role of Tax Intermediaries', at pp.4–5. As illustrated by the cum-ex example, banks can enter into tax-driven transactions on their own account, or facilitate and finance transactions for their customers, or both.

[22] It is nonetheless important to recognize that one by-product of the increased scrutiny on the conduct of banks since the Global Financial Crisis has been an increase in internal efforts at self-regulation by banks in relation to tax matters. This has led to internal codes of conduct, enhanced tax risk management procedures, etc, which in some banks has led to a marked decrease in structured tax avoidance activity. The issue is discussed in Chapter 5.

[23] A recent report describes the regulatory review of banks as the enablers of tax abuse as being 'geographically uneven and politically slow'. See Anastasia Nesvetailova, Andrei Guter-Sandu, Ronen Palan, and Yuval Milo, 'Tax Evasion and Avoidance Through Financial Engineering: The State of Play in Europe', City Political Economy Research Centre report, October 2018, at p.13, available at https://www.google.com/url?sa=t&rct=j&q=&esrc=s&source=web&cd=1&cad=rja&uact=8&ved=2ahUKEwiVoNGgtqXkAhUbRBUIHcXQD5IQFjAAegQIARAC&url=https%3A%2F%2Fwww.city.ac.uk%2F__data%2Fassets%2Fpdf_file%2F0010%2F450487%2Fd.1.7-tax-evasion-and-avoidance-by-financial-inniovation-wp.pdf&usg=AOvVaw0J_4yPfzAHdM81WKEXrVYB. There has been some recognition of the role of the 'financial sector' in tax planning by the European Parliament—see, for example, European Parliament, 'The Role of the Financial Sector in Tax Planning', Study for the TAXE 2 Special Committee, May 2016, available at http://www.europarl.europa.eu/RegData/etudes/STUD/2016/578980/IPOL_STU(2016)578980_EN.pdf. However, the focus of the study is on a wide variety of tax-driven schemes and arrangements, some of which are quite general and not specific to the financial sector, rather than on the providers of those schemes.

[24] Dominika Langenmayr and Franz Reiter, 'Trading Offshore: Evidence on Banks' Tax Avoidance', CESifo Working Paper Series No. 6664, 25 September 2017, at pp.1–2, available at https://ssrn.com/abstract=3057458.

trade, by contrast a bank acting as the short seller (where the bank originates the trade and monetizes the generated tax credit) will see no impact on its effective tax rate, although its revenues will be boosted by its receipts from participation in the cum-ex trade. It is also common for a bank's tax-driven activities to relate to taxes other than income taxes with the result that there is no impact on its effective tax rate.[25] In short, banks generate profits directly from the tax system, in addition to reducing or avoiding the incidence of tax for themselves and their clients. A further reason why the role of banks may not be fully understood is that, in formulating a response to tax-driven products or schemes, the primary focus of tax authorities is generally geared towards dealing with the specific product or scheme in isolation. Such an approach does not encourage the tax authorities to take a wider view of the transaction, or series of transactions, and to consider either the pattern of activity overall or the source of the activity.[26] All of these factors explain why the unique challenges posed by banks have not been fully recognized.

Nonetheless, there are some isolated examples where states have identified the unique issues raised by the banks in relation to the tax system. One such example is the UK, where banks alone were singled out by the UK tax authorities and asked to sign up to a code of practice regulating their behaviour in relation to tax planning and the promotion of tax products.[27] The UK Government's case for introducing the code to apply to banks only was both specific and general. The specific point made was that 'some banks have been involved in tax avoidance that goes well beyond reasonable tax planning'.[28] The more general motivation stems from what is referred to as the unique position of banks in that they 'can seek to avoid their own tax liabilities; . . . provide financial services to customers, many of which services are sensitive to tax and some of which can be used for tax avoidance; and . . . have access to large amounts of capital which they can use to facilitate avoidance schemes designed and implemented by others, for example by providing loans of billions of pounds for periods sometimes as short as a few hours'. The point was also made that, in the light of the significant taxpayer support to stabilize the banking system, taxpayers are entitled to expect that banks

[25] Examples relating to transfer duties are discussed in the next section.

[26] Some tax authorities have sought to tackle the position of promoters or enablers of tax avoidance schemes (for example, the Australian promoter penalty law now inserted into Parts 4–25 of the Taxation Administration Act 1953) as well as the position of serial users of avoidance schemes (for example, the UK tax authority, HMRC, set up a Serial Avoiders Unit to identify and tackle users of multiple avoidance schemes).

[27] See further HMRC, 'Code of Practice on Taxation for Banks', a collection of HMRC papers giving information and guidance on the code, available at https://www.gov.uk/government/collections/the-code-of-practice-on-taxation-for-banks. For a critical discussion of the code, see Richard Collier, 'Intentions, Banks, Politics and the Law: The UK Code of Practice on Taxation for Banks', *British Tax Review* 4 (2014), 478–508.

[28] HMRC, 'Code of Practice on Taxation for Banks, Consultation Document', 29 June, 2009, Foreword.

and their customers will pay their fair share of tax.[29] Part of the case made by the UK government for the introduction of the code was that the aggressive tax planning behaviour by banks was more aggressive than that of companies in other sectors.[30]

A similar approach of singling out banks for special treatment has been taken in South Africa. In 2009, the South African Revenue Service (SARS) signed an accord with the Banking Association of South Africa, which is the main representative body for South African banks. The motivation for the accord was the very low effective tax rate of banks notwithstanding the industry's high level of profits. Particular concerns of the government were that the banks' structured finance activities were eroding their corporate income base and that their tax base was being utilized for the benefit of their clients.[31] The goal of the accord was therefore to require from South African banks a higher commitment to tax compliance and a reduction in what were regarded as 'harmful and unacceptable tax practices'. The concerns of SARS about banks dated back to the mid-1990s.[32]

These examples of individual countries singling out banks are the exception, not the rule.[33] Neither has there been much discussion of the roles which banks play in tax systems by the tax-policy-setting international bodies. Prior to the Global Financial Crisis, there was some discussion of banks and taxation by such bodies, but it was mainly concerned with how the general tax rules might be adapted to more comprehensively tax banks with international operations, rather than with the activities of banks in the context of the tax system per se.[34] The

[29] HMRC, 'Code of Practice on Taxation for Banks, Consultation Document', at p.7.

[30] See HMRC, 'A Code of Practice on Taxation for Banks—Consultation Response Document', 9 December 2009, at p.8.

[31] The relevant background and the South African accord are discussed in OECD Forum on Tax Administration, 'A Framework for a Voluntary Code of Conduct for Banks and Revenue Bodies', September 2010, at pp.17–20. Although the accord was only signed in 2009, the concept dated back to the early 2000s and a first draft of the accord had been circulated in 2004.

[32] For example, in his 2001 Budget speech, the then South African Minister of Finance commented that 'Government is concerned about the low effective tax rate on banks. Banks are able to defer and avoid tax by using derivative financial products and structured asset-based finance techniques, amongst other devices.' OECD Forum on Tax Administration, 'Framework for a Voluntary Code of Conduct', at pp.17–18.

[33] Although not explained, there is a statement in a 2010 document of the OECD Forum on Tax Administration that some states have also responded to banks by limiting the scope for the avoidance of tax by introducing alternative minimum taxes or presumptive taxes on easily identifiable and audited tax bases, for example, on gross assets. See OECD Forum on Tax Administration, 'Framework for a Voluntary Code of Conduct', at p.18.

[34] For example, the 1984 report by the OECD 'The Taxation of Multinational Banking Enterprises', in *Transfer Pricing and Multinational Enterprises, Three Taxation Issues* (OECD, 1984), 44–70, and also the later report 'The Taxation of Global Trading of Financial Instruments' (OECD, 1998) were largely concerned with applying the income allocation rules under the arm's-length principle in the case of international banking and the global trading of financial instruments respectively. Another strand of discussion involving banks (and again of little relevance in the current context) was concerned with improving access to bank information for tax purposes to counter tax evasion practices of bank customers—see, for example, OECD, 'Improving Access to Bank Information for Tax Purposes' (OECD, 2000).

position changed as a result of the increased attention paid to taxation in the financial sector following the Global Financial Crisis. Most of the immediate focus then was on the development and application of additional measures such as bank levies or financial transaction taxes that might be used to tax banks in order to recoup bailout costs and the continuing implicit ('too-big-to-fail') state guarantees.[35] However, a strand in the discussion was a concern expressed about aggressive tax planning by banks, particularly in relation to financial transactions, and tax avoidance 'by engineering'.[36] This was perhaps not surprising given the similarities between the complex bank-engineered 'collateralized debt obligation' financial instruments that were regarded as an important factor in triggering the financial crisis and the highly structured financial instruments designed for tax purposes. Whilst it was generally acknowledged that the financial crisis was not caused by tax issues, the crisis nonetheless served to highlight some important issues relating to tax.[37] These included the adverse impact of complexity and limited transparency and the fact that uncertain tax treatments of innovative financial products could impact the risk-taking positions of banks.[38]

There was some consideration of the role of banks by the OECD (strictly, by the OECD's Forum on Tax Administration, 'FTA') in the course of its work on 'tax intermediaries'. This, as noted above, was intended to explore the supply side of aggressive tax planning.[39] The initial 2008 OECD 'Study into the Role of Tax Intermediaries' was intended to investigate the role and types of tax intermediary (including accounting firms, legal firms, banks, in-house tax teams, boutiques, promoters, and insurance companies) and their impact on tax compliance. Included in particular was the role of intermediaries in 'unacceptable tax

[35] See, for example, Julian Alworth and Giampaolo Arachi, eds, *Taxation and the Financial Crisis* (Oxford University Press, 2012). It is also true that another important strand in the discussion concerned the structure of incentive payments. The IMF opened up a wider debate on the subject and the UK and France introduced taxes on bank bonuses. See at pp. 2 and 12.

[36] See, for example, International Monetary Fund, 'A Fair and Substantial Contribution by the Financial Sector, Final Report for the G-20', prepared by the Staff of the International Monetary Fund', June 2010, available at https://www.imf.org/external/np/g20/pdf/062710b.pdf. The report comments that aggressive tax planning in the financial sector could be addressed more firmly and gives an example of engineered tax results through the use of swaps (see at pp. 5, 21, 26).

[37] See Douglas A. Shackelford, Daniel Shaviro, and Joel Slemrod, 'Taxation and the Financial Sector', *National Tax Journal* 63:4 (2010), 781–806, at p.783. However, Eddins suggests a more significant impact in the Financial Crisis from tax rules. This is on the basis that collateralized debt obligations (CDOs) organized as pass-through entities were made more attractive by structuring them to permit more tax offsets leading to a higher after-tax level of return. See Samuel T. Eddins, 'Tax Arbitrage Feedback Theory', mimeo, IronBridge Capital Management LP, 2009, available at https://ssrn.com/abstract=1356159.

[38] OECD, 'Building Transparent Tax Compliance by Banks' (OECD, 2009), p.18. It was also argued that the income tax rules in many countries encouraged excessive corporate leverage and, in some countries, highly leveraged home ownership.

[39] OECD, 'Study into the Role of Tax Intermediaries', p.4. The Forum on Tax Administration (FTA) was created in 2002 as a forum for tax commissioners from OECD and non-OECD countries. Its membership currently comprises tax commissioners from fifty-three countries. Further information on the FTA is available from the OECD website at http://www.oecd.org/tax/forum-on-tax-administration/.

minimization arrangements'.[40] The main output of the study was the proposal for developing an 'enhanced relationship' (now referred to more commonly as 'cooperative compliance' and also called 'horizontal monitoring').[41] Essentially, the proposal advances the concept of a real-time relationship between taxpayer and tax authority based on cooperation and trust, with both parties going beyond their statutory obligations.[42] The study distinguished banks from other tax intermediaries for a number or reasons. Amongst these were the reduced transparency of their dealings, and the fact that some banks engage in aggressive tax planning in the inter-bank market and trade for their own account.[43] The discussion of banks notes that they design, promote, and facilitate tax-driven financial strategies. It also recognizes that aggressive tax planning deals by banks can be very large, with single deals involving funding in the billions and tax advantages counted in the hundreds of millions of dollars. It is also noted that much aggressive tax planning involves cross-border structuring of transactions and the use of financial instruments such as repos, stock loans, and derivatives.[44]

This initial work on banks ran into difficulties due to the limited knowledge on the part of the tax authorities of aggressive tax planning by banks. Because of these obstacles, the OECD concluded that a further separate study was required. That followed a year later in the form of the 2009 FTA report, 'Building Transparent Tax Compliance by Banks'.[45] This report was concerned with, and included various examples of, complex structured finance transactions entered into, or promoted by, banks. It included a chapter on tax evasion transactions involving banks. The report made a number of recommendations among which were the need for greater transparency on the part of banks, more banking industry knowledge on the part of tax inspectors, greater cooperation and exchanges of information between tax authorities, etc. However, as with the earlier 2008 study on intermediaries, the main thrust of the discussion was building the case for the application of cooperative compliance arrangements between banks and tax authorities.[46]

[40] OECD, 'Study into the Role of Tax Intermediaries', p.6. The nature of 'unacceptable tax minimization arrangements' was not defined, but two areas of concern were identified (at pp. 79 and 80). These were (1) tax planning involving a position that is legally tenable but has unintended tax revenue consequences and (2) the adoption of a tax position where it is not disclosed that there is significant uncertainty as to whether it accords with the law.

[41] For more recent work on the topic, see the OECD reports 'Co-Operative Compliance: A Framework—From Enhanced Relationship to Co-Operative Compliance' (OECD, 2013) and 'Co-operative Tax Compliance: Building Better Tax Control Frameworks' (OECD, 2016).

[42] OECD, 'Study into the Role of Tax Intermediaries', at pp. 4, 72–3.

[43] OECD, 'Study into the Role of Tax Intermediaries', at p.5.

[44] OECD, 'Study into the Role of Tax Intermediaries', at pp. 12, 42–4.

[45] OECD, 'Building Transparent Tax Compliance by Banks'.

[46] See OECD, 'Building Transparent Tax Compliance by Banks', at pp.43–5. The 2009 study led to a later meeting in Rome between the OECD, a number of banks, and revenue officials to explore how the cooperative compliance relationship could be built. See OECD, 'Revenue Bodies and Banks Move Towards Transparent Compliance', discussing the meeting of 10–11 October 2011 in Rome, Italy, available at http://www.oecd.org/ctp/revenuebodiesandbanksmovetowardstransparentcompliance.htm.

The tax authority–taxpayer cooperative compliance model recommended in this second study was in essence the same as that recommended in the initial 2008 OECD study for a wider group of tax intermediaries. Unfortunately, there is little exploration of whether the same model can in practice be applied to banks. Consequently, there is in little in the report by way of consideration of the relatively greater difficulty of implementing this approach to banks as compared to other taxpayers as a result of the variety of factors raised earlier in this chapter. For example, because tax is relevant to many of the commercial products of a bank, such as leasing, structured notes, derivatives, equities, and prime brokerage, many different front-office trading desks, organized on a global or regional basis and dealing on global markets, are involved directly in the management of tax risk. It cannot, therefore, be assumed that the bank's tax department is—as is the case for most large corporates—the sole or even primary custodian of tax risk within the organization. However, the OECD study did note that the bonus culture in a bank would increase the motivation for tax structuring, although it did not explore the implications of this or how it might be addressed under the cooperative compliance model.[47]

There was another OECD report focused on banks in the following year, 2010. This was solely concerned with aggressive tax planning involving losses suffered by banks as a result of the Global Financial Crisis.[48] The main recommendations of the report were connected to themes aired in previous reports, particularly the merits of cooperative real-time engagement between tax authority and taxpayer, the need for better transparency and disclosure, and the desirability of better industry knowledge on the part of the revenue authorities dealing with banks, etc.[49]

Throughout its work on tax intermediaries (including the two separate studies on banks) the OECD has placed a strong emphasis on building the case for wider adoption of the cooperative compliance model between tax authorities and taxpayers.[50] Whether or not this is the most useful manner of dealing with banks may be debated, though the additional difficulties of applying that model to banks were hardly explored. In any event, the attention given to banks and their impact on the tax system was short-lived. By 2012, the attention of the OECD, as well as other bodies that have an international tax policy mandate such as the European Commission, had shifted to the wider and politically high-profile concerns about tax avoidance by MNCs, which led to the OECD's Base Erosion and

[47] See 'Building Transparent Tax Compliance by Banks', at pp.17–18.

[48] OECD, 'Addressing Tax Risks Involving Bank Losses' (OECD, 2010).

[49] OECD, 'Addressing Tax Risks Involving Bank Losses', at pp.65–6.

[50] This is also the main theme reflected in OECD Forum on Tax Administration, 'Framework for a Voluntary Code of Conduct'. This 2010 document was modelled on the work in the UK on the Code of Practice on Taxation for Banks and in South Africa on the Accord with the South African Banking Association. The approach of the framework for a voluntary code has not been widely adopted.

Profit Shifting (BEPS) project. The concerns about banks and tax that had been triggered by the Global Financial Crisis were not so much subsumed into the BEPS project as entirely displaced by it and the focus on banks largely disappeared.[51]

Even as the BEPS project was getting under way, the focus of policy makers had reverted to the more usual approach of concentrating on individual structured tax products rather than the source of these products. Two OECD reports produced on the eve of the BEPS project exemplify this. In the first, 'Hybrid Mismatch Arrangements', there are references in the discussion to the involvement of banks in hybrid structures. These include the comment that the hybrid issues have already been raised in the context of international banking activities in the earlier work on banks.[52] There is also a reference to multi-billion-euro settlements on hybrids, including with four banks in New Zealand.[53] In the second, 'Aggressive Tax Planning based on After-Tax Hedging', there is a passing reference to the fact that the complex structured product which is the subject of the report (and which it is stated involves multi-billion-dollar transactions and hundreds of millions of tax dollars at stake) originated in the banking sector.[54] In neither case is the significance of the role of banks recognized or pursued. Neither is it recognized in relation to the concern with hybrids that the products had their origin in financial instruments developed by banks to raise capital for regulatory purposes, nor that the OECD itself had considered this point some twenty years earlier in its work on new financial instruments.[55] Instead, the entire focus is on the structured tax product itself, taken in isolation, rather than on the provider or source of the product. Not surprisingly, the serial nature of the problem faced by tax regulators is therefore obscured.

The Features of Tax Systems—Introduction

The previous section has explored the potentially unique position of banks to exploit tax systems. As indicated earlier, it is also necessary to consider certain features of tax systems which routinely also contribute to, or facilitate, that exploitation process.

[51] The OECD BEPS project started in the latter part of 2012, by which time the European Commission had already commenced its work, including a public consultation, on the topic of 'double non-taxation'—see European Commission, 'Tackling Double Non-Taxation for Fairer and More Robust Tax Systems', press release, 29 February 2012, available at http://europa.eu/rapid/press-release_IP-12-201_en.htm. An extensive description of BEPS and the BEPS reports is available from the OECD website at http://www.oecd.org/tax/beps/.

[52] The specific reference is to the consideration of the topic in the 2010 OECD report, 'Addressing Tax Risks Involving Bank Losses' (which is discussed below)—see OECD, 'Hybrid Mismatch Arrangements' (OECD, 2013), at p.5.

[53] OECD, 'Hybrid Mismatch Arrangements', at pp.5–6.

[54] OECD, 'Aggressive Tax Planning Based on After-Tax Hedging' (OECD, 2013), at pp. 7, 41.

[55] OECD, 'Taxation of New Financial Instruments' (OECD, 1994), p.101.

Here, reference to certain 'features of tax systems' denotes not only the substantive tax rules but also the administrative procedures or arrangements by which tax systems are managed. Paradoxically, both substantive tax rules and their management through the operation of administrative regimes have the potential to facilitate exploitation of the tax system, a point that is amply demonstrated by the case of cum-ex.

Substantive Rules of a Tax System that Facilitate their Own Exploitation

Tax rules may be exploited across the tax system but, for the reasons discussed below, that exploitation is more acute in relation to tax rules dealing with financial markets and financial products. In that context, the exploitation necessarily flows from the substantive tax rules. However, the argument developed here is that these rules actually facilitate their own exploitation.

The assertion here that substantive tax rules 'facilitate their own exploitation' is intended to be more than simply a reference to the fact that the systemic complexity of tax systems creates conditions which may facilitate abuse—though complexity is clearly a significant problem for tax systems, and particularly for tax rules dealing with financial products and markets. It is also taken as a given that many tax rules are not robust to abuse, meaning that they are not effective in preventing abuse, including manipulation or exploitation of the tax base.[56] Rather, what is intended by the reference to tax rules facilitating their own exploitation is the proposition that certain features of the tax rules themselves actually contribute to their susceptibility to abuse, or, in different terms, lend themselves to manipulation at the taxpayer's will.[57] Here, the terms 'abuse', 'manipulation', and 'exploitation' all refer to cases where the intended operation of a tax rule is avoided by taxpayer actions, whether that is a tax benefit intended for a narrow category of taxpayers being made available to a wider group or whether it is an intended tax charge being avoided. The proposition is therefore that certain features of the tax system actually contribute to, or facilitate, the process by which substantive tax rules can be exploited in this way.

[56] The 'robustness to abuse' test is often used as one of the measures to assess how well tax systems, or components of tax systems, work in practice. See for example, in a derivatives context, Charles Plambeck, David Rosenbloom, and Diane Ring, 'General Report', in International Fiscal Association, *Tax Aspects of Derivative Financial Instruments*, Cahiers De Droit Fiscal 80b (Kluwer Law International, 1995), at p.690.

[57] It is considered that the discussion here is equally applicable irrespective of whether the underlying legal system is based on a civil- or a common-law system. For example, similar issues are raised in relation to the debt–equity distinction in both civil-law and common-law jurisdictions—see Wolfgang Schön et al., 'Debt and Equity in Domestic and International Tax Law—A Comparative Policy Analysis', *British Tax Review* 59:2 (2014), 146–217.

Two major features of substantive tax rules may deliver this result. These are: (1) the existence of what may be termed 'tax differences', being broadly distinctions that are made in the tax rules which for one reason or another are problematic and (2) the unsatisfactory treatment in the tax system of derivatives and other complex financial products.[58] These two features are separate and independent of each other but, as will be seen, their effect when used in combination is amplified. Though relevant on a wider footing, the idea that tax rules may facilitate their own exploitation is explored here in the narrower context of financial products and financial markets. That context is, of course, the focus of this book, but it is also considered that, for a number of reasons, the failure of the tax rules identified here is especially acute.

Tax Differences

Nearly all tax systems rely extensively on the use of distinctions or categories that are created or adopted in the detailed rules of the tax system. These distinctions or categories will, in any particular case, determine the application of a tax rule. Examples of them include: whether, when, and how income is taxable; whether expenditure is deductible; whether allowances and credits are available; and so forth. Such distinctions commonly apply right across the tax system. For example, common distinctions exist in relation to the categories of taxpayers (e.g. pension funds versus hedge funds, employees versus the self-employed), transactions (e.g. a gift versus a sale), income (e.g. interest income versus discount), expenditure (e.g. business expenditure versus non-business or personal expenditure), income recognition (e.g. realized and unrealized gains), financial products (e.g. debt versus equity), assets (e.g. moveable versus fixed property), etc. This use of distinctions or categories is also central to the types of distinct taxes that exist, for example the separate taxes dealing with income or designated types of income, taxes which apply to capital gains, taxes that apply to capital transfers, stamp taxes, etc. In the particular circumstances of each case, the distinction or category into which a taxpayer, cash flow, element of capital, transaction type, or expense falls will determine which set of tax rules will apply, and how they will apply.

This extensive use of distinctions and categories within tax systems is widely recognized.[59] It has been expressed as a process of 'line-drawing' within tax

[58] Though the discussion here focuses on tax differences, there may be other factors that lead to exploitation or abuse of the tax system, such as the differences in tax and accounting treatment, loopholes in the tax law, etc. The state of alignment of accounting standards and tax legislation is discussed in Oktavia Weidmann, *Taxation of Derivatives*, Series on International Taxation, No. 52 (Wolters Kluwer, 2015), Chapter 6.

[59] This use of distinctions and categories is the backdrop to Wolfgang Schön's argument based on a 'continuity approach', namely that for tax purposes (and to deliver neutrality and therefore efficiency of resource allocation and the prevention of tax arbitrage) similar activities should be treated similarly and

systems.[60] It is also commonly referred to as the 'cubbyhole' approach, with activities or transaction types being assigned their own cubbyhole with separate tax rules for each relevant cubbyhole.[61] It has also been described as a 'formalistic' approach adopted by tax law,[62] as well as in terms of 'legal fictions'[63] or 'mapping'[64] in the tax law.

The same line-drawing approach is also evident in the tax treaty rules of the international tax system. For example, such tax treaties are normally available only to the class of 'residents' of particular states who meet various specific tests. The treaties apply different rules to each of certain separate categories of income and capital such as dividends, interest, rent, royalties, etc.

As a practical matter, the use of distinctions or line-drawing in any individual tax or in any tax system is inevitable.[65] There are two major reasons for this. First, the nature of a tax requires the need for a *legal* definition of what is to be taxed and how it is to be taxed, the practical reality being that the line-drawing delivers (or at least is intended to deliver) a tax system that can be readily administered and applied with a degree of legal certainty so that taxpayers know in advance the tax consequences of their actions.[66] Even under tax systems that are designed to be as simple as possible, recourse to some distinctions, categories, and line-drawing is

different activities should be treated in accordance with the substantial features of the difference. For Schön, tax rules should reflect the range or 'continuum' of taxpayer options and choices and 'discontinuous' and distorting provisions which would have a sudden and economically unrelated effect on alternatives are to be avoided—see Wolfgang Schön, 'International Tax Coordination for a Second-Best World (Part I)', *World Tax Journal* 1 (2009), 67–114, at pp.94–9.

[60] See, for example, David Weisbach, 'Line Drawing: Doctrine and Efficiency in the Tax Law', *Cornell Law Review* 84 (1999), 1627–81. Weisbach argues that this line-drawing in the tax system should be based on the grounds of efficiency, rather than on doctrinal concerns or traditional tax policy. The efficiency of a tax is measured by the 'deadweight loss' or 'excess burden' of the tax. This is equal to the loss in value to consumers in excess of the revenue raised by the government. An efficient tax is one with a low deadweight loss. A more detailed explanation and worked example are given by Weisbach at pp.1650–3.

[61] See, for example, Edward Kleinbard, 'Equity Derivative Products: Financial Innovation's Newest Challenge to the Tax System', *Texas Law Review* 69 (1991), 1319–68, at p.1329.

[62] See, for example, Daniel Shaviro, 'Income Tax Reform Implications of the Financial Crisis', in Alworth and Arachi, eds, *Taxation and the Financial Crisis*, 174–89, at p.185.

[63] See, for example, H. David Rosenbloom, 'Banes of an Income Tax: Legal Fictions, Elections, Hypothetical Determinations, Related Party Debt', *Tax Notes International* 32 (December 2003), 989–1000.

[64] The problem of swaps as a mapping problem is discussed in Henry Hu, 'Swaps, the Modern Process of Financial Innovation and the Vulnerability of a Regulatory Paradigm', *University of Pennsylvania Law Review* 138 (1989), 333–435, at p.394.

[65] The implication is that it is unlikely that any tax system can be perfectly robust to exploitation. Nonetheless, as will be discussed below, existing tax systems are particularly weak in this regard given the enormous scale of tax differences that have been created.

[66] For example, *de minimis* thresholds may be required in cases where there are disproportionate compliance costs for taxpayers with smaller levels of income, etc. Line-drawing may also be justified on policy grounds, such as to deliver tax exemptions for charities, etc.

inevitable.[67] Second, some of the distinctions used by the tax system, such as the separate legal personality of a company from its shareholders, or the distinction between debt and equity, have important consequences outside the sphere of tax. Nonetheless, under most present-day tax systems, the reliance on separate distinctions and categories is ubiquitous. Further, this pervasive use of distinctions and categories is in turn applied—and policed—by numerous definitions, thresholds, and ceilings. The result is that tax systems are often built on a truly colossal amount of line-drawing,[68] making them highly fragmented and inordinately complex. The systemic fragmentation of tax rules within each jurisdiction and from jurisdiction to jurisdiction dealing generally with taxpayers, transactions, types of income, ownership tests, etc accentuates the tax exploitation opportunities discussed in this chapter.[69] The complexity of tax systems leads to two additional problems. First, the detailed rules creating that complexity will often lead to more opportunities for exploitation of the system. Second, highly intricate and prescriptive rules generally make it more difficult to deploy and apply broad or purposive anti-avoidance rules, exacerbating the difficulties of maintaining an efficient tax system.

Much of the line-drawing or formalism in the tax system relies on legal distinctions.[70] In the case of the debt–equity distinction, for example, the original

[67] The proposal for a flat tax developed by Robert Hall and Alvin Rabushka was designed to be as simple as possible to administer but nonetheless the tax was broken into two parts: one for business income and one for wages and salaries, meaning that employees and independent contractors will be subject to different rules—see Robert E. Hall and Alvin Rabushka, *The Flat Tax* (Hoover Institution Press, 2007), available at https://www.hoover.org/research/flat-tax. The example is discussed in Weisbach, 'Line Drawing', at pp.1633–4. The destination-based cash-flow tax, also designed to be as efficient as possible, would apply to corporates and it distinguishes between financial and non-financial cash flows. See Alan Auerbach, Michael Devereux, Michael Keen, and John Vella, 'Destination-Based Cash Flow Taxation', Oxford Legal Studies Research Paper No. 14/2017, available at https://papers.ssrn.com/sol3/papers.cfm?abstract_id=2908158.

[68] For example, this is reflected in a significant body of work of the UK's Office for Tax Simplification (OTS) related to this issue. This includes findings relating to the UK tax system such as the existence of 1,989 legal definitions in three tax acts reviewed (see Office for Tax Simplification, 'Definitions in Tax Legislation and their Contribution to Complexity', February 2017 at paragraph 2.7.1). Various OTS papers on complexity are available at https://www.gov.uk/government/publications/ots-papers-on-aspects-of-complexity-in-the-tax-system. It is also worth noting that a UK tax authority document in 2009 acknowledged the existence of over 200 anti-avoidance purpose tests in the UK tax law. Many of these tests have substantial similarities, but there is a wide variation in the detailed design. See HMRC, 'Simplifying Unallowable Purpose Tests', discussion document, 31 July 2009, at p.7. The issue is also discussed in Weisbach, 'Line Drawing', at pp.1631–2.

[69] For example, a repo of shares from, say, a Ruritanian branch of a UK company to a Ruritanian bank is equivalent in economic terms to a stock loan from a UK company to a UK branch of a Ruritanian company but the tax treatment of the two transactions may be very different. On the policy implications of cross-border arbitrage, see Diane Ring, 'One Nation Among Many: Policy Implications of Cross-Border Tax Arbitrage', *Boston College Law Review* 44 (2002), 79–175.

[70] For example, a tax deduction for interest paid relies on the existence of an underlying 'debt' or 'indebtedness' for legal purposes for the relevant cash flow to be characterized as interest, irrespective of any accounting treatment of the payment. Similarly, the legal characterization would be essential in the case of identifying a 'dividend' received. On the other hand, a tax deduction for money spent or costs incurred places much less emphasis on the legal status or nature of the payment (though even here it might be argued that whether or not monies have been 'spent' or costs 'incurred' raises legal issues).

rationale was a legalistic one, namely that the corporation is so enmeshed with its shareholders that payments to them in respect of their capital should not be deductible whereas payments on debt are to 'real' third parties and so should be. By contrast, from an economic perspective, both kinds of payment represent a return to capital, and it is their combined treatment at the corporate and personal levels that matters.[71] A similar emphasis on the importance of legal concepts can be seen in the international tax sphere. This is reflected in the separate tax treaty articles for different legal forms of cash flow, such as interest, dividends, royalties, etc.[72]

Notwithstanding the very extensive use of line-drawing in tax systems, in many cases it is difficult to identify a clear normative rule that provides the rationale for the line-drawing—or at least a rationale that continues to be valid.[73] For example, in the case of the debt–equity distinction, which is such a prominent feature of most tax systems, it is difficult from a tax policy perspective to see why debt finance should be favoured in comparison with equity finance, particularly given the huge impact of the distinction. In the case of cross-border payments of interest this can in practice lead to the reallocation of taxing rights relating to profits from one country to another. Also relevant is the fact that there are many financing instruments that are not easily classified by reference to the binary categories of debt and equity.[74] The residence test for tax treaties is similarly anachronistic, being based originally on an analogy to individual taxpayers in the jurisdiction concerned on the presumption that the residence of a company reflects the residence of its underlying shareholders.[75] The test has remained decisive despite

[71] See International Monetary Fund, 'Debt Bias and Other Distortions: Crisis-Related Issues in Tax Policy', 12 June 2009, available at https://www.imf.org/external/np/pp/eng/2009/061209.pdf, at p.5. The debt–equity distinction is discussed in detail in Wolfgang Schön, 'The Distinct Equity of the Debt–Equity Distinction', *Bulletin for International Taxation*, 66:9 (2012), 490–502.

[72] The emphasis on legal concepts is aptly illustrated in the words of Mitchell B. Carroll, whose work on the international approach to income allocation proved highly influential in the development of the international tax rules: 'Economic fact must inevitably give way to the definite principles and provisions of law under which business is conducted.' Mitchell B. Carroll, *Taxation of Foreign and National Enterprises Vol. IV, Methods of Allocating Taxable Income* (League of Nations, 1933), at pp.176–7. The comment was made in support of the view that subsidiaries should not automatically be regarded as creating a permanent establishment of the parent corporation.

[73] See Weisbach, 'Line Drawing', at p.1640. John Kay goes further in analyzing more generally the cause of the complexity in tax systems: "It is not politicians who have messed up with the system we have. It is administrators, trying to make the best of fundamentally unworkable principles. . . .It really is not the case that the system is complex because it is a finely-honed instrument of sophisticated economic management, or that it is so complicated because it is fair. It is mainly complicated because of attempts to buttress bits of the system that do not work and probably never could have worked." John Kay, Is Complexity in Taxation Inevitable? IFS Working Paper 57, February 1985.

[74] See IMF, 'Debt Bias and Other Distortions', at p.12.

[75] The early discussion concerned the 'domicile' test for both individuals and corporate bodies: League of Nations, 'Double Taxation and Tax Evasion'. This later became the 'fiscal domicile' test: 'League of Nations Fiscal Committee London and Mexico Model Tax Conventions, Commentary and Text. C.88.M.88.1946.II.A.', p.11. 'Fiscal domicile' was then defined by reference to the residence in Article 4 of the 1963 OECD Model Double Tax Treaty before wholly giving way to the residence concept in the 1977 Model. See also the discussion in Schön, 'International Tax Coordination', at p.69.

the significant shift in the composition of shareholders in quoted companies and the material reduction in the percentage of shares held by domestic shareholders.[76] Further, in the international sphere, the extensive reliance on tax structuring based on legal concepts (and contracts) by MNCs has come to be seen as highly problematic.[77] It is also questionable whether the basic presumption that tax law should attach to the legal nature of a transaction and not to its economic effect is generally correct. There are various instances in which tax law is concerned with the economic or financial outcomes of particular arrangements rather than with transactions as such.[78]

The result is that the line-drawing in the tax system may be anachronistic, incoherent, based on incorrect or faulty assumptions, or at variance with economic reality.[79] For the purposes of the discussion here, such problematic distinctions in the tax system are referred to collectively as 'tax differences'. It is, of course, the job of tax policy thinking to root out these anachronistic or inappropriate distinctions so that similar activities, transactions, and taxpayers are taxed in a similar way, removing behavioural distortions and unfairness in the tax system and reducing compliance costs. However, as the earlier discussion of the pervasive line-drawing in the system demonstrates, that is easier said than done. The current reality is that extensive use of line-drawing and distinctions is baked in and permeates tax systems.

There are two immediate consequences that flow from the existence of these tax differences. First, they will often fail (at least partially) in their intended effect because of the phenomenon of 'tax shifting' (as explained below) and, second, they

[76] In 2015, about 26 per cent of US stock was held by foreigners in portfolio investments of $5.8 trillion. Foreign multinational companies owned a further $4.6 trillion of direct non-portfolio investments in US companies. See Steven M. Rosenthal and Lydia S. Austin, 'The Dwindling Taxable Share of U.S. Corporate Stock', *Tax Notes*, 16 May 2016, 923–34, at p.928. The same article also charts other significant shifts in the US shareholder population, for example the share of US corporate stock held in taxable accounts has fallen by more than two-thirds in the last fifty years, from 83.6 per cent in 1965 to 24.2 per cent in 2015. The position is even more pronounced in Germany, with 53 per cent of the DAX being owned by foreigners, according to the EY survey of the ownership of the DAX of April 2018, available in German at https://www.ey.com/de/de/newsroom/news-releases/ey-20180425-dax-konzerne-mehrheitlich-in-auslaendischer-hand.

[77] Much of the transfer pricing work in the recent G20/OECD 'Base Erosion and Profit Shifting' was geared to countering the ease with which legal agreements and legal 'booking' arrangements could be used by multinational companies to shift profits to tax havens. The recognition of these problems is not new. For example: 'Legal constructs, which are largely elective and easily manipulated, play too great a role in determining international tax consequences of business arrangements.' Michael Graetz, 'Taxing International Income – Inadequate Principles, Outdated Concepts, and Unsatisfactory Policy', Faculty Scholarship Series, Paper 1618 (Yale Law School, 2001), at p.316.

[78] See Gammie, 'Moral Taxation, Immoral Avoidance', at p.595. Gammie argues that to accord particular tax consequences to the legal characterization of particular transactions where the subject matter of the law is concerned with economic or financial outcomes can be a particularly disastrous way of proceeding.

[79] See, for example, the discussion of the US rules for taxing international income tax as now involving inadequate principles and outdated concepts in Graetz, 'Taxing International Income'.

create opportunities for tax arbitrage.[80] These consequences are especially relevant in relation to financial products.

The first consequence concerns the intended tax treatment of particular categories of taxpayer or transaction or income type, etc. For example, a tax statute may provide an exemption from tax for one category of taxpayer, offer a reduced withholding tax for another, while giving a tax credit to a third. However, the differential treatment of taxpayers intended by the tax law may not be delivered in economic terms. This is because (1) the immediate consequence of a tax benefit (or tax charge) in relation to an asset or income stream may be its impact on the market pricing of that asset or income stream and (2) changes in market pricing therefore have the potential to benefit a wider population than the categories of taxpayer targeted by the tax system. Thus, if a tax benefit is created to apply to a specific asset and in relation to a designated class of taxpayers only (e.g. income from certain specified government bonds is exempt in the hands of a specified class of pension fund), the price of those bonds will increase by virtue of the existence of the tax benefit as the market recognizes and prices in the positive effect on expected cash flows from the bonds. This means that current holders of those bonds, whether they are pension funds or not, will benefit from the tax effect in the market pricing. It also means that if a pension fund designated as exempt from income tax purchases the bonds from a non-pension-fund seller, the income the pension fund will receive on those bonds will be tax exempt, but some of the tax benefit will be shared with the seller through the increased purchase price paid by the pension fund for the bonds. The example illustrates what economists refer to as 'tax shifting' and specifically the distinction between the statutory incidence of a tax measure and its economic incidence.[81] There are many examples of this phenomenon across tax systems.[82] As a general matter, such shifts in the incidence of tax measures reflect a conflict between what is intended by the legal distinctions

[80] An arbitrage in this context refers to a financial strategy which delivers a riskless profit and which requires no investment. See further footnote 4 of chapter 1.

[81] Tax shifting reflects the fact that a tax measure designed to apply to a particular class of persons and at a specific point in the production and distribution chain may affect the economic welfare of other people at different points in that chain. The statutory incidence of a tax identifies the person who is obligated by law to remit a tax payment to the government, while the economic incidence refers to changes in economic well-being resulting from changes in behaviour and equilibrium prices induced by taxation. See B. Essama-Nssah, 'Assessing the Redistributive Effect of Fiscal Policy', The World Bank, Policy Research Working Paper 4592, April 2008, available at http://documents.worldbank.org/curated/en/213081468322746159/pdf/wps4592.pdf, at p.4. Discussion in the economics literature tends to discuss these issues in the context of the imposition of a tax burden, but the theory is equally relevant in the case of a tax measure creating a tax benefit at a specific point in the production and distribution chain.

[82] In a financial products context, see Patrick Honohan, 'Avoiding the Pitfalls in Taxing Financial Intermediation', The World Bank, Policy Research Working Paper 3056, May 2003, at p.16. The discussion in V. Nanda and R. Singh, 'Bond Insurance: What is Special about Munis?', *The Journal of Finance* 59:5 (October 2004) , 2253–79 suggests that tax-exempt municipal bonds can fuel the bond insurance market. For an analysis in the context of corporate income tax, see Arnold Harberger, 'The Incidence of the Corporation Income Tax', *Journal of Political Economy* 70 (1962), 215–40.

made in the tax system and the economic consequences (and therefore also changes in behaviour) that may flow from the impact of taxation.

The reason why there is a particularly high potential for such 'tax shifting' to occur in relation to financial products is that they are (1) very often subject to tax measures that aim to discriminate between different classes of owner (such as different stamp or transfer duty rules or withholding tax rates, or income tax exemptions for certain classes of owner) and (2) traded in high volume in highly liquid markets.[83] The pricing of the DAX futures market, for example, has historically implied that dividends on the German shares that comprise the DAX are valued at 95 per cent or more of the *gross* amount of the dividend, notwithstanding a withholding tax obligation applicable to those dividends for some classes of shareholder which would result in a payment to them of a lower *net* dividend. This means that the bulk of any tax credit benefit relating to a dividend received by classes of tax-advantaged shareholder is already priced into the market value of the share.[84] This in turn means that a shareholder that is not entitled to that tax credit may nonetheless benefit significantly from it in the event that the shares are sold in the market before the dividend is paid.[85]

The incidence-shifting that is discussed above is directly relevant to the discussion here because the phenomenon fuels transactional activity, particularly in financial products, by creating opportunities—whether deliberately or unwittingly—for parties to profit from or monetize tax benefits. Indeed, the shift in market pricing that reflects the tax benefit in any particular case flows from the existence of an assumption on the part of market participants that the tax benefit will be accessed, and this in turn creates an incentive to transactional activity on the part of any non-entitled holder in order to share in that benefit. It therefore contributes to, or facilitates, the process by which tax rules may be exploited.[86]

The second, and perhaps more obvious, consequence of tax differences is that the tax treatment intended by the relevant line-drawing may often be frustrated by arbitrage or manipulation. There will often be transactions on either side of the

[83] As is explored further below in the discussion of derivatives, tax benefits reserved to some classes of investor may be shared not only where the asset concerned is or can be traded but also include cases where risk in the asset can be traded even if the asset is not (e.g. through the pricing of hedging contracts).

[84] A similar situation existed under the previous German dividend imputation system, which was eliminated in 2000. McDonald estimates that approximately one-half to two-thirds of the value of the dividend imputation tax credit is reflected in market prices of German stocks (and related equity derivatives). See Robert L. McDonald, 'Cross-Border Investing with Tax Arbitrage: The Case of German Dividend Tax Credits', *The Review of Financial Studies* 14:3 (Fall 2001), 617–57.

[85] For a detailed discussion of the theoretical implications of differently taxed investors on the equilibrium price of securities, see Suleyman Basak and Michael Gallmeyer, 'Capital Market Equilibrium with Differential Taxation', *European Finance Review* 7 (2003) 121–59.

[86] As will be seen below, it is also true that derivatives can be used to deliver incidence-shifting effects.

line, wherever it is drawn, that will be substantially similar, in other words, substitutes for each other. Given the economic impact of tax attributes as discussed above, taxpayers will be influenced by these tax factors and modify their behaviour to achieve the best result in after-tax terms.[87] The result is that, in effect, the tax system offers up many choices of legal or transactional form. Distortions are thereby created and, in the process, taxpayers are given some levers of control over how much tax they pay. Taxpayers that are not targeted by the law will, if possible, seek to take advantage of any beneficial tax provision and taxpayers that are targeted will seek to avoid any penalizing or disadvantageous provision.[88] The opportunities for arbitraging tax differences are also further expanded as a result of the possibility of exploiting the interaction between tax systems in a cross-border setting.[89]

In many cases, it is the legal form of a transaction, arrangement, entity, etc that is particularly open to manipulation by the taxpayer.[90] This explains why, in cum-ex, 'shell' pension funds, which under certain tax treaties were uniquely able to reclaim the entire amount of the cum-ex tax credit, were so often employed as buyers in the strategy.[91] A consequence of this kind of activity is often the

[87] Any such tax-influenced change in behaviour will also have efficiency effects and an impact on revenues raised through the tax system. Slemrod and Gillitzer give an example of such a tax-influenced change in behaviour, namely that following the US Tax Reform Act of 1986 there was a large shift from consumer loans, the interest on which ceased being deductible, into still-deductible mortgage or home equity loans. See Slemrod and Gillitzer, *Tax Systems*, at p.59.

[88] The position in relation to the debt–equity distinction alone has given rise to a whole industry seeking to skirt the distinction. See, for example, the discussion of monthly income preferred securities ('MIPS') as a tax-deductible substitute for preferred shares in Weisbach, 'Line Drawing', at p.1673. MIPS were also used by Enron to issue tax-deductible debt to offshore subsidiaries which in turn issued securities considered to be equity on the firm's balance sheet—see David L. Brumbaugh, 'Enron and Taxes', in Theodore F. Sterling, ed., *The Enron Scandal* (Nova Science, 2002), 151–4, at p.154. A more recent (and global) example is represented by the advent of bank 'bail-in' bonds and similar contingent capital which is structured as debt but converts into equity in certain circumstances. These instruments have emerged since the Global Financial Crisis of 2008–9 under the framework of measures to strengthen the capital base of banks developed by the Basel Committee on Banking Supervision and they have led to much discussion on how they should be treated for tax purposes—see, for example, the HMRC discussion paper 'The Tax Treatment of Regulatory Capital Instruments', 2011, available at https://assets.publishing.service.gov.uk/government/uploads/system/uploads/attachment_data/file/366055/discussion.pdf.

[89] The multiple different rules from one tax system to another hugely expand the available line-drawing or 'cubbyholes' that may be arbitraged, for example by structuring cross-border cash flows to bring together the most tax-optimized payor cubbyhole with the most tax-optimized recipient cubbyhole.

[90] The position is magnified by the differences in tax rates between different taxpayers on different types of income, and the differences that exist from one jurisdiction to another. For example, instances of company directors flying to tax haven locations where the company otherwise has no or a very limited presence in order to fix the residence of the company for tax purposes are common.

[91] See further the discussion in chapters 2 and 3. In fact, the cash flows representing the dividends (and tax credits) legally owned by such pension funds may be passed on to other legal entities (for example in the form of payments under a swap). This emphasizes the critical significance for tax purposes of the formal legal status of the immediate recipient of the cash flow as a recognized 'pension fund', irrespective of the real economics of the transaction. Note also that the apparent tax benefits in the case of cum-ex derived from the fact that the dividend compensation payment was, for German tax

enactment of anti-avoidance rules, often extremely complex, and designed to support and police the intended tax distinction or category and counteract arbitrage activity. This adds further complexity to the system and the cumulative complexity may also produce further mismatches that can be arbitraged. The paradox is that the greater the complexity, the more opportunities there will be for arbitrage.[92]

Whilst what is described above is generally the reality of most tax systems, the consequences of tax differences being open to abuse or exploitation are especially acute in relation to the tax rules applicable to financial products and markets. There are a number of reasons why this is so. First, some of the most fundamental and common tax line-drawing relates to financial products (e.g. the debt versus equity distinction) or financial markets participants (e.g. the trader or market professional/ intermediary versus investor distinction). These distinctions often lead to other important tax distinctions and asymmetries, such as the distinction between income/profit recognition on a mark-to-market basis as distinct from income/profits being recognized on a realization basis. Other cardinal distinctions, such as that between income and capital, feature prominently and are therefore also recurrently important in the taxation of financial products. This is reflected in what may be termed the 'independent instrument' approach adopted by most tax systems which seeks to maintain the differences from a *legal perspective* in the character of cash flows from financial products. A second reason is that the amounts involved in financial cash flows (such as interest, dividends, cash flows under derivatives, etc) are often very large. Further, many types of financial product are highly liquid and are issued and traded in huge volume. The consequence is that where tax exploitation opportunities exist in relation to financial products or markets, the relevant financial product 'raw material' will be available in very large quantities, potentially allowing large-scale trades.[93] This means that the resulting tax effects and the value to be derived from exploiting the tax system are potentially very significant. Third, financial markets are global and very highly integrated. On the other hand, tax systems are jurisdictional/domestic and therefore necessarily fragmented. With operations crossing domestic borders, banks can use financial products to access huge pools of capital and access a wide span of

law purposes, treated (or at last thought by cum-ex traders to be treated) in a short sale situation in the same way as a real dividend.

[92] There are many cases where an anti-avoidance provision has been introduced into the tax law only for it subsequently to be used as the basis for a tax arbitrage transaction. An example in the UK was the practice of issuing debt with a tiny fraction of the return dependent on the results of the business in order to take advantage of the anti-avoidance provision in Corporation Tax Act 2010, Section 1000 (1) where an interest deduction could not be used (e.g. due to losses). This led to a further anti-avoidance provision, Section 1032 of the same Act.

[93] It is also possible that, once used in a tax arbitrage arrangement, a financial product may become available for immediate reuse in the arbitrage, as was seen in the recycling of securities in the case of cum-ex.

global investors in order to exploit domestic tax systems. This makes it easy to commoditize and distribute financial products developed in one market to other markets. Fourth, the contractual nature of financial products means that product innovation can be very rapid, given that product modification to deliver tax-driven goals can often be delivered simply by varying the contractual terms of a legal instrument.[94] Further, both the speed of innovation and the complexity of financial products and financial markets present potent barriers to the tax authorities' understanding of such business, products, and markets and contribute to a lack of transparency for tax purposes. It is, therefore, no surprise that the issue of tax avoidance has been described as being nowhere more problematic nor economically important than in relation to the taxation of financial products.[95]

There is one other major factor which contributes to the process by which the tax rules for financial products and markets may be exploited. This relates to the way in which derivatives and other new financial products have been dealt with by the tax system. This is discussed in the following section.

The Tax Treatment of Derivatives and Other Financial Instruments

It will be evident from the discussion in Part I of this book that derivative transactions in some form have existed for many years.[96] However, the financial derivative markets as we understand them today emerged in late 1970s and early 1980s following the emergence of the first swap products and in response to the lifting of exchange controls, deregulation and globalization of markets, and developments in information technology.[97] The real growth in these markets emerged in the mid-1980s. There are now trillion-dollar markets in derivatives such as futures and forwards, options and swaps relating to currencies, interest rates, commodities, share and other indices, credit default, etc. The nominal value of derivatives outstanding (in other words, the total value of assets referenced by derivative contracts) is many times greater than the value of the actual assets themselves.[98]

The growth of derivatives markets and the globalization of securities markets has also led to an expansion in the use of other financial products, such as stock

[94] In the banking sector, there is also a pronounced industry focus on product innovation, as explained in the previous chapter.

[95] Slemrod and Gillitzer, *Tax Systems*, at p.61.

[96] See further the discussion in Chapter 6 at footnote 49.

[97] A thorough discussion of the nature and uses of derivatives is available in Das, *Swaps and Financial Derivatives*.

[98] A raft of BIS triennial and regular OTC derivatives market statistics showing the enormous size of derivative markets is available at https://www.bis.org/statistics/derstats.htm.

lending, repo, structured notes, securitization, etc.[99] Together, these products have often been (and commonly still are) referred to as 'new' or 'innovative' financial instruments, although, as the products have now been a staple feature of financial markets for more than three decades, those labels seem no longer appropriate. However, it is useful to have some collective reference point for these products and so in the discussion that follows they will be referred to collectively as 'complex financial products'.

Challenges for Tax Systems

There are various features of derivatives that make them problematic for tax systems, but the heart of the problem is that tax systems typically rely on distinctions that can readily be undermined, if not eliminated altogether, by financial innovation.[100] Of particular significance is the ability of a derivative contract to designate almost any underlying reference 'asset' by reference to which cash flows under the derivative contract will be paid or received. This might include a specific asset or assets, an event or transaction, a designated cash flow, etc. Derivatives can therefore replicate the economic effects or characteristics of other financial products. Cash flows under derivatives are therefore highly flexible. Derivatives can be used to convert one type of income into another or into a combination of different types of income or to roll up cash flows or change their timing.[101] Derivatives can also be embedded in other financial products, such as a debt product with an embedded option.

What flows from these features is that derivative products present a number of significant challenges to the traditional approach adopted by many tax systems.[102] These include the following:

[99] I include in this category a wide variety of products and instruments, including the dividend adjustment mechanism in the cum-ex trade, the pre-release mechanism that is discussed at p.253, etc.

[100] See Alvin C. Warren, 'US Income Taxation of New Financial Products', *Journal of Public Economics* 88 (2004), 899–923. There is also a thorough discussion of the problems for the UK and German tax systems caused by derivatives in Weidmann, *Taxation of Derivatives*. There are many ways in which derivatives can pose difficulties across the tax system. For example, transactions in options contracts have been used to defeat rudimentary control tests over shares couched in traditional terms relating to the ownership of shares and voting control (as in the UK case of J Sainsbury plc v O'Connor [1990] BTC 363). However, the discussion in this chapter is concerned particularly with their impact on the tax rules relating to financial products.

[101] Das gives a compelling example of the way in which traditional financial instruments may be decomposed and reconstructed by the use of derivatives—see Satyajit Das, *Derivative Products and Pricing* (John Wiley, 2006), at pp.5–8.

[102] It is not surprising that derivatives are potentially problematic for tax systems because they are used to transfer risk in ways which cannot be achieved by traditional instruments. For a more detailed discussion of the specific challenges of derivatives for the tax system, see OECD, 'Taxation of New Financial Instruments', at pp.29–31; United Nations, 'Taxation of New Financial Instruments', presented at the Ad Hoc Group of Experts on International Cooperation in Tax matters, tenth meeting,

- *Timing and amount of income asymmetries*—e.g. a cash flow under a derivative transaction may be structured to yield a tax deduction for the payer but the recipient may not be taxed or taxed on a deferred basis, such as where a single 'balloon' payment under a swap is deductible for the payer but taxed in hands of the recipient on an accruals basis. The different recognition bases that are typically relevant in this context are the payment basis, accruals, and mark-to-market.
- *Characterization asymmetries*—e.g. where one country treats cross-border payments under a derivative as arising on income account and therefore as tax deductible, but the other state treats the receipt as a capital gain, taxable at lower rate, and possibly on a deferred basis.[103]
- *Application of 'source' for tax purposes*—determinations as to the source of cash flows under derivatives are important in establishing whether to apply a withholding tax and, in the case of cross-border payments, may dictate which of two countries have primary taxing rights under a double tax treaty.
- *Traditional distinctions drawn by tax systems*—the design flexibility of derivatives poses some significant challenges to traditional distinctions reflected in the tax system, such as the debt–equity distinction and the notion of realization of income.[104]
- *Challenges to determining the 'owner' of an asset for tax purposes*—traditional ownership tests for tax purposes are often premised on the right to receive income from an asset and the right to dispose of the asset. However, derivatives transactions can shift the relevant risk and return from an asset without any transfer of the asset itself. This means it is possible to have legal ownership of an asset without the attendant risk and reward associated with it, and equally that it is also possible to be entitled under a derivative

Geneva, 10–14 September 2001; and OECD, 'Innovative Financial Transactions: Tax Policy Implications', Special Sessions on Innovative Financial Transactions, presented at the Ad Hoc Group of Experts on International Cooperation in Tax Matters, tenth meeting, Geneva, 10–14 September 2001, ST/SG/AC.8/2001/CRP.8 at pp.3–4, ST/SG/AC.8/2001/CRP.10, at p.2. This OECD document is available at http://unpan1.un.org/intradoc/groups/public/documents/un/unpan002448.pdf. Seven major problems in taxing derivatives are identified in Weidmann, *Taxation of Derivatives*, Chapter 3. Julian Alworth deals with the challenges in different terms as: the distinction between certain and uncertain income flows; the non-uniform characterization of transactions; non-linear rate schedules; and timing. See Julian S. Alworth, 'Taxation and Integrated Financial Markets: The Challenges of Derivatives and Other Financial Innovations', *International Tax and Public Finance* 5 (1998), 507–34, at pp.512–13. A detailed discussion in a US context is available from Joint Committee on Taxation, 'Present Law and Issues Related to the Taxation of Financial Instruments and Products', JCX-556-11, 2 December 2011, available at https://www.jct.gov/publications.html?func=startdown&id=4372.

[103] The same arbitrage may also work within the tax system of a single country where the parties are subject to different tax rules.

[104] For example, Alvin Warren discusses the traditional reliance of realization income taxation on the distinction between fixed and contingent returns and demonstrates that this is no longer tenable in the light of financial equivalences arising under financial innovation. See Warren, 'US Income Taxation of New Financial Products', at p.902.

instrument to the reward and be subject to the risks from an underlying asset without being the formal legal owner of it.[105]

These challenges are exacerbated by a number of additional factors, including: the diversity of cash flows under derivatives, with some cash flows certain, some contingent, some capped or subject to a floor; the wide range of derivative products, including dynamic portfolio swaps, structured first-to-default products, etc; the embedding of derivatives in traditional financial products, as seen in the expansion of the structured notes market; the leverage typically inherent in derivatives;[106] and the fact that different derivative products can be substituted for each other or combined to form new products (for example, an interest rate swap is equivalent to a series of cash settled interest rate forward contracts, and a swaption consists of an option on a swap). Further, these challenges are not restricted to derivatives but are also relevant to other complex financial products, such as stock loan and repo transactions. For example, under a stock loan or repo transaction the legal ownership of a parcel of securities may be transferred to another person but the relevant risk and reward will be retained by the transferor.[107] Also, debt instruments with unusual features (such as equity kickers or warrants)[108] and other instruments with features of both debt and equity (such as convertibles, non-voting preferred shares, perpetual debt, bail-in bonds, etc) raise difficult borderline issues in relation to the traditional debt–equity distinction. Another feature of the challenges posed by derivatives is that in tax planning their use is frequently combined with a tailored accounting and legal (and sometimes regulatory) treatment.[109] The challenges of derivatives and complex financial products are not restricted to domestic-law tax systems but also raise similar difficulties and inconsistencies, such as those relating to characterization and ownership, under double tax treaties.[110]

[105] This explains the difficulties presented by derivatives to the concept of 'beneficial ownership' which is used widely in double tax treaties. See, for example, 'Commentary to Article 10 of the OECD Model Tax Convention on Income and on Capital' at paragraph 12.4 and the decisions in the Swiss swaps cases, Federal Supreme Court decisions 2C_364 and 377/2012 and 2C_895/2012.

[106] Derivatives commonly involve significant leverage in their terms. This means that a relatively small initial monetary outlay on the contract may nonetheless involve exposure to price movements on a significantly larger underlying asset.

[107] The relevant risk and reward is retained by the original owner because of the obligation on the borrower to redeliver to the owner (the lender) securities that are equivalent to those borrowed or repo'd.

[108] An equity 'kicker' is an incentive in the form of a right which in certain circumstances will allow the holder to acquire shares at a future time. It is often issued in combination with subordinated debt. A warrant is similar to an option in that, until its expiry, it entitles the holder to acquire shares at a given price.

[109] Michael P. Donohoe, 'Financial Derivatives in Corporate Tax Avoidance: A Conceptual Perspective', *Journal of American Accounting Association* 37:1 (Spring 2015), 37–68, at p.39.

[110] Problems under tax treaties have been recognized for some years—see OECD, 'Taxation of New Financial Instruments', pp.31–9. Some of the difficulties are caused by the fact that the treatment of

All these challenges naturally lead to the question of how derivatives have been dealt with by tax systems.

Response of Governments

At a very generalized level, the response of governments to derivatives in a tax context has typically been to pursue a dual agenda. First, authorities seek to remove tax impediments to the development of derivatives markets, so that artificial tax barriers to new risk management techniques are removed or minimized. Second, they simultaneously endeavour to counter or remove opportunities for tax exploitation using these products.[111] There is an obvious tension between these objectives, and the manner in which many tax systems have sought to deal with derivatives has in practice exacerbated this tension, as is explored further below.

Tax systems have wrestled with derivatives and complex financial products. An early and recurrent pattern was that the tax law struggled to keep pace with developments in financial products including derivatives, worsening the significant challenges they posed to tax systems. This was clear when derivatives were emerging in the 1980s, but, even though derivatives have now been a core part of the financial markets landscape for the last four decades, the point that the tax law struggles to deal with derivatives has been made emphatically, and at regular intervals, ever since.[112]

There are generally three particular problem areas relating to the treatment of derivatives within the tax system:

derivatives under tax treaties is usually determined by their treatment under domestic law. See OECD, 'Taxation of New Financial Instruments', pp. 11, 18, 22, 24.

[111] See generally OECD, 'Taxation of New Financial Instruments', OECD, 'Innovative Financial Transactions', and Plambeck, Rosenbloom, and Ring, 'General Report'.

[112] See, for example, OECD, 'Taxation of New Financial Instruments', at pp. 3, 8. The OECD report was based on a survey of countries that was conducted in 1989. The same point that tax systems struggle to deal with derivatives has been made ever since. In the 1990s, for example, see International Fiscal Association, *Tax Aspects of Derivative Financial Instruments*, Cahiers De Droit Fiscal 80b (Kluwer Law International, 1995), at p.657. The point was also the first point of comment in a 2001 paper prepared by Victor Thuronyi of the IMF for the United Nations' Ad Hoc Group of Experts (see United Nations, 'Taxation of New Financial Instruments'). The point was also repeated by the OECD, which made it clear that tax rules and policies have generally been developed to address more traditional financial instruments and are not suited to deal with modern financial instruments (see OECD, 'Innovative Financial Transactions', at p.8). A decade later, in 2011, the point is made with equal force in a United States Government Accountability Office Report (US GAO, 'Financial Derivatives, Disparate Tax Treatment and Information Gaps Create Uncertainty and Potential Abuse', GAO-11-750, September 2011).

- The slowness of tax systems to adapt, or even respond, to derivatives.
- The reliance on general principles of tax law.
- The tendency to address the taxation of the derivative/financial product in isolation rather than to consider what derivatives can accomplish in the context of the tax system.

The first point relating to the slowness of tax systems to deal with derivatives and complex financial products is illustrated by the comments made above on the very lengthy period over which tax systems have attempted to come to terms with them. Connected with this are certain capacity constraints within tax authorities discussed later in this chapter in the context of tax administration issues. The slowness of tax authorities to respond was apparent in relation to the cum-ex trade. In that case, the appreciable time lag was caused by a failure on the part of the tax authorities to understand the real effect of the composite cum-ex transactions, including the degree to which derivatives trades in combination with short sales and stock borrows could be used to exploit the glitch in the settlement system and export the financial benefits among the participants. A slow response to dealing with complex financial products is not confined to Germany. In the US, for example, this was the main theme of a 2011 report of the Government Accountability Office which observed that in some cases the Internal Revenue Service will identify derivatives-based tax arbitrage strategies 'long after they have been introduced and gained considerable use'.[113] There are many cases where perceived weaknesses or gaps in the tax system exploited by derivatives take many years to be plugged.[114] This is an important issue, because actions to arbitrage the tax system often benefit from a first-mover advantage. That advantage is obviously intensified by a slow response on the part of the tax authorities.[115]

The slow and faltering response to derivatives is evident in an international context relating to tax treaties. Twenty-five years ago, the OECD discussed the treaty position and recognized 'a great many problems involved in the taxation of financial instruments in general'. The lack of consensus among tax authorities meant no compelling solutions could be found. The OECD concluded that preservation of the then status quo (which is broadly what still remains) was unacceptable and unattractive because of the opportunities available for tax

[113] See 'Highlights of GAO-11-750', a report to congressional requesters, p.1 summarizing the US GAO report, 'Financial Derivatives, Disparate Tax Treatment and Information Gaps Create Uncertainty and Potential Abuse' referred to in footnote 112 of this chapter.

[114] For example, in the UK 'deep in the money' options have been widely used to avoid stamp taxes since the mid 1990s at least. It was only in 2016 that the mischief was closed by a statutory change (Finance Act 2016, Section 138), at least 25 years after the strategy first emerged. For further instances of the slow response to tax planning involving derivatives, see Donohoe, 'Financial Derivatives in Corporate Tax Avoidance', at p.38.

[115] The issue also means that responses to abuse relating to derivatives and complex products will often be made on a piecemeal basis, so that even if one instance of abuse is dealt with it can be replaced by others.

avoidance.[116] The OECD report was pessimistic about the prospect of any consensus approach being achieved and suggested the tax avoidance problems were very likely to persist and increase.

The second problem identified refers to the broad assimilation of derivatives into tax systems through a reliance on existing general principles of taxation.[117] These general principles in tax systems and the distinctions they draw were formed long before the advent of derivatives and other complex financial instruments. What is more, those principles and distinctions are often not altered to accommodate derivative financial products.[118] Since derivatives will often not readily fit in the 'cubbyholes' of existing tax systems (or will fit into more than one), a choice often needs to be made as to how they are to be accommodated in the existing tax rules. This may result in inconsistencies in the tax treatment of transactions that have the same economic result.[119]

The third problem is that the approach of tax authorities has often been geared to identifying a single tax treatment for a derivative on the basis it is seen as separate and independent both from the underlying asset or financial instrument (of which it is a derivative) as well as any related transaction.[120] This approach is often intended to ensure that the tax treatment of the derivative is clear, thereby removing any tax impediment to the use of the instrument for risk-management purposes.[121] (It is true that tax law does sometimes look at the relationship of a derivative to another asset or transaction, for example where the derivative is a

[116] OECD, 'Taxation of New Financial Instruments', at pp.37–8. The conclusion of the report was to continue to study the issues.

[117] OECD, 'Taxation of New Financial Instruments', pp. 16, 20. See also Plambeck, Rosenbloom, and Ring, 'General Report', at p.660. The general principles of taxation often rely on the relevant accounting treatment and, at least in the early days, this has also struggled to keep up with developments in derivatives in relation to disclosure and accounting standards—see OECD, 'Taxation of New Financial Instruments', p.27. A good example of a state which has no detailed tax rules for derivatives but simply applies the general corporate tax rules is Germany—see Weidmann, *Taxation of Derivatives*, at pp.83–6. However, there are also some examples where states have sought to develop more comprehensive rules to deal with derivatives. For example, there is in the UK tax legislation a highly detailed tax regime that seeks to deal with derivatives for the purposes of the corporate income tax. The UK Derivative Contract provisions are contained in Part 7 of CTA 2009 and comprise approximately 150 sections of law.

[118] For example, although the debt–equity distinction is made increasingly tenuous by the emergence of a range of derivatives and structured financial products, there has been very little appetite on the part of governments to abandon the sharp distinction between the two that is normally seen in the design and operation of tax systems.

[119] The process will often lead to new rules (with an emphasis on anti-avoidance) that are intended to cope with the issues, but which create more arbitrage opportunities. The inconsistencies are also a feature of the treatment of derivatives in double tax treaties—for example, where interest subject to a withholding tax is replaced by an economically equivalent cash flow under a swap, the interest article in the tax treaty would normally have no application on the basis that the derivative involves no underlying debt obligation. See OECD, '2017 Model Tax Convention on Income and Capital' (OECD, 2017), commentary on Article 11, at paragraph 21.1.

[120] See Plambeck, Rosenbloom, and Ring, 'General Report', at p.667. This approach is referred to in the IFA Cahier as the 'separate transactions principle' (see at p.667). The OECD 1994 report refers to it as 'the independent instrument approach'. See OECD, 'Taxation of New Financial Instruments', at p.8.

[121] OECD, 'Taxation of New Financial Instruments', p.34.

hedge or part of a composite transaction, and provide that in such a case the relevant tax treatment is determined by reference to that related transaction, though this is less common.[122]) This means that tax systems tend not to address the *multiple* uses of a single derivative financial product. Consequently, tax systems will generally not vary the relevant tax treatment according to the diverse uses to which the derivative instrument may be put.[123] Neither is it common to see a derivative bifurcated or disaggregated into its component parts under the rules of the tax system.[124]

Consequences

Not surprisingly, the result of the way tax systems deal with derivatives and complex financial products is often the inadvertent creation of an array of avoidance opportunities for taxpayers.[125] These opportunities stem from a number of factors, such as inconsistencies in the rules where one product with similar economic outcomes to another may be taxed differently because the applicable tax rules were introduced at different times and without coordination. As the bifurcated or disaggregated treatment of the constituent elements of derivatives is not common in tax systems, it is also easy for taxpayers to combine different elements within the same derivative product. This allows taxpayers to exploit differences between the economic fundamentals of financial products and the categories or cubbyholes used by the tax system. For example, the economics of holding an equity product such as a parcel of shares can be replicated by entering into a total return swap, buying a call option, selling a put, investing in an equity-linked note, buying a forward, borrowing the shares, entering into a reverse repo over the shares, etc, with all these different options potentially being subject to quite different tax rules. There is also the problem that tax rules dealing with derivatives themselves can be quite diverse. The rules may vary by the type of derivative product, but they may also differ according to the underlying asset or financial instrument referenced by the derivative, the type of taxpayer, the purpose of the

[122] See Plambeck, Rosenbloom, and Ring, 'General Report', at p.668.

[123] OECD, 'Taxation of New Financial Instruments', at p.13.

[124] The greater use of bifurcation of the constituent elements of derivatives and financial products by the tax system has been seen as a possible strategy to deal with the tax problems from these instruments, but various practical problems have rendered such an approach uncommon. See OECD, 'Innovative Financial Transactions', at p.3, and also Plambeck, Rosenbloom, and Ring, 'General Report', at p.670.

[125] US GAO, 'Financial Derivatives', pp.10–21. The plentiful supply of avoidance opportunities created by derivatives has been recognized for some time—see OECD, 'Taxation of New Financial Instruments', pp. 23, 31, 32, and passim. A similar conclusion is reached in a more recent study—see Nesvetailova, Guter-Sandu, Palan, and Milo, 'Tax Evasion and Avoidance', at p.6.

transaction, and so on.[126] This inevitably adds complexity and further enlarges the opportunities for tax exploitation. It has been suggested recently that the rapidly growing financial technology (Fintech) sector, including cryptocurrencies, peer-to-peer lending, initial coin offerings, and crowdfunding, will add a further world of opportunities for tax avoidance and evasion.[127]

The situation described above explains why an inadequate tax treatment of derivatives may often contribute to the process by which tax rules can be exploited. This can be seen in two principal ways.

First, derivatives can be used by a taxpayer to replicate the economic effects of owning a traditional instrument or entering into a transaction, yet in each case without the normal tax disadvantages of doing so.[128] An example relating to a financial instrument is a 'synthetic' investment in equity shares in the form of a total return swap, which, by virtue of the designation in the contract of the underlying reference assets, replicates the economic effect of a combined investment in shares and the financing of that investment with a loan. This is reflected in the cash flows under the instrument, which, for the period of the swap, involve the party which is 'long' under the swap (i) *receiving* amounts equivalent to increases in the market value of the underlying shares as well as any dividends on them and *paying* amounts equivalent to any fall in the market value of the shares (commonly referred to as the 'equity leg' of the swap), and (ii) paying amounts equivalent to interest to finance the acquisition of the shares (the 'financing' leg). An example of this type of swap is given in Figure 7.2 which is discussed later in this chapter. For some investors, the swap may be more advantageous from a tax perspective, for example because the dividend-equivalent swap cash flows are not subject to the withholding tax that would apply to dividends on real shares.[129]

An example relating to a transaction is the use of a forward contract over a portfolio of shares combined with a stock loan to replicate the effect of selling those shares. Such structures have been widely used and may be illustrated by the US example of a variable pre-paid forward contract.[130] The motivation of the

[126] An example of different tax rules for different taxpayers in relation to the same transaction (meaning a mismatch is inevitable if there is a dealer on one side and a non-dealer on other) is given in US GAO, 'Financial Derivatives', at pp.11–12.

[127] See Nesvetailova, Guter-Sandu, Palan, Milo, 'Tax Evasion and Avoidance', at pp. 8 and 56–62.

[128] The OECD has described this ability of derivatives to replicate the economic properties of other financial instruments as perhaps their most fundamental challenge to existing tax systems. See OECD, 'Innovative Financial Transactions', at p.22.

[129] Withholding taxes illustrate a number of issues raised by derivatives. Such taxes are highly susceptible to tax planning using derivatives given that: different withholding tax rates apply to different legal forms of cash flow (but usually not to cash flows under a derivatives contract); the individual cash flows are taxed in isolation and without regard to their economic connection with other financial transactions; and the withholding mechanism assumes one-way payments of gross income (whereas many derivatives involve payments being made by both parties to a contract).

[130] An earlier similar structure in the US, though based on a short sale rather than a derivative, which was designed to achieve the same after-tax result was the 'short against the box' transaction. This

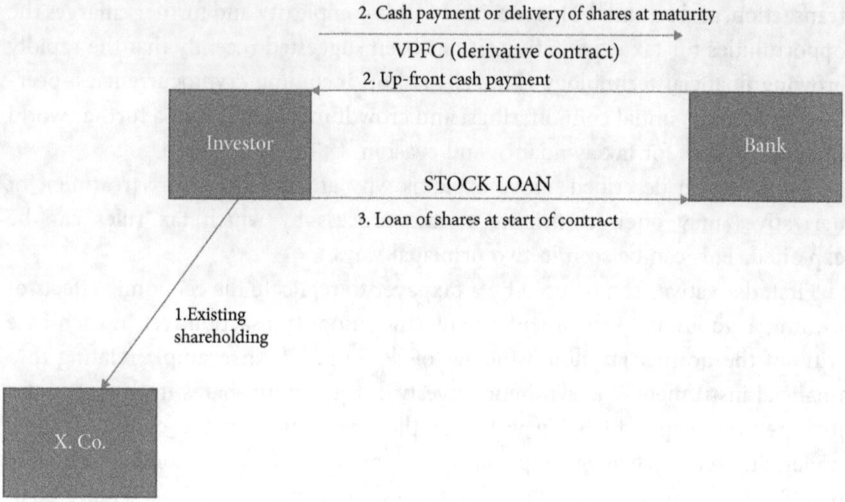

Figure 7.1. Replication effect of derivatives

transaction from a tax perspective is to defer a tax bill that would otherwise arise on a true legal sale of shares which have appreciated in value since being acquired. The structure is illustrated in Figure 7.1. It shows an investor that owns a parcel of appreciated shares entering into a forward contract to sell the shares, typically at a point three to five years in the future. At the same time, the investor lends the shares to the bank. By means of the forward, the investor has in economic terms transferred its risk in the shares, while simultaneously through the stock loan it has transferred the shares themselves. The up-front cash payment received from the bank allows the investor to reinvest in other assets. For tax purposes, however, the stock loan would not be treated as a taxable disposal of the shares, while the sale of the shares (and therefore any taxable gain) would not be recognized until the expiry of the forward contract and the actual delivery of the shares under that contract.[131]

involved a taxpayer entering into a short sale of securities which were identical to appreciated securities that the taxpayer already held. The effect of the short sale would be that in economic terms the taxpayer sold its interest in the appreciated shares (as the taxpayer would be insulated from the effects of further market price movements in the price of the shares through the short sale). However, the transaction 'worked' for tax purposes because the gain on the appreciated shares would not be recognized until the close-out of the short position as a result of the separate analysis under the tax rules of the taxpayer's offsetting positions. See Kleinbard, 'Equity Derivative Products', at pp.1357–8.

[131] The simplified example here is based on an example in US GAO, 'Financial Derivatives', at pp.18–19. Certain other details would be important under a US tax analysis, including the inclusion of a cash settlement option in relation to the forward and the use of a detailed formula to fix the number of shares to be delivered (or cash settled). This variability in the number of deliverable shares is included to avoid certain anti-abuse rules that do not permit deferred recognition of prepaid sales—see IRC Section 1259 on constructive sales.

There are many other instances in which derivatives have been or can be used to deliver a tax-optimized substitute for a more traditional instrument or transaction.[132] The ability to deploy derivatives in this manner has the same effect as a taxpayer election in the tax law, in the sense that it allows the taxpayer to choose the most favourable of two possible treatments under the tax law. However, in the case of derivatives, the 'election' is generally not intended under the tax rules.

The second way that the tax treatment of derivatives may contribute to the process of exploiting tax rules is through their use as a transfer or distribution mechanism in connection with tax benefits that are intended by the tax system to be restricted to some taxpayers only. The manner in which a tax benefit may be 'shared' through such a transfer or distribution mechanism will vary from case to case, but the sharing is often achieved through the on-payment of a monetary amount which corresponds to some or all of the relevant tax benefit derived by the payor.[133] An example that has already been seen in the structuring of the cum-ex trade is the use of swaps or similar derivatives, such as single stock futures. These were used in the cum-ex trade for two distinct purposes: first, to insulate the cum-ex buyer from the effect of market price volatility whilst temporarily holding the shares after purchasing them; and, second, as a mechanism to share the tax benefit arising to the cum-ex buyer. It is this second purpose that is of relevance here. In the cum-ex trade, the sharing of the tax benefit was delivered through the pricing of the derivative transaction, meaning that an amount reflecting some portion of the tax credit derived from the cum-ex trade by the cum-ex buyer would be included in the cash flows paid away to the derivative counterparty by that buyer.

The function of a swap as a transfer or sharing mechanism relating to a tax benefit can be illustrated with a simple example. Figure 7.2 illustrates certain cash flows that legally (and usually also for tax purposes) are quite different even though they may be similar in economic terms. These are the dividends received by Bank at Step 1 as compared with the dividend-equivalent payments it makes under the swap at Step 2. The different treatment of these cash flows for tax purposes provides the potential for any tax benefit to be shared. Assume that Bank derives a tax benefit at Step 1 as it is entitled to an exemption from the withholding tax in respect of dividend payments on the shares it holds. Assume further that the

[132] A UK example concerns the acquisition of UK shares through a 'deep in the money' call option, the idea being that the stamp tax charge that normally applies to a straight purchase of the shares can be largely removed. This is achieved by the seller granting a call option over the shares with a very low strike price. The premium for the grant of such an option would be very large, reflecting the low strike price for the shares on exercise. However, until a recent change in the law, the premium consideration would not be subject to the stamp tax charge. This means that any stamp tax would apply only to the consideration for the shares paid by way of the strike price. This structure was used widely for many years until its recent abolition. See Richard Collier, 'Finance Act Notes: Section 138: Stamp Duty: Transfers to Depositaries or Providers of Clearance Services' *British Tax Review* 5 (2016), 635–6.

[133] There are also cases where the tax 'benefit' is the avoidance of a tax cost such as a charge to transfer duty, in which case some or all of the tax cost avoided may be passed on in the pricing of the instrument that delivers the sharing of that tax benefit.

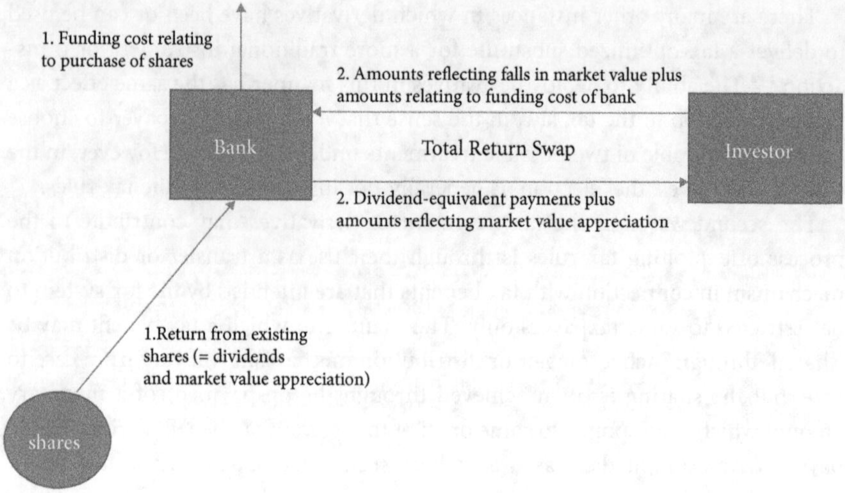

Figure 7.2. Distribution effect of derivatives

exemption is not available to Investor (instead, Investor would be subject to the withholding tax if it received a dividend). Bank is able to share the tax benefit through the cash flows under the derivative because the derivative is subject to different tax rules. Critically, the 'dividend equivalent' amounts paid under the derivative incorporating some or all of the tax benefit derived by Bank are not subject to withholding tax even though they are equivalent in economic terms to the dividend payment itself (which, of course, is subject to withholding tax).[134] The result is that the tax benefit can be shared between Bank and Investor. Derivatives contracts are frequently used in this way because they are normally not subject to withholding tax.[135]

In Figure 7.2, Bank may be willing to pass on the entirety of the tax benefit to Investor to secure a spread or 'turn'—that being the difference between its funding cost relating to financing the derivative hedge (i.e. the shares) and the financing leg payments received by Bank under the swap. The incentive to share the tax benefit in the way discussed here becomes more obvious when the asset giving rise to the tax benefit is supplied by the other party, who is then rewarded (by sharing economically in the tax benefit) through the swap. This was of course a common feature of cum-ex trades.

[134] The example also illustrates the point that the two main ways for a taxpayer to use derivatives may be seen in the same transaction: in the example given, the investor in the swap benefits from the ability of the derivative to replicate a traditional financial product (here, shares in a company), whereas for the bank which holds the real shares and enters into the swap, the derivative functions as a distribution mechanism. More detailed examples of the use of derivatives in tax planning are given in Donohoe, 'Financial Derivatives in Corporate Tax Avoidance'.

[135] For a discussion of the reasons why it is difficult to apply a withholding tax to the cash flows of derivative contracts, see Plambeck, Rosenbloom, and Ring, 'General Report', at pp.684–6.

The ability to use derivatives as a sharing or 'distribution' mechanism in relation to tax benefits obviously adds significant flexibility to the process of exploiting a tax benefit, whether it be tax-exempt income, a tax credit, a stamp or transfer tax exemption, reduced withholding tax, etc. This is because the cash flows under the derivative can be tailored to fit the tax preferences of the investor. It is also possible to insert intermediate entities between the investor and the payor under the derivative to achieve additional flexibility. For example, an intermediate vehicle could be used to convert the return under a derivative into a return on equity or debt where such an intermediate entity was equity or debt funded by the ultimate investor.

It is useful to consider the process by which a derivative may act as a sharing or distribution mechanism in relation to a tax benefit by analogy with the process of securitization. As discussed in the previous chapter, the securitization process can transform bank loans into a marketable transaction or product.[136] Significantly, the loan itself is a bilateral contractual relationship specific to two parties. It will contain bespoke elements and is relatively illiquid. It may never have been contemplated that it could be converted into a tradable asset. However, this is precisely what is achieved in economic terms, given that the securitization vehicle can issue securities to global investors that are freely tradable, with the return on those securities reflecting the return on the underlying loans.[137] Likewise, a tax benefit will typically be intended as bespoke and restricted to a specific taxpayer (or class of taxpayers) alone. Nonetheless, in a similar way that a loan is made economically tradable by a securitization, a derivative may be used to distribute and share in economic terms some or all of a tax benefit intended for a specific taxpayer (or class of taxpayers). In principle, this 'distribution' can be to any person or class of persons in the world.[138]

The analogy between the distributive features of derivatives and those of the securitization structures suggested above is imperfect. In the securitization, the loan asset is actually transferred to a special purpose vehicle, whereas a tax benefit cannot itself usually be transferred directly to another party in this way. However, for various reasons (such as a bank not wishing to let its customers know their loans are being sold), a similar constraint may also be relevant in the case of a loan in a securitization, meaning that the loan asset cannot be sold. In the field of

[136] See the discussion of securitization in Chapter 6.

[137] The terms of the bonds would in this case normally pass on all risk and return in the underlying loans to the bond holders (or possibly reconfigure the entitlements to the underlying risk and income by reference to different tranches of bonds issued).

[138] The basic tax structuring that is illustrated by the securitization analogy has very wide practical application. For example, it is central to the cum-ex trade, as seen in the very extensive use of, for example, cum-ex buyers structured as pension funds or other tax-favoured entities which would use and price derivatives contracts to pass on or share the tax benefits with other investors. It is also a staple feature of dividend-arbitrage transactions, and is endemic to certain businesses (such as synthetic prime brokerage) or markets (such as the contracts for differences market over UK shares). In all these cases, there is the same wholesale 'securitization' of tax benefits that is illustrated by the above analogy.

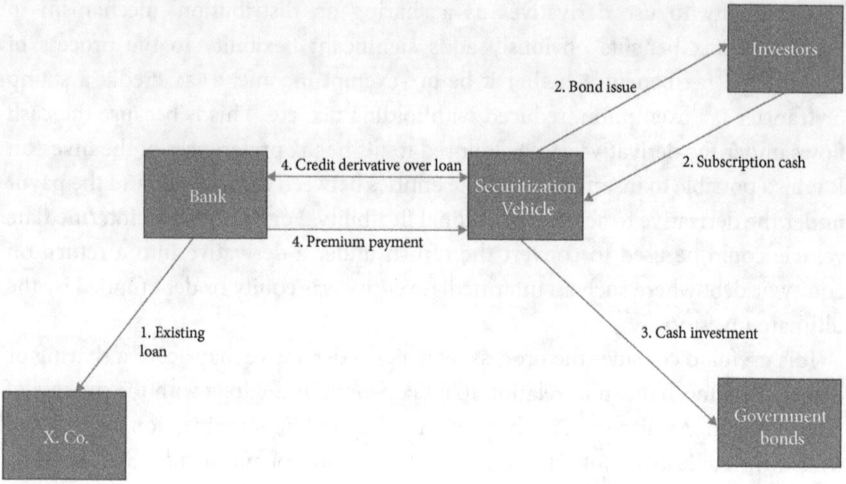

Figure 7.3. Synthetic securitization

securitization, the problem may be overcome by the use of a 'synthetic securitization', which is illustrated in Figure 7.3.

In a synthetic securitization there is never any transfer of the loan. The borrower will most probably be unaware of the transaction. Instead, the economic risk in the loan is shifted to a securitization vehicle by means of a credit derivative such as a credit default swap. Under the terms of the credit default swap, the securitization vehicle would make good (effectively, insure) a loss on the loan suffered by the bank (such as a default). In return it would be paid a premium by the bank for bearing this risk. By investing the cash subscription proceeds it receives from the bond issue in a risk-free asset such as government bonds, the risk profile of the securitization vehicle is exactly the same as it would be had the vehicle purchased the loan directly (as it would have done in a traditional securitization). The return derived by investors in the bond comprises the risk-free return on the invested cash plus the premium income paid under the credit derivative. Again, their risk profile is the same as if the securitization vehicle had purchased the loan.[139]

This example completes the analogy with derivatives and tax benefits. In place of a borrower from a bank whose loan is securitized without that borrower knowing, there is a tax authority giving a tax advantage to a taxpayer (or class of taxpayers) in respect of an asset or transaction, unaware that risk and benefit in

[139] For a more detailed discussion of securitization, see Darrell Duffie, 'Innovations in Credit Risk Transfer: Implications for Financial Stability', Bank for International Settlements, Working Paper No. 255, July 2008, available at https://www.bis.org/publ/work255.pdf.

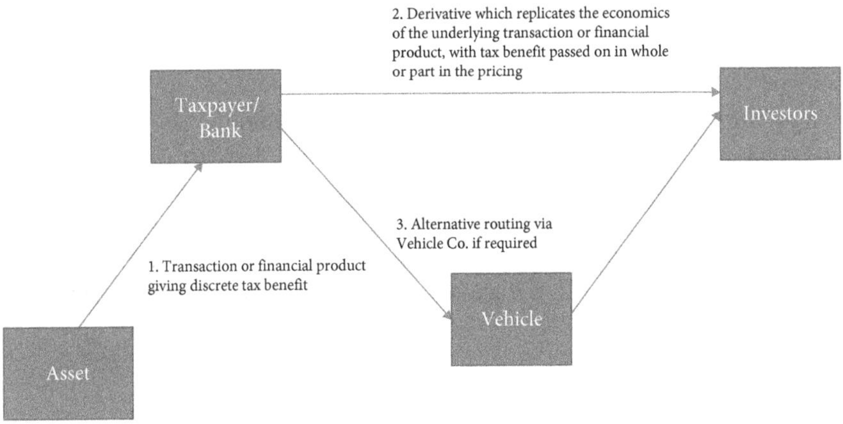

Figure 7.4. Distribution effect: analogy to synthetic securitization

that asset or transaction has in economic terms been passed on in whole or part to one or more other parties through the derivative. The position is shown in Figure 7.4.

This example also shows an alternative possibility of routing the return to the investor by way of a separate legal entity which converts the return into a return on equity or debt, as required by the investor.

In the example, all parties, apart from the state conferring the tax benefit, gain economically from the arrangement. The investor accesses the relevant financial product and participates in some or all of the tax benefit derived by the taxpayer/bank in the pricing of the transaction and does so in a way which ensures that the cost of the asset is less than it would be on a direct investment in the asset. The taxpayer/bank will either charge explicitly for its 'intermediation' role or retain some portion of the tax benefit. In either case, it will gain from the transaction, even though the derivative transaction would normally mean it has hedged its risk in the relevant underlying asset. Put another way, some or all of the tax avoided by the use of the derivatives structure is 'monetized' by the taxpayer/bank and contributes to the profitability of the structure. The loser is, of course, the state conferring the tax benefit, since this is made available on a potentially much wider basis than had been intended.[140]

The discussion so far has considered the difficulties in the taxation of derivatives separately to the implications of the tax differences that were discussed earlier. However, there is also an effect from the combination of these two features of tax systems. Due to their flexibility as a possible distribution mechanism, the

[140] Efforts to circumscribe the unintended use of tax systems, often leading to complex anti-avoidance legislation, are of course a major feature of tax systems and may often frustrate attempts to exploit the tax system. However, the ability of the tax authorities to administer and police the tax rules in the financial sector represent a particularly difficult challenge, as discussed in the next section.

use of derivatives in tax-structured products will often expand the scale of the 'tax shifting' discussed earlier. They may also be used (and are in practice used extensively) to expand the scope of exploitation opportunities arising out of the line-drawing in tax systems. This is because the line-drawing may be made more problematic or even untenable by virtue of the fact that derivatives can be used to recreate the effects of other traditional financial products at will, in a way that immediately places the transaction outside the scope of the line that has been drawn. Derivatives may also be used to create new categories of instrument or transaction for tax purposes, posing further difficulties to existing line-drawing in the tax system.

Tax Administration Issues

The administration of tax systems may and, in the context of financial products and markets, often does contribute to the process by which the tax system facilitates its own exploitation.

The importance of administration issues, which in this context include policing and enforcement, are an essential element in the design of tax systems. This would seem obvious. In practice, however, tax administration issues are rarely given much priority or weight in the discussion and appraisal of tax systems.[141] This is despite the fact that the inherent complexity and fragmentation of tax systems makes it all the more important to consider administration issues carefully. As a practical matter, it is also common for administration arrangements to fall into disrepair over time.[142]

The cum-ex case study illustrates the significance of administration issues. The treatment of the dividend adjustment mechanism in the settlement system that was the linchpin of the cum-ex trade was an administrative response to the issues created by the two-day lag in the operation of the settlement system. It is also significant that the exploitation of cum-ex was perpetuated, and probably expanded, by the serial unsuccessful attempts of the tax authorities to close the trade down in the course of administering the tax system. The cum-ex trade was finally closed down with the enactment in the law of a simple administrative change, namely the alignment of the functions of the withholding tax agent and

[141] The traditional analysis of tax systems is concerned with the tax rate and the tax base, but much less with administration issues such as the costs and viability of administering and enforcing the tax system. See Slemrod and Gillitzer, *Tax Systems*, at p.5.

[142] A good example of this relates to the discussion of Denmark in Chapter 4. In that case, internal tax authority audit reports from the year 2000 revealed that in an examination of two banks, only 37 per cent of tax reclaims were supported with the required documentation. In other words, in 63 per cent of cases documentation was either incorrect, incomplete, or missing. See the report of DR News of 25 August 2015 by Mette Simonsen, available at https://www.dr.dk/nyheder/penge/40-procent-af-skats-refusionsudbetalinger-skatteudbytte-gik-til-svindlere.

the writer of any tax credit voucher. The cum-ex example demonstrates that trades involving billions of euros can be created and then curtailed purely by actions associated with the administration of the tax system.

These administration issues involve two additional complications in relation to financial products and financial markets. First, the tax system will contain a large body of tax law that applies only in a financial-sector context (for example, tax provisions dealing with manufactured or synthetic payments, repo transactions, dividend washing transactions, derivatives taxation, etc). Second, and probably more important, the inherent complexity of financial-sector business and markets requires the application of specialized knowledge such as knowledge of the detailed features of a derivatives trading business or of how transactions are actually structured and settled. This industry knowledge is relevant because the significance of some tax issues cannot be understood, meaning that the system cannot be administered, without a solid appreciation of the sector, including the operation of the market, its settlement arrangements, regulatory issues, and market practice.[143] Again, this point is aptly illustrated by cum-ex, where it was many years before the tax authorities realized that what they had previously seen as an apparently obscure glitch in the settlement system was in reality a major opportunity to exploit the tax system that was marketed on a global scale. The scale of the opportunity flowed directly from a very low deterrence effect presented by the enforcement function of the tax system administration.[144]

If tax authorities are to have the means or capacity to successfully administer the taxation of the financial sector, they must have (1) specialized industry-focused tax technical expertise and (2) a deep knowledge of the sector.[145] Acquiring the necessary 'sector' knowledge is much more challenging than it may sound. It will vary by the type of taxpayer concerned and the type of business

[143] This point is not restricted to the financial sector, though it is especially relevant to that sector. In the cum-ex example, the relevant tax law was relatively straightforward (though raised some difficult points of interpretation). However, the significance of that tax law turned on a number of non-tax factors such as the mechanics of the settlement system, relevant delivery mismatches, etc. There are, of course, other sectors in which a specialized knowledge of matters going beyond the tax rules may be important for tax authorities (e.g. the oil and gas sector).

[144] There is a significant literature on the deterrence impact of effective tax audits and similar enforcement actions—see for example Michael Allingham and Agnar Sandmo, 'Income Tax Evasion: A Theoretical Analysis', *Journal of Public Economics* 1 (1972) 323–38, whose model studies the choice of a taxpayer who rationally trades off the benefits from evading taxes and the risky costs from detection and incurring penalties; and more recently Christian Traxler, 'Deterrence of Tax Evasion' in G. Bruinsma and D. Weisburd, eds, *Encyclopedia of Criminology and Criminal Justice* (Springer, 2014), 1005–14.

[145] Administrative capacity is broadly defined as the means that an administration disposes of to fulfil its mission—see Frederik Heitmüller, Moran Harari, and Markus Meinzer, 'Tax Administrations' Capacity in Preventing Tax Evasion and Tax Avoidance' (17.10.2018 version), Tax Justice Network, Coffers EU Horizon 2020 Project, at p.11, available at https://www.taxjustice.net/wp-content/uploads/2018/11/Tax-administrations'-capacity-in-preventing-tax-evasion-and-tax-avoidance.pdf. This paper discusses the scope of data on tax administrations, current initiatives in the field, and the 'output' measures that might be used to assess or measure administrative capacity.

lines operated. In the case of a bank, for example, it will require a knowledge of the operation of many sub-sector businesses, such as securitization, prime brokerage, securities trading, and structured credit products, among many others. It will also be important to understand the features and practices associated with a wide range of transactions such as financing, stock loan, repo, swap, option, futures, and collateral transactions that may be relevant to a number of business lines conducted by a particular taxpayer.[146] The point is that, to take an example, it is not possible for a tax authority to police the inter-bank market armed only with a knowledge of the tax rules. Rather, it is essential to understand the application of the tax system in the context of the practical operation of the market and the business carried on by players in the industry.[147] This is understandably a major challenge for tax authorities. For a tax inspector to develop the required industry expertise takes a considerable amount of time and this can be hard to deliver given the difficulties of retaining specialist staff within the tax authority.[148]

The seriousness of these industry issues has been recognized by tax authorities. In the series of reports on tax intermediaries (including banks) that was considered earlier in this chapter, the OECD's Forum on Tax Administration emphasized the importance of industry knowledge in securing tax compliance in the banking sector.[149] This focus by the Forum on Tax Administration on the

[146] Quite different issues will be relevant for different types of financial-sector business. Many of the businesses carried on, and transaction types used, by an investment bank will be irrelevant to the business of a retail bank. The issues (and tax law) for an insurance business will again be different and, depending upon the tax system concerned, may need to be broken down by sub-sector, such as the distinction of life versus non-life business. The issues that are relevant to the business of the investment management/fund sector are again likely to be different to those of banks and insurance companies.

[147] In relation to cum-ex, it is recognized by Spengel that tax knowledge alone on the part of the tax authorities was never sufficient for the task of dealing with the trade. See Spengel, 'Expert Opinion', at p.39. A similar point is made in the German parliamentary investigation into cum-ex, specifically the difficulties of knowledge required at the interface of the tax system and financial markets law and practice—see German Parliamentary Report at p.344.

[148] There are various reasons for this. Industry-specialized tax inspectors may become more marketable and in consequence be hired by banks or tax advisory firms. There is also the problem that the tax inspector's own career within the tax authority concerned might be enhanced by periodic changes in posting to gain different experiences due to a prevailing institutional preference for broadly-based generalist experience in the career structure of the tax authority concerned. This would inevitably undermine attempts to build deep industry-specialist knowledge. The latter point is referred to in OECD, 'Study into the Role of Tax Intermediaries', at p.62.

[149] The 2008 OECD study into the role of intermediaries, for example, acknowledges that revenue bodies need to know much more than tax and accounting, and this includes the context in which taxpayers do business, an understanding of the industry concerned, etc. See OECD, 'Study into the Role of Tax Intermediaries', at p.30 and Appendix 7.1 at pp.62–4. The later 2009 OECD study, 'Building Transparent Tax Compliance by Banks' makes similar recommendations for tax authorities in relation to the banking sector and explores ways in which a better understanding of the sector could be secured, including working with regulators and banking industry associations. See OECD, 'Building Transparent Tax Compliance by Banks', at pp. 9, 49–50. The point is also emphasized in a later OECD publication from 2013 which states that to detect aggressive tax planning schemes based on after-tax hedging, it is important that the tax authority staff have a 'first rate understanding of finance and hedging' and also 'the relevant background and expertise to understand the rationale and key industry drivers...to understand these very complex and engineered...schemes'. See OECD, 'Aggressive Tax Planning Based on After-Tax Hedging', p.38.

importance of industry knowledge has, following the OECD's BEPS project, to some degree been supplanted by more generalized concerns with avoidance by multinationals, particularly in relation to the tax rules dealing with cross-border income allocation.[150] In any event, recognizing a problem or issue and dealing with it are two different matters. The reality is that there is a great variation in the degree to which tax authorities recognize the industry knowledge issue and, for those that do, there is invariably a problem with the adequacy of resources.[151]

Germany's experience in attempting to deal with cum-ex illustrates the difficulties. Though it may seem hard to believe given the realities of cum-ex activity at the time, in 2009, at the heyday of cum-ex, a study on banks by the OECD's Forum on Tax Administration held up the German tax authority as a model of how to deal successfully with the banking industry specialization and industry knowledge issues.[152] In a discussion of the need for better banking industry expertise on the part of tax officials, the study referred to the extensive formal education schemes run by the German tax authorities and their various 'special training programmes, exchange events and comprehensive written information on the specific problems involved in bank taxation'.[153] The report also contained a discussion vaunting the advanced cooperation between the German tax authorities and the banks. This was said to work 'very well' and involve 'constant dialogue' which 'gives auditors the information they need', and it was observed that 'in performing their work, bank auditors draw upon the knowledge and skills gained in their intensive initial and further training'.[154] As was seen in Chapter 4, a much less rosy picture of the position of the German tax authorities is painted by the German parliamentary investigation into cum-ex: this suggests that, within the tax authority, there was in reality a generally poor knowledge of financial markets and that the highly industry-specific nature of the issues caused a real problem for them. By any measure, the tax authorities were very slow to understand the scale of the issues. They also did not understand the obvious impacts of their attempts at corrective measures (for example, the real consequences of excluding foreign

[150] See, for example, the focus on transfer pricing and permanent establishment issues (and the absence of any emphasis on industry knowledge in the discussion of tax risk analysis) in OECD, 'International Compliance Assurance Programme: Pilot Handbook' (OECD, 2018), available at www.oecd.org/tax/forum-on-tax-administration/publications-and-products/international-compliance-assurance-programme-pilot-handbook.pdf. It is arguable that, even before the advent of the BEPS project, FTA concerns in relation to the banking sector had been channelled into efforts to develop what was then called the 'enhanced relationship' (now 'cooperative compliance') between taxpayer and tax authority. See, for example, the 2010 OECD report 'Addressing Tax Risks Involving Bank Losses'.

[151] Some tax authorities have made significant efforts to create specialized resources to deal with specific industry sectors such as the banking sector, but the task of creating and maintaining an adequate level of suitably qualified people within the revenue authority has proved problematic. There is a good summary of the difficulties in a US context (including staff turnover, the time taken to understand specialized business, etc) in US GAO, 'Financial Derivatives'.

[152] OECD, 'Building Transparent Tax Compliance by Banks'.

[153] OECD, 'Building Transparent Tax Compliance by Banks', p.88.

[154] OECD, 'Building Transparent Tax Compliance by Banks', Annex B2, pp.87–8.

custodians from the 2007 countermeasures that were enacted). The complexity of the arrangements and the dearth (if not total absence) of specialist resources to deal with the problems being thrown up were also factors that materially hampered the tax authority investigation.[155]

The two sharply contrasting pictures of the same set of facts: one from the Forum on Tax Administration publication and the other from the German parliamentary report on cum-ex might be taken to indicate that the tax authorities, or at least their Commissioners, do not have a clear grasp of the real scale of the challenges for administering the tax system in the area of financial markets and financial products. The cum-ex case study illustrates those challenges, but the example is hardly necessary. The inherent complexity and fragmentation of the tax system, compounded by the additional issues in the taxation of the financial sector that have been discussed so far in this chapter, make it inevitable that tax authorities will always struggle with the challenges presented by the sector.[156] In contrast with most other sectors, the financial sector also presents some difficult conflicts between anti-avoidance tax rules and regulatory rules.[157]

[155] See German Parliamentary Report at pp. 145, 151, 157, 239, 243–4.

[156] A high-profile example of the degree to which tax authorities have struggled with the taxation of financial products and financial markets is given by US attempts to regulate substitute (or 'dividend equivalent') payments relating to dividends on US shares. Such payments may be a feature of stock loan and repo agreements and they may also be embedded within the cash flows of derivatives, such as swaps. The example is particularly relevant as the US has the most developed tax law on complex financial instruments and derivatives, and the treatment of substitute payments has received enormous political scrutiny following the report of the US Senate Permanent Subcommittee on Investigations, 'Dividend Tax Abuse'. The example of the US treatment of substitute payments may therefore arguably be regarded as the most that realistically can be done by a tax administration to deal with a particular financial product issue. The history of attempts to deal with substitute payments is complex and lengthy, going back more than twenty years (and the process remains unfinished). Features of that history include: (1) a complete change of established policy on the sourcing rules for such substitute payments; (2) the issue of an IRS Notice (Notice 97-66, 1997-2 C.B. 328) which was applied by the banking industry for more than ten years (apparently based on the plain words of the Notice) before the IRS concluded that the manner of its application was inconsistent with what had been intended; (3) the issue of an advisory memorandum (AM 2012-009) which seems to be based on a misunderstanding of the cross-border securities lending market on the part of the IRS; and (4) recurrent difficulties on the part of the IRS in providing promised regulations to provide clarity and guidance on the application of the relevant statutory rules in IRC Section 871 (m) (for example, regulations were promised in 2012 in connection with Notice 2010-46, 2010-24 IRB 757 but have yet to appear, leaving the scope of the substitute payment withholding rule unclear). In October 2018, the IRS issued Notice 2018-72, which further extends the date for dealing with these regulations to 2020. For a detailed discussion of the issues, see Mike Gaffney, 'Stock Lending Notices, Unwritten Intent and Economic Substance', *Tax Notes*, 22 December 2014, and Mike Gaffney, 'Cross-Border Securities Lending and Qualified Securities Lender Regime', *Tax Notes*, 8 August 2011.

[157] Some of the difficulties are illustrated by the German tax reform to deal with cases of perceived dividend tax credit abuse arising on 'cum-cum' transactions. These new rules are discussed in Chapter 4. They have been criticized on a number of fronts as giving rise to a conflict with banking supervisory rules. See for example, Baker & McKenzie, 'German Dividend Withholding Tax Credit to be Substantially Limited', Hot Topics release, January 2016, available at https://www.bakermckenzie.com/-/media/files/insight/publications/2016/01/german-dividend/al_germany_withholdingtaxcredit_jan16.pdf?la=en, at p.3. Similar views in respect of these rules (and specifically the expectation they will create 'uncertainty, complexity and collateral damage that affects…numerous other stock-related

The Consequences of Inadequate Administration of Tax Systems

The implications of the situation described above for the administration of tax systems in relation to financial markets and financial products are not difficult to identify. They go some way towards explaining why it is that tax administration issues may contribute to the process by which tax rules, particularly those relating to financial products and markets, are often readily exploited.

First, the task of policing the tax rules is obviously made difficult by the combination of the specialized, complex, and fragmented nature of the technical tax rules, coupled with all of the issues discussed relating to the importance of industry, as opposed to tax, expertise. These difficulties facing the tax authorities in monitoring compliance with and enforcing the rules are likely to encourage the exploitation of tax rules. Second, this state of affairs in turn means that, where abuse does take place, it will often not be readily identified by the tax authorities, or it will be identified only after a lengthy passage of time. Third, in those cases where an abuse is identified, it may take the tax authorities some time to get to grips with the issue and mount an effective response.[158] A fourth consequence is that, in taking action to counter abuse that has been identified, fresh mismatches may inadvertently be created. The financial sector's ability to respond flexibly and rapidly to a new rule may in turn lead to further opportunities for exploitation, creating a whole new cycle of abusive activity. A fifth consequence is that the sharing of intelligence on specific tax-driven structures or arrangements between

transactions with a genuine business purpose') are expressed in Volker Junge and Ingo Kleutgens, 'New German Tax Rules to Reduce Cum/Cum Trades', *Tax Notes International*, 29 August 2016, at p.801.

[158] Data on the slowness of the US Internal Revenue Service to deal with complex tax issues arising out of the US taxation of derivatives is available from US GAO, 'Financial Derivatives'. This shows that between 1996 and 2010 the Treasury and IRS did not deal with fourteen out of fifty-three guidance projects (just over 26 per cent) related to derivatives that they had designated as a priority on their annual Priority Guidance Plans. (The Priority Guidance Plan was established by IRS Chief Counsel and US Treasury's Office of Tax Policy to act as a prioritization schedule for developing and issuing guidance. The Plan is issued each year and identifies the guidance projects that are the current IRS and Treasury priorities to be completed over a twelve-month period that runs from 1 July to 30 June each year.) Also, some projects were removed from the list without being completed and some took longer to complete. The completion rate for projects related to derivatives on the plan for one or more years was just above 50 per cent for projects on the plan for one year falling to a completion rate of approximately 20 per cent for projects on the plan for three years or more. This is discussed at p.27 of the report. There is also a discussion of the 'glacial pace of legislative and regulatory responses to financial innovation' in Kleinbard, 'Equity Derivative Products', at p.1351. Even where the tax authorities respond to cases of aggressive tax avoidance, the response may be misconceived. For example, in some states it has been common for tax authorities to deal with such structures by a process of negotiated settlement with the taxpayer concerned. However, such an approach is arguably misconceived on the basis it (1) reaffirms the business strategy of the taxpayer implementing such structures, (2) removes any downside or deterrence, (3) sets or consolidates a precedent in the treatment of such structures, and (4) in some cases influences overseas tax authorities to adopt a similar approach.

the tax authorities of different states cannot operate as it should: the tax authorities in one state may not be able to initiate any sharing process nor use data that is received from another state in cases where data has been shared with them.[159] The development and evolution of the cum-ex trade illustrates every single one of these features.[160] There are very many other examples.[161]

The discussion thus far has centered on the appreciable obstacles which a tax administration must confront in a financial services industry where highly detailed and fragmented tax rules are applied to highly specialized financial services markets with complex products, structures, and practices. There is, however, one further aspect of tax administration that needs to be considered. This concerns the investigation and pursuit by tax authorities of cross-border tax-driven structures,[162] for example where a specific case of misconduct is uncovered, and the parties concerned have been identified.

It is generally not possible for a state to pursue revenue claims in the courts of a foreign jurisdiction. This is because of the existence of a well-established and almost universal rule against foreign revenue enforcement (the 'revenue rule').[163]

[159] It also seems that the existing international mechanisms or bodies which are designed to fulfil this sharing function (such as the OECD's Aggressive Tax Planning Directory or the Joint International Taskforce on Shared Information & Collaboration (JITSIC) network) struggle with the required level of sector specialism to be effective in relation to highly structured financial-sector trades. Both points are illustrated by the example of cum-ex, though in the latter stages in Germany the German tax authorities did initiate attempts at cross-border cooperation targeted at the cum-ex trade.

[160] The discussion in Chapter 4 has shown that the authorities were hampered in their dealings with the cum-ex trade by a lack of industry knowledge and also that they were slow to understand and deal with the trade. The impact of their unsuccessful attempts to deal with the trade in 2007 and 2009 in fueling participation in the trade has also been discussed. With regard to the sharing of relevant experience of cum-ex, it was reported by the Bloomberg news service on 5 November 2018 that Kristian Jensen, the Danish finance minister had stated that Denmark could have avoided losing billions of dollars in tax revenue through cum-ex if it had been warned about the trade by other states that were already cracking down on it. See https://news.bloombergtax.com/daily-tax-report-international/staggering-case-of-bank-tax-fraud-has-danes-questioning-eu-1.

[161] Various examples are given in the US GAO report 'Financial Derivatives'. At pp.24–5 of the report there is a discussion of the growth in use of total return swaps for tax purposes due to the lack of guidance from the IRS, which was interpreted as acquiescence in the tax treatment adopted by taxpayers. Credit default swaps are discussed at pp.22–4. Although the product was developed from the early 1990s, it is reported that the IRS first heard about them in 2000 and produced no guidance until 2004. It is also noted that the tax rules remained unclear, with taxpayers using different approaches which yielded different tax results in practice. A case involving the unintended consequences of guidance issued by Treasury and the IRS where new opportunities for tax abuse were created is given at p.29.

[162] The issue discussed here concerns the difficulties arising in cross-border cases. Where the parties are located in the same jurisdiction as the relevant tax administration, the ordinary domestic process by which tax authorities investigate, collect evidence, and, in tax evasion cases, prosecute will be followed. There have been a number of such cases in Germany in relation to cum-ex. The domestic process is often not a swift process, but typically may be completed within, say, a couple of years. Cross-border cases are also highly relevant to cum-ex. For reasons explained in Part I of this book, the actions of the German tax authorities led to significant participation in cum-ex trades by non-German banks, funds, and intermediaries.

[163] L. Collins et al., eds, *Dicey and Morris on the Conflict of Laws*, 13th edition (Sweet and Maxwell, 2000), Vol.1, p.97. There are two reasons behind the rule: first, such enforcement of a claim for taxes would represent an extension of sovereignty, and, second, it might also clash with public policy in the

However, the rule does not prevent significant cooperation between states, and there are extensive arrangements for the exchange of information and mutual assistance in the collection of revenue claims.[164] These are the primary mechanisms that are relevant to the investigation and pursuit by tax authorities of cross-border cases involving evasion and aggressive avoidance.[165]

There are various different mechanisms and arrangements between states relating to the exchange of information and mutual assistance in the collection of taxes, although space does not permit an extended survey of these here.[166] Some of these mechanisms are particularly focused on gathering and sharing information on tax schemes entered into by corporates, including banks.[167] There have been a number of significant recent developments, reflected particularly in the

jurisdiction concerned—see Lord Keith in Government of India, Ministry of Finance (Revenue Division) v. Taylor (1955) AC 491. The rule is common in many common law jurisdictions—e.g. USA (Milwaukee County v. M.E. White Co. 296 U.S. 268, 268 (1935)), Canada (United States v. Harden (1963) SCR 366). In civil-law jurisdictions, foreign revenue claims are generally regarded as public laws that cannot be enforced outside the state in which they are enacted. The rule can be abrogated on a bilateral basis in a double tax treaty, but this is not common. On the revenue rule generally, see Brenda Mallinak, 'The Revenue Rule: A Common Law Doctrine for the Twenty-First Century', *Duke Journal of Comparative & International Law* 16:1 (2006), 79–124, available at https://scholarship.law.duke.edu/cgi/viewcontent.cgi?referer=&httpsredir=1&article=1107&context=djcil. The scope of the revenue rule has featured in recent US litigation relevant to the issues discussed in this book. This concerns the pursuit by the State of Denmark of millions of dollars which it regards as secured by fraudulent tax reclaims on the part of a large number of US pension funds. See In Re Skat Tax Refund Scheme Litigation, Memorandum Opinion, No. 1:2018cv04047—Document 80, US District Court, Southern District of New York, 2019, 18-md-2865 (LAK), available at https://law.justia.com/cases/federal/district-courts/new-york/nysdce/1:2018cv04047/493285/80/.

164 These two mechanisms are both reflected in the OECD Model Tax Treaty, with Article 26 dealing with the reciprocal exchange of information and Article 27 with mutual assistance in the collection of taxes. These two mechanisms have been discussed and developed from the start of the international tax system—see League of Nations, 'Double Taxation and Tax Evasion', at pp.34–5.

165 See, for example, the discussion of the institutional response to fraud in De La Feria, 'Tax Fraud and the Rule of Law', at p.21.

166 For example, exchanges of information may be made in three different ways: on request, automatically, or spontaneously. Article 26 of the OECD Model is intended to allow bilateral treaty information exchanges 'to the widest possible extent'. A similar approach is taken in the Multilateral Convention on Mutual Administrative Assistance in Tax Matters (available at https://read.oecd-ilibrary.org/taxation/the-multilateral-convention-on-mutual-administrative-assistance-in-tax-matters_9789264115606-en#page1), on which see the commentary to Article 2 at paragraph 2 (p.38).

167 For example, there is the Joint International Taskforce on Shared Intelligence and Collaboration (JITSIC), which is hosted by the OECD and which comprises forty of the world's national tax administrations. The purpose of JITSIC is to enable its members to collaborate (by sharing their experience, resources, and expertise) within the framework of bilateral and multilateral conventions and tax exchange arrangements in 'more effective and efficient ways to deal with tax avoidance'. This is normally done through a nominated single point of contact appointed by each JITSIC member to coordinate and manage that state's JITSIC interactions. See further the JITSIC website at http://www.oecd.org/tax/forum-on-tax-administration/jitsic/. The OECD itself seeks to play a leading role in improving international cooperation between states in countering international tax avoidance and evasion. The OECD seeks to identify relevant trends and help governments in dealing more quickly with emerging risks. In that context, a confidential library of over 500 aggressive tax planning schemes is maintained by a sub-group of countries that are members of the OECD's Working Party 11 (Aggressive Tax Planning).

push for greater transparency in the international tax sphere,[168] and also including mechanisms aimed directly at aggressive tax avoidance structures.[169]

All these processes and procedures are no doubt of assistance to tax authorities in the investigation and pursuit of cross-border cases of evasion and aggressive avoidance. However, they fall a long way short of providing even a satisfactory response when it comes to dealing with the practical realities of very complex cases like cum-ex where there are some obvious difficulties relating to the nature and scale of the activities comprising the trade.[170] These difficulties include: the extremely large number of complex and inter-connected transactions; the large number of parties; the range of different roles of the parties (for example, buyer, seller, intermediary, hedge counterparty, stock lender, prime broker/financer, investment fund, investment manager, etc) and, sometimes, the interchangeable role of those parties from one transaction to another; the range and specialist nature of the law that may be involved (which may include securities law, legal provisions relating to the market operation and infrastructure, etc); and the deep complexity of the composite arrangements or structure (and again the variations from one transaction to another). This includes the inordinate complexity in the type of instruments used, the manner in which they fit together, and the manner of execution. As an example, the ability to use swaps, forwards, and options as alternative instruments to deliver the same economic result by way of both on-exchange and OTC execution greatly widens the ambit of enquiry by tax authorities. Features such as these bear directly on the efficacy and speed of cross-border tax investigations. The most obvious impact is on the scale, and the specialist nature, of the information that needs to be communicated from a state requesting

[168] Principles of transparency and effective information exchange have been developed through the work of the OECD's Global Forum on Taxation consisting of OECD and non-OECD countries and jurisdictions. The standards for exchange of information are set out in Article 26 of the OECD Model Convention and the 2002 Model Agreement on Exchange of Information, on which see http://www.oecd.org/dataoecd/15/43/2082215.pdf.

[169] A good example is the recent European Union Directive on Administrative Cooperation in Taxation Number 6 (DAC6) dealing with the mandatory automatic exchange of information in the field of taxation in relation to reportable cross-border tax planning arrangements (Directive 2018/822 of 25 May 2018). The Directive sets out the hallmarks of reportable cross-border arrangements that intermediaries must report to the tax authorities to allow them to be assessed by those authorities. This is the latest in a series of EU Directives and follows earlier Directives dealing with: the automatic exchange of tax rulings (Directive (EU) 2015/2376 of 8 December 2015, DAC3); the exchange of country-by-country reports between tax authorities (Directive 2016/881 of 25 May 2016, DAC4); and the access to anti-money-laundering information by tax authorities, beneficial ownership, and other customer due diligence (Directive 2016/2258 of 6 December 2016, DAC5).

[170] There may also be variations in the standards of what states are prepared to agree to in relation to mutual assistance with the collection of taxes. Article 27 of the OECD Model provides for comprehensive collection assistance. However, as noted in the Commentary to the Article (see at paragraph 1), there may be obstacles that frustrate such assistance (such as practical difficulties arising from different tax systems, national law or policy which precludes such assistance, etc). It is normally left to states to agree in the bilateral negotiation process the extent to which assistance is to be given and the practical details of what is covered.

assistance to a state whose help is requested (the 'requested state'). The case of cum-ex serves as a good example of what is involved in this process.

Requests for assistance from German authorities have involved massive amounts of data and extensive descriptions of the matters under investigation being provided to the requested states. German domestic law has to be explained and translations of the relevant provisions supplied. This includes tax law provisions, criminal law provisions relating to various aspects of fraud (such as attempts and recurrent acts), and provisions under the German Code of Criminal Procedure concerning what may be searched and seized, and in what conditions, as well as legal provisions relating to the rights of the accused and witnesses. Securities law provisions may also be included. The relevance and applicability of various tax treaty provisions must also be demonstrated, and the relevant text included. Complex structures involved in any particular case would have to be carefully described in the correspondence between authorities. This includes the creation and use of multiple vehicles, including pension funds in various jurisdictions outside Germany and often located in jurisdictions other than the requested state. The network of market operators involved in the scheme would need to be identified and their roles and interactions explained, including custody banks, brokers and agents, inter-dealer brokers, prime brokers, funds, and fund managers. Detailed background documents are typically provided, such as copies of numerous court decisions which would demonstrate that any requested search and seizures would be lawful if the objects to be searched were in Germany.

Where a request relates to search and seizure, this may include a request relating to multiple residential and business properties (of individuals and their employers including advisory firms, law firms, intermediaries, banks, and funds), and relating to the confiscation of evidence and interrogation of witnesses and the persons accused. In each separate case where such a request is made, justification for the request would need to be provided, together with a detailed list of the possible items that are sought. There may also be a lengthy list of questions to be raised in the interrogations with the accused persons and witnesses. These would need to be tailored for each person and would include a long list of questions relating to relevant interactions with a large number of other involved parties.

Not surprisingly, letters sent by the requesting state and dealing with the matters discussed above may, with relevant attachments, be hundreds of pages long. The task of assembling the relevant data, refining it on a case-by-case basis so that it is adapted to the particular circumstances of each of a potentially large number of parties, and then translating all of this material into the official language of the requested state will need to be repeated for each of the other requested states. Each case that is initiated also, of course, requires an ongoing commitment to the pursuit of the case, which may include regular exchanges with the requested state, providing further information or clarifications, dealing with the impact of local law in the requested state, and other developments as the case advances. The demand for specialist resources in both the requesting and requested state to initiate and pursue these cases is therefore appreciable. Given that such cases may, due to the nature of the process, involve very lengthy periods of enquiry, a dogged and determined perseverance on the part of the investigating officials is also essential.

For such cross-border investigations to be successful, it is also necessary that there are adequate specialist resources and a cooperative and committed attitude on the part of those involved in the requested state. This may not always be forthcoming, given the variation and availability of specialist resources in requested states. Even if there are adequate resources available, the requesting state may find it difficult to secure meaningful cooperation.[171] There may also be time limits or other checks that have been agreed between the states which constrain the process.[172] The mere passage of time itself may create a problem. For example, common difficulties experienced in the cross-border investigations into cum-ex trades entered into by banks include systems constraints such as an inability on the part of the bank to access trading data and problems created by the fact that the cum-ex traders with knowledge of the scheme and the systems which supported it have long since left the bank. Both factors can make it hard to locate the data that is sought.[173]

It will be evident from the above discussion that the investigation and pursuit, on a cross-border basis, of complex cases of misconduct involving multiple parties and thousands, if not hundreds of thousands, of financial product transactions is problematic. The available mechanisms, coupled with the constraints that are regularly encountered, mean the process will be, at best, slow.[174]

[171] For example, it is reported that the US authorities answered requests from Germany for certain confirmations relating to the cross-border investigation of cum-ex with one-word answers. See German Parliamentary Report at p.247.

[172] The requesting and requested states may have agreed a time limit after which a request for assistance may no longer be made as regards a particular revenue claim (see the Commentary to Article 27 of the OECD Model at paragraph 9), and there is generally no obligation to assist under Article 27 if the requesting state has not pursued all reasonable measures of collection under its own laws and administrative practices (Article 27 (8) (c)) or where the administrative burden is disproportionate to the benefit (Article 27 (8) (d)). It is also possible that the costs of any assistance may become an issue. Usually, the ordinary costs of the requested state (being those expected in normal domestic collection proceedings) are not reimbursed by the requesting state but extraordinary costs over this are potentially recoverable. A host of other constraints may also arise in practice, such as the impact of the legal standards in the requested state relating to adequate cause for search and seizure, or to the precision of the description of items sought.

[173] Some data requests have involved searches across very large pools of electronic data, relying on search word parameters, or specific data fields, which cannot always be accurately identified by those who are unfamiliar with the relevant underlying transactions or arrangements. Given the delays in the investigation process, it is also possible that the data may have been destroyed under a data retention policy.

[174] It is expected that the pursuit by the German authorities of cross-border cum-ex cases will take many years. The existing exchange of information and mutual assistance mechanisms are better suited to one-off cases where the problems discussed here—such as multiple parties in different (and interchangeable) roles, vast numbers of transactions, etc—do not feature.

The discussion in this chapter is concerned with an exploration as to why tax is so often a feature of complex structured transactions entered into by banks. As outlined above, the answer lies partly in the unique position which banks occupy in relation to tax systems and partly in the features of tax systems themselves, especially as these relate to financial products and financial markets. The fragmentation and inordinate complexity of the rules and the manner in which they are enforced and administered often have the collective and paradoxical effect of facilitating, rather than hindering, the exploitation of the tax system. There are various implications that arise from this discussion and these will be considered further in the next chapter.

8
Conclusions

Regulatory and tax policies towards the financial sector have been formed largely independently of each other. A more holistic approach is needed to ensure that they are properly aligned in both the incentives and the overall burden they imply for the sector.

International Monetary Fund, 'A Fair and Substantial Contribution by the Financial Sector', June 2010

Finance is not only an economically unsafe and violently pro-cyclical sector but also part of a democracy that is not working.

Ewald Engelen et al, *After the Great Complacence*, 2011

Introduction

This book is a study of failure. It might be argued that the failure lies in the inability of the banks to control their traders and front-office staff, or alternatively that the source of failure is that of the regulators and tax authorities in being unable to control the banks. However, each of these interpretations is an inadequate explanation of the nature of the problem and underestimates the scale of the much more pervasive failure at all levels of the system.

As is demonstrated by the cum-ex case study in Part I of this book, the conventional mechanisms of regulatory control, as exercised by the regulators and tax authorities, were either ineffective or broke down completely: the regulatory authorities seemed barely aware of what was going on, despite the transaction reporting of daily movements of shares around dividend dates measured in the hundreds of billions of euros. The actions of the tax authorities were no less of a failure, both with regard to the time (measured in years) that it took them to realize the scale of what was happening and the failed attempts to close the trade down. Paradoxically, those efforts to stop the trade had the effect of actually encouraging or even tacitly endorsing the activity that they were seeking to curtail. Based on the discussion in Part II of the wider banking-sector and tax-systems issues, it is concluded in this final chapter that this failure should not be regarded as some sort of isolated aberration but as rather the practically inevitable

Banking on Failure: Cum-Ex and Why and How Banks Game the System. Richard S Collier, Oxford University Press (2020). © Richard S Collier.
DOI: 10.1093/oso/9780198859673.001.0001

consequence of the operation of the system as a whole.[1] From the perspective of banks entering into cum-ex trades, the failure of the system was not just a feature of the system that might be taken advantage of, but rather the foundation of an entire business model.

The analysis in Part I of this book draws on a single case study. The case of cum-ex is a useful example of misconduct by the banks at the intersection of financial markets and tax systems. This is so for various reasons, including the massive monetary amounts involved, the scale of the participation across the financial sector, the nature of the complex financial product structuring that was involved, and the number of states affected. However, the discussion could have centred on any one of a number of other trades or schemes, all of which are examples of a similar 'banking on failure' business model, whose objective is to monetize deficiencies and vulnerabilities of the financial system.[2]

The reasons that account for this systemic failure at a more general level have been addressed in chapters 6 and 7 and emerge from the answers to the questions posed in those chapters about why it is that banks and tax systems are so often involved in these incidents of misconduct. In the case of banks, the incentives to enter into such transactions are high, the control structures to prevent such incidents are inadequate or deficient, and there seems a ready confidence on the part of banks that the prospects of detection and therefore sanction are low. As seen from the discussion of tax systems in Chapter 7, in the context of the tax rules on financial products, the reality is that failure is baked in, particularly given that the nature of those rules and the failure to deal with the impact of derivatives means that tax systems actually provide the means to facilitate their own exploitation.

The only 'control' mechanisms that seem to have operated successfully in the cum-ex case are those that lie outside the normal controls infrastructure, namely those that arise from the investigative efforts of the press and the determination of whistle-blowers.[3] These have arguably made a more immediate and direct

[1] References in this context to the 'system as a whole' are intended to refer to the combined operation of, including the interaction between, financial market systems and tax systems.

[2] For example, Chapter 7 refers to a spate of recent cases involving exploitation of the 'pre-release' mechanism in connection with depositary receipt arrangements which emerged as this book was being written. These cases have a number of similar features to the cum-ex case. See the discussion at Chapter 7, p.253. Another example that has been reported recently is the 'heartbeat' trade used by exchange traded funds (ETFs), with the assistance of banks, to avoid capital gains tax on redemptions. The arrangement is described as involving a sequence of share transfers designed to remove capital gains tax through the operation of Section 852(b)(6) of the US Internal Revenue Code. It has been reported that, in 2018 alone, the fund industry avoided tax on more than $211 billion in gains (using heartbeat trades and other methods). 'Section 852(b)(6) went from a footnote in the tax code to the cornerstone of a new industry', according to the report of Zachary R. Mider et al., 'The ETF Tax Dodge is Wall Street's "Dirty Little Secret"', Bloomberg Businessweek, 29 March 2019, available at https://www.bloomberg.com/graphics/2019-etf-tax-dodge-lets-investors-save-big/. A further example concerning a basket of options trade is given in Nesvetailova, Guter-Sandu, Palan, and Milo, 'Tax Evasion and Avoidance', at pp.38–41.

[3] The various instances of the involvement of whistle-blowers are explained in the German parliamentary report on cum-ex. The German press has been responsible for extensive investigative

contribution to the task of holding the banks to account than all of the other conventional mechanisms of control. However, though that result has been achieved in the now high-profile case of cum-ex, there are many other instances of misconduct where no corresponding transparency or public visibility has been achieved through the acts of the press and whistle-blowers, making these informal levers somewhat unreliable as checks on the system.

As to the significance of the issues highlighted here, if in any particular case the number of those banks, funds, or other market participants gaming the system is small, then the immediate issue is the revenue loss to states. The cum-ex case study indicates that the numbers can be comfortably in the billions or more likely tens of billions of euros.[4] Where, however, there is a more significant gaming of the system (for example, on an industry-wide scale), there may in addition be more fundamental distortions created to the integrity and efficient functioning of markets themselves.

In this concluding chapter, I first comment on what I take to be the significant lessons or implications, including the more important policy issues, from the discussion in the earlier chapters. I then make some suggestions of directions that might be explored to address these points, recognizing that fundamental reform in this area will not be easy. Finally, I offer a last word.

Lessons

A number of lessons emerge from the discussion in this book, both from the case study in Part I and the discussion of broader issues concerning the nature of banking business and tax systems in Part II. In this concluding chapter, I do not attempt to summarize every single one of these points but rather aim to draw out what I consider to be three major themes that are reflected in much of the earlier discussion. I then seek to conclude on the impact of these themes in combination. These themes relate to: (1) particularities of the banking business landscape and the tax rules for financial markets and products; (2) the nature and consequences of systemic complexity; and (3) the failure of governance and control mechanisms. These themes are discussed below. Collectively, the themes explain not merely the recurrence of misconduct by banks in relation to tax systems but also support the

reporting on cum-ex and there have also been some television documentaries on the topic. The European Parliament's Special Committee on Financial Crimes, Tax Evasion and Tax Avoidance has called for safeguards and protections relating to both journalists and whistle-blowers—see European Parliament Resolution of 26 March 2019 on Financial Crimes, Tax Evasion (2018/2121 (INI)) at para.s 382–403, available at http://www.europarl.europa.eu/doceo/document/TA-8-2019-0240_EN.html.

[4] See further the discussion of the financial impact in Chapter 4 at pp.159–61. There has for many years been a recognition of the potential for highly remunerative exploitation of tax systems using financial products. See, for example Plambeck, Rosenbloom, and Ring, 'General Report', at p.657.

starker conclusion that, in the absence of significant change, it is practically inevitable that misconduct of the sort seen in cum-ex will continue to occur.

Particularities of the Landscape Relating to Banking Business and the Tax Rules for Financial Markets and Products

The particularities of the landscape that are relevant here include a number of features that have been discussed in this book. These particularities are important because collectively they create a set of conditions in which trades like cum-ex are both *stimulated* and *facilitated*.[5]

The nature of banking business

Chapter 6 describes the advent in the 1970s of the 'originate to distribute' model of banking business and the laissez-faire approach adopted by regulators which accompanied it. The transformation of the bank business model to one in which credit transactions were continually originated and then sold off by the banks began to replace the traditional relationship of bank and client shifting the focus to the generation of transactions. The financial sector was liberalized on both sides of the Atlantic, greatly increasing the number of market participants. Together with the advances in technology which made high speed communications and computing possible, the banks found themselves at the forefront of a wave of globalization which continued for decades. As the reach and capabilities of banks expanded, these changes increased competition among banks, driving down margins on the banks' standard credit offerings. As a consequence, the mainstream loan, credit-card-receivable and mortgage products became commoditized. In almost any other industry these changes would have led to lower long-term returns.[6] However, the banks, and particularly those with investment

[5] The manner in which trades like cum-ex are encouraged and facilitated by features of the financial markets and tax landscape, including the nature of banking business and banking products, is explored in the discussion that follows. In broad terms, however, it is argued that the shift in the banking business model has encouraged the pursuit of such transactions and a number of features such as the privileged position of banks, their access to the system, and the highly abstract nature of the banking product, as well as the tax treatment of derivatives and the weak governance controls on the system, facilitate such transactions.

[6] As discussed in Chapter 6, such low returns have occurred in the financial sector in relation to highly standardized products such as retail banking and stock brokerage. Each continues to be subjected to lower fees and commissions, with innovations such as 'bank on an app' lowering the profitability of the former and commission-free brokerage doing the same in the case of the latter. An example of this trend is given in the report of Tom Warren, 'Monzo Launches its "Bank of the Future" in the US', *The Verge*, 13 June 2019, available at https://www.theverge.com/2019/6/13/18677298/monzo-bank-us-launch-date-availability. It is widely recognized that, in many industries, competition magnifies diminishing returns on investment. See, for example, Feng Li et al., 'The Impact of Competitive Intensity on Future Profitability and Future Stock Returns', The University of Chicago Booth School of Business, Working Paper 11–30, available at http://ssrn.com/abstract=1908338.

banking operations, were able to find and exploit new opportunities within the market system that had been created. That they were able to do so was made possible largely by the features of the financial market landscape that are discussed in this section.

As described in Chapter 6, banks have innovated by deconstructing traditional financial assets into their constituent parts, or by pooling assets into securitized products, enabling cash flows or risks embedded in them to be packaged into new types of claim and sold off. On the theory that the circulation and trading of these claims yields benefits to the system through the global distribution or sharing of risks, banks were able to innovate relatively free of regulatory restriction. Derivative and securitized products proliferated.

However, these changes, which became widely appreciated in the aftermath of the Global Financial Crisis, tell only part of the story. It is also true that banks, by virtue of their institutional role, have been able to access and utilize features of the financial system which are generally not available to other market participants. The point is illustrated in a number of ways in the case of cum-ex.[7] Complex financial systems incorporate anomalies and differences, timing disparities, or suffer from 'glitches' and other gaps and inconsistencies. These quirks and disparities are the raw material which banks can access, exploit, and monetize. They are able to do so partly because of certain inherent features in the banking 'product' and partly because they benefit from a set of privileges which collectively are not available to other market participants. The result is that banks can use a range of tools at their disposal to unlock and extract value from the system for themselves and their clients.

The disparities, anomalies, and glitches that are referred to above may relate to a wide variety of factors, such as differences in the pricing of similar assets across different markets, restrictions on the ability to access one market in comparison to another, and variations in the treatment of similar assets in different jurisdictions. However, tax differences are also highly relevant in this context and feature prominently in schemes and arrangements designed by banks, which may also be marketed to their clients. That is because the tax rules (particularly those involving financial instruments) represent fertile ground for the banks. This is so for a number of reasons.

First, the sheer scale of assets and cash flows subject to taxation, as well as the financial amounts at stake due to the impact of taxation, are significant.[8] A second reason relates to the nature of any 'difference' that is being exploited. The very act of exploiting many financial system differences can work to reduce the financial

[7] Examples of this in the cum-ex trade include the ability of banks to use accelerated settlement times in relation to the borrowing of securities and their delivery to the cum-ex buyer, the ability to enter into bespoke and highly flexible futures contracts, etc.

[8] See further the discussion in Chapter 7 at pp.256–7, 264 and 274–5.

opportunity being exploited. For example, where a security trades at a low price in one market and a high price in another, market participants will purchase the lower-priced security and sell the higher-priced security, driving up its price in the former market and down in the latter. As the two prices converge, an equilibrium is established where it becomes increasingly less profitable to trade or 'arbitrage' the two securities. By contrast, schemes to extract value from tax differences do not generally work in this way. Although tax schemes are, as in cum-ex, often presented within banks as a form of 'arbitrage', any tax difference is in fact merely redistributed or shared among those participating in scheme, rather than reduced by the process of that sharing or redistribution. The tax difference which is the focus of the trade consists in a permanent difference created by tax rules rather than a 'mispricing' of two assets created by market forces. Third, financial schemes which exploit tax differences are inherently less risky, at least from a trading perspective.[9] Open-market arbitrage trades whose subject matter is asset mispricing involve participation in volatile markets and may expose participants to a multitude of risks.[10] In cum-ex and similar tax-driven schemes, participants enter into interlocking and predetermined steps that are expressly designed to eliminate risk.[11] These factors therefore explain why banks and their clients may be attracted to tax-based structures or trades: such trades often present the highest risk-adjusted returns.[12]

[9] The relevant tax risks under the law may nonetheless be significant. These may include a variety of risks such as those arising out of multiple detailed anti-avoidance rules, general anti-abuse provisions, specific provisions aimed at facilitators of tax schemes, tax disclosure and reporting rules, etc. The complexity of navigating such tax rules should not be underestimated. This also explains why legal opinions dealing with tax issues can be very long and why the relevant tax technical analysis will often impact on the detailed structuring of any arrangements. Where these technical risks are ignored or simply not addressed, this suggests that the perpetrators of misconduct are relying on the non-detection of the arrangements, as in some varieties of the cum-ex trade.

[10] Depending on the arbitrage, the risks may include foreign exchange risk, interest rate risk, default risk, and price risk, among others. Further, the arbitrage itself may incorporate risks which traders fail to appreciate. For example, West Texas Intermediate crude oil and Brent crude oil typically trade at very similar prices. However, in 2011, the difference in price between the two spiked to over $25 per barrel of oil, owing in part to difficulties transporting less expensively priced oil to the market in which it would fetch a higher price. See the report of David Sheppard and Bruce Nichols, 'Insight: Oil Convoy Blues: Trucking Game Foils Crude Traders', Reuters, 14 October 2011, available at https://www.reuters.com/article/us-cushing-trucks/insight-oil-convoy-blues-trucking-game-foils-crude-traders-idUSTRE79D0OP20111014.

[11] In cum-ex transactions, this would often be achieved through the use of derivatives as hedging contracts and, at the conclusion of the transaction, by returning the securities to their point of origin, possibly the initial lender of the securities.

[12] It is self-evident that the financial markets are volatile and even those trades which are apparently low-risk are fraught with hazard. For example, consider the events of early 2017, when the Swiss National Bank, having assured markets that it would hold the Swiss franc steady against the euro, decided to abandon that policy, causing the euro to fall as much as 41 per cent against the Swiss franc. Two global banks were estimated to have lost $150 million each, while one hedge fund lost upwards of $800 million, which destroyed its business. See the report of Proinsias O'Mahony, 'Traders Staring at Unimaginable Losses from Euro–Franc Peg Abolition', *Irish Times*, 27 January 2017, available at https://www.irishtimes.com/business/personal-finance/traders-staring-at-unimaginable-losses-from-euro-franc-peg-abolition-1.2080096.

The existence of financial system anomalies is a necessary but not sufficient condition for a successful scheme to extract value from the anomaly. The ability of the banks to monetize differences, inconsistencies, and gaps in the financial system is materially assisted by two other features of the financial market landscape, namely the nature of the banking product itself and the privileges accorded to banks.

The nature of the banking 'product'

The nature of the banking industry product differs in important ways from the products generated and sold by other sectors of the economy. A financial product or instrument is abstract, being a legal construct, namely a set of legal rights and obligations which govern cash flows or claims between one or more parties.[13] This has two important implications. First, financial products are highly malleable. Because they have contractual form, banks can implement them, or alter their characteristics, very quickly. This means product innovation is rapid: a new financial instrument can be conceived and even executed in hours. The ability to innovate rapidly can allow banks to restructure products so as to mitigate, avoid, or even exploit the impact of new legislation, which can be especially relevant in a tax context.[14] Second, the abstract nature of financial products, particularly where they are entered into away from the view of public markets, renders them more opaque and less observable. A financial transaction carried out

[13] The highly abstract nature of the modern banking business raises some concerning questions about the state of our system of law. The banking sector in particular is able to take advantage of legal concepts and constructs which were developed in a time where the law regulated and adjudicated issues directly connected to the real economy, such as the transfer of property, the sale of goods, and simple intangible claims. A further layer of legal concepts emerged later, such as the netting of payments and the setting-off of obligations. The process of product structuring can commandeer these rules and concepts and apply them to financial structures in ways that can bring about significant financial consequences despite few, if any, tangible changes going beyond a mere legal agreement. For example, parties may enter into a legal agreement whereby one person may deliver shares to another but with a corresponding simultaneous obligation on the part of the person receiving the shares to immediately deliver them back by way of stock loan. Those delivery obligations could be netted, with the consequence that no shares move at all. The effect could be that a multitude of different effects ensue, some recognized by tax rules, some not; some recognized by regulatory capital and accounting rules, others not. In a further abstraction, the parties have transformed the character of their legal rights merely by agreeing to do so. Underlying these examples is the paramount importance of legal form, a matter that is considered in the context of certain US tax rules in Jeff Maddrey, 'Respect for Form: Securities Loans and Hedged Positions in Fungible Stock', in Matthew Stevens, ed., *Taxation of Financial Products and Transactions* (Practising Law Institute, 2007). The idea that mere legal form may in itself create new sources of economic wealth is not new. It was discussed and illustrated by reference to various examples as long ago as 1935 in an article (by the American legal scholar Felix Cohen) which challenged the formalist idea that legal principles could or should be construed in the abstract, separate from their enforcement, judicial interpretation or impact on society. See Felix Cohen, Transcendental Nonsense and the Functional Approach, Columbia Law Review, Vol. XXXV, June 1935, No. 6, pp. 809-849.

[14] Chapter 3 illustrates this point in the context of the cum-ex trade. As that chapter explains, driven by the ingenuity of the cum-ex traders and their advisers, there were repeated refinements and restructurings of the trade that were designed to continually boost its financial and operational efficiency and ensure that any obstacles that were created by the tax authorities were sidestepped to the extent possible.

on a bilateral basis between a bank and an inter-dealer broker, for example, will be private. Even complex 'structures' are (despite the word connoting a physical form) nothing more than a composite set of bilateral and often private contracts between parties. In the absence of any legal requirement to disclose them, all such contracts will also be private.[15]

The privileged position of banks and bankers

Banks (and bankers) are privileged in a number of ways. Although some of these privileges are available to the smaller banks, the full suite of privileges is the exclusive preserve of the larger banks. The available privileges can be broken down into various categories. There are privileges conferred upon banks explicitly by statute, such as access to a central bank lending facility and deposit insurance. These give banks ready access to liquidity and confer what is in effect a government guarantee upon a portion of their liabilities (i.e. deposits). These are important advantages, not available to other market participants, because they give banks ready and reliable access to high levels of funding.[16] Large banks will also normally be members of, and therefore have direct access to, numerous financial markets and exchanges around the world.[17] Banks also operate and participate in the payment system which connects corporates, individuals, and banks to the financial infrastructure and to each other.[18] There are also certain components of market infrastructure that are effectively only accessible to the banks because of

[15] The private status of contracts is relevant because it brings potential secrecy, and secrecy is relevant because even in the absence of high payoffs and strong incentives to cheat, a system which conceals conduct can be turned to advantage. In a setting far away from the 'culture' and 'greed' of banking, the peer review process by which academic research is subjected to scrutiny by a researcher's peers has been the subject of major abuse in recent years. It is reported that researchers were able to exploit the secrecy and anonymity of the process to pressure authors whose work they were reviewing to cite the reviewer's own work in the paper under review. In that way, the reviewer's work received a greater number of citations, boosting its apparent importance. See further Jonathan D. Wren et al., 'Review-Coerced Citation: Case Report, Update on Journal Policy and Suggestions for Further Prevention', *Bioformatics*, 30 January 2019, available at https://academic.oup.com/bioinformatics/advance-article/doi/10.1093/bioinformatics/btz071/5304360.

[16] As described in Chapter 6, cum-ex and other similar trades require leverage to magnify the benefits of transactions. Large stock borrowings must also be collateralized, an obligation which would place significant stress on smaller balance sheets. In practice, custody banks which lend out large quantities of shares for pension funds and other institutional lenders will only deal with a select list of top-tier banks.

[17] The banking sector is characterized by formidable barriers to entry. A bank must be generally be licensed or permissioned to conduct specified financial services in a country market. Maintaining operations and connections to market infrastructure in dozens of countries around the world itself is a major undertaking. There are over 140 stock exchanges around the world, many of which are supported by central clearing houses. A complete list is available at https://www.stockmarketclock.com/exchanges. Membership is a prerequisite for participation in the relevant market.

[18] Each country in which a bank operates has its own set of market conventions and practices. Each has its own laws and regulations governing capital adequacy, liquidity, market conduct, etc. Consequently, a very large investment in people and systems is essential. Devising and implementing complex trades such as cum-ex raises the bar further. As Chapter 6 described, a deep concentration of experts in a range of disciplines such as accounting, tax, and legal is necessary to be able to manage an 'originate to distribute' business model.

practical considerations or established conventions. Banks manage and take responsibility for large parts of the financial system: setting interest rates, fixing gold prices, and acting as recognized trading counterparties to central banks. In the latter role, they act as facilitators for government debt issuance as well as market makers in the trading of such debt and are the institutions through which important aspects of monetary policy are conducted.[19] In many jurisdictions, banks are also charged with functions connected with the operation of the tax system, such as the confirmation of a taxpayer's tax status, the withholding and collection of taxes, discharging reporting obligations, and the preparation of documentation such as tax vouchers.[20] This may vest banks with a privileged role under the operation of the tax system as a practical matter (as in cum-ex, where only the local German custodian banks could write the tax voucher for the cum-ex buyer). It may also consist in banks being formally accorded privileged status under the tax system, for example to facilitate their role in the operation of financial markets.[21] Further, as discussed in Chapter 7, banks occupy a unique position to exploit tax systems because of their nature and attributes, including the ability to access capital and financial markets and provide financial leverage.[22]

A further important privilege from which banks benefit is political protection. It may take the form of an implicit government backstop, flowing from the perceived importance of the role of banks in the economy (for example, in relation to the formation of credit in the economy or their operation of the payment system). Their standing as organizations which are 'too big to fail' may influence other realms of regulatory endeavour, for example by attenuating the willingness of authorities charged with the enforcement of banking laws and regulations to bring actions against them. When misconduct by banks and their staff does lead to enforcement action against them, settlements and fines negotiated in secret by financial authorities without full disclosure of the facts is the rule rather than the exception.[23] By contrast with the Dieselgate example discussed in Chapter 6 (where numerous corporate executives were quickly arrested), there appears to be a reluctance to hold individuals, particularly bank executives, accountable. A system that is too weak to effectively and publicly enforce its own rules provides

[19] As an example, in the United States approximately twenty-four banks, headquartered in the US and elsewhere throughout the world, act as primary dealers for the New York Federal Reserve. For more information, see https://www.newyorkfed.org/markets/primarydealers.html.

[20] Banks may have a wide variety of reporting obligations. For example, under the FATCA and Common Reporting Standard (Automatic Exchange of Information) requirements rules, banks are required to report instances of tax evasion.

[21] A good example is the UK stamp taxes provision that exempts 'intermediaries' from the stamp tax (strictly, stamp duty reserve tax and stamp duty) that otherwise applies to purchasers of UK equities. See Finance Act 1986, Section 88A and Section 80A. The exemption applies to 'intermediaries' (broadly, market makers) rather than to banks per se, though there is a significant overlap between these two categories of taxpayers.

[22] See further the discussion in Chapter 7 at 256–7.

[23] See further the discussion in Chapter 6 at pp.223–4 and 249.

banks with greater latitude in their dealings and amounts to a further de facto privilege.

Banks are also privileged in that, as noted above, they can by virtue of their institutional role both access and utilize features of the financial system which are generally not available to other market participants for their own benefit. This confers upon them a dual capacity (and therefore also potentially a conflict) in the conduct of their affairs. They both operate and control the system and yet are simultaneously participants in it. If the conflict is not appropriately managed, the result is the creation of an incentive to game the system.[24]

The effect of the factors discussed above is that banks comprise a financial system which confers powers and privileges upon its constituent members, the banks themselves, creating an exclusive domain whose operation the banks are in the best position to comprehend. Their degree of control and the absence of effective independent checks upon their conduct closes their activities off to a large extent from incisive examination. In the context of the competitive pressure on margins in their standard business lines, their position of privilege and the nature of the banking business product incentivizes and facilitates exploitation of the system. Differences among financial instruments, opportunities for self-dealing, system peculiarities, anomalies, and glitches can all be unlocked to create value by banks. They can redeploy or repurpose these privileges to their own advantage and in ways in which those who devised the features of the financial system never considered.

The Tax Rules for Financial Markets and Products

As is explored in Chapter 7, a central problem for tax systems is that fundamental distinctions and differences in those systems are readily subverted by financial product innovation, meaning that financial innovation also magnifies the adverse impact of inconsistencies and asymmetries that exist in the system. The position is made more acute by a number of factors: the scale of different regimes or 'cubbyholes' in tax systems (many of which seem hard to justify); the general tendency to respond to individual new developments on a piecemeal basis within the existing architecture of the system (which creates significant systemic complexity and means that economically similar products may be taxed in different

[24] At the time of writing, the risks and dangers of a conflict arising in such circumstances are becoming apparent in the Boeing 737 Max 8 scandal, where Boeing, the aeroplane manufacturer, simultaneously produced the defective 737 while having a prominent role in self-certifying its airworthiness. See the report of Aaron C. Davis and Marina Lopes, 'How the FAA Allows Jetmakers to "Self Certify" that Planes meet U.S. Safety Requirements', *Washington Post*, 15 March 2019, available at https://www.washingtonpost.com/investigations/how-the-faa-allows-jetmakers-to-self-certify-that-planes-meet-us-safety-requirements/2019/03/15/96d24d4a-46e6-11e9-90f0-0ccfeec87a61_story.html?noredirect=on.

ways, creating further tax arbitrage opportunities);[25] and the inadequate attention paid to the administrability of any response in the form of new tax rules. Inevitably, this creates opportunity for exploitation of the tax system. Tax authority efforts to counter such avoidance activity can create further complexity in the system and therefore more scope for abuse.[26] The position is fuelled by the speed of product innovation,[27] the recurrent use of derivatives in tax-driven transactions,[28] and the significant financial amounts that are routinely at stake.[29] The usual result as regards the tax rules dealing with financial products is therefore a high level of systemic complexity that does not lend itself to effective administration by the tax authorities. The features discussed above relating to the banking business landscape are also relevant in boosting the ability of banks to game the system because of the close connections between tax systems and the financial system as a whole.

Systemic Complexity and Its Consequences

The systemic complexity that is referred to in this book arises from the nature of financial markets, the nature of tax systems, and particularly from their interaction.

There are numerous financial markets which trade a wide range of traditional securities such as shares, bonds, currencies, and commodities. Beyond these conventional assets, however, a vast array of financial instruments incorporating, fusing, or referencing elements, cash flows, or risks of both traditional assets as

[25] As has been discussed in Chapter 7, the difficulties from derivatives are exacerbated by the fact that not only can derivative contracts be used to replicate underlying instruments such as debt or equity products, but they can also be used interchangeably with the same economic result.

[26] A good example is the UK tax regime created to deal with 'manufactured' payments (the rules of which are discussed in Chapter 3). These rules (which, ironically, were originally developed to help the banks manage their cash flows relating to tax requirements) were recurrently used to facilitate complex tax arbitrage structures (see, for example, HMRC v Bank of Ireland Britain Holdings Limited (2008) EWCA Civ 58). The result was that over their twenty-year life, the statutory rules were continually being amended and reformulated, making them extraordinarily complex. Largely due to the appreciable difficulties of coping with their continual exploitation, the rules were finally removed from the statute book. See the discussion in footnote 88 of Chapter 3.

[27] See further the discussion in Chapter 6. Innovation in relation to financial products is delivered by changes to the contractual terms of legal instruments, which can be achieved rapidly. This contrasts with other industry sectors (such as the pharmaceutical or automotive sector) where the process of product innovation takes many years. Not surprisingly, tax structuring in those other industry sectors will often revolve around the manipulation of abstract assets and legal arrangements which can be achieved rapidly—such as in relation to the ownership of assets such as intangible property or the creation of re-invoicing arrangements.

[28] US GAO, 'Financial Derivatives' notes the widespread use of derivatives in transactions designed to avoid and evade tax liabilities.

[29] The point is of course illustrated by the cum-ex case. Other examples of the significant financial amounts involved in tax-structured products involving derivatives and complex financial products are included in Chapter 7.

well as novel ones are traded.[30] Price differences among these many and diverse products are only one feature which may give rise to financial opportunity. The trading or settlement systems which administer them may not have taken full account of certain of their features, opening up the potential for exploitation.[31] As the number of instruments grows, the systems and rules for managing them expand proportionately, and so the complexity of the system also rises, creating yet further opportunities.

Tax systems are usually inherently complex, sometimes inordinately so. Also, they vary significantly from state to state. As discussed in Chapter 7, there are, in almost every state, special difficulties that arise from the attempts of the tax rules to deal with financial products, including their variety and proliferation. The result is many different financial instruments with different tax treatments or concepts,[32] from state to state and within each state. The position is compounded further by the many different categories of taxpayer, each with their own tax status and attributes.[33] All of these differences involving states, taxpayers, and financial products create a vast range of possibilities and permutations, with each potentially having a different after-tax result.

The systemic complexity referred to above is probably inevitable. The infrastructure and component elements of both tax systems and financial markets is almost invariably highly complex and it is unrealistic to expect this to be otherwise. The 'complexity issue' here is therefore not concerned with the mere existence of systemic complexity, but rather with the point that the regulatory and tax authorities have struggled to get to grips with that complexity and been ineffective in understanding and managing it. Complexity has, in other words, erected a material barrier to the enforcement of laws. This in turn has fuelled tax avoidance and evasion opportunities. An additional point is that tax systems have in many cases failed to deal with complex financial instruments such as derivatives and therefore often made the complexity issue worse by the response that they

[30] Hybrid instruments (such as convertible bonds) fuse features of both bonds and shares. Structured deposits may have cash flows contingent on the occurrence of certain events. There are also products like tradable certificates that represent the right to emit carbon dioxide, weather derivatives which enable parties to lay of the risk off an adverse weather event, and so on. These are among many financial products priced and traded on exchange and off exchange in different marketplaces around the world.

[31] In recent years, the system of trading carbon credits was targeted by gangs who used the services of large banks to iteratively sell and resell carbon credits in a form of carousel fraud which was estimated to cost EU governments €5 billion. See the report of the Bureau of Investigative Journalism, 'Deutsche Bank Scandal: Courts Still Chasing Billions through Tax Scams and Carbon Credits', *City AM*, 7 May 2019, available at https://www.cityam.com/tax-scammers-and-carbon-credits-decade/.

[32] For example, different countries may have quite different concepts of legal, tax, and economic ownership (so for some countries in a given transaction (such as a transfer of shares) ownership may move for tax as well as legal purposes—in other countries it may not).

[33] Particular tax attributes of a taxpayer may be derived from the domestic tax law of one state or under the double tax treaties entered into by that state.

have adopted.[34] The complexity issue in this light is all the more important given that tax systems create material value by allocating tax benefits or privileges to certain taxpayers, yet do not always deliver, manage, or contain that allocation very well, often because they fail to deal with the effects of financial instruments or recognize the potential for 'tax sharing'. This point was explored in the discussion in Chapter 7 of the way tax benefits can easily be shared and traded by the use of derivatives. The risk is that uncontrolled systemic complexity creates an uncontrolled money machine, which is arguably exactly what cum-ex turned out to be.

The interplay among financial system actors, particularly banks, inter-broker dealers, and their clients with diverse financial instruments, numerous systems for taxing and managing financial instruments, and regulators is not static. Each not only exerts influence on the other, but the actions of regulators and banks are subject to continuous change. As posited by complex adaptive system theory,[35] the effect is that even a comprehensive appreciation of the individual components of the system may not convey an adequate understanding of the working of the whole, much less how, through the adaptive behaviour of market actors and feedback mechanisms, the system will behave in unexpected ways and respond to changes imposed upon it.

Significant systemic complexity therefore makes it hard for the regulator (whether bank regulator or tax authority) to monitor and police the system and to constrain any undesirable behaviour. The difficulties in dealing with that complexity explain why in cum-ex the trade was not fully understood for such a lengthy period despite being 'in plain sight' of both the bank controls and the regulators, and why the attempts to curtail it repeatedly floundered.[36] The wider lesson is that misconduct might never be detected or be detected only long after the banks have moved on to other business (or bankers to another bank), potentially leaving the authorities with an uphill battle in pursuing it, especially where there are cross-border issues, as exemplified by the difficulties experienced by prosecutors in cum-ex.[37]

Another important lesson from the cum-ex trade is the existence of many specialized tools or mechanisms that are available (or that can be made available by the banks) to create or unlock 'value'. These include market mechanisms,

[34] The discussion in Chapter 7 that seeks to demonstrate that the tax rules dealing with financial instruments actually facilitate the exploitation of tax systems is of immediate relevance to this point.

[35] See John H. Miller and Scott E. Page, *Complex Adaptive Systems: An Introduction to Computational Models of Social Life*, (Princeton University Press, 2007).

[36] This is not to diminish the impenetrability of the cum-ex trade itself. The point is simply that its outline and constituent parts were there for all to examine. Cum-ex traders portrayed the trade as a market mispricing or arbitrage opportunity and, as discussed in Chapter 6, were able with the aid of legal opinions to have it approved. The trade was also discussed in general terms with regulatory authorities. As a trade, the term 'cum-ex' was widely known throughout the industry. How precisely it was carried out was less well understood.

[37] The difficulties for the tax authorities in investigating the cum-ex trade are discussed in Chapter 7 at pp.295–301.

timing disparities, an array of financial products, and tax exemptions. The tools at their disposal also include the use of instruments or market conventions that may be repurposed or 'hijacked', meaning used for a purpose other than the one for which they were intended. Examples of this in cum-ex include the lengthening or shortening of settlement conventions at will and the reliance on the stock lending mechanism, as well as the use of flexible futures contracts with extended settlement periods or infinitely variable terms which converted what were essentially off-exchange and private bilateral contracts into overt on-exchange transactions processed by clearing houses. The ability to use (or 'hijack') these mechanisms is made possible by the banks' deep understanding of, and expertise in, the system as a whole.

Expertise is a by-product of the systemic complexity. Participation in complex systems obviously requires specialist expertise—the more complex the system, the more specialist the expertise required.[38] This leads to the question of how those exploiting, and those controlling, the system respond to complexity and which group can best manage it. The unsurprising response to that question is that the group of people with an established track record of dealing with that complexity is the group with a financial incentive—and therefore the resources—to actively exploit it. That financial incentive, and therefore that expertise, is concentrated in the banks and provides them with a formidable advantage.

Another feature of the complexity that is also abundantly evident in the cum-ex case is the high relevance of the (often mundane) mechanical or administrative aspects of the system, namely the multiple processes and operational devices that underpin the system as a whole. The exploitation of the different settlement times in cum-ex (i.e. T+2 settlement between the buyer and seller, yet with T+0 settlement for the stock loan and the delivery of the borrowed shares to the buyer by the bank), which is a core feature of the cum-ex trade, demonstrates the profound importance of these otherwise mundane mechanisms. In that case, a once-yearly settlement-system anomaly from deep within the clearing system gave birth to a multi-billion dollar industry. Notwithstanding their importance, these routine or mundane operational and administrative mechanisms are rarely the subject of scrutiny. The mechanisms, and the relative lack of attention paid to them, expand the 'toolbox' of possible instruments at the disposal of the product structurer. The interaction of tax systems and financial markets creates three possible planes in which the product structurer can operate, these being the domains of the legal, economic, and physical (as, for example, in the physical possession of securities). Given that tax systems largely operate by reference to the

[38] Arguably, the very requirement and authority of such 'expertise' was hijacked in the cum-ex trade. This can be seen in the role of the legal opinions that dealt with the detailed tax analysis and that were presented as authoritative support for the trade, yet which were actually ultimately somewhat meaningless given the failure to include within those opinions the full picture of the arrangements for the execution of the trades.

legal sphere, albeit with some limited reference to economic concepts, the ability to exploit these three different planes in structuring complex transactions—for example in relation to different concepts of ownership—is significant. For example, a taxpayer may hold the legal title to securities (i.e. legal ownership, which is usually followed for tax purposes) and enter into a swap transaction under which all the relevant economic risks and rewards of ownership are transferred to another person without disturbing that legal ownership.[39] It also explains the significance of the ability to move the physical and beneficial ownership of shares among parties (through devices such as stock loans, repo, and collateral transactions) without creating acquisitions or disposals of the subject securities for tax purposes. This is because of the existence of tax exemptions that will normally be available for such transactions.

The systemic complexity also gives rise to gaps and 'glitches' which emerge in the operation of those systems.[40] These will be identified first (and therefore also lend themselves to exploitation) by those with deep systems know-how and experience. The opportunities for exploitation created by such gaps and glitches in the system may not be attributable to a single individual factor but may arise due to a particular combination of factors which come together in an unexpected way. Again, this is a point illustrated by cum-ex, which was made possible by the simultaneous existence of various factors in concert: the particular mechanics of the settlement system, the treatment of stock lending, the ability of intermediaries to vary the standard settlement times, the differential tax treatment of the derivative compared to the underlying shares and dividend, etc.

This discussion of systemic complexity suggests some obvious learning points, starting with the cardinal point that it is never advisable to create a complex interlocking system that cannot be effectively policed, especially when banks are more adept at exploiting the system, and have enormous financial incentives to do so.[41] It also suggests that much greater consideration should be paid to the practicalities of operating, maintaining, and policing the system. It reveals that responding to misconduct in a way that does not take account of these systemic features but instead focuses on the conduct of the individual perpetrators (the 'bad apples' response described in Chapter 5) is both inadequate and directed at

[39] Under tax systems, it is frequently true that different financial instruments may have a similar economic result yet be taxed in an entirely different way. The example referred to demonstrates how this situation might be exploited using derivatives.

[40] A recent example concerns a software glitch within one of several (and overlapping) anti-financial crime systems of Germany's biggest bank that for almost a decade prevented some potentially suspicious transactions being flagged to law enforcement authorities. The glitch was reported to have been created by two of 121 parameters within the particular system being defined incorrectly. See Olaf Storbeck, Glitch revelation is fresh Deutsche blow, 23 May 2019, Financial Times at p. 14.

[41] Cum-ex shows that banks can exploit the interconnections between parts of the system in unexpected ways, using mechanisms that were arguably never intended to have the effect to which the banks put them, and adapting to changes in the system (changes which potentially create new trading opportunities).

proximate rather than root causes of the mischief. Possible responses to deal with these points are explored later in this chapter.

The Failure of Governance and Control

A central feature underpinning a number of the problems referred to in this book is that the business and operations of the modern bank have evolved and outgrown the existing system for its governance and control. This is not simply a reference to an inadequate external regulatory regime, but is rather to be understood at three levels, namely as referring to: (1) the internal structures for governance and control at banks, including those bearing upon the activities of bankers/traders and the management of products and businesses lines; (2) the structures that are external to the bank, specifically in relation to the bank regulators (which are charged with market surveillance, instituting market reform, and enforcing compliance in the finance sector) and the tax authorities (which are responsible for operating and enforcing the tax system), and where, to a large extent, the core problems concern insufficient penetration of the banks' business affairs, inadequate knowledge of specialist areas, and reliance on a piecemeal approach lacking a comprehensive framework for understanding the complex, cross-border inter-bank markets; and finally (3) the market infrastructure which supports banking business, where the issues concern elements of the system that are antiquated, opaque, or simply inadequate and not fit for purpose.

(i) Failure of Internal Governance and Control

The discussion in Chapter 6 identified a number of difficulties with the bank's internal governance and control model. The difficulties include an *interdependency* problem consisting of financial and competency issues. In the financial sphere, the banks' staff including those employed in the control functions rely on the revenues generated by the 'front-office' bankers and traders since their own compensation is derived from that same revenue. The competency issue is that the dependence of the bank on the front office derives from the trader's specialized skill, expertise, and knowledge of markets. By contrast, staff within the bank's control functions are very unlikely to have had any direct experience of the line of business. This means that the intelligent and effective operation of control functions in the bank (for example, the implementation of business risk assessments) relies to a large degree on the specialized knowledge of the front-office producers. There is also an *intermingling* problem which also consists of two elements. 'Leakage' of staff occurs from the control groups (e.g. tax, legal, and accounting functions) into the front-office due to the need for specialized knowledge in the line of business to devise transactions and assist with the sign-off or approvals process. There is a strong incentive for control staff to transition to front office, where the pay is generally much higher. That transition further strengthens the skill set of the business line. Second, members of the bank's senior management team are generally drawn from the ranks of the front office. They may be more sympathetic to the desire of the front office to get business done than to expressions of concern raised by the control functions. The imbalance of substantive financial power, as well as the competency weaknesses referred to above, are powerful obstacles to the intended operation of the bank's internal governance and control. In a business model where a conveyor belt of transactions is the lifeblood of profitability, efforts to suppress the machine starve the bank of oxygen. In the case of cum-ex, for example, many in senior positions would not have understood the trade. For those who did the calculus applied may have been that in the portfolio of similar trades, the expected gains would on average outweigh the likely losses over time. These internal conditions go a long way towards explaining the ease with which the cum-ex trade was able to navigate the control infrastructure of the bank and receive official blessing.

(ii) Failure of External Regulators

In relation to the external regulators, namely bank regulators and the tax authorities, it is hard to avoid the conclusion that they are unable to get to grips with the complexity of the system as a whole in the area which is the focus of this book, namely at the intersection of the financial markets systems and tax systems. This includes failing to appreciate the implications that arise from the multidisciplinary nature of that complexity.[42] In the case of the bank regulatory authorities, it seems their role has evolved in a manner which is not suited to understanding and capturing the complexity of transactions carried out by modern banks. Some important factors in that evolution are discussed below and include the patchwork of regulators, which in some jurisdictions include product-based regulatory responsibility, as well as the boundaries of effective regulation that arise due to geography and discipline.

An important issue is the requirement within both bank regulators and tax authorities of sufficient expertise. Problems arising from the lack of sufficient specialist knowledge on the part of the tax and regulatory authorities surface at a

[42] It has been argued that there is a wider problem with complexity and that complexity itself needs to be addressed and managed. For example, the *Financial Times* reported the warning given by Andy Haldane, executive director for financial stability at the Bank of England, in relation to the Basel III rule book, that the complexity of current regulation is preventing regulators from spotting and averting financial crises: 'Modern finance is complex, perhaps too complex . . . As you do not fight fire with fire, you do not fight complexity with complexity. Because complexity generates uncertainty, not risk, it requires a regulatory response grounded in simplicity. Less may be more.' See *Financial Times*, report of Brooke Masters, 31 August 2012. That theme is also pursued in Awrey, Dan and Kathryn Judge, Why Financial Regulation Keeps Falling Short, Cornell Law School Legal Studies Research Paper No. 20-03; European Corporate Governance Institute (ECGI) Law Working Paper No. 494/202; Columbia Law and Economics Working Paper No. 617 (2020). Available at: https://scholarship.law.columbia.edu/faculty_scholarship/2604

number of levels. They limit the authorities' ability to identify cases of misconduct at the earliest possible time and also impair their capacity to devise and implement effective responses. In cum-ex, for example, the potential practical implications of the very early indication of a technical 'glitch' in the system were only understood years later, meaning the opportunity to close down any mischief before it was industrialized was not acted on. There are very many similar cases where instances of misconduct are identified at an early stage but not dealt with, or dealt with only after an appreciable delay.[43] The same is true in developing an effective response, as shown by the repeated but failed efforts to close down the cum-ex trade, or the failure to shut down the mischief posed by the LIBOR rate-setting system, or even inhibit the burgeoning lending to persons who did not have the means to repay the debt in the lead up to Mortgage Crisis, a situation which was self-evidently unsafe and unsustainable. The lack of sufficient expertise also means that sharing of intelligence between regulators, whether on a domestic or cross-border basis will be constrained. This is because the channels for the capture and dissemination of intelligence on schemes within the jurisdiction and the receipt and distribution of intelligence on schemes from other jurisdictions that might be relevant locally are unlikely to be resourced with suitably experienced staff.

An important element in the failure of external governance and control is the neglected importance of operational and administrative issues. As illustrated by the cum-ex case, systems and rules may be designed and implemented with inadequate control on how they might operate or how their operation might evolve, as well as how they will be maintained and policed. This obviously means that intended control and governance mechanisms may prove to be inadequate.

There is also an obvious problem from the fragmentation of regulatory oversight and control. Fragmentation of oversight leads to an external control framework for banks which fails to comprehend in a unified manner the diverse uses to which financial instruments may be put. It opens up the possibility, if not the likelihood, of diverging priorities for regulators, creating an incoherent and unsystematic surveillance, examination, and enforcement regime. The ease with which cum-ex moved outside Germany to involve the participation of entities from around the world and the use of a wide array of financial instruments traded on different global markets may be contrasted with the absence for a considerable time of any penetrative regulatory regime and any understanding either within Germany or internationally of the relevant cross-border structuring of the cum-ex trades. The execution of the cum-ex business was fluid and seamless, yet the control mechanisms were organized on a fragmented basis, and in accordance with thinking that predated modern finance. This resulted in a strict division of

[43] The slowness of the response by tax authorities to cases of tax abuse involving financial products is a general theme of US GAO, 'Financial Derivatives'. Some further specific examples are also given later in this chapter as well as discussed in chapter 7 at pp.280–1.

responsibilities concerning tax issues (the preserve of the tax authorities, but organized on a strictly jurisdictional basis) and market issues (the preserve of the market regulator), meaning that no regulator knew what was going on.[44] This is not to say that divisions of responsibility among regulatory bodies or within tax authorities is necessarily undesirable. The issue lies in whether compartmentalization serves a purpose or is counterproductive. Within regulators, multiple regulatory roles are commonly spread across one or more regulatory bodies. These will include supervisory functions such as oversight for safety and soundness of banks or scrutinizing the manner in which they conduct their business.[45] These same regulators may simultaneously have responsibility for investigation and enforcement. A conflict often lies in the fact that the former functions are directed at enabling the development and growth of the financial sector while the rigorous prosecution of the latter functions will impede the sector's progress or shine a light on the failure of the regulator to properly carry out its supervisory role. Separation of the supervisory function from the enforcement function serves to ensure that an insistence on conformity with the rules is not contaminated or overridden by considerations of the regulator's reputation, the importance of the banking sector for the wider economy, or for that matter the large contribution which banks make to the tax base. This conflict of aims can act as a further hindrance to the penetrative investigation of issues coming to the regulator's attention.

(iii) Failure of Market Mechanisms

Finally, in relation to market infrastructure, the discussion of cum-ex reveals that a number of aspects of that infrastructure suffer from weaknesses which can be exploited by the banks operating the system. For example, in a time when executions by banks and their customers on stock exchanges are measured in microseconds, it is hard to understand why a settlement system cannot operate in shorter time frames than days (as in the T+2 or T+3 settlement conventions discussed in Part I). Certain subsections of the market also seem to operate in a

[44] See further the extensive discussion of the role in cum-ex of the German financial market regulatory authorities and the tax authorities in the German Parliamentary Report. The matter is also discussed in Chapter 4 at pp.162–3. The issue is by no means a matter for Germany alone. The US GAO report recounts the failure of the US Internal Revenue Service to interact with regulators including the SEC and CFTC (see US GAO, 'Financial Derivatives', at pp.38–41). The observation that 'collaboration between federal agencies is especially important for federal agencies to maximize performance and identify and resolve problems faster' was also identified as a specific recommendation (see at p.42) and is supplemented by the suggestion to go further and explore partnerships with bank regulatory agencies. On the fragmentation caused by product- and geography-based regulation, see further the discussion in Chapter 6 at pp.220–2 on the role of the CFTC and SEC.

[45] There are many possible supervisory models and space does not allow for an examination of each of them here. For an overview written during the Global Financial Crisis, see, for example, Group of Thirty, 'The Structure of Financial Supervision: Approaches and Challenges in a Global Marketplace' (Group of Thirty, 2008), available at https://www.legco.gov.hk/yr08-09/english/panels/fa/papers/fa0223cb1-837-3-e.pdf.

relatively archaic manner. For example, the stock loan mechanism was a core feature of the cum-ex trade and features in many other tax-structured transactions. Stock lending tax exemptions available in most markets allow securities to move freely as well as privately around the financial system, transferring legal ownership in the lent securities without creating a disposal of them by the lender for tax purposes. Yet as the loaned securities move through the system, they do so without the strictures and transparency imposed by open exchanges, price discovery, and the required reporting of transactions that are routine in other product markets.[46] Where it is required, transaction reporting itself may be inadequate to mitigate the kinds of problems posed by trades like cum-ex. While countries like the United States and the United Kingdom have in recent years greatly enlarged the scope and scale of transaction reporting, these efforts are focused at an individual financial instrument level. The regimes do not take account of composite transactions such as structured trades, which bring individual transactions together to achieve a combined effect.

The Inevitability of Misconduct

Taken together, the consequence of the main themes discussed above is that market structure and conditions both incentivize and facilitate system exploitation by the banks.

With margins on many standard banking product lines declining by virtue of intense competition, banks have been motivated to seek out profit elsewhere in the system where value could be unlocked.[47] Complexity and subtle differences among assets, such as in relation to their differential or inconsistent tax treatments, have offered up a fertile opportunity set, particularly given that tax benefits are not arbitraged away (and therefore diluted) by the process of trading or

[46] The opaque, private, and antiquated nature of the stock loan market is currently the subject of class action litigation in the United States. See: Iowa Public Employees' Retirement System v. Merrill Lynch, Pierce, Fenner & Smith Inc et al, U.S. District Court, Southern District of New York, No. 1:17-06221. The action alleges that the defendant banks 'conspired to keep stock loan trading frozen in an inefficient and opaque OTC market in order to preserve their privileged position as intermediaries on every trade'. It continues, stating that 'unlike many other financial markets, the stock loan market has not evolved to reflect the ways in which modern technology can facilitate efficient and transparent electronic trading. Instead, the stock loan market remains an inefficient, antiquated and opaque over-the-counter ("OTC") trading market dominated by large dealer banks'. See paragraphs 2 and 3 respectively. The position is set to change in the European Union with the advent of the Securities Financing Transaction Regulation, which, among other things, will compel holders of stocks who lend them out to disclose the details of such lending. For a summary of the regulation, see the website of the London Stock Exchange at https://www.lseg.com/markets-products-and-services/post-trade-services/unavista/regulation/securities-financing-transactions-regulation.

[47] For the reasons advanced in Chapter 6, banks and bankers will gravitate towards business opportunities that offer the highest return and lowest level of risk for the bank. Where the bank both participates and retains an interest in a transaction for its duration, as in the case of cum-ex, they will endeavour to ensure that it is as close to risk-free as possible.

distributing them. The complexity of the financial and tax systems, and the ability to innovate rapidly, acts to the advantage of the banks and plays to their strengths, while the system of regulation and enforcement struggles to cope with the complexity and the possibilities presented by features, anomalies, or flaws that arise from the manner in which financial products are accommodated within tax systems or by market infrastructure. An inability or disincentive for authorities to intervene together with an often soft and secret sanctions regime in the event of enforcement is also significant. Further, the high incentives available, based on the compensation model for bank traders and the high returns for banks and their customers, leads to a significant asymmetry of deployed resources on the part of banks and regulators. The systemic complexity also provides an array of tools to help in the exploitation process, especially given the paucity of controls on operational and administrative mechanisms. The privileges enjoyed by banks add to the toolbox.

Extracting the opportunities for profit offered up by the system does not require the involvement of participants from outside the system. Participation is both closed and largely unobservable. This conglomeration of factors incentivizes cooperative behaviour among banks, inter-dealer brokers, and their clients. Over time, it drives their collective conduct towards a collusive state where the payoff for the banks is higher than would be the case in the event they were each to pursue the strategy independently. This hypothesis seems to offer a much more satisfactory explanation of the persistent cooperative conduct of numerous banks in the LIBOR rate-setting example and the collusive behaviour of hundreds of banks in the cum-ex example (to name just two examples among many) than the 'bad apples' theory that was discussed earlier in this book.

It seems hardly surprising that the conclusion drawn here is that misconduct such as that seen in the cum-ex trade is practically inevitable. Of course, this is not to say that the particular cum-ex glitch in Germany was inevitable, but rather that the consequence of hugely complex and interlocking financial and tax systems means that similar sorts of glitch will inevitably arise and that gaps or inconsistencies in those systems will be open to exploitation. This conclusion suggests that the focus on addressing misconduct in this area by a response based on personal culpability and sanctions (i.e. the 'bad apples' theory) is an inadequate response, or at least one that needs to be bolstered significantly. Yet a focus on personal accountability and culpability is arguably the dominant direction of current reform.[48] My conclusion suggests that the responses so far proposed to deal

[48] As a general matter, personal culpability measures are being toughened up, and this includes the imposition of greater penalties. For example, the European Parliament's Special Committee on Financial Crimes, Tax Evasion and Tax Avoidance reiterates in its recent draft report that financial institutions, advisers, and other intermediaries that knowingly, systematically, and repeatedly facilitate, engage, or participate in money laundering or tax evasion activities should face effective, proportional, and dissuasive penalties, and, where applicable, be restricted from operating in the single market. See

with these issues may not be what is required and offer little new in getting to grips with the issues. It is, of course, recognized that the conduct of many of those in the banks and the funds that have participated in schemes like cum-ex is to be challenged in the strongest possible terms. Nonetheless, an exclusive focus on the protagonists will create obstacles to some important responses that are required. Cum-ex was never about 'isolated' conduct by some small group of miscreants. As the facts demonstrate, there were *hundreds* of banks (and clients of banks) involved. This confirms that the method and opportunity, and the willingness and ability, to exploit the flaw is endemic to the existing financial system. The existence of this widespread misconduct involving hundreds of parties and crossing numerous geographies is evidence that the system, not just the individual bank or taxpayer, stands in need of reform, a matter that is addressed in the next section.

Possible Responses

Introduction

The nature and scale of problems identified in this book indicate that a material rethink of the current situation is required. A careful analysis of reform options would be a sizeable undertaking and would also raise the need for a review of the advantages and shortcomings of the major reform possibilities, whether relating to the wider governance of banks or to tax systems. Such an analysis would require at least another volume in its own right and so is beyond the scope of my undertaking here. Nonetheless, the discussion which follows seeks to make a number of observations about the possible directions such reform might take. It first considers improvements that might be made in the arrangements for the governance and control of banks before addressing issues relating to tax systems.

(i) The Governance and Control of Banks

The discussion earlier in this chapter of the failings in control and governance identified problems arising in three separate areas: internally within the bank;

European Parliament, 'On Financial Crimes, Tax Evasion', Resolution of 26 March 2019 (2018/2121 (INI)), at para 179, available at http://www.europarl.europa.eu/doceo/document/TA-8-2019-0240_EN.html. This trend is also reflected at a domestic level, as illustrated by, for example, the UK rule introduced from 2017 dealing with the corporate offence of failure to prevent the criminal facilitation of tax evasion, guidance on which is available at https://assets.publishing.service.gov.uk/government/uploads/system/uploads/attachment_data/file/672231/Tackling-tax-evasion-corporate-offences.pdf.

externally with bank regulators; and in relation to certain market mechanisms. Measures to address these deficiencies need to be considered at all three levels.

In relation to the internal structures at banks for governance and control, a recurrent feature of the many individual cases where banks entered into cum-ex trades is the apparent failure of senior management to understand and properly evaluate the trade. Senior managers either did not understand the transactions which were generating high levels of profit or they did understand but failed to raise concerns. If the former, this suggests consideration should be given to ways to boost relevant business knowledge, for example, through a mandatory qualification scheme for bank employees such as senior management and compliance personnel, who have not historically been required to have any specific skills, experience, or qualification.[49] If they are to assess complex financial transactions independently, they should possess the means to do so. If the latter, then assigning senior management greater personal accountability may be required.[50] However, in the absence of admission that the senior manager knew there was a problem but pressed on with it in any event, personal accountability presupposes the existence of a mechanism that the manager ought to have known, throwing the solution back at least in part on a training, examination, and qualification regime.

Another common feature of the cum-ex trading was the very high level of autonomy of the banks' traders. This can be seen in the ability of the traders to hire their own dedicated middle-office staff or 'desk support', engage their own external counsel, and corral the approval process, including concealing vital aspects of the structure of the trade in presenting it for sign-off. In all these cases, they were able either to bypass the controls or render them ineffective. These examples suggest a stricter approach to the segregation of duties is necessary, including a bar on access to external counsel by front-line trading staff and the denial of any ability to manage, influence, or control other resources of the bank. This points to a broader concern, namely that trading desks or product lines have come to be treated within banks as 'businesses' in their own right and with their own funds to deploy. This intermingles their proper execution role, whereby they manage the profit and loss directly associated with their book of business, with a wider executive function which extends their powers in ways which are unchecked by the bank's control mechanisms. For example, the selection and

[49] This is the case in many but not all jurisdictions. In the US, a broad syllabus of Registered Representative and Registered Principal examinations is administered by FINRA. See https://www.finra.org/industry/qualification-exams.

[50] There is a sharp contrast between the high number of bank scandals uncovered in the aftermath of the Global Financial Crisis and the low number of individuals to whom personal liability has been attached. Some steps have been taken in an effort to remedy this problem. In the UK, for example, the Senior Managers and Certification Regime is an effort to hold senior managers of banks to account for the businesses under their watch. See the Financial Conduct Authority's publication 'Senior Managers and Certification Regime: Banking', 26 July 2017 (updated 29 November 2018), available at https://www.fca.org.uk/firms/senior-managers-certification-regime/banking.

engagement of external legal counsel should be managed by the bank's legal team, to ensure that counsel are mandated based on their competence and independence. Equally, hiring a middle-office team to support trading activity would normally be the remit of the operations group, whose primary role is to safeguard the integrity of the bank's processes, not to serve and facilitate the peculiar needs of a structured trading desk. Restoring an effective control and challenge process to the trading desks is therefore a priority. One way in which this could be achieved is through the formation of an independent organ of the bank whose responsibility it would be to comprehend both *what* it is that the trading desks are engaged in and *how* it is that their business is conducted, not only at the outset of a transaction but also over its lifetime. Ideally, this production management control would include the bank's chief risk officer, chief technology officer, and senior representatives from the bank's operations, legal, and compliance groups. Reporting to the bank's chairman, it would be assigned the task of the independent analysis, management, control, and challenge of trading desk activity.[51] Such an organ of corporate governance would bring the senior roles into more direct contact with the business carried out by the bank, removing what in many cases may be ten or more reporting levels. The determinations of this group would be retained in written form and available for inspection and review by regulators.

Another major trait of the cum-ex trade was the relative ease with which it would be signed off within banks, suggesting that the controls process in which various functions such as legal compliance, tax, regulatory capital, and others within the bank subjected the trade to reputational and substantive scrutiny was ineffective and requires bolstering.[52] A number of responses should be considered in order to embed more effective control. These would include a greater focus on the operational manner and real-world implementation of transactions given that the internal controls review of complex structured trades tends to be at an early conceptual level, when the transaction structure is being formed.[53] This could be achieved by introducing legal and compliance controls within the operations group at the bank. At most banks, the operations group has no dedicated advisory function, meaning that it cannot mount an effective challenge to transactions or requests emerging from the business line at the bank. Such a structure would

[51] Such an approach would also mitigate the interdependency issue discussed earlier in this chapter.

[52] Chapter 6 discusses some of the reasons behind this result, including the inadequate market and operational knowledge within the legal and compliance functions, the uncritical acceptance of transactions (which was exacerbated by the misleading presentation of the transactions given that aspects of the cum-ex trade were omitted from the approval process), the power of the trading desk/front office bankers, and the role of opinions from specialist outside legal counsel supporting the trade.

[53] The importance of this point is underlined by the fact that the manner of the actual implementation of the cum-ex trade could potentially transform the transaction into a fraudulent trade yet the precise arrangements for implementation would typically not have been discussed in the controls and approvals process. As noted earlier, expert legal opinions are normally based on an abstract or conceptual analysis of any proposed structure and do not deal with detailed operational or implementation issues.

introduce a counterbalance to the high level of advisory resources and technical skills to which the line of business has access. The operations group advisory function's role would include regular review and verification of transactions by the bank's compliance staff, focusing on implementation and process issues and ensuring that they conform with process requirements imposed by the original transaction approval. The introduction of formal reporting to regulators specifically on complex structured trades is another possibility.[54] A further option is a more strongly bifurcated reporting structure within the bank, such as an arrangement whereby legal and compliance functions report up into a chairman who is responsible for regulatory compliance. The CEO would retain responsibility for oversight of the lines of business and the day-to-day running of the bank.[55] Such a structure would greatly limit the extent to which bankers on front-office trading desks could exert influence over control functions (which in some banks extends to the hire-and-fire decisions and even the level of pay of staff with a control function). It would also reflect the fact that the bank has two purposes each with its own constituents: one to turn a profit for the benefit of shareholders, the other to serve broader social functions which both justify its special privileges and require that they be deployed lawfully for the benefit of the public at large.

As discussed in the previous section, the cum-ex discussion reveals that external bank regulators have significant difficulties identifying, investigating, and enforcing misconduct by banks. Despite substantial variation in the organization and mandate of regulatory authorities by jurisdiction, similar problems of detection and enforcement are common across jurisdictions.[56] A cross-border element to the banks' activities greatly exacerbates these problems. The consequence of this situation is clearly a reduction in the disincentives to misconduct. Addressing these problems will not be a simple task but would require some basic changes in the scale of resources available to regulators and the training they receive. This might include specifically qualification and certification according to a syllabus that incorporates the multi-disciplinary aspects of complex banking transactions so that regulators may be better able to identify and respond to questionable transactions. That might include significant time spent in the control apparatus of banks. Other desirable improvements would include enhancing the examination regime. For example, the making of false, misleading, or incomplete statements in

[54] This might be mandated prior to trade execution. The scope and definition of any such requirement would need to be considered.

[55] The separation of CEO and Chairman roles has been the subject of much debate. See, for example, David F. Larker and Brian Tayan, 'Chairman and CEO: The Controversy over Board Leadership Structure', The Rock Centre for Corporate Governance, Stanford University, 24 June 2016, available at https://www.gsb.stanford.edu/faculty-research/publications/chairman-ceo-controversy-over-board-leadership-structure, and Robert C. Pozen, 'Before You Split That CEO/Chair', *Harvard Business Review*, April 2006, a summary of which is available at https://hbr.org/2006/04/before-you-split-that-ceochair.

[56] See further the discussion and examples of misconduct in Chapter 6.

the context of a formal examination is not commonly prosecuted. A significant strengthening of what is today a rather cumbersome system of cross-border cooperation and coordination for mutual enforcement would also be a welcome improvement.[57] The practice of negotiating and agreeing secret settlements with banks, which only come into public view ex post facto and in summary form, should also be brought to a close or heavily discouraged to promote a fair and effective sanctions regime.[58]

The discussion earlier in this chapter notes the frailties or shortcomings of certain market mechanisms, such as relating to settlement conventions, stock lending, and transaction reporting. In all such cases, it seems likely that improvements could be made. There has been significant investment in electronic execution platforms in the financial system, such as high-speed electronic trading venues and the emergence of transparent order-driven markets. Much less attention has been paid to the system's administrative or operational workings which are long overdue for modernization.[59] Given the difficulties which system timing issues can create,[60] exploration of a more rapid means of recording securities entitlements should be carried out.[61] In light of the issues raised by the stock loan

[57] It is remarkable, for example, that in the European Union there is a 'passporting regime' under which an authorized financial institution may freely conduct business throughout the European Union having been authorized by its home state regulator with authority to do so. There is then cooperation and coordination in the supervision of that bank. However, as cum-ex reveals, there is no mechanism having corresponding force to investigate and prosecute banks which abuse this authority. On the EU passporting and supervision regime, see European Banking Authority, 'Passporting and Supervision of Branches', available at https://eba.europa.eu/regulation-and-policy/passporting-and-supervision-of-branches.

[58] The current system in which penalties are negotiated and agreed in secret and in which a summary enforcement notice emerges upon the conclusion of those negotiations would appear to contravene some fundamental principles of the justice system (particularly where fines are levied for conduct that is never explained publicly). These include a process of adjudication which is open to public inspection and which allows participants in the system to learn details of the misconduct which gave rise to the enforcement so that they may correct their own behaviour or pursue private remedies for redress flowing from misconduct of which they may be unaware.

[59] Banks have underinvested in back-office and administrative systems for decades. Consulting groups have extensively documented the problem and the costs and risks associated with it. A 2013 report by Capgemini describes how an average mortgage application passes through thirty-five manual steps before completion and how at one well-known US bank, the benchmark of paper per employee per year is 10,000 pages. See Phil Falato et al., 'Backing up the Digital Front: Digitizing the Banking Back Office', (Capgemini Consulting, 2013), p.4, available at https://www.capgemini.com/consulting/wp-content/uploads/sites/30/2017/07/backing_up_the_digital_front26_11_0.pdf.

[60] Timing issues were at the heart of the cum-ex trade given the ability of the cum-ex seller to exploit the difference between the timing of the sale to the cum-ex buyer (under the T+2 delivery convention) and the timing of the stock borrow and the delivery to the buyer of the borrowed securities (both of which were virtually instantaneous).

[61] Efforts to modernize other aspects of the financial system and ensure more rapid settlement of transactions among financial institutions have been successful in recent years. In the United Kingdom, for example, the banking industry implemented 'Faster Payments' (FPS), a system which reduced payment times from days to seconds. Faster Payments grew out of the Cruickshank Report, a UK Treasury review of the payment system in the UK, which recommended that an independent payment system commission be introduced precisely to take the place of payment infrastructure privately controlled by the banks through the inter-bank market, where banks were 'able to write their own rules', see Don Cruickshank, 'Competition in UK Banking: A Report to the Chancellor of the

mechanism, consideration should be given to whether it is time for this market to move to the use of centralized exchanges where loans of securities can be bid for and executed in an open, transparent, and competitive manner. Stock loan transactions could then be reported and recorded in indelible distributed ledgers. Finally, the failure of the current highly detailed transaction reporting regimes to deal with composite transactions seems an obvious failing that needs to be addressed as it is hard to see what meaning can be extracted from the constituent transactional components when they are reported in isolation.[62]

The options for reform discussed above are directed at possible areas of improvement to the current system of banking governance and control in the absence of material change in the structure of the banking industry itself.[63] A consideration of options for such wider structural change in the banking sector is outside the scope of this book. However, it is nonetheless relevant to refer to a broader structural problem in the functioning of financial systems that is a recurring theme in this book, yet which has to date been given almost no recognition in the calls for wider systemic change in the banking sector. This is the point that the banks are able to participate (i.e. not only trade, but utilize infrastructure) in a system which they simultaneously control and operate. As has been seen, that issue gives rise to a number of difficulties and conflicts. It enables the banks to operate the system for their own benefit.[64] For example, in the

Exchequer' (HMSO, 2000), p.vii, available at https://www.vocalink.com/media/1603/cruickshank_report_2000.pdf. Regulators might consider whether the financial industry should transition to the use of a similar independent body whose responsibility would be to implement a modern system to ensure that there is, as near as possible, a direct correspondence between changes in the ownership of shares and the register of shareholders.

[62] This is on the basis that the transparency achieved by reporting transactions is intended to facilitate the detection and investigation of market abuse, a point that is confirmed by, for example, the UK's Financial Conduct Authority (FCA) transaction reporting regime, details of which are available at https://www.fca.org.uk/markets/transaction-reporting. The FCA describes the regime as one in which the FCA is able to detect and investigate market abuse, among other purposes.

[63] Nonetheless, it is recognized that options to address the structure of the banking sector may have a significant bearing on the issues discussed in this book. For example, a proposal which has gained prominence in recent years is a return to Glass–Steagall, mandating the separation of commercial banking from investment banking (trading) activity. Glass–Steagall, as it is commonly known, was a set of provisions contained in the United States Banking Act of 1933 (Pub.L. 73–66, 48 Stat. 162, enacted 16 June 1933). It was passed in the aftermath of the banking scandals of the Great Depression and mandated the separation of commercial banking from investment banking activities. In doing so, it sought to isolate speculation (associated with the operations of investment banking) from the creation of bank credit backed by government-insured deposits. Another possibility would be to mandate a return to a more traditional banking model with commercial payment and securities settlement infrastructure being carried out by one or more independent infrastructure operators with the banks engaging in the origination of credit decisions only (such as credit-card lending, mortgages, commercial loans). Under this approach, banks would be limited to a client-only role, and not permitted to engage in proprietary trading. The securitization of credit transactions, hedging transactions, and secondary-markets trading would be the realm of financial services organizations, privately owned and funded by private capital.

[64] The Dodd–Frank legislation passed in the aftermath of the Global Financial Crisis specifically addressed the issue of proprietary trading within banks—see § 619[1] of the Dodd–Frank Wall Street

context of cum-ex, the banks were able to exploit subtle timing differences in the settlement of securities available only to the banks and custody banks as operators of the system. In the context of LIBOR, as another example, they were able to exploit self-referential aspects of the rate-setting system, enabling them to modify the rate at which they borrowed through their own rate-setting activities, an issue explored in Chapter 6.[65] This leads on to the point that in controlling the system, the banks are able to modify or greatly influence the way that system is shaped. The earlier discussion of the new products that facilitated cum-ex further illustrates the point. These include the flexible futures contract mechanism that was designed to convert off-exchange into on-exchange contracts and that was engineered to allow custom expiry dates, strike prices, and extended settlement periods.[66] In cum-ex, banks were able to act in the capacity of both a proprietary trader and as agent for their clients more or less simultaneously. This included planning and marketing cum-ex as a trade opportunity and, in some cases, carrying out both the short-selling role (on their own behalf) and the role of buyer (on behalf of their customers), by relying on mandates to trade provided by the client. This issue is relevant to the wider debate about the structure of the banking market and options to address the issue are likely to involve some simplification in the role and operations of banks.

(ii) Tax Systems

Turning to the discussion of tax systems, it seems clear that the cum-ex and other financial product tax structures discussed in this book reflect some profound problems in existing tax systems.[67] These problems have existed—and also became more acute—over a lengthy period.[68] Given that many of these problems

Reform and Consumer Protection Act (12 U.S.C. § 1851) (the 'Volcker Rule'). However, it did not apply a blanket ban to proprietary trades. Instead, banks could trade on their own account in specified circumstances (and continue to do so). In any event, to the extent banks are operating in concert with their clients, it becomes difficult to disentangle what is a true proprietary trade from what is a trade which facilitates client business or (in the words of the Volcker Rule) 'the reasonably expected near-term demands of clients'.

[65] See further the discussion of LIBOR in Chapter 6 at pp.197–9.

[66] See further the discussion of these products in Chapter 3 at pp.106–10.

[67] There are, of course, variations in the degree to which individual tax systems have sought to deal with financial products, but the problems discussed in this book are generally relevant to virtually all tax systems. It would be difficult to argue that any country has fully grappled with the issues posed by derivatives and other new financial instruments. Rather, a few countries (typically those with developed capital markets) have developed an at best partial response which has inevitably created a highly complex tax system. Neither has the system of double tax treaties been revised to deal with derivatives and other new instruments in a satisfactory manner. See further United Nations, 'Taxation of New Financial Instruments', at p.2.

[68] The current position of tax systems reflects limited progress on required reform actions since the opening up of the derivatives markets in the late 1980s.

flow directly from the basic nature of tax systems and the way they seek to accommodate financial products, one possible direction would be to remove some of the difficulties by simplifying the way the tax system deals with financial products. This would require fundamental tax system reform.[69]

The major options for the wholesale reform of tax rules relating to financial products are relatively well-established.[70] Those reform options have recently been summarized as reducing to, broadly, three alternative approaches.[71] These are: tax rules that are based on an 'anticipatory' approach; a 'retroactive' approach; or a mark-to-market approach. An 'anticipatory' approach would involve taxing all income and allowing all deductions based on anticipated returns, with the goal being to eliminate income deferral and other exploitation of tax rules in a realization-based (i.e. capital-gains-based) regime.[72] Retroactive taxation, on the other hand, would tax returns by retroactively spreading gains or losses over the term of the relevant financial contract, with tax liabilities that thereby arise in earlier periods then bearing an interest charge (correspondingly, earlier period

[69] The case for reform should be clear based on the discussion so far in this book, but is also addressed in OECD, 'Innovative Financial Transactions'; Timothy Edgar, *The Income Tax Treatment of Financial Instruments: Theory and Practice* (Canadian Tax Foundation, 2000); and Alvin C. Warren, 'Financial Contract Innovation and Income Tax Policy', *Harvard Law Review* 107 (1993), 460–92. The discussion of tax reform here focuses on reform options relating to corporate income tax systems of the type operated by most states. It is also true that tax reform of financial sector transactions might also be delivered by radical change to the tax system as a whole, for example as delivered by the destination-based cash flow taxation proposal, though such options are not considered further in this book. For an explanation of the destination-based cash flow tax, see Auerbach, Alan, Michael Devereux, Michael Keen and John Vella, Destination-Based Cash Flow Taxation, said Business School Research Paper, 2017-09, February 2017.

[70] Much of the reform discussion has taken place in the context of the US tax rules but given that the problems arising from the taxation of financial products are broadly similar in many countries, the reform discussion has a wider relevance to tax systems around the world. On the US position, see, for example, Joint Committee on Taxation, 'Present Law and Issues'. Most of the academic research and proposals discussed here also relate to the US taxation rules on financial products, though the reform principles addressed have a broader relevance to many states (though taxes not seen in the US—such as stamp or transfer duty taxes on financial products—are not dealt with in the US discussion).

[71] See Alex Raskolnikov, 'Tax Reform and the Tax Treatment of Financial Products', Statement before the Joint Hearing of the US House Committee on Ways and Means and US Senate Committee on Finance, Washington DC, 6 December 2011, at pp.511–15. However, possible reform options have been considered in different ways by other commentators. For example, Patrick Honohan discusses three proposals: first, the possibility of simply not taxing capital income; second, the use of financial transaction tax; and third, the use of a VAT. See Honohan, 'Avoiding the Pitfalls', at pp.6–11. Five possible income tax policy responses are considered by Alvin Warren (mark-to-market, integration of related investment positions, deductibility limitations, disaggregation of financial products into their constituent parts, and formulaic taxation of contingent returns). See Warren, 'Financial Contract Innovation and Income Tax Policy', at pp.474–82. A different perspective on possible policy responses (including a number of different options) is given by the OECD. See OECD, 'Innovative Financial Transactions', at pp.27–39.

[72] This approach would be most suitable for time-value of money returns but could also be used for risky or contingent returns, though in that event would become appreciably more complex as it would then be necessary to determine the expected return for each such contingency notwithstanding the uncertainties of future contingent events. See Raskolnikov, 'Tax Reform and the Tax Treatment of Financial Products', at pp.511–12.

losses would accrue an interest entitlement).[73] Finally, under a mark-to-market approach, financial products would be taxed as if the relevant product or contract had been sold at the end of the tax year and reacquired at the beginning of the next tax year. The result is therefore to tax annual fluctuations in value, irrespective of whether there has actually been a disposal or realization in the period.[74] The three different approaches proposed would not necessarily be restricted to derivatives, but the broader the scope, the greater the implementation issues that would need to be addressed.[75]

Central to all the reform proposals for the taxation of derivatives and complex financial products is the need for a drastically simplified system which replaces the current patchwork of measures (including the simultaneous operation of tax rules addressing income on the one hand and realization (capital gains) on the other). The three reform proposals referred to above achieve this by discarding the distinctions between the various forms of return accruing to financial assets. Instead, the approach is in each case based on an aggregated or total return from financial products.[76] Another fundamental feature of these approaches is the recognition that if such systemic reform is not implemented, then the existing problems will inevitably remain.[77]

Wholesale reform of the type discussed above would represent a material improvement to the treatment of financial products under any tax system, with the potential to deliver an effective and efficient capital income tax. This would clearly reduce the scope for exploiting mismatches and complexity in that system through tax-structured products. However, there are three problems with any

[73] This approach would not present the same difficulties from risky or contingent events that are faced by an anticipatory taxation approach. However, it would bring an obvious credit risk problem—i.e. a taxpayer making losses in an early period would be confident of recouping interest from the government, but the government may in practice be less confident of collecting tax and interest from a taxpayer making large returns in earlier periods. To avoid this issue, it might be possible to apply a retroactive taxation approach based on presumed, rather than actual, returns—see further Alan J Auerbach, 'Retrospective Capital Gains Taxation', *American Economic Review* 81 (1991) 167–78.

[74] This feature gives rise to a concern that the mark-to-market approach would require taxpayers to pay cash tax on 'paper' gains in relation to financial products that had not actually been disposed of. Another concern commonly voiced in relation to mark-to-market taxation is the availability (and complexity) of reliable valuations for all financial products. See Raskolnikov, 'Tax Reform and the Tax Treatment of Financial Products', at pp.514–15.

[75] If the reform is limited to derivatives, that would need the scope of derivatives to be demarcated. Given the embedding of derivatives into more conventional financial products (e.g. a structured note), the process could prove complex, though the required line-drawing would displace multiple existing line-drawing in tax systems. See further Raskolnikov, 'Tax Reform and the Tax Treatment of Financial Products', at p.511.

[76] As indicated by Alworth, the approach adopted is more in line with the economic (Haig–Simons) concept of income. See Alworth, 'Taxation and Integrated Financial Markets', at p.508.

[77] See IMF, 'Debt Bias and Other Distortions', at p.26: 'Complex financial instruments exploit tax distortions—differential treatment across types of income, investors and jurisdictions—that are deeply embedded in current practice. Tax arbitrage opportunities, and hence scope for creative ways to exploit them, will remain unless all forms of capital income are taxed at a single marginal rate—internationally as well as domestically.' A similar point is made in Raskolnikov, 'Tax Reform and the Tax Treatment of Financial Products', at p.506.

reliance on this approach in isolation. First, for various reasons, any such reform would in practice be difficult and there is in any event little evidence that there is the appetite on the part of states to prioritize the complete overhaul of their financial-sector tax rules in the manner that would be required. Second, any overhaul of the tax rules would probably still need to be accompanied by a sharply increased attention to the administration aspects of tax rules dealing with financial markets and complex financial products. Third, virtually all reform proposals have been advanced in the context of a single, domestic tax system. This means they do not address cross-border mismatches between the tax systems of different states (and also that they may if implemented, generate new opportunities for tax-structured financial products).

In relation to the first problem, any tax reform relating to financial products would not be straightforward. Inevitably, there would at a policy level be difficult decisions relating to the trade-offs involved in possible reform options,[78] as well as challenging implementation issues, such as drawing the technical boundaries of any new rules and preventing avoidance activity. In addition, potential conflicts with regulatory objectives would need to be managed.[79] This would include recognizing and addressing the fact that some tax reform options may be closed off by regulatory constraints.[80] A further issue for most states is the difficult balance between controlling tax avoidance and allowing financial markets to operate efficiently. This is particularly so given that for many states a macroeconomic policy of not disrupting financial markets normally overrides tax policy considerations. More fundamentally, however, there is little evidence on the part of states to suggest the wholesale reform of the type discussed above is realistically on any mid-term—let alone near-term—time horizon.

On the second issue, even if a fundamental reform route were pursued, it would need to remove the prevailing patchwork approach in its entirety. This would include addressing mismatches and vulnerabilities created by tax rules dealing with the collection and administration mechanics of any new system. Cum-ex and similar structures show that mechanical administration and collection mechanisms can readily be hijacked and turned against the system,[81] yet these

[78] The significant policy trade-offs required in any effective and efficient tax system to deal with financial products are discussed by the OECD in 'Innovative Financial Transactions' at pp.3–4.

[79] The tensions between tax and regulatory policies are illustrated by the general tax bias to debt, which runs counter to regulatory objectives as the latter, unlike the former, generally penalize debt. The tension led to the development of (tax-deductible) debt-like instruments that could qualify for regulatory purposes as 'Tier-1' capital, such as trust preferred securities or 'TruPS'. See Alworth and Arachi, eds, *Taxation and the Financial Crisis*, at p.7. The issue is also discussed in IMF, 'Debt Bias and Other Distortions', at p.12.

[80] Also, the 2011 US Government Accountability Office Report refers to tax policy options that are precluded by commercial factors or market realities. See US GAO, 'Financial Derivatives', at p.32.

[81] The cum-ex trade exploited an asymmetry in the separation of basic mechanisms to (1) apply withholding tax and (2) give a corresponding credit for it. The trade was finally ended by changing those mechanical arrangements. Similarly, the 'pre-release' trade that is referred to in Chapter 7 (see the

mechanisms are often largely ignored in rethinking tax systems.[82] It is true that any significantly simplified reform response would assist the position. However, systemic reform proposals are largely concerned with a conceptual response to existing problems and do not cater for possible tax evasion responses where administration issues relating to the protection of the system are especially important. Accordingly, it would be important to pay particular attention to the administration issues in any reformed tax system.

The third issue is that a wholesale tax reform to remove distortions in the tax treatment of financial products and investors will not be an answer to the problems discussed in this book unless it is achieved on a domestic *and international* basis. If, as suggested above, the prospects for wholesale reform in individual states seem generally rather distant, then the prospects of states acting in concert to deliver unified global reform in this area would seem remote indeed. A wholly unprecedented level of tax cooperation between states would be required at a time when global tax reform already has a quite different set of (much more limited) priorities and is already under strain.[83]

Given that, unfortunately, the current position is unlikely to be altered by wholesale systemic reform of the tax rules on financial products, it is useful to turn to possible responses that might more realistically be considered to achieve some level of improvement at least over the current state of affairs. However, in the absence of comprehensive systemic reform, these are largely geared to managing the symptoms, rather than dealing with the causes of the existing problem areas highlighted in chapters 6 and 7. As long as there is, as now, a high level of complexity in a significant number of fragmented but interlocking systems (such as multiple tax systems, banking and settlement systems, etc), and as long as there is no change to the current incentive structures, the fundamental issues that have been highlighted seem very likely to remain.

Nonetheless, there are some obvious points that can be made relating to the periodic amendment of tax system rules, such as the principle that any reduction

discussion in footnotes 7 and 8 of that chapter) hinges on the exploitation of simple mechanical arrangements on the border of the tax and capital markets systems.

[82] The pressing need for a much greater awareness of the importance of administration issues and their design in tax systems is discussed generally in Slemrod and Gillitzer, *Tax Systems*.

[83] Since 2012, the main focus of international tax reform has been on the BEPS project (described in footnote 51 of Chapter 7) with a particular concern on the digitalization of business emerging latterly out of that project. The scale of cooperation that would be required to deliver a globally unified approach to the treatment of financial products would go far beyond what has been seen in the BEPS project and in respect of the digitalization issues and would also present a number of acutely difficult issues, such as the ability to achieve any consensus direction, etc. Further, the experience of developing a consensus solution between states in order to police transfers of wealth to offshore locations is hardly encouraging. The most important economy in the world, the US, has demonstrated no intention to join, or cooperate with, the global initiative represented by the Common Reporting Standard. See Elisa Casi, Sara Nenadic, Mark Dinko Orlic, and Christoph Spengel, 'A Call to Action: From Evolution to Revolution on the Common Reporting Standard', *British Tax Review* 2 (2019), 166–204.

of disparities in the tax system (e.g. equalizing the tax treatment of income and capital gains that reflect returns that are economically similar) will reduce the pressure from derivatives.[84] This suggests that even some limited application of the reform proposals discussed earlier, such as the use of the mark-to-market basis of taxation, might prove helpful.[85] A similar effect to the reduction of disparities in the system is achieved by a general reduction in the tax rate, or the lowering of differentials between different tax rates, because in either case what is at stake is correspondingly reduced. The general point is, of course, that derivatives and complex financial products magnify the effect of any anomalies in a tax system, which means that any tax system should be frugal in recognizing tax differences and avoid a proliferation of distinctions based on legal differences or which operate by reference to one class of taxpayer rather than another. This means thinking about the tax rules in a much more defensive way, with a specific focus on how they might be 'hijacked' or exploited, and recognizing that distinctions already made in the system cannot be assumed to function in a static or predictable manner. It also includes the preparedness on the part of the fiscal authority to make hard trade-offs in the design or amendment of tax rules to close off the possibility of abuse.[86]

The discussion in this book underlines the obvious need within a tax system for sufficient tax authority staff with deep specialist knowledge of both financial products and financial markets, a point that is equally relevant both when tax rules are designed and when they are administered. Staff in the tax authority with specialist industry, as well as tax, expertise will be much better at engaging with financial market associations on topical issues and understanding potential areas of weakness in the system. They will also be better placed to understand the interaction of the tax system and financial products and make an assessment of whether there is in practice a strong enough reason to retain features of the tax system that give rise to asymmetries or gaps in the face of the exploitation

[84] The reverse is also true so that if disparities are widened or rates or rate differentials are raised then the problems caused by the tax-driven use of derivatives will grow. The implications are that obvious asymmetries that generate tax differences should where possible be purged. An example of where this point is highly relevant can be seen in the OECD's 2013 report, 'Aggressive Tax Planning Based on After-Tax Hedging', in which it was recognized that if the tax treatment of hedging transactions and the reference asset was the same, there would be no scope for the highly complex arbitrage transactions that were the subject of the report and which were reported as having hundreds of millions of tax dollars at stake. See the discussion of the report in Chapter 7 at p.264 and OECD, 'Aggressive Tax Planning Based on After-Tax Hedging', p.39.

[85] Nonetheless, in the absence of an across-the-board response, there is a risk of introducing a new opportunity for tax structuring by such a measure (such as using a mark-to-market basis to deliver an immediate deduction for income paid out under an instrument and relying on a realization-based rule to defer taxation on the corresponding return).

[86] Examples of such an approach include the pragmatic UK decision to abolish the possibility of obtaining tax credits under the much-exploited manufactured dividend legislation that is referred to in footnote 26 of this chapter.

opportunities.[87] In nearly all tax systems with which the author is familiar, this point concerning the need for greater financial market and product expertise needs much greater recognition, particularly in the way it is delivered in practice. In order to give effect to such greater focus, a number of actions might be explored to bolster specialist technical resources within the tax authority, drawing on internal and external opportunities. These include the development of specialist roles within the tax authority as a career-enhancing route, and developing ways such as secondments to access the expertise of specialist practitioners in the banks and advisory firms and hiring them as consultants when they retire. As the case study discussion has shown, confident claims by a tax authority to have this specialist level of expertise already in place will often run far ahead of the underlying reality.[88]

Whilst the deployment of specialist staff by a tax authority improves the prospects of identifying existing problems in the tax system and as they emerge, there are also considerations that arise in relation to the appropriate response to such problems. These do not concern just a legislative response but might include, for example, more immediate warnings being publicized by the tax authorities on areas of concern, recognizing that any legislative response will inevitably be appreciably slower. There is also an important point relating to the way in which tax-structured trades are dealt with. The automatic response of some tax authorities has been to seek to negotiate a compromise settlement based on any disputed areas of the law, yet this is an approach that in effect endorses or at least encourages the banks' structured products business model.

One particular feature that should be an area of greater focus for the administrators of tax systems is cooperation between tax authorities in different states targeted at financial products.[89] There are various reasons for this: greater cooperation could help the possible movement towards building an international consensus on the tax rules for financial products, reducing opportunities for cross-

[87] Though tax officials with specialist industry and product knowledge will generally be better equipped to understand where the concerns are—or might be—in a tax system, this should not be taken as underestimating the task of reliably identifying those problem areas. According to Raskolnikov, 'Our knowledge of revenue losses from derivatives-based tax reduction strategies is largely anecdotal, wholly unsystematic, and woefully incomplete'—see Raskolnikov, 'Tax Reform and the Tax Treatment of Financial Products', at p.506.

[88] See in particular the discussion in Chapter 7 at pp.293–4.

[89] Recognition of this point is emerging. A Special Committee on Financial Crimes, Tax Avoidance and Tax Evasion was created by the European Parliament following media reports of tax misconduct. The committee has proposed a raft of measures to overhaul the system for dealing with financial crimes, particularly by improving cooperation between the multitude of authorities involved and by creating new bodies at EU and global level. See European Parliament, 'Tax Crimes: Special Committee Calls for a European Financial Police Force', press release, available at http://www.europarl.europa.eu/news/en/press-room/20190225IPR28727/tax-crimes-special-committee-calls-for-a-european-financial-police-force. There is also a separate initiative on tax crimes involving the UK, US, Canada, Australia, and the Netherlands. See HMRC, 'Tax Chiefs Unite to Tackle International Tax Crime', news report of 2 July 2018, available at https://www.gov.uk/government/news/tax-chiefs-unite-to-tackle-international-tax-crime.

border arbitrage. Other practical benefits could be expected to materialize, such as the potential availability of early warnings about the spread of tax-structured products that could, as in the case of cum-ex, be implemented in multiple jurisdictions.[90] More targeted cooperation with other states in this area would also help a jurisdiction understand if there are features of an overseas tax system, or any differing approach to administration issues in that overseas tax system, that are creating the opportunity for tax-structured transactions in its own jurisdiction.[91] Notwithstanding these points, there seems to have been relatively little learning by states from the experiences of other states. Rather, there are many examples where problems arising in one state merely repeat what has already happened in another state (or sometimes numerous other states). Cum-ex is an obvious example where communication between different tax authorities could have been significantly improved.[92] Equally, the US Permanent Subcommittee on Investigations responded to the phenomenon of what it referred to as 'dividend tax abuse' as though it had never been seen before, notwithstanding the same issues (and structures) had been dealt with in many jurisdictions previously, most notably in Italy, where the tax authorities began their own challenge by targeting the activities of US banks.[93] Even in the relatively more obscure case of the recent structuring by banks of 'pre-release' arrangements (referred to in Chapter 7),[94] tax authority concerns about the pre-release mechanism and the way it might be exploited for tax purposes emerged in the UK in the early 1990s, almost thirty years ago.[95] Thus, notwithstanding the obvious point that tax authorities should be able to learn from each other, these examples illustrate there is limited sharing of relevant experiences between states. It is true that there exist certain mechanisms for sharing information on tax schemes between states. These include the JITSIC arrangements that were referred to in Chapter 7.[96] However, these mechanisms do not seem to work very well in cases involving financial products and financial markets, as such cases demand highly specialist knowledge. If tax

[90] The case study in Part I is concerned with Germany alone, but, as has been noted, a number of other jurisdictions have also reported similar tax-structured activity. These jurisdictions include Austria, Belgium, France, the Czech Republic, Denmark, Germany, Finland, Italy, the Netherlands, Norway, Poland, Spain, and Switzerland. See European Parliament, 'Cum-Ex Tax Fraud Scandal'.

[91] The OECD has noted that attempts to prevent tax arbitrage relating to financial instruments need to take account of differences not just in tax law but also in differing approaches to the administration of tax. The OECD also see administrative coordination amongst tax authorities as a way to reduce such exploitation opportunities. See OECD, 'Innovative Financial Transactions', at p.27.

[92] As noted in Chapter 7, it has been reported that the Danish finance minister has stated that the billions of dollars of financial damage caused in Denmark (which is discussed in Chapter 4) could have been avoided if cum-ex activity had been relayed to that state by other states that were already cracking down on the trade. See the discussion in footnote 160 of Chapter 7.

[93] See the discussion of Italy in footnote 5 of Chapter 7. [94] See Chapter 7 at p.253.

[95] The concerns about the pre-release mechanism emerged in the early 1990s and concerned schemes to exploit the UK stamp duty reserve tax rules in their application to depositary receipt arrangements.

[96] See the discussion in Chapter 7 at footnote 167.

authorities are to learn from each other more efficiently and effectively, it will be necessary to build into any cooperation arrangements a materially better understanding of financial markets and financial products. In practice, this will require the involvement of people with the relevant specialist expertise. It will also be important that the channels for both gathering and disseminating relevant information within individual jurisdictions are similarly resourced with expertise in both tax and financial products and markets.

The existence of multiple different tax systems across jurisdictions raises the question of how a tax authority might respond to asymmetries of tax treatment (which could include administrative features) between tax systems that might be relevant to the tax-driven use of financial products. These asymmetries are important because so long as they exist, there will be scope for tax arbitrage and exploitation arrangements. Given the number of tax systems and the wide variation among them, it would not be realistic for a tax authority to attempt a rigorous examination of all possible cross-border asymmetries. This means that a tax authority normally has no choice but to adopt a largely reactive strategy to specific instances of abuse. Nonetheless, some priorities may be identified. Not surprisingly, the most important priority is the need for specialist staff within the tax authority with good market and financial-product knowledge, as well as tax knowledge. Financial markets experts (regardless of their expertise in tax) within the tax authority would enable it to better assess emergent as well as potential indications of abuse. If appropriately deployed, these broader skills would also help a tax authority to monitor market developments and identify trends and shifts in cross-border activity that might be relevant to its own tax system.[97] There may also be particular features of that tax system that are commonly relevant to cross-border transactions and that warrant careful policing.[98] The same point is also relevant to double tax treaties, whether when a treaty is first negotiated or in monitoring its application. In either case, consideration should be given to the degree to which scope for tax arbitrage or exploitation is created by the treaty itself when the asymmetries between the tax systems of the respective treaty signatories are borne in mind. An obvious example (and again a common feature of the structuring in cum-ex) is the exploitation of pension fund exemptions from withholding tax which appear in some double tax treaties.[99]

[97] A tax authority will be better able to monitor market developments if it deploys suitably qualified staff to build relationships with individual banks, specialist advisers, and banking associations, for example by ensuring there is an active dialogue on, say, the interpretation and application of complex parts of the tax law, the design of future changes in the law, and in relation to the general tax policy affecting the financial sector.

[98] An example that is relevant to cum-ex but which has also been a common feature in other cases is the case of the tax credit provisions in tax systems.

[99] See, for example, the discussion of pension funds in Chapter 2 at pp.51–2 and p.69.

The Last Word

The discussion in this book centres on the case study of a single highly structured financial products tax trade. The book seeks to examine the wider relevance of cum-ex by explaining the forces that create and incentivize the use of such tax-driven structures. It may be concluded that the cum-ex trade is emblematic of a state of affairs in which systemic complexity within the financial sector has bourgeoned and banks have evolved beyond the capacity of the system to control them or the capacity of banks to control themselves. A similar point can also be made in relation to the operation of the rules in tax systems that deal with financial products and financial markets. In both cases, the intended mechanisms of control have become inadequate and faulty. The existence of these faulty controls, coupled with the forces that create and incentivize the use of highly structured financial products, explains the recurrent instances of misconduct—as well as explaining the ability on the part of banks to industrialize exploitation opportunities based on tax systems, as the cum-ex case study in Part I of this book clearly illustrates. The bizarre result is that functioning tax systems, particularly in the way in which they deal with financial products, create a subsidy to the banks. Further, the tax-system-based exploitation opportunities discussed in this book are available only to banks and their invited clients, financially privileging only those with access. In acting as the administrators of the financial system, the banks can be seen to provide an overt public role, and one widely recognized by policy-makers to be vital. What is less well known is that they are the quiet dispensers of the financial system's hidden special benefits. It seems self-evident that the financial and tax system should not be allowed to work in this way in support of the banking on failure business model.

APPENDIX

German Institutions, Legislation, and Official Sources

Institutions

Federal Central Tax Office, Bundeszentralamt für Steuern (BZSt)

Federal Financial Supervisory Authority, Bundesanstalt für Finanzdienstleistungsaufsicht (BaFin)

Federal Ministry of Finance, Bundesministerium der Finanzen (BMF)

Frankfurt Stock Exchange, Frankfurter Wertpapierbörse (FWB)

Legislation

Annual Tax Act 2007, Jahrsteuergesetz 2007

Banking Act, Kreditwesengesetz (KWG)

Commercial Code, Handelsgesetzbuch (HGB)

Corporation Tax Act, Körperschaftsteuergesetz (KStG)

Criminal Code, Strafgesetzbuch (StGB)

General Tax Code, Abgabenordnung (AO)

Income Tax Act, Einkommensteuergesetz (EStG)

Investment Act, Investmentgesetz (InvG)

Investment Tax Act, Investmentsteuergesetz (InvStG)

Trade Tax Act, Gewerbesteuergesetz (GewStG)

Official Sources

Decree on the General Tax Code, Anwendungserlass zur Abgabenordnung (AEAO)

Federal Tax Gazette, Bundessteuerblatt (BStBl)

Federal Law Gazette, Bundesgesetzblatt (BGBl)

Bibliography

Advizen, 'European D&O Insurance Market', October 2011, available at https://www.advisenltd.com/wp-content/uploads/europeanDandO.pdf

Agence France-Presse, 'We Didn't Expect EPA to Go Public So Quickly', *Industry Week*, 7 March 2016, available at https://www.industryweek.com/corporate-culture/vw-we-didnt-expect-epa-go-public-so-quickly

Allen & Overy, 'European White Collar Crime Report', Q2, 2017

Allen & Overy, 'European White Collar Crime Report', Q3, 2017, available at http://www.allenovery.com/SiteCollectionDocuments/Allen-Overy-European-White-collar-Crime-Report-Q3-2017.pdf

Allingham, Michael, and Agnar Sandmo, 'Income Tax Evasion: A Theoretical Analysis', *Journal of Public Economics* 1 (1972), 323–38

Alworth, Julian S., 'Taxation and Integrated Financial Markets: The Challenges of Derivatives and Other Financial Innovations', *International Tax and Public Finance* 5 (1998), 507–34

Alworth, Julian, and Giampaolo Arachi>, eds, *Taxation and the Financial Crisis* (Oxford University Press, 2012)

Andorfer, Isabella, and Andrea Minto, 'The Four Lines of Defence Model for Financial Institutions', Financial Stability Institute, Occasional Paper No 11 (Bank for International Settlements, December 2015), available at https://www.bis.org/fsi/fsipapers11.pdf

Arnold, Brian, 'Responses to Tax Avoidance', in Malcolm Gammie, ed., *Striking the Balance: Tax Administration, Enforcement and Compliance in the 1990s*, Conference Report of the Institute for Fiscal Studies Sixth Residential Conference, 1993 (Institute for Fiscal Studies, 1996), 201–208

Association of Certified Fraud Examiners, 'Report to the Nations on Occupational Fraud and Abuse, 2014 Global Fraud Study', available at https://www.acfe.com/rttn/docs/2014-report-to-nations.pdf

Auerbach, Alan J, 'Retrospective Capital Gains Taxation', *American Economic Review* 81 (1991), 167–78

Auerbach, Alan, Michael Devereux, Michael Keen and John Vella, Destination-Based Cash Flow Taxation, said Business School Research Paper, 2017–09, February 2017, available at https://papers.ssrn.com/sol3/papers.cfm?abstract_id=2908158

Austrian National Bank, 'Facts on Austria and its Banks', October 2015, available at https://www.oenb.at/en/Publications/Financial-Market/Facts-on-Austria-and-Its-Banks.html

Awrey, Dan and Kathryn Judge, Why Financial Regulation Keeps Falling Short, Cornell Law School Legal Studies Research Paper No. 20–03; European Corporate Governance Institute (ECGI) Law Working Paper No. 494/202; Columbia Law and Economics Working Paper No. 617 (2020). Available at: https://scholarship.law.columbia.edu/faculty_scholarship/2604

Baker & McKenzie, 'German Dividend Withholding Tax Credit to be Substantially Limited', Hot Topics release, January 2016, available at https://www.bakermckenzie.com/-/media/files/insight/publications/2016/01/german-dividend/al_germany_withholdingtaxcredit_jan16.pdf?la=en

Bank for International Settlements, 'International Banking and Financial Market Developments', *BIS Quarterly Review* (March 2008), available at https://www.bis.org/publ/qtrpdf/r_qt0803.pdf

Bank for International Settlements, 'Statistical Release: OTC Derivatives Statistics at End-June 2018', 31 October 2018, available at https://www.bis.org/publ/otc_hy1810.pdf

Basak, Suleyman, and Michael Gallmeyer, 'Capital Market Equilibrium with Differential Taxation', *European Finance Review* 7 (2003), 121–59

Basel Committee on Banking Supervision 'Principles for the Sound Management of Operational Risk' (Bank for International Settlements, June 2011), available at https://www.google.com/url?sa=t&rct=j&q=&esrc=s&source=web&cd=1&ved=0ahUKEwirxKSs7LnbAhXBLlAKHfXVAxUQFggpMAA&url=https%3A%2F%2Fwww.bis.org%2Fpubl%2Fbcbs195.pdf&usg=AOvVaw0OA46f8_T2HkpZodWhZ8XG

BBC, 'UBS Fined €3.7bn in Tax Fraud Case', 20 February 2019, available at https://www.bbc.co.uk/news/business-47305227

Bender, Rene 'Fünf Mal Haft, 70 Beschuldigte – Diese Manager sitzen wegen Dieselgate', *Handelsblatt*, 19 June 2016, available at https://www.handelsblatt.com/unternehmen/industrie/vw-audi-porsche-fuenf-mal-haft-70-beschuldigte-diese-manager-sitzen-wegen-dieselgate/22708740.html?ticket=ST-735853-1ihC9bxci36dbHerxzdE-ap5

Bernstein, P.L., *Capital Ideas: The Improbable Origins of Modern Wall Street* (The Free Press, 1992)

Black, F., and M. Scholes, 'The Pricing of Options and Corporate Liabilities', *Journal of Political Economy* 81:3 (1973), 637–54

Black, William K., *The Best Way to Rob a Bank is to Own One* (University of Texas Press, 2005)

Bloomberg Editorial Board, 'Where Have All the Public Companies Gone', *Bloomberg Opinion*, 9 April 2018, available at https://www.bloomberg.com/opinion/articles/2018-04-09/where-have-all-the-u-s-public-companies-gone

Bognanni, Massimo, 'Gier frisst Hirn', *Tagesschau*, 24 March 2019, available at https://www.tagesschau.de/wirtschaft/cum-ex-skandal-101.html

Boston, William, 'Investor Test Case in Volkswagen Emissions Scandal Goes to Court Next Week', *Wall Street Journal*, 6 September 2018, available at https://www.handelsblatt.com/unternehmen/industrie/vw-audi-porsche-fuenf-mal-haft-70-beschuldigte-diese-manager-sitzen-wegen-dieselgate/22708740.html?ticket=ST-735853-1ihC9bxci36dbHerxzdE-ap5

Brumbaugh, David L., 'Enron and Taxes', in Theodore F. Sterling, ed., *The Enron Scandal*, (Nova Science, 2002), 151–4

Buettner, Thiess, Carolin Holzmann, Felix Kreidl, and Hendrik Scholz, 'Stock Market Behavior on Ex-Dividend Dates: The Case of Cum-Ex Transactions in Germany', 13 March 2018, available at https://ssrn.com/abstract=2960015

Bureau of Investigative Journalism, 'Deutsche Bank Scandal: Courts Still Chasing Billions through Tax Scams and Carbon Credits', *City AM*, 7 May 2019, available at https://www.cityam.com/tax-scammers-and-carbon-credits-decade/

Carrington, Damian, 'Four More Carmakers Join Diesel Emissions Row', *The Guardian*, 9 October 2015, available at https://www.theguardian.com/environment/2015/oct/09/mercedes-honda-mazda-mitsubishi-diesel-emissions-row

Carroll, Mitchell B., *Taxation of Foreign and National Enterprises: Vol. IV, Methods of Allocating Taxable Income* (League of Nations, 1933)

Casi, Elisa, Sara Nenadic, Mark Dinko Orlic, and Christoph Spengel, 'A Call to Action: From Evolution to Revolution on the Common Reporting Standard', *British Tax Review* 2 (2019), 166–204

Cassis, Youssef, Richard Grossman, and Catherine Schenk, *The Oxford Handbook of Banking and Financial History* (Oxford University Press, 2016)

Center for Automotive Research, 'Automotive Product Development and the Need for Balance with the Regulatory Environment', 20 September 2017, available at https://www.cargroup.org/automotive-product-development-cycles-and-the-need-for-balance-with-the-regulatory-environment/

Chavez, Michael, 'The Power of Purpose in Financial Services' *Forbes*, 31 July 2018, available at https://www.forbes.com/sites/michaelchavez/2018/07/31/the-power-of-purpose-in-financial-services/#361c0152323f

Christensen, Barbara, 'GRAFIK Skattesvindel: Det kan vi få for 6,2 milliarder kroner' DR News, 27 August 2015, available at https://www.dr.dk/nyheder/penge/grafik-skattesvindel-det-kan-vi-faa-62-milliarder-kroner

Clearstream, 'Compensation Handbook, Corporate Action Transaction Management for Customers of Clearstream Banking AG', Frankfurt document number F-CMG04, January 2018

Clearstream, 'Customer Handbook in English', available at https://www.clearstream.com/clearstream-en/keydocuments-1-/icsd-1-/customer-handbook

Clearstream, 'Income Processing CSD', available at http://www.clearstream.com/clearstream-en/products-and-services/asset-services/income-processing/income-processing-csd

Click, Christopher J. 'Death of a Benchmark: The Fall of LIBOR and the Rise of Alternative Rates in the United Kingdom and the United States', *North Carolina Banking Institute* 22 (2018), 283–307, available at http://scholarship.law.unc.edu/ncbi/vol22/iss1/16

Cohen, Felix, Transcendental Nonsense And The Functional Approach, Columbia Law Review, Vol. XXXV, June 1935, No. 6, pp. 809–849.

Collier, Richard, 'Section 77 and Schedule 29—Manufactured Payments: General', *British Tax Review* 4 (2013), 473–4

Collier, Richard, 'Intentions, Banks, Politics and the Law: The UK Code of Practice on Taxation for Banks', *British Tax Review* 4 (2014), 478–508

Collier, Richard, 'Finance Act Notes: Section 138: Stamp Duty: Transfers to Depositaries or Providers of Clearance Services', *British Tax Review* 5 (2016), 635–6

Collins, L. et al., eds, *Dicey and Morris on the Conflict of Laws*, 13th edition, 2 vols (Sweet and Maxwell, 2000)

Commodity Futures Trading Commission, 'CFTC Orders UBS to Pay $700 Million Penalty to Settle Charges of Manipulation, Attempted Manipulation and False Reporting of LIBOR and Other Benchmark Interest Rates', CFTC Release Number 6472-12, 19 December 2012, available at https://www.cftc.gov/PressRoom/PressReleases/pr6472-12

Contag, Moritz et al., 'How They Did It: An Analysis of Emission Defeat Devices in Modern Automobiles', IEEE Symposium on Security and Privacy (SP), 22–26 May 2017, available at https://cseweb.ucsd.edu/~klevchen/diesel-sp17.pdf

Conti-Brown, Peter, 'Why Wells Fargo Might Not Survive Its Fake Accounts Scandal', *Fortune*, 31August 2017, available at http://fortune.com/2017/08/31/wells-fargo-fake-accounts-scandal-2017-tim-sloan/

Crawford, David, 'Germany Probes UBS Staff on Tax-Evasion Allegations', *Wall Street Journal*, 8 November 2012

Cruickshank, Don, 'Competition in UK Banking: A Report to the Chancellor of the Exchequer' (HMSO, 2000), available at https://www.vocalink.com/media/1603/cruickshank_report_2000.pdf

Curcuru, Stephanie, 'U.S. Cross-Border Derivatives Data: A User's Guide' (United States Treasury Board Division of International Finance, May 2007), available at https://ticdata.treasury.gov/Publish/frbulmay2007.pdf

Danckert, Sarah, 'Westpac to Fight ASIC Allegations after ANZ, NAB Settle Rate-Rigging Case', *Sydney Morning Herald*, 20 October 2017

Das, Satyajit, *Swaps and Financial Derivatives*, 3rd edition (John Wiley, 2004)

Das, Satyajit, *Derivative Products & Pricing*, 3rd edition (Wiley Finance, 2006)

Datalend, *The Purple: A Datalend Research Publication*, Issue 1, September 2016, available at https://issuu.com/equilend/docs/data_magazine_digital_issuu?e=25574162/38985667

Davis, Aaron C., and Marina Lopes, 'How the FAA Allows Jetmakers to "Self Certify" that Planes meet U.S. Safety Requirements', *Washington Post*, 15 March 2019, available at https://www.washingtonpost.com/investigations/how-the-faa-allows-jetmakers-to-self-certify-that-planes-meet-us-safety-requirements/2019/03/15/96d24d4a-46e6-11e9-90f0-0ccfeec87a61_story.html?noredirect=on

De La Feria, Rita, 'Tax Fraud and the Rule of Law', Oxford University Centre for Business Taxation, Working Paper 18/02, January 2018, available at https://www.sbs.ox.ac.uk/sites/default/files/2018-08/WP1802.pdf

Desai, Mihir, Testimony before the US Senate Committee on Finance, 10 March 2015

Desax, Marcus and Martin Busenhart, 'Swiss Tribunal Rules on Ownership and Treaty Abuse Issues regarding Total Return Swaps', *Tax Notes International*, 7 May 2012, 557–64

Devereux, Michael, Judith Freedman, and John Vella, 'Tax Avoidance', report commissioned by the UK National Audit Office (Oxford University Centre for Business Taxation, 2012)

Division of Supervision and Regulation, 'Bank Holding Company Supervision Manual' (Board of Governors of the Federal Reserve, as supplemented in January 2017), available at https://www.federalreserve.gov/publications/files/bhc.pdf

Donohoe, Michael P., 'Financial Derivatives in Corporate Tax Avoidance: A Conceptual Perspective', *Journal of American Accounting Association* 37:1 (Spring 2015), 37–68

Donohoe, Michael P., 'The Economic Effects of Financial Derivatives on Corporate Tax Avoidance', *Journal of Accounting and Economics* 59:1 (2015), 1–24

Dourado, Ana Paula, 'Tax Avoidance Revisited in the EU BEPS Context', in Ana Paula Dourado, ed., *Tax Avoidance Revisited in the EU BEPS Context*, EATLP International Tax Series, Volume 15 (IBFD, 2016) pp. 3–24

Duffie, Darrell, 'Innovations in Credit Risk Transfer: Implications for Financial Stability', Bank for International Settlements, Working Paper No. 255, July 2008, available at https://www.bis.org/publ/work255.pdf

Easson, A.J., *Cases and Materials in Revenue Law* (Sweet and Maxwell, 1973)

Eddins, Samuel T., 'Tax Arbitrage Feedback Theory', mimeo, IronBridge Capital Management LP, 2009, available at https://ssrn.com/abstract=1356159

Edgar, Timothy, *The Income Tax Treatment of Financial Instruments: Theory and Practice* (Canadian Tax Foundation, 2000)

Egan, Matt, '5,300 Wells Fargo Employees Fired over 2 Million Phony Accounts', CNN Business, 9 September 2016, available at https://money.cnn.com/2016/09/08/investing/wells-fargo-created-phony-accounts-bank-fees/index.html

Eisenberg, Jon. 'Brother Can You Spare $8.9 Billion? Making Sense of SEC Civil Money Penalties', K&L Gates Legal Insight, 13 February 2014, available at https://www.jdsupra.com/legalnews/brother-can-you-spare-89-billion-maki-87533/

Engelen, Ewald et al., *After the Great Complacence: Financial Crisis and the Politics of Reform* (Oxford University Press, 2011)

Essama-Nssah, B., 'Assessing the Redistributive Effect of Fiscal Policy', The World Bank, Policy Research Working Paper 4592, April 2008, available at http://documents.worldbank.org/curated/en/213081468322746159/pdf/wps4592.pdf

European Banking Authority, 'Passporting and Supervision of Branches', available at https://eba.europa.eu/regulation-and-policy/passporting-and-supervision-of-branches

European Central Bank, *The Payment System, Payments, Securities and Derivatives and the Role of the Eurosystem*, ed. Tom Kokkola (European Central Bank, 2010)

European Commission, 'Tackling Double Non-Taxation for Fairer and More Robust Tax Systems', press release, 29 February 2012, available at http://europa.eu/rapid/press-release_IP-12-201_en.htm

European Commission, 'Aggressive Tax Planning Indicators', Taxation Papers, Working Paper No. 71 (European Union, 2017), available at https://ec.europa.eu/taxation_customs/sites/taxation/files/taxation_papers_71_atp_.pdf

European Commission, 'Antitrust: Commission Confirms Inspections in the Car Sector in Germany', press release, 23 October 2017, available at http://europa.eu/rapid/press-release_STATEMENT-17-4103_en.htm

European Commission, Study on Aggressive Tax Planning and Indicators, Final Report, Taxation Papers, Working Paper No. 61-2015, (European Union, 2016) Ramboll Management Consulting and Corit Advisory, available at https://ec.europa.eu/taxation_customs/sites/taxation/files/resources/documents/taxation/gen_info/economic_analysis/tax_papers/taxation_paper_61.pdf

European Parliament, 'Understanding Securitisation: Background – Benefits – Risks'. (European Parliamentary Research Service, October 2015), available at http://www.europarl.europa.eu/RegData/etudes/IDAN/2015/569017/EPRS_IDA%282015%29569017_EN.pdf

European Parliament, 'The Role of the Financial Sector in Tax Planning', Study for the TAXE 2 Special Committee, May 2016, available at http://www.europarl.europa.eu/RegData/etudes/STUD/2016/578980/IPOL_STU(2016)578980_EN.pdf

European Parliament, 'Draft Report on Financial Crimes, Tax Evasion and Tax Avoidance' (2018/2121(INI)), 9 November 2018, available at http://www.europarl.europa.eu/cmsdata/156723/TAX3%20Final%20draft%20report.pdf

European Parliament, 'The Cum-Ex Tax Fraud Scandal: MEPs Call for Inquiry, Justice, and Stronger Tax Authorities', press release, 29 November 2018, available at http://www.europarl.europa.eu/news/en/press-room/20181120IPR19552/cum-ex-tax-fraud-meps-call-for-inquiry-justice-and-stronger-tax-authorities

European Parliament, 'Tax Crimes: Special Committee Calls for a European Financial Police Force', press release, 27 February 2019, available at http://www.europarl.europa.eu/news/en/press-room/20190225IPR28727/tax-crimes-special-committee-calls-for-a-european-financial-police-force

European Parliament, 'On Financial Crimes, Tax Evasion', Resolution of 26 March 2019 (2018/2121 (INI)), available at http://www.europarl.europa.eu/doceo/document/TA-8-2019-0240_EN.html

European Union, 'Directive on Administrative Cooperation in Taxation', Directive 2018/822 of 25 May 2018, (DAC6)

Ewing, Jack, 'Volkswagen Denied Deception to EPA for Nearly a Year', *Houston Chronicle*, 21 September 2015, available at https://www.houstonchronicle.com/business/article/Volkswagen-denied-deception-to-EPA-for-nearly-a-6520476.php

Ewing, Jack, 'Volkswagen CEO Martin Winterkorn Resigns Amid Emissions Scandal', *New York Times*, 23 September 2015, available at https://www.nytimes.com/2016/07/25/business/vw-wvu-diesel-volkswagen-west-virginia.html

Ewing, Jack, 'Researchers Who Exposed VW Gain Little Reward from Success', *New York Times*, 24 July 2016, available at https://www.nytimes.com/2016/07/25/business/vw-wvu-diesel-volkswagen-west-virginia.html

Falato, Phil et al., 'Backing up the Digital Front: Digitizing the Banking Back Office' (Capgemini Consulting, 2013), available at https://www.capgemini.com/consulting/wp-content/uploads/sites/30/2017/07/backing_up_the_digital_front26_11_0.pdf

Fama, E.F., 'Efficient Capital Markets: A Review of Theory and Empirical Work', *Journal of Finance* 25:2 (1970), 383–417

Fama E.F., and M. Miller, *The Theory of Finance* (Holt, Rinehart and Winston, 1972)

Fastrup, Niels, and Thomas Svaneborg, 'Politi i fire lande jagter Sanjay Shah', DR News, 12 December 2016, available at https://www.dr.dk/nyheder/penge/politi-i-fire-lande-jagter-sanjay-shah

Fastrup, Niels, and Thomas Svaneborg, 'Milliardkuppet', Webfeature report on DR News, undated, available at https://www.dr.dk/nyheder/webfeature/milliardkuppet

Federal Ministry of Finance (Austria), 'Information on Capital Yields Tax Refunds for Dividends Received by Taxpayers with Limited Tax Liability (Non-Resident Taxpayers)', undated, available at https://english.bmf.gv.at/taxation/Relief_Austrian_Withholding_Tax_on_Dividends_2.pdf?67rqd9

Federal Reserve, 'Statistical Release: Large Commercial Banks', 31 March 2018, available at: https://www.federalreserve.gov/releases/lbr/current/default.htm

Ferguson, Adele, 'Banking Bad', ABC News, Australia, 5 May 2014, transcript available at https://www.abc.net.au/4corners/banking-bad/5433156

Ferris, Stephen, Gregory Noronha, and Emre Unlu, 'The More the Merrier: An International Analysis of the Frequency of Dividend Payment', *Journal of Business Finance and Accounting* 37:1–2 (2010), 148–70

Finaccord, 'D&O Insurance in Europe', December 2014, available at http://www.finaccord.com/documents/rp_2014/series_prospectus_dando_insurance_europe.pdf

Financial Conduct Authority, 'Market Watch', newsletter, June 2017, available at https://www.fca.org.uk/publication/newsletters/marketwatch-52.pdf

Financial Conduct Authority, 'Senior Managers and Certification Regime: Banking', 26 July 2017 (updated 29 November 2018), available at https://www.fca.org.uk/firms/senior-managers-certification-regime/banking

Financial Crisis Inquiry Commission, 'Crisis Inquiry Report: Final Report of the National Commission on the Causes of the Financial and Economic Crisis in the United States', Submitted by The Financial Crisis Inquiry Commission Pursuant to Public Law 111-21, January 2011, available at http://fcic-static.law.stanford.edu/cdn_media/fcic-reports/fcic_final_report_full.pdf

Financial Services Authority, 'The Turner Review: A Regulatory Response to the Global Banking Crisis', (Financial Services Authority, 2009)

Freedman, Judith, 'Beyond Boundaries: Developing Approaches to Tax Avoidance and Tax Risk Management' (Oxford University Centre for Business Taxation, 2007), available at http://eureka.sbs.ox.ac.uk/3563/

Friedman, Milton, 'The Social Responsibility of Business Is to Increase its Profits', *New York Times*, 13 September 1970, 32

Frigessi di Rattalma, Marco, ed., *The Dieselgate: A Legal Perspective* (Springer Nature, 2017)

Gaffney, Mike, 'Cross-Border Securities Lending and Qualified Securities Lender Regime', *Tax Notes*, 8 August 2011

Gaffney, Mike, 'Stock Lending Notices, Unwritten Intent and Economic Substance', *Tax Notes*, 22 December 2014

Gammie, Malcolm, 'Moral Taxation, Immoral Avoidance—What Role for the Law?' *British Tax Review* 4 (2013), 577–90

German Parliament, German Parliamentary Report 18/12700, 18th Electoral Term, Recommendations and Report of the 4th Committee of Enquiry under Article 44 of the Basic Law, 20 June 2017 (German language text)

Gibbs, Margot et al., 'Brisante Spur nach Dubai', *Suddeutsche Zeitung*, 13 June 2018, available at http://www.sueddeutsche.de/wirtschaft/steuerflucht-brisante-spur-nach-dubai-1.4012419

Graetz, Michael, 'Taxing International Income – Inadequate Principles, Outdated Concepts, and Unsatisfactory Policy', Faculty Scholarship Series, Paper 1618 (Yale Law School, 2001)

GreenbergTraurig, German Cum-Ex Verdict: What This May Mean for UK Firms, March 26, 2020, available at https://www.gtlaw.com/es/insights/2020/3/german-cumex-verdict-what-this-may-mean-for-uk-firms

Group of Thirty, 'The Structure of Financial Supervision: Approaches and Challenges in a Global Marketplace' (Group of Thirty, 2008), available at https://www.legco.gov.hk/yr08-09/english/panels/fa/papers/fa0223cb1-837-3-e.pdf

Haldane, Andrew, 'Rethinking the Financial Network', speech given at the Financial Student Association, Amsterdam, 28 April 2009, available at https://www.bis.org/review/r090505e.pdf

Haldane, Andrew, 'Small Lessons from a Big Crisis', Federal Reserve Bank of Chicago 45th Annual Conference, 8 May 2009

Hall, Robert E., and Alvin Rabushka, *The Flat Tax*, (Hoover Institution Press, 2007), available at https://www.hoover.org/research/flat-tax

Harberger, Arnold, 'The Incidence of the Corporation Income Tax', *Journal of Political Economy* 70 (1962), 215–40

Heitmüller, Frederik, Moran Harari, and Markus Meinzer, 'Tax Administrations' Capacity in Preventing Tax Evasion and Tax Avoidance' (17.10.2018 version), Tax Justice Network, Coffers EU Horizon 2020 Project, available at https://www.taxjustice.net/wp-content/uploads/2018/11/Tax-administrations%E2%80%99-capacity-in-preventing-tax-evasion-and-tax-avoidance.pdf

HMRC, 'Code of Practice on Taxation for Banks, Consultation Document', 29 June, 2009

HMRC, 'Simplifying Unallowable Purpose Tests', discussion document, 31 July 2009

HMRC, 'A Code of Practice on Taxation for Banks—Consultation Response Document', 9 December 2009

HMRC, 'The Tax Treatment of Regulatory Capital Instruments', discussion paper, 2011, available at https://assets.publishing.service.gov.uk/government/uploads/system/uploads/attachment_data/file/366055/discussion.pdf

HMRC, 'Tax Chiefs Unite to Tackle International Tax Crime', news report of 2 July 2018, available at https://www.gov.uk/government/news/tax-chiefs-unite-to-tackle-international-tax-crime

HMRC, 'Code of Practice on Taxation for Banks', available at https://assets.publishing.service.gov.uk/government/uploads/system/uploads/attachment_data/file/566119/The_Code_of_Practice_on_Taxation_for_Banks___HMRC_consolidated_guidance.pdf

HM Treasury, 'Government Action Halts Banking Tax Avoidance Schemes', press release, 27 February 2012, available at https://www.gov.uk/government/news/government-action-halts-banking-tax-avoidance-schemes

Holder, Eric, 'Transcript; Attorney General Eric Holder on "Too Big to Jail"', *American Banker*, 6 March 2013, available at https://www.americanbanker.com/news/transcript-attorney-general-eric-holder-on-too-big-to-jail

Honohan, Patrick, 'Avoiding the Pitfalls in Taxing Financial Intermediation', The World Bank, Policy Research Working Paper 3056, May 2003

Hu, Henry, 'Swaps, the Modern Process of Financial Innovation and the Vulnerability of a Regulatory Paradigm', *University of Pennsylvania Law Review* 138 (1989), 333–435

Institute for Fiscal Studies, *Dimensions of Tax Design, The Mirrlees Review* (Oxford University Press, 2010)

International Compliance Association, 'Begin a Career in Compliance', available at https://www.int-comp.org/careers/a-career-in-compliance/begin-a-career-in-compliance/

International Fiscal Association, *Tax Aspects of Derivative Financial Instruments*, Cahiers De Droit Fiscal 80b (Kluwer Law International, 1995)

International Monetary Fund, 'Global Financial Stability Report', April 2006

International Monetary Fund, 'Global Stability Report: Financial Stress and Deleveraging', October 2008, available at https://www.imf.org/en/Publications/GFSR/Issues/2016/12/31/Financial-Stress-and-Deleveraging-Macro-Financial-Implications-and-Policy

International Monetary Fund, 'Debt Bias and Other Distortions: Crisis-Related Issues in Tax Policy', 12 June 2009, available at https://www.imf.org/external/np/pp/eng/2009/061209.pdf

International Monetary Fund, 'A Fair and Substantial Contribution by the Financial Sector: Final Report for the G-20', prepared by the Staff of the International Monetary Fund, June 2010, available at https://www.imf.org/external/np/g20/pdf/062710b.pdf

International Organization of Securities Commissions and Bank for International Settlements, 'Securities Lending Transactions: Market Development and Implications', report prepared by the Technical Committee of the International Organization of Securities Commissions and the Committee on Payment and Settlement Systems of the central banks of Group of Ten countries, July 1999

Ishi, H., 'National Report on Japan', in International Fiscal Association, *Tax Avoidance and Evasion*, Cahier de Droit Fiscal International 68a (Kluwer, 1983) at pp. 477–489

Iwersen, Sönke, and Volker Votsmeier, 'Razzia im Cum-Ex-Skandal Hauptverdächtiger soll 43 Millionen Euro hinterzogen haben', *Handelsblatt*, 10 April 2019, available at https://www.handelsblatt.com/finanzen/banken-versicherungen/cum-ex/steuerhinterziehung-razzia-im-cum-ex-skandal-hauptverdaechtiger-soll-43-millionen-euro-hinterzogen-haben/24203002.html?ticket=ST-1007876-Ri99bLkgioeN5ToqpTf4-ap2

Jacobs, Otto, Dieter Endres, Christoph Spengel, Andreas Oestreicher, Andreas Schumacher, Hannah Nusser, Pia Dorfmuller, and Barbara Zuber, *Internationale Unternehmensbesteuerung* (C.H. Beck, 2016)

Janus Henderson, 'Global Dividend Index', Edition 15, August 2017, available at https://az768132.vo.msecnd.net/documents/109355_2017_11_21_11_44_28_033.gzip.pdf

Jensen, Michael, and William Meckling, 'Theory of the Firm: Managerial Behavior, Agency Costs and Ownership Structure', *Journal of Financial Economics* 3 (1976) 305–60

Jimenez, Adolfo Martin, 'Tax Avoidance and Aggressive Tax Planning as an International Standard—BEPS and the "New" Standards of (Legal and Illegal) Tax Avoidance', in Ana Paula Dourado, ed., *Tax Avoidance Revisited in the EU BEPS Context*, EATLP International Tax Series, Volume 15 (IBFD, 2016), 25–62

Joint Committee on Taxation, 'Present Law and Issues Related to the Taxation of Financial Instruments and Products', JCX-556-11, 2 December 2011, available at https://www.jct.gov/publications.html?func=startdown&id=4372

Jorion, Philippe, *Value at Risk, The New Benchmark for Managing Financial Risk*, 3rd edition (McGraw Hill, 2007)

Junge, Volker, and Ingo Kleutgens, 'New German Tax Rules to Reduce Cum/Cum Trades', *Tax Notes International*, 29 August 2016

Kay, John, *Other People's Money* (Profile Books, 2016)

Kay, John, Is Complexity in Taxation Inevitable? IFS Working Paper 57, February 1985.

Keenan, Douglas, 'My Thwarted Attempt to Tell of LIBOR Shenanigans', *Financial Times*, 26 July 2012, available at https://www.ft.com/content/dc5f49c2-d67b-11e1-ba60-00144feabdc0

Kleinbard, Edward, 'Equity Derivative Products: Financial Innovation's Newest Challenge to the Tax System', *Texas Law Review* 69 (1991), 1319–68

Knellwolf, Thomas, and Klaus Ott, 'Schweiz hilft deutschen Ermittlern mit Razzia', *Sueddeutsche Zeitung*, 29 October 2014, available at https://www.sueddeutsche.de/wirtschaft/steuerfall-schweiz-hilft-deutschen-ermittlern-mit-razzia-1.2187897

Laffer, Arthur, and Jan Seymour, *The Economics of the Tax Revolt: A Reader* (Harcourt Brace Jovanovich, 1976)

Langenmayr, Dominika, and Franz Reiter, 'Trading Offshore: Evidence on Banks' Tax Avoidance', CESifo Working Paper Series No. 6664, 25 September 2017, available at https://ssrn.com/abstract=3057458

Larker, David F., and Brian Tayan, 'Chairman and CEO: The Controversy over Board Leadership Structure', The Rock Centre for Corporate Governance, Stanford University, 24 June 2016, available at https://www.gsb.stanford.edu/faculty-research/publications/chairman-ceo-controversy-over-board-leadership-structure

Laukkanen, Antti, 'Taxation of Investment Derivatives', IBFD Doctoral Series (IBFD, December 2007)

League of Nations, 'Double Taxation and Tax Evasion', Report and Resolutions submitted by the Technical Experts to the Financial Committee of the League of Nations, Document F.212 (League of Nations, 1925)

Levi, Michael, 'The Media Construction of Financial White-Collar Crimes', *British Journal of Criminology* 46:6 (2006), 1037–57

Levi, M., and J. Burrows, 'Measuring the Impact of Fraud in the UK', *British Journal of Criminology* 48:3 (2008), 293–318

Lewis, Michael, *Flash Boys*, (Penguin, 2015)

Lewis, Sara, 'New EU Guidance Meant to Prevent Dieselgate Repeat', *WardsAuto*, 10 February 2017, available at: https://www.wardsauto.com/engines/new-eu-guidance-meant-prevent-dieselgate-repeat

Li, Feng et al., 'The Impact of Competitive Intensity on Future Profitability and Future Stock Returns', The University of Chicago Booth School of Business, Working Paper 11–30, available at http://ssrn.com/abstract=1908338

Lindley, Joanne, 'Wage Growth and Human Capital in the UK Finance Sector', University of Surrey, School of Economics Discussion Papers 0313, March 2013, available at https://ideas.repec.org/p/sur/surrec/0313.html

Llewellyn, David T., 'Fifty Years in the Evolution of Bank Business Models', in Morten Balling and Ernest Gnan, eds, *Fifty Years of Money and Finance—Lessons and Challenges* (Suerf, 2013), 319–54, available at https://www.suerf.org/books-and-colloquium-volumes/217/50-years-of-money-and-finance-lessons-and-challenges

Logue, Kyle D., 'Optimal Tax Compliance and Penalties When the Law Is Uncertain', *Virginia Tax Review* 27:2 (2007), 241–96

Lokken, Lawrence, 'Taxation of Derivatives and New Financial Instruments', paper prepared for the United Nations, contained in the report of the Ad Hoc Group of Experts on International Cooperation in Tax Matters on the Work of its Eighth Meeting (UN 1998) ST/ESA/258

Luyendijk, Joris, 'Former Private Banker: "Making Money is the Easy Part"', *The Guardian*, 19 September 2013, available at https://www.theguardian.com/commentisfree/2013/sep/19/private-banker-investment

McDonald, Oonagh, 'The Repeal of the Glass–Steagall Act: Myth and Reality', Policy Analysis No. 804 (Cato Institute, November 2016)

McDonald, Robert L., 'Cross-Border Investing with Tax Arbitrage: The Case of German Dividend Tax Credits', *The Review of Financial Studies* 14:3 (Fall 2001), 617–57

McGee, Patrick, 'How VW's Cheating on Emissions Was Exposed', *Financial Times*, 11 January 2017, available at https://www.ft.com/content/103dbe6a-d7a6-11e6-944b-e7eb37a6aa8e

McGee, Susan, 'Wells Banking Scandal a Crisis We Can Finally Understand', *The Guardian*, 7 October 2016, available at https://www.theguardian.com/business/us-money-blog/2016/oct/07/wells-fargo-banking-scandal-financial-crisis

McKelrath, K., 'The Volkswagen Scandal Wasn't Exposed by Regulators, but by Two Engineers Working at a Small Non-Profit Lab', *Alternet*, 6 October 2015, available at https://www.alternet.org/2015/10/volkswagen-scandal-two-engineers-who-exposed-massive-deception/

McKinsey & Co., 'Retail Banking Insights', March 2015

Maddrey, Jeff, 'Respect for Form: Securities Loans and Hedged Positions in Fungible Stock', chapter 3 in Matthew Stevens, ed., *Taxation of Financial Products and Transactions* (Practising Law Institute, 2007)

Mallinak, Brenda, 'The Revenue Rule: A Common Law Doctrine for the Twenty-First Century', *Duke Journal of Comparative & International Law* 16:1 (2006), 79–124, available at https://scholarship.law.duke.edu/cgi/viewcontent.cgi?referer=&httpsredir=1&article=1107&context=djcil

Markowitz, H., 'Portfolio Selection', *The Journal of Finance* 7 (1952), 77–91

Merton, R.C., 'The Theory of Rational Option Pricing', *Bell Journal of Economics and Management Science* 4:1 (1973), 141–83

Mider, Zachary R. et al., 'The ETF Tax Dodge is Wall Street's "Dirty Little Secret"', *Bloomberg Businessweek*, 29 March 2019, available at https://www.bloomberg.com/graphics/2019-etf-tax-dodge-lets-investors-save-big/

Miller, Hugo, and Karin Matussek, 'VW Executive Tally in VW "Dieselgate" Grows with Stadler Arrest', *Bloomberg*, 18 June 2018, available at https://www.bloomberg.com/news/articles/2018-06-18/vw-executive-tally-in-vw-dieselgate-grows-with-stadler-arrest

Miller, Joe, 'Mopping up Dieselgate: The Boss Transforming Volkswagen', BBC News, 17 March 2019, available at https://www.bbc.co.uk/news/business-47524588

Miller, John H., and Page, Scott E., *Complex Adaptive Systems: An Introduction to Computational Models of Social Life* (Princeton University Press, 2007)

Miller, Merton, and Franco Modigliani, 'Dividend Policy, Growth, and the Valuation of Shares', *Journal of Business* 34 (1961), 411–33

Mitchell, Martin, 'Citicorp and Travelers Plan to Merge in Record $70 Billion Deal: A New No. 1: Financial Giants Unite', *New York Times*, 7 April 1998

Modigliani, Franco, and Merton Miller, 'The Cost of Capital, Corporation Finance, and the Theory of Investment', *American Economic Review* 48 (1958), 267–97

Moffett, Michael, 'Volkswagen's Defeat Device Debacle', Thunderbird School of Global Management, 2017, available at https://thunderbird.asu.edu/faculty-and-research/case-series/id/a07-17-0009-author-michael-moffett

Mollenkamp, Carrick, and Mark Whitehouse, 'Study Casts Doubt on Key Rate', *Wall Street Journal*, 29 May 2008

Morgenson, Gretchen, and Louise Story, 'Banks Bundled Bad Debt, Bet Against it and Won', *New York Times*, December 23 2009, available at https://www.nytimes.com/2009/12/24/business/24trading.html

Munksgaard, Kresten Morten Thye, and Katrine Birkedal Frich, 'GRAFIK Skat snydt for 12,3 milliarder: Det kunne vi have fået...', DR News, 14 December 2016, available at https://www.dr.dk/nyheder/penge/grafik-skat-snydt-123-milliarder-det-kunne-vi-have-faaet

Nanda, V., and R. Singh, 'Bond Insurance: What is Special about Munis?', *The Journal of Finance* 59:5 (October 2004), 2253–79

Neighbour, John, 'Innovative Financial Instruments Challenge the Global Tax System', *Tax Notes International* , March 17, (1997) pp. 931–936

Nesvetailova, Anastasia, Andrei Guter-Sandu, Ronen Palan, and Yuval Milo, 'Tax Evasion and Avoidance Through Financial Engineering: The State of Play in Europe', City Political Economy Research Centre report, October 2018, available at https://www.google.com/url?sa=t&rct=j&q=&esrc=s&source=web&cd=1&cad=rja&uact=8&ved=2ahUKEwiVoNGgtqXkAhUbRBUIHcXQD5IQFjAAegQIARAC&url=https%3A%2F%2Fwww.city.ac.uk%2F__data%2Fassets%2Fpdf_file%2F0010%2F450487%2Fd.1.7-tax-evasion-and-avoidance-by-financial-inniovation-wp.pdf&usg=AOvVaw0J_4yPfzAHdM81WKEXrVYB

Noonan, Laura, 'The Landesbanken: Inside Germany's Trillion Euro Banking Blind Spot', Reuters, 17 September 2013, available at https://www.reuters.com/article/us-banking-germany-landesbanken/the-landesbanken-inside-germanys-trillion-euro-banking-blind-spot-idUSBRE98G06720130917?feedType=RSS&feedName=topNews

O'Donnell, Bob, 'Your Average Car is a Lot More Code-Driven than You Think', *USA Today*, 28 June 2016, available at https://eu.usatoday.com/story/tech/columnist/2016/06/28/your-average-car-lot-more-code-driven-than-you-think/86437052/

OECD, 'The Taxation of Multinational Banking Enterprises', in *Transfer Pricing and Multinational Enterprises, Three Taxation Issues* (OECD, 1984), 44–70

OECD, 'Taxation of New Financial Instruments' (OECD, 1994)

OECD, 'The Taxation of Global Trading of Financial Instruments' (OECD, 1998)

OECD, 'Improving Access to Bank Information for Tax Purposes' (OECD, 2000)

OECD, 'Innovative Financial Transactions: Tax Policy Implications', Special Sessions on Innovative Financial Transactions, presented at the Ad Hoc Group of Experts on International Cooperation in Tax Matters, tenth meeting, Geneva, 10–14 September 2001, ST/SG/AC.8/2001/CRP.8, available at http://unpan1.un.org/intradoc/groups/public/documents/un/unpan002448.pdf

OECD, 'Principles of Corporate Governance' (OECD, 2004), available at http://www.oecd.org/corporate/ca/corporategovernanceprinciples/31557724.pdf

OECD, 'Study into the Role of Tax Intermediaries' (OECD, 2008)

OECD, 'Building Transparent Tax Compliance by Banks' (OECD, 2009)

OECD, 'Addressing Tax Risks Involving Bank Losses' (OECD, 2010)

OECD, 'Revenue Bodies and Banks Move Towards Transparent Compliance', 11 October 2011, available at http://www.oecd.org/ctp/revenuebodiesandbanksmovetowardstransparentcompliance.htm

OECD, 'Aggressive Tax Planning Based on After-Tax Hedging' (OECD, 2013)

OECD, 'Co-Operative Compliance: A Framework—From Enhanced Relationship to Co-Operative Compliance' (OECD, 2013)

OECD, 'Hybrid Mismatch Arrangements' (OECD, 2013)

OECD, 'Co-operative Tax Compliance: Building Better Tax Control Frameworks' (OECD, 2016)

OECD, 'International Compliance Assurance Programme: Pilot Handbook' (OECD, 2018) available at www.oecd.org/tax/forum-on-tax-administration/publications-and-products/international-compliance-assurance-programme-pilot-handbook.pdf

OECD and Council of Europe, 'Convention on Mutual Administrative Assistance in Tax Matters', 1998, available at https://www.oecd.org/tax/exchange-of-tax-information/convention-on-mutual-administrative-assistance-in-tax-matters.htm

OECD Committee on Fiscal Affairs, 'Tax Evasion and Avoidance' (OECD, 1980)

OECD Forum on Tax Administration, 'Seoul Declaration', (OECD, September 2006), available at www.oecd.org/ctp/ta/seouldeclaration

OECD Forum on Tax Administration, 'A Framework for a Voluntary Code of Conduct for Banks and Revenue Bodies', September 2010

OECD Secretariat, 'OECD Work on Tax Avoidance and Tax Evasion', in Council of Europe, *International Tax Avoidance and Evasion* (1981)

Office for Tax Simplification, 'Definitions in Tax Legislation and Their Contribution to Complexity', February 2017, available at https://assets.publishing.service.gov.uk/government/uploads/system/uploads/attachment_data/file/246081/ots_review_of_definitions_in_tax_legislation.pdf

Oltermann, Philip, The men who plundered Europe: bankers on trial for defrauding €447m, The Guardian, 21 September 2019, available at https://www.theguardian.com/business/2019/sep/20/the-men-who-plundered-europe-city-of-london-practices-on-trial-in-bonn#img-1

Oltermann, Philip, Former London bankers convicted after Germany's "greatest tax robbery", The Guardian, 19 March 2020, available at: https://www.theguardian.com/world/2020/mar/19/former-london-bankers-convicted-after-germany-greatest-tax-robbery

O'Mahony, Proinsias, 'Traders Staring at Unimaginable Losses from Euro–Franc Peg Abolition', *Irish Times*, 27 January 2017, available at https://www.irishtimes.com/business/personal-finance/traders-staring-at-unimaginable-losses-from-euro-franc-peg-abolition-1.2080096

Overesch, Michael, and Hubertus Wolff, 'Financial Transparency to the Rescue: Effects of Country-by-Country Reporting in the EU Banking Sector on Tax Avoidance', February 2019, available at https://papers.ssrn.com/sol3/papers.cfm?abstract_id=3075784

Plambeck, Charles, David Rosenbloom, and Diane Ring, 'General Report' in International Fiscal Association, *Tax Aspects of Derivative Financial Instruments*, Cahiers De Droit Fiscal 80b (Kluwer Law International, 1995) pp. 653–690

Podkul, Cezary, 'Wall Street Stock Loans Drain $1 Billion a Year from German Taxpayers', *ProPublica*, 3 May 2016, available at https://www.propublica.org/article/wall-street-stock-loans-drain-1-billion-from-german-taxpayers

Pozen, Robert C., 'Before You Split That CEO/Chair', *Harvard Business Review*, April 2006 pp. 26–28

Raskolnikov, Alex, 'Tax Reform and the Tax Treatment of Financial Products', Statement before the Joint Hearing of the US House Committee on Ways and Means and US Senate Committee on Finance, Washington DC, 6 December 2011

Reuters, 'This Former FBI Director Will be Volkswagen's "Settlement Master"', *Fortune*, 19 January 2016, available at http://fortune.com/2016/01/19/volkswagen-robert-mueller/

Reuters, 'VW Has Still Not Fixed One in Three Dieselgate Cars in Britain', 8 November 2017, available at https://uk.reuters.com/article/uk-volkswagen-emissions-britain/vw-has-still-not-fixed-one-in-three-dieselgate-cars-in-britain-idUKKBN1D828L

Ridley, Kirstin, Clare Hutchison, and Aruna Viswanatha, 'ICAP Fined $87 Million over LIBOR, Three Former Staff Charged', Reuters, 25 September 2013, available at https://www.reuters.com/article/us-icap-libor/icap-fined-87-million-over-libor-three-former-staff-charged-idUSBRE98O0BX20130925

Ring, Diane, 'One Nation Among Many: Policy Implications of Cross-Border Tax Arbitrage', *Boston College Law Review* 44 (2002), 79–175

Roe, Mark, and Michael Tröge, Containing Systemic Risk by Taxing Banks Properly, 35 Yale J. ON REG. 181 (2018)

Rosenbloom, H. David, 'Banes of an Income Tax: Legal Fictions, Elections, Hypothetical Determinations, Related Party Debt', *Tax Notes International* 32 (December 2003), 989–1000

Rosenthal, Steven M., and Lydia S. Austin, 'The Dwindling Taxable Share of U.S. Corporate Stock', *Tax Notes*, 16 May 2016, 923–34

Ross, S.A., 'The Economic Theory of Agency: The Principal Problems', *American Economic Review* 63 (May 1973), 134–9

Royal Commission into Misconduct in the Banking, Superannuation and Financial Services Industry, 'Interim Report', 28 September 2018

Royal Commission into Misconduct in the Banking, Superannuation and Financial Services Industry, 'Final Report', 1 February 2019, available at https://financialservices.royalcommission.gov.au/Pages/reports.aspx#final

Rumble, Tony, Mohammed Amin, and Ed Kleinbard, *The Taxation of Equity Derivatives and Structured Products* (Palgrave Macmillan, 2003)

Sandmo, Agnar, 'The Theory of Tax Evasion: A Retrospective View', *National Tax Journal* 58:4 (December 2005) 643–63

Segal, David, It May Be the Biggest Tax Heist Ever. And Europe Wants Justice. New York Times, 23 January 2020, available at: https://www.nytimes.com/2020/01/23/business/cum-ex.html.

Schön, Wolfgang, 'International Tax Coordination for a Second-Best World (Part I)', *World Tax Journal* 1 (2009), 67–114

Schön, Wolfgang, 'The Distinct Equity of the Debt–Equity Distinction', *Bulletin for International Taxation* 66:9 (2012), 490–502

Schön, Wolfgang et al., 'Debt and Equity in Domestic and International Tax Law—A Comparative Policy Analysis', *British Tax Review* 59:2 (2014), 146–217

Schopflocher, Tom et al., 'Global Structured Finance 2019 Securitization Energized with $1T in Volume', S&P Global Ratings report, 7 January 2019, available at https://www.spglobal.com/en/research-insights/articles/global-structured-finance-outlook-2019-securitization-continues-to-be-energized-with-potential-1-trillion-in-volume-expected-ag

Schreiber, Meike, 'Bafin sorgt sich um Stabilität vieler Bankene'. *Suddeutsche Zeitung*, 18 July 2017, available at http://www.sueddeutsche.de/wirtschaft/cum-cum-geschaefte-bafin-sorgt-sich-um-stabilitaet-vieler-banken-1.3592721

Schuetz, Marcus, 'Dieselgate – Heavy Fumes Exhausting The Volkswagen Group', The University of Hong Kong, Asia Case Research Centre, Ref: 16/572C (ACRC, 2016)

Schwarcz, Steven L. 'Securitization Ten Years after the Financial Crisis: An Overview', *Review of Banking and Financial Law* 37:2 (2018), 757–69, available at https://papers.ssrn.com/sol3/papers.cfm?abstract_id=3169839

Sell, Sarah Skidmore, 'Ray Tomlinson: Programmer Who Invented the Email System and Chose the @ Symbol to Connect Senders and Addresses', *The Independent*, 7 March 2016, available at https://www.independent.co.uk/news/obituaries/ray-tomlinson-programmer-who-invented-the-email-system-and-chose-the-symbol-to-connect-senders-and-a6917536.html

Shackelford, Douglas A., Daniel Shaviro, and Joel Slemrod, 'Taxation and the Financial Sector', *National Tax Journal* 63:4 (2010), 781–806

Shafer, J., and J. Solursh, 'National Report on Canada', in International Fiscal Association, *Tax Avoidance and Evasion*, Cahier de Droit Fiscal International 68a (Kluwer, 1983), 296–7

Sharpe, W.F., 'Capital Asset Prices: A Theory of Market Equilibrium Under Risk', *Journal of Finance* 33 (1964), 425–42

Shaviro, Daniel, 'Income Tax Reform Implications of the Financial Crisis', in Julian Alworth and Giampaolo Arachi, eds, *Taxation and the Financial Crisis* (Oxford University Press, 2012), 174–89

Shea, Terry, 'Why Does It Cost So Much for Automakers to Develop New Models?', *Autoblog*, 27 July 2010, available at https://www.autoblog.com/2010/07/27/why-does-it-cost-so-much-for-automakers-to-develop-new-models/

Shenfield, Arthur, 'The Political Economy of Tax Avoidance', IEA Occasional Paper 24 (IEA, 1968)

Shepardson, David, 'Volkswagen Settles U.S. Diesel Owner Lawsuit on Eve of Trial', *Forbes*, 23 February 2018, available at https://uk.reuters.com/article/uk-volkswagen-emissions/volkswagen-settles-u-s-diesel-owner-lawsuit-on-eve-of-trial-idUKKCN1G72SY

Sheppard, David, and Bruce Nichols, 'Insight: Oil Convoy Blues: Trucking Game Foils Crude Traders', Reuters, 14 October 2011, available at https://www.reuters.com/article/us-cushing-trucks/insight-oil-convoy-blues-trucking-game-foils-crude-traders-idUSTRE79D0OP20111014

Shriber, Todd, 'The Best ETFs 2019: A Comprehensive Guide' *Investopedia*, 22 April 2019, available at https://www.investopedia.com/investing/best-etfs-2018-comprehensive-guide/

Simonsen, Mette, '40 procent af Skats refusionsudbetalinger for skatteudbytte gik til svindlere', DR News, 25 August 2015, available at https://www.dr.dk/nyheder/penge/40-procent-af-skats-refusionsudbetalinger-skatteudbytte-gik-til-svindlere

Slemrod, Joel, and Christian Gillitzer, *Tax Systems* (MIT Press, 2014)

Smith, Adam, *The Wealth of Nations* [1776], ed. Edwin Cannan (Modern Library, 1937)

Smith, Geoffrey, and Roger Parloff, 'Hoaxwagen', *Fortune*, 7 March 2016, available at http://fortune.com/inside-volkswagen-emissions-scandal/

Spengel, Christoph, 'Expert Opinion pursuant to s. 28 PUAG for the 4th Investigative Committee of the 18th Legislative Term', 28 July 2016 (German language text)

Spengel, Christoph et al., 'Estimate of Tax Liability Incurred by Cum / Ex short Selling Transactions', University of Mannheim report, 31 March 2017, available at https://spengel.bwl.uni-mannheim.de/fileadmin/files/spengel/Dokumente/PDF/Projekte_u_Gutachten/Steuerschaden_Cum-Ex__2017-03-31_.pdf

Spengel, Christoph, and Thomas Eisgruber, 'Die nicht vorhandene Gesetzeslücke bei Cum/Ex- Geschäften', *Deutsches Steuerrecht* 16 (2015), 785–848

Spurgeon, Charles E., 'Ethernet: The Definitive Guide', available at https://www.oreilly.com/library/view/ethernet-the-definitive/1565926609/ch01.html

Stigum, Marcia, *The Money Market* (Dow-Jones Irwin, 1983)

Strasburg, Jenny, 'European Probe Widens into Tax Maneuver', *Wall Street Journal*, 29 October 2014, available at https://www.wsj.com/articles/european-regulators-expand-probe-into-tax-avoidance-stock-trades-1414604558

Strasberg, Jenny, 'Officials Expand Probe of Tax Move', *Wall Street Journal*, 30 October 2014

Stumpf, Robert, 'VW Dieselgate Graveyards Grow to Over 300,000 Cars Across U.S.', *The Drive*, 30 March 2018, available at http://www.thedrive.com/news/19768/vw-dieselgate-graveyards-grow-to-over-300000-cars-across-u-s

Svaneborg, Thomas G., 'Milliardsvindel mod Skat: Dansk politi mistaenker finansmand i London', DR News, 1 November 2015, available at https://www.dr.dk/nyheder/penge/milliardsvindel-mod-skat-dansk-politi-mistaenker-finansmand-i-london.

Svaneborg, Thomas, 'Skat på mission i New York: Kraever milliarder tilbage til statskassen', DR News, 26 June 2018, available at https://www.dr.dk/nyheder/penge/skat-paa-mission-i-new-york-kraever-milliarder-tilbage-til-statskassen

Tett, G., 'Silos and Silences. Why So Few People Spotted the Problems in Complex Credit and What That Implies for the Future', *Banque de France Financial Stability Review* 14 (July 2010), 121–9

Thielman, Sam, 'Volkswagen to Pay $14.7bn Settlement and Buy Back Cars from Consumers', *The Guardian*, 28 June 2016, available at https://www.theguardian.com/business/2016/jun/28/volkswagen-settlement-buy-back-cars-emissions-rigging

Traxler, Christian, 'Deterrence of Tax Evasion', in G. Bruinsma and D. Weisburd, eds, *Encyclopedia of Criminology and Criminal Justice* (Springer, 2014), 1005–14

Uckmar, V., 'General Report', in International Fiscal Association, *Tax Avoidance and Evasion*, Cahier de Droit Fiscal International 68a (Kluwer, 1983)

United Nations, 'Taxation of New Financial Instruments', presented at the Ad Hoc Group of Experts on International Cooperation in Tax Matters, tenth meeting, Geneva, 10–14 September 2001

United Nations Department of International Economic and Social Affairs, 'International Co-operation in Tax Matters', Guidelines for International Co-operation Against the Evasion and Avoidance of Taxes (with Special Reference to Taxes on Income, Profits, Capital and Capital Gains) (United Nations, 1984)

United States Department of Labor, 'Employee Benefits Security Administration Fact Sheet', available at https://www.dol.gov/agencies/ebsa/about-ebsa/our-activities/resource-center/fact-sheets/what-is-erisa

United States Department of Labor, 'History of EBSA and ERISA', available at https://www.dol.gov/agencies/ebsa/about-ebsa/about-us/history-of-ebsa-and-erisa

United States Department of Justice, 'Volkswagen AG Agrees to Plead Guilty and Pay $4.3 Billion in Criminal and Civil Penalties; Six Volkswagen Executives and Employees are Indicted in Connection with Conspiracy to Cheat U.S. Emissions Tests', press release, 11 January 2017, available at https://www.justice.gov/opa/pr/volkswagen-ag-agrees-plead-guilty-and-pay-43-billion-criminal-and-civil-penalties-six

United States Department of the Treasury, 'Treasury Announces Final Suspicious Activity Rule for Broker-Dealers', 28 June 2002

United States Environmental Protection Agency, Office of Enforcement and Compliance Assurance, 'Notice of Violation by letter to Volkswagen AG, Audi AG and Volkswagen Group of America', 18 September 2015, available at https://www.epa.gov/sites/production/files/2015-10/documents/vw-nov-caa-09-18-15.pdf

United States Government Accountability Office, 'Financial Derivatives, Disparate Tax Treatment and Information Gaps Create Uncertainty and Potential Abuse', GAO-11-750, September 2011

United States Government Directorate of Intelligence, 'Globalization of Financial Markets: Implications, Vulnerabilities and Opportunities', October 1986, declassified in part, available at https://www.cia.gov/library/readingroom/docs/CIA-RDP87T01127R001100940003-0.pdf

United States of America Before the Securities and Exchange Commission, 'Order Instituting Cease and Desist Proceedings, Pursuant to Section 8A of the Securities Act of 1933, Making Findings, and Imposing Remedial Sanctions and a Cease-and-Desist Order', Administrative Proceeding File No. 3-18605 In the Matter of Deutsche Bank Trust Company Americas, 20 July 2018, available at https://www.sec.gov/litigation/admin/2018/33-10523.pdf

United States Senate Permanent Subcommittee on Investigations, 'Tax Haven Banks and U.S. Tax Compliance', Staff Report, 17 July 2008, available at https://www.hsgac.senate.gov/imo/media/doc/REPORTTaxHavenBanksJuly1708FINALwPatEliseChgs92608.pdf

United States Senate Permanent Subcommittee on Investigations, 'Dividend Tax Abuse: How Offshore Entities Dodge Taxes on U.S. Stock Dividends', Staff Report, 11 September 2008, available at https://www.hsgac.senate.gov/subcommittees/investigations/hearings/dividend-tax-abuse-how-offshore-entities-dodge-taxes-on-us-stock-dividends

United States Senate Permanent Subcommittee on Investigations, 'Caterpillar's Offshore Tax Strategy', Majority Staff Report, 1 April 2014, available at https://www.hsgac.senate.gov/imo/media/doc/Caterpillar's%20Offshore%20Tax%20Strategy%20(4-1-14,%208-28-14%20FINAL).pdf

University of California–San Diego, 'Researchers Find Computer Code that VW Used to Cheat Emissions Tests', 22 May 2017, available at https://phys.org/news/2017-05-code-volkswagen-emissions.html

US Securities and Exchange Commission and US Commodity Futures Trading Commission, 'Memorandum of Understanding Between the U.S. Securities and Exchange Commission and the U.S. Commodity Futures Trading Commission Regarding Coordination in Areas of Common Regulatory Interest and Information Sharing', 11 July 2018, available at https://www.cftc.gov/sites/default/files/2018-07/CFTC_MOU_InformationSharing062818.pdf

Valladares, Mayra Rodriguez, 'Deutsche Bank Needs Serious Laundering'. *Forbes*, 7 April 2019, available at https://www.forbes.com/sites/mayrarodriguezvalladares/2019/04/07/deutsche-bank-needs-serious-laundering/#4465c7bd42d4

Votsmeier, Volker, and Sönke Iwersen, 'Tax Law Experts Played Along', *Handelsblatt Global*, 1 August 2017, available at https://global.handelsblatt.com/finance/tax-law-experts-played-along-806313

VRT Nieuws, 'Topman UBS België in verdenking wegens fraude', 19 June 2014

Walsh, Paul, 'Global Securities Lending Hits $2 Trillion Mark', *Global Custodian*, 13 March 2017, available at https://www.globalcustodian.com/global-securities-lending-hits-2-trillion-mark/

Warren, Alvin C., 'Financial Contract Innovation and Income Tax Policy', *Harvard Law Review* 107 (1993), 460–92

Warren, Alvin C., 'US Income Taxation of New Financial Products', *Journal of Public Economics* 88 (2004), 899–923

Warren, Tom, 'Monzo Launches its "Bank of the Future" in the US', *The Verge*, 13 June 2019, available at https://www.theverge.com/2019/6/13/18677298/monzo-bank-us-launch-date-availability

Weber, E.J., 'A Short History of Derivative Security Markets', in W. Hafnerand H. Zimmermann, eds, *Vinzenz Bronzin's Option Pricing Models* (Springer, 2009), 431–66

Weidmann, Oktavia, *Taxation of Derivatives*, Series on International Taxation, No. 52 (Wolters Kluwer, 2015)

Weisbach, David, 'Line Drawing, Doctrine and Efficiency in the Tax Law', *Cornell Law Review* 84 (1999), 1627–81

Wheatcroft, G.S.A., 'The Attitude of the Legislature and the Courts to Tax Avoidance', *Modern Law Review* 18 (May 1955), 209–30

Wilenius, Paul, 'Enemies Within: Thatcher and the Unions', BBC website, Friday 5 March 2004, available at http://news.bbc.co.uk/1/hi/3067563.stm

Wood, Robert, 'French Criminal Tax Probe Of UBS—Talk About Déjà Vu'. *Forbes*, 4 June 2013, available at https://www.forbes.com/sites/robertwood/2013/06/04/french-criminal-tax-probe-of-ubs-talk-about-deja-vu/#1db14e8a5ccd

Wood, Robert, 'New UBS Tax Evasion Probe, Again Over Americans', *Forbes*, 5 February 2015

Wren, Jonathan D. et al., 'Review-Coerced Citation: Case Report, Update on Journal Policy and Suggestions for Further Prevention', *Bioformatics*, 30 January 2019, available at https://academic.oup.com/bioinformatics/advance-article/doi/10.1093/bioinformatics/btz071/5304360

Yeates, Clancy, Sönke Iwerson, and Volker Votsmeier, 'Germans Don't "Blame and Shame"; Emails Reveal Macquarrie's Mind over Tax Deals', *Sydney Morning Herald*, 22 July 2019

Index of Names

For the benefit of digital users, indexed terms that span two pages (e.g., 52–53) may, on occasion, appear on only one of those pages.

Subject Index

Note: Figures are indicated by an italic "*f*", respectively, following the page number.

For the benefit of digital users, indexed terms that span two pages (e.g., 52–53) may, on occasion, appear on only one of those pages.

The manufacturer's authorised representative in the EU for product safety is Oxford University Press España S.A. of el Parque Empresarial San Fernando de Henares, Avenida de Castilla, 2 – 28830 Madrid (www.oup.es/en or product.safety@oup.com). OUP España S.A. also acts as importer into Spain of products made by the manufacturer.

www.ingramcontent.com/pod-product-compliance
Lightning Source LLC
LaVergne TN
LVHW011821200926
848484LV00005B/1274

9780198859673